INTERSECTING TANGO

Cultural Geographies

of Buenos Aires,

1900–1930

Adriana J. Bergero

Translated by Richard Young

UNIVERSITY OF PITTSBURGH PRESS

Published by the University of Pittsburgh Press, Pittsburgh, Pa., 15260

Library of Congress Cataloging-in-Publication Data

Bergero, Adriana J., 1953-

Intersecting tango : cultural geographies of Buenos Aires, 1900-1930 / Adriana J. Bergero ; translated by Richard Young.

p. cm. — (Illuminations)

Includes bibliographical references and index.

ISBN-13: 978-0-8229-4318-1 (cloth : alk. paper)

ISBN-10: 0-8229-4318-2 (cloth : alk. paper)

ISBN-13: 978-0-8229-5985-4 (pbk. : alk. paper)

ISBN-10: 0-8229-5985-2 (pbk. : alk. paper)

1. Buenos Aires (Argentina)—History—20th century. 2. National characteristics, Argentine. 3. Buenos Aires (Argentina)—Social conditions—20th century. I. Title. II. Series: Illuminations (Pittsburgh, Pa.)

F3001.3.B543 2008

982'.11—dc22

2007049543

Frontispiece: New arrivals at Immigration Hall (Archivo General de la Nación, n.d.)

The author has made all reasonable effort to find and contact the holders of rights for the works analyzed and to obtain their permission. The author wishes to thank the National Archive of Argentina (Archivo General de la Nación) in Buenos Aires for permission to reproduce the photographs made available by the photography department and the Detroit Institute of Arts for permission to reproduce *The Nightmare,* by Johann Heinrich Füssli.

For the Bergeros,
the Miguel-Amoreses,
Juárezes, Piccos, Zelayas,
Borgarellos, Catenas,
and Gherleros, and for
the tango singer
Sofía (Bergero) Bozán,
"La Negra"

For the immigrants
who came to Buenos Aires
at the beginning of the 1900s

and for all immigrants
everywhere of any time

CONTENTS

Illustrations follow pages 106, 250, 406

ACKNOWLEDGMENTS

I would like to thank John Beverley and Sara Castro-Kláren, editors of the Illuminations series, who were the first to place their trust in what would become my personal cognitive map of Buenos Aires of the beginning of the twentieth century. I also wish to thank Peter Kracht and Deborah Meade, who steered the publication process with patience and care, and Carol Sickman-Garner, for her exquisite, thorough copyediting.

My gratitude also goes to Richard Young, who with untiring patience translated the taut silence written on the skin of the *muñecas bravas* and defeated men of Buenos Aires from Spanish, Cocoliche, and Lunfardo into English.

The encouragement and generosity of Andrés Avellaneda, David W. Foster, John King, Neil Larsen, Jorge Ruffinelli, Diana Sorensen, and Saúl Sosnowski gave me the energy to continue my work. I am profoundly grateful to each of them.

I also owe thanks to Raquel Arostegui and Luisa Valenzuela, in Buenos Aires, for generously opening their homes, sharing their delightful gardens and balconies and the riches of their human and intellectual friendship. I thank Jorge Bergero, José Bergero, Esteban Carrizo, and Pedro Chanta for helping me continue to assemble the puzzle of Buenos Aires from the perspective of all our personal diasporas.

During the rainy cold of *porteño* winters and springs, Tomás González Naveyra, Cecilia Lagos, José Luis Scalercio, and Mónica Scordamaglia, of the Photography Department at the National Archives in Buenos Aires, were an inexhaustible source of assistance. My thanks to them for offering me a treasure from archives they know better than anyone. My appreciation also goes to the Academic Senate Faculty Grants Committee at the University of California, Los Angeles, for its strong and continuous support of my research over many years.

My profound gratitude to Gladis Yurkievich and Saúl Yurkievich, who is still at Rue Pernety and will always be in Saignon.

My gratitude also goes to Daniel Deutsch for his extraordinary ability to deductively understand cities and spaces, his unwavering support, and his refreshing sense of humor. I thank him, too, for accompanying me to Scarlenghe, Cumiana-Turin, Alba de Tormes, Abony, Montevideo, and Buenos Aires—ports of departure and entry for our migrant families. And for showing me the way to Delft.

INTERSECTING

TANGO

INTRODUCTION

Bisogna farsi argentino/a.
[You must become Argentinian.]

Popular saying

BY THE TIME I REALIZED THAT TO
study a city, especially Buenos Aires, in the midst of radical transition might
be overambitious, it was already too late to change my mind. The photos at
Argentina's National Archives had started me on a path from which there
was no return. The expectant faces of the new arrivals at Immigration Hall
(figure 1) stared at me unflinchingly, as if asking for something. And the
announcement in Italian I read in an old issue of *La Nación* brought the
plight of these new arrivals even closer: "Michele Belote, Italian, son of
Francesco Belote and Margarita Alfonso, seeks news of his father. Anyone
knowing of his whereabouts or able to provide information about him is
requested to go to Via Salta, no. 290, for which his son will be very grateful"
(*Argentina, la otra patria* n.d., 39).

Michele Belote was forced to rely on others to help him find his father in
a chaotic city whose residents and boundaries were in constant transition. If
Michele Belote could strive to find his father in this way—to rearrange his
family map, pulled apart by departures and disencounters within a city still

without personal maps—then, I resolved, I too could map Buenos Aires, attempting to decipher the city's dramatic changes at the dawn of the twentieth century. Indeed, in many ways, this study is about maps—both urban maps and the cognitive and affective maps that diasporas, exile, and cities confuse and reassemble.

From today's perspective, Buenos Aires in the early 1900s was a place where intersecting discourses spoke about the city and its women. To listen to those discourses in all their simultaneity is both a fascinating and a disturbing experience. From them emerge the contortions of bodies in pain: the unemployed wandering the streets in fear and anguish, without soles on their shoes; women swallowed up into social invisibility through dishonor or prostitution; anarchists awaiting deportation or execution; fathers selling daughters to sinister pimps or bordello madams; consumptive women; cynical, cruel women; women guilty of infanticide; women workers exploited to the limit of their bodies; solitary lovers and weeping men; and above all people—especially women—who took their own lives. Daily life in Buenos Aires between the beginning of the twentieth century and 1930—what took place in the city's private and public domains—was absorbed into countless social texts and imaginaries that spoke of crises, fractures, and chaos from kaleidoscopic points of view. These texts and imaginaries also spoke of *casos:* private social affairs that were raucously laid, with all their details and sanctions, before their public "judges," found in the audiences of the press and the popular theater.

The linking of identity and space implies stable communities, homogenized through shared networks of daily practices. The processes of modernization, however, brought about the separation "of time and space, disembedding mechanisms, and institutional reflexivity" (Giddens 1999, 92) —profound dissymmetries caused by a new cycle in the relentless expansion of capitalism, and violent crises in political participation caused by a broadening of the "range of individuals . . . seeking to take part in political decisions" (Bobbio and Matteucci 1985, 1040). My study is framed by the first presidency of Hipólito Yrigoyen (1916–22), the presidency of Marcelo T. de Alvear (1922–28), Yrigoyen's second term (1928–30), and the takeover of General José Uriburu (1930–32), although some of the texts discussed here reach into the presidency of Agustín P. Justo (1932–38). From an economic point of view, this is the first period of industrialization, when light industry for the internal market developed alongside foreign trade, associated with the agricultural/ranching economy that brought Argentina into global markets. From a sociological standpoint, this period featured the emergence of new historical agents from the process of modernity, including women and the first urban-industrial proletariats in Latin America.

To speak of modern Argentina is to speak, above all, of Buenos Aires, a hypertrophy described in Martínez Estrada's *La cabeza de Goliat* (Goliath's Head) and, before Martínez Estrada, in the utopian dreams of Domingo Faustino Sarmiento: "She [Buenos Aires] is alone in the vastness of Argentina . . . [and] in her contact with the nations of Europe; she alone exploits the advantages of foreign trade; she alone has power and income" (Sarmiento 1993, 59). By the second half of the nineteenth century, the Frontera Sur (Southern Frontier), which borders on indigenous Patagonian territories, had become not only the first frontier of Argentina's nationalist imaginary but the foundation of the new nation. As an unassailable concept, this frontier facilitated the double agenda of genocide and cultural assimilation, which empowered the hegemony of "civilization" over "barbarism," of city over desert, and of industrialization as the sole model of economic growth. According to Norberto Bobbio and Nicola Matteucci, Argentina's first period of modernity unfolded during the second half of the nineteenth century, with the penetration and subsequent integration of those national territories left uncontrolled by colonial authorities, the centralization of political power, the founding of the state bureaucracy and the national army, the unification of markets and currency, and the designation of a national capital. The spectacular military success of the Conquest of the Desert would be ensured by a railway infrastructure that would consolidate the occupation of the conquered territories. Since the 1845 publication of Sarmiento's *Facundo: Civilización y barbarie* (Facundo: Civilization and Barbarism), the elite had responded to the cultural challenge of defining national identity by endorsing the image of an Argentina committed to modernity and to the four pillars of liberalism: the promotion of immigration, industrial growth as the underpinning of economic progress, statism, and public education (Bobbio and Matteucci 1985, 1040).

No iota of doubt could be found in the elite's implementation of modernity: "The dominant class . . . agreed, almost arrogantly, that it allowed for the faithful reproduction of a way of life from an outside world that was worthy of being imitated and even surpassed" (Botana 1977, 235). The Generación del Ochenta (Generation of 1880), in the Conquest of the Desert, unleashed military genocide and a devastating economic disruption.[1] At the same time the elite were brandishing hard evidence to claim that frontiers were forever, however, Buenos Aires was already beginning to lose whatever stable form it had, becoming a fluid, porous urban space. Instead of guaranteeing absolute frontiers, then, the Generation of 1880 and the Generación del Centenario (Centennial Generation)—in the city that served as the space of their self-beguilement—gambled in a game whose moves would eventually provoke the spectacular polymorphism that characterizes modern Buenos Aires.[2] While Miguel Juárez Celman (1886–90) may have epitomized the maximum expression of absolute political rule, the economic modernization led by his Conservative Order unleashed an unprecedented social explosion.[3] The resulting frenzy of collective life had to be resolved within the city itself, where the likelihood of crisis was most extreme. One hundred partial and six general strikes were held during the first decade of the twentieth century, because of the activism of unions and opposition organizations, headed mainly by foreign leaders. The government declared a state of emergency five times, perpetrated five massacres of workers, and passed the Ley de Residencia (Residency Act) in order to control foreigners' residence and establish the state's powers of deportation. Workers' protests, such as the general strike of May 1909, known as Semana Roja (Red Week), drew attention to the profound disparities in the uneven economic insertion of different social sectors in the capitalist system, but the dominant class suppressed the strike brutally and sought to erase the resulting bloody scenes from the city's imaginaries. After all, the elite had a much more engrossing pursuit at hand: the flamboyant celebrations held in 1910 to honor the May Revolution of 1810. These events were intended as an ostentatious showcase, open to the world and to the rest of Argentina, to exhibit two elements of the Conservative Order's most idiosyncratic symbolic capital: its unbridled prosperity and its lavishness. But the opposition had something else in mind: taking advantage of the momentum generated by the Centennial to uncover the elite's political manipulations, electoral fraud, and administrative corruption. Even at the heart of the oligarchy, the benefits of a reformist response to the ethical and political challenges posed by anarchists, anarcho-syndicalists, socialists, and communists—mobilized in Buenos Aires and in the rest of the country—

was becoming clear. The oligarchy began to break apart from within, but its fragmentation reflected the intervention of a sector that, according to Natalio Botana, was aware that these social threats could be met with "strategic intelligence," that it was possible "to concede a bit of privilege and thereby save a way of life or remain in power" (1977, 235). This astute evaluation crystallized with Roque Sáenz Peña's ascent to the presidency (1910–14). Sáenz Peña, an internal opposition candidate, distanced himself from Argentina's most conservative factions in an attempt to maintain control of the democratic game within the oligarchy. His reform of electoral laws (10 February 1912) demonstrated that the elites could stay afloat even in the most testing tides and storms. The new laws specified which people were citizens and what criteria defined citizenship, in terms of nationality, age, gender, financial assets, and education. With the support of Interior Minister Indalecio Gómez, the most essential measure for enabling social modernity became reality under Sáenz Peña. The 1912 reforms guaranteed universal male suffrage. They made the vote secret and obligatory from the age of eighteen and guaranteed representation to political minorities, but women, the mentally ill, drunks, and foreigners were left out in the cold. For immigrants, these reforms were a maneuver that reinforced the stipulations of the earlier Residency Act against a highly politicized proletarian population that, by 1914, included 59 percent foreigners (Vargas 1999, 19). Nevertheless, the 1912 Ley Sáenz Peña made it possible for the Unión Cívica Radical (Radical Civic Union), or Radicalismo, to come to power in 1916, under Hipólito Yrigoyen, whose political clientele was drawn from the middle and popular classes previously disregarded by the Conservative Order. But nothing would unfold without a hitch. The Radical government stumbled forward, dealing with pressure from the working class and the ensuing panic among conservatives, calming the anxieties of the middle class, extinguishing dissidence from within the Radical ranks, and overcoming the economic crises of the postwar period—all based on the state's role as a mediator of social conflict, a role that, historically, the state pursued only tepidly. In 1922, Marcelo T. de Alvear succeeded Hipólito Yrigoyen, benefiting from the Paz Social (Social Peace) resulting from the country's economic recovery.

This study examines, first, how the modernization of Buenos Aires produced profound identitary dislocations of all kinds. It might be said that the nation's cognitive maps were yet to be drawn, since they had still to absorb not just the complex political heteroglossia embodied in the city's many anarchist, anarcho-syndicalist, socialist, feminist, communist, radicalist, union, and neighborhood associations, but also a fundamental linguistic, cultural, and ethnic diversity so dense that it earned Buenos Aires the nickname Babilonia. It could not have been easy to piece together social meanings in a Nation House that was truly in a state of full-blown transition. Thus, the consolidation of a national imaginary became a political matter of the highest priority. As Burton Pike points out, "The city is, on one hand, incomprehensible for its inhabitants; as a whole it is inaccessible to the imagination unless it can be reduced and simplified" (1996, 245). But this kind of simplification, which seeks to make things coherent, is an entirely fluid process, in a state of constant adjustment. The Buenos Aires of the early twentieth century will thus be approached here through its imaginaries, through the theoretical convergence of urban geography, sensorial geography, cultural studies, gender studies, and social history. I will examine a variety of social texts, including literature, journalism, popular culture in the theater and tango, serial novels and melodrama, public health and industrial medicine, parliamentary debates and political discourse, professional and amateur photography, the culture of the market, architecture, interior design and furniture, the value attached to perfume, and the secrets hidden in home remedies—all of these texts addressing and commenting on the cultural recruitment of modernization and the process of Argentineanization.[4] Donnatella Mazzoleni wonders, "Why the city and the imaginary?" and concludes that approaching a city through its imaginaries is the only methodology allowing us to touch not only "the [different] levels of the conscious, but also, necessarily, those of the collective unconscious" (1985, 7). Such a study of the city demands a nontraditional framework. Structuralism, Mazzoleni points out, draws attention to the multidiscursive nature of the city's languages and to the semiotic artifacts spread throughout its geography, their signifiers, the syntax of their locations, and their invariables (typologies) and variables (morphologies) —"the discontinuous body of the urban habitat, cells, tissues, organs, systems of organs, and systems of systems" (Mazzoleni 1985, 8). Although the city's materiality is synchronically displayed within its spatial convergence, however, Mazzoleni notes that historicism is instrumental to understanding urban languages along diachronic axes, which in turn allows new conceptual frameworks to be unveiled. The city, then, is not static content, but pure movement, history, process, "a narrative that identifies . . . processes and laws of trans-formation, chains of cause and effect, genealogies" (Mazzoleni 1985, 9). At the same time, there are also pivotal moments when researchers begin to detect *discursive nodes*—centers of tension where all kinds of aspirations, concerns, and anxieties converge with pressing urgency, coinciding fortu-itously with attempts to control social meaning, which is precisely the task of imaginaries. In Buenos Aires, these discursive nodes acted upon incandes-cent evidence of upheavals, crossroads and dilemmas, marches and counter-marches, consolidations, detours and failures—all eventually projected not just onto events marking the grand history of the country but also onto everyday life.

Modernity unleashed unprecedented laws of exchange. It was such a new social construction, and it altered so many patterns of daily life, that it gave rise to perplexity, hilarity, and pain, but above all to excess: an excess of social interaction, uncontainable by traditional frames and boundaries. The grotesque body is, essentially, the material world at its most extreme. It is open and conducive to hyperbolic disorder. It disregards the stigmatized value of social deviations in physical or identitary spaces and pays no heed to the negativity attached to social transgressions, improvisations, and experi-mentation. As a decentered signifier, the grotesque body empowers participa-tory imaginaries that have no borders. Hence the nomadism of the identities it unleashes. Mazzoleni, recalling Bakhtin, sees grotesque space as an irrup-tion of the messiness of organic life: "Waves of food, drink, sperm, excre-ment, urine wash together and mingle inside that carnivalesque receptacle and then burst outward from there as far as the ends of the universe" (1985, 19). In urban culture, the grotesque body appears in opposition to architec-ture, but the city is itself inclined to be a grotesque body, because of the con-nectivity of its communicating vessels, which mix together the flows of public and private life. In fact, deviations and alternatives, difficult for even the most vigilant political, religious, and sexual institutions to spot, may emerge from private life. How could such institutions detect the dissym-metries and social disorder generated behind the closed doors of intimacy and subjectivity?

Sensorial cognitive maps occupy center stage here. So much in Buenos Aires speaks of bodies. So many cognitive maps of the city unfold through corporeal registers. Mazzoleni argues for the body as habitat, as the first and original dwelling place, so much a part of each individual that its sensuous-cognitive experience is nonnegotiable and nontransferable. Moreover, she proposes that "the body is, with respect to language, a fluctuating signifier, a zone of semantic disorder, anything that is located, as it were, 'below' language" (1985, 19). My analysis of early twentieth-century Buenos Aires approaches the representation of the body in three ways: first, as the realm most closely allied to subjectivity and to the physical-symbolic space of interaction with the new labor culture of industrialization; second, as the space through which the objects of market culture enter and remain; and third, as the interceptive space of new sociosexual practices.

The difference between modern cartography and empirical geography is everyday life—in other words, decoding and interpreting the knowledge that, in the modern city, is above all knowledge gained from a culture in motion. Rossana Reguillo proposes that everyday life is a privileged place, allowing us "to consider society in its complex plurality of symbols and interactions." It is the space where the structures of social reproduction and the structures of social innovation come together: "Assembled with the certainty that it will be repeated, everyday life is, above all, a fabric of times and spaces that guarantee the existence of the constituted order" (Reguillo 1998, 99). And yet everyday life is also the place where social actors detect periods of exception or the passing of the "constituted order" once they have sensed that the reliability of certain measures is in crisis.

The expanding cycles of capitalism offer the clearest demonstration of the notion that there is no such thing as essential everyday life. The modernization of Buenos Aires was indeed a reconfiguration of certainties and rituals. The logic underlying daily life in preindustrial times gave way to copious alternative narratives, although the city's reactive imaginaries tended to resist *acontecimientos,* "disruptive events that upset the continuum of everyday life" (Reguillo 1998, 101). Repetition and rupture order daily life, but a social praxis becomes legitimized as a habitus not through repetition, but because *it makes sense* to a collective subjectivity—in other words, when social actors grant it a subjective sense, which in turn can modulate the patterns of interpersonal interaction (Reguillo 1998, 101).

Mazzoleni remarks that something lies beyond the visible in the experience of empirical geography, something that "is difficult to represent with concepts and words because it belongs to a pre-logical field of experience, to non-verbal communication" (1993, 289). How is it that the polycentric experience of the city—with the body of each one of us moving through space—leads to the development of axes of subjective meaning that coexist with the invisible language of the imaginaries and their silent task of organizing everyday life and the grotesque body of the city? Where can we detect the tension between daily life as a site of the reproduction of social normality and daily life as a shelter for the *social exception*—for new venues and scenarios nurtured by the subjectivity and intersubjectivity of the city's social actors?

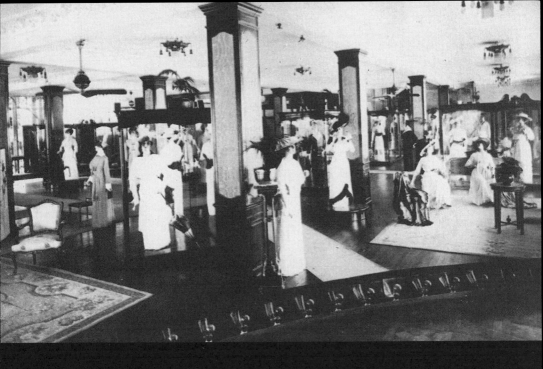

Urban

Ceremonies

1 THE JOCKEY
CLUB

IN *ANTES DEL NOVECIENTOS* (BEFORE
the 1900s), Adolfo Bioy identifies urban social spaces with the streets of
Buenos Aires: "I would look at a house and understand . . . what the life of
the family [that lived there] was like." He must have been very taken with
this game and relates a personal experience from when he was nine years
old, and he caught out a classmate who claimed to live at Belgrano 1045,
recognizing that "that number did not exist [and that] the Plaza de Montserrat occupies the place corresponding to it." Bioy continues: "They had us
write out . . . our name and address. I was able to see through the screen
made by his head and arm, behind which Forcadas was trying to hide what
he was writing on the paper. I read 86A Street, no. 59. In a fit of indignation
I told him: 'You're a snob, don't ever talk to me again!' He went quite red
and said nothing. We never spoke again. Poor Forcadas. He lived on a backstreet and was ashamed to admit it" (Bioy 1958, 11). For Bioy, then, urban
space is an identitary mechanism. Indeed, in the Buenos Aires of 1900, very
precise boundaries set apart the backstreet area of the barrio of Montserrat,
and Bioy put his finger right on them.

Urban space is in one sense a map, profusely imbued with the meanings and criteria of social stratification that become especially visible during times of disorder and confusion, when categories of classification and representation go into crisis. Modern cities are broad points where innumerable interpretative communities converge, where different forms of representation are constantly endeavoring to make the city comprehensible and map it cognitively. These cognitive maps configure criteria for understanding the social dimensions of space, identitary strategies, and degrees of sociocultural separation or proximity ("proxemic distance") arising from the "use man makes of space as a specialized product of culture" (Hall 1985, 6). But the city is also a place inviting diachronic slippage, a juxtaposition of pasts and presents—"frozen forms of energy fixed at different times in the past and around which the busy kinetic energy of the present swirls" (Pike 1996, 243). Every city, then, is a palimpsest created by many different hands at many different historical moments, although the fact that these moments coexist becomes much more evident and interactive during periods of transition.

The Buenos Aires of the earlier twentieth century was essentially in a state of constant transition. The never-ending transformations of its internal relations and its urban and cultural substance made its citizens into empirical semioticians, experts in observing, comparing, recognizing, and ordering their perceptions. Every inhabitant of the city was a potential agent of representation who organized the labyrinth of the near and the far, the self and the other, the private and the public: the city's streets, squares, and public spaces; its passageways, bodies, dwellings, lodging houses, mansions, and bordellos; its paradises and infernos.

This study is largely a symbolic undertaking, intended to recover the intersection of literary texts, photographs, letters, urban chronicles, and other writings left behind by inhabitants of Buenos Aires. But how should we approach the evolution of the city's material fabric between 1900 and 1930 and the many languages through which the city expressed itself? Henri Lefebvre would begin by warning us that, although "nature's space is not staged," capitalism partitions urban space and gives it, in contrast, an "active— operational or instrumental—role . . . as knowledge and action" (1995, 70). The Buenos Aires that we are examining was a spatial/symbolic site of tensions and representations, in contact and contradiction with one another, all expressing the intense class struggle that marked Argentina's first stage of modernization. We will begin, then, by examining Buenos Aires's representational complexity, as well as the meanings communicated by its buildings; the layout of its streets; the design of its public spaces and means of transportation; the rise and fall of real estate values in different areas of the city; and the locations of its ports, parks, residential areas, and commercial centers.

The representation of every city is articulated around rhetorical commonplaces, constructed on the basis of archetypes, and destroyed or forgotten in relation to new social paradigms and the rituals they generate. Compared to the Gran Aldea (Great Village), as it was called in colonial times, Buenos Aires seemed during the first period of industrialization to have just been founded. Everything still remained to be done, but the city's paradises and infernos first had to be designated. The official representation of Buenos Aires enjoyed great visibility because of the city's privileged discursive position compared to the nation's backward areas. The city would become the surface on which the elites of 1880 and the Centennial would write their most emblematic version of modernity. As if by a stroke of magic, a new and spectacular city emerged, destined politically and culturally to legitimate the Argentinean oligarchy.

The 1880 and Centennial elites used both political and urban discourses to emphasize Buenos Aires's Parisian character, especially in Barrio Norte, the oligarchy's residential area, where the buildings' architectural homogeneity, the urban planning, and the artistically designed use of space were instrumental in marking this area as superior to the city's other cultural geographies. This was especially true with respect to the untidy, awkward "other" Buenos Aires, growing from an organic demographic expansion. The elite's Parisian urban archetype was turned into an icon that stood for Buenos Aires as a whole, stripping all value from the disordered appearance of the grotesque city. Barrio Norte was equated with a place of enchantment, a landmark for the entire nation. However, the boundary between the two cities was a strange one. Although Barrio Norte was founded on economic exclusion, it was nonetheless able to enlist admirers and imprint its paradigms of urban uniformity on the national imaginaries in consort with the tight political monopoly of the Conservative Order. How did it win the cultural allegiance of groups who had no share in the symbolic capital of the elite, represented by a Parisian Buenos Aires?

The Jockey Club, its original building on Calle Florida an initiative of President Carlos Pellegrini (1890–92), provided a model for Buenos Aires's social life that was based on an apparent paradox—the possibility of being aristocratic and heterogeneous at the same time: "It will be an aristocratic club, if by aristocratic we understand what can only be understood in our times . . . a wide and open selection of members from society that includes . . . all educated and honorable men" (Newton and Newton 1966, 109). And indeed, the club's membership list embraced the city's heterogeneity, including both third-generation Argentineans and foreigners (English, Irish, Basque, Scottish, and German). But not just any foreigner who reached the port of Buenos Aires could be nominated for membership. Jockey Club members were all linked to farming and ranching—that is, to the great Argentinean landholdings at the turn of the twentieth century. Membership, in reality, restricted heterogeneity by class origin, and thanks to this constraint, the Jockey Club's members developed a closed esprit de corps, aware of belonging "to a superior political stratum composed of a particular kind of individual: an outstanding one" (Botana 1977, 73).

The modern elite thus replaced the patrician elite by consolidating its economic and cultural position. It became the intermediary for foreign (especially British) capital and brought the country into the new global order through the industrialization of farming and the exportation of cattle and agricultural products. With respect to culture, the members of the new elite became insatiable devourers of the sumptuous styles of modernity, imported from Paris, which they emulated so uncritically that the old patrician class was scandalized, viewing them as a noisy gang of Frenchified spendthrifts. I can find no better way to illuminate the rift between the two oligarchies— between the Gran Aldea and cosmopolitan Buenos Aires—than through the objects that furnished their respective sacred spaces. While the austere patrician realm of Jorge Luis Borges featured sabers and daguerreotypes of the Founding Fathers, the spaces of the modern oligarchy were marked by chinoiserie, mistresses, ostentatious stairways, and statues bought in Paris and loaded aboard transatlantic liners bound for Puerto Madero.

In fact, what drew the most attention in contemporary accounts of the spectacular ball held to inaugurate the Jockey Club, on 30 September 1897, were a Diana sculpted by Falguière and a staircase. Teófilo E. Díaz, writing for *El Diario* in Montevideo, was overwhelmed: "I have seen three giant staircases: one in the Paris Opera, another in the Berlin Art Gallery . . . and the staircase of the new Jockey Club mansion with green marble handrails" (qtd. in Korn 1983b, 55). The staircase would shine even more brightly because it was located in a sacred place: "'We could see the effect,' Pellegrini explains to Miguel Cané. 'It was immediate. With overcoat collars turned up, hats on their heads, and their pants rolled up, men . . . pushed through the inner door and came in off the street without any ado, took a few steps, and were struck dumb, slowly pulled off their hats and looked around in amazement'" (Newton and Newton 1966, 110). Miguel Cané and Carlos Pellegrini, these two prominent politicians from the new elite, were delighted to verify that the persons whom the architectural discourse of the Jockey Club staircase was meant to address—the people whom they expected to be struck dumb—were indeed taken aback so completely that they stood with their hats in their hands and their eyes wide open. These dazed spectators were not members of the club, but people off the street, from the *other* Argentina, as Pellegrini's letter to his colleague Miguel Cané goes on to explain: "As soon as [he saw the staircase], even the most brutish Indian was overcome and dominated, and all he wanted was for no one to realize he was out of place" (Newton and Newton 1966, 110–11).

Indeed, once they were inside the club, the inhabitants of the other Buenos Aires would be totally displaced by a transculturizing, sublimating experience that established the boundaries of exclusion and privilege in silence, with no need for words. That moment when the staircase held these outsiders spellbound was enough to induce acts of reverence—they removed their hats, as if entering a sacred place—while also evoking feelings of being overpowered, dominated in the context of a class struggle now being fought with capitols and symbolic capital. And if some of those whom Cané and Pellegrini sought to hold spellbound did not physically enter these golden halls, the extended arm of the press and its florid society columns, placed at the elites' disposal by modernity, would provide an opaque nation with imaginaries enlightened by the glitter of the club's galas.

It is further remarkable that Pellegrini's assessment is still firmly positioned within the discourse and ideological framework of the Frontera Sur, whose indigenous population Pellegrini equates with the mix of migrants in Buenos Aires.[1] Through the language of sophisticated stairways, Pellegrini achieves exactly what Julio Argentino Roca had accomplished with the weapons of genocide. The language might have changed, but the purpose remained the same. Pellegrini's intended recipients were no longer Pampas, Guaiminíos, Ranqueles, Guenaquenes, Araucanos, Vorogas, Pehuenches, Huilliches, or Manzaneros, but urban toughs and proletarians, mestizos/as, blacks and mulattos/as, and European immigrants fleeing from hunger.

Carlos Pellegrini and Miguel Cané—the first a president of the republic, the second a senator of the Conservative Order—were elite cultural agents caught in the act of producing new talismans. And as their private correspondence reveals, they went about their task after carefully pondering every detail, one in Buenos Aires, the other in Paris, where Cané took notes on improving service at the Jockey Club by comparing it to such exclusive Parisian clubs as the Cercle de la Mediterranée and L'Épatant. Even the choice of chef concerned Cané, who invited Pellegrini to imagine the level of sophistication at L'Épatant: "It has the best service I know, and there is an extraordinary profusion of servants." The mâitres d'hôtel, he remarks, wore especially tailored black tails, black knickerbockers, white stockings, and shoes. The valets de chambre wore dark brown or coffee-colored livery, while the valets de pied were clad in blue livery, white stockings, and shoes. All were spotlessly clean. Those valets de pied who did well were promoted to valets de chambre, and from among these the mâitres d'hôtel were chosen (Newton and Newton 1966, 108). Significantly, Cané's insistence that all personnel wear shoes would have ruled out practically the entire serving class in the Gran Aldea. He elaborates further: "Here ... at the Cercle de la Mediterranée, where 15 to 20 persons dine every day, they've been looking for and trying out chefs recommended [to them] ... for six months. They have one now ... who earns 600 francs a month, but he also has a *saucier*— someone to do the sauces—at 250 francs, [and] a *rôtisseur* at 300 francs" (Newton and Newton 1966, 108).

As Cané points out, L'Épatant wouldn't hire "a single servant below a particular height, and they have them submit to the *toise* [a measuring apparatus used for conscripts, etc.]. That's why you'll see quite a few well-formed, young, and very well-groomed *gaillards*" (Newton and Newton 1966, 108). He goes on: "You should be very concerned with the bearing of the service personnel at the club"—a concern that could be easily dispelled by strictly enforcing criteria for the mâitres d'hôtel, valets de chambre, valets de pied, and the chef. Cané adds that "short, fat, ill-formed servants" should also be avoided, "because service is an important matter; it conveys the essence of a club and *teaches* the habits of social culture to those who have none" (108; emphasis added). The social hierarchy of the connoisseur is clearly in evidence, as is the exalted discursive position of his teaching (Paris and the Jockey Club). Of course, these closed criteria implied discarding the entire workforce represented by the decrepit Fetente in Roberto Arlt's *El juguete rabioso* (Mad Toy, 1926) or *El jorobadito* (Little Hunchback, 1933), or by the protagonists of Elías Castelnuovo's *Vidas proletarias* (Proletarian Lives, 1934), as well as innumerable workers whose hands and arms had been mutilated as a result of the lack of safety measures in Buenos Aires's unregulated factories.

However, we should not think that this exclusion was categorical. We have already seen how the Jockey Club's socioarchitectural impact was calculated to induce a sense of captivation in the country's economic and ethnic others, who were defeated and dazzled by the material and symbolic codes of an elite with a mind so close to Paris that many of them maintained a family residence there. But Cané wanted to establish unambiguous proxemic distances in Buenos Aires, to specify who could cross the new social borders, whether defined by the Jockey Club or by the nation he and his class imagined and built. As a senator, Cané had, after all, been the force behind an antianarchist law that permitted the deportation of undesirable foreigners with just three days notice.

Why then did these two celebrated politicians and writers invest so much energy as diligent administrators and punctilious decorators? Cané's careful instructions are like those of a businessperson setting up a restaurant, but a businessperson under great stress, perhaps because he knows that this is not just any restaurant, but one that will stage refinement for the rest of the nation. In order to carry out their many self-imposed objectives, these new Founding Fathers would have to do everything themselves, from passing new national legislation to designing menus. As Cané explains, the menus of exclusive Parisian clubs were very particular. In a place like the Cercle de la Mediterranée, "it wouldn't occur to anyone to order two steaks topped with fried eggs as a main course, then a plate of chitterlings, and finish off with an omelet" (Newton and Newton 1966, 107). Gourmet gastronomy is one of the most class-ridden, pyramidal institutions in the entire service industry, and Cané wanted nothing more than to reproduce its structure in Buenos Aires. At the same time, he wanted to educate his own class so that its uncouthness and excesses would, with a bit of luck, be attenuated by the refinement of the great French bourgeoisie. Cané no doubt was gazing through a bifocal lens. He understood that he was speaking from the perspective of a country still afflicted by a "barbarism" that the sophistication of Paris was expected to correct, replacing it with proper manners and eliminating the uncouth behavior of an upstart elite unsure of the imported social graces it was both making its own and imposing on others. It was essential that the nation's habits not be a source of embarrassment when brought under the severe scrutiny of French etiquette.

Cané, who seemed to be losing sleep over the pile of dilemmas yet to be resolved, committed himself to leaving no detail to chance: "Think it over carefully," he advises Pellegrini, "and let me know if you are still keen on the idea of bringing in a chef; I think it better to look for a good one over there, one who already knows a bit about *our* habits" (Newton and Newton 1966, 107; emphasis added). "Here" and "there" define unsymmetrical cultural and identitary locations. While a standard has been set based on ex-centric metropolitan criteria, it still has to reach accommodation with the local. Why defer so much to Paris? And what does Cané mean when he says "our habits"? To begin with, "our" tradition will not stem from the popular gastronomy of Buenos Aires's immigrant population, predominantly associated with the culinary culture of poverty sustaining Italian, Spanish, Russian, Yiddish, and Polish rural immigrants: casseroles, stews, pizza, pasta, garlic soups, tripe, potages, and sausages—"macaroni soup, meat stew à la Garibaldi with carrots, onions, potatoes, parsley, and cloves" (Bucich 1962, 118). Such staples defined the carbohydrate-laden menus of the many inns and food stands along the *cammin vegio* (old road) in the immigrant district of La Boca, a gastronomic heteroglossia beginning to make itself forcefully known alongside the bastardized Spanish spoken in Argentina. Nor could the Jockey Club envisage "our" tradition as coming from the tables of the creole proletariat, with their "corn stew with bacon and maté . . . noodles fried in fat with maté" (Castelnuovo 1934, 44).

Something quite different would emerge from the chef's kitchens at the Jockey Club. This would be Cordon Bleu cuisine, approved by the cultivated palate of the French bourgeoisie, and now to be spread by the Argentinean elite not only "to the culture of the upper classes but also to the new middle classes" (Romero 1983, 16). This cuisine, more than ideal, was like a hand in

Urban Ceremonies and Social Distances

a glove, reinforcing gastronomically the power of the elite's ranching economy and its vast estates.

What kind of chef was finally taken on at the Jockey Club? The one who already knew "a bit about our habits" came from Mar del Plata, the exclusive summer resort of the elite. Thus, no matter how much Cané and Pellegrini strove to copy Paris cuisine, they could not, in the end, avoid negotiating between Paris and "our" ways, between purity and hybridity. It shouldn't be surprising, then, that Cané deemed it necessary to translate *saucier* for Pellegrini as "someone to do the sauces." In fact, Buenos Aires's proximity to Paris seemed to be characterized by dissymmetry and slippage.

And while it might be tempting, speaking of slippage, to conclude that Cané and Pellegrini had ended up in a traditionally feminine place—zealously controlling every household detail, cogitating obsessively on the servants' profiles and uniforms and the menu's contents—we should not imagine them sporting a kitchen apron. We must not lose sight of the fact that the Jockey Club was a strictly male preserve, a sanctuary for straitlaced men going about the serious business of putting the Nation House in order. Both Cané and Pellegrini were acting out of the conviction of their class's foundational role in a country where much still remained to be done.

At the time of the Centennial (1910), the elite were conscious of the importance of fixing their own scenario on the national stage, in order to display their symbolic capital. Thus, the Jockey Club served as an emblematic piece of the elite's mise-en-scène. *Caras y Caretas, La Nación,* and *La Prensa* would provide the means for spreading the new order of the modern elite's transculturation project to the public, with respect to cuisine, decor, and social functions. These mass publications served as bridges between the private and the public. Everything consumed, worn, and preferred within the elite's private sphere was transferred to the public domains by the *notas sociales* (society columns).

The Guatemalan Enrique Gómez Carrillo was the *modernista* chronicler par excellence of the Buenos Aires of the privileged and, without a doubt, also the most adept at negotiating the unstable professional space of the writer at the fin de siècle.[2] He was the perfect flaneur, observing the city and the new languages of modernity from a select, transitional discursive position "on the threshold of city life as of the bourgeois class. Neither has yet engulfed him; in neither is he at home" (Benjamin 1986, 156). In Gómez

Carrillo's *El encanto de Buenos Aires* (The Charm of Buenos Aires, 1921), modernist pure art is intertwined with consumer advertising. Carrillo caresses the new objects of consumption, conferring relevance and beauty on them like the best of window dressers. Nonetheless, his urban chronicles do not portray the social praxis of just any area of the city. In order to bestow style on the "the utilitarian vulgarity of money, . . . the 'gilt' (lexicon) of *modernismo* is applied to adorn the city" (Ramos 1989, 114).[3] Gómez Carrillo "adorns" Buenos Aires with Argentinean women walking lithely with "short, springy steps, swaying . . . with the *allure souple* of the latest fashions . . . as if they were paid by some great couturier *to make the world see* what the living poem of a beautifully worn toilette is like" (Gómez Carrillo 1921, 165; emphasis added).

Gómez Carrillo's chronicles, whether published in *Caras y Caretas* or *La Nación,* projected the *porteño* elite's desire to be looked upon as models of the new rituals that placed performers and their audiences in hierarchical order (Carrillo's women made the whole world *see*) and defined proxemic frontiers within the space of the city.[4] The swaying, studied gait of the women of the elite seems to inscribe a circle around them, a body bubble that shields them from physical proximity to the common breed of *porteños* and *porteñas:*

> Oh, daughters of Palermo, you delightful dark-haired girls who stroll like mannequins from the Rue de la Paix, what a pity you don't resolve to give up your habits . . . [and] walk along the streets in the center as well! As you know, those streets are reputed to be ugly. If you were to enliven them, they would become delightful. . . . How can you not understand that you are patriots, that you can best give prestige to your city by adorning it with the constant gift of your graces? How can you not feel enough compassion to cast the beauty of your eyes on the terrible prose of a town devoted to business and struggle, tensions and envy? (Gómez Carrillo 1921, 166)[5]

The urban chronicler here contributes to the process of semanticizing the new maps of Buenos Aires's cultural geography. He asks the "daughters of Palermo" to distribute "the constant gift" of their "graces" more widely and more fully, to show compassion for ordinary people "devoted to business and struggle, tensions and envy," to "enliven" streets "reputed to be ugly." He must have known this was an impossible request. The daughters of Palermo did not tread the streets of the center, but Calle Florida and the elegant gardens of Palermo. Proxemic distances are thus being recognized here, the preventive caution of Buenos Aires's exquisite beauties beginning to endorse invisible but zealously guarded frontiers in the city's imaginaries. These "daughters" adorn dioramas and sacred settings with their silky eyes and arrogant graces. It was not for nothing that Gómez Carrillo rightly compares them to "mannequins from the Rue de la Paix," strutting along the runway of the streets of Barrio Norte, showing off *ad honorem* the glamour of their class.

Why did Gómez Carrillo want the daughters of Palermo to venture into other sectors of Buenos Aires when it was vital to maintain the specificity and symbolic function of Barrio Norte as sublime? Calle Florida and Palermo would become expressly semanticized areas of privilege, marked by the comings and goings of the oligarchy's chic women. Their languorous strolling, therefore, would become a means of spreading cultural models—as well as political hierarchies—that every *porteño* would notice when walking along Florida. For cultural recruitment to be effective, in other words, the city's spaces had to be uneven, had to preserve proxemic markers and distances.

Countless texts at the close of the nineteenth century emphatically highlighted the unprecedented moment when women erupted into public space. However, there were public spaces of all kinds, some of which became stages for the display of the private. To produce differential spaces in Buenos Aires, Gómez Carrillo would turn to the marketing strategies of the fashion industry, mainly the concept of the feminine. The real runways for fetishizing the feminine—Gómez Carrillo's feminine worlds were linked to the women of the elite—were the society columns and the commercial advertising appearing in specialized periodicals, which exhibited mannequin bodies, festive women delicately dressed in luxurious objects of desire. In this respect, the chronicler did not exaggerate, for although he recorded the everydayness of the city, he managed to keep his focus on the exceptional. Thanks to Julio Ramos's remarkable study, we have learned that the most contradictory aspect of *modernismo*'s texture surfaces in chronicles like Gómez Carrillo's. As a stratagem of modernity, the chronicle must swing between the marketplace and art, between pure and applied art, between massive readership and the solitary artist. And what is necessary to join these two spheres together is a synthesis of the aesthetic of waste, which Gómez Carrillo pulls off to perfection: "Luxury . . . might be read as a subversion of the utilitar-

ianism of other discourses that are proper to capitalism (including information)" (Ramos 1989, 116).

I believe that the two-faced discursive position of *modernismo* might also
be understood through a close examination of how it worked in relation to
the production of urban space. Seen from this perspective, *modernista* aesthetics would provide a salve for the bourgeoisie's anxiety over differential
spaces. The city of luxury is an exceedingly differential space. Given that
modernista aesthetics proposed progressively higher paradises, more inaccessible and further removed from the basic rituals and habitats of the masses,
its models of the world were a perfect fit for the semantics of the capitalist
economy: only the differentiated is profitable. In Buenos Aires, differential
spaces were *produced* through social distinction and fashion, which are especially associated with the feminine. For this reason, Gómez Carrillo's
writing cannot allude to just any women. Only aristocratic women can se-
manticize urban geography and stigmatize the vulgar, ugly, dangerous spaces
of the center, inhabited by men degraded by the mercantilism of money,
strained by the effort of their muscles, soaked by the sweat of their labor, and
not smelling too good either. This imaginary concludes that the feminine
space of the city is located in the society galas held at the Teatro Colón,
where the daughters of the elite wore glamorous diamond tiaras, or in the
parks, where they moved "with swans . . . [and] smiles . . . [where] everything is light as air [and] has a soft touch of artificiality . . . where every
detail is delicate, almost fragile" (Gómez Carrillo 1921, 166). The signifier
woman is thus completely dissociated from work and attached instead to
leisure, to an excess of artifice and sumptuous consumption—the cultural
trademarks of the new elite. It is not hard, then, to foresee the unfailing
tribulations that were the lot of working women, who, excluded from the
gossamer of silks and satins, nonetheless desperately tried to fit into identitary
molds of femininity. During the Belle Époque, aristocratic women such as
Magdalena Ortiz Basualdo de Becú (figure 2), Eugenia Huici de Errázurriz,
Rosita Alcorta, and Victoria Ocampo were admired as much for their affiliation to haute couture as for their intellectual sophistication. After spending
much time in their Paris residences, "they had been ordained to select and
supervise what others ordered from dressmakers like Worth, Pauin, Doucet,
and Poiret" (Moreira 1992, 180). But by 1914, several important Paris fashion

houses (Astesiano, Henriette, Jean et André, Palau, Tomé, Madame Suzanne) had opened *maisons* in Buenos Aires, in the same areas favored by the elite.

While Domingo F. Sarmiento wanted a homogenous country leveled by public education, Pellegrini and Cané resorted to monumental staircases, slim servants, and classes taught by Bavarian fencing masters to place high culture and the languages of social distinction at the top of a hierarchical scale. Their emphasis, therefore, was not exactly on the popular classes' access to public education; after all, they saw Sarmiento's dreams as the root of a vast liberal error, with alarming consequences. While 1884's Bill 1420, concerning public and universal education, was strengthened by the University Reform Act of 1911 and further broadened under Hipólito Yrigoyen, opening "university faculties and administrations, as well as the liberal professions and, hence, government services to greater middle class participation" (McGee Deutsch 1993, 48), the elites of 1880 and the Centennial were more excited by spectacle, by promoting their illuminated mansions, the iridescence of their velvets and the brilliance of their family jewels, than by cultivating Argentina's intellectual lights. The effect of this emphasis on spectacle was pure gestalt, like window dressing: the spaces and objects of privilege were illuminated, while the other Buenos Aires and the other Argentinas sat in the dark, against the light, in the background. Perhaps that is why all representations of these other Buenos Aires—whether Borges's Palermo, Gálvez's La Boca, or the tango's *arrabal*—are seen by the dim light of streetlamps or *a media luz* (in the half light), to use an expression from tango itself.[6]

2 PALACES AND
RESIDENCES

WHEN THE OLIGARCHY MOVED FROM
the southern district of Catedral Sur to Barrio Norte, it unveiled the architectural style most associated with it: the *petits hôtels* or palaces in the French
manner, which required much more space than regularly sized lots, sometimes occupying as much as half or even a full city block (Scobie 1974, 132).
The *petits hôtels* were in sharp contrast with the rest of the city, notoriously
scarred by dwellings characterized by severe overcrowding and promiscuity.
While the patrician elite had drawn its legitimacy from swords, uniforms,
and war, the new generation relied on society galas, but required settings
appropriate to that purpose. Among these grand settings were the Pereda
Palace (Arroyo 1130) (figure 3); the Alzaga Unzué Palace (Cerrito 1430);
the Duhau Residence (Avenida Alvear 1671); the Unzué de Casares Residence
(Avenida Alvear 1345); the Center for National Culture (Avenida Alvear
and Rodríguez Peña); the Center for the National Academies (Avenida
Alvear and Rodríguez Peña); the Alvear Palace Hotel, now the Jockey Club
(Avenida Alvear y Chacabuco); and the Anchorena Palace (Avenida Alvear

and Montevideo), which was offered to President Marcelo T. de Alvear in 1922 and, through one of the turns of political life, eventually became the residence of an illegitimate daughter of a rancher from the pampas—María Eva Duarte de Perón. If the repetition of street names here makes us feel we are walking in circles, this impression is accurate. The buildings are aligned with each other, set close together along Avenida Alvear and Plaza Pelle-grini, a triangular plaza in the space between two square blocks of land set at 45 degrees to each other. Plaza Pellegrini, originally part of a subdivision of small farms established by city founder Don Juan de Garay (Calcagno et al. 1992, 56), and shaped by angles preventing the rapid flow of traffic, lies beyond the cultural time and space of the modern city. In other words, it is an exclusive space that deliberately evades the language of the mass city.

The significance of *Caras y Caretas'* role as an intermediary between middle-class and proletarian readers, and the new rituals and ceremonies of the Argentinean elite, cannot be overemphasized. Unlike the unstable pub-lications of marginal social actors, *Caras y Caretas* stroked urban imaginaries weekly, like a punctual clock—one of the new certainties introduced by modernity. In its *notas sociales* for 10 January 1920, a chronicler writing under the pseudonym "La Dama Duende" (Lady Imp) reported on the mar-riage ceremony of Miss Josefina Errázuriz Alvear, held at "the bride's family mansion, a sumptuous palace . . . whose austere architecture evokes the splendors of the court of King Louis": "Inside the Errázurriz palace . . . the aristocratic crowds mill around. . . . The diaphanous laces, the dark and brightly colored soft silks, the translucent pearls, the sparkling diamonds, and, above all, the dreamy flowers, covering tables and consoles, blend their beauty into a harmony of suggestive enchantment. . . . The solemn tones of the orchestra throb. . . . Now the snow-white silhouette of the bride, her graceful head veiled in a film of tulle, crosses the gallery."[1] Like one of Rubén Darío's butterflies, La Dama Duende is yet another *modernista* who flits from silks and flowers to the music of the orchestra, describing the palace furnishings in detail in the course of her flight: "The vase of fine Venetian crystal, antique porcelain chimeras from China, multicolored stan-dards once brandished by victorious regiments in Flanders, the chest that held the riches of some historic great house in Burgos, and the forged railing . . . from a mansion in Salamanca on whose bars is displayed the holy invo-cation: *Ave Maria, Gratia Plena.*"

Hungry for the past as an escape from modernity, La Dama Duende dismantles the lordly houses of the Spanish Empire and bestows their adornments on the tawdry city of Buenos Aires. In the midst of the symbolic capital of an ostentatiously secular elite, the chronicler places the setting under the vigilant eye of the Catholic Church, which was never to withdraw from the Argentinean political scene. In the syntax of the society column, the maternal authoritarianism of Josefina Alvear de Errázurriz figures alongside the severe, persuasive word of the priest, a detail that social historian José Moya would read as a resurgence of Hispanism, which provided the nationalism of Manuel Ugarte and Enrique Larreta with the spirituality necessary to oppose "the mediocrity of Anglo-Saxon utilitarian democracy" (Moya 1998, 359).[2] The palace celebration thereby combines the ostentation of luxury with a certain restraint: the polychromatic lasciviousness of red and white roses, pale gladioli, and haughty orchids with the reserve of aristocratic guests; men in tails who talk about business in British English and about love in French with sober Spanish coats of arms and their delicate corollas. The chronicler links the "subtle charm of works of art of different periods and styles" with the charm of the gathering: "The arrogant figure of María Luisa Constanzó . . . the slender, fine silhouettes of Mercedes Ortiz de Basualdo [and] Beatriz Gallardo, the Misses Flores Pirán, Muñiz Livingston, . . . Christophersen, and so many others . . . are the principal charm of the lively reception."

The cultural recruitment of Buenos Aires's citizens began by venturing into the city's most lucrative areas: gendered spaces and liaisons founded on desire. Female figures in the palaces are displayed as part of the decor, property, and symbolic capital of the elite. The women are distinguished and exquisite, set in arrogant gestures and poses, static signifiers of immutable privilege. As it did with its fenced-in estates and branded cattle, the oligarchy put its mark on its women—a gesture not without cause.[3] And not in vain: according to Eugenio Cambaceres's xenophobic descriptions in *En la sangre* (In the Blood, 1887), the specter of exogamy affected the minds and inflamed the insatiable bodies of the upstarts arriving in Puerto Madero.

Although La Dama Duende highlighted the women's haughtiness, the term most frequently used to describe them was *encanto* (charm). Gómez Carrillo's *El encanto de Buenos Aires* had set that coin rolling through the city's imaginaries, and it subsequently spread everywhere, especially in the cosmetic industry. On 19 July 1919, for example, Madame Charlotte Rouvier explained in *Caras y Caretas* that "the charm of a face should not vary even with the passing of the years, but you need to preserve it." *Modernismo* wove strands of gold from this word. Beginning at the sumptuous balconies along Avenida Alvear, these strands would enter the pores of the cultural life of Buenos Aires and infiltrate the dirt and desperation of the dark tenements in La Boca, like strands of cruelty circulating throughout such contrasting areas of the city. Every week, alongside the urban chronicles—"Notas del tranvía" (Notes from a Tram), "Los estrenos cinematográficos" (New Films), "Ejercicios físicos de la mujer" (Physical Exercises for Women), or "Campaña en defensa de la salud pública" (Public Health Campaign)—*Caras y Caretas* also published fairy tales—attached, significantly, to the society columns. To the right of the report on the wedding at the Errázuriz-Alvear palace, for example, Luis María Jordán locates readers in the heady ages of magic, the spaces allowing escape from the coarseness of everyday life: "There was once a king . . . who lived in a magnificent court surrounded by the pomp, ceremony, and splendor of his palaces." The resemblance between the king in the fairy tale and the gentlemen in Buenos Aires's palaces is clear: "He had princes who fawned on him . . . women who loved him for his beauty or his power, poets who wrote rounded quatrains and sonorous couplets in his honor, ships that brought him men and jewelry from all corners of the earth."

The possessions of Jordán's king also parallel those of the Buenos Aires elite, who were celebrated in panegyrics such as Rubén Darío's "In Memoriam: Bartolomé Mitre" (Paris, 1906), a pompous paean for the president of Argentina (1862–68), who also owned *La Nación:* "Happy . . . patriarch, wreathed in laurel, who . . . sees the towers rise . . . and amidst great sights the future dawn" (Darío 1977, 329–31). Like Jordán's *modernista* king, those in the *porteño* palaces also have ships at their disposal to bring them men and jewelry—men from all over Europe to labor in their factories, and jewelry for their wives and lovers. The "once upon a time" formula removes the reader from the everyday crassness of tramway robberies, vending machines, street noises, and the fashionable Swedish exercise that even Emma Zunz, the eponymous character of a Jorge Luis Borges story, practiced with her friends. Dreamy tales were not needed to find enchantment in Buenos Aires. The photos in the *notas sociales* confused the daughters of the Argentinean oligarchy with Darío's princesses and the queens of the European royal families, whose steps were closely followed in *Caras y Caretas,* although it was not necessary to go very far to touch the glamour of nobility: Buenos Aires's palaces played host to the Infanta Isabel, the Duke of Windsor, the Maharaja of Kapurtala, Humberto of Savoy, and Louis Ferdinand of Hohenzollern (Moreira 1992, 178).

Through such an effective cultural network, the oligarchy created sensually textured spaces that were deliberately at odds with the massive, inescapable world of industry and cement. Every time their palaces were opened, allowing society columnists to display their happiness and "aesthetic disposition," their "capacity to neutralize the ordinary urgencies and to bracket off practical ends, a durable inclination and aptitude for practice without function" (Bourdieu 1996, 54), the worlds of the elite cast spells of exclusivity, leisure, and extravagant fantasy. Such an imaginary disrupted the conventional separation of everyday urban life and literary imaginaries. The glamour of the aesthetic was transferred to the mass-circulation press, which turned the magic of elite ceremonies into reality. Their synchronic immediacy superimposed a time of enchantment on the time of work. Richard Sennett contends that "in the modern capital the relentless continuity of its ceremonial fabric seemed insulated from equally vast scenes elsewhere in the London of poverty and social distress" (1994, 319). In Buenos Aires, however, the dream industry brought fairy tales to life in the newspapers alongside the classifieds, where work was offered and sought, in the midst of a city stricken by the hunger resulting from countless economic crises, by the brutality of the bordellos, and by the burden of piecework.

Seen from the outside, the economic excess of the palaces' unusual architectural features—ornamentation, corbels, molding, turrets, ironwork, dormers, pilasters and pilastered window openings, cornices and balustrades, curved surfaces, lintels, and mansard roofs—provided an adept means of seizing the attention of passersby. Inside the palaces were oak paneling, Chippendale staircases, marble from Carrara and Portoro, oak from Slovenia, great pieces of porcelain, Baccarat crystal, tapestries, sculptures and statues, and chandeliers. In "Vida moderna" (Modern Life, 1899), Eduardo Wilde wrote from the provinces to a friend: "Do you know why I'm here? To get away from home where I couldn't take a step without cracking my skull against some work of art or other. The living room looked like a bazaar, so did the anteroom, and let's not talk about the study! . . . The twenty bedrooms . . . the corridors and even the kitchen were jam-packed. . . . The light couldn't get in because of the drapery. . . . The air couldn't circulate for folding screens, statues, vases, and every other blessed thing" (1899, 217). The accumulation of objects must have struck a particular contrast for this *costumbrista* writer, who was also a keen observer of the city's sordid tenement buildings.[4] His untimely flight to the open air of the pampas perhaps allows us to infer that Wilde was claustrophobic, but we might also recognize that a place like the one he describes could easily trigger such symptoms in anyone. "Vida moderna" contemplates the countryside as a place where the relationships of intimacy and premodern (paternalistic) contact with the local, long disappeared from the city's palaces, are still preserved: "At last I am alone with my servant and the cook, a hefty woman from the town, who knows all about politics and creole cakes" (Wilde 1899, 213). The objects that have turned the family home into a cosmopolitan museum, showing off the acquisitive power of the oligarchy, have come between Wilde and his urban habitat. Living space had become theatrical, fit for a stage, ready for the grand society scene. Even the identity of its inhabitants was in danger of disappearing: "Not so long ago, in the house of another friend, a child who had gone there with his mother was lost. . . . The poor child had got himself into a corner that he couldn't escape because his way was blocked by a chiffonier, two folding screens, and an amphora from who knows where, the Twelve Peers of France, eight crusading knights, . . . and a life-sized bronze of Demosthenes" (Wilde 1899, 221–22).

Rubén Darío must have had the palaces of the elite in mind when he both repudiated and flattered the ostentatious accumulation "of wealth and marvelous works of art" (1986, 74) in "El rey burgués" (The Bourgeois King). Darío lived in Buenos Aires from August 1893 until December 1898, when *La Nación* sent him to Spain and then to Paris, where he met Gómez Carrillo. In 1896, *La Nación* threw him a spectacular banquet. He had just published the *Oda a Mitre* (Ode to Mitre), dedicated to the owner of his most important source of employment, and in 1912, another reception was held in his honor. It may thus be assumed that he was quite familiar with all the paraphernalia of the aristocratic, bourgeois kings of Buenos Aires: "Good taste. He ascended a stairway lined by alabaster and smaragdite columns. . . . Refinement . . . Japonerie! Chinoiserie! . . . Bronze chimeras . . . lacquer from Kyoto encrusted with the leaves and branches of great flora . . . rare fans, like butterflies, on the walls . . . yellow silk costumes . . . centuries-old porcelain. . . . Moreover, there was a Greek room filled with marbles: deities, muses, nymphs, and satyrs; [there was] a room from the age of gallantry with paintings by the great Watteau and Chardin; [there were] two, three, four, so many different rooms!" (1986, 74).

The aesthetics of *modernismo* and art nouveau were adopted by the new elites with respect to three sociocultural fields at odds with conventional ways: architecture, interior decor, and feminine adornment. When Wilde asserted that the light could not get in and the air could not circulate, he was merely describing the semiotics of a claustrophiliac aesthetics, underlying a utopia based on isolation and exclusion. Within the same cultural consortium/language, *modernista* architecture sought to increase the distance between the interior of the house and the world outside. It used heavy curtaining, which served to deaden the noise from the street, soften the light, and lend texture to a muffled and melodious interior. Julián Martel's *La Bolsa* (The Stock Exchange, 1891), perhaps the first text to endorse this imaginary of the semiotics of the interior and its xenophobic distances, describes another palace on the Avenida Alvear: "Those Aubusson carpets . . . those walls swathed in pale pink silk like a jewelry box; that thick curtaining . . . those great mirrors, with their jardinières . . . filled with flowers, as if extending a prize to the beauties trying to see themselves in the beveled glass" (1979, 63). Countless examples from literature, newspapers, serial novels, photographs, and films made Buenos Aires familiar with the syntax of glamour. In Martel's palace, the mirrors focus attention on the interior, muffled by silks and carpets, turning away from the bustle of the streets.

Ramos cites María Luisa Bastos to explain how the second phase of literary *modernismo* shaped the taste of the bourgeois kings, even as it railed against the bourgeois kingdoms of industrialization (1989, 116). Nevertheless, writers had no option but to depend on these kings for employment. They understood that once they were banished to anonymity, they would suffer the same economic vulnerability as the masses. The artist who spoke of privilege from its periphery would soon discover, not without pain, that the restricted, exclusive maps of social patronage had irreversibly expired. The exclusivity of art was available only to members of the one class with sufficient power of acquisition—to the Güells, who hired Antoní Gaudí, or to the Mitres, who hired the pens of Darío and Gómez Carrillo. However, the Argentinean oligarchy must have made the professional ambiguity of *modernista* writers a little bit more tolerable, by combining new money with the older symbols of privilege. The Argentinean oligarchy was always situated halfway between the ancien régime, with which it was associated through its country estates, and the bourgeoisie, to which it was economically joined as an agent of industry. Between the country estate and industry, the elite were both aristocratic and bourgeois, politically conservative and culturally liberal, cosmopolitan, urban, and landowning. They lived on their estates in Buenos Aires and Paris and never failed to invoke the authority of the Church, even if they were the ones responsible for the secular Act of Universal Education. In Buenos Aires, the landowner Celedonio Pereda commissioned the Catalan painter José María Sert, who had decorated the Rockefeller Center (1933), to endow his palace with spectacular ceilings. The landowner's dinner guests could then admire internationally renowned art each time they looked up with forks in their hands. In this way—and in any other way they could—the Peredas of Buenos Aires made sure they were close to the Rockefellers.

Like a common language, luxury drew cosmopolitan elites together, while also internalizing global culture. The Argentinean elite was an economic oligarchy and an agent of cultural mediation that played its favorite game: turning Buenos Aires into Paris, or perhaps Manhattan. As Noé Jitrik points out, one of *modernismo*'s key features was the exploitation of a subjectivity focused on showing not "the images of things but the impressions they leave . . . a search that leads to . . . the strange, as in the unusual . . . the infrequent, the aristocratic" (1978, 7–6). In this way, *modernismo* reasserted the criteria of dissimilarity, genius, and talent—all indispensable for separating the elect from the anonymous and the elite from the multitude. Catalan *modernismo* inspired works in Buenos Aires that also served as manifestos, such as the Confitería del Molino (The Windmill Café), the Barolo building (at Santa Fe and Callao), and the Fevre and Basset Company (at Figueroa Alcorta and Ocampo). Its prime mover between 1906 and 1916 was Julián J. García Núñez, a student of Domènech i Montaner and Antoní Gaudí.

The urban historian José María Peña points to *Caras y Caretas* as a promoter of art nouveau in Buenos Aires because of the magazine's cosmopolitan avidity for new aesthetic languages.[5] Beginning with the cover of its first issue (1898), entitled "Números calendarios" (Calendar Numbers), featuring prints by the Spaniard Castro Rivera, the magazine's illustrations consistently connected popular culture with art nouveau. Not all of Buenos Aires, however, was enamored of the movement: "According to some, it is the most refined blooming of aesthetic sensibility; according to others, it is only a ridiculous style characterized by an extreme lack of taste, calling attention to itself by its vulgarity and the irregular extravagance of its lines" (Peña 1992, 233). Without going quite so far, one caustic detractor of the Francophile oligarchy and their well-known and pitiless dislike of the premodern city, Jorge Luis Borges, attacked this globalized taste in *Evaristo Carriego* (1930). Concerning art nouveau's tentacular encroachment on the city's local, organic cultures, he remarked, "Palermo was heading for silliness in a hurry: the dreaded art nouveau buildings were springing up like swollen flowers even in the swamps" (1974, 130).

At the other end of the scale, Armando Discépolo's comedy *El movimiento continuo* (Perpetual Motion, 1916) describes a typical proletarian room in which immigrants mingle with "white clothing and ironing boards. . . . A sewing machine and two or three opera prints. A portrait of Alfonso XIII." Out of pure excitement, the tenement's residents speculate on how they will spend their earnings once their perpetual motion machine is a success. The power of the examples coming from above, as well as the parody of resistance coming from below, may be appreciated in their dream of owning their home:

> PEPA: I'd like a cottage with unplastered walls . . . and a crowd of little ducks like painted yellow cotton wool; then a chicken coop with laying hens and a little Catalan rooster. . . .
>
> ASTRADA: Nonsense! . . . You ask for fluffy ducks instead of flamingos, pelicans, swans from Australia or ostriches from Africa, and a pair of elephants for amusement. . . . Aim higher! . . . Ask for more! . . . Ask for a palace with modern furniture.
>
> CASTAÑEDA: That's the way! . . . Modern Styl. A living room in Italian walnut; a bedroom in hardwood; olivewood marquetry; a railway-style writing desk; rugs from Smyrna; tapestries, paintings, chandeliers, planters, and the rest. (Discépolo 1987b, 317)

For their own home, the characters combine "Modern Styl" with an exotic *modernista* inventory and art nouveau decor, although the graceful flamingos and the bulky elephants are a bit over the top. I wish to emphasize, however, that the scenography of the popular theater, like the newspapers, contributed greatly to familiarizing audiences with the interiors of mansions, apartments, clubs, professional offices, summer villas, and *garçonières*.[6] Some stage directions are sketchy in this regard ("a luxuriously appointed room with divans, sofas, mirrors, piano, large chandelier in the center" [Dolard and Rillo 1922; *El amor que no se vende* (Love Not for Sale)]), while others are so detailed that the author seems to be pulling our leg: "The upholstery on magnificent carved cherry and walnut furniture is by Aubusson. The folding screen . . . with figures faded by its patina is a genuine Coromandel, and the large tapestry . . . is one of those pieces of work that established the reputation of the artistic industries of Bauvais. In a corner, its flowing lines standing out against the dark tone of the cherrywood base, . . . may be seen a white marble nude. . . . [There is] a large fireplace . . . a portrait of Mr. Helguera attributed to Turmer and a pastiche of Felisa by Sigali" (Saldías 1927, 2; *Primavera en otoño* [Spring in Autumn]). Such crossovers between high and low culture must have been so numerous and widespread that many stage directions could take for granted that the director would know what was meant: "Hall or elegant entranceway. . . . Appropriate furniture" (Gutiérrez and Alberti 1927, 1; *Yo me hago el loco* [I Pretend to be Crazy]); "A room with expensive furniture, upholstery to match the color of the carpet" (Tabanillo 1927, 3; *La moral del gringo* [Italian Morality]).

It was all the same anyway. The mansions of the elite were as much stage settings as were the sets designed for the popular theater. Rigid codes of social distinction and specialization gradually penetrated the daily habits of the Buenos Aires elite. In *Prometeo y compañía*, a character caught in the motion of cultures in transition explains that in his house in Buenos Aires, "the meal took two hours because the servant wouldn't let me use the silverware I had in my hand but only the special pieces intended for each dish" (Wilde 1899, 217). By contrast, on his Río Cuarto ranch, he had eaten "olives with a spoon because he wanted to [and paid no attention to] silverware for fish, for asparagus, for oysters, for salads and desserts, or to centerpieces that would not allow me to see the people opposite, or different-colored glasses. . . . [There] anything goes" (214). He complains about new social rituals such as Christmas cards and the rigid control exercised over the time allowed for social interaction, a process discussed by Beatriz González Stephan (1995) regarding

Manuel Antonio Carreño's *Manual de urbanidad y buenas costumbres* (Manual of Etiquette and Good Manners, 1854).

A keen awareness of both body and mind must have been required to organize the cognitive maps of the labyrinthine, confusing palace interiors. They were claustrophiliac, darkened spaces, crammed with objects and divided by screens doubtless in the Japanese style: "One night as I was going into my study in the dark I almost put out an eye on a bust of Gladstone; on another occasion Venus de Milo gave me a bruise that's still painful," complains Wilde's narrator (1899, 218). Far worse, however, was to work in such places, as Spanish maidservants discovered to their cost:

> There were scenes between [the servants] and the ornaments all the time.
> "Madam," said the servant, "Francisco has broken one of Phydias's fingers."
> "How did he do that?"
> "That Phydias is very hard to dust, Madam."
> And the bust of Praxiteles turned up without a nose. Francisco had brought the bust down with one sweep of the feather duster. . . . A large porcelain elephant carrying a tower on its back loses its trunk once a week; fortunately it's stuck back on with glue.

Although Wilde admits, "I'd like to see you clean a house like that," he doesn't hesitate to add: "I've spent the last few years taking care of vases, curtains, paintings, clocks, candelabras, bronzes, and marbles and throwing Spaniards into the street with their feather duster and all their belongings so they can go break their own grandmothers' noses" (1899, 220–22).

Article 17 of the Ordinance Regulating Domestic Service (1887) required domestic employees to answer "for losses and damages suffered through their fault by the employer." Article 19 adds, "The employer may discount from his servant's wage the value of damages and losses caused by the servant's fault" (Oficina de Servicio Doméstico 1877, 7–8). Given the high cost of the palace's furniture and works of art, Wilde's servant expected to be dismissed for being unable to assume responsibility for breakages caused with his feather duster. The new discourse framed around the home fetishized the object, placing so much value on its status and care that domestic employment depended on it. In fact, between the servants and their labor stood a work of art accorded more social value than either of them. The new urban culture required profound efforts of adjustment from the inhabitants of the modern city and, as in the bourgeois king's palace, demanded constant refinements to sensorial maps. Residents and workers had to tread carefully. They had to look out for obstacles suddenly stuck out in their path in spaces that had so many centers and focal points that their attention was constantly being drawn in various directions at once. Such a sculptural treatment of interior and exterior spaces did not come about by chance; its dramatic profile was central to the transformation of elite residences into settings for the national stage.

What can we read from the architectural plans of Buenos Aires's palaces? In my view, they enact a perfect spatialization of the oligarchy's outlook of the world. In the Gran Aldea, the colonial house had been shared by servants and masters who mingled in the paternalistic social space of the patrician order. In the shift from the colonial house to the typical residence of the Francophile elite, the three central patios—with their columned galleries, orange blossoms, ferns, and cisterns—were sacrificed. Class division in the colonial house, of course, had certainly been unmistakable: the first patio contained a receiving room and bedrooms for the adults, the second rooms for the children, and the third the kitchen and servants' quarters. But thanks to the continuity of open space in the three patios, which were all on the same level, noises from the kitchen combined with noises from the children's games and from the living room. By contrast, the palaces of the new elite, "of several floors, with the kitchens in the basement, changed the internal order of every home . . . at the same time as servants had to attend on apartments that were spaced widely apart" (Carretero 1974, 82). However it is considered, this architectural design began by placing more space, more floors, more height and breadth between the classes.

The mansions' floor plans featured excessively large reception halls "that disconcerted members of the previous generation, accustomed as they were to being treated and received more intimately" (Carretero 1974, 83). These halls ended in an imposing staircase leading to the more inaccessible private rooms on the second and third floors, thereby erecting a partition that increased the proxemic distance between the street and the intimate spaces of the family. Analyzing the sexualization of space in the houses of the *modernistas* Moller and Müller, Beatriz Colomina concludes that the bedrooms were a "threshold of the private, the secret . . . where sexuality is hidden away," which explains why their decor was given over to feminine tastes. On the other hand, the houses' social spaces, such as the library, were masculine ones: "The leather sofas, the desks, the chimney, the mirrors represent a 'public space' within the house—the office or the club invading the interior" (Colomina 1992, 81). Therefore, the idea of the "public" was accepted only when mediated by the codes of exclusion practiced in the club or the professional office. Bourgeois individualism and its concept of intimacy, which strictly and obsessively negated any sort of collectivism, were materialized in the gendered language of architecture. Paul Rodaway remarks that interpersonal contact is always reduced in developed cultures, where "public spaces are large and open, such as large hotel foyers, roomy airport lounges, broad corridors in buildings, boulevards and large open areas in public parks" (1994, 59–60).

The archetypical bourgeois house of the Centennial Generation adopted these spatial languages, bureaucratizing interpersonal relations and compartmentalizing the social groups interacting inside the mansion. Each level of the house functioned as a separate world. The servants frequented the upper floors only for the time strictly necessary for cleaning them. In a word, spatial/identitary distances in the domestic world of privileged Buenos Aires began to echo the proxemic separations that the Conservative Order imposed on the public domain. There was no possibility of confusion, as Armando Discépolo's *Babilonia* (1925) clearly illustrates. This grotesque farce takes place in the kitchen and servants' quarters in the basement of a mansion: "an underground factory for servants where deformity is confirmed—and fixed —under the employers' surveillance: seen from above [the servants] seem tired and humiliated" (Discépolo 1996, 204).[7] At ten-thirty on a winter's night, the servants are waiting exasperatedly in the basement kitchen for the leisurely gathering upstairs to finish. One of them comments, "Be patient. Tonight's an exception, a banquet." A maid from Madrid protests, "It's daft having to wait until they've finished before we can eat" (165). In reply, the German chauffeur reminds her she is sacrificing the most important period of her life: "She's stuck down here wasting away her youth that'll never come back and she'll be sorry for it later . . . when she can't be a servant no more and then she'll cry." To leave the basement would be an uncertain step—"I'm scared of falling into a void," one of the servants remarks—because the kitchen is in fact the only identitary space they have, even though their life in the basement is hardly a desirable one: "They've got their hands all over you down here and would as soon spit on you. We all wallow in the mud. We all boil in dirty water" (199). In fact, the workers' identity is shaped by the space they occupy within the three structures of consumption attributed to the configuration of bourgeois identity: "food, culture and presentation (clothing, beauty care, toiletries, domestic servants)" (Bourdieu 1996, 184).

The impotence of the servants in *Babilonia* is treated sensorially by Discépolo. They are confined to a space below ground, where the air from the world above, especially for those who do not go upstairs to work, is only accessible when the door to the stairs is opened, as if it were a hatch. The basement is narrow and low, stacked with shelves loaded with demijohns, boxes, and tins, which visually reduce the amount of space above still further —where the air should be and where an opening is most needed. The benches and chairs have short legs, on account of the low ceiling, and—to add even greater discomfort—the oven and its burners raise the temperature, which confinement also increases. All this contributes to the anxiety prompted by claustrophobia. The space is narrow and asphyxiating, made smaller still by the accumulation of objects and the constant comings and goings of eleven servants who bump into each other, argue, and fight while they work. The basement's entire space is focused on work completed or yet to be completed. Upstairs, dinner is not over, and the servants continue to wait expectantly to serve the hot desserts and take up the liqueurs. The inescapable acoustic and visual perceptions of oppression and irritability derive from multiple sources and heighten the inevitability of confrontation among the basement's inhabitants. This group embodies proletarian Buenos Aires, its cultural heterogeneity and its Babylonian linguistic mosaic. Crowded together and exhausted from a long day (sixteen hours of continuous work for one "exceptional" night), uncomfortable because of the confined space, the kitchen's unbearable heat, and the frustratingly long wait to eat, why wouldn't the servants' stress turn into irritation with each other? Edward Hall would certainly have anticipated such a conclusion (1985, 46), based on John Calhoun's experiments, which demonstrated that the biochemistry of bodies in close quarters can lead to aggressive and unbalanced behavior, even trigger miscarriages and infant mortality. As we will see with respect to the *conventillos* (tenement buildings), communications in the basement, strained by overcrowding, inclined toward an interpersonal dynamic based so much on violence and irritability that any chance to build up social laterality—empathy among people sharing similar experiences—was severely compromised.

Spatial polarization in the residences of the elite consigned the colonial city to the past. In addition to creating obstacles to the imagination, and to the search for more egalitarian social and spatial utopias, the semiotic structure of the elites' residences, in my view, was instrumental in reconfiguring domestic interpersonal relations. Indeed, the radical realignment of society introduced by social modernity was regulated by an impressive array of means in many spheres of public and political life—including the floor plans of mansions, which gave material form to the internal frontiers the elite sought for Buenos Aires and for the rest of the country. With this end in mind, the oligarchy resorted to stairways and stories; degrees of accessibility; the sociophysical partitioning of groups and their circulation, habits, and working hours; even variations in temperature and sociolinguistic registers. While those in the kitchen gradually came to communicate more and more in Cocoliche and Lunfardo—the hybrid versions of Spanish spoken by immigrants—the ladies and gentlemen of the house spoke French and English.

In sum, the architectural plans of the mansions of Babilonia–Buenos Aires revealed the intentionality of an irreconcilable watershed between two cities. On the one hand, above stairs, the oligarchy, disdainful and unconcerned about what was happening below, enjoyed its leisure in the new city it had created from nothing. On the other hand was the basement, associated with sweat, labor, the social blight of *conventillo* culture, and the contamination coming from contact with sweating bodies. The two cities did not rub against each other, every contact between them channeled by the division of work and the semantization of spaces. As Rodaway has stated, of all the senses, touch is the one most avoided in advanced cultures because "to touch is . . . a corporeal situation rather than a cognitive position" (1994, 44). Thus, beginning in the domestic sphere of the mansion, the modern city promoted the development of preventive and defensive cognitive maps in which touching became inadvisable, an action to approach only with caution. Since touching always implies being touched, the xenophobia of the elites and their nationalist discourses was most powerfully expressed in elite repugnance at rubbing shoulders with those in the street and the unbearable caresses of exogamy.

3 PARKS, PLAZAS, AND CALLE FLORIDA

THE FIRST MAYOR OF BUENOS AIRES, Torcuato de Alvear, changed the Barrio Norte into a distinctive green space for leisurely strollers and outdoor enjoyment. This was a semirural area that had by 1890 become a residential zone where summer estates spread into Palermo Park and lavish mansions were built far back from the standard setbacks the city council required for the rest of Buenos Aires. Plaza Pellegrini, Avenida Alvear, and the district of Recoleta, where Alvear initiated remodeling, proudly flaunted a solemnly uniform urban architectural style. Many points of access were available exclusively to pedestrians and, in several cases, only by means of magnificent staircases. The Recoleta zone, open to everyone in theory, was in reality designed to remain an enclosed preserve in the midst of the noisy modern city, away from the circulation of public transportation.

David Harvey argues that public spaces were instrumental to the cultural geography of the Enlightenment and its intention "to construct a new, more democratic, healthier and more affluent society" (1993, 249), while Diana Balmori links the streets to modernity's most democratic, egalitarian, open, and unrestrained urban forms (1991, 84). Hence municipal regulations intended to prevent blockage in the streets, a space where collective interests could prevail over private. However, as Richard Sennett points out, the urban design of modern Paris "enabled the movement of large numbers of individuals in the city, and disabled the movement of groups. . . . The nineteenth-century urbanists imagined individuals protected by movement from the crowd" (1994, 324). Wide boulevards and arteries allowing the rapid circulation of traffic served perfectly to thwart any threat from concentrated Paris masses converging on these same spaces for revolutionary purposes. The mid-nineteenth-century reform of Paris by Baron Georges Haussmann, Napoleon III's minister for urban affairs, adopted the same goal as the London Underground and Regent's Park: regulating the gathering of crowds in the new public spaces of modernity. Analyzing the ring road around Regent's Park, Sennett notes a fundamental paradox: a place intended for public gatherings—a park—ended up having quite the opposite purpose: "A great, flat, grassy open space might seem the perfect invitation to organized groups. . . . Yet [John] Nash's plan worked against such use of open space by creating a wall of rapidly moving traffic around the park. . . . Many natural outcroppings and stray buildings along the belt were removed in order to make sure the carriages could move without interruption. . . . Dickens thought the belt road around the park resembled a racetrack" (325–26). Areas ringed with roads allowed for fast-moving traffic, so that they could not be entered easily. These were places for circulation, but not for contact. As perimeter traffic accelerated, it discouraged crowds of pedestrians from entering them and, more pointedly, from staying long.

Another strategy used to regulate public access is suggested in Buenos Aires's municipal records for 13 November 1895, concerning public transportation fares in Barrio Norte: "Intendente Emilio V. Bunge eloquently underlined the dangers of lower fares to such upper-class locations in his arguments against a concession for an electric streetcar along Avenida Alvear. . . . Such a line, he argued, would bring an invasion of *conventillos* and cheap worker residences and depreciate the exclusiveness of Palermo Park" (Scobie 1971, 172). By 1895, Bunge seemed to understand what the languages of the modern city, such as public transportation, were capable of unleashing. He knew that in order to preserve Palermo, it was "necessary" to divert the flow of pedestrians and crowds conveyed by public transportation. An article in *La Prensa* had warned in 1871 that "trams that have already brought the outskirts into active communication with the center threaten to make all those [outlying] locations part of the center of Buenos Aires" (Calcagno et al. 1992, 22). Meanwhile, Palermo adhered to the rhythm of the oligarchy's weekend estates, its back turned to the relentless rhythm of the industrial city, its loud center and standard checkerboard grid designed to regulate the spaces of the mass city. We could very well infer that the languages of money and commercial frenzy were completely absent from the iconic sites of Barrio Norte. Nor was it by chance that Palermo enjoyed the urban luxury of green spaces. In addition to tree-lined streets, Barrio Norte abounded in plazas (Plaza Francia, San Martín de Tours, Ramón J. Carcano, Bartolomé Mitre, República Oriental del Uruguay, Dante), gardens, open spaces, and parks, especially the elegant greenery of Palermo Park. But were these parks actually "public," or were they merely garden settings, embellished landscapes for the residences of the elite?

In his fascinating *Sensuous Geographies,* Paul Rodaway notes that, in spite of a general tendency to associate geography with cartography, there are also other matters to consider. Geographic maps become cognitive maps through a process of conferring meaning (*making sense*). On the other hand, geography is first organized in light of information derived from how the body senses (touch, smell, taste, sight, hearing, balance, synesthesia). Thus, Rodaway uses the word *sense* with two meanings—cognitive and corporeal—meanings that Cartesian rationalism unfortunately dissociated, even though they are intimately related and mutually involved: "The sense(s) is (are) both a reaching out to the world as a source of information and an understanding of the world so gathered" (Rodaway 1994, 5). This process—sensorial/cognitive mapmaking—is both "a relationship to the world and a decision-making process with respect to that world" (11). Rodaway's sensuous geography deviates from the classical behaviorist/positivist approach by incorporating transrational models from Gestalt psychology and phenomenology, replacing the understanding of geography as the simple functional organization of space (cartographic geography). Instead, Rodaway's sensuous geography turns toward a geographic understanding from the perspective of identity and subjectivity, a *site* that will process our mental maps, starting with the body's registers and memory. Our cognitive maps have their point of departure in the body and its sensors. From this source, there emerges a representation of reality and its myriad different stimuli and sources that captures, assesses, and orders the value of objects, textures, temperatures, colors and volume, abundance, ambiguity, and redundancy. Our directional system (our sense of gravity and balance) combines with our hearing, olfactory and gustatory systems, and visual sensors to bring significant nuance to the cognitive map, adding stereoscopic information about depth, surface, volume and texture, degrees of absorbency or resonance, and haptic data derived from the body's tactile receptivity. From this perspective, Rodaway's definition of geographic space questions eidetic reductionism and universalized perceptions of space. In his view, bodyscape is a sociohistorical construct (127). Each geography and cognitive map—an all-encompassing definition of life at a given moment—is organized according to local and subjective sensorial systems, complemented by the interaction of cultural semanticizers. In other words, cognitive maps are built from the intersection of spaces culturally associated with each other through their attachment to the systemic reproduction of social meaning and the organic/local/subjective production of social meaning.

At a sensorial/cognitive level, changes in the texture of the city are sensed most swiftly in its green spaces. These include substantial thermal changes, because of the ecosystem of plants, which displace the monochromatic, monothermal city of cement with the polymorphism of textures, colors, and fragrant smells. In a stroll through Palermo and Recoleta, for example, the mass city was replaced by a distinctive syntax articulated as a whole by sumptuous gardens with delicate floral settings, areas densely lines with trees, dramatic sculptural groupings, monuments, intimate plazas, imposing stairways, and even fountains, such as the one inconspicuously located at an inner corner of Arroyo and Esmeralda. These areas are located where fast-moving traffic slows down, opening into intimate, unforeseen corners and green zones of silence. They offer permanent residents calm havens of contemplation, of separation from the city. Borges would say that here even sighs may be heard. And as for the occasional passerby, she enjoys a temporary yet significant change in the subjective, spatial relationship between her body and the city. In Recoleta, she breathes better and even experiences a silent *recoleto,* or sense of reverence, similar to the quiet feeling of belonging inspired by the semiotics of churches and temples.

Urban Ceremonies and Social Distances

The gardens, parks, and green corners are an extravagant use of real estate that would have been unthinkable, too expensive, for the unimaginative, sterile texture of the urban center. In 1874, during the debate over the proposed law to authorize the construction of Palermo Park, Nicolás Avellaneda stressed the public character of parks, intuitively acknowledging the scope of their power to transform. Such public promenades would serve "to mollify, improve, refine, and ennoble the sentiments of the masses, thereby giving a gentler form to the harsh struggles engendered by democracy. . . . Once . . . [the parks] are more frequented, our elections will be less agitated" (qtd. in Gorelik 1998, 157). However, as Adrián Gorelik points out, the problem with Palermo Park was its distance from the center. The difficulty of reaching it on foot did not help to transform the urban practices of those sectors of society for which it was presumably intended (Gorelik 1998, 156).

This situation is common to modern cities. The symbolic attraction of New York City's Central Park lay, in principle, in its "central" location—in the intention to locate this important means of improving the city's sanitation and social well-being in a spot that is democratically equidistant from every part of the city. However, Central Park is also located where real estate speculation was at its worst (Gorelik 1998, 157), so that it ended up as a green rectangle fronting the exclusive penthouses of Wall Street millionaires. With respect to the reforms in Paris, Baron Haussmann's *Memoires* lamented, somewhat unconvincingly, that "in spite of all my efforts at making these splendid promenades easily accessible to all classes, I didn't succeed in making their use more generalized, except on Sundays and . . . holidays . . . because of the distance and the cost of transportation" (qtd. in Gorelik 1998, 159). In Buenos Aires, while real estate speculation had made it impossible to locate green spaces in the center, invisible social frontiers and urban languages such as transportation fares also made it difficult to access those public green spaces that, by careful calculation rather than chance, bordered on areas of privilege: the Palermo of the landscaper Charles Thays (1875), the Zoological Gardens (1875), and the Botanical Garden (1882).

The "other" Buenos Aires would have something quite different to say when evaluating the results of public urban reform. In his poem "Rosedal" (Rose Garden), the tango poet Homero Manzi redesigns Palermo Park, making some significant additions:

If it were me, just 'cause I'm a bum,
I'd give you streetlamps
and tin shacks
and dark doorways
filled with moist kisses and the scent of basil.
And in your streets, smoothed by a road roller,
I'd place a barrel organ and a lame grinder.
Every time I look at your lake . . .
I feel a wild need to fix it up with metal drums,
tin cans,
old boots . . . and a spittoon
like the mudflats in Pompeya. (Salas 1968, 197–98)

For Manzi, Palermo Park is a landscape, "like it was done by a barber / as affected as a pergola or a packet of pastries tied up in blue and white ribbons," so artificial and out of sync with the organic city that the poet prefers "the arches under the bridge / where bums spend the night philosophically." In contrast to the architectural language that mimics European-style parks, with their statues of lily white virgins—"three ascetic skinny women," as Manzi calls them, that go with benches like "eunuchs painted in meringue" —he proposes other cultural geographies for Buenos Aires that include the tin shacks of La Boca, old boots, spittoons, and a lame Neapolitan organ grinder from the barrio. Only in this way might the inhabitants of the "other" Buenos Aires feel somewhat at home. Palermo was a synthesis of urban styles with so many exclusions it called out to be rewritten and resemanticized, so that this emblematic place, once intended for everyone, would not incite discomfort or a lack of a sense of belonging in the residents of Pompeya. The authorial voice in "Rosedal," loudly opposing the elite's aesthetics, would opt instead for those of barbarism and the grotesque city, insisting on adding and mixing urban spaces, returning to the fragrance of lowly basil from Italian cooking, and creating intimate spaces amenable to love under the dim light of the streetlamps, rather than the eternally ornate spaces where society showed off in public.

The workers' city grew like unrelieved jungle. The proletarian classes' sensorial and cognitive maps of Buenos Aires lacked the healthy, relaxing spaces with which urban reformers sought to improve quality of life. There were no recreation areas in which one could breathe purer air more deeply, places that would somehow mitigate the heartless rhythms of the vertiginous city in which the workers were trapped. There were, in effect, no places allowing them to alternate between work and leisure at no cost to themselves. Furthermore, there were no tranquil settings inviting human contact beyond the oppressive tenements and the deafening frenzy of the factories. In my opinion, working Buenos Aires was thus *subtly* demoralized, denied the leisure time and relaxation of parks and plazas. It was far from natural light, fresh air, the aroma of flowers, the breeze wafting through jacaranda foliage, the green serenity of English lawns—resources that would have created some degree of respite and a quite different identitary relationship between the city and the bodies of men and women brutalized and battered by unregulated factory work. The city, clearly, was not generous with everyone. Uneven accessibility to public transportation and public sites was an urban language of inequality, highlighting the fallacy and ambiguity of an urban planning that deprived "the most congested sectors" (Gorelik 1998, 157) of a lung that would benefit those most exposed to tuberculosis, the archetypical disease of the proletariat during the first period of industrialization.

The *La Prensa* columnist's concern that the trams "threaten to make all those [outlying] locations part of the center of Buenos Aires" reveals a very clear understanding of the risks, shifts, and faux pas brought on by urban expansion. In his alarm at the leveling and massification of urban space, the writer opposes the pronoun "we" (as in "we at *La Prensa*") to the heteroglossic multitude of the grotesque city, who doubtless smell unpleasant and have little charm. Such cautions not to mix, evident in the interventions of Intendente Alvear and his successors, were to be expected in an elite whose liberalism accommodated modernity, especially its economic revolution and transformations, while never disguising their conservative control. In fact, having seen that trains and tramways create too much movement, the columnist argues for containing the displacements of the masses through some kind of measure designed to prevent the frontiers from collapsing, to resist too much fraternizing. The political pragmatism of the conservative elite shows through here, in the notion that different classes would inhabit the same city, but separately.

How were these urban frontiers conveyed? Commenting on the kind of visitors who went to Palermo Park, the columnist Roberto Gache asks: "Where does our good stoic male go [on the weekend] with his wife and children? The ordinary man goes on foot to Palermo with his 'lawful,' 'fat' wife and their children . . . all dressed alike in the modest fruits of the same liquidation sale." And this makes Gache nervous: "Beside the lake [at Palermo] at another aristocratic hour, [a thousand similar families] stop and enjoy their party. Where are the lovely, graceful figures that gave this very place such a unique and elegant charm in the morning? The holiday [is] very different now. . . . There are weary faces, hard, callused hands. . . . Why, out of a sense of painful emulation, come to this spot that is the peaceful refuge for those who have a more pleasant and happy life? The holiday these people have in this place is absurd. An absurd holiday" (1919, 76). To judge from Gache's vicious remarks, he is bothered by changes to places. The holiday "these people" enjoy in "this place" is absurd, a painful attempt to emulate a pleasant, happy Buenos Aires. He is somewhat relieved that these excursions have a time limit, since everyone returns to their own place at six P.M.: "The scullery maid [with] her bright red dress and two unshapely, suffering feet clad in extraordinarily tight shoes [is] taken by the hand by her beau; she listens to him and allows herself to be desired. Isn't this an uncouth affair that really belongs in a doorway?" (Gache 1919, 76).

Perhaps Gache senses that, through the interplay of different lifestyles, the homogenization of social practices threatens to impoverish the aesthetics of the exclusive city, swallowing up its high-class profile. Perhaps he senses the danger of the grotesque city invading ceremonial spaces, such as Plaza San Martín, another of the icons of the geography of privilege. By about 1914, the area around the plaza was distinguished by the architectural homogeneity of its palaces, in the style of L'École de Beaux Arts. By 1920, it was the elites' residential commercial center (in Calle Florida). The gently sloping plaza stood out as a truly delightful place of repose, under the spreading shade of the jacaranda and acacia trees. Jorge Luis Borges celebrated this space with heartfelt emotion in the poem "La Plaza San Martín." He knew every inch of it, perhaps his favorite spot in the whole of Buenos Aires.

From 1894, the oligarchy began to make public a private custom whose social value permitted them to take over Calle Florida, as described by Luis de Cánepa in *Buenos Aires de antaño* (Buenos Aires of Yesteryear): "The luxurious carriages of the ruling class rolled along the elegant Calle Florida in the late afternoon toward the new Palermo Park. . . . At nightfall . . . they returned as if in a ritual procession" (qtd. in Carretero 1974, 92). The parade's participants "were all dressed up, more to show off their refinement and good taste than to enjoy the stroll" (Carretero 1974, 91). What stands out in these comments is the fact that all reference to the world of work is absent, precisely because the well-to-do go out for a drive at just the time of day when the "other" city is working. At the same time, their new ritual takes control of the public space of the street, writing a text intended more for the rest of the city than for those who are writing it. This is a spectacle whose cultural actors are knowingly taking part in a ceremony, investing their time, gestures, clothes, and carriages. We might say that the participants enjoy their drive while others are working precisely because they do indeed belong to a group of economic parasites. Yet if we look more closely, they might also be seen as working in their own fashion, investing their effort in making a spectacle of privilege. They are working, in effect, to produce self-legitimating social rites. Thus, in Buenos Aires's cultural geography, Calle Florida becomes a public space transformed into a site for the private/public ostentation of the elite.

In "Dos palabras del autor" (Two Words from the Author), the prologue to *Pot Pourri (Silbidos de un vago)* (Potpourri: Whistlings of a Vagabond, 1881), Eugenio Cambaceres describes the elite's never-ending routine: "I get up at noon, lunch at one, wander like an aimless ball along Calle Florida, eat when the time takes me . . . play a hand of bezique at the Club . . . etc. I thought I might very well fancy changing direction . . . one crazy thing occurs to me much like another; I contribute to enriching the national literature . . . [and] between a yawn . . . and a jar of *caporal* [tobacco], I manage to come up with the bundle of nonsense with which you are familiar" (1956, 15). The product of this "nonsense"—his writing—provides an alternative to the yawns induced by the never-ending routine between the Club and Calle Florida, which includes literature, "one crazy thing . . . much like another." Cambaceres's remark traces the continuity between appropriation of the urban spaces of privilege (Calle Florida, the Club) and appropriation of its cultural spaces (writing). Moreover, both activities—wandering and writing —are described as adventures and, hence, as outside the discipline of intense hourly labor. Yet nothing Cambaceres does will fall into a void. What he writes will find a solid place in the national literature, while what he does (meandering) will inject transcendence into a vulgar city, furnishing rituals for a city in need of them because earlier ones have dissipated entirely.

Between 1880 and 1914, the great department stores opened in London and Paris, as well as on Calle Florida in Buenos Aires—Au Bon Marché (1891), Gath y Chávez (1913), and Harrods (1914): an intrinsic "part of the bourgeois culture and its historical flux" (Michael B. Miller 1981, 6), linked to the euphoria of the prewar period and the development of new strategies in mass consumption (see part 2). The design of the department store Gath y Chávez, built in the style of Avenida Alvear's *petits hôtels,* was not without purpose: its objective was to attract customers with purchasing power, as well as the wider population of curious passersby who merely wished to browse. Nor was it accidental that the store emulated the interiors of the palaces of the elite, with their domes and windows of colored glass, like those in Galeries Lafayette in Paris; their curved stairways in iron and bronze; their chandeliers and frosted lamps; their plush carpets, comfortable armchairs, and cozy corners decorated with little tables and plants (figures 4 and 5). As Karal Ann Marling points out, the interior of Los Angeles's Bullocks Wilshire department store was made up of "a series of artfully decorated rooms in a private home, themed to the merchandise casually displayed—without price tags or sale signs—in areas devoted to sporting goods, kitchenware, and so forth. Lighting came from the floor and table lamps, customers were encouraged to settle into easy chairs" (1997, 57). The objective of such thematic spaces was clear. In Buenos Aires, the elegant stores on Calle Florida—unlike the Jockey Club, where the exogenous were excluded—not only welcomed outsiders but modified their identitary maps in the process. It was as if, on entering these stores, the customer, crossing the threshold of a palace, was allowed to remain inside. Gómez Carrillo describes them: "We are now at the end of Calle Florida. . . . I go into a store. . . . How surprised I am to find myself transported to the true capital of elegance! Is it Le Printemps department store? . . . Is it the Louvre and its unending exhibition of precious objects? Is it Les Galeries Lafayette with its swarm of pretty girls who try on the most eccentric hats with perfect ease?" (1921, 62). The chronicler links art and money, Buenos Aires and Europe, *porteño* stores and French commercial icons. The commercial modernization of Buenos Aires would end by privileging global culture over local, fetishizing consumer merchandise, and hierarchically categorizing the new geographies of its place of production.

Urban Ceremonies and Social Distances

4 PASSAGES, PUBLIC SPACES, AND CULTURAL CROSSINGS

EVEN ERDOSAIN, THE PROTAGONIST of Roberto Arlt's *Los siete locos* (Seven Madmen, 1929), stands in awe before the stunning storefronts. In spite of his highly precarious employment situation, he has frittered away part of the six hundred pesos and five cents he has stolen: "He lunched on crabs and turtle soup . . . in restaurants where the price of sitting next to the well-heeled is very high, he drank expensively . . . although he lacked the bare necessities, such as underwear, shoes, or a tie, for living even a mediocre life" (Arlt 1981c, 1: 140). Arlt's characters are skillful semioticians of the city, seasoned interpreters of the messages conveyed by its architectural discourses and different zoning districts. They are among the quickest to catch disappearing, shifting, or hallowed signifiers and to reinterpret their meanings. Indeed, perhaps it is such people, those most acutely affected, who feel the city's language systems most keenly: they are their intended recipients. The city of privilege speaks to the middle and proletarian classes, trapped in the double bind of recent cultural recruitment and permanent economic instability.

But is Erdosain a flaneur? To begin with, he simply trudges tormentedly through the city in an anguished state of mind, unlike the Paris flaneur described in *Vida de hoy* (Life Today) in January 1937: "He is not the businessman who goes about his affairs by the shortest route . . . [but] an intelligent, often ironic individual, with nothing to do . . . who spreads his wandering, smiling curiosity along the streets. . . . [The flaneur] is an example of a placid, European lifestyle, and one must pay tribute to the elegant uselessness of that phlegmatic, decorative citizen who . . . gives flair and class to the streets." Nothing could be further from the desperation of Arlt's madmen than the indifferent, placid, elegant, European saunter of the flaneur. While Erdosain works as a deliveryman, he overlooks none of the places marked on the cultural geography of the city through which he passes. He recognizes them from the perspective of his bitter understanding of the meanings and displacements they imply. One of his journeys takes him along Arenales and Talcahuano, Charcas, and Rodríguez Peña, ending in Montevideo and Avenida Quintana (Barrio Norte). It is enough for him to notice the homogeneity of the buildings and zoning to realize that he has entered a different territory—indeed, a different city, noted for "the spectacle of the magnificent architecture on those streets, forever denied to the unfortunate" (Arlt 1981c, 1: 133). From this point on, the organization of his geographic map will rely on only one of his senses: the city of the privileged is indeed a spectacle to be admired, but only through Erdosain's sense of sight—in other words, through a sense perception Rodaway associates with the greatest sensorial distance. Yet it is one thing to be permitted to see this *frontera norte* (northern frontier) and quite another to be allowed to linger there, to interact, because proxemic meanings establish barriers that prevent Erdosain from touching anything. It is barely permissible for him to remain in this space, let alone transgress its boundaries, especially with the bravado of his "improper" sexual desire. So why does Erdosain visit these forbidden zones so often? I believe that he does so in order to pay homage in a painful pilgrimage.

By the end of the 1920s, boundaries and the daily practices they contained were already clearly recognizable within Buenos Aires's cultural geography. Although he was only allowed to look, when he peered in from the street outside, Erdosain was nonetheless torn apart by two conflicting identitary spaces: his fascination with the sacred geographies of the "other" and the self-repudiation of his condition as an outsider: "That world was another

Urban Ceremonies and Social Distances

world within the vile city he knew, another world for which his heart now beat with slow, heavy palpitations" (Arlt 1981c, 1: 133). Erdosain's cognitive social maps trigger a strong emotional response of anxiety and unease. Such palpitations, and altered cardiovascular rhythms, permeate the urban maps of Arlt's city, charting unbearable levels of anxiety.

Erdosain describes the *petit hôtel* to which he is able to gain access only by looking—only through those sense perceptions that do not entail crossing property lines. His gaze is not unresponsive, however: "He looked at . . . the green plumes of the cypress trees in the gardens defended by walls with serrated cornices, or thick railings strong enough to hold off the charge of a lion. . . . A governess in a gray wimple strolled along the pathways. And he owed 600 pesos and 5 cents! He stared for a long time . . . at the windows painted pearl gray. . . . How different love must have been in the shade of those tulle drapes that deaden the light and muffle the sounds" (Arlt 1981c, 1: 134). He stares at length, admiring the garden, because he is not indifferent to the sharp contrast it makes with the soulless, deserted central areas of the city where he lives. Similarly, the sober tones of black and gray strike him as sharply distinct from the chromatic, unregulated heterogeneity of El Sur. As figure 6 shows, a residence's proxemic distance from the street increases by degrees according to the building's style. Access varies depending on whether houses are located directly at the edge of the sidewalk; distanced from the street by a garden; or wholly separated from the street by semiotic markers such as a semicircular driveway, a wall, railings, a tall fence, or a hedge. Those who construct these semiotics evidently want their residences to be well secluded behind noticeable boundaries. However, in the case of the mansions Erdosain views, they are not designed to be completely hidden from passersby. Closed and well defended, but open to public admiration, they stake out a defensive demarcation of social distance, seduce by being seen, and yet remain untouchable behind imposing iron railings. Their tantalizing semiotics seem to profile a remarkably sociophobic and hysterical mind. As Erdosain notes, moreover, the barrier between the mansion and the street is fortified even further by the watchfulness of majordomos and governesses keeping an eye on the interior gardens—also protected, incidentally, by lions. In other words, this geography is constructed as a proxemic safeguard, ideal for agoraphobes. By contrast, Erdosain's urban cognitive map shapes his perception of the palaces from the outside, and through the overpowering weight of his *mapas del dolor*—the maps of his own pain. Perhaps this explains why Arlt never published in *Caras y Caretas,* where writers like Gómez Carrillo would have papered over the dissymmetries of urban life in order to launch the imaginary of a city without conflicts, devoted only to its charms. We might say that Arlt and Gómez Carrillo write from discursive positions located on opposite sides of the palace railings.

Nevertheless, there are mansions and mansions—or, at least, mansions as signifiers with variable meanings. Adela Di Carlo's *folletín* "Justa recompensa" (Just Rewards) was published on the Day of the Worker in 1920, appearing during that decisive interregnum in Argentinean history between 1919's so-called Semana Trágica (Week of Tragedy) and the suppression of the anarcho-socialist strikes in Patagonia in 1922–23, when the Radical Party governed in full sway.[1] "Justa recompensa" tells the story of "a poor immigrant of Turkish nationality who came to our country with no more capital than a will to work, excellent health, in spite of deprivation, and a few coins that . . . amounted to just three pesos."[2] Unable to speak Spanish, the immigrant sold oranges in "one of our main squares [until] a beautiful woman from one of the lordly-looking houses signaled to him to approach." She is the new vendor's first customer, and their transaction is completed in spite of language barriers and the predictable proxemic apprehensions. The kindly woman "out of compassion paid more for the oranges than they were really worth." Moreover, her compassion and generosity seem not to end there. When the immigrant comes to rearrange his oranges, "how surprised he was to find a highly valuable jeweled ring in one of the baskets! Whose could it be? Its owner could be none other than the woman who bought the oranges." The man's scruples trouble him during a sleepless night until he can endure it no longer. At four A.M., he goes to the door of the mansion and wakes up the owners: "The Turk only had to show them the ring, which the woman recognized immediately." The immigrant who had seen the house from the outside will now be welcomed, not just into the mansion, but into the imaginary of the Nation House: "From that moment on, [the owner of the house] took him under his wing, gave him money to set up a small business, and encouraged him so much that today the poor Turk is the owner of one of the most opulent stores on Calle Independencia. He lives happily, not only because he sees the efforts of his continuing work rewarded, but also because his protectors still lavish their moral support on him."

Urban Ceremonies and Social Distances

In Di Carlo's story, all the characters add something meaningful: the woman her sensitivity, and her husband the power of decision granted by his wealth. A very profound change has occurred here, but certainly not in the gendered spaces of the sexist imaginary, where the lady of the house is expected to perform charity while the gentleman is the true agent of social habilitation. The "beautiful woman" intercedes for the immigrant without leaving her house because, while there are women of every stripe on the streets, the virtues of wealthy women belong inside. Although the owners of the mansion bring power and kindness to the situation, the "Turk" also has virtues without which he could not possibly fit into the new society. "Justa recompensa" thereby alludes to a new political ambiance associated with the imaginary of socioethnic reconciliation, introduced during the Radical Party's three governments, which took full shape toward 1922–28, during President Alvear's Acuerdismo (Social Accord). "Turks" belonged to the most despised group in the tide of immigrants. They had been described with revulsion by a prominent member of the Conservative Order and the Generation of 1880 in a serial novel published in *La Nación* beginning in 1891 entitled *La Bolsa,* part of a series called the "Ciclo de La Bolsa" (Stock Exchange Cycle): "Filthy Turks, with their red fezzes and shabby slippers, expressionless faces, and trays of gaudy trinkets, vendors of cheaply colored oleographs, aimless charlatans . . . beggars who stretched out mutilated hands or made a show of the repulsive sores on their crippled legs" (Martel 1979, 7). Here, Julián Martel's imaginary intermingles the racism and the classism of a conservative elite whose irritation at having to live alongside the poor and the mutilated from the grotesque city is triggered by the errors of an ill-conceived immigration policy that ought to have had stricter criteria with respect to ethnicity and work skills. Yet although the Stock Exchange Club or Miguel Cané's Jockey Club would never have hired a *turco* in 1891, another tune would be playing by 1920.

It should be said that Di Carlo's *turco* was totally defenseless when it came to dealing with the conditions of his own migration. Given his vulnerability, this newcomer's chances of survival were so scarce that it was essential for the new owners of the Nation House to rescue and welcome him, actions that would have been unthinkable earlier, behind the social armor shielding the mansions of the Conservative Order, but had become entirely possible at the time of transition from conservative to radical imaginaries. "Justa recompensa" introduces a new political clientele among the middle class, whose hardships would now be overcome through the generosity of the Argentine republic. In the story of a ring fallen out of the sky over a palace, the immigrant embodies the new imaginary. Although Di Carlo claims that the immigrant "is the main author of his own well-being," that "his integrity was greater than his poverty and inspired the act that led him along the path to his good fortune," his prosperity in fact results from habilitation from above, thanks to the protection of unsuspected judges who, in fact, verify his ability to adapt to democratic, bourgeois civility and, above all, his respect for private property. It is not work that makes it possible for the *turco* to leave Martel's despised crowd, but the messianic intervention of social regulators, bourgeois populists living in palaces.

However, not all imaginaries endorsed the social habilitation suggested in "Justa recompensa"; others served as reminders that entry into the Nation House was considerably tougher, as proves to be the case for Arlt's Erdosain, much to his dismay, shattering the futile hope he rested on the whim of a "gloomy and melancholy millionaire": "He imagined that behind . . . the blinds of one of those palaces a certain 'gloomy and melancholy millionaire' (I use Erdosain's terms exactly) was studying him through opera glasses. . . . When he thought that the 'gloomy and melancholy millionaire' might be watching him, he put on a sad and thoughtful face and stopped gazing at the arses of the maidservants passing by, pretending to be fixed by the attention he was giving to a great mental task. . . . Erdosain hoped that the 'gloomy and melancholy millionaire' would summon him at any minute, after seeing the muscles in his face hardened by so many years of suffering" (Arlt 1981c, 1: 134). Erdosain imagines the interior of the palace: "A lamp shone in a corner of the room. . . . [On top of a piano] some sheets of music gave off the fragrance of pages touched only by feminine hands. The bust of a woman stood on a windowsill draped with net curtains the color of pretty violets" (1: 135). Arlt's character wonders: "Under what circumstances had he been inside that room . . . ? He couldn't remember" (1: 135). Even though he has the "worn boots, threadbare tie, and stained suit [of one] who earns a living on the street," entry into such mansions is not a matter for the body, but for the successful work of imaginaries. In Di Carlo's story, the actions of those living in the palace take the form of hard cash that allows the "Turk" to own a high-class store. No wonder Erdosain resorts to such habilitating imaginaries: "He would triumph. Yes! He would triumph. With money from the 'gloomy and melancholy millionaire,' he would set up an electro-plating laboratory" (1: 136). Erdosain's scientific knowledge and inventions are his only hope of gaining social recognition for his entrepreneurial virtues, of getting closer to the professional classes, but making this transition still depends in any case on being "seen" by the lords of the mansions. From be-hind their blinds, they seem disposed to watch—perhaps even with binoculars —for passersby deserving of social and economic rewards, including the sexual trophy of one of those languid-headed women. But first Erdosain must win the noble hearts of the gentlemen of the palace.

The protagonist of Roberto Arlt's *El juguete rabioso* (Mad Toy) easily as-certains the nature of Buenos Aires's invisible borders through an accurate scrutiny of the values and meanings of material signifiers and social actors. Observing "empty streets, discreetly lit, with flourishing plane trees . . . tall buildings with beautiful facades and windows draped with heavy curtain-ing" (Arlt 1981b, 105), his attention is drawn to a silence in which only whis-pers and muffled sounds seem appropriate: "A young boy and a girl talked in the shadows; the melody of a piano came from the orange room. I thought I would never be like them . . . never live in a beautiful house or have an aris-tocratic girlfriend" (105). From the other side of half-opened windows, the exogenous passerby will never be allowed to enter the body of the mansion/ woman; he can only dwell on sex from afar. When the protagonist, Silvio Astier, reaches a luxury apartment building on Charcas 1600 (Barrio Norte–Recoleta), this new type of housing in the cityscape of high-rises not only in-creases the proxemic distance between the street and the private but also provokes a mood of pretense in Silvio's behavior. He describes the building using a vocabulary somewhat too sophisticated for a street vendor exhausted from walking so far: "From outside, with the harmonious lines of the metopes emphasizing the sumptuousness of the magnificent, complex cornices and their broad windows protected by rippled glass, [the luxury apartment build-ings] cause poor wretches to dream of unreal refinements of luxury and power" (106). Silvio uses the symbolic language-capital of the other, shrink-ing the proxemic distance of the apartment buildings and repositioning himself on relational maps, so that when he alludes to "poor wretches," he no longer occupies his own place, but the identitary site of the ventriloquist. The voices of privilege speak through Silvio, and, at least for the moment, he speaks on their behalf and with their purposes, although he will never be one of them. Is there any place in Arlt's writing where the speech of the other is not intermittently woven into an *almost* fruitless search for self-expression?

As he enters Charcas 1600, Silvio goes through doors jealously guarded by an alert doorman: "He surveyed me from head to foot like a guard dog; then . . . with a sense of indulgence that could only have come from his gold-braided blue cap, he let me in" (Arlt 1981b, 107). Just as the doorman disguises himself under his blue cap, Silvio uses his ventriloquist's voice to project disdain for and distance from subalterns like himself. By coming into contact with ambiguous spaces, physically and culturally contaminated by the submission of dependence on employment, the two proletarians acquire amphibious identities. Once inside, Silvio crosses the silent, solitary hallways, protected by a doorman and a door that seems to belong outside "a huge steel vault" (107), both shielding much more than "ceilings decorated with Valhalla clouds" and rippled glass in the style of Sezesion: "A piano, fancy trinkets, bronzes, flower vases . . . a most delicate perfume heralded her presence. . . . I found myself before a woman with a childlike face, long, soft hair curled around her cheeks, and a low neckline. A fuzzy, cherry-colored robe didn't quite cover her white and gold slippers" (109).

If Wilde sought to flee, Silvio wants to remain in this privileged space. It is no surprise that the young lady of the house speaks French and fills her languorous leisure time reading in that language. Nor is it surprising that her sexuality is a possession that has been seized by the men who own those whispering, sensual, protected spaces, a possession beyond the reach of bodies wracked by the tempests of the aroused city. However, it should be noted that not everything is static in the kaleidoscopic geography of the city, nor do all *porteños* endure Silvio's broken heart, his painful pilgrimage on swollen feet. If the city planners of the Centennial, and the network of *modernista* artisans, thought they had endowed the oligarchy with a solemn and static national stage, the setting described in Humberto Notari's *Aquellas señoras* (Those Ladies, 1923) suggests, by contrast, that symbolic values change when the signifiers are placed somewhere else. The setting is a room: "On the walls are sheaves of evergreen plants entwined with artificial flowers . . . [that] form garland-like festoons, from which there hangs a splendid lamp." At first sight, the description makes one think of the facade of Jules Dubois (at Avenida de Mayo 1297) or the balconies by Pablo Pater (Riobamba 1175), but the artificial flowers catch our attention, and the sheaves entwining them are also somewhat suspicious. This is the residence of Madame Claudia, a house of courtesans ("those ladies"), and the cultural crossings to be found here are simply outrageous:

> MARCHETTA: My dressmaker is one of the best there is; my hairdresser attends on all the aristocracy; my shoemaker lived in London for seventeen years.... I have a manicurist, a masseuse, and an old fortune-teller who reads my cards.... I go to the theater when the *premières* are interesting; I subscribe to *Figaro* and *Journal Amusant;* I have ten days at the shore in winter and two weeks in the summer on a beach by the sea.... I play the stock market, drink Vichy water... eat fish on Fridays because I like tartar sauce.... I do-nate to charity.... When it rains, I read Bouget, ... and although I have so many things to do, I do what I can to spend a little time on Art, and I paint liberty postcards. (Notari 1923)

The elite's sacred areas and rituals may inspire pilgrimages, but the grotesque city handles such matters in its own way. Marchetta, an avid reader of the society columns in *Caras y Caretas* and *La Nación,* has followed French society rituals to the letter, but when all of Buenos Aires imitates these rituals, their power to command declines. No one can guarantee that the masseuse will not be confused with fortune-tellers on the Avenida de Mayo, or the exclusive French Riviera with the proletarian *ribera* (shore) of the unappealing River Plate. Marchetta's daily habits may be read as cultural crossings; as evidence of how unstable messages become when they undergo massification; or as confirmation that the organic city hybridizes objects and messages, which are falsified or resignified in the city's haphazard, awkward bid to embrace the modern condition. After all, as the populist imaginary of Radicalism suggested, there is room for everyone.

If the promise of Di Carlo's story still depends on mediation from the palace, Notari's *sainete* (popular farce) positions the members of the middle class as social actors able to grant a second cultural wind to products conse-crated from above by giving them new, irreverent, lopsided, and parodic meanings. Everything changes place in the city, and the street contributes to this process in more than one sense. The editor of *Martín Fierro,* Evar Méndez, laments the wide circulation of Rubén Darío's poetry, irreparable once his work had been appropriated by the masses: *milonguitas* (tango dancers) in the barrios of Boedo and Chiclana, and *malevos* (thugs) and grocers in greasy local pizzerias, "will recite [his verses], perhaps in factories and cabarets, in the driver's seat of their carts, and over tables with *barbera* [wine] spilled on them" (Sarlo 1969, 119). In a *sainete* by Carlos Mauricio Pacheco, *La patota* (The Gang, 1922), an orchestra plays the tango "La morocha" (Mulatta) on a *porteño* night in an open-air café, while the all-night carousers alternate between drinking and turns at cabaret:

> AGUSTÍN: Come on Sardetti, I mean Rodríguez . . . let's have a poem. . . .
>
> WOMEN (*applauding the request*): Yes . . . yes.
>
> RODRÍGUEZ: Well, since you insist! Do you know Rubén's [Darío's] "The Princess"?
>
> ALL: Yes, of course. . . . I'll say so! Let's hear "The Little Princess."
>
> RODRÍGUEZ (*in a high-pitched voice*):
>> The little princess is sad
>> the little princess is pale
>> she no longer wants to be a rose
>> she no longer wants to be a chrysalis
>> the little princess is sad
>> the little princess is pale . . .
>
> EDUARDO (*feigning sadness*): Ah!
>
> WOMEN (*they clap*): Very good, very good. . . . (Pacheco 1964, 87–88)

Modernista aesthetics were affirmed by dazzling society galas and languid pianos, but their allure went awry when adopted by the popular classes, where their negligible relationship to the facts of everyday life was soon exposed. In the bustling café where *la patota* meets, the sighs of Darío's poetry are interrupted by drunks thumping the table and jostling the poet, who retreats in disarray after enduring the jibes thrown at him for his affected manners. While Silvio Astier undertakes pilgrimages to aristocratic Buenos Aires, here the discourses of high culture come to grief in the derisive and irreverent grotesque city. As Evar Méndez complains, "It inevitably reaches the multitudes, [where] the unlettered rabble takes over this treasure of the mind and rhythm" (Sarlo 1969, 19). The streets of Buenos Aires became a shifting space, where a culture in motion was constantly redefined in light of the interaction, tension, and cultural replication of the city's many social agents.

As Richard Sennett points out, the development of modern capitals such as London "consistently razed housing and shops inhabited by the very poor to create homes for the middle class or the rich" (1994, 321). In Buenos Aires, none of the energy used to reform the center was ever invested in relocating the displaced population. Hence the inevitable importance of *conventillos,* cheap accommodations, boardinghouses, and *villas miserias* (shanty towns), as well as the later massive relocation to barrios on the periphery, in a diasporic displacement that gradually dismantled some urban environments while creating others.[3] Another aspect of development underlined by Sennett is the concentration of property "in the hands of great landowners who privately controlled large tracts of land in the city" (321). The cultural agents of the Centennial pursued the class struggle in many ways, including tight control over urban space. Their mega-project accelerated the transformation of Buenos Aires into a modern city by eliminating unused spaces and open-air markets, by building or enclosing vacant lots in the center (Matamoro 1982, 32), by zoning it and removing any deviation from the public eye, but particularly by imposing a grammar and consistency that displaced the languages of the grotesque city. Huge blocks of flat walls in perfect architectural continuity stood out above all (figure 7). Compact walls lined streets that facilitated the rapid flow of traffic in imitation of Haussmann's utopia: "new, uniform street walls of enveloping, straight streets that carried high volumes of carriage traffic" (Sennett 1994, 329). The cultural actors associated with urban heterogeneity did not go unnoticed in the elite's obsession to modernize Buenos Aires: the strong arms of municipal agencies cast their spontaneity into the shadows. Just as in transitional London, when poverty did remain in the center, it was held in pockets hidden from public view (Sennett 1994, 322). Yet in spite of the diglossic demarcation of urban cultures, cultural discontinuity survived in secret, behind the uniformly walled streets of central Buenos Aires. These streets provided passageways and tunnels through which to reach *otros cielos* (other skies), as Cortázar would call them, and hinted at the city's resistance to the modern homogenization of time and space. The avant-garde's irrationalist imagination would unleash the uneasiness of unknown passageways, concealed tunnels and spaces that wriggled away from urban and cultural control as countermaps of the visible city.[4]

How would attention be drawn to the commercial zone? During the Centennial, the elite transformed the center into a permanent fiesta.

Sarmiento proposed public lighting as a way to banish the uncivilized night of barbarism, but electric lighting gave life to a continuity that dramatically accelerated biological rhythms in public and private spaces and profoundly changed senses of intimacy. The transition from the center's illumination by gaslight to the starkness of electric light was felt intensely by the inhabitants of Buenos Aires, as a voluminous body of writing confirms: "It's a big mistake to place arc lamps outside store windows. The irritation caused to pedestrians by such intense light is impossible to avoid. Lamps of 1000 candlepower or more should not be used. . . . The public stays away from windows similarly lit. Besides, the glass pane of the storefront is an excellent reflector of lamps set up like this and increases the annoyance caused by the intense light" (*PTB,* 2 January 1918).

Whether through the starkness of the light or the grid design of the city streets, urban transformations in Buenos Aires required complex processes of adaptation. The new city desubjectivized its inhabitants by imposing a homogenizing identity on them in many ways. According to Adrián Gorelik, the decision to divide urban space into a checkerboard was a major aspect of urban reform. The 1898 proposal to reshape Buenos Aires according to "a predominantly uniform squared grid . . . defining every block precisely" (Gorelik 1998, 128) was an expression of a *voluntad de la forma* (desire for uniformity).[5] Mariapola Fimiani maintains that "the urban grid was introduced in the context of a great historical change in power" (1985, 230). Citing Foucault, she comments on restrictions placed on individuals, who "are enclosed in a prescribed space, in which the slightest movement is controlled and all events are recorded." The grid layout is a cartographic abstraction that threatens the organic nature of knowledge in motion and any empirical or dialogic relationship between social actors and urban space. It is a prosthesis that preordains how the body and the subject move through the city, thereby aggravating tensions between empirical knowledge and urban cartography. *Porteños* felt the frustration of walking according to designs forced upon them, deprived of something vital. For this reason, like a dissident opposed to modernity, the space of identity in avant-garde writing became totally spontaneous in reaction to the rationalist and systematized cultural mapping of the city. The post-*modernista* poet Fernández Moreno complains:

> My brain is a grid
> like your streets, oh Buenos Aires. . . .

Urban Ceremonies and Social Distances

If I am asked why my verses
are so precise, so regular
I'll tell everyone I learned to write them
over the geometry of your streets. (1921, 9).

Some avant-garde writers delved into the languages of modernity, as Francine Masiello suggests in *Lenguaje e ideología* (Language and Ideology), with respect to Oliverio Girondo's *Kodak desafiante* (Kodak Challenge) (Masiello 1986, 123). Some resorted to haphazard syntax to disorder the city, while others took refuge in the *arrabales* as a way of preserving subjectivities and enduring the violence of the dislocating transition.

In *El conventillo: Costumbres bonaerenses* (The Tenement: Customs of Buenos Aires, 1917), Luis Pascarella records the traces of an evanescent old city as viewed by newcomers: "Brick after brick, the ramshackle building, its great window railings torn off, disappeared slowly beneath the destructive pickaxes of the masons, almost all of whom were foreigners and to whom the old colonial building meant only a pile of useless debris that had to be removed to leave the space free for the palace planned for that site" (1917, 60). Even in 1936, with the widening of Corrientes Street, there was no room for urban and cultural dissonance, as reported on the city page of *Vida de hoy* (October 1936): "At last it's open . . . Calle Corrientes. Buenos Aires is changing, and the rhythm of the times must be followed, excitedly and avidly. . . . Dr. de Vedia y Mitre has had . . . the strength to strike a great blow and do away with the ridiculous empty spaces of a project that was half finished. . . . Now it's time to build. . . . The same tax levied on big buildings will be applied . . . to old houses belonging to the holdouts who . . . persist in preserving them." Vacant spaces, empty lots, or houses out of sync with the city's new standards, times, and languages would not be tolerated. Invoking the public good and general interest, the journalist demands that the municipality take appropriate measures against the "egos or whims of the minority." Architectural homogenization had become another identitary strategy of modern culture, against whose demolition, eradication, and eviction there was no appeal: "the best way is to remove existing buildings, old walls in ruins."

The scarce recognition this unfeeling writer gives the affective value of urban spaces is astounding. By contrast, the protagonist of Borges's "La señora mayor" (The Elderly Woman), in *El informe de Brodie* (Brodie's Report), asserts the preciousness of space within the dynamic of place/identity better than anyone. After the epidemic of 1871 forces Señora Rubio de Jáuregui to move from the barrio of Catedral (San Pedro Telmo and Monserrat) to Palermo, the city, she finds, is never the same again. She is a living memory of other cultural times, still recalling the year of the epidemic and the Infanta's visit during the 1910 Centennial. She continues to use names that have become obsolete, talking about "the Calle de las Artes, Calle del Temple, Calle Buen Orden, Calle de la Piedad, the two streets named Larga, the Plaza del Parque and de los Portones. What were affected archaisms for her family, who still referred to Uruguayans as Orientales, came naturally to her" (Borges 1974, 1050). It might be inferred that she is agoraphobic, because the story is set in 1953 and she has not been able to bring herself to leave the house since 1929—perhaps so as not to face her fading city: Buenos Aires "has been changing. . . . The city that the woman imagined on the other side of the door to the street was much earlier than the one belonging to the time when they had to move away from the center. The oxen that pulled the carts still stood in Plaza Once, and the dead violets perfumed the farms in Barracas" (1050). By 1929, Barracas had already become an impoverished working-class neighborhood of noisy Genoese immigrants, a rough area smelling of the polluted Riachuelo, without a single violet to perfume the river breezes.

In those times of transition, the key word was *adaptation*: adaptation to a culture in motion. That daily life might be experienced as a perplexing drama, replete with surprise turns, novelty, crises, and constant upsets and accidents, is confirmed by the black humor of Carlos Mauricio Pacheco's *Los tristes o gente oscura* (The Sad Ones; or, Dark People, 1906). One of the characters explains: "I was site foreman. I fell off the top into the lime. . . . After that, everything went wrong, as it does when you're poor. My poor wife died, we had no food. . . . Today I got tired of begging and was on my way back when we got caught in the rain." In *El diablo en el conventillo* (The Devil in the Tenement, 1906), also by Pacheco, the character Tránsito lists recent events in his *conventillo*:

> Look at what's happened around here in just a month and a half. The dressmaker's son, poor thing, was killed by a tram right here at the door. . . . The woman in the shop died of pneumonia, and today they're taking out Don Tomás, who'd been hail and hearty. Let's keep counting. Doña Anita's hus-

band has come home drunk a hundred times . . . without a scratch. The day before yesterday, he turned up stretched out on the stairs with his face all bloodied. Someone set fire to Doña Asunción's little boy's crib, and he almost burned alive. Yesterday the Andalusians on the second patio went at each other with knives and chairs.

The urban remodeling that opened streets to fast traffic also reflected the accelerated rhythm of production. In the city section of the magazine *Buenos Aires* (January 1937), Carlos Sanguinetti expressed concern for the almost two hundred dead and six thousand injured because of the speed of the cars and the carelessness of victims: "It would be good to impose . . . a slower speed on central streets" (13). We can deduce that the population had not yet adjusted to the new urban rhythm by 1937. As much is evident in the complaint of Miguel, an old Italian in Armando Discépolo's *Mateo* (1923), who symbolizes the transition that is turning the city upside down. A carriage driver who resists entering the new world, he is reluctant to respond to the dictate of the day: *hay que entrare* (you must move up)—that is, shift to motorized transportation. His refusal will inevitably cost him his livelihood: "The automobile! A fine discovery! Whoever invented it should feel proud of himself. We should put up a statue . . . on top of a pile of corpses, no less! Diabolical vehicle; a revolting machine I'm condemned to watch come and go, always full of crazy-looking passengers, while the bugle, the horn, the hooter, and the squeals all leave me confused or make me deaf" (Discépolo 1987a, 317). Mateo, Miguel's horse, is as old and useless as his master. Horses, drivers, and pedestrians were expected to adjust their bodily geographies as they moved through this new urban space that imposed its rules on them instead of containing them. Certain cognitive frames of reference and assumptions about identity are made obsolete in a daily life possessed by speed:

> MIGUEL: There's nothing more for me to do in Bona Saria with my old bone shaker. The carriage is finished. . . . The automobile has killed it. People are witnessing a terrible spectacle on the street, the death of the carriage . . . and nobody turns a hair. (320)

The adjustment of identity the new culture required of the workforce is defined by Miguel's son Carlos ("You have to start, Dad, you have to become a chauffeur" [318]), by his friend Severino ("You have to start, my friend" [324]), and by Miguel himself ("I have to start, I have to start" [339]). The alternative is unemployment, or crime and imprisonment—a fact of which Miguel is perfectly aware, as he exclaims in his Italian dialect: "I'm sorry. Our peace is finished. I am lost! I am lost!" His son, on the other hand, opts for the chauffeur's uniform: "I've been practicing at the wheel for some time . . . but kept it quiet so I could surprise you with the good news" (341). In 1923 Buenos Aires, the retooling of the workforce required training not always accessible to those living in tenements. Since Carlos lives with his father, he is economically able to adjust by learning to drive but, above all, by understanding the inevitability of the new culture of labor. His father, in contrast, resists and pays the consequences.

Irritation against the "poor old carriages" triggered the rampant intolerance of urban chronicler Roberto Gache: "I wonder why the horses in the poor old carriages never walk in a straight line. Wouldn't it be the shortest and the easiest? . . . These zigzagging nags are always the skinniest and the feeblest. See how profound my question is: do they stretch out the route because they are weak, or are they weak because they stretch out their route?" (1919, 75). Gache's use of a *vosotros* imperative in the phrase "See how profound my question is" (Advertid lo profundo de mi duda) betrays the speaker's pomposity and antiorganic rigidity: he can only conceive of walking a route in straight lines.[6] Others, including the likes of Miguel and Mateo, he simply dismisses. Discépolo, in contrast, through his attention to the different tempos of two generations out of sync with each other, clearly understands the tension between two coexisting cultures of work whose respective skills designate quite different social and identity spaces. Inclusion and exclusion are the two poles that clearly belie the truth of inclusive imaginaries proclaiming an open city with a place for everyone.

Tramlines were electrified in 1892, and the Argentina Railway's Central Station opened in 1915. The first trains ran between Plaza Once and the docks in 1916. Between 1928 and 1930, the Lacroze subway line was built, and the Constitución-Retiro line opened in 1936. To judge from the network and extent of fast surface and underground lines, the city would eventually have very good transportation from the center to the suburbs, as the mobilization of the masses that brought Peronism to power on 17 October 1945 would show. However, before 1945, transportation systems were also used as another urban political language of civil control. James Scobie comments: "In 1895 in an effort to enable workers to travel further, and to relieve the con-

Urban Ceremonies and Social Distances

gestion in downtown *conventillos,* the municipality ordered companies to run 'worker cars,' for one hour in the early morning and one in the evening, in which laborers could travel at half price. The companies neutralized the measure by using open or broken-down vehicles and by having such irregular and infrequent runs that no workers could be assured of the promised savings or of getting to work on time" (1974, 171). As Scobie explains, fares dropped in 1900, making the spread to the suburbs possible, but still, not everything ran on rails. On 7 January 1909, *La Vanguardia* ("Organ of the Socialist Party, Defender of the Working Class") criticized "the abysmal service of the [tram] companies": "Looking out for the interests of shareholders, the companies don't hesitate to defraud the public ... preventing the number of workers to benefit from reduced fares from being very high. . . . With the complicity of the municipality, they use cars with a capacity for only 20 seated passengers instead of 'window-box' cars [jardineras], with a capacity of 32." According to *La Vanguardia,* the Anglo-Argentina Company "would not allow the guards to carry passengers from the center to Flores." They understood that they were required only to "bring" workers, not to "take them back"—to the intense frustration of the workers, given the distance between where they lived and the factories, workshops, and docks: "[The trams] run in insufficient numbers and give rise to all the eventualities caused by such a service associated with the problem of getting to work on time. . . . The same thing happens in the evening. In order to get home promptly, we find ourselves having to pay 10 cents instead of 5 cents, which makes the company very happy, forcing people to travel in first-class cars. . . . Passengers who take second class have to travel in 'window-boxes,' small, closed trailers that are veritable ovens on wheels in summer."

In this regard, I would like to refer to *El viaje aquel* (That Journey, 1914), reworked as *El guarda 323* (Guard No. 323, 1915), by Armando Discépolo and Rafael José de la Rosa. This *sainete,* set in a tramcar held up in traffic at six P.M. one winter's evening, examines public and social uses of the tram, reading it as a microcosm reflecting the social crossroads of modern life. On the one hand are the regulations imported by British capital and the powerful Anglo-Argentina Company: "The bell here, the trolley there, the ticket machine here, the schedule there, one inspector getting off and another getting on" (Discépolo 1987b, 97). The guard on the tram, Don Pascual, must impose strict rules on the passengers; on newspaper vendors and readers;

on prostitutes ("tramline turtledoves"); on men looking for "tramline turtledoves"; on girls working in fashion houses; on mailmen; on seamstresses employed by milliners; on dozing passengers he wakes up because it is forbidden to sleep on board; on old men who sigh, "Ah, what a slender woman, what a snake of a woman!"; on cheeky passengers slapped by indignant ladies; on "the noisy rabble, thieves at work, someone smoking, another one spitting . . . someone else complaining" (97). Here is a bubbling cauldron of life contained within the space of public regulation, including the prohibition on spitting, which was part of a public health campaign against tuberculosis, the disease of the age:

> DON PASCUAL: We know the ordinance forbids spitting inside the car because of infection. This means you have to spit outside, but on that side only, since the sidewalk is on this side and mustn't be infected either. Oh . . . you can't open the window in case one of the passengers doesn't like it. . . . Oh . . . you can't open the door at the front in case the passengers catch pneumonia or there's an accident of some sort.

Even Don Pascual himself is reduced to being a *máquina de lo boleto* (ticket machine), who "hands out a ticket, takes the money, and that's it." Since "he has to fulfill his duty . . . talking on his own behalf is not part of his job" (97). His interaction with the passengers precludes everything that "is not part of my job" (88, 90). He is as mechanized as the tram. When a passenger explains, "I need to spit," and asks what to do because "my mouth is watering," the guard contains the spontaneity of the situation by referring to the letter of the law: "We concluded that saliva is not covered under ordinances . . . you can't spit": "Has the world gone crazy then? On board this car, full of warnings against fake products and pawnshops, that goes on its way, forever, struck by rain, wind, sun, and stones, sounding the bell, giving off sparks . . . stopping with a pull on the bell . . . lurching without warning . . . killing people and never arriving on time with its rules" (97). But on his way home, Don Pascual stops in a dark street in the barrio of Vélez Sarsfield. Standing at the center of the stage, he addresses the audience. Far from the unrest of the city center, his lucid and incisive speech warns that the profound change brought by the new culture has begun to have an effect on personal relations: "We see something that makes us think and think again because, by comparison, the tramcar is a world. . . . There are sad people and happy people, but everybody is indifferent. No one looks at anyone. They're all enemies. They pay for their ticket staring at the machine with a face like a tiger and go on their way" (97).

Osvaldo Pellettieri argues that "it is easy to see the nature of [*El guarda* 323] as a *sainete* from the *dramatis personae:* only 9 of its 42 characters are named, and the rest are defined by their function within the text: 'The snorer,' 'The smoker,' 'The spitter.'" In addition, I would note the authors' success in taking full advantage of the genre's dual focus. Their task was to portray modern public space as interactive: as a world regimented by strict ordinances on the one hand and, on the other, by the vagaries and sloppiness of the grotesque city and its fickle minds, which relentlessly undo these ordinances. The interior industrial/social design of the public transportation system must have added further to the process of depersonalization, as Don Pascual incisively remarks: the seats were rigid, "without compartments, the . . . carriage had all passengers facing the front, staring at one another's backs rather than faces" (Sennett 1994, 344). Places of public encounter had become deterrents to social connectivity. Yet although trains, subways, and avenues diverted the conflictive city to the exterior and the socialized city to the interior, urban space was still open to intersecting identities, overlapping boundaries, overflow, and excess. The best example of such hybridity is Don Pascual, who, in his capacity as a tramcar conductor, is required to enforce the same practices in transculturation he criticizes, inspired by empirical wisdom.

Don Pascual opens a channel of communication to the great theater audiences of Buenos Aires by addressing them *cara a cara* (face to face). He confronts them directly from the stage, protected by the intimacy of a suburban street in the calm of ten o'clock at night, confident that the laterality of shared experiences in the barrio will draw him closer to his listeners.[7] Indeed, he creates a social setting for the audience that dramatically reverses the imposition of practices aimed at the socialization of individualism and endorses the interpersonal connectivity of an organic society. His address evinces an awareness of how much modernizing forces have already begun to affect him and the city. The "familiar faces" of his listeners encourage him to talk about "two or three matters that have been overlooked." But what has been overlooked? This "traveler in urban time" (the phrase is García Canclini's) retrieves a dialogic space in social/collective identities disconnected from the socializing forces of modernization. When he asks "Has the world gone crazy, then?" he does so from the utopian standpoint of a dissident social subject evaluating the transformation of his present.

Don Pascual's candid speech clearly exceeds the rule that forbids everything "not part of my job" (Discépolo 1987b, 85), and he succeeds, at least for the duration of his address, in overturning the restrictions of his new working identity: "Excuse me if I chatter a little, but when I can speak without the uniform . . . I feel a different man. . . . I'm no longer a guard. . . . I'm a man and I like to talk" (97). Talking *zenza l'uniforme* (without the uniform) is like touching the other. Sennett recalls Alexis de Tocqueville's dismayed remark about the modern city: "Each person . . . behaves as though he is a stranger to the destiny of all others. . . . He may mix among them; but he sees them not; he touches them, but he does not feel them" (1994, 323). The masses do not feel united by their proximity; they feel only physical contiguity. Many urban systems put a progressive scale in place in order to manage the gradations of social distance. Yet even though transportation, zoning regulations, housing floor plans, and identities imposed by the culture of labor led to the shores of modern sociability, everything depended on where you wanted to go. Discépolo's character is a truly unique subject: he changes several of these gradations and arrives at where he wants to be by stopping the rhythm of the city and embracing others in the quiet stillness of the suburb.

In *La cabeza de Goliath* (1940), Ezequiel Martínez Estrada describes how "tramcars and passengers are swept along [in Buenos Aires] like particles of metal in electric whirlwinds. This infinitely complex, living mass is in a state of perpetual unrest" (1940, 32), throbbing with restlessness, kinetic passion, and tachycardia "in the chauffeur, in the pedestrian, in the tradesman behind his counter, in the person talking on the phone, in someone waiting for his girlfriend, and in someone drinking coffee determined not to do anything" (33). We infer from Discépolo's *sainete* that, by 1914 or 1915, the interpersonal distances set by urban culture were already heavily demanding and experienced as a source of frustration. Just because public transportation systems had expanded did not mean that *porteños* felt closer to each other. Perhaps the speeding up of physical circulation, the intensity of the work schedule, and the little spare time left for wandering and improvisation might be read as *distractions* meant to regulate threats unleashed by the grotesque city from its spontaneous edges.

To speak of uniforms—and of the process of creating cultural uniformity —is to speak of disguises. Perhaps this is why the theme of carnival is so evident in the imaginary of the turn of the twentieth century. The *conventillo* in Carlos Mauricio Pacheco's *sainete Los disfrazados* (In Costume, 1906) is like every *conventillo:* a privileged space for analyzing the intersection of rural and urban worlds. Gauchos (horsemen) from the pampas mix with *compadres* from the suburbs and Cocoliche immigrants, in the sentimental culture of the *folletín,* the tango, and the ballads of the *payadores.*[8] One gaucho character makes fun of the new uniform worn by his neighbor, a driver for the Anglo-Argentina Company: "A little kid suit . . . all tin buttons like a porter at the Congress building. . . . That's why I prefer to go without and stay hungry. . . . You've given up like a sap. You, the tough guy from Floresta . . . you used to wear your cap at an angle, and your red silk handkerchief spilled out over your pocket like an open knife wound in your heart. . . . You too have put on a disguise" (Pacheco 1964, 20). In *Los disfrazados,* either "we all live in disguise" or we sell ourselves out, like the driver who has "gone the way of the gringos and electricity, which makes everything as easy as pie" (20). The subjective, the spontaneous, and the alternative are blocked by disguises as a way of internalizing the new socially appropriate behaviors. Sennett concludes that urban planning in transitional cities is aimed at discouraging "the movement of organized groups through the city. Individual bodies moving through urban space gradually became detached from the space in which they moved, and from the people the space contained" (1994, 323). Thus, time and place are perceived as an expression of displacement in *Los disfrazados,* as an obsession with disguises: "On account of its size and its dynamic, many-sided life, Buenos Aires . . . is one city within another. No one can know it well. Its pace of change is too violent to follow. To visit it from one end to the other is, for us *porteños,* to seek out the unknown within our own home" (Sanguinetti 1937, 12).

Beginning with the city's expansion and the drop in public transportation fares in 1900, the working class relocated from the center to the suburbs, while commercial and financial activities remained concentrated in the center, a space under the tight control of capital. The center of Buenos Aires thus became an immense setting intended to induce modern social practices in a citizenry relentlessly persuaded to take them all in. Cinemas, theaters, cafés, patisseries, racetracks, dancehalls, restaurants, cabarets, and so on were the new cultural spaces for new social habits that prompted blatant consumption. Now it became "necessary" to acquire a whole new wardrobe for each habit. The range of merchandise available was therefore more diversified, and the pressure consumers felt to acquire the new fashions and manners was increased through the press, literature, and the *folletín,* which became socializing agents in the massification of practices endorsed by local elites acting as the intermediaries of global culture.

In his report *La fatiga y sus proyecciones sociales* (Fatigue and Its Social Consequences), Alfredo Palacios, the Socialist representative in Congress, circulated an impressive body of writing on debates over shortening the workday in industrialized countries. He alluded to reports by the Lombardy Heart Institute; *La fatigue intellectuelle* (Intellectual Fatigue); *Les journées de huit heures* (Eight-Hour Days); *Use of Factory Statistics in the Investigation of Industrial Fatigue; Le Mouvement Syndical Internationale* (The International Union Movement); *La Revue International du Travail* (The International Labor Review); *Ekonomischeskaia Zhizn* (Economic Life); *Nya Daygligt Allehanda* (New Daily News), by the Chamber of Commerce in Scaine, Sweden; *Information Sociale,* by the Croatian Committee of the Federation of Employers in Industry and Commerce; *The Franco-American Report to American Manufacturers,* and many more. Palacios detailed resolutions from the Congress of Workers in Baltimore (1916), the International Congress of Workers in Geneva (1917), the International Conference at Berne (1913), the Conference of Trades Unions at Leeds (1916), the International Trades Unions Congress (1921), the Conference of the Trades Unions of the Confederation of Danish Unions (1919), and the latest meetings of the International Bureau of Labour. He also referred to decrees reducing the length of the workday in France (1915); the Soviet Union (1917); Germany (1918); Austria, Czechoslovakia, Poland, Holland, Norway, Spain, Switzerland, and Sweden (1919); and other countries.

Texts like Alfredo Palacios's, along with congressional debates, are proof of the internationalism of Argentina's citizenship. The National Congress was not functioning in a political vacuum, but was attentive to an impressive body of thought directed at understanding the social impact of transition in the industrial mode of production. Political life followed the international trajectory of movement and countermovement, not only to implement new social and labor rights but above all to establish evidence of the strength of the country's highly participatory public sphere. Studies in the new science of industrial medicine were the source of proposals for laws, parliamentary discussions, union resolutions, demands, and strikes, at the same time as they were at the core of labor associations, international congresses, and exchanges among different social agents. Public life brought together a broad spectrum of social actors, including doctors, biologists, lawyers, workers, legislators, traders, public administrators, scientists, and educators. A cartoon appearing in *Caras y Caretas* (figure 8) characterized the Argentinean public sphere as a place for chatter and the open exchange of opinions and writings, seemingly indistinguishable, during the Radical government's reign, from the public sphere of any country of metropolitan modernity. It was flexible, changeable, and above all interactive. Such political hyperventilation was vividly represented in the imaginaries of the first part of the twentieth century, corresponding to the liberal image that Argentinean society proudly held of itself—as a porous, progressive, and evolving space where social agents enjoyed a place of honor.

Such enabling imaginaries prepared the citizenry to accept any kind of novelty in any context, such as vending machines and Coca-Cola (a term also used to describe idle women: "You're more useless than a Coca Cola").[9] Even vegetarianism flourished, inspired by Rousseau's rationalism and endorsed by Echeverría's and Sarmiento's revulsion at the "carnivorous atavism" of the gaucho's barbarian barbecue,[10] although it nonetheless constituted a scandalous offense to the national(ist) diet.[11] The milieu was equally propitious for shifts in gender identity, as in Florentino B. Chiarello's *Hay que conservar la línea* (Keep in Shape, 1927), in which a military man, with his sleeves rolled up, recites a recipe for fried tongue. Or for cultural crossings, as in *El hombre del frac* (The Man in the Morning Coat, 1927), a *sainete* by Ives de Mirande and André Picard, in which Bebe Domínguez, a *bacán*— a typical fat-cat oligarch, a wastrel man-about-town, his hair slicked down with gel—ventures into the area of Buenos Aires known as El Sur (the South): "At noon I went for a stroll around the docks. You know how important our docks are, what? How the people work like dogs! I don't know what they can be thinking! In La Boca I was caught in a downpour and spent two hours watching it rain and putting up with a sailor who wanted to sell me a used umbrella. . . . They were eating on the ships and barges. My nostrils feasted on a symphony of aromas from soups and stews, pastas, minestrone, and meat roasted *a la criolla.*" As Bebe strolls in his tailcoat along Puerto Madero, he is condescending enough to appreciate the economic importance of the docks, the strenuous work of the stevedores, and the other goings-on in La Boca. Just to be on the safe side, however, he doesn't eat on one of the barges, but at an elegant restaurant where the menu allows him a choice of "roast boar's meat," "golden capybara cooked slowly," "duck preserved in its own fat," "roast beef," wine from Romanée, even tripe. The *other* Buenos Aires was in reality several, and the fact that these overlapped facilitated transfers and intense cultural hybridity, as in gastronomy, parody, and many other ways of crossing cultural frontiers. When Bebe's circle of friends decides to organize an outing, "there's nothing like a ballroom in a barrio outside the city center. The ladies will think they're off on an adventure." Outside their usual haunts, they listen to *tonadilleras* (popular singers) and dance the tango, in a scene that is by itself enough to confirm imaginaries in which social bridges were extended from the Conservative Order to Radicalism and beyond. What is implied by these men in tailcoats and slicked-down hair who cross over into the other Buenos Aires? What does this movement into the urban fringes of the tango mean?

The geographical and cultural expansion of tango suggests an infinitely open, fluid city where the cultural, ethnic, and linguistic heterogeneity of the *arrabal* could slip into other districts of Buenos Aires, into the rest of Argentina, and even into Europe. But it was not just a matter of turning up and fitting in. In *Memorias de un viejo* (Memories of an Old Man, 1888), Víctor Gálvez (Vicente G. Quesada) analyzes and stigmatizes the social agents of tango, from his perception of an ethnically and culturally unified nation:

> The transformation of the *compadrito* is always difficult because he is affected by nature and vain enough to believe himself better than others. . . . The person, either man or woman, who has not learned how to choose colors, how to dress, how to speak or to walk, is considered *guarango* [uncouth] in popular language. He lives in a small town, never in the city centers; he prefers the suburb . . . between town and country. . . . He is persuaded that putting his knife in his mouth, fighting with it . . . smoking black tobacco in the parlor, at the table, in the patio, and on the street are features of distinction. . . . He very likely has yellow-stained fingers and walks with a sway from right to left" (qtd. in Ulla 1982, 20).

Besides being a militant nonsmoker, Gálvez attacks the total lack of social composure of the suburbs with regard to standards in the socialization of dress, cultured speech, and posture. What is this swaying, effeminate gait!?

Tango originated in about 1877 in "*candombe* societies made up of men and women of color [whose] headquarters were set up in the barrio of Mondongo . . . on the western side of the barrio of Montserrat" (Gobello 1980, 10–11). José Gobello cites Francisco Romay, who describes the Afro-Argentinean mutual societies founded with the objective of collecting funds for freeing slaves: "Mud huts with thatched roofs. . . . They also celebrated their holidays, . . . [which] were dances, kinds of savage rituals performed to the sound of primitive instruments; the sensual dances that went on for hours and hours were almost always immodest and were often a cause for intervention by the authorities" (qtd. in Gobello 1980, 11). And if the authorities did not show up to restore order, Romay was certain to intervene discursively, in order to put things in their place with racist pronouncements. The "uncouth" suburb (*guarango arrabalero*) was stigmatized for its loud colors; its hybridity; its lewd, lascivious dancing; and its inhabitants' penchant for practicing dental hygiene with knives instead of toothpicks.

The barrio of Mondongo had taken its name from an association of former slaves. According to Fernando Ortíz, "a certain region in the Congo . . . was called *Dongo. Mu Dongo* is obtained from the addition of the Bantu native prefix *mu,* to give Mondongo, which was also influenced by the Spanish *mondongo* (meaning 'stomach lining of cattle')" (qtd. in Gobello 1980, 11). From such syncretism, the most spectacular cultural, linguistic, choreographic, and corporeal hybridization to occur in Argentinean culture was achieved. The swaying gait (*caminar canyengue*) and stops and turns (*cortes y quebradas*) of the dance became the emblematic discourse of the vulgar, insolent, and fractious grotesque city. Its social agents, "not easily transformed," succeeded in evading the modern city. Just look at them! They walk in a "strange," "suspicious" way! As Gobello points out, the music and choreography of tango is an Africanization of the *milonga* and the mazurka from the outskirts of the city, the pampa, and the world of the gaucho, who was on his way to being drawn into urban culture. Gaucho literature, or *criollismo,* would turn him into a national(ist) icon whose purity would counter the transculturalization of the gaucho-turned-*compadrito,* a subject irreversibly "tainted" by the fluid edges of the city.[12] The tango, by contrast, became linked to the circus, life in the bordello, the dance's eroticism sending normal criteria of judgment into crisis. Thus, the border crossings negotiated by Bebe Domínguez's friends (to Boedo, El Sur, and the tango) imply a slippage through the cracks of the unifying city, at least from the standpoint of enabling imaginaries. After a life of unrestrained profligacy, Bebe ends up as an usher in a Boedo cinema, a fact that turns no one pale in Buenos Aires. He wears a tailcoat, is a man-about-town by day, and works in Boedo by night. His friends (and this imaginary) suggest, however, that he is not exactly on the road to wrack and ruin, because he will soon be back at his elegant *garçonière:* "There are cases like his every day in Buenos Aires. Today they fall, tomorrow they rise again." In fact, a timely inheritance does indeed allow him to "rise" again.

When the ne'er-do-wells (*bacanes*) visited El Sur, they were, in effect, making an excursion into a different urban time, which still survived in 1927. Their outings were made possible thanks to the impressive layers of the social archive compressed into tango, including the substratum of Afro-Argentinean identity, although this ethnicity's presence in the city had been diluted by miscegenation and the amnesia of racism and nationalism. When the *bacanes* listened to the *tonadilleras,* they were hearing the voices of demographic diversity preserved in the syncretic space of the tango. In 1927, everything seemed possible in Buenos Aires. The sons of the Fatherland rubbed shoulders with Nation's bastards, while enabling imaginaries assured everyone that people fall and then rise again—never the other way around.

5 THEATERS
AND CAFÉS

W HEN THE URBAN TRAVELER
reached the center, the city gained another consumer for the stunning array
of choices from the entertainment industry. Corrientes Street was at the core:
"From all the barrios, squashed together inside a hundred tramcars . . . a
yelling, laughing multitude travels en route for the night. . . . The night is
on Corrientes Street . . . awaiting them with open theaters, cinemas, and
brightly lit cafés" (Marechal, *Historia de la Calle Corrientes;* qtd. in Troncoso
1983, 303). The dazzling street, studded with lights and illuminated signs,
stood in for Buenos Aires as a whole in the urban imaginary, becoming the
setting for the Golden Age of popular theater (1897–1910), which brought
together an eager public and an impressive output of dramas, comedies,
sainetes, grotescos, and revues. In 1910, the year of the Centennial, 97 dramas
and comedies were performed in Spanish, before an audience of 1,001,638.
There were 414 performed in Italian, with 580,848 spectators, and 119 in
French, with 327,628 spectators (Diego 1983, 146). And of course, the number
of theaters multiplied to accommodate this enthusiasm: the Doria Theater
(1887), the Onrubia (1890), the Odeon (1892), the Mayo (1893), the Politeama,

the Teatro della Alegría, the Teatro della Victoria, the Colón Theater (1901), the Apollo, the Cervantes (1921), the Ateneo and Mitre (1925), the Theater House (1927), and so on. Thus, the twentieth century began with a complement of theaters ready to accommodate a massive public in unprecedented numbers.

The theater industry was supported between 1910 and 1934 by the professionalization of writers and journalists and by forty different magazines and periodicals. Popular publishing established culture for the masses through *folletines* such as *La novela semanal* (The Weekly Novel, 1917), *La novela para todos* (A Novel for All, 1918), *La novela femenina* (A Novel for Women, 1920), and *La novela universitaria* (The University Novel, 1921) (Mazzioti 1990, 71). Modernity had inaugurated new public spaces—the street, the newspaper and *folletín,* the factory, the workshop, the Congress, the *conventillo,* the cabaret, the *garçonière,* and the great department stores—but it was the theater that brought all these spaces together. Next to tango, the theater was the most all-embracing of cultural spaces because of its capacity to include a wide array of allusions to urban areas, social types, everyday customs, and languages: cynical political committee men, fragile children selling newspapers, proletarian women bent over sewing machines, adulterous and virtuous women, fugitive anarchists, organ grinders from the barrio, drug traffickers, *bacanes,* naive provincials, aristocrats facing bankruptcy and suicide, exploited prostitutes and shady pimps from the sinful city, street vendors, "Turks with handbarrows, Jews with their pitiful suitcases, Andalusians carrying baskets, Italians selling peanuts" (Posada, Speroni, and Vignolo 1982, 151).

I would highlight that as modernity gathered momentum, it broke the traditional molds of representation in its path and created new ones. It is interesting to note that the performance of the material experience of the quotidian became the core of modernity and shaped the emergence of a vast display of discourses aimed at absorbing its complex texture and simultaneity. Among them, the *género chico*—consisting of short pieces of one or two scenes that might be musicals, revues, comic or satirical plays, *costumbrista* scenes, or dramas—responded best to the challenge. The *género chico* restructured how the aesthetic and the social interacted, reflecting the crises in political participation and the visibility acquired by new social agents from the middle and proletarian classes. This form captured a world and events that were immediately and easily recognizable to the audience. In the *sainete Primero en la colorada* (First Past the Post), for example, the characters consult actual racing schedules from the newspapers. Anarchists in the drama *Puerto Madero* read in the morning paper about their own participation in the previous night's strike. The female characters in *La buena vida* (The Good Life) read the popular Piedmontese author Carolina Invernizio, and *La mujer que odiaba a los hombres* (The Woman Who Hated Men) alludes to Dr. Julieta Lanteri's suffragette protest in the center of Buenos Aires. In *El marido de mi novia* (My Girlfriend's Husband), an upholsterer sings a hit tango, and in *Nadie la conoció nunca* (No One Ever Knew Her), a character remembers his last meeting with the poet Evaristo Carriego in El Inmortal, a well-known *porteño* restaurant.

Nemesio Trejo, perhaps the most brilliant and innovative of all the *sainete* writers, led the way with such immediate, contemporary references. Opening on 21 October 1907, his groundbreaking play *Los inquilinos* (The Tenants) alluded to events from the end of August, just two months before the work's first performance. Trejo's astute eye undoubtedly caught the sociohistorical transcendence of the first strike by inhabitants of the *conventillos,* which for the first time politically mobilized new social agents, especially proletarian housewives (figure 9). The reviewer for *La Prensa* wrote that "the audience filling the theater did not spare its applause," recognizing the "highly topical" theme (qtd. in Pellarollo 1997, 186). Trejo aimed his spotlight remarkably well, highlighting a landmark in the city's social history at the same time as he opened the history of Argentinean literature to a consideration of how everyday reality could indeed effect changes in discursive and aesthetic paradigms. The public even recognized every trick and maneuver property owners like Timoteo used to evict their tenants:

> TIMOTEO: I'll report the house to the Department of Health and say there have been cases of bubonic plague and yellow fever so they'll order it vacated. I've no intention of dropping the rent by a cent. . . . Property is inviolable. The law and the constitution protect the rights of the owner. (Trejo 1912, 21–22)

Moreover, when *Los inquilinos*'s characters sang "El tango de los inquilinos" (The Tenants' Tango), the theater audience joined in:

> Down with extortion
> and down with abuse.
> Up with the rights

of the poor man too.
With our song we ask
for justice, justice.

Set to the music of "La morocha" (written by Enrique Saborino and Ángel
Villoldo in 1905), this tango's lyrics were adapted as "La suba de los alquil-
eres" (The Rise in the Rents), referring to the 1907 strike, and circulated as
such along the porous channels of popular culture. Such a pioneering authorial decision converted Trejo into a mindful compiler of the products of
popular culture and a cultural catalyst who understood the importance of
recording the instantaneous reactions of social agents commenting on their
immediate surroundings.

The *sainete*'s imaginaries offered a view of the everyday, seeking to bring
coherence to the spectator's sense of social laterality within the urban experience. It seemed that any event in the everyday history (*petite histoire*) of the
city could resonate in theater performances. The *sainete* was verbose, stereotypical, populist, and melodramatic. It was the first modern discourse to
record the immigrant city and to offer an image of a collective in a constant
state of definition, transition, and change. Audiences at the popular theater
also saw themselves represented in the *sainete*'s innumerable subgenres,
speaking their own loose colloquial languages: "There are as many dialects
as there are different groups of people, all of which just adds to the confusion" (Posada, Speroni, and Vignolo 1982, 154). Alberto Vacarezza referred
to the *sainete* as "the joy, the grace, and the color of Buenos Aires placed in
your heart," summarizing it as follows:

> A tenement patio
> an Italian manager,
> a headstrong Spaniard, an attractive woman, a scheming man,
> two toughs with knives, an exchange of words, a fit of passion,
> a conflict, jealousy, an argument,
> a challenge, a stabbing, high emotions, a shot,
> a call for help, the cops, . . . the curtain.
>
> (Qtd. in Posada, Speroni, and Vignolo 1982, 154)

Abel Posada, Marta Speroni, and Griselda Vignolo explain that new plays
opened every week, with up to five performances a day, during the Golden
Age, Argentina's first example of mass culture and an advanced culture in-

dustry, which, in the 1920s, began to compete with Hollywood cinema and later with radio (Posada, Speroni, and Vignolo 1982, 158). It mingled events of everyday life, music, dancing, and tango, creating a network of discursive crossings in which reciprocal exchange, even with the cinema, was commonplace, as in DeFilippis Novoa's *sainete La vendedora* (The Salesclerk), adapted for the screen as *La vendedora de Harrods* (The Salesclerk at Harrods, 1921).

With such a wide assortment of subgenres in popular theater, the eclectic *género chico* created a social and representational space for the middle and proletarian classes that was denied in high culture. It embraced both the optimism/conformity of the *sainete* and a gallery of dispirited, pitiful souls, left stranded on the city's margins by economic crises and the crises in identity that followed. The action of the *sainete* unfolds in public spaces (tenement courtyards, streets, and bars), while that of the *grotesco* takes place in dark interiors and wretched store back rooms—spaces so oppressive they seem more like caves or prisons. This specialization addressed different objectives. Signs in the *grotesco* are ambiguous and uncertain because they are intended to demonstrate that institutions such as the family and the state have deteriorated. By contrast, the *sainete* proposes encounters, truces, and hopes, metaphorized in the racial and linguistic mix found in the *conventillos,* from which Argentina's *razza forte* (mighty breed) will emerge. The *género chico,* then, represents intersecting spaces, allowing the exchange and realignment of identities. If we trace the evolution and networks of imaginaries of that time, however, we might conclude that the stereotyping popular theater incurred in the wake of its Golden Age prevented it from countering dominant imaginaries. While it did tackle everyday issues, and was for this reason alone highly explosive, because of its remarkable audience appeal, its appropriation by mass culture nevertheless meant that often situations "that had turned out to be successful, moving, or pleasing to the public" (Mazziotti 1990, 75) were merely repeated. The Italian immigrants in the *sainetes* would always be nostalgic Cocoliches, and although they pronounced severe and well-reasoned criticisms, the hilarity provoked by their linguistic shortcomings ended up dissolving any authorized place there may have been for their truth.

The leisure industry also promoted the establishment of cafés and bars in Buenos Aires, which led to habits adopted for after work or for when the theaters turned out. Borges's character in "El Zahir" (1949) enters an old-style bar on the corner of Chile and Tacuarí: "To my misfortune, three men were playing cards in the shop. . . . I ordered a glass of orange juice and was given a *zahir* with the change." Shops (*almacenes*) like these sold not only wine "but every kind of rough alcohol" (Scenna 1977, 111). However, Borges's scene is a pure anachronism, because these *almacenes,* once typical of the *arrabal* in the Gran Aldea, had been replaced by cafés by 1930. As the city stretched into the pampa, the country bars (*pulperías*) gave way to the suburban *almacenes* and then to the cafés. On Avenida de Mayo, there was no trace left of the evanescent past. The strict zoning in the center explains the density of the cafés along this street, including the Café Tortoni, the only one to survive. There were, at one time, forty-five cafés in ten blocks alone, from Cabildo to Congreso: La Prensa, Nueva Prensa, Confitería París, Montevideo Chico, La Cosechera, Café Madrid, La Querencia, Gaulois, Café Eslava, Paulista, Café and Bar Yokohama, American Bar, Café La Castellana, Café La Puerta del Sol, Café La Toja, Café Iberia, Café del Hotel París, Café Español, Café del Centenario, Cervecería Berna, Café Avenida Keller, Ciudad de Londres, and so on. Their names act as an archive of nostalgic memory for immigrants of all origins, especially those from Spain.

The dynamic of the center's daily activity has not been better reconstructed than in *Buenos Aires* (1919), a *sainete* by César Iglesias Paz. And what better way to appreciate the impact of the Avenida de Mayo than to see it through the astonished eyes of the members of a provincial family, who succumb to the novelties of the city as soon as they arrive and find themselves enjoying a coffee while sitting in a café on a public sidewalk that was uncommonly wide for the Gran Aldea. As the man from the provinces declares, "Buenos Aires is full of temptations": riding on a streetcar, using the post office, joining the bustle on the street, taking five o'clock tea or drinking a bottled soda, asking for room service, riding elevators, talking on the telephone, meeting on street corners, handing out visiting cards, and above all watching women on the streets at any hour of the day—especially "those aged seventeen . . . because there are so many of them here":

FILIBERTO: The way they look!

FEDERICO: I can see one from here dressed in pink, and I'm gazing at her now! What an adventure! Have another little cup of coffee, father-in-law. I know what I'm talking about.

FILIBERTO (*giving in*): But, son . . .

Urban Ceremonies and Social Distances

FEDERICO: . . . What have you come to Buenos Aires for? Nobody knows about anything here. It's not like back home where you can't even stick your nose out onto the street.

The shamelessness of the *porteñas* and the anonymity of the city excite the fantasy of the provincials to the point of flirting with adultery. In the eyes of the rest of Argentina, the capital is synonymous with single men leading a dissipated life "amid the clubs and late-night revels, friends and girlfriends," and anonymity intensifies this feeling. Although "carnival is necessary" in the provinces, so that people are not recognized, in Buenos Aires, by contrast, "disguise is not needed," "because people don't know each other that well." Given "the reputation of Buenos Aires for fantasy," people arrive with "the illusion that . . . it's an enchanted city," like a magnet that draws people in with promises of making a wealth of personal fantasies and dreams come true: a husband for a single woman, for example, or an affair for a married man. The experience that has the most impact, however, is the feeling of being part of the crowd in the street: "Look how the people move in crowds, *in waves,* at these rowdy fiestas" (emphasis added). That this is a new corporeal experience, there is no doubt: "Close control is impossible in this world of people where some unscrupulous type is always ready to outsmart your vigilance":

FILIBERTO: I'm a wreck. . . . I was pushed, squeezed, trampled, bitten. . . . There were moments when my feet no longer touched the ground. I was walking on air. . . . "Don't shove," "Let me by. Are you going to walk over me or something?" . . . Fortunately, two attentive gentlemen at my side held me up. How attentive they were . . . two very polite gentlemen!

FEDERICO: Could they have been thieves? . . .

FILIBERTO: My watch! They've pinched my watch! How can this be?

Buenos Aires submits the newcomers to noise, sin, and distraction. The women finally conclude that "Buenos Aires drives men mad" and decide "never to come back." Sanity will return when the family takes itself home to their uneventful province: "If you ask me, we can leave right now . . . nothing but car horns . . . sheer noise, that's Buenos Aires."

When he died, the writer Conrado Nalé Roxlo (1898–1971) declared, he wanted to be in a room "with dark wood and clear mirrors . . . with huge windows . . . overlooking an avenue where it is still possible . . . to follow the natural flow of the seasons . . . watching the rustling flight of the chestnut-colored leaves [falling from the old plantain trees]" (qtd. in Ostuni and Himschoot 1994, 32). His description alludes to the interior of the café La Cosechera, once frequented by Roberto Arlt, Roberto Mariani, Jorge Luis Borges, the Logroño poet Pedro Herreros, Carlos de la Pua, Enrique and Raúl Tuñón de Lara, and others. And Roxlo even includes a reference to Safón, "an adventurous Catalonian waiter, well read and attracted to literature, willing to serve coffee on credit and to loan money without interest" (qtd. in Ostuni and Himschoot 1994, 32). The cafés brought waiters and intellectuals together, as at Los Inmortales, where Florencio Sánchez, Evaristo Carriego, Horacio Quiroga, Alberto Gerchunoff, José Ingenieros, Ricardo Rojas, Alfredo Palacios, Rubén Darío, Jean Jaurés, and Ramón del Valle Inclán used to meet.

The *confiterías* were another novelty. When a character in "El Aleph" named Borges enters a *confitería* out of misplaced nostalgia, a single glance is enough to confirm the cruel metamorphosis of a city that has robbed him of his sacred places, the love of Beatriz Elena Viterbo, and even the National Prize for Literature. The victorious rival in his fight for Beatriz's love and for the prize is Carlos Argentino Daneri, a strident fan of modernity who writes panegyrics in praise of "the principal stores in the parish of Concepción," "the estate belonging to Mariana de Cambaceres de Alvear on Calle Once de Septiembre in Belgrano," and "a gasometer to the north of Calle Veracruz." Daneri has invited him for "a glass of milk in the salon-bar next door that Zunino and Zungri, out of a sense of progress, . . . have opened on my corner. It's a *confitería,* you should know. I accepted more out of resignation than enthusiasm" (Borges 1974, 1: 612). The owners' names refer to Italian immigration, as does the name of Carlos Daneri himself. However much he considers himself Argentinean, "the Italian 's' and frequent gesticulation still persist in [Daneri] at a distance of two generations" (1: 618). Zunino is a lawyer "of proverbial seriousness" and, unfortunately, also the owner of a noisy but highly successful business. Borges heads out for his meeting calculating the reasons why he should not go and, worse still, the risks of remaining in that "inexorably modern salon-bar [that] was hardly less awful than I expected. At neighboring tables, the patrons animatedly discussed how much Zunini and Zungri had invested, without sparing a dime" (1: 621).

In such bars and cafés, Borges finds himself caught up in the vulgarity of social others who drink milk (*toma leche*). As we realize, modernity tends to mix everything together, so that any establishment that flaunts its public character only exaggerates Borges's sociophobia, in which even the telephone exposes him to the unwelcome outside world.[1] Once he is forced to accept Daneri's invitation, Borges will have to put up with "the man's" immigrant accent and the versatility, passion, and triviality of the products of his mind. Inside the *confitería*, Borges's suspicions ("the salon-bar [that] is hardly less awful than I expected") only triple his phobias, his fear of confronting situations that are far too open—namely immigrant Argentina; the *confitería* full of rowdy customers; and the pain he still feels at having been abandoned by Beatriz Viterbo, Daneri's cousin, who, although dead since 1929, is nonetheless a measure of Borges's failure and Daneri's success.

Although they have only recently opened the *confitería,* the "inexhaustible Zunino and Zungri" are already planning to expand it. Borges feels that everything and everyone, except himself, is in a state of total expansion, especially the modernity of the likes of Zunino-Zungri-Daneri, the new money, and Italian upstarts who are upsetting everything by winning the second National Prize for Literature in a field of cultural endeavor that was once the sole province of Borges's class and its Writers Club. This is modernity at its most extreme, a space as intolerably open and boundless as that "outrageous *confitería*." An overwrought Borges, then, feels protected by his agoraphobic and claustrophobic sensorial geography. For this reason, he distances himself from Daneri, who has already gotten his hands on so many sacred sites. His poems dare to degrade not only the Cambaceres estates, a stalwart against modern exogamous socialization, but also the world of literature and the beloved Beatriz, who surrendered to her boisterous upstart of a cousin in spite of her membership in the aristocratic Club Hípico (Riding Club). In order not to run into him—in order to regain some kind of self-control—Borges needs to forget the city that has betrayed him with such careless metamorphoses, embodied in flighty women like Beatriz.

Going back to less private stories, the Café Germinal, the Café Feminista, and El Revolucionario Español were anarchist centers where "the waiters, whom we always used to address as 'comrades,' were men versed in politics and readers of progressive newspapers" (Larroca, Soler Cañas, and Scenna 1977, 132). Artistic gatherings and meetings of militants were also held in these spaces of cultural consumption. Books by intellectuals and bohemians were launched. Journalists from *La Nación* and *La Prensa* used them as offices, and sessions of Congress were discussed over their marble-topped tables. José Antonio Saldías summarized the atmosphere: "You could spend the whole afternoon with just one coffee without anyone daring to remove you. Can you imagine what that meant for someone who was unemployed or gloomy, for whom it was torture to go back to an unwelcoming room, where the only attraction was a bed, when worn out with fatigue at midnight or in the small hours of the morning?" (qtd. in Scenna 1977, 127). The typical café waiter is compellingly conjured in Juan Guijarro's "Mozo de café":

> Waiter: Coffee!
> (The automaton returns with the coffee poured and inspires these
>   verses in me.)
> Waiter, you live buried
> inside the lugubrious luxury of your party suit,
> that pressed tuxedo, coffin of your soul . . .
> you're the strangest of workers,
> to whom everyone speaks familiarly for a ten-cent tip.
> Although the glasses on your tray give false cheer
> (they are women after all),
> don't tarnish your smile
> and give cause to consume you from within! . . .
> one day you'll cast off your prison garb,
> which even has a number on it, and on that day, young man,
> your heart will beat manfully. (Qtd. in Ostuni and Himschoot 1994, 22)

The coffin, the automatism, the depersonalizing costume, the prison garb—all evoke a necrophiliac city. This "strangest of workers" would fit very well into Burton Pike's explanation of the nineteenth-century city as a metaphor of disintegration: "[The] character or narrator typically presents himself alone, against the city, an isolated individual consciousness observing the urban community" (1996, 247). Like Balzac's Vautrin, the new heroes and heroines are marginal figures (Rastignac, Lucien Chardon), linked to the orphanage in Dickens, to the neurotic in Baudelaire, and to the underground in Dostoyevsky. Roberto Arlt's Erdosain summarizes them all, at the same time as he embodies urban imaginaries as social fragmentation. He always feels like "a stranger in a city where he missed the train" (Arlt 1981c,

1: 133). Every personal contact forces him to distance himself in order to avoid the closeness and enmity he feels "for people to whom too many confidences have been made" (1: 133). And he has good reason for feeling this way: "[Erdosain] entered the Japanese bar. Drivers and pimps sat in circles around the tables. A black man . . . plucked parasites from his underarm, and three Polish pimps, with heavy gold rings on their fingers, talked about bordellos and procuresses in their jargon. . . . The black man . . . looked about him . . . but no one paid him any attention" (1: 129). Even though the patrons share a common area, every table in the bar is a sociospatial cubicle, which is perfectly suitable for Erdosain. After ordering "a coffee, he leaned his forehead on his hand and sat staring at the tabletop" (1: 129). Such an imaginary suggests that public spaces are not precisely meeting places and that any intimacy is unbearable. In Buenos Aires, an immense quantity of cultural texts was concerned with flight from social contact. Proxemic distances, paranoiac perceptions, and phobias imposed a compulsive withdrawal from the slightest touch, contact, or interaction. They advised distance and precautions of every kind, including, of course, misogyny. Remember, no women are found in the cafés mentioned above—which is, perhaps, for the best. As Guijarro remarks to the waiter, almost in passing, "your heart will beat manfully," and "the glasses on your tray give false cheer / (they are women after all)."

How were the enthralling lights of the center seen by an outsider? The "English Saturday," the result of a piece of imported legislation, came into effect in 1932. The journalist Miguel Navas interviewed seven office workers, as well as the author of the legislation, Dr. Enrique Dickman, who had proposed that work should stop at midday on Saturday "so that . . . a quicker recovery from the wear and tear on the muscles and nerves might be obtained" (Navas 1932b, 23). Nevertheless, as one worker explained, even after a business closed, "the personnel are almost always kept on until after 8 P.M., and since we all start work before 8 A.M. . . . this means that we work about 10 hours a day" (15). Such were the precariousness of Law and the uncertainty of the working environment. In *Las aguafuertes porteñas (Porteño Sketches)*, Roberto Arlt describes another side to the reform in "La tristeza del sábado inglés" (The Misery of the English Saturday), namely the relation between the citizen and the space of the city center, which acquires meaning, and embraces its subjects, only when it is attached to systemic/market functions: "The silence of the tomb hangs over the city. . . . without any money, place to go or desire to go anywhere" (Arlt 1981a, 74): "I was out walking one Saturday . . . when, on the opposite side of the road, . . . I saw an office worker, with stooped shoulders, who was walking slowly, leading a three-year-old child by the hand. The child was sporting, quite innocently, one of those little ribboned bonnets, not an old one, but a nonetheless pitiable one. . . . The little girl was walking slowly and her father even more so. And in a flash I caught a room in a boardinghouse and saw the child's mother, a young woman withered by penury, ironing the ribbons on the little girl's bonnet" (2: 75). As already noted, the working class did not frequent public parks. Hence this typical scene on a day of rest for a family in the 1920s: the soulless stroll of a father and daughter along treeless cement streets, carrying the weight of exploitation in every step. There is no place for them to go. Yet another of Arlt's characters also walks, overwhelmed, through the desolate city center: "Sad. Bored. I saw in him the product of twenty years working fourteen hours a day in a tiny room for a pittance, twenty years of privation, meaningless sacrifices, and the unholy fear of being thrown into the street" (Arlt 1981a, 75). Arlt's implacable gaze turns off the center's cheerful lights and strips the skin from its facade, exposing "its fearful nakedness" and "the aggressive rigidity" of its metal shutters. Alluding to Roberto Mariani's *Cuentos de oficina* (Office Stories), Arlt explains, "There is no sadder day than the English Saturday . . . [and nothing sadder than] the office worker who, on one of those Saturdays, at 12 o'clock at night, is still looking for an error of two cents in the end-of-month balance!" (75). Alfonsina Storni's "Domingos" (Sundays), included in *Languidez* (Languor, 1920), describes a similar weekend stroll along "the quiet streets of the center":

> Sometimes I walk and the dark closed doors
> Of the offices are like sepulchers
> On the sidewalks.
> If I were to knock one of those Sundays
> On the cold doors
> Of gray metal, a hollow sound
> Would answer me. (Storni 1984, 157)

Arlt's text speaks of the tomb, Storni's of silent barriers, sepulchers, and death. Such dramatic allusions reveal that the new practices were indeed felt as an unbearable burden. Passersby seemed to have been grafted onto the systemic space of the market culture like uncomfortable marionettes performing rites that robbed both public spaces and subjectivities of any suppleness and vitality.

In transitional Buenos Aires, the spontaneous practices of cultures in motion ran adrift when they found no resonance in the symbolic languages of the city or when their capacity to shed meaning was weakened within the imaginaries that had produced them. Other practices, on the other hand, would produce important shifts within the controls over the interpretation of daily life. My definition of the term *imaginaries* addresses them as representations and reflections of cultural flows, absorbing the richness unfolded by the social simultaneity of the quotidian and by the multidiscursive positions forged by the subjectivities and bodies moving throughout the city. They are *culturas en movimiento,* cultures in motion, that capture the everyday, process it, and elaborate on its events in narratives and representations.

Although the oligarchy had endowed the city with imaginaries and ceremonies through which to venerate what was not to be touched, the market displayed a wide array of new social habits in the rest of the city, such as the rituals of coffee and entertainment, which conferred a collective feeling of belonging, but without erasing social tensions. Urban fragmentation and simultaneity force meaning to reestablish itself through a sense of intersubjectivity that seeks "new hypotheses . . . understandable at a cognitive-linguistic level in order to guarantee the continuity of the group" (Reguillo 1998, 102). Daily life cannot exist without discourses to explain it, and this is the task of the imaginaries. They highlight, conceal, and rearrange certain phases of the everyday, semanticizing both the normal and the exceptional through constant adjustments and tensions between institutional and private meanings. The competence of social actors consists of their ability to reflect on and evaluate socializing models and quotidian events, on which they confer meanings based on their own subjectivity (Reguillo 1998, 198). This process of testing/assessing/signifying contributes to subjects' rationalization of how they place and perceive themselves in the world and the logic they confer on their actions. In this sense, the writings of Storni, Borges, Arlt, and Guijarro are careful evaluations of the meanings, values, and models imposed by modernity, the maneuvers of social agents positioning themselves in relation to the socially appropriate, allowing agents to search for their own identity while they were also contesting modernity.

6 CONVENTILLOS

The key assumption of Buenos
Aires's enabling imaginaries was the idea that everything coming from the
conventillo was upwardly mobile, like tango: "There goes the tango, from
slum to skyscraper . . . from tenement to palace. . . . Yes, indeed!" wrote
Florencio Chiarello in *Así se escriben los tangos* (How Tangos Are Written,
1929, 9). The Buenos Aires of the Centennial could present the traveler with
an image of opulence and wealth because it set out to erase from public view
whatever remained of its immense, underground, undervalued social diversity: the anarchists, prostitutes, blacks and mulattos and mulattas, pimps,
women factory workers and seamstresses, stevedores and newsvendors, alcoholics, the mentally ill, newly arrived immigrants, and *compadritos* who
had just crossed the border between the pampas and the city. As in London,
urban growth in Buenos Aires sought "to reap the benefit of capitalism without the challenge of revolution" (Sennett 1994, 322) through the oligarchy's
concentration of capital in real estate in the city center. Such processes produced overcrowded tenements and allowed the elite to keep a city pervaded

by dramatic social, ethnic, gender, and ideological inequality as far as possible from revolutionary transformations.

The Paris Commune was a movement of the urban proletariat that gained the consent of the industrial bourgeoisie, who wished to oppose the rural aristocracy of the nineteenth century. Although Haussmann's redevelopment during the Second Empire had displaced the impoverished sectors of the population, demographic growth soon outstripped available housing. The majority of *communards* worked, paradoxically, in construction, and one of their first measures was to abolish rents in reaction both to high-priced overcrowding in tiny rooms and to the merciless eviction policies that guaranteed landlords immediate profits without risk. The Buenos Aires uprising of July 1890 was a protest against financial speculation, protected by a corrupt government that turned a blind eye to the infamously unsanitary conditions of the tenements. The Department of Public Health's interventions in this regard went beyond mere regulations. Its narratives of germs and of *conventillos* as silent sources of endemic illness were so compellingly spread that characters in the *sainetes* saw the agency as controlling life in Buenos Aires, even a visit from the president of Brazil. In Nemesio Trejo's *Los devotos* (The Devotees, 1900), Lucas claims, "If you ask me, I think his arrival's up to the Health Department":

MELITÓN: Why the Health Department?

LUCAS: Because when quarantine is lifted for outbreaks over there, it's imposed over here. . . . When there's no bubonic plague here, they've got it there. If we've got some animal disease here, they have yellow fever there and fifty other similar epidemics, when there's not a threat of revolution all over. That's why his visit is being put off day after day.

The tenement population was stigmatized by such narratives and subjected to relentless intervention, inspection, and surveillance. By the end of the nineteenth century, advances in medicine and public health had shaped a discourse that drastically altered perceptions of public spaces and how people thought about the body. Ever since Louis Pasteur discovered anthrax microorganisms (1866), and Robert Koch the tuberculosis bacillus, interpersonal contact, sweat, odors, exhalation, and bodily fluids and discharges were seen as channels for spreading microorganisms. The conventional method for preventing plague had long been quarantine, but in a densely populated city, this required the full intervention of the state. By 1900, the fear of contagion, triggered again and again by every epidemic, had been translated into a general dread of interpersonal contact. Even if individuals defended themselves against the threat of disease through personal hygiene, isolation was still the preferred form of battling an invisible enemy that lurked in the bodies of others. Contagion was the transmission of an undetectable, invisible signifier that could not be seen or that only became palpably visible when it was already too late. Thus, medical discourse legitimized the need for prophylactic measures and preventive proxemic distances. Stephen Kern perceives this process in developed cultures, which goes from precaution to obsession, as characterized by "the antisexual instinct, the instinct of personal isolation, [and] the actual repulsiveness to us of the idea of intimate contact with most of the persons we meet" (1975, 38). This obsession easily reaches extremes: "To most of us, it is even unpleasant to sit down in a chair still warm from the occupancy of another person's body. To many, hand-shaking is disagreeable" (Kern 1975, 39). Public health discourses at the end of the nineteenth century operated metaphorically like a cartographer, mapping conditions of sanitation and marking areas contaminated by social diseases, usually associated with poverty. Those with the greatest impact on the growing cities were the venereal diseases used as a pretext to justify the shackles placed on the bodies of proletarian women. These were the demons that stalked the institution of marriage and lurked in the threat of exogamy.

Between 1880 and 1915, the *conventillos* were the "unavoidable" form of housing for working-class Buenos Aires. After 1900, however, the reduction of public transportation fares made movement toward the new suburban barrios possible. The following description of a tenement at Salta 807 appeared in *La Prensa:* "[It was] occupied by 48 people. In room no. 4, measuring 15 feet by 18, slept a married couple, a girl 15 years of age, and 6 men. In room no. 5, 15 feet by 15, slept a woman whose husband was in a hospital for infectious diseases, and 6 other men. Two kitchens sheltered 11 men, and room no. 7 had 6 more" (qtd. in Leandro H. Gutiérrez 1983b, 72). By 1901, 140,000 tenants—17 percent of the city's population—lived in just 35,000 rooms (Oved 1978, 129), an average of four persons to each small, dark, unventilated, unsanitary space (see figures 10 and 11).

Sainetes, dramas, and tangos made the *conventillo* a key element in the representation of urban life. It was enough to allude to the *conventillo* to invoke a deterministic place/identity. The *conventillo* was a mark of origin, a frame of reference so trenchantly embedded in popular culture that just a mention of it would release sinister images of fatalistic narratives in the listener's mind. Rent costs consumed 16.4 percent of the average worker's income in about 1886, 19.2 percent in 1896, and 30.1 percent in 1912. The residents of the tenements worked in construction, on the railways, and at the port; they were office workers, domestic servants, butchers, shoemakers, shop assistants, stevedores, and above all the proletariat of industries processing raw materials, such as meatpacking and wool plants, tobacco factories, flour mills, and grain elevators. The economic attraction of Buenos Aires remained intact for forty years in spite of repeated, devastating crises in 1880, 1890, 1913–14, and 1929 (Scobie 1974, 136). During the Great Depression, "bread cost three times as much as it did in England, fuel four times, and groceries twice as much" (Scobie 1974, 138). At the beginning of the twentieth century, as a result of an abundant immigrant workforce, unemployment rose sharply. In August 1900, "thousands of unemployed paraded along the Avenida de Mayo to the Plaza de Mayo. President Roca himself appeared on a balcony of the Casa Rosada, but his promises to study the problem were drowned out by the whistles . . . of the angry crowd. A year later, again in the plaza, another . . . crowd gathered to protest the President's failure to even look into the situation" (Scobie 1974, 140).

A letter from the neighbors of a building located at Laprida 642, published in *La Vanguardia* on 13 January 1909, warned of the threat of "centers of infection": "[This] is a *conventillo* with 94 rooms . . . in a deplorable state. There are 6 toilets (two on each floor), and the plumbing for all 6 is broken, so that those on the upper floors are flooded and unusable and drip onto the floors below. . . . The baths don't work either." To speak of a sensuous geography is to speak of the body and its irrevocable place in the construction of identity. How does a body feel when it is forced into contact with overcrowded and promiscuous spaces, polluted water, and nauseating smells?

In Enrique González Tuñón's story "Camas desde un peso" (Beds for a Peso or More, 1932), there is a powerful description of the undesirable nocturnal intimacies of the boardinghouse:

> There were five of us, but we never spoke except to say goodnight. My companion to my right had the cloying smile of a mannequin. He approached

his bed on tiptoe so as not to disturb our sleep and greeted us with the friendly nod of a store clerk if he caught us with our eyes open. The one on my left . . . lived as if he were perpetually smuggling something. He hid his clothes under his mattress for fear of having them stolen or seized, and he huddled guiltily beneath his sheets. . . . The last of the group [was] formerly a petty lawyer adept . . . at living off others, a shyster on a run of bad luck, suffering from rheumatism and a chronic cold that broke the silence of our hospital lodging with a hoarse cough. (González Tuñón 1999, 53)

Nobody would expect to see social laterality flourish in such overcrowded spaces. And nobody knows such promiscuity better than the main character of Roberto Arlt's *El juguete rabioso,* who experiences it in the irredeemably seedy attic/storage room in the city center that he shares with the starving old man Dío Fetente: "[It was] an absurd, steep triangle tucked under the roof, with a dirty round window that looked onto Calle Esmeralda and through which the voltaic arc lamp could be seen. . . . The porthole was broken, and gusts of wind whistled through it" (Arlt 1981b, 85–86). The attic affords no protection from the chilly *porteño* winter or the din of the city that never sleeps, but only exacerbated feelings of vulnerability and agoraphobia. There is no electric light. Astier's roommate goes out to urinate on the terrace, and then, "ready to confront the cold of the night, . . . he climbed onto his cot, covering himself . . . with blankets—burlap sacks stuffed with useless rags" (86). His bed is "so poor it's a castoff from the ghetto."

These hellholes of marginality trapped stigmatized ethnic groups inside places where any degree of compassion or social concern seemed unthinkable. Astier does not confer a single positive value on poverty. He views it from so far above that he feels justified in distancing himself from his equals in the hopes that such separation will allow him to reach a different place in life. It torments him that "the owners of businesses slept peacefully in their luxurious bedrooms while . . . [he] wandered aimlessly through the city like a dog." Trembling with hatred, he throws a burning cigarette end at "a human shape sleeping huddled in a doorway; a small flame flickered in its rags" (Arlt 1981b, 156).

Not all urban imaginaries considered tenements and boardinghouses socially unsalvageable. Other representations associated them with spaces where new collective identities could be generated. Geographical and cultural dislocation did not necessarily imply fatalism or total loss. In fact, the social

Urban Ceremonies and Social Distances

actors living in these infamously unsanitary spaces gave birth to the most widespread linguistic product of twentieth-century Buenos Aires: a new language—a devilishly bastardized Spanish that perhaps became the urban proletariat's most pivotal source of identity. Spanish had intermingled with the many languages of Buenos Aires's Babylonian migration at a time when the social spaces of modernity were entirely permeable, engendering bastardized hybrids. Cocoliche and Lunfardo are just two of the dialectal variants produced by this linguistic contact and slang usage, barely scratching the surface of the innumerable linguistic registers that were ostentatiously displayed in popular culture, the theater, and tango, registers that would eventually foster different degrees of identitary relocation.

In a country that had always thought of itself as exclusively European, it must have been perplexing to hear a greeting spoken in an indigenous language. In Pablo Suero's *La vida comienza mañana* (Life Begins Tomorrow, 1926), one of the characters offers the greeting, "Temk Kausta," and another replies, "Kunata. Presentamaru amigu makaparu, pues," in a form of Aymara, phonetically and graphically Castilianized. Every language that passed through the intersecting filters of immigrant Buenos Aires—Galician, Andalusian, Catalan, German, French, Polish, Yiddish, Russian, Arabic, Greek, Turkish, and so on—was subjected to a frenzied metamorphosis, and of course, no one expected any subsequent purity or consistency in spelling or adherence to grammatical norms. In *La restauración nacionalista* (The Restoration of the Nation, 1922), the nationalist Ricardo Rojas refers to the imperative imposed on education to nationalize new arrivals and homogenize social languages, although he has serious reservations: "What will be the point . . . if the teacher teaches grammar and says that Spanish is the national language if the pupil sees the sidewalks on the way home from school full of signs in French, English, and German?" (1922, 315). Seeing the difficulty of imposing "one of the marks of our nationality" on immigrant Buenos Aires, Rojas appeals to the high-minded M. Remy Gourmont by curtly claiming that "bilingual peoples are almost always inferior," incapable of "defending our own language in our own home"; he explains the need to preserve Spanish against "those who come not only to corrupt it but to supplant it. Since the street is a public domain where the state intervenes for reasons of health and morality, it ought also to intervene for reasons of nationality and aesthetics" (315–16). Not only was Rojas right to tie home and language together, as major pieces of the identity puzzle; he was also right to be concerned about the streets, that hectic, popular kitchen, where language transfers created tasty stews seasoned with a large dash of humor and a "grammatical liberty" that defied all expectations of linguistic purity (Castro 1991, 46).

The first description of the spontaneous speech of Buenos Aires's popular classes—variously called argot, *caló, germanía,* or Lunfardo—dates from 1879, identifying it as the jargon of hoodlums and professional criminals, the working class, and the mentally ill. According to Mario Teruggi, however, this emphasis on the argot's cradle as "material and moral poverty, its nursemaid as a life of crime" (1978, 23), is a misrepresentation popularized by self-appointed lexicologists Benigno B. Lugones, Antonio Dellepiani, Luis Villamayor, and Luis María Drago, who came into contact with Lunfardo between 1878 and 1894 in their rather biased capacity as criminologists and police officers. Whether writers, criminologists, or police, however, these individuals were certainly xenophobic. For instance, Lugones doesn't hesitate to attribute greater skill at break-ins and robberies to Italians than to Spaniards or native-born Argentineans (Castro 1991, 19), and Drago, in the first positivist study of criminality (known as the "Drago doctrine"), links language to criminality (i.e., to the underworld and prostitution). It was the naturalist Eugenio Cambaceres who introduced Lunfardo to literature for the first time in *En la sangre* (In the Blood, 1887), making his protagonist speak in a way that reflects who he actually is, the son of a deprived immigrant from Calabria and a child of the street—conditions enough to validate the feelings of repugnance for social upstarts that this emblematic novel endorses.

The economic processes of industrialization created the *arrabales* and populated them with cultural agents who produced their own linguistic subsystem as a counterpart to the *langue polie.* Even Rubén Darío used Lunfardo words when writing for *La Nación* (Castro 1991, 28). Lunfardo is an entirely capricious and unpredictable floating form of communication, not fixed by writing but rather affiliated with the elasticity of oral speech, which disregards the pressures of linguistic standards and the notion of "correct" forms. It is pure phonetic travesty, indiscriminate transgression. Like every argot, it is deeply attached to the sociological sediment from which it arose. Initially, it was typically a male subsystem, using African, Argentinean *criollo,* and immigrant elements, and was restricted to working-class areas, but radio broadcasting soon spread it to the rest of the country, especially through tango. Beginning in the 1920s, female vocalists—Manolita Poli, Ada Falcón, Azucena Maizani, Rosita Quiroga ("La ñata gaucha"), Sofía Bozán (Sofía Isabel Bergero), and Libertad Lamarque—also made Lunfardo familiar to female listeners (Castro 1991, 180), who were able to hear both Lunfardo and tango on the radio without having to enter a cabaret or some other place of ill repute. This was a long journey, from cultural obscurity and ignominy in Afro-Argentinean, working-class barrios to massive diffusion via radio and cinema, the international stardom of Carlos Gardel (1917–36), the founding of the Academia Porteña del Lunfardo at the initiative of José Gobello (1968), and the classical status achieved by Astor Piazzolla's tango.

By 1914, the cultural assimilation of the immigrant masses was giving shape to a homogenous city where differential social agents and spaces nonetheless never failed to thrive. Lunfardo lost the social negativity with which it had initially emerged to become a new space of identity, insolently affirming its difference in order to encompass the many subaltern groups who spoke it. This linguistic hybridity asserted the grotesque city's marks of identity so vividly that Rojas saw the city as a denationalizing space, one that escaped the cultural homogenization of *one* nation with *one* language and imaginaries bound together by *one* set of unifying meanings. Along with creating neologisms, left to the unruly spontaneity of individuals and groups, Lunfardo has many other sources of linguistic transgression. Among them are semantic changes in words taken from a base language and embedded in another language; loan words with a restricted meaning (specialization), a broader meaning (generalization), or semantic shifts; and other changes made involuntarily or on purpose (metaplasms, anagrams) (Teruggi 1978, 44). Lunfardo's anagrammatic forms, created by reversing syllable order, are another of its linguistic games. Thus, *vesre* is a syllabic anagram for *revés*. Nonetheless, while *feca, dorima, jermu, llobaca, gotán, lorca,* and *sope (café, marido, mujer, caballo, tango,* and *peso)* can be easily reversed, this is not so for *tordo (doctor)* or other more complex formations. For example, *tové* is the reverse (*vesre*) of *vento* (money)—a word that is already Lunfardo, not Spanish. Similarly, *shomi* is *vesre* for *misho,* from the Lunfardo *mishiadura* (poverty), just as the Lunfardo *brame* and *bramaje* come from the Spanish *hembra* and *hembraje* (female, females).

Conformity to some linguistic norm could not be further from the minds of Lunfardo speakers, more attracted to sharing knowing winks prompted by their appreciation of aberrant deviations. As agents of culture, they worked in a fluid, arbitrary bricolage of borrowings and phonetic, morphological, syntactic, and semantic crossovers. The social text that most successfully documented this loose and liberating linguistic space was the *género chico,* although its plays never sought to standardize Lunfardo. Every *sainete,* comedy, or off-color combination was not intended to fix sociolinguistic variants, which were as elusive as slippery fish. With its mix of *compadritos,* native-born gauchos, immigrants, and mulattos, with its bordellos and criminal underworld, the urban space of the *arrabal* benefited from being allowed to grow without too much surveillance from the police—or with their acquiescence—and certainly without much linguistic policing. Julián Centella, an immigrant from Parma who lived in the barrio of Calle Oruro, describes the aesthetics of his Lunfardo verse: "I discover nothing and invent even less. I repeat. I remember . . . not without lending an ear to whatever is current, immediate, or recent, [or] without considering myself a mystic or one who uplifts people" (Furlán 1995, 92). His formation, he adds, was that of a "desperate, lonely man of the street; a long-time renter of seedy rooms." By drawing attention to orality, daily life, and poverty, Centella emphasizes three essentials of the new discursive forms, discursive positions, and cultural agency of modern life in Buenos Aires:

> Batuquero
> candombero
> sos el pique que aparece ¡sacatraca! y escabulle
> Sos así, grone, finito
> y lo bato la sordina que es un modo despacito
> de solfearle a la bartola lo que el cuore me sacude.
>
> (Qtd. in Furlán 1995, 94)

> African rowdy
> African dancer
> you're the thief who shows up at the door—rat-a-tat-tat!—and is gone
> That's you, fancy blackman,
> and I'll give away your secret which is an easy way
> to steal from you whatever my heart desires.

Porteño audiences of popular theater not only ended up speaking Cocoliche or Lunfardo in their daily lives, but, if the parenthetic direction by

Eliseo Gutiérrez and León Alberti in *Yo me hago el loco* (I Pretend to Be Crazy, 1927) is any indication, were even capable of recognizing the dialectal variations of immigrants:

> GIROLAMO: Scusi, siñora, buen giorno, ío volevo darle la scátola in mano, a lei. . . . (*Gives her the box.*) Quería star sicuro que la caca andava al suo destino. (*Although a Milanese pronunciation has been suggested [in the preceding stage direction], the actor Ruggero, who first performed the work, spoke with a Neapolitan accent. The actors are authorized . . . to perform in a southern dialect if it is more convenient.*)

Girolamo speaks Cocoliche, a Castilianized version of Italian, although at times it corresponds more to an Italianized Castilian.

It is interesting to note that the term *Cocoliche* and its linguistic characteristics came about as a result of pure improvisation, when one of the actors in *Juan Moreira,* a vaudeville staged by José Podestá in 1890, spontaneously began to caricature the speech of an Italian actor named Antonio Cocoliche, ever since destined to lend his name to the hybrid language: "Me quiame Franchisque Cocoliche, e sono cregollo gasta lo güese" (Castro 1991, 47) (My name is Francisco Cocoliche, and I am *criollo* to the bone). The patois Cocoliche was *cregollo* (*criollo*) because it had been born in the immigrant city. Phonetic transferals in Cocoliche, like Girolamo's *caca* (excrement) instead of *caja* (box), were repeatedly exploited in *sainetes* for humor and the festive atmosphere they created. Popular theater thus used its collective space to proclaim the well-worn truths of its self-enabling imaginaries about life and survival in a tough, heartless city that, nevertheless, like Lunfardo itself, was also a living archive of many cultures and social agents.

In Nemesio Trejo's *Los políticos* (The Politicians, 1907), a Basque, standing in the middle of the street, rails in his own language against the city mayor:

> Agurneré biotreco
> amacho maitiá
> laiste recorri conaiz
> consola saítea (Trejo 1979, 25)

In Babylon–Buenos Aires, then, a neighbor from Galicia replies to what he believes the Basque has said in Euskera, although his reply, spoken in Galician and understandable only to Galician speakers, has absolutely nothing to do with anything:

Francisquiño son o xastre
e son neto de meu abuelo
fillo son de Padro o xastre
quien a naide lle ten medo
que cos seus arroxus feitos
salga o aceiro a brillare
fará temblar o inferno (1979, 25)

This character reacts as the audience would when confronted with life's daily interactions in the linguistic confusion of the city—by guessing at the meaning of the words and venturing an answer. In *El novio de mamá* (Mama's Boyfriend, 1914), by Armando Discépolo, Rafael José de Rosa, and Mario Folco, a Brazilian named Da Ferro, living in Doña Petrona's rooming house, has fallen for Doña Petrona's daughter Desdemona. The fact that he does not speak Spanish, Lunfardo, or Cocoliche is of no consequence, and when he sighs for the girl, he sings a popular Brazilian love song that features a stereotypical lovesickness, conveyed in a sort of Portuguese-Lunfardo:

Se anuviada mea fúlgida estrella
por evespao dos colores eo vi
se tan solo chorar a um ingrato
me aguarda sombrí, fatal porvenir;
se a vivir da lembranza que mata
a esto mondo tan solo nascí,
e es a vida uma senda de abroxos
que triste es a vida eo quero morir.

(Discépolo, de Rosa, and Folco 1987, 139)

But the problems really begin to arise when Petrona receives Da Ferro's friend Abreu, and they talk at cross-purposes, he in Portuguese and she in Spanish:

ABREU: Trago pra Joaquín Da Ferro, un sincero abraxo, puro, forte, de viñao mais as boas de seu paes.

PETRONA: ¿Qué dice? . . . ¿Las boas nuevas de su país?

DESDÉMONA: No, mamá. . . . ¡Confundís!

PETRONA: ¿Y se viene con las víboras? ¡No faltaba más!

ABREU: Nao. . . . Eo trago as boas. . . .

PETRONA: ¿Se las traga? . . .

ABREU: . . . As boas noticias de sua mae e pae.

PETRONA: ¡Ah, las boinas nuevas! . . . ¡Pero qué barbaridad! ¡Fale mellor, hombre!

ABREU: A siñora nao fala o portugués.

PETRONA: Eo falo de outra manera. (1987, 147)

Taking "boas," meaning "good" in Portuguese, to refer to snakes (i.e., "boas" in Spanish), Petrona wonders why Abreu is swallowing snakes when she interprets "Eo trago as boas" ("I bring good news" in Portuguese) as "Yo trago las boas" ("I swallow the snakes" in Spanish)—in other words, understanding "trago" (I swallow) instead of "traigo" (I bring) and "boas" (snakes) instead of "buenas" (good). Similarly, instead of "as boas noticias" (good news), she hears "las boinas nuevas" (new berets). In the end, when Abreu, who is from Portugal, says he is surprised that Petrona does not speak his language ("A siñora nao fala o portugués"), she asserts that she certainly does speak Portuguese, although hers is a distorting, hybrid variant: "Eo falo de outra manera."

While some people throw up walls around themselves, others are more prepared to cross bridges. Pajarito is the only Argentinean-born resident of the boardinghouse represented in *Mañana será otro día* (Tomorrow's Another Day, 1930), by Alberto Vacarezza, Alejandro Berruti, and José González Castillo. Yet when speaking to fellow boarders, all of them immigrants, he takes words from Lunfardo and mixes them with terms picked up from the society columns. For example, he asks: "Pero ¿cuándo será il giorno que lo dejan a uno apolillar veinticuatro horas seguidas en esta residencia?" (Vacarezza, Berrutti, and González Castillo 1930, 3) (When will the day come they'll let us sleep twenty-four hours at a stretch in this residence?), using the Italian "il giorno" for "day" instead of the Spanish "el día," and using "apolillar" (from the Italian slang "poleggiare," crossed with the Spanish "polilla," meaning "moth") instead of the Spanish "dormir" for "to sleep." His lexical forays inevitably create difficulties of understanding that affect everyone, but this linguistic jumble soon becomes humorous, as when Pajarito explains that he is temporarily strapped for cash:

PAJARITO: A propósito de ventolín. . . . ¿Ustedes saben que yo también voy prendusqui a la oreja del tellebí?

CATALDO: ¿Cóme dijiste? . . .

RAMITO: ¿Cómo es jezo? . . . ¿Cómo es jezo? . . .

PAJARITO: Pero en qué idioma tendré que chamuyarle a estos aparatos pa'que me entiendan. Quiero decir, que aunque mi falta transitoria de recursos no me permitió oblar mi parte correspondiente . . . yo también porto. (4)

Pajarito uses the Lunfardo "ventolín" for "money" and the phrase "voy prendusqui a la oreja del tellebí" to express his dilemma. Then, realizing his interlocutors' confusion, he has to translate: "In what language do I have to talk [chamuyarle] to these characters so they'll understand me? I mean that although my temporary shortage of funds has not allowed me to donate my share . . . I'll also contribute."[1] As the only tenant born in Argentina, and therefore the only native speaker fully knowledgeable of Spanish, the *compadrito* Pajarito later takes the trouble to arbitrate a point of confusion arising from communication between a Galician and an Italian when one of them has used the verb "imputar" (to impute) and the other has heard "puta" (prostitute):

MADEIRO: Pirmítame señora que eu no he hecho . . . todu esu que usté imputa. . . .

CATALDO: ¿Cóme, cóme dice? Retire inmediatamente esa palabra que ofende mi diñítá.

PAJARITO: Un momento. . . . Permítaseme que en mi carácter de letrado de este llotivenco aclare ese concepto: "Imputa", del verbo "imputar." . . . Significa simplemente atribuir, culpar. . . . La señora ha imputado al yoyega la seducción de esta infeliz . . . ¡Y esto es todo! ¡Que siga el debate! (25)

Pajarito explains: "In my capacity as the only literate one in this *conventillo*"— which he inverts, saying "llotivenco," in typical Lunfardo style—"let me clarify this concept: 'Impute,' from the verb 'impute.' . . . It simply means to attribute, to blame. . . . The lady has blamed the Galician for the seduction of this unhappy girl. . . . And that is all! Let the discussion continue!"

Lunfardo words, in a constant state of flux because of their oral nature, change phonetically, morphologically, semantically, and stylistically. They are like carousel horses (*caballos de vuelta*), endlessly circling back and forth between languages.[2] This unstable linguistic alterity creates the hybrid space where cultural agents take full charge of their language, changing official/ institutionalized Spanish into an outmoded gesture. Italian immigrants, hearing Italian forms already altered by Cocoliche and Lunfardo, recognized these words and used them, at first with a sidelong glance, as if to make sure no newly arrived compatriot within earshot would reproach them for betraying their mother tongue. Nevertheless, they incorporated these words into their Spanish vocabulary, aware of the communicative and affective advantages with respect to integration into the new community. Needless to say, all this implies, in fact, a remarkable array of tolerance, a sharp sense of humor, complicity, play, the capacity for negotiation, flexibility, and the ability to maneuver. The users of these hybrids knew full well that the words were not from their "original" language but belonged to the "new" language that they were forging as a collective identity.

Lunfardo and Cocoliche speakers also acquired a keen sense of sociolinguistic awareness about how their lexical choices marked their identity in such cultural intersections. In Alejandro Berruti's *Cuidado con las bonitas* (Beware the Pretty Ones, 1931), Rosalía's mother reacts when her daughter uses the word "chorro" (Lunfardo for "thief"), and the girl corrects herself, saying: "Disculpá. . . . ¡Ladronzuelo!" (Sorry. . . . Petty thief!). In Alberto Nović's *El rincón de los caranchos* (Vulture's Corner, 1919), in a shack made of old wood and tin located on the shore, a father and son are mulling over the latter's scant chances for work. When the son says he would be good at selling newspapers because he can shout like "un otario" (a "mug" or "sap" in Lunfardo), his father corrects him and suggests he not use that word because it is "muy del arrabal" (typical of the *arrabal*). There is also an awareness that linguistic usage serves to indicate a speaker's social level. When confronted with the phrase "la metempsicosis de la vida" (the metempsychosis of life), a character from a shack in a poor neighborhood responds: "Did you hear him? He said 'metempsychosis.' What a difficult word. . . . Let's have another little word like that." In *El guarda 323* (Guard No. 323), the immigrants' complex relationship to their new language is summed up by Don Pascual's keen irony: "In this country with its pure language, the truth is that what we speak is what the language is missing, for heaven's sake. . . . So, carry on [talking] . . . child of this country!" (Discépolo 1987b, 275).

Don Pascual alludes to "this country with its pure language," and Pajarito asks, "In what language do I have to talk to these characters so they'll understand me?" In what language or in what variant should the "child of this country" be addressed? And with which speakers could linguistic variants be used? For no matter what the *arrabal* derived from its place at the margins, its inhabitants still had to interact with the other Buenos Aires, where the formal registers of "the pure language" were indeed spoken as a key allowing access to the economic and formal culture of modernity. Social spaces were heavily contested, and at the heart of the class struggle, imaginaries and representations, languages, identitary profiles, spaces, and passages interacted with each other. A gaucho character in Alberto Novión's *Los primeros fríos* (The First Winter Days) explains to the woman he loves, "If you look down on me because I'm not Italian, I'd learn to play *murra* [an Italian card game] for you, get drunk on Barbera, and even play *bocha* [bowls]" (1977a, 48). For a *criollo* to thus adopt Italian identity demanded the same open-mindedness and level of effort as for a Cocoliche to adopt a new language and identity. For both, that intermediary language was simultaneously a source of alienation and a source of belonging, like the city itself. For immigrants, this was more than just a matter of turning up and everything coming up roses. The city opened its port and customs houses to them, but it closed innumerable borders. The same might be said of mestizos, *compadritos,* and Afro-Argentineans who had entered Buenos Aires by the back door. Here again, even though the language marked them, it also gave them a sense of liberty and self-determination, expressed in every *caballo de vuelta.* Every word in Lunfardo sheltered its speakers beneath the deliberately cryptic hermeticism of slang, which, coming from the underworld of crime, somehow obstructed surveillance and persecution by the police and the courts.

The imaginary associated with the palaces of the Conservative Order was categorically discriminatory, but it unleashed a deep pool of desires and reactions that ended up molding many dreams in Buenos Aires, contested by anarchists, socialists, and feminists and later capitalized on by the democratizing imaginaries of Radicalism. The streets were spaces freely accessible to all, but they also marked out distances intended to separate. Nevertheless, the public space of the streets never failed to facilitate urban journeys and crossings, social interaction, and explorations in social spontaneity. The new languages of the street both separated and united. The *conventillo* was a space that harbored violence and contagious epidemics, but it was also the place where many found their new urban identity. What was Buenos Aires?

As yet it *was* nothing, if "to be" implies an essentialism fixed by identities and routines. It was pure cultural intersection.

For Pierre Bourdieu, daily life is historical because it is formulated on the basis of a process that goes from practices (culture in motion) and structures (objectified culture) to the consolidation of habit (assimilated culture). Habits are "systems of durable, transposable dispositions, structured structures predisposed to function as structuring structures" (1990, 53). Every new paradigm incorporated into transitional Buenos Aires arose from an acute awareness of making a break with the past. The past—and earlier identitary habits—became a cognitive reference, actively present but constantly reenvisaged, affirmed, rejected, or replaced. In the social texts of the 1920s, the city was still a physical and symbolic artifact that offered no fixed urban or identitary maps because they were still in the process of taking shape. Don Pascual, the character from *El viaje aquel* and *El guarda 323,* is a cautious, reflexive example of a social actor who spots the points at which paradigms emerge. These paradigms, however, were still being formulated, and they depended on the plausibility of their structure to justify the incorporation of the new models they proposed. There are at least two principles that serve to legitimize everyday habits: regularity—a comforting source of continuity against extraordinary events that could interrupt the journey toward innovative models and values—and consensual objectivism. Such a sense of continuity became all the more relevant in view of the groundbreaking transition that was under way. Rossana Reguillo argues that control over the definitions of life implies possibilities for new agreements that will remain valid until they lose their power to persuade. In the interstices between paradigms, "the circulation of certain themes (the structures of domination in the family, the meanings attributed to work . . . [and] sexual conduct) demand that social actors decide between what is *appropriate* and what is *true*" (1998, 103; emphasis added).[3]

Nemesio Trejo's *La quinta de los reyes* (The Estate of Kings, 1916) conceives of flights of fancy beyond the sordidness of the tenement: "This squalid boardinghouse may again be what it was. I hope to wander along these corridors at night . . . without hearing people snore or arguing in strange languages, [without] the smell of cooking—all that ruckus hateful to my sensibility. You'll become the owner, you'll empty the tenement, and

perhaps the notes of a piano will echo again among the trees of the estate."
Pacheco's work alludes to preimmigration Buenos Aires, which had already
become an impossible anachronism, while Armando Discépolo's *Mustafá*
(1921) speculates about what will emerge from the confusing world of
the tenement:

> Don Gaetano: Doesn't a race of the strong result from mixing? Why is the
> strong race coming about in Buenos Aires? . . . Because this is a hospitable
> country. It takes in all the migrants, puts them all in a *conventillo*, mixes
> them all up, and out onto the street come all those nice kids kicking, punch-
> ing, beating people over the head, and attacking women. (1969, 257)

Where Trejo alludes to regressive utopias, Discépolo envisages the identity
of the immigrant city. Either way, both see the *conventillo* as the seed of a future Argentina and wonder what the historical fate of its new social agents
will be. Confronted with the emergence of new imaginaries to interpret its
subjectivities, Buenos Aires itself seems to wonder how and where it will re-
formulate its rites, sociability, sexuality, subjectivities; its place for dreams; its
models of the family, the national, the collective, the political, and utopias—
in other words, the complex juggling between imaginaries that advocate
the "truth" (*lo verdadero*) of spontaneity and subjectivity and those that strive
for the "correctness" (*lo acertado*) of social normalization.

Señora Magdalena Ortiz
Basualdo de Becú (*Caras y
Caretas,* 7 February 1920)

Pereda Palace, 1130 Arroyo
Street, Buenos Aires

Grand Hall at Gath y Chávez (Archivo General de la Nación, 1913)

Fourth-floor annex at Gath y Chávez (Archivo General de la Nación, 1914)

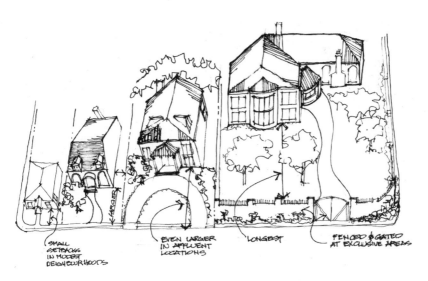

Municipal building setbacks (Daniel Deutsch, drawing)

Diagonal Norte (Avenida Roque Sáenz Peña), Horacio Cóppola (Archivo General de la Nación, 1936)

Bill posting prohibited (*Caras y Caretas,* 22 March 1919)

Tenants' strike (Archivo General de la Nación, 1907)

Patio in a *conventillo*
(Archivo General de
la Nación, 1906)

Room in a *conventillo*
(Archivo General de
la Nación, 1912)

Muñecas

Bravas

7 PARADIGMS AND DEVIATIONS

> But the smart woman becomes a juggler
> who plays with the pretensions of wolves.
>
> Nemesio Trejo, *Las mujeres lindas*

CATALINA H. WAINERMAN AND Rebeca Barck de Raijman are justifiably perplexed by the longevity of school textbooks in Argentina. Pedro Blomberg's *El sembrador* (The Sower, 1925) went unchanged until 1956, Luis Arena's *Hermanito* (Little Brother, 1936) was left untouched until 1965, and A. Ferreya's *El nene* (The Baby, 1895) was still in use in 1959. As Wainerman and Raijman remark, this longevity provided a way of "freezing society in time while shamelessly displaying it as manifestly archaic and distanced from reality" (1984, 16). Juan García Puron's *Lector nacional* (National Reader, 1910) confirms that gender identity was one such source of social normativity: "Through games based on washing, ironing, and cooking, [girls] learn and become fond of many domestic tasks that may be useful or necessary to them much later" (qtd. in Wainerman and Raijman 1984, 27). What Puron wrote in 1910 was right on target.

By 1910, middle-class and proletarian women had begun to join the labor force, earning their livelihoods as nannies and domestic servants, pressers and seamstresses. Primary-school textbooks recycled "universal" truths in an attempt to intersect the effects of the unprecedented spiral of transformations caused by modernity. The insertion of women into the working world unleashed new social paradigms as much as it fostered imaginaries set on orienting and resemanticizing the collective actions they inspired. The shift in female identities was initially intersected by reactive imaginaries that refocused them in light of consumer culture. "Narratives of perdition" (*historias de perdición*) were also formulated in order to strenuously reinforce female domesticity and counteract the appeal of novelty with the "good" conduct represented in the paradigm of the "socially appropriate" (*lo acertado*).

The transitional turmoil wrought by modernity severely tested the persuasive power of social imaginaries. In fact, these imaginaries were "compelled" to absorb and interpret the new forms of urban life and the full spectrum of daily events in order to maintain themselves as the representations best equipped to interpret the quotidian. Reactive imaginaries could thus be instrumental in protecting "the social" from *acontecimientos*—"that is to say, from disruptive events that upset the continuity of daily life" (Reguillo 1998, 101). For women to work entailed a deviation from practices long socialized by civil law and biological criteria. What would become of young and adult *porteñas* who had no choice but to work when they had been warned that to do so was "a cruel fate, a source of misery . . . painted in dramatic hues of deep black" (Wainerman and Raijman 1984, 33)? *Alma recta* (Righteous Soul) recommended work only in the event of a husband's death. In other words, only after life had been turned inescapably upside down should women be exposed to the "fatal" and "irreversibly dramatic surrender" that work entailed: "The love every mother feels for her children . . . gave courage to the spirit of the poor [widow] who, . . . remembering the fine sewing she had learned during her childhood, before poverty knocked on the door of her home, looked for work and dedicated all her time to it" (qtd. in Wainerman and Raijman 1984, 32).

The narrators of *Alma recta* and *Lector nacional* both confirm the suitability of a background in domestic skills when poverty struck those who were physically and emotionally weak by nature, forcing them to confront the demands of the workplace. How did such imaginaries narrate empirical reality under the transformations being brought about by transition? The ideal would have been for women not to work at all, but when no other solution seemed viable, the best option was for them to work within the home at manual tasks, without budging an inch from the physical and symbolic place that marked their gender identity. Descriptions of the plight of single proletarian mothers were melodramatically loaded with personal misfortunes, while endearing diminutives emphasized their "vulnerability" and their "inability to react": "Day and night the poor woman sat with her sewing frame on her lap and a needle in her hand, managing with the paltry product of her work to provide the essentials for her *hijitos* [little ones]" (*Alma recta,* qtd. in Wainerman and Raijman 1984, 33).

The school texts are particularly long on discouragement when it comes to work outside the home, because this entails a more radical "abandonment of women's 'natural' habitat . . . that forced them to undertake 'masculine' tasks in contact with men and machines" (Wainerman and Raijman 1984, 23). The factory was seen "as a dangerous place in which women were at the mercy of all kinds of demands and abuses because of their delicate nature" (Wainerman and Raijman 1984, 33). *Alma recta* praised schools where women received job training and recommended saving girls from the "painful and often humiliating methods invariably awaiting . . . [those] forced to learn their trade in the workshop or the factory" (qtd. in Wainerman and Raijman 1984, 33). In other words, in the adjustment to social practices brought about by transitional modernity, working women were viewed with considerable hesitation as an inevitable result of industrial development, as a threat to both the family and social order (Feijoó 1990, 286), and as an open invitation to unspeakable immorality. While the exploitation of women and children, and the highly dangerous, violent nature of the factories, were indeed burning realities, here I wish to trace how the dominant imaginaries "prepared" working women to confront their new identity in industrial Buenos Aires and to examine the imaginaries with which they were burdened when they crossed the threshold of factories and workshops.

In "The City Image and Its Elements," Kevin Lynch states that margins are "linear breaks in continuity . . . which close one region off from another . . . a crossing or convergence of paths, moments of shift from one structure to another" (1996, 99), adding that the observer may identify their markers through the contrast they present with the rest of the city. In the absence of an all-embracing map of the city (totally impossible for the citizen to obtain), these markers act as a biased, stereotypical aid to recognition. Geographical landmarks are points of reference in the organization of urban maps. Government buildings, churches, towers, monuments, administrative centers, hospitals, commercial centers, plazas, bridges, parks, and public spaces may be recognized at a distance, as medieval and Renaissance urbanists understood very well by using them to distinguish urban spaces. What, then, are the markers of the *arrabal* in Buenos Aires?

The flood of migration produced profound demographic changes and new concerns: unemployment, prostitution and pimping, begging and vagrancy, delinquency, drugs, and new social and gender identities, all of which gave rise to xenophobia, racism, sexism, and homophobia. The first moment in the representation of the *arrabal* came in *Vida y costumbres en el Plata* (Life and Customs of the River Plate, 1888), by the Franco-Brazilian Emilio Daireaux, who portrayed the city through polarizing two of its faces: "the Buenos Aires of Don Torcuato [de Alvear]," as opposed to "that horde of blacks, mulattos, Indians, old people, and former soldiers, all harbingers of the Apocalypse, who surround and bother you . . . as you leave the churches": "You see them wandering the streets, in unending, strange lines, limping, dragging shapeless shoes . . . talking, laughing, muttering broken sentences into which all the languages of the world seem to have spilled words . . . that common decency has banned from use. . . . They are all mixed together so that it's impossible to tell to which sex each of them belongs" (qtd. in Leandro H. Gutiérrez 1983a, 86). Daireaux, a successful financier, describes the crowd with dismay as a social space where polymorphism has opened the door to hesitation and ambiguity, as much with respect to shoes as to language and sexuality. These people are all shapeless (or *new*) forms, and it bothers him to be unable to identify "to which sex each of them belongs." The hybrid forms are indecent, and he is concerned about their growing numbers. The grotesque city is provoking a crisis among the maps, categories, and univalent identities, which are no longer effective means of understanding the flood of new and unpredictable forms of social configuration.

The social body needed to be closely watched and set on the right path, an interdisciplinary task to be undertaken by the many forms of policing that the city would develop. In 1891, Dr. Donovan, Buenos Aires's chief of police, proposed a vagrancy law to control beggars and vagrants. On 1 December 1890, Fabio Carrizo clarified the concerns in *Caras y Caretas:* "They are not the product of our soil, but the castoffs of a poorly managed, discourag-

Muñecas Bravas *of Buenos Aires*

ing immigration policy." Since "Torrans" was the brand of the sewage pipes used where the homeless lived, they were called *atorrantes* (vagrants) and associated with inclement weather, unemployment, and the sewers. Moreover, since they fed off "boxes of garbage placed at the doors of the houses . . . bits of meat that had been thrown away, bare bones, and all the filthy remains from the kitchen," as Daireaux explains, (Leandro H.Gutiérrez 1983a, 86), the *atorrantes* were associated metonymically with garbage. Given the outcry in Buenos Aires calling for "the disappearance of such spectacles" (Leandro H. Gutiérrez 1983a, 86), a memorandum from the mayor's office proposed the expansion of the almshouse. Whether because of their defiance of the law through criminal behavior or because of their begging, these leftovers of urban society had to be processed in a way that would make them disappear. They were an element of dissymmetry that the city had to smooth over. But how to make them go away? By 1888, Emilio Daireaux had already begun this task through his representation of the *arrabal*.

Modern Buenos Aires was a veritable Babylon, a mecca for prostitution, a port for trafficking in women intended for a predominantly adult working population, aged between fifteen and fifty-nine years. Prostitution—the circulation of women, men, and children at the service of public sexuality— was considered an unavoidable evil. It was not made illegal until 1936, all the efforts of the state before that date merely directed at maintaining legal controls. The equation of prostitution with the *conventillos* appeared already in the first national census (1887) and thereafter remained. Proletarian women were among those principally threatened with being forced into prostitution, for reasons that are not difficult to figure out. Unskilled *obreras* (working women), mostly foreigners, with low wages and minimal protection against abuse, constantly found themselves on its threshold. The following figures from the 1887 census tell the story for Buenos Aires:

	Argentineans	*Foreigners*
Domestics	10,012	10,727
Laundresses	954	3,390
Pressers	2,125	2,488
Unspecified	34,115	42,195
Total	38,206	59,674

Source: Carretero 1995, 44–45.

I would highlight in particular the *nonsocial place* hidden by such terms as "unspecified," "without a profession," and "various." Two years after prostitution was made illegal, in 1938, prostitutes continued to figure significantly among the federal police's arrest statistics, revealing how little the culture of modernity had done to equip these noncitizens for the workforce:

Profession	Number arrested (1938)	Percentage
Without a profession	1,921	59.60%
Prostitutes	615	19.08%
Various	308	5.98%
Housemaids	272	8.47%
Industrial workers	40	1.24%
Business workers	25	0.72%
Students	21	0.65%
Professionals	17	0.52%
Day laborers	4	0.02%

Source: Carretero 1995, 158.

As Andrés M. Carretero points out, most of the names on the municipal registers belonged to women of Slavic origin, which also reveals that *criolla* women had been ousted by male tastes for blond women (1995, 45). Men also preferred younger women, as the following figures reveal:

	Age	Percentage
Younger than	18	2.16
	20	7.66
	22	14.91
	24	23.70
	25	17.33
	28	16.53
	30	12.09
Older than	30	5.62

Source: Carretero 1995, 51.

Carretero stresses "the vulnerability of underage women, the social abandon to which they were submitted, [and] the mercilessness of the system

Muñecas Bravas *of Buenos Aires*

that drew women into prostitution" (1995, 52). The rise in prostitution was justified unequivocally by the high rate of male immigration, to the extent that one public health physician, Emilio Coni, referred to it in his memoirs (*Memorias de un médico higienista,* 1918) as a social palliative. According to Susan S. M. Edwards, such an explanation covers up the essentialist thesis that "male sexuality is considered instinctual, not social, not learned; thus rape, sexual assault and the use of prostitute women by men is exonerable" (1993, 92). The fact that a public health official "understood" the "natural" inevitability of prostitution, then, endorsed a social contract that granted impunity to a structure of criminal exploitation.

Carretero describes several categories of female prostitution in Buenos Aires:

> 1. *Cocottes* (mistresses) were usually foreign women noted for "their beauty, youth, education, and refined manners." They had expensive tastes and were kept in luxury apartments, with a car, a chauffeur, and a box at the Colón Theatre: "They could compete on equal terms in appearance and social deportment with women having the most distinguished last names. . . . Some of them ended up costing well-known men a good part of their fortune or a piece of the country from their father's estate." Cambaceres himself made one of them an heiress (Carretero 1995, 88).
>
> 2. *Mantenidas* (kept women) had an apartment provided by a lover whom they discreetly accompanied to parties and the theater: "They were the temporary lovers of comfortable middle-class men . . . [and] were employed in public offices or businesses to cover up their status" (88).
>
> 3. *Cabareteras* or *milonguitas* were dancers who sat at the tables of male customers in the cabarets and encouraged them to drink. Both they and male and female homosexuals went to *fiestas negras* (literally "black parties") where drugs were taken and couples changed partners. Since the pace of their life quickly wore them out, they soon had to leave the cabaret and "choose between the bordello, illegal prostitution, and crime" (88).
>
> 4. *Prostibularias* (bordello prostitutes) toiled without rest, without family or money. They were prey to madams and pimps, taken "from brothel to brothel . . . as objects who made money." Beautiful women were seldom found in the brothels, according to Carretero: "The most unfortunate were young. . . . The majority . . . the mainstay of the profession" had fallen from other categories of prostitution through exhaustion, age, and overwork. They bore the brunt of social revulsion, judicial sanction, police roundups, and the cold, prophylactic eye of the public health physician (89).

5. *Yirantas* (streetwalkers) were physically and emotionally exhausted, no longer acceptable in the brothels. Having lost their youth and beauty, they were alcoholics and/or drug addicts and involuntary collaborators with criminal organizations: "Lacking any means . . . they walked the plazas, public baths, [and] railway stations," where they were arrested for vagrancy (89).

6. *Prostitutas libres* (unattached prostitutes) moved between the world of prostitution and the "straight" life, their professions as various as *"vitroleras* [women who played records in cafés], dancers, *cupleteras* [singers], . . . models, pedicurists and manicurists, . . . waitresses in cafés, bars, [and] canteens, [and] hotel chambermaids" (89–90).

7. *Alcahuetas* (procurers) were the women who facilitated prostitution.

The public eye was ever alert to reading new modes of female sexuality in the social conduct and body language spreading ungovernably through urban space, where even the most imperceptible signs were cause for alarm or anxiety. There were single mothers, single mothers pretending to be widowed, women who chose to remain single, professional women, *grotesque* women, lesbians, femmes fatales, flirts, flighty women, vampires, vamps, courtesans, and prostitutes. Prostitution served as a form of both upward and downward social mobility. In *Otra cosa es con la guitarra* (It's Something Else with the Guitar, 1921), by Antonio Mones Ruiz and Arturo de Bassi, champagne and drugs flow freely in a high-class cabaret where two *milonguitas* allude to the thin line that separates prostitution from the condition of women working in factories and domestic service:

> MILONGUITA 1: I don't know what those poor things are doing, wasting their youth toiling as maids or factory workers, instead of enjoying this party.
>
> MILONGUITA 2: There are many dummies in this world.
>
> Milonguita 1: That's why, you know, on any day, I . . . The son of the house where I was working as a chambermaid set me up in an apartment, presented me with a dress, and showed me the ropes. And frankly, you know, I'm grateful to him. Because of him, I am what I am. You only have one life, and you have to enjoy it. What the hell! (qtd. in Lara and de Panti 1961, 243)

Adela, in Carlos M. Pacheco's *Tangos, tongos y tungos* (Tangos, Cards, and Racing Nags, 1918), follows a similar trajectory, from which it may be deduced that such changes in identity and social practices had already started to "make sense" in the search for social advancement: "He's fixed me up

Muñecas Bravas *of Buenos Aires*

well, don't you think? A nice apartment. I have a player piano, heating. . . . At night his friends come along, the best kind of boys. . . . We play poker. I've changed a lot, my dear. I'm not the person you knew. . . . I smoke Turkish cigarettes now, and I'm learning French. One has to learn French. One has to improve oneself" (Pacheco 1964, 110). Roberto Gache, in *Baile y filosofía* (Dance and Philosophy, 1922), summarizes the mechanistic narrative that irrevocably links the factory to the cabaret through a story that, because of its vulgarity, "comes as no surprise to anyone":

> This woman was born in a *conventillo*. She worked, alongside her parents, as a laborer in a factory. She was pretty, attractive; on her curvaceous, firm body her modest cotton dress looked luxurious. . . . This sad and sensual woman expected something more of life, without knowing what. . . . Since life is not happy in a palace, it's foolish and naive to believe it might be so in a *conventillo*. . . . This young woman did well, then, to leave poverty behind. . . . A man deceived her. Then, when she had grown used to her fall, many men . . . made her happy for an instant. In addition to teaching her how to forget, they gave . . . her foolish heart the consolation of money (qtd. in Lara and de Panti 1961, 239–40)

In 1900, the lawyer Manuel Gálvez was appointed usher at the Chamber of Commerce, Crime, and Corrections. Consequently, by the time he published *Nacha Regules* (1919) and *Historia de arrabal* (*Arrabal* Story, 1922), his cultural geography of the criminal underworld was strongly conditioned by a threefold proxemic distance: through his position as an official of the justice system, through his connection to the laws and policies of the Conservative Order, and through his association with naturalist orthodoxy. Naturalism posits environmental influence as the very essence of character, arguing in favor of a consciousness that is always externally derived. It also presupposes a sense of analytical objectivity, which was decisively endorsed in Gálvez's case by his institutional knowledge. Naturalist aesthetics generally draw attention to the darker spaces of the city; they do not address its pathologies dispassionately, but rather as deviations from bourgeois normativity and the purity of its truth. Social "cases" and their subjects constitute the center of naturalism's fatalistic narratives of social deviation, which beg for the preventive intervention of the state. As David W. Foster points out, in contrast to European conventions, Argentinean naturalism was intended not to "criticize a destructive social dynamic, but to confirm a specific social order and to condemn any deviation from it by misfits and outcasts who are unable to abide by its conditions and profit from its benefits" (1990, 78). *Historia de arrabal* reaffirmed the stigmatizing imaginary previously activated by Daireaux. Like Daireaux, other urban technocrats were also ready to react promptly as soon as they caught any signs of the grotesque city, spotted scenes of "deviation," and remarked on them as repositories of sin and abnormality. Among all possible discursive positions, theirs was a view from above, mercilessly obsessed with the world of the *arrabal*.

To begin with, let us focus on two authorial decisions Gálvez made in *Historia de arrabal.* On the one hand, he chose to set his story in La Boca, in order to draw the forbidden city into the mapping of urban spaces; on the other hand, he chose to use a female character, Rosalinda Corrales, in order to speak of female sexuality and poverty as negative spaces, ghettos that he describes as unsalvageable abysses. The attribution of symbolic meaning constitutes the first step in the production of social space. It is therefore no coincidence that Gálvez's narrator has the reader's first contact with Rosalinda take place as she is leaving a "meatpacking plant whose monumental buildings stretch along the Riachuelo" (1989, 7). As the most segregated cultural perimeter of Buenos Aires, the manufacturing area on the city's southern edge, in Boca and Barracas, was a world where poverty never ceased to breed hybrid social forms. The tenements of La Boca and Isla Maciel were home to European immigrants, especially Italian Genovesi, who worked initially on the construction of Dock Sur. Gálvez lingers endlessly on their dwellings, the "shantytowns of hovels raised on piles and made of boards and sheets of metal. Once painted in garish colors, they were now faded and filthy" (1989, 10). With its uneven lines of discarded materials, this area is linked by the narrator to the culture of marginalization, to the prostitutes and beggars "who wear the old rags of the well-to-do, just as the hovels of the *arrabal* were made from the old and useless materials of the city" (1989, 10). Working men and women, immigrants, anarchists, gauchos, black men and women, mulattos and mulattas, *compadres, compadritos, malevos* (violent individuals), criminals, pimps, and of course male and female prostitutes—the brothels were concentrated in the *arrabales* of Buenos Aires—completed the political and sexual heteroglossia of the new Frontera Sur, the *external* borders of the modern city.

Along with hybrid languages in the process of formation, Mikhail Bakunin, Pietr Alexeievich Kropotkin, Leo Tolstoy, and Charles Malato Hennequin also figured in the many tongues spoken in the *arrabal*. Work in La Boca was brutal, as even a *bacán* as frivolous as Bebe Domínguez noted: "Dock workers were hired each morning between 5 and 6 A.M. . . . This work might entail twelve trips an hour down a gangplank, unloading 220-pound bags of sugar, or 150 trips a day from ship to shore, balancing unwieldy, 130-pound stacks of lumber on one's shoulders" (qtd. in Scobie 1974, 143). This was an urban space where the city was growing rapidly, in association with the textile industry and the *frigoríficos* (meatpacking plants). Everything that the other Buenos Aires, with its new urban languages, was striving to become was completely withheld from the *arrabal*. With its muddy streets, uneven sidewalks, and drainage that held unpleasant surprises for passersby, the *arrabal* must have provoked flashbacks to the times of the Gran Aldea. In other words, it was an inconvenient by-product of the grand city dreamed of for the Centennial.

Let us remember that the homogenization of the center required the systematic elimination of the *baldíos* (vacant lots) spontaneously used as public spaces for open-air markets, circuses, the informal economy, and the gathering of the working class. Hueco de Lorea thus gave way to the Avenida de Mayo, lined with offices, hotels, and cafés, although since 1865 it had been a stopping place for transient laborers and the site of "lodgings, eating houses, and cafés, the Teatro della Alegría, . . . the squalid rooms for pleasure used by the black servants" who worked in the Gran Aldea and the aristocratic Club Progreso (Matamoro 1982, 27). Daily life in such "empty" spaces so excited transgressions of social frontiers that even Adolfo Alsina, the patrician landowner and later president, used to visit El Alcázar and the Café Oriental, where African choreography, with decidedly tango-style *cortes,* was already featured. "Empty" spaces like Lorea and Miserere were disruptive in more than one sense: they questioned coherence and opened contact zones, permitting a crossing of boundaries in the sense of tactile contact that was a particularly thorny signifier for the imaginaries of surveillance.

By 1923, it was evident that the urban reforms pushed by the Generation of 1880 and the Centennial Generation were not for everyone. An untidy, disordered city insolently resisted such efforts. Innumerable texts refer to the grotesque city, the dark background behind the bright lights of formal modernity, which challenged the control of the socializing technologies of the legal, medical, and judicial systems. It is tempting to conclude that Buenos Aires was tautly stretched between two polarized spaces, the central north and the southern *arrabal,* but this restricts the understanding of urban space to binary categorizations. Gálvez, I believe, wrote *Historia de arrabal* precisely because he was aware that the experience of everyday life did not meekly fit into narrow, reassuring categories that set the mind at ease. If, as an usher, he witnessed repeatedly how every crime diminished the law, as a writer, he could not fail to gamble on what writing could conjure. To judge from *Historia de arrabal,* what most obsessed him was the city's volatile behavior, the impossibility of making clear-cut separations in the conceptual planning of urban space: "Disgusting taverns and hovels, many of them the refuges of *malevos,* where it seemed impossible for human beings to live, alternated with decent houses, in an extreme poverty inhabited by the workers of Isla Maciel" (Gálvez 1989, 10). It was precisely this alternation and proximity that triggered panic in the reactive imaginaries of the transitional city. As described in Luis Pascarella's *El conventillo: Costumbres bonaerenses,* fear of disease paralyzed the family living in a colonial mansion placed alongside a *conventillo:* "A bite, an insignificant scratch, or a cold became major events . . . requiring pharmaceutical intervention. . . . They lived under perpetual siege by an enemy of their health: tetanus, diphtheria, and even bubonic plague would suddenly appear and embitter their happiest moments" (1917, 135). This is reminiscent of the public health alarms parodied by the character in *Los devotos* who recounts the countless quarantines called for to deal with bubonic plague, cholera, yellow fever, and lice.

Urban coexistence was regulated by sluice gates, opened and closed in turn, with contact zones controlled by the proxemic distances embedded in the paranoia and xenophobia of medical, sanitary, literary, and legal discourses. As Stephen Kern points out, the bourgeoisie asserted itself as a social model through the extreme distances it established from violence and sexual promiscuity, concepts that their imaginaries successfully managed to associate with the lower classes: "Consequently their sexual morality began to become ever more restrictive" (1975, 5). What, then, does the mansion owner in *El conventillo* have in mind when he builds a ghetto in reverse? He orders "the walls of the room to be stuccoed . . . and douses even its invisible pores, 'relentless incubators of treacherous microbes,' in disinfectant." And to be certain of minimizing the risks of infection from outside, he forbids "entry to the servants, the main vehicle by which pathogens travel" (Pascarella 1917, 139).

In *Historia de arrabal,* Rosalinda is one such "vehicle." She is twenty years old, blond, sensual, and therefore the embodiment of what men look for in a brothel: "She had fair skin; thick, red lips; a body that was not firm, but not soft either; her expression was warm and caressing. She was extraordinarily attractive to men on account of the gentle, long sway of her hips . . . and as she passed along the streets she left many sensual thoughts in her wake" (Gálvez 1989, 9). Like most female characters in tango, Rosalinda lives on the outer edge of the city's borders. In the transitional city, her body displays the same uncomfortable alternation as did respectable and nonrespectable houses. Adding ambiguity to ambiguity, she has a warm, caressing expression on her face; walks with a sway; and has thick, red lips. However, her proletarian condition finally resolves all ambiguity unhesitatingly: Rosalinda is where she ought to be and where, according to naturalist determinism, she will always remain. She ends her engagement to the anarchist Daniel to become Chino's sexual slave and a member of the chorus of pitiful women at El Farol Rojo (The Red Lantern). She is repeatedly assaulted by sailors and *malevos,* by "loathsome words and gestures, the voices of drunks, the songs of the sailors in unintelligible tongues, and above all [by] the tragic light that turned the ground of the street and the walls of the neighboring houses the color of blood" (11). Indeed, the color red assails her unremittingly, as in the many "visions of blood she has had in her life. Chino bloodied her face at the age of sixteen. Her delirious father talked about blood all the time, about battles and knife wounds. Then there were the rivers of blood at the *frigorífico* and that horrible light at The Red Lantern" (59).

The association of the *arrabal* with blood brings us to Esteban Echeverría's *El matadero* (The Slaughterhouse), the first text to connect the municipal slaughterhouse and its social agents to the hated Rosas federation,[1] equating them all with the brutal work of the butcher quartering a carcass under the blows of an axe: "He hung . . . the quarters on hooks . . . skinned one of them [and] cut the fat off another; from among the rabble that looked on, waiting to seize the offal, a grubby hand emerged now and then to steal a piece . . . amid shouts and explosions of anger" (Echeverría 1963, 23). Echeverría was not exactly interested in the process because of the suffering of the cattle, but because he wished to persuade the reader to transform the sacrificed animal allegorically into a Unitarian hunted by Juan Manuel de Rosas. It was Domingo F. Sarmiento, in *Facundo,* who equated the sequence "red-Rosas-slaughterhouse" with "*colorado* [red]-Mazorca [Rosas's secret police]," recalling how the *colorado* emblem was in evidence during the Te Deums sung in honor of Rosas "as an insignia of adherence to the cause" and of "the terrible Mazorca" (Sarmiento 1993, 316). Consequently, Gálvez knew full well which colors to use for his horrifying imagery—how to get the most from well-established Argentinean imaginaries. Not coincidentally, he also alludes to yet other features fundamental to the imaginaries of the new nation: the mud and mire of the roads on the outskirts of Buenos Aires (Echeverría 1963, 9).

Rosalinda "was accustomed to blood on account of her work at the *frigorífico,* and yet that purple light [outside the brothel] made her dwell on crimes and evil nightmares" (Gálvez 1989, 46). Nevertheless, she soon becomes used to prostitution and to the shady Barrio de las Ranas. In a chronicle entitled "El Barrio de las Ranas" (1907), R. I. Ortiz links social agents in this southeastern corner of the city to the incineration of garbage and much else: "In all that sewer known as the Barrio de las Ranas, there is not the smallest thing, matter, or individual that is not nauseatingly disgusting, and anyone visiting the place . . . has to put phenic acid on his handkerchief and ice in his spirit. It infects everything, the pituitary and the soul" (Ortiz 1967, 81). The prophylactics necessary to enter these "human swamps" are phenic acid and a suitably armored sensibility. Ortiz's urban map was designed to induce shivers at these "visions of hell" by simply seeking the reader's revulsion: "One should only look and pass by . . . for there are sights of such disgust and horror that the mere mention of them is enough . . . to bring on fits of nausea" (81).

The packing plant where Rosalinda works is an industrial version of Echeverría's slaughterhouse. In Echeverría's and Gálvez's texts, the workers who cut up the carcasses and handle the bloodied meat are unmistakably associated with the popular classes. But they have something else in common as well: their urban geographies highlight the symbolic meaning of the city's outskirts. After the displacement of local cottage industries, political unification, and ranching's dominance after the defeat of Rosas (1852), the *arrabales* of Buenos Aires were converted into areas for processing cattle. As a result, the city was ringed "at every point by this belt of bloody killing fields"

(Matamoro 1982, 26). *Historia de arrabal* brings La Boca's belts of blood and crime (*cinturones rojos*) to life, marking them in red on the new cultural maps of Buenos Aires. Thus, the city adopted the standard typology of urban geography, whereby brothels, garbage, cemeteries, psychiatric asylums, and slaughterhouses—everything that city officials sought to conceal—were located outside the city's limits. These were places frequented by the likes of unemployed soldiers returning from the war with Paraguay and the Desert Campaign, or by the slaughterhouse laborers who provided the workforce for the *frigoríficos*.[2] Urban imaginaries strove to establish preventive social distances. Representatives of public health and hygiene linked the *arrabales* in parliamentary debates to the happy hunting grounds of venereal disease, while popular clamor allowed no one to forget the blight of their bordellos, such as one on Calle Junín known as El Siniestro (The Menace).

In *Flesh and Stone,* the cultural geographer Richard Sennett, in an extraordinary, horrifying description of Venice's sixteenth-century ghettos, analyzes the proxemic mechanisms of the ghetto that the city's mercantile aristocracy imposed on Jews, Germans, Persians, Greeks, Dalmatians, Armenians, Albanians, and Turks. He explains that these spatial/cultural constructions served to hide all physical traces of the ghetto's inhabitants, thereby socially eradicating them from the daily life of the city. These constructions put a fence around them, removed them from sight, and calmed fears of touching or smelling them. Sensory communication through smell is eminently chemical, involving contact with the breath, odors, sounds, heat, and warmth of the other (Hall 1985, 143). Confronted by the mixing of bodies coexisting in the same urban space, Venetian (and *porteño*) city authorities accomplished at least two goals: the regulation of social interaction through strategies of segregation and the imposition of their own nightmares on the rest of the city. Sennett adds that the three ghettos intended for Jews housed an irresolvable paradox: "If the touch of Jews seemed like a physical, sexual infection, as Jews become associated in the public mind with the spread of syphilis, Jewish doctors were also called to treat the disease" (1994, 225). As physicians, they would diagnose, prescribe treatments, and inevitably touch bodies, just like the prostitutes in Buenos Aires's *arrabales,* who were linked to syphilis and gonorrhea. Unlike the Jews of Venice, however, the prostitutes of Buenos Aires were not escorted from their homes to their places of work. Nor they were bolted in from evening until the following morning—or perhaps they were, in fact, as much is implied by the etymological roots of the word *lupanar* (brothel), which refers to a cell that housed slaves imported to ancient Greece (Sau 2000, 252). In Buenos Aires, a series of city ordinances naturalized sexual servitude: "Those who lived in bordellos were treated like part-time jail inmates. Madams (*regentas*) could not leave for more than twenty hours, and prostitutes had to return within two hours of sunset. . . . All prostitutes had to carry identity cards" (Guy 1991, 50). Strict police and sanitation controls, combined with discourses of social fear, totally alienated the prostitute within the heart of the nation, while her double punishment as a woman and as a member of the proletariat also served to strengthen "appropriated patriarchal and class values and [. . . determined] the gender structure of urban labor" (Guy 1991, 38).

Excluded from the ranching economy of the pampas, which was reserved for gauchos, the native female labor force migrated to Buenos Aires and joined the process of industrialization, providing an alternative to working men, who had become highly politicized by anarchism and unionism. Women earned "wages lower than the average: dressmakers and seamstresses received between $0.50 and $1.00 per day when the average wage for men was between $1.50 and $2.50. The wages of domestic servants may well have been lower" (Molyneux 1986, 125). This was exploitation so severe that it was akin to a new form of slavery. By the end of the nineteenth century, the average domestic servant worked twelve hours a day, seven days a week. Two strikes, in 1888 and 1890, protested the complete lack of time for rest and the employers' practice of keeping "conduct books," which were indispensable for an employee wishing to move elsewhere: "A negative judgment made it almost impossible to find another job" (Molyneux 1986, 125).

In her remarkable *Plotting Women,* Jean Franco analyzes this period of transitional "threats" in Mexico under Porfirio Díaz and alludes to the public health doctor Luis Lara y Pardo, who "possibly exaggerated when he estimated that one hundred and twenty of every thousand women were registered prostitutes and declared venereal disease to have reached 'epidemic proportions.'" Still, Franco points out, "his warning that men should take the maximum precautions during intercourse could scarcely be considered radical at a time when sexuality and death were so closely associated in literature" (1989, 95).

Gálvez's urban map connected the port, La Boca, Isla Maciel, Dock Sur, and Avellaneda to sexuality, death, social disease, and infection. No wonder the eugenic fears of municipal agencies and cultural actors made them react heartlessly to prostitutes like Rosalinda, whose promiscuity, blood, and sexual fluids touched homes, immaculate matrimonial chambers, wives, and children—in other words, the nation. For although Rosalinda only frequents La Boca at the beginning of the story, she later "came to know . . . the ignominy of Buenos Aires as a whole. Her body rested on the filthiest of beds. All the cheap hotels had been host to her. She had been along Callao and Pueyrredón, along the Paseo de Julio and San Juan. . . . She was a regular at disreputable cinemas, in cafés where girls went looking for men. . . . The streets were all familiar with her slender figure, her swaying hips that aroused the men, her thick lips, her blond hair" (Gálvez 1989, 75–76).[3] In 1894, a municipal memorandum noted the problem of "unlicensed prostitutes . . . [who] wandered the streets, theaters, and public footpaths; in effect, where . . . they find the opportunity, they are ready to ply their trade" (Leandro H. Gutiérrez 1983a, 89). Following such a pattern of expansion, Rosalinda crosses the avenue Almirante Brown to "the poverty-stricken streets of southwest Barracas: Puentecito, Limay, Perdiel, California." She crosses Avellaneda and heads from La Boca to the port area of Paseo de Julio (el Bajo and la Recova) and then to the center (Suipacha and Viamonte, Corrientes and Libertad), Cochabamba, and Constitución. She reaches Callao and goes even further, as far as Pueyrredón. On Gálvez's urban map, this exaggerates her statement of defiance even further: Rosalinda has entered Barrio Norte.

Every city has its frontiers, its border agents, and its controllers of the transit of interlopers. Rosalinda is certainly an interloper, her slippery, unhindered circulation throughout the city a concern for Gálvez's imaginary. To associate this young woman (living in Isla Maciel and working in Dock Sur) with the plague was to tie together persistent collective memories of cholera brought back by troops from the Paraguayan War (1867), typhoid fever (1869), and diphtheria and yellow fever (1871). However much public health authorities attributed these scourges to objective causes, such as unsanitary living conditions, a hazardous sewage system, and improper garbage disposal, public opinion continued to link them to the poverty of the *conventillos* in El Sur, specifically San Telmo and La Boca. Yellow fever had spread from the *conventillos* to the rest of the city, leaving fourteen thousand dead. Venereal disease was the other nightmare, although in this case, the public health official's imaginary found a much more precise carrier in the female proletarian. *Historia de arrabal* is impregnated with the court usher's zealous training in detecting the gaping holes in social normativity and the advance of Buenos Aires's sinister, dark corners and illegal backrooms, where social epidemics were furtively incubating. Gálvez was ever alert to the movements of the grotesque city because he feared its outbreaks and the unpredictability of its organic passages. Jean Franco recalls the analogy drawn between the city and the human body by Stallybrass and White: "Whilst the 'low' of the bourgeois body becomes unmentionable, we hear an ever-increasing garrulity about the *city's* low—the slum, the rag-picker, the prostitute, the sewer—the 'dirt' which is 'down there.' In other words, the axis of the body is transcoded through the axis of the city, and whilst the bodily low is 'forgotten' the city's low becomes a site of obsessive preoccupation, a preoccupation which is itself intimately conceptualized in terms of discourses of the body" (qtd. in Franco 1989, 96).

In this spatial polarization of the city's subjects, a woman is either "a living work of art" (Gómez Carrillo 1921, 58–59) or a proletarian condemned to predetermined social tragedy. According to the reductionist thesis of *Historia de arrabal,* as described by Rosalinda's friend Isaura, there are two options for "snatching that girl from the *malevo*'s clutches," and both entail "having her protected by Daniel Forti, replacing one man with another" (Gálvez 1989, 57). The young woman is to be cared for by the anarchist and by marriage, in contrast to the predatory "protection" of the *malevo* and prostitution. Harrington, Rosalinda's boss at the factory, is a third option, also placing her in the care of a man, but in spite of her pleas ("I'll be your servant, sir, if you don't love me. But save me. Do it for your mother" [44]), he backs away when he hears about Rosalinda's life in the brothel. As the narrator explains: "To take her from the *malevo* was to expose himself. . . . Better not to stick his nose into anything. . . . His only ambition was to live quietly and enjoy the charms of the prettiest girls at the packing plant" (45). Even if Rosalinda walks street after street and remains employed at the factory, she will never get far. The more she moves around, the more she is trapped, as Donna Guy explains, pointing to a crucial aspect of the gender mapping of the early stage of industrialization: "Women who sought work in . . . public places were always suspected of supplementing their income with the proceeds of sin. In this way, neighbors stigmatized women who operated tobacco stores, forerunners of contemporary kiosks, or who owned cafés and music halls or worked there as waitresses. Those who took in laundry or sewing were also suspect" (1991, 45). Access to work in Buenos Aires, or any transitional city under modernity, conferred an ambiguous condition on women. Being a worker/prostitute was an algebraic equation, both classist and androcentric. But what identitary place could Gálvez construct for Rosalinda other than her submission to the ferociously gendered structure of the sex trade and the deterministic imaginaries of naturalism? Rosalinda "lost all sense of her personality. Accustomed to that way of life, she came to have no idea of good or evil. . . . She could not conceive of ever being able to leave that life. It was the end, the only thing possible for her. . . . She even believed she felt some tenderness for her *malevo*. . . . She considered him her man, her male, and obeyed him blindly as such, completely submissive to his will (Gálvez 1989, 77).

The novel follows the gradual and irreversible extinction of Rosalinda's sensory awareness and ability to react. Sunk in lethargy, Rosalinda internalizes her space of interpellation and confinement in the ghetto. Was this, however, the only destiny available to proletarian women in transitional Buenos Aires? Among the many alternative environments avoided by the imaginary of *Historia de arrabal* are the libertarian movements of anarchists, feminists, and socialists, whose political activism was centered precisely in Dock Sur and La Boca. Such women are right at Rosalinda's side, nearby. In fact, a song of freedom is repeatedly heard from barges and wharfs as she passes by:

> Son of the people, chains oppress you
> and this injustice cannot go on,
> if your life is a world of pain,
> prefer death to slavery. (Gálvez 1989, 55)

Why doesn't Rosalinda hear it? Why doesn't Gálvez conceive of Rosalinda's social salvation by resorting to other possibilities, already historically active in the daily life of the city?

As a product of the first and second stages of industrialization, anarchism surfaced in Argentina in response to (1) rapid economic growth and the demand for labor; (2) the wave of European immigration (by 1900, 60 percent of the working class was of immigrant origin, and they brought political militancy along in their baggage, especially from Spain, Italy, France, and Germany); (3) an electoral system that gave no political representation to the proletariat; (4) blockage of land tenure for immigrants and their subsequent overcrowding in conditions of urban poverty and exploitation; and (5) severely restricted access to naturalization under the Residency Act. At the height of the anarchist movement, of the 345,493 immigrants who landed in 1895, only 715 were eligible for naturalization: "The immigrant population was kept in a precarious situation economically and politically. The double disqualification (electoral and national) that allowed minimal political expression . . . encouraged it to have expression in a combative and often revolutionary way" (Molyneux 1986, 122).

Alternative historical models were, then, already at hand, such as feminist anarchism centered on the publication *La voz de la mujer* (The Voice of Women, 1896–1901). With all the hallmarks of a minority publication, written in Spanish and Italian, it declares on its cover that it "publishes when it can." Because its contributors used pseudonyms, their real names remain unknown, except for writers Irma Ciminagli, Ana López, Teresa Marchisio, and Virginia Bolten—the only woman ever deported under the Residency Act. They were followers of Spanish feminists Soledad Gustavo (Teresa Mañé), María Martínez, and Teresa de Claramunt; French feminist Laurentine Sauvrey; and Italian feminist Maria Mozzoni. Although it appeared irregularly and had a pamphletlike style, *La voz de la mujer* was widely distributed, popular among *obreras* and women in domestic service. In spite of its short life span, it succeeded in attracting even the attention of the cosmopolitan *Caras y Caretas,* which, like the press in general, referred to its editors in sexist terms as "the two beautiful women who edit *La voz de la mujer*" (Molyneux 1986, 130). In its seventh issue, the journal gathers testimonials against prostitution, proposes free love, denounces discrimination against illegitimate offspring, and criticizes marriage as class oppression and conjugal anonism—a one-sided contract based on virginity and fidelity to which only one party subscribes. It also condemns domestic violence, focusing on one case in particular that had arisen in the very heart of the anarchist movement.[4] Nevertheless, Gálvez's naturalist agenda left him deaf to these cries for such political breaks. There are no female models of resistance in *Historia del arrabal,* only confirmation of the thesis of *deformación sin retorno social,* which sees no second chance for social "deformation."

For Rosalinda, the Frontera Sur is a space without alternatives. This frontier, from which there is no return, is also crossed by Emma Zunz when she surrenders to the sailor off the *Nordstjärnan,* tied up at dock number three in Puerto Madero. Jorge Luis Borges was quite precise when he gave his narrative "Emma Zunz" the date 22 January 1922—also *Historia de arrabal's* year of publication. Consistent with the workplace context of Gálvez's proletarian *porteña,* Emma Zunz works in Tarbuch and Loewenthal's textile factory, located in the "rundown *arrabal*" near Warnes. However, the direst frontier in 1922 Buenos Aires is the one Emma crosses when walking from Almagro to El Bajo. Emma's times are also those of union struggles and anarchist strikes—turmoil that Emma takes advantage of in order to get close to Aaron Loewenthal and to uncover his murder of the factory owner, not exactly to claim labor rights but for much more personal reasons. Emma finds the place/motive for her sacrifice, her self-immolation, and the mutilation of her sexuality precisely in the sinful city traversed by Rosalinda. In doing so, she becomes Rosalinda, as well as all the countless workers in the brothels of Buenos Aires: "Emma lived in Almagro, on Liniers Street. We know she went to the waterfront that evening. Perhaps she saw herself multiplied in the mirrors along the infamous Paseo de Julio, displayed under the lights, and undressed by hungry eyes, but it's more reasonable to suppose that at first she wandered unnoticed along the indifferent arcade. . . . She went into two or three bars, saw the routine or technique of other women. Finally, she came across men from the *Nordstajärnan*" (Borges 1974, 1: 565).

While Temple was the red-light district of the upper middle class, the lower classes frequented La Boca, Paseo de Julio, Tierra del Fuego, Miserere, and Corrales Viejos (Matamoro 1982, 33). Paseo de Julio (the present-day Leandro Alem) was the center of prostitution in the port. Rosalinda worked there, and Emma sacrificed herself in its tantalizing shadows. The tango "Allá en el Bajo" (Down in El Bajo), by Ismael Aguilar and Gerónimo Martinelli Massa, set to music by Agustín Magaldi and Pedro Noda, associates this area with bloody encounters and fights between *malevos:*

> The struggle is fierce,
> no quarter is given. . . .
> An arm feints,
> the blades clash,
> and the eyes glisten
> filled with rage.[5]

Similarly, in "Paseo de Julio," Pedro Herreros describes the area with a truly amazing power of synthesis:

Arcades. Shady shoplifters.
Pillars. Dirty silhouettes.
Popular dances. Poets.
Vagrants. Sailors.

A movie theater. [Pornographic] postcards. Shopfronts.
Pipes. Tobacco. Cheap places to eat.
An employment agency.
Cafés with music. Prostitutes.

Hunger. Books. Clothes. Mud. (qtd. in Lara and de Panti 1961, 240)

Herreros gives us a glimpse of some of the most characteristic features of the *arrabal*'s hybrid culture: brothels, music halls, rooms let by the hour, prostitutes, employment agencies, pornographic postcards, vagrants, shady silhouettes, sailors, exchange bureaus, gun shops, popular dancing, tango, street organs, poets, hunger, and dirt. In "Del Buenos Aires exótico" (From Exotic Buenos Aires; *Revista PBT,* 2 January 1918), Eçe Del Clé describes the *arrabal*'s arcades: "To walk along the arcades of Paseo del Julio is to be unexpectedly transported . . . to an exotic, ugly, dirty city in which every language is spoken and through which the strangest, most extravagant types parade. It's the barrio of the poor . . . crews off ships . . . the unemployed looking for work or wandering in disillusion with a stoic look of resignation among that conglomeration of humanity eating on the sidewalks and throwing their leftovers into the street." The article concludes: "Dirty men, dirty women, dirty children, with dirty bodies and dirty mouths. This, in a word, is the picture of Paseo del Julio." In contrast to the Barrio Norte, where a stroller might wander in and linger to gaze around longingly, the irredeemable cultural geography of the sinful Frontera Sur calls for a rapid retreat in the name of decontamination.

I believe that the only way to understand the magnitude of Emma Zunz's passage across social frontiers is to reconstruct the unspeakable revulsion inspired by Paseo de Julio and the dismay that readers must have felt at her ignominious passage from decent *obrera* to a woman trapped in the filth of the brothel. Like Rosalinda, Emma becomes a woman of the forbidden city, inferring the business and routine of removing her clothes, the gestures and contortions in unknown, malodorous beds. The intertextuality of Borges's story and the sociourban discourses of the Paseo de Julio allow the horror of this frontier crossing to be imagined more vividly, as an abomination that, in Emma's case, is all the more horrendous because it is voluntary and deliberate. And, speaking of deliberate crossings, Borges's lyric voice in "El Paseo de Julio," from *Cuaderno San Martín* (San Martín Copybook), allows the reader to suspect that he has crossed these frontiers himself, at least in the imaginary realm of his writing: "I swear that I have not *deliberately* returned to the street / with the high arches repeated as if in a mirror / . . . Paseo del Julio, although my memories . . . know you / I never felt you as my homeland" (1974, 1: 95; emphasis added):

> Barrio, clear as a nightmare . . .
> your curved mirrors betray the ugliness of your faces,
> your night warmed in brothels hangs from the city.
> You are ruination, forging a world
> from reflections of the world and its deformities;
> you suffer from chaos, you are sick with unreality,
> you insist on gambling your life with crumpled cards;
> your alcohol incites fights,
> your Greek women jealously finger their books of magic. (1: 95)

Certainly, *that* part of Buenos Aires was not Borges's "homeland." Since his description of the Paseo de Julio coincides with that offered in other social texts, it may be deduced that his knowledge was derived only from "readings." Nevertheless, one detail is out of place in his writing: while the lyric voice proclaims, "I have only a blinding ignorance of you," it contradicts itself when it admits to having "returned to the street." Although the speaker's blinding ignorance is "insecure," it is sufficiently powerful to urge his return and to trigger his writing: "my verse is question and proof." He says, "I never felt you as my homeland," and yet explains that his writing comes from "obedience to what has been glimpsed." I suspect that Borges has these shameful borders very much before him. He has glimpsed them in the blinding light and revisited them through conjecture. He has even had Emma, one of his major literary characters, walk through them. These are veiled crossings into the forbidden city by the "other" Borges, a double whose ambiguity never ceases to reverberate.

Emma is taken by the faceless sailor to "a door and then to a murky hallway and then to a winding stairway and then to a lobby . . . and then to a passageway and then to a door that closed behind her" (Borges 1974, 1: 566).

It could be said that Borges's entire production is pure conjecture about frontiers. Borgesian texts focus on frontiers crossed with varying degrees of horror, curiosity, fear, and resignation, and "Emma Zunz" is unquestionably one of these texts. The enumeration of the many frontiers Emma crosses (passageways, doors, hallways, stairways, lobbies, corridors) stresses a materiality that is irreversibly divisive. The young woman takes a trail of blood—her own—with her from the brothels, where she loses her virginity, to mark her last fatal meeting with Lowenthal: "A sudden flow of blood burst from his obscene lips and stained his beard and clothing" (1: 567). Emma has just killed him. But how can she cover up the crime? We have seen how the culture of work in transitional Buenos Aires entails sexual harassment, like that of Rosalinda's slimy boss, who offers his "friendship" to the young female workers in the *frigorífico* in exchange for sexual "favors." So Emma disguises her crime with the social text of sexual assault precisely because such a text is absolutely believable in her circumstances: "She disarranged the armchair, unbuttoned the dead man's jacket, took off his spattered spectacles, and left them on the filing cabinet. Then she picked up the telephone and repeated what she would repeat many times in these and other words: *Something terrible has happened. . . . Mr. Lowenthal had me come to see him about the strike. He assaulted me, and I killed him*" (1: 568; original emphasis). Emma will no longer be Emma, but a woman contaminated by the Frontera Sur, whose sexuality has been ruined by the unspeakable horror of the brothel's rituals. I believe that Emma's crossing is all the more fearful since she undertakes it *in reverse,* the opposite of what was recommended on the preventive urban maps of public health physicians and naturalist writers. Even though she could have avoided it, Emma crosses the frontier like Borges's captive in "Historia del guerrero y la cautiva" (History of the Warrior and the Captive), making an irrevocable choice that would doubtless have left Manuel Gálvez and Sarmiento speechless—but, evidently, not Borges who, unlike Sarmiento and Gálvez, takes the opposite direction through his fiction and "regains" that speech in order to go deeper into ignominious territories.

The most spectacular condemnation of prostitution in grotesque theater of the time is Feruccio Tosoni's drama *En un rincón de la quema* (In a Corner of the Dump, 1922). Its action unfolds in a barrio next to the city's incinerator whose inhabitants survive amid the rubbish cast off by the city. The drama takes place on the eve of a son's return after fifteen years in jail, ready to begin his "rehabilitation and a new life." In the last few years, his mother has lived with a *malevo* who has forced her and her young daughter into prostitution, a situation unknown to the son. Renato, released a day ahead of schedule, wanders through the city he no longer recognizes and strikes up a conversation with a young woman he meets when he rests on a bench in a square: "She told me to follow her, . . . [and] since it was late, I went with her and spent the night with her." Immersed in an imaginary that regarded urban dumps as metonyms for a life of relentless condemnation, the audience of *En un rincón de la quema* must have been quick to realize that the prostitute Renato meets is his own sister:

> RENATO: This is dreadful! . . . Horrifying! It has a name! It's called incest! Oh!
>
> ELVIRA (*crying bitterly*): Fate has punished us . . . punished us.

If we could visualize in its entirety the immense body of texts that represent women sold by parents or guardians; women subjected to melancholic or voracious gazes of desire; women punished in the name of honor or the preservation of the family; women murdered out of jealousy or suspicion; women abandoned and thrown to the inclemency of the streets; women condemned by implacable judges and exemplary verdicts, by tango narratives, or by fathers, brothers, husbands, boyfriends, or neighbors, we would certainly conclude that women in Buenos Aires—from the femme fatale, with her seductive clutches, to the prostitute, with her inevitable social death—were unavoidably susceptible to suspicion or sanction because of their sexuality. As sanctioning imaginaries gained ground, their truths asserted what was considered "socially correct" (*lo acertado*), while attributing the prevalence of prostitution to malformed family structures. Such is the case with Rosalinda after her father dies, leaving her at the mercy of Saturnina and her son, who soon becomes her *cafisho* (pimp). One night, Saturnina's son "seized her head in both hands and banged it against the ground. . . . The exasperated *malevo* . . . hit her in the face and body. Rosalinda was shaking all over. She was crying, moaning hoarsely. Finally, she could take no more. She had no strength left. . . . Then El Chino raped her. . . . Nobody helped her. Saturnina had seen everything her son was doing, but went back to sleep" (Gálvez 1989, 20). With a single stroke, this imaginary attributes the social scourge of prostitution to the fragmentation of the family resulting from the physical displacement and economic/cultural dislocation of the proletariat searching for work. In other words, it blames the ecology of poverty for the erosion of moral and ethical principles.

The scene of family members and guardians, or neighbors and prostitutes in league with a pimp, surrendering young women is a commonplace of popular theater. In Carlos Mauricio Pacheco's *Los tristes o la gente oscura* (The Sad Ones; or, Dark People, 1906), two *malevos* discuss the details of the transaction to purchase María:

> PINOTO: It's a good deal for you.
>
> LECHUGA: I told her about a sister living in Palermo.
>
> PINOTO: Why didn't you talk clearly to her? After all, she wasn't born to be . . . respectable. . . . Didn't you say her mother was crazy and her father a drunk?
>
> LECHUGA: I haven't dared explain it to her. She has such an innocent face! But she'll give in like all of them. . . . Two hundred pesos. . . . In any case, she could well take off with a *malevo* any day. (Pacheco 1977b, 40)

The young woman has been beaten and bloodied by her drunken godfather:

> MARÍA: I'm used to it; I hardly feel anything anymore; I can't even cry. . . . They hit me, they push me, and not even a tear. (*With total disillusion.*) It's all the same to me. . . . Sometimes I'd like to let myself die of hunger or cold. . . . The only thing I feel all the time is being very afraid.

Narratives of the road to ruin (*narrativas de perdición*) ordered social meanings in light of the emergence of such deviations by endorsing female domesticity as the most appropriate conduct (*lo acertado*). María's future in the brothel is a foregone conclusion. She will follow in the footsteps of Rosalinda to become an accomplice to criminals, bought and sold dozens of times, bloodied by blows intended to teach her a lesson as each *malevo* inscribes his territory and power to terrorize on her body. She will even betray her family and potential redeemer at the command of her pimp, just like Rosalinda: "She, who adored . . . [Daniel Forti]; she, who would be freed by him; she had killed him herself." Rosalinda is led everywhere with no choice of her own: "The *malevo* . . . pushed her to make her leave. Without looking at Daniel lying dead, she left hesitatingly, as if unaware of everything, with slow, awkward steps" (Gálvez 1989, 70). It is remarkable how this imaginary compulsively represents the proletarian woman as a subject who has totally

Muñecas Bravas *of Buenos Aires*

given up on herself, who has no control over her reaction and no room to maneuver. Gálvez's narrator remarks that Rosalinda "could not conceive of ever leaving such a life. This was the end, the only thing possible for her." Similarly, Carlos Pacheco's María states, "They hit me, they push me, and not even a tear. It's all the same to me," confirming a wealth of images that are all too familiar in the sado-misogynistic imaginary.

In the fluid dialogue between classical mythology and patriarchal thought, the figure of the incubus stands out. Incubi are demons whose nocturnal work consists of taking control of sleeping women. They possess the women, smother them, and sit on them until they choke. Johann Heinrich Füssli captures this figure with the extraordinary suggestive power of chiaroscuro in his 1790 painting *The Nightmare* (figure 12), which shows the illuminated body of a woman lying supine and half naked on a bed, a grotesque monster crouched on her stomach. Incubi must have sharpened the erotic imagination of the Marquis de Sade and undoubtedly opened the way for the violence of pornography and sado-eroticism, stimulated by the utter *defenselessness* of women. Bereft of strength, the woman's passive body is exposed to the observation of a voyeur, easily penetrated under the sovereignty of absolute possession by a male who, according to this misogynist imaginary, sees the female body as a passive locus for the consummation of his fantasies. The female *petite mort* in Füssli's scene encapsulates the exercise of this sovereignty perfectly. Pornography is precisely defined in legal discourse as "the graphic, sexually explicit subordination of women, in pictures and/or in words that also included women presented dehumanized as sexual objects . . . who enjoy pain or humiliation . . . who experience sexual pleasure in being raped" (Dworkin 1989, xxxiii). It outlaws imaginaries in which women are "presented in postures or positions of sexual submission, servility . . . [or] as whores by nature. . . . [It outlaws] women presented in scenarios of degradation, injury, torture, shown as filthy or inferior, bleeding, bruised, or hurt in a context that makes these conditions sexual" (Dworkin 1989, xxxiii). This definition invites us to wonder whether texts like Gálvez's openly border on the pornographic. Sheltering beneath an agenda obsessed with the identification of "social" ills, perhaps such texts in reality contribute to perpetuating them, especially since the intense sexual tension that ripples through *Historia de arrabal* invariably culminates in descriptions of sexual violence against Rosalinda's body.

In *Sexual Anarchy: Gender and Culture at the Fin de Siècle,* Elaine Showalter deduces that the objectives of public health discourse with respect to prostitution turn women into case histories "to be opened and shut. The criminal slashes with a knife. The scientist and the doctor open the woman up with the scalpel or pierce her with the stake. The artist or writer penetrates the female case with a sharp-honed imagery and a phallic pen" (1991, 134). The naturalist writer therefore becomes an impassive anatomist, dissecting a body that represents deviation and social anarchy—much like Gálvez, whose writing acts upon the corpse of the prostitutes of Buenos Aires while they are still alive. Such an imaginary is like Füssli's painting. It creates a night without dawn for proletarian urban women who are paralyzed and defeated by the futility of any possible escape. It feeds fantasies of unending, brutal penetration in the sado-misogynist imagination that had turned prostitution into an acceptable social institution. It relocates the perversion of the city in the female body, while reaffirming the right of masculinity/the masculine subject to watch over and prey upon it. The *malevo rufián* (pimp) destroys the woman's body; the public health physician sets the legal rules that permit continued circulation of this prostituted body; and the writer decrees its social death, ensuring that prostitutes are "lost forever" (Gálvez 1989, 57) at the same time as he makes it possible for the reader to enter the scene as a voracious voyeur, as in Füssli's painting. Public health regulations concerning prostitution turn the prostitute into a space where the sickening violence of sado-misogynism is legalized and left unpunished.

How is it possible to escape the coherence of an imaginary so well assembled? How can we spot other models to contradict it? A female character in Pacheco's *Los tristes o gente oscura* exclaims hopefully, "There must be another life beyond this darkness." In 1922, Roberto Gache told a very "ordinary" story about "a mysterious, sad woman who, in the midst of all the *sainetes* and reviews at the national theater, . . . burst out in tears . . . with a tango telling of her own suffering" (Lara and de Panti 1961, 239). Whenever the singer of *tonadillos* sings tangos, she relates the story of her own downfall, echoing the innumerable social texts of the city. Perhaps Gache refers to the story as "ordinary" in order to block, yet again, the residue of social sensibility and dissent welling up in the city. This is, after all, a story from the "other" city, and no truth can ever emerge from its mire. Hence the relevance of texts that vacillate or that blatantly invert paradigms sympathetic to conventional narratives.

In Carlos Pacheco's *Tangos, tongos y tungos,* Tiburcio whispers discouragingly that, like any femme fatale, Teresita "has a heart of stone. Believe me. She doesn't love anyone." But Teresita explains her iciness: "[From my childhood] I remember nothing but beatings, the pangs of hunger and the cold. All I remember is sadness and darkness. . . . We [women] don't love anyone. . . . Let them all go to hell" (Pacheco 1964, 103). Now that Teresita has moved up in the world, from *milonguita* to aristocrat's lover, Claudina surrenders her niece Isabel to her. She hopes her niece will emulate Teresita's success, although she is hardly more than a child. "This is the lady you are going to be with, the only true friend you'll have besides your aunt," she says sarcastically after assuring Teresita that the young girl is a virgin, an "innocent [who only knows how to] cook and sew." Later, Teresita and her accomplices morbidly check Isabel out from head to toe before deciding how to set her up as a prostitute: "We'll package her as a French woman. She has the figure. . . . Does she know how to dance? . . . With that look and the *milonga* school . . . we'll see how she runs." But Isabel has touched something in Teresita's heart, and when the transaction is almost complete, she suddenly reacts:

> TERESA: You want to take the girl away from me. . . . You know what kind of blood I have in my veins. . . . Look, first you'll have to kill me; I'll defend her against them, against you, against old Claudina . . . against everyone! (115–16)

The metamorphosis of Teresita into Teresa is not frivolous: changing the name that once linked her to prostitution implies that she has taken control and has reflexively chosen to follow a different path.[6] Instead of staging the sado-erotic scene that makes the female body available to the pornographer or the rapist, as in Füssli's painting, Teresa chooses for Isabel what she could not choose for herself. Her surprising decision abruptly breaks with the road to ruin, offering a luminous alternative. Some extraordinary questioning and realignment have undoubtedly taken place. Teresa has become a social actor who has reflected on the common assumptions of daily life and social patterning and has set herself against them, pressed perhaps by a thirst for social imaginaries far removed from the claustrophobic narratives of the mire and perdition of prostitution. Interventions such as Teresa's, however, are exceptional, literally crushed under the monumental weight of the imaginaries of predetermination fed by naturalism and other social texts.

8 WORK, THE BODY, AND DISLOCATIONS OF IDENTITY

DURING THE FIRST PHASE OF industrialization, the process of selecting factory workers began with a hiring boss who looked them over for evidence of physical strength. A medical exam then excluded all those with deformities, hernias, varicose veins, and mutilations, the main objective being to assess a worker's capacity to adapt to the demands of the job. The touchstone for scientific "objectivity" in capitalist labor culture was *The Principles of Scientific Management* (1911), by the Pennsylvania engineer Frederick Winslow Taylor. Taylor's philosophy was denounced in Argentina early in the industrial era by anarchist, socialist, and communist organizations and especially by the socialist senator Alfredo Palacios, who wrote *La fatiga y sus proyecciones sociales* (Fatigue and Its Social Consequences) and made the matter a subject of parliamentary debate. One of Taylor's experimental methods was to time women who removed defective parts from an assembly line, with the objective of eliminating slow or inattentive workers. Having demonstrated that some "women wasted time talking, conversation was forbidden and they were separated from each other," and "piecework at differential rates was introduced" (Palacios n.d., 71). This experiment was designed to expose those who were inept or simply unable to adjust to estimates for productivity and physical endurance (i.e., to the duration and intensity of the work). The results were more than encouraging to the interests of capitalism: "35 women could do the work previously done by 120; they earned more and increased the accuracy of the job by one third" (Palacios n.d., 71). This method rewarded the workers who adapted with bonuses (initially of 10 percent) and eliminated the weak and lazy of both genders, as well as *habladoras,* or "chattering women." From Taylor's point of view, the unions were left to represent the "incompetent" or those whose physical condition, age, or exhaustion had made them rejects of an industrial machine that demanded only young fodder and strong, complete bodies.

On Sunday, 3 January 1909, under the headline "Por las mujeres y los niños" (For Women and Children), the socialist newspaper *La Vanguardia* denounced failures to comply with Article 12 of Law no. 9,688, requiring every factory to provide an enclosed room where *obreras* could change their street clothes in privacy, although the failure to comply continued to expose women's bodies on open factory and workshop floors. This increased public familiarity with the body of the working woman effectively made it a sort of an extension of the "public body" of the prostitute. On Monday, 25 January, and Tuesday, 26 March, *La Vanguardia* reported on a "paper factory located at Montes de Oca 2290 . . . [where] women and children are atrociously exploited . . . doing piecework in an unhealthy environment without a room in which to change their clothes so that they have to do so in full view of their male coworkers." These aspects of the new work culture profoundly disturbed the relation of men and women workers to their own bodies, altering personal interactions and playing a crucial role in the definition of new gender identities. As Foucault might have concluded, factory labor culture consisted of a set of measures shaped to class and gender, arbitrarily imposed by each industry without any possibility of appeal. The state was simply "slow" to enforce labor legislation.

From the very beginning of industrialization, once the chattering *obreras* had caught the attentive ear of Taylor's inspectors, the social history of work has pointed to silence as one of the measures that disrupts female identity. Manuel Chueco, a contemporary, wrote that "the deafening noise makes it impossible to hear a human voice, but it doesn't come from the chatter and whispering of that swarm of women and girls: order and the harshest discipline are supreme" (qtd. in Feijóo 1990, 296). The illustration "El taller: Orden y silencio" (The Factory: Order and Silence) reveals, remarkably, how decisions about the organization of space resulted in a conventlike atmosphere, so that the young working women, sitting erect and spotlessly dressed, could apply themselves to their task without any distraction (figure 13). This was how the factories and workshops controlled the norms of social exchange. Both the identity of the new social class (i.e., the proletariat) and its gender identities were heavily intersected by the new capitalist labor culture. Whether they were men, women, boys, or girls, workers were acquiring a face and a social place in light of that culture. Women were made to undress in public, and children were docile fodder to be exploited by bosses —a condition made all the more dramatic in the children's case because it was compounded by their parents' acquiescence.

In Argentina, these conditions were present most notoriously in the meatpacking industry, which employed women between eighteen and thirty-seven years of age, their factory work strongly reinforcing the traditional social roles of both single (50 percent) and married women (46 percent). In "Women Workers in the 'Cathedrals of Corned Beef,'" Mirta Zaida Lobato underlines the significance of the meatpacking industry for the insertion of the landowning oligarchy at the leading edge of the industrializing process and the export market, as well as its centrality in the daily life of the proletariat: "A cultural icon, the packing plant was the site where the dramas of the poor were woven . . . where men showed their strength, their skills, their masculinity; and where women could only be victims of the infernal machines, of the squalor, and of evil" (1997, 55). Hence, it was not by chance that Manuel Gálvez placed Rosalinda in the most territorial environment sexist imaginaries could muster. This was a patently unequal space, where the higher salaries given to male workers rewarded physical strength and dexterity with the knife. In my opinion, however, we should not lapse into an examination of this issue based solely on gender differences. Physical strength, roughness, and endurance—the markers that the paradigms of the time used to define virility—were Darwinian conditions that also marginalized those members of the male population unable to contribute the physical strength, mental concentration, retention of reflexes over long periods of time, and coordination of movements demanded by the never-ending rhythm of the production lines (see chapter 16).

As Lobato concludes, "To kill animals, stack the quarter sections of cows, or simply to keep up with the rhythm of the assembly line called for machos" (1997, 63). These "machos" were the auctioneers, handlers, slaughterers— men who cut up the shanks, butchered the head, worked with the saw, gutted the animal, quartered its carcass, cut up the hindquarters and the flanks, and hanged the butchered carcass up on hooks. In "Una visión del mundo del trabajo: El caso de los obreros de la industria frigorífica Berisso, 1900–1930" (A View of the Working World: The Meatpackers of Berisso, 1900–1930), Lobato describes the production line from the moment when the animal was felled: "It went through the hands of about 35 workers, one after another, who slaughtered, bled, skinned, amputated heads, hooves, and legs, or eviscerated in turn, and who differed from each other in their ability to handle a knife in some 30 specialties, each paid a different salary" (1990, 325).

The *frigorífico* acted as a powerful endorsement of the traditional spaces of gender, the nature of its production rewarding violence and forcibly leading to the numbing of sensibilities through an unavoidable familiarity with the cutting and dismemberment of carcasses. In other words, it naturalized suffering and death. It is to be expected that the culture of work in the country's most dominant industry would profoundly influence social relationships inside and beyond its factories. The men's work certainly called for greater physical strength on the slaughterhouse floor and in the high-temperature rooms and the ovens. Nevertheless, although the work assigned to women was sedentary and required less physical strength, it also demanded manual skills and careful handling, necessary to preserve the texture of the meat. Lobato points out that no recognition was given to the strength needed to strip the fat from tripe without tearing it or to remain seated hour after hour grinding meat and stuffing it into sausage skins (1997, 63). Women were assigned "female" jobs: handling the offal, grinding the meat, preserving, dying, packaging, and sausage making. Instability was another characteristic of women's work in the factories. In addition to being physically confined and earning patently lower wages, women workers were constantly being transferred from one sector of the production line to another: "'I entered the sewing department,' explains a Polish woman, 'from sewing they sent me to meat cutting, from there to canning, from there to oil, [and] later I returned to canning'" (Lobato 1997, 64). In each case, it is relevant to note, the transfers from one station to another demanded new efforts of adjustment and a redrawn sensorial/cognitive map, essential to undertake new tasks. Adjustments of the kind advised by Taylor with respect to production quotas—taking into account the position of the body and the necessary mental and physical effort—required workers to develop specific reflexes for each work station, intended to eliminate wasted time and effort and enhance the rationalization of labor. The result of the companies' unending rotation was a "nonspace/-place" for unskilled workers.

In *Historia de arrabal,* right from the outset, Rosalinda is identified with the vulnerability and penetrability of the terrified female body: "She was frightened not only by those men who reeked of blood, but by the ironwork on the huge, black bridge . . . and as the ferry moved from one shore to another . . . it let out a fearful noise, shook, and even made the piers along the Riachuelo shudder" (Gálvez 1989, 7). Lobato argues that cement, iron, and steel were used "to give greater strength and solidity to structures" (1990, 327), but Rosalinda's visual/haptic perception records the other side of that function—namely, the sensorial/cognitive impact of the violence of noise and the volume of heavy masses. Immense structures and buildings beyond human scale, giant chimneys, massive cargo barges, and colossal machines all contributed to a geography made doubly aggressive because it was never static, the sudden movements of gears and machinery making it imperative to react promptly within the full range of sensory fields. Inside, the plant was like a gigantic city. Its "streets permitted movement in one direction only and had signs that prohibited otherwise": "The different segments of the factory were built on several floors, on each of which one phase of the production process was carried out, and materials were moved by gravity along gutters and pipes. For this reason, slaughtering was located on the upper floors . . . so that offal, tripe, heads, skins, and tongues were moved by the effect of gravity" (Lobato 1990, 328).

Can we imagine ourselves moving along these slippery, slimy spaces soaked in blood, grease, and organic matter? Personal space is defined as "an emotionally charged space bubble around each individual which is regarded as private and personal space. It is effectively an extension of this self's presence in space and violation of this space, or territory, by another is felt like the violation of the body itself" (Sommer 1969, 57). Imagine this personal bubble in a constant state of alertness, threatened by the sudden fall of heavy objects, innards, cattle heads, streams of blood, and unrecognizable parts from the bodies of animals.

According to Paul Rodaway, behaviorist theory combines complex models of multiple, alternate stimuli: "thresholds (levels of stimulus necessary before expected behaviour occurs), habituation (reduced response after repeated exposure to a stimulus) and chance" (1994, 17). Thus, Rosalinda must construct a sensorial/cognitive map with which to process sensorial perceptions, allowing her to react as quickly as possible throughout her long and arduous day. Even though an eight-hour workday had been legislated in 1929, noncompliance was the norm. Work in the packing plants began at seven A.M., seven days a week. Rosalinda works Monday through Saturday, from seven A.M. until five P.M.: "It wasn't pleasant, ten hours preparing the small cans, and not so much because of the length of the day or the work itself, but because of the atmosphere of the place, the insufferable heat, the smoke, the steam from the meat cooking . . . the persistence of a coworker whose propositions bothered her, not having an hour free during the day, and the cruelty of some of her companions [who were] jealous of her because she was pretty" (Gálvez 1989, 14). The overall multisensorial haptic perceptions caused by sharp metals, bloody hooks, and meat hanging over her send chilling flashes throughout her body. A woman who worked in a meatpacking plant explains: "In the tripe sections, jobs were performed in a very humid environment, with floors covered with water, in a constant contact with raw material that impregnated clothes, shoes, and even bodies with a strong odor. In conserva, where they diced meat, workers frequently cut their hands and contracted infections. Some women worked in conditions of great heat; the women in the hides section who classified wool were subjected to acids. . . . The wool had poison in it that irritated your skin. Often, I couldn't even wash the dishes because of the pain" (Lobato 1997, 65). The space in the *frigorífico* is semanticized by the violence of the work done there—the ritual of death; the dismemberment of carcasses through the wielding of knives, pincers, and hooks; the disemboweling of the cattle; the handling of offal, entrails, and intestines—but I wish here to emphasize smells in particular. The smells of the *frigorífico* are absolutely essential for understanding Rosalinda and the other young female workers of Buenos Aires.

Lobato emphasizes that work in the meatpacking industry was particularly dirty, the floors covered in blood and the decomposing animal remains giving off nauseating smells (1990, 329). One male worker remembered these smells on his wife's body: "When she'd come out of the tripería she had a smell that was awful, I remember her hands, nails, because however much she'd wash and perfume it was a smell that penetrated the skin" (Lobato 1997, 60). A woman from the Armour plant agreed: "We used to come out of the tripería with a smell that was so bad that you couldn't even travel by bus" (Lobato 1997, 60). The *obrera* stood apart from fellow travelers on the bus because her body trailed the smell of the factory, while her husband, too, kept his distance from his wife's body and from intimacy with her. We might read this smell, impregnated on the skin, as a sort of writing left on the body of the worker by the culture of the factory, as well as the signifier of a degraded working and social space. The repulsive odors of industry seem to trace the outline of a ghetto whose inhabitants must be equally repulsive because of the smell that has been transferred to them. How is it possible to dilute this branding? How is it possible to bear a body that reeks of blood? How is it possible to escape from that ghetto?

Rosalinda's sensorial geography picks up semiotic indicators through smells. In fact, she is terrified of "men who reeked of blood." I believe that the extraordinary importance attributed to perfumes at that time can be understood within the context of the impact of smells transferred from factories to proletarian bodies. Cheap or expensive, elusive or long lasting, perfumes became yet another type of disguise. The perfume industry marketed a "corrective" to identity and interpersonal distances, the imaginaries of perfume allowing women workers to "erase" the stamp of their underlying sociospatial origin in the *conventillo* and to leave their proletarian peers behind, along with the factory's nausea and violence.

The subjectivity of female workers was also reconfigured by uniforms that redrew the female body in terms of the factory's cultural space: "It was clothing that disfigured you, that hat down to here . . . and white square overalls" (Lobato 1997, 60). The new clothing made of *percal* (hard cotton) gave a male stamp to the masculine territory of the factory, although this desexualization (or resexualization) did nothing to desexualize labor relations. On the contrary, the imposition of a uniformed shape on the working body of the *obrera* was just another way to reinforce gender hierarchies. This was another way the meatpacking industry, which already gave women different jobs and lower wages, resolved the tensions resulting from the arrival of women in the workforce. The sexual harassment and brutal working conditions therefore reminded women constantly that they were out of place: "If women's primordial function was motherhood and care of the home, their wage labor could only be understood as something they were condemned to, a fatality whose negative consequences had to be forestalled" (Lobato 1997, 64).

The social disciplining of workers at their jobs was achieved through restrictions on movement, the impossibility of stopping the production line, continuous work, and a strict system of control that forbade both men and women from talking or moving away from their assigned work stations. This discipline was the task of the overseer, who kept an eye on every individual throughout the day, monitoring how they applied themselves to their work and used their time. The factory doors were guarded: "They patrolled the entire site and even showed up in the latrines in order to prevent unnecessary delays and, needless to say, conversations considered dangerous" (Lobato 1990, 327). This situation must have been doubly distressing for women, especially when we consider that absolute immobility, the impossibility of moving away from their work stations, must have been unbearable during menstrual periods, pregnancy, and after childbirth—conditions completely disregarded by management's lack of sensitivity. Thus, petitions for better hygiene and drinking fountains first appeared in the first years of the twentieth century, but the big factories, like Armour and Swift, only began to install bathrooms and changing rooms between 1910 and 1914.

In *Niñez abandonada y delincuencia en Buenos Aires* (Abandoned Childhood and Delinquency in Buenos Aires, 1924), Dr. Artemio Moreno declares that "this moment is ripe with ideas . . . that give dignity to life." Since "the meaning of perfection in civil society is its humanitarian foundations," he argues for corrective measures, such as compensating expectant workers and facilitating "maternity . . . [by] moving them off certain jobs that because of their nature and duration lead to pelvic deformity and make reproduction difficult" (1924, 14). The legal world was beginning to connect hazardous labor practices with premature births, miscarriages, and sterility: "Saturnism, or poisoning from the inhalation of lead fumes, has had terrifying results: Among 77 married women, 17 were sterile. In 212 pregnancies, there were 90 miscarriages (42.5%), 10 premature births, and 61 children who died within the first year. . . . Encouraged by such deadly experiences, women working in those industries have taken to using certain lead-based compounds to induce abortions" (Moreno 1924, 30). Moreno contended that in matters of labor law, everything remained to be done. Laws had perhaps been established, but daily experience revealed great irregularities and contradictions in their enforcement. Such was the double bind of modernity, caught between parliamentary political discourse and the interests of capitalism. In the world of the packing plants, inspectors in industrial medicine raised the alarm about falls and trauma caused by slippery floors; amputations resulting from knives, saws, and hooks; and the transmission of brucelosis and anthrax from infected animals. By that time, too, it was already known that the decompression caused by sudden changes in temperature could trigger "severe respiratory complaints with implications for the heart and kidneys [and that] the constant humidity was conducive to rheumatism and subsequent cardiac complications" (Carreño 1931, 33).

This was all part of a new social setting, its signs noted by experts and lawmakers only when they were already clearly and irreversibly present in the bodies of the working population. Yet Rosalinda prefers the factory a thousand times over the hell of prostitution, which exposed her to the lethal dangers of life as a streetwalker. Donna Guy argues that for proletarian women who could be rehabilitated, the trend was "to reshape the lower class family to fit more bourgeois models, and define women's work as reproduction and nurturing rather than production" (1991, 44). Such a model is proposed by Isaura, an old friend of Rosalinda, who lives "in a sad, wretched house in Barrancas . . . behind which articles of clothing were hung out to dry" (Gálvez 1989, 53). Once the young woman is "protected" by matrimony, she opts to work in the home environment (washing clothes) and is fully resigned to her misery. But not all the proletarian women of Buenos Aires opted for the path of resignation chosen by Isaura. Indeed, a striking number of women elected instead to abandon the ghetto of the *conventillos*. These women would be sung about obsessively with irremediable nostalgia by the tearful men of the tango, who wept once they realized that they had lost them forever.

9 CHAINS OF
DESIRE

Splendors . . . but where did you learn such
a pretty word?

Roberto Arlt, *Los siete locos*

"SPLENDORS" IS THE TERM SO APTLY
chosen by Enrique Gómez Carrillo to describe "the good taste, the refinement, the absolute chic" of Calle Florida. He writes: "All the gems are there
. . . the Laliques, the Brindeaux, the Tiffanies. . . . Those hats most certainly
come from a Lewis, a Carolina Reboux. . . . Those clothes . . . those laces, into
which so many dreams are sewn, are precious. . . . Those delicate, translucent
little trinkets are jewels; those whispy scarves . . . those sheer, mesh, and colored stockings that spread their elegant temptation over silken calves" (Gómez
Carillo 1921, 54–55). An advertisement for "The South American Stores Gath
& Chávez Ltd." in *Caras y Caretas* (4 January 1919) displays a cornucopia of
luxury items spread at the feet of a woman in a languid, playful pose:

GIFTS FOR THE LADY

Bottles of Perfume, Manicure kits, Dressing-table sets, Fans, Parasols, Wallets,
Purses for Combs, Fabric for dresses and blouses, Lingerie, Novelty Kimonos

and Pyjamas, Pearl, Amber, and costume Necklaces, and many more new items impossible to list.

GIFTS FOR THE GENTLEMAN

Splendid stands for Walking Canes and Umbrellas, Wallets and Billfolds, Cigarette and Matchbox Cases, Luxurious boxes from Block & Co. Cigarettes, a Magnificent Pipe rack, Wristwatches in gold, silver, and nickel, Handsome Penknives, Charming Colognes, Manicure kits and Hairbrushes, Boxes of Ties, Suspenders, Stockings, and a large quantity of items for Gifts in good taste.

This cornucopia was fed by a steady diastolic rhythm.[1] Market-oriented imaginaries suggest that anything anyone could possibly desire is available, displayed in fact in full view, an open invitation to dream. The advertiser must have thought these objects sacred, to appear in capitals and deserving no less, for they unleashed a chain of desires that touched the purchaser with the magic of fantasies waiting to be fulfilled. A month later, in an advertisement for "Face Powder by Grissac of Paris" (*Caras y Caretas*, 23 February 1919), a woman sits in her boudoir gazing at the items from the earlier cornucopia, now spread out on her dressing table. She leans over them in a pose that conveys total tenderness and delicacy. In the intimacy of her boudoir, her proximity to these objects of desire bestows a perfect feminine identity on her.

In "La revancha del Frac. Su vuelta a la vida mundana" (Tailcoat Comeback: Evening Dress Back in Society), an Argentinean living in Paris comments on the Great War's impact on fashion: "Gentlemen attend the principal London theaters . . . in evening dress. On the nights of 1 January 1917 and 1 January 1918, with war still at its height, you could see hundreds of tailcoats in the best cafés in Paris and London as the champagne flowed in rivers" (*Caras y Caretas,* 25 August 1919). The author of this urban chronicle, Manfredi, is perplexed by the thoughtlessness with which consumer culture reacts in such a time of crisis: "They dance, make music and sing. . . . All the theaters are packed with people. . . . And, needless to say, nothing but the twinkling of jewels, smiles, and coleoptera against white backgrounds could be seen at the Opera." And something else also bothers him: "Many of the brand-new tailcoats belong to people who got rich from the war, who just look ridiculous when trying to pass themselves off as aristocrats. An expensively dressed couple, totally lacking in elegance, enter an aristocratic café. He wears a new tailcoat, she an expensive dress worn without any grace." Manfredi is displeased at the massification of the fashion industry, which no longer shows any sense of loyalty. As Georg Simmel argues in *Filosofía de la coquetería* (Philosophy of Coquetry), fashions "are indicators of class because those of the upper class are different from those of the lower and are abandoned once the latter begins to appropriate them" (1945, 68). Further, Simmel points out, fashion is abstract because of its indifference, and it contributes to accelerating the rhythm of capitalism: "The more agitated a period is, the more rapidly its fashions change" (1945, 72, 81).

In his rapturous description of privileged women in Buenos Aires, Gómez Carrillo confesses that his remarks refer only to the elite or the moneyed aristocracy, admitting that there is "a much more numerous class of women" that he labels "young women without fortune": "Anyone who out of necessity or for pleasure is walking the streets of Buenos Aires in the early hours of the morning will have seen them filled with an extraordinary crowd of women. Thousands of women . . . hurried along by time, counted in minutes, spill onto the street and catch the streetcar from their barrios. They walk more quickly on rainy mornings because the streetcars run later" (1921, 92). Unlike the chic strollers, these "women without fortune" followed routines they had not chosen, forced to dash to work, dependent on streetcars, and exposed to inclement weather: "This is the legion of working women. It grows every day. They head demurely for the factory, where they are gradually taking over all the jobs performed by men. . . . Others go to take their place in stores, bureaus, banks, businesses, or public offices. The night before, they will have taken a course in typing, language, or stenography" (Gómez Carrillo 1921, 92). It would be difficult today to re-create the general bewilderment at the presence of women in the streets, although it is revealing that Gómez Carrillo portrays working women as a "legion," relentlessly committed to taking over "all the jobs performed by men."

With these thoughts in mind, I would like to follow Rosina's steps in Pascarella's *El conventillo*. Akin to the countless seamstresses portrayed by Carriego and in the tango, at fourteen she is already "dreaming of new dresses, combs, accessories, and makeup. The workshop was changing her from an obedient daughter into a vain, rebellious young woman. When she was paid for the week on Saturdays, she hid a few coins for creams and ribbons"

(Pascarella 1917, 95). She visualizes her place/identity in terms of flight from the promiscuous environment of the *conventillo,* but where does she find the models of identity that so compellingly feed her dreams? "Although the shop where she worked was modest," we are told, "the wealthy girls from the barrio would order fashionable dresses, alterations . . . that Rosina was charged with delivering to their homes. The long hours spent waiting in drawing rooms, the handling of fine fabrics, the personal lives of those girls with their faces covered in creams and cosmetics all excited her adolescent imagination" (1917, 95).

As an ensnaring paradox, the working world of Buenos Aires *obreras* drew them from the beginning into chains of desire. In Alejandro E. Berruti's drama *Madre tierra* (Mother Earth, 1920), the daughter of a wealthy landowner is on edge, waiting to receive the clothes for her holidays:

> LAURITA (*by telephone*): Madam Renard? Well, look, the outfits are urgent because we are leaving for Mar del Plata on Sunday, you know. What . . . they're ready to be tried on? OK, I'll send the car right away so you can send the assistant with the dresses. (Berruti 1920, 20)

Once they entered the lavish living spaces of wealthy señoritas, assistants were introduced to tantalizing chains of desire that exposed them to a cultural space of intersecting identities. After she makes clothes destined for others but inaccessible to her, all that remains in Rosina's hands is the starlight of imaginaries of consumption, which exclude her economically but enthrall her culturally. To cap it all off, her distinguished customer occasionally presents her "with garments she no longer needed that [Rosina] fitted to her juvenile body and then displayed with visible pride" (Pascarella 1917, 105). Her access to garments worn by the privileged is always secondhand. Her body is dressed in someone else's body.

Rosina begins to somatize the distances demanded by these identitary crossings, "feeling disgust for the *conventillo.* What a contrast between the bedrooms of some of her customers and the little box of a room with its old and dirty furnishings she had to see every night! In the patio, she sought the company of other dressmakers and seamstresses to talk about fabrics, hairdos, and boyfriends" (Pascarella 1917, 95). In this imaginary, however pathetic it seems, "fabrics, hairdos, and boyfriends" are entwined; keeping up with fashion leads to marriage, and the dressmaker's trade becomes a means of transmission for the new logic and identity of modernity.

In Carlos Mauricio Pacheco's *sainete El diablo en el conventillo* (The Devil in the Tenement, 1916), the cultural crossover derives from an elegant lady who befriends two sisters:

Zulema: As you know, we work at an exclusive store.

Sara: One afternoon . . . [an elegant woman] came in to try on some boots.

Zulema: She began talking to us, so friendly. . . . She's so nice. . . .

Vieja: She's really taken to these two. You should see the presents she's given them. (Pacheco 1977a, 106)

Night after night, the elegant woman provides the inspiration for the seamstresses to display an appetite for consumption that is unthinkable in relation to their wages. In a city where young girls seemed forever on the edge of sexual demands or rampant prostitution, where minors were sold for profit, even by their own families, the generosity of this woman must have sounded an alarm for more than one member of the audience, especially when Zulema explains: "Well, the other night, after the show . . . you should have seen what a drive, on an amazing moonlit night. . . . They took us by car as far as . . . where shall I say, as far as Tigre." The warning from an old woman in the *conventillo* is not long in coming: "Beware of misfortune. . . . There's a devil on the loose in the parish." In fact, the whole tenement is on the lookout for a *jettatore* (Lunfardo: "evil influence"), but the threat doesn't come from the neighbor who is most suspected:

Sara: When we left the theater . . . we lost sight of her. . . . We've lost her forever!

Mateo: You shameful girl!

Angelo: Something incredible is happening! . . . The devil has got in!

Mateo: Yes, sir. . . . But the devil who's got into the patio . . . isn't the one they're taking off to the police station. . . . The devil was a woman . . . that friend. That friend was the devil! (Pacheco 1977a, 113)

An advertisement or an unsuspecting encounter was enough to awaken a powerful temptation to become "other." How could such persuasive invitations to shift identity, and the promise of redemption from the sinister poverty of the tenements, possibly be ignored? The new paradigms of consumption floated in the air of the city's imaginaries, crossing every frontier, and showed the way out of life as a seamstress (*salir de costurera*). Why such urgency?

Seen from the outside, the system of home-based sweatshops prevalent in Buenos Aires's garment industry seemed to elude the discipline, time, and pace of production of factory work. Nevertheless, "the conditions of extreme exploitation in which it developed, the geographical fragmentation that resulted from its implementation in thousands of homes, excessive competition, and the impossibility of the majority of workers undertaking any activities that would take them away from their place of domicile prevented any attempts at union organization and resistance by workers until the century was well advanced" (Feijoó 1990, 300). According to the 1904 municipal census, women were restricted to jobs linked to the cultural construction of femininity (Feijoó 1990, 293). It is also revealing that, among all factory workers, women textile workers amounted to 39.8 percent, in a sector that had a clear gender imbalance: 9,946 men and 37,416 women. Literally legions of seamstresses, embroiderers, and hat makers led a life of misery and poverty. And along with numerous tangos, melodramas, and films, poems such as "La que hoy pasó agitada" (The Anxious Woman Who Passed By Today), "¿No te veremos más?" (Shall We See You No More?), "La inquietud" (Anxiety), "La costurerita que dio aquel mal paso" (The Seamstress Who Went Wrong), "Cuando llega el viejo . . ." (When Her Husband Returns . . .), "Caperucita Roja se nos fue" (Little Red Riding Hood Is Gone), and "De sobremesa" (Around the Dinner Table), from Evaristo Carriego's *El alma del suburbio* (Soul of the Suburb, 1913), all consolidated the seamstress as the most emblematic representation of women during early industrialization.

In "Las trabajadoras porteñas a comienzos de siglo" (*Porteño* Working Women at the Beginning of the Century), María del Carmen Feijoó takes issue with the progressive imaginary that attributed greater numbers of women working in the factories than really occurred. The situation made it possible for laws for the protection of women and children in the workplace, such as Law no. 5291 (1907), to focus on more modernized groups of workers and thus to disregard those in environments that continued to be overlooked (Feijoó 1990, 291). Contemporaries had difficulty recognizing work at home (*trabajo domiciliario*) as work. This recognition would not come until 1913, when Eduardo Rojas presented his doctoral thesis in jurisprudence, "El *Sweating System*: Su importancia en Buenos Aires" (Sweatshops and Their Importance in Buenos Aires), to the Faculty of Law and Social Sciences. Mario J. Portela's dissertation, "El *Sweating System*. Definición. Origen. Importancia del mismo" (Sweatshops: Definition, Origin, Importance), followed in 1914. But parliamentary debate on regulating *trabajo domiciliario* was not opened until 1915, thanks to the initiative of Deputy Del Valle Iberlucea.

The scant visibility of this type of labor was a consequence of its development in homes and clandestine workshops, where it was unregulated, with no links to union solidarity or action, factors that accounted for its success and survival: "The worker toiled in her own home, submitting the price of her labor to the arbitrary estimate of her employer" (Portela 1914, 9). With respect to their social profile, "70 percent of women in the sweatshop system were mainly unmarried, and the rest were widows, divorced women, and women abandoned by their husbands. . . . The age of the workers showed that industry located in homes was not an occasional or transitory activity, but a working way of life" (Portela 1914, 19). Both Rojas and Portela allude to the *obreras'* social isolation. Portela refers to the lack of a work schedule and the lack of security against fire and accidents, as well as to problems of health and hygiene due to poor ventilation and light. In Buenos Aires in 1914, 75 percent of those working at home, often "groups of large families," lived and worked in "wretched dwellings, damp cellars in which the air capacity was never more than 12 cubic meters" (Portela 1914, 29), when twenty cubic meters per room were recommended. Portela also alludes to work-related illnesses, such as tuberculosis, "curvature of the thorax, eye complaints brought on by working under artificial light, lymphatism in women, rickets in children."

Both Portela and Rojas also highlight the presentation of the day's work at the day's end, an all-too-frequent event in the lives of the women in the *sainetes,* comedies, and dramas of the time. One example is Discépolo's *La fragua* (The Forge, 1912), in which the seamstress Santa's nightly handover (*entrega nocturna*) of her work is doubly loaded, both fraught with premonitions of sexual endangerment and even tragedy and tainted by a sense of weakness and exhaustion after an intense day's work. The two authors also cite the lack of economic stability: "A worker," Portela tells us, "could find herself without work for 5 or 6 weeks in a row" (1914, 21). Portela further draws attention to the impact of religious scruples on home industries: "Mothers, fearful of the influence of life in the factory on their daughters, or wanting to hide their true economic situation, prefer to make silent home-workshop laborers of their daughters, who work an exhausting schedule" (1914, 13). Eduardo Rojas adds: "Embroiderers work from 12 to 13 hours a day at home to earn a wage of 1.40 pesos. Seamstresses, with between 12 and 17 hours, earn between 0.35 and 6 pesos a day, of which 0.10 to 0.30 is deducted for expenses. The majority of workers pay 30 pesos monthly to rent a room, which is commonly used as bedroom, workshop, and dining room. Tiemakers work from 9 to 15 hours a day, and research shows there are many children under 9 years of age among them" (1913, n.p.). The figures for these wages are beyond our comprehension, but not so the physical exhaustion after nine or fifteen hours of work every day, exposed to the most unhealthy conditions. Rojas cites the example of a home "containing 6 persons who live, sleep, work, and eat in a single room measuring 5 x 5.2 meters. The head of the family is tubercular, and his 12-year-old daughter is visibly lymphatic" (1913, n.p.).

In *La tristeza de los viejos* (The Old Folks' Sorrow, 1927), by Juan Manuel Curat Dubarry, the shoemaker's daughter Aurora tells whoever wants to hear her: "How revolting! . . . Always looking at this hateful barrio and smelling the stink of the shoe polish that's poisoning me" (Curat Dubarry 1927, 3). Interestingly enough, strong feelings of claustrophobia ("I'm choking . . . I need air" [4]) alternate on her sensorial/spatial map of the *conventillo* with agoraphobic behavior ("I can't bring myself to go out" [17]). After leaving home, Aurora will be prostituted by an individual described as "a poisonous insect dragging you along in order to take control of you again and sate its hateful intentions" (19). In other words, *staying* and *leaving* seem to have been the same for proletarian women in Buenos Aires: both choices that would only confine them. And between the hyperventilation brought on by the street and the wretched oppression of the *conventillo* was an intermediary state described by Aurora: "I'm afraid, very afraid" (14). How could she overcome the dread of fleeing the *conventillo*?

The cultural marriage of *modernismo* and art nouveau thoroughly reshaped the representation of the "feminine" by bestowing on it a "natural" softness and lightness, which the textile industries artfully exploited with silks and chiffons—"fabrics as light as spring clouds. One of them achieved

Muñecas Bravas *of Buenos Aires*

the miracle of manufacturing such a light veil that three hundred and twenty meters were needed to weigh one pound" (Gómez Carrrillo 1919, 48). Three hundred and twenty meters weighing one pound. This antigravity setting for the feminine was encapsulated by the whirl of high society and by *marquesas* like Eulalia, in "Era un aire suave" (There Was a Gentle Breeze), who knew how to laugh more than anything else:

> With her pretty eyes and her red mouth
> the divine Eulalia laughs, laughs, laughs.
> She has blue eyes; she is cruel and beautiful.
> She casts a strange, living light with her gaze.
> In her moist, starlike pupils there appears
> the golden crystal soul of Champagne. (Darío 1977, 181–82)

Modernismo and art nouveau together emphasized the feminine as a woman's natural inclination, characterized by artificiality, frivolity, carefulness, detail, ornament, and posturing. From the floralism of Adolphe Mucha and the Pre-Raphaelites Joseph Maria Olbrich and Charles Rennie Mackintosh, to the work of the Catalan Gaspar Camps Junyent, art sublimated images of women surrounded by delicate lilies, mysterious irises, and soft violets in trompe l'oeil. The cultural agents of the modernist aesthetic—such as Jeanne Paquin (Jeanne Marie Charlotte Beckers), Elsa Schiaparelli, Madeleine Vionnet, Coco Chanel, and Jeanne Lanvin in the world of fashion, and René Lalique, Cartier, Boucheron, Chaumet, George Fouquet, and Gerard Sandoz in the world of jewelry and perfume bottles—gave this aesthetic material form. Art, then, was applied to daily life through the intersection of aesthetic and commercial languages. And thanks to the ascension of impressionist coloring, *modernistas* turned to pastel shades, suggesting the immaterial worlds of daydreaming, whimsy, fantasy, and the darting flights of dragonflies. These softened shades would appear in bourgeois homes in interiors intended for women (at dressing tables, in dressing rooms), as well as in the women's departments of large stores. They would provide the colors for fashions in women's underwear, while asserting the docility and softness of the "feminine."

This fetishization of the feminine contrasted with the solid, massive, gravity-bound bulk of the new urban environment, while the alluring froufrou of the dishabille's rustling silks changed the chemistry of the pri-

Chains of Desire

vate scenarios of the bourgeoisie. Everything had to be light if it sought to be feminine, a strategy for resisting harsh, complaining identities. This paradigm of female identity was so vividly imprinted on social imaginaries that it was visible even in worlds heavily burdened by anguish, such as Alfonsina Storni's "Resurgir" (Resurrection):

> To go through life with wings on my soul
> Wings on my body, wings on my thoughts . . .
> To forgive, to forgive, to hold no resentment.
> To confine it all to oblivion and weep in the quiet
> Solitude of night with tears of pearls. . . .
> Pearls of sweetness and joy of feeling at peace
> And understanding life as a silken rhythm. (Storni 1984, 16)

One must weep if there is no other recourse, but only shedding warm, feminine "tears of pearls" and "understanding life as a silken rhythm." Art extended an invitation to fashion, nature gave shape to its flights, and it was manifested in the receiving rooms of bourgeois homes, in advertising posters, and in department-store windows. Valerie Steele traces this aesthetic of the evanescent in the fashions of 1908–10: "Evening dresses, tea-gowns, and lingerie were made of soft, light, clinging and even semi-transparent materials (such as chiffon, lawn, muslin, faille, and thin silks like *crêpe de chine,* as well as a lot of lace). The most popular colours were tender, delicate pastels. Fashion journalists described dresses as 'simple evening seductions . . . irresistible confections of tulle and net . . . painted *mousselines de soie,* delicate tinted chiffon' that were intended to produce an effect of 'adorable frothiness and delicacy'" (1985, 218).

From this industry, which employed the greatest number of women, came "underage lymphatic girls bowed under the weight of huge bundles of clothes" (Rojas 1913, n.p.). Yet while Rojas is pained by the heavy loads that deformed the bodies of young girls, Gómez Carillo prizes the immateriality of the dreamy fabrics and exquisite fashions displayed on Calle Florida. *El encanto de Buenos Aires* is a manifesto proclaiming new standards in feminine beauty, defined in terms of luxury objects. The author constructs an imaginary of the mannequin-woman that equates her with a doll. Endlessly exposed to the voyeurism of males, who observe her from the privileged point of knowing she is unable to move or speak, the mannequin-woman feeds male fantasies of possession. She is always portrayed in profile, never full-faced, highlighting the spareness of a languid, anorexic profile, a body totally untouched by metabolic changes, hormonal imbalances, pregnancies, nursing, or malformations. Never looking to the front, but toward some remote point, the mannequins caused a new world of gestures, measurements, height, and volume to circulate from department-store windows or the society pages of *Caras y Caretas*.

Juan José's "Los zapatitos trágicos" (The Tragic Little Shoes), a *folletín* published in *Caras y Caretas* (15 January 1921), narrates the mishaps of a young worker who "at great sacrifice and with an even greater dream" manages to save fifteen pesos: "What a pair of shoes she will buy with them!" explains the narrator. She imagines them "in patent leather, narrow, high-heeled, of excellent quality, with exquisite white trim." In this web of imaginaries, shoes like these promptly transport her from the *conventillo* to the scene of lavish receptions like the one held "in honor of the embassies . . . to commemorate the fourth centenary of the discovery of the Straits of Magellan." Photos of this reception appeared in *Caras y Caretas* on the page opposite Juan José's story, making it easier to weave these imaginaries together. Her purchase of the shoes is a kind of betrayal of the class condition reflected in her worn-out shoes and torn, discolored stockings. The new shoes shine, "dazzling, irresistible," like *true* princes, in the shop window, and the clerk is at pains to turn them carefully "on their heel to show off the shine of the patent leather and the elegance of the design." But the customer is concerned when she tries them on:

> "They seem a bit short to me."
> "What do you mean? Short? . . . No, they suit you marvelously! Can't you see how tiny your feet are, very tiny (*she blushes*), you'd hide them if you wore a big shoe! . . . This shoe makes your foot look small."

The clerk "reshapes" the body and feet of the customer with his flattery, adjusting them to the new aesthetics of the body. Thus, the young worker purchases not just one but several forms of betrayal. In addition to exceeding her acquisitive limits as a factory *obrera,* the young woman also betrays her own body. Although intended to be worn only on Sundays, because of their sumptuous elegance and price, the shoes are a "real agony. It's painful to see her walk. She steps so carefully, she seems to be walking on fine crystal glasses." At home, at seven A.M. on Monday—in her working-class identity, not as a starstruck consumer—she correctly concludes: "What a bitter disappointment! . . . And to think she'll not be able to buy another pair for so, so long."

The title of Juan José's *folletín,* "The Tragic Little Shoes," strikes an intertextual contrast with those "magic slippers" that the *modernista* pantheon of princes—saviors of the Cinderellas of Buenos Aires—embedded in an imaginary that promised a spectacular rise in social standing. But the buyer succumbs to the short-term effects of fantasy. While Saturday shopping promises wonder, the gloss has already dulled by Sunday and Monday. Before revealing the price, the clerk shows off the shoes as if they were exquisite *modernista* vases. In effect, he is, as the story goes, "a great, intuitive psychologist. He knows that nothing fills the heart like difficulties in obtaining an object of desire, especially doubts about obtaining it," as the narrator of "Los zapatitos trágicos" explains. An illustration by Gouche de Larco entitled *La canción romántica* (The Romantic Song), in the same issue of *Caras y Caretas,* recalls fairy-tale settings that gracefully place a regal-looking couple in each other's arms, strolling at night through the landscape surrounding an enchanted palace that could belong to the princess Cinderella. Why combine "The *Tragic* Little Shoes" with a romantic fairy tale? The reader of *Caras y Caretas* would not be far off if she thought she was being ensnared in a game where one thing was switched for another. Like the magic slippers, imaginaries are openly displayed in all kinds of showcases. After all, the problem of the fantasy's compatibility with real-world wages is not one for the market or for *Caras y Caretas,* which has the effrontery to promote the fantasy anyway, unconcerned with the fact that it excludes working women with "inappropriate" feet from the ranks of redeemable Cinderellas.

Where can the tentacles of this chain of desire be traced? To begin with, it is intriguing to note that not all of its coincidences are symmetrical. Records for entry into the workforce show that, by 1904, women and girls were working in houses of fashion and dressmaking, in workshops manufacturing clothes and hats, shirts and stockings, corsetry and embroidery. There was a huge population of tailors and dressmakers, pressers, washerwomen, hat makers, shoemakers, window dressers, and shirt makers, manufacturing the daily attire and the uniforms of state employees. As for commercial outlets, those most frequented by female workers—aside from stores that sold food (24.15 percent)—were shops selling dresses and dressing-table products (26.58 percent); haberdasheries (29.95 percent); shoe stores (27.46 percent); clothing stores (13.08 percent); and stores selling fabrics, leather, furs, and accessories (18.18 percent) (Feijoó 1990, 294). In other words, at both ends of the production chain, in the factory and at the store, women occupied three places highlighted by the division of the market according to gender. As workers in factories, workshops, and tenement rooms, they assembled, stitched, and sewed products for women. Then, as store employees, they sold these articles/promises of "femininity"—items they would have loved to buy themselves as women consumers.

How should we define "femininity" in this chain of desire? Is it the glove or the hand that gives it shape? For Gómez Carrillo, feminine beauty "demands constant vigilance, unending effort." It is a subtle art "that allows you to choose the tilt of the head, the smile, the gesture, as well as the most provocative hat—the art of adjusting your gaze and arranging your hair . . . perfecting your complexion or your figure, and . . . [having] that awareness of your own physical flaws that makes you able to hide them with a pose, a trick of the appearance, a little tulle or a lot of ingenuity" (1919, 60). There was a gap between the women adored by Gómez Carrillo and the proletarian women of Buenos Aires that, according to the diastolic, self-affirming imaginaries of modernity, could be bridged only if it was perfectly understood that access to the spaces of luxury entailed severe breaks with identity. If a working woman were to follow Gómez Carrillo's model, she would indeed have a long road ahead of her, beginning with body language, as noticed by *El conventillo*'s narrator: "Like every imitator, the poor thing was unaware of the virtue of a nuance. She was ignorant of the slow apprenticeship, the patient toil, the infinite variety of resources used by a 'society woman.' . . . She was only familiar with the barest external features of the art of the toilette: the strokes of a pencil, the liner on the eyebrows until they were all sticky, the cheap powder applied to her face with a trowel" (Pascarella 1917, 110). Once the new corporeal practices were emulated by factory and shop workers, these women were criticized as social climbers by commentators in the women's section of *PBT* (6 February 1918), denigrated as imposters: "Those postures of self-importance, arrogance, and smugness are intolerable. They do not belong to distinguished people celebrated in the real world, but to the upstarts and all those who lack true merit and look for ways to appear important. . . . The social climber demands respect and does not trouble to be warm and gentle, fearing that her importance will be doubted."

What manners and body language should be adopted in order not to be caught out as an impostor? Rosina understands the need to "soften her voice, movements, and look. The join of her lips, which harbored blasphemy and vulgarity, spread in a smile that turned to a grimace because it didn't match the rest of her expression" (Pascarella 1917, 111). The challenge of this powerful imaginary forces Rosina to think of herself laughing, like Darío's *marquesa,* or like Storni's lyric voice going through life with wings on her soul: "Pearls of sweetness and joy of feeling at peace / And understanding life as a silken rhythm." It's not that Rosina never touches silks. In fact, she certainly handles and fondles them in her job as a seamstress. She is acutely aware that a change in identity is not just a matter of merely leaving the cultural space of the *conventillo* behind: "What should she do to become a real young lady? What should she do to present herself, to move, to speak like those young women to whom she used to deliver dresses and hats? The soft, rustling silks, furs as soft as a caress, ribbons and laces drenched in perfume that must have driven the men crazy, those men with such white hands and polished nails" (178).

Similarly, in *Los siete locos* (Seven Madmen), Hipólita, a good reader of Carolina Invernizio, watches "the manners of the young ladies all the time" at the houses where she works: "She studied how they inclined their heads and how they said goodbye to their friends at the doors of their houses, later repeating the greetings and gestures she remembered in front of the mirror. The actions she performed in the solitude of her wretched room left a feeling of nobility and delicacy on her lips and in her soul for several hours. Then she reproached herself for her former clumsy manners, as if they . . . were detrimental to the real personality of a young lady she now possessed" (Arlt 1981c, 1: 273). For a short while, Roberto Arlt's character rubs shoulders with paradises not meant for her, in which her life appears to be "stirred by an elegance as penetrating and soft as a cream scented with vanilla. . . . She seemed to feel mellifluous voices coming out of her throat saying 'yes' and 'no' until she deluded herself that she was responding to a delightful speaker wearing a blue fox fur around her neck" (1: 273). Yet however much the cultural borrowings are performed, the new spaces to be negotiated (the body, the mansion, the interaction with the woman in the blue fox fur) soon reveal themselves to be "nonplaces" where painfully troubling identities ferment. Hipólita is just a chambermaid in a mansion on Avenida Alvear, who enters and leaves these identity games, but not without being affected by their disquieting shortcomings: "There were three young women and four servants. I woke up in the morning and couldn't believe it was I moving around furniture that didn't belong to me, that those people only spoke to me so that I'd wait on them. And . . . I felt that the others were firmly attached to their life and their homes, while I felt loose, lightly tied to life by a string" (1: 263).

Just like Hipólita, Rosina resorts to sociolinguistic variants in order to assemble her new identity. She puts on a "soft and tender" voice and tries to distance herself from the tongues of the immigrant heteroglossia ("the *farrago* on the patio"), which "larded . . . its untranslatable slang with horribly distorted *criollo* sayings" (Pascarella 1917, 52), and the language of the tenement children who "spoke words from the brothel with the same indifference as they recited poetry to the flag or prayers to the Virgin, so that newly arrived foreigners thought they were peoples' names" (108). As a seamstress, an expert in the art of patching things together, Rosina takes away here and adds what is missing there, trying to fit the profile of her customers, whom she thinks of as her true, albeit impossible, interlocutors. She despises the hybrid patois of the margins, positioning herself in an identity that displaces and rejects her origins.

Borges's *El tamaño de mi esperanza* (The Size of My Hope) defines this linguistic hybridity as "a loathsome gibberish in which the castoffs of many dialects cohabit, words shove against each other offensively and are as tricky as a worn playing card" (1993, 122). However, such linguistic code switching is but one of the many farewells and separations demanded of young *arrabal* women on their way to the center of Buenos Aires or determined country girls en route to an unforgiving Paris, as exemplified by the 1925 Alejandro Scarpino/Juan Calderella tango "Canaro en París" (Canaro in Paris). The emblematic scene of the young woman's flight (*espiante*) from home at night is described in the tango "9 de Julio":

> Whisked away in the car
> where your pimp awaited;
> everyone in the tenement
> has wept at your flight. (José Luis Padula/Ricardo Llanes)

What imaginaries could have had the power to make these impulsive breaks a painful but "necessary" evil—leaving families behind; burying the memory of the barrio and abandoning tenement boyfriends; forsaking aged parents worn down by life and younger, helpless siblings, like the little brothers in Evaristo Carriego's melodramatic verses who cry: "We are left alone . . . / No need to say how much we'll miss you! / And you . . . will you really miss us?" (Evaristo Carriego 1985, 87) Abandon, *amurar*, flee, leave, never to return—these commands must have been so imperative that their compulsion attenuated the pain they triggered: the unbearable fear of absolute rupture and the guilt at wrenching oneself away from the only identity one has ever known.

In her struggle to erase every trace of her origins, Rosina begins by distancing herself from her father: "That man with the grimy face, who spoke a language that was mocked everywhere, couldn't be her father, and when she approached him to give him a kiss, she blushed to her roots with shame" (Pascarella 1917, 188). Similarly, "whenever she met . . . [anyone from the *conventillo*] she grimaced with disgust and tried to get away, to remove herself from their approach" (178). Overly optimistic imaginaries of social and cultural mobility encourage Rosina to leave everything she knows behind. But where do these imaginaries take her? What scenes and narratives of splendor persuaded proletarian and middle-class *porteñas* to push back their fear of falling into uncharted territory? The label on the bottle of "L'Heure du Rimmel" (1925) shows a young blond woman at her dressing table putting on her makeup (figure 14). In this interior, personal space, the woman is wearing a brief, transparent nightgown. The mirror on the dressing table reflects her image, and the label's encircling shape is intensified by other circles. The scene's enclosing circles—the label and the frame around it—portray not only the most interior space in the house—the bedroom—but a telling model of female identity founded exclusively on feminine self-absorption.

In "Women, Desire and Bibelot," Rèmy G. Saisselin describes the cultural meaning of the dressing table, where women sit "surrounded by bibelots, and expensive objects of desire, to be possessed and cherished, but also exhibited" (1984, 65). To the extent that they "encompassed everything from an object of beauty and art for the aesthete, of pride of possession for the successful speculator, financier, and banker" (Saisselin 1984, 65), women became valuable pieces in the bourgeois male's personal art collection. And bibelots played

Muñecas Bravas *of Buenos Aires*

an important role in the new "feminine" scene, the compulsion to accumulate small, exquisite, "feminine" objects. These were a woman's own collection. In addition to cushions, the typical "room was littered with little sofas ... little tables, with plants flowering in porcelain jars, and flowers flaunting themselves in cut-glass bowls, photographs in silver frames ... magazines ... faint watercolours ... slanting mirrors in showy frames" (Saisselin 1984, 65). The compulsion to possess—to have innumerable small objects full of beauty nearby, close at hand—fed the pleasure of consumption. As a furnishing for the dressing table (*tocador* in Spanish), the bibelot was meant to be touched (*tocado*), the bottles of perfume and cosmetics to be caressed, their possession right there, within reach, furnishing the woman who sat waiting with a burning urge: to beautify herself.

The typesetters for *Caras y Caretas* repeatedly played at combining advertisements for gonorrhea medications with advertisements for cosmetic creams and ermine wraps, sometimes even on the same page. The logic of their impish syntax resides perhaps in their intention to polarize the contrasting cultural spaces implied. The illustration for "L'Heure du Rimmel" is all the more conspicuous for this contrast. Such interior scenes at dressing-table mirrors were apologies for a paradigm of female self-centeredness that would have met entirely with Gómez Carrillo's enthusiasm: "Of one hundred women who beautify themselves, ninety-nine of them in fact don't have a man in mind at all. A psychologist once said: 'Elegant women don't dress for us to see them, but to see themselves. Women dress up without thinking of friends, without thinking of anything'" (1919, 60–61). Such *ensimismamiento femenino* (female self-absorption) sublimates interior spatialities. The self-absorbed woman, "enclosed in her home, doesn't pass up any means within her reach to beautify herself. She adorns herself because she adores herself, because in some obscure, unconscious, tyrannical way she thinks of herself as a mystic icon. She adorns herself for the sake of adornment" (Gómez Carillo 1919, 61).

Having become a fetish of herself, and engaged in the task of her own sublimation, this female Narcissus was very common in the visual arts of the time, especially on the covers of publications intended for women. Such an aesthetic is captured in George Barbier's *Shéhérazade* (1914), Georges Lepape's *Le miroir rouge* (1919) or *Gabriel Ferrot* (1925–30), Frank Mackintosh's *Asia* (1932), and William Welsh's *Summer* (1931), and on the covers of *Women's*

Home Companion, Vanity Fair, Harper's Bazaar, and *Vogue.* Only one of these images endorses maternity: George Barbier's illustration for *Femina* (1922) of a woman lifting a child. An illustration by Sylvain Sauvage (figure 15) perhaps presents this model of self-indulgence most pointedly. It shows a young woman examining herself closely in a mirror held close to her face by a slender, delicate hand. She is caught in a perfect, self-engrossed bubble, clothed in a majestic coat trimmed in the softest white marten and wearing a wide-brimmed black hat. Both accessories delicately encircle the female figure. No trace of the external world is present, the illustrator having dispensed with any element that might have competed with the centripetal centrality of this chic, elegant young woman and her expensive attire. Copied to the point of saturation by advertisers, especially in *Caras y Caretas,* this new paradigm of womanhood diminished the model of self-effacement associated with maternity and, in doing so, made it easier for proletarian *porteñas* to avoid looking at what they left behind on their hazardous journey to the city center.

Women in front of mirrors, wearing jewels, exquisite lingerie, or stunning furs for the cocktail hour—blond women, from the upper class, we infer. It could be said that the woman on the label of "L'Heure du Rimmel" doesn't work for a living, just like the woman depicted by Sylvain Sauvage, who invests all her energy in examining herself in the mirror. But if we look more closely, we might say instead that both are actually working *on themselves.* As Gómez Carillo remarks, "She adorns herself because she adores herself, because in some obscure, unconscious, tyrannical way she thinks of herself as a mystic icon." The capriciousness and impulsiveness of such women were affirmed by magazine covers and product labels, thereby emotionally removing *porteñas* further and further from the factories and the sewing machines. I believe that several strands of utopianism flow into the cultural geographies of these delightful, unruffled interiors. The body is delicately preserved in a corporeal bubble of centripetal detachment and hedonism. Fashion and other languages of the market had turned the new objects of desire into a means of physical embellishment and sociocultural mobility. Just as cities were being almost entirely transformed, it was the perfect moment for a diastolic imaginary, for all manners of euphoria to spread narratives of overcoming difficulties and hardship. As an instrument of modernity, art nouveau transferred an aesthetics of the purely ornamental to the market, thereby inciting levels of consumption widely exceeding the basic. And these new levels of the chains of desire went yet further, compellingly inducing new daily practices and promising identitary shifts: everything to which the *milonguitas* of the tango desperately aspired. Moreover, the new consumerism was never static, but more and more arbitrary and more and more unattainable: "And how easy it is to understand such intoxication from so much temptation! . . . From the white glove to the more intimate camisole and the luxurious ermine. . . . There is no woman, no woman at all, who could resist this abundance, this luxury, this feast that seems the work of the devil" (Gómez Carrillo 1921, 64).

Manuel Romero's tango "Aquel tapado de armiño" (The Ermine Coat) captures the scene of a woman enthralled by a shop window. Believing that a good fur coat might keep out the cold nights of a *porteño* winter, she makes an opportunistic request of her companion. "It was the highest point of our affection," the *amurado* (jilted man) later complains:

> I had no money,
> you loved the ermine.
> How often the two of us
> shivered at the window.
> You whispered to me:
> Oh, my love, if only you could!
> After a thousand sacrifices
> I could buy it for you at last;
> I borrowed from friends, I went to loan sharks.
> I went a month without smoking!
>
> That ermine coat
> all lined in lamé
> that covered your body
> as you left the cabaret.

According to this imaginary, the woman ensures her ascent to the cabaret and the company of other men precisely by showing off her ermine and shedding the man who had paid for it:

> That ermine coat
> was in the end

more durable than your love;
I'm still paying for the coat,
but your love long since expired!

Aside from the emptiness that follows his jilting (*amuramiento*), all the man has left of his sacrifices, including giving up smoking for a month, are payments. The cornucopia of the market grew even more bountifully—outfits, shoes, gloves, and above all hats: "the woman's hat, the fantastic, whimsical, smiling hat that . . . seduces, that surprises, is slightly mad and so coquettish; the artistic hat is a product of Paris" (Gómez Carrillo 1919, 138). Gómez Carrillo contemplates these hats, and Teodelina Villar knows them all too well, in spite of the Borges of "El Zahir."

What Borges most detests is the capriciousness and surrender to Paris fashion of the woman he has fallen for in spite of himself. The setting of the narrative in "El Zahir" is Buenos Aires in 1932, the year when Teodelina Villar dies. Pictures of the woman, who flitted between Paris and Hollywood, and was a regular at palaces of temptation such as Richmond, Harrods, and Gath y Chávez, had been "cluttering the society magazines" since 1930: "She experimented with one change after another. . . . The color of her skin and the style of her hair were famously changeable. She also altered her smile, her complexion, the slant of her eyes. She had been scrupulously thin since 1932. . . . The war gave her much to think about. Once Paris was occupied by the Germans, how could she keep up with fashion?" (Borges 1974, 1: 590). Teodelina is decidedly frivolous. The war concerns her only because it interrupts the export of fashion. She is an insatiable, anorexic mannequin who cares about nothing. She adopts and discards styles in the same way she changes the color of her hair. On account of this capacity for metamorphosis, Simmel would have argued, it is natural for her to join the world of fashion as an advertising model. The narrator remarks of this unthinking consumer that she incurs two solecisms: having to work and dying in Barrio Sur. However, I think she also incurs a third and that the three together are of such intolerable magnitude that Borges withdraws his love.

The first solecism is the "misfortune" that forces Teodelina to work: "Dr. Villar had to move to the Calle Aráoz, and his daughter's picture adorned advertisements for beauty creams and cars. (The creams she applied so lavishly on herself, the cars she *no longer* owned!)" (Borges 1974, 1: 590; original emphasis). Teodelina thus becomes a further link in the chain of desire. The "dark apartment on the Calle Aráoz," an inferior area of Buenos Aires, links Teodelina to other members of the elite now down on their luck. The second solecism, "dying right in Barrio Sur," may be read in other ways, because Teodelina's "death," at least as far as Borges's love is concerned, could have happened "elsewhere." The narrator comments that during the Great War, "a foreigner whom she had always distrusted took the liberty of presuming on her good faith by selling her a number of stovepipe-shaped hats. Within a year it was rumored that those monstrosities *had never been worn in Paris* and therefore were not hats, but arbitrary, unauthorized caprices" (Borges 1974, 1: 590; original emphasis). I believe this is her third solecism: yielding ingenuously to the fashion/seduction offered by the foreigner. She surrenders to him, opening herself to his "arbitrary, unauthorized *caprices,*" much as Gómez Carrillo's compulsive women allow themselves to be swept up by the "undeniable intoxication [that] possessed women's minds" and turned them into Füssli's abandoned female bodies.

In a highly xenophobic society where the idea of the foreign was heavily charged with negative connotations, the allusion to the dishonest dealer also refers us to Eugenio Cambaceres's Genaro in *En la Sangre* (In the Blood), preying on inexperienced society girls whose innocence has left them open to manipulation. Teodelina thus joins the legions of "unreliable" women who are seduced by fashion and deceived by foreigners. Máxima's humiliation in Cambaceres's *En la sangre* is no less when she falls for a master of deception who exchanges his Barrio Sur tenement (on Bolívar and Defensa) for the Barrancas mansion in Belgrano when he marries. He has risen in the world, his direction opposite that of Teodelina, who has fallen—from the Barrio Norte to Calle Aráoz, from high society to "having" to work. Such were the vicissitudes, reaccommodations, and misalignments in times of transition that were so frightening to nationalists.

To judge from the above, Borges's text would see the insertion of women into the working world as a somehow unavoidable fall in the turbulent maps of social relocation in Buenos Aires. Borges (i.e., the character in "El Zahir") punishes Teodelina with his disdain and distance in order not to live alongside those areas of contact with the vulgar world of commerce she has wholly embraced. In contrast to Gómez Carrillo, for whom "the only aspect [of progress] that entails complete perfection is the supreme art of those who know how to create industries for the beautification of women" (1921, 64), Borges's text rejects consumption, perhaps because it identifies it as the mediator for the cosmopolitan, spendthrift oligarchy that deposed the austerity of patrician nationalism. With its fashions and its many hats, the new culture of consumption made converts everywhere, especially among its most susceptible customers and weakest links—namely women, who are viewed as an abstract category, without regard for their differences and independent of their power of acquisition.

In her *folletín* "Las chicas de enfrente" (The Girls across the Way; *Caras y Caretas,* 12 February 1921), Cleopatra Cordiviola wonders what lies behind the curtains of a house with three young women: "They are the best-dressed girls on the block. By saying they are the best dressed I mean they follow fashion the closest. The reader knows . . . what 'well dressed' means in today's language. In summer they are not without a dress in voile, one in coarse linen, one in cotton, one in washable silk, one in raw silk, one in taffeta . . . and one in sheer crepe for special occasions. Clothes are their greatest concern. . . . A person's worth according to them . . . depends on how many dresses she has in her . . . wardrobe." Since the three sisters live in a small, modest house, Cordiviola has cause to dwell on the profound discrepancy between the barrio in which they live and their style. Their father is "a shoe repairer who works on the patio bent over a strange array of worn soles and old boots. He always has the sad look of a tired animal in his eyes. His daughters don't bother with him."

The question posed in the text is: "How does this poor old man with aching bones manage to pay for all his daughters' luxuries?" And how, in turn, can we read *Caras y Caretas* as a cultural agent of consumption at the same time as it published critical texts like the *folletín* "The Tragic Little Shoes"? The story shows off the glitter of the market with a diastolic beat but at the same time systolically warns of limits. Those who "deserve" to follow fashion are certainly not the daughters of shoemakers. *Caras y Caretas's* ambivalent agenda reinforces the unavoidability of the market's objects/desires, which must be pursued whatever the circumstances. The tension, however, does not reside here, but in the gap between the chain of desire and the acquisitive capacity of *porteñas,* between socioeconomic identity and the universal and abstract identity of the consumer. In this gap, trembling hearts beat sorrowfully over the desperate flight from the tenement and the predictable abyss that followed: prostitution for women, crime and deception for men *amurados* for an ermine coat.

In a *sainete* by Armando Discépolo, *El vértigo* (Vertigo, 1919), some Italian immigrant jewelers work at home at a table spread with tools for filing and engraving, while their wives work with sewing machines and fabrics:

> ISABEL: I've sewn even more today! . . . I'm so tired! . . . And it's all just so we can eat, nothing more than eat! . . . How I'd like to have a diamond and ruby barrette! . . .
>
> MARISA: Diamonds, why?
>
> ISABEL: What a question! . . . To show them off! Diamonds are so shiny! They make you beautiful. . . . So that people look at you and are jealous of you and think you pretty. (Discépolo 1987a, 280)

Then Isabel remembers Julia, the shopkeeper's ex-wife, who "instead of peddling maté and kerosene in shabby clothes, now dresses in the best, rides in a car and wears diamonds":

> SILVESTRE: You like them too much; and a woman who likes these bits of glass is trouble.
>
> ISABEL: Don't say that! . . . Bits of glass! . . . Are you blind?
>
> SILVESTRE: You're the blind one. Don't you know men go to prison for stealing stones like the ones you're asking for? . . . The sparkles you like so much are a will-o'-the-wisp, an abyss into which the ambitious, the giddy, and the blind all fall. They cheat and do dirty deals in exchange for their shine. (1: 283–84)

Innumerable texts deal with the "feminine" obsession for jewels, relating it to the unmoved femmes fatales whose desire causes "men [to] risk their lives at the bottom of mines to bring out the diamonds" (Discépolo 1987a, 280). But the allure was so overpowering that in *El vértigo,* Isabel looks longingly at the precious stones: "The butterfly [Miguel] finished yesterday . . . seemed alive. Diamonds, rubies, emeralds, sapphires . . . how they shine! . . . All it was missing was the ability to fly (*laughing*). What if it flew and pinned itself on me here" (1: 281).

I believe this *estética del vuelo* (aesthetic of flight) suggests the ease of the social climb for women, thanks to the antigravitational cultural geography represented in modernity by art nouveau. I am convinced that the delicate texture of the chiffons, silks, and muslins helped to furnish an imaginary in which everything was possible through laughter, indifference, unconcerned frivolity, and the spectacular rise of those "butterflies" to newfound freedom. As Francine Masiello points out, "The marketing of gender images and dress served the liberal state as a vehicle to modernize culture. Dress, when monitored under the aegis of fashion, created the illusion of choice and freedom" (1997, 220), while simultaneously confirming the truth of the affirmative imaginaries of modernity.

Nevertheless, the lyric voice in the Pedro Maffia/Celedonio Flores tango "La mariposa" (The Butterfly, 1921) has a few caustic words on the subject:

> After treacherously sipping
> at the rose of my love
> you fly off deceivingly
> to find
> the charm of another flower.

The heart of the tango centers on a fall from flight. Its dysphoric imaginary warns *porteñas* that after their climb, nothing is left but a fall: "Be careful, butterfly . . . / don't let the bright lights dazzle you . . . / for then you'll pay / for all your sins / for all your treachery."

Writings like Carolina Muzilli's address the social costs of flights engineered by the industries of desire from a rather different perspective. In her outstanding report *El trabajo femenino* (Women's Work, 1913), Muzilli draws attention to the fact that the making of artificial flowers—an industry "that seems to have been created especially for women"—has by "happy" coincidence been assigned to proletarian women: "Does it occur to the happy brides who braid their hair with the traditional orange blossom how many tears, how many sleepless nights, how much sorrow is contained in each of those little white flowers? . . . Does it occur to them that anemia and tuberculosis will exact their tribute by making prey of the poor working women who spend the day fashioning them?" (1913, 8). The feminist activist knows that for women to work with wax is contrary to Law No. 5291, which outlaws work by women in industries harmful to their health. Sustained exposure to fumes from melted wax produces a gradual blocking of pores in the skin and the lungs. With this in mind, I thought of two photographs of working women, both seated in harmful postures, that can help us imagine the reality Muzilli saw (figures 16 and 17). Their taut muscles and stressed spinal columns, after long hours of work and immobility, are, I believe, what Muzilli wanted us to be thinking of when she deconstructed the process of production to focus on the harmful costs of the finished product. She sought to force the consumer/reader to visualize the high social price exacted on the bodies of workers, as in the manufacture of gloves—a complex, meticulous task that leads to severe eye disorders and induces lumbago and/or sciatica, with workers forced to bend over for long hours. The tobacco worker's chair also requires a posture that places the entire weight of the body on one group of muscles, ligaments, joints, nerves, and vertebrae, producing, among other conditions, cystic degeneration, anchylosis, herniated disks, atrophy of the muscles, and partenthesia. I believe that Muzilli's objective, surely, was to make the consumer choke at the moment of purchase—or at least pause for an instant to consider the pain, deformities, and industrial illnesses resulting from nine hours of work in the same position (figures 18 and 19), with bent necks and backs; to imagine the trauma of compression, resulting first in inflammation and then in the degeneration evident in sciatic scolioses.

As a counterweight to the triumphalist languages of modernity, Muzilli's writing attempts to awaken women from the romantic daydreams of weddings, orange-blossom wreaths, and lace, trying to reverse the social insensibility induced by the culture of consumption, which offers products as if they have fallen from the sky or arisen from limbo, totally dissociated from the bodies that endure the effort of production. When contemplating "the laces, gauzes, veils, ribbons, furs, and everything that is part of the adornment of a feminine icon," touched by tender "pale, nervous hands," Gómez Carrillo asks, "How is it possible to resist what is so attractive?" (1921, 62). We can imagine Muzilli's reply. It is also interesting to note that Gómez Carrillo associates the object of consumption with desire, using the vocabulary of eroticism when he speaks of the relation between silks and the Eves who wear them: the "domination of the enslaving desire" that "causes the heart to race"; "tyrannical, imperious desire"; the "true intoxication [that possesses] the female mind"; "the flame that shines"; "to touch, to stroke"; "temptations" (1921, 62). *El encanto de Buenos Aires* speaks of the temptations of consumption as penetrating defenseless subjects, who succumb to a fall or uncontrolled surrender. Gómez Carrillo portrays a pale-skinned consumer— which is to say, a Caucasian woman, never a proletarian—whose delicate hands are never deformed by the manual work carried out by seamstresses, pressers, and domestic servants. The three strands of his logic—patriarchal, classist, and racist—circumscribe aspects of the body as a source of identity that must be kept securely out of sight in order to erase any traces of shame. And since the body is a signifier that also reveals social place, the erasure of its markers is not guaranteed just by wanting them to be erased.

In ¡Siga el corso! (Follow the Parade!, 1920), by José Antonio Saldías, Rosa intends to remake herself:

> ROSA: I'd wear those boots with the stitching and those low-cut dresses. A feathered hat and I'd paint my eyes with a little of the shoe polish women at the dancehall use. . . .
>
> MARIO: She says she wants to be queen of the cabaret. With those hands like sandpaper, feet with three bunions on each foot, and bandy legs like parentheses two squabbling dogs could run through. (Saldías 1922, 246)

Mario makes fun of Rosa's "hands like sandpaper." How can she hide them when even poems by the socialist Alfonsina Storni convey the belief that "the hand is the aristocracy of the body" (Storni 1927, 5)? *Porteñas* seem physically and culturally trapped, halfway between the offer and the purchase, at a crossroads, as agents of production, sale, and consumption. The most dramatic contradiction in identity, however, is borne by the mannequin who is caught between the graceful message spoken by her body and the uncomplaining silence she must preserve. Even Gómez Carrillo alludes to the mannequins' many contradictions: "They are paid like servants, but dress like queens. . . . They wear the ermine coats, the lace bodices, the velvet skirts, the tulle shawls before the wealthiest of women try them on. They are the first to wear the magnificent hats. . . . Yet, although they dress up like this, they have to find the humblest dairy counter at lunch time so as not to spend more than the poor factory workers" (1919, 116). He wonders how, with their scant wages, they can satisfy the desire encouraged by direct contact with such sumptuous attire, which they have to put on and take off "every two hours." Or perhaps, he speculates, they put these clothes on and take them off of their own accord: "The young mannequins are not content with what their employees pay them to put on luxury clothes. There are others who'll pay them more just to take them off" (1919, 116).

In the photo "Jewelry-store employees" (figure 20), five solicitous salesclerks smile at the photographer, just as they undoubtedly smiled at their customers. Similarly, in "Interior of notions store" (figure 21), a salesclerk displays silk stockings with an insinuating smile in spite of the nine or ten hours she spends on her feet every day. The salesclerks in the first photo work in a prestigious jewelry store and are uniformed in black, with an impeccable white blouse and yoke. The clerk in the second wears no uniform and seems to work in a less prestigious store. In both photos, the saleswomen are young, suggesting discrimination in employment criteria. Carolina Muzilli remarked on the identity displacements occasioned by these forms of "feminine" work: "Whoever saw them behind the counter attired in the classic black dress, identified by their livery, with complicated hairdos that made their heads look like confectionery towers or minor works of art, might think of them as the workers who enjoyed the best working conditions. The fact is that luxury and vanity make mannequins of them, managed by their department boss, and there is no cause for concern that any complaint will come from their lips when they are mistreated" (1913, 20).

In Roberto L. Cayol's *La chica de la guantería* (The Girl in the Glove Shop, 1920), a woman is harassed by a shop owner and his son. Since she moves quietly about the shop, there is nothing to suggest any discrepancy between her personality and the softness of the suede gloves she sells, a reflection of the tendency to equate the body language of the saleswoman with the merchandise for sale. It's not surprising that her name has been shortened from Josefina to "Fina," as if she were simply another docile feminine adornment of the shop. Similarly, she is not inclined to speak much, and what little she says is constantly cut off by her superiors: "Yes sir, yes," "Sir, I . . . ," "It's . . . ," "Whatever you say, madam," and so on. She accepts "deductions for damages" (two pesos off her salary of ten pesos) without a word, as well as a "lesson" "to be more careful about her work." The father and son's sexual harassment in *La chica de la guantería* is treated with the hilarity proper to a *sainete* until the young woman's last, unexpected intervention: Fina blurts out the fact that she is married, a fact that she has kept hidden. When questioned about her secret, she replies in a tone of recrimination, in a way that contrasts with the semimuteness and submission imposed by the culture of work: "Three months after our marriage my husband lost his job, like many others. . . . I saw him dying of shame and need and thought it wasn't right to let him die like that. (*With sorrowful anger.*) Buenos Aires is hard on honest poor people. When I took to the streets in search of a job that wouldn't tarnish my reputation, I was still Mrs. Fernández. . . . 'No madam,' they said at every door I knocked on, 'we prefer single women.' . . . My heart was breaking, and the bread wasn't coming in. . . . We had to eat, even at the cost of a lie. . . . (*A look of bitter surprise on their faces.*)" Fina angrily outlines the explicit reasons why employers prefer single women ("they apply themselves more to the job, they are punctual"), as well as the implicit ones ("their warped motives"). Her outburst, which must have seemed more transgressive then than now, denounces a culture of work that overtly shelters sexual harassment.

In *Nacha Regules* (1918), Manuel Gálvez describes the labor practices of department stores, where employees were as controlled as they were in the factories: "[Nacha Regules] had been exhausted for days. Eight, nine hours without sitting down!" Like their counterparts in the factories, salesclerks were made to stand at their work for ten hours at a stretch. Law No. 5291, requiring the provision of a chair for workers, passed in 1913 but went unobserved. Employers did not deem it necessary to comply with the law just because Congress had debated and passed it. It was not for nothing that when Arlt's seven madmen gathered in Temperley to consider the elements of a "good" dictatorship, kept in place "through the terror imposed by numerous executions" (1981c, 1: 280), they had the discipline of Harrods in mind. The view provided in Muzilli's *El trabajo femenino* uncovers the dark side of those dazzling cathedrals of consumption, turning our attention from Gómez Carrillo's consumers to the workers: "Hurried and breathless, they have to go up and down the stairs goaded by inspectors located on the various floors, and when any of them is slowed by overtiredness . . . the department head is there to admonish her in more or less vulgar terms, given that any sense of polite speech and gallantry has been lost" (Muzilli 1913, 20). Muzilli explains that labor practices submit "saleswomen to the brutality and arrogance of managers, inspectors, department chiefs, assistant chiefs, and head saleswomen, because their greatest urge is to boss people around . . . differing from each other only in the scope of their vulgarity" (20). While the shop-window mannequins display bodies from the world of dreams, Muzilli's writing makes us look at bodies from the world of work (*cuerpos del trabajo*): "The saleswomen in the tailoring department are responsible for carrying the heavy mannequins up and down the stairs. In one of the department stores, two saleswomen, who were taking one of these mannequins down the stairs, fell awkwardly because of the heavy weight they were carrying, injuring themselves and breaking the mannequin. The store deducted the cost of the mannequin from their meager wages" (20).

In *Nacha Regules,* Gálvez takes advantage of the exchange and borrowing among social discourses, carrying Muzilli's report along with him as he takes us inside one of the department stores where his main female character works:

> They forced her, loading her down with the heavy wooden object. [Nacha] went down one floor, almost collapsing with the effort. She was going to leave it on the staircase landing when they sent to say that if she didn't continue she would be fired from the store. She went down another floor. Some employees laughed as they saw her go by. Others took pity on her in silence. She was exhausted. She gathered her strength . . . and went down some steps. Then, without knowing how, she rolled down to the landing. She lost consciousness, and when she came to . . . the manager was looking at her with his watch in his hand. (Gálvez 1950, 132)

They explain to Nacha that they will deduct the time she was unconscious from her wages and that "she must pay for the mannequin. Pay? She didn't understand clearly . . . Pay the full amount for the mannequin in monthly installments. . . . Every month she would earn ten pesos less. Ten pesos less!" (132). Since she earns only thirty pesos, and "everyone knows how impossible it was for a shop assistant to live on thirty pesos," they suggest that she "sell her body": "She was not young and pretty for nothing" (131). Such irony and hypocrisy were indeed widespread. The municipal census of 1887 defines formal work as a "safeguard for the innocence of women . . . [because] prostitution preferably recruits those who practice it from among the idle and the poverty-stricken" (qtd. in Feijoó 1990, 289)—a strategy for social engineering that had no foundation in reality. Muzilli states that store models "managed by the department head . . . sought to supplement their meager wages through vice. Painful, but true" (1913, 21). She concludes that the severe job demands created a demoralizing atmosphere, "a monstrous altar built on pain and humiliation," as the narrator of *Nacha Regules* would add.

One of the texts that represents such cries in the silence of the wilderness most comprehensively is Josefina Marpons's novel *44 horas semanales* (44 Hours a Week, 1936), rediscovered by David W. Foster in *Social Realism in the Argentine Narrative*. It traces the life of women office workers through the person of Camila Cellis: "The employers see accessible prey in working women, and their male coworkers see enemies who challenge them for jobs in exchange for a lower wage. Neither the one nor the other could imagine the painful effort needed to summon up . . . the effort required to impose conditions of equality" (qtd. in Foster 1986, 143). Muzilli wonders "what those pretty heads exquisitely covered in curls are really thinking": "It is . . . futile for them to delude themselves that they are not workers" (1913, 20). The saleswomen inhabited ambiguous spaces in the new working practices of the stores, halfway between consumers and workers, links to products offered with gestures that insinuated accessibility and docility, thus making them easy prey to sexual consumption. Let us remember that direct inter-action between the customer and the saleswoman was an entirely new experience. In Buenos Aires, as elsewhere in the modern world, the new working practices reinforced an intensely misogynistic imaginary from innumerable sources: factory women were made to undress in public; forced to put up with the sexual advances implied by their subalternity; moved from here to there in the factories at the whim of management; and required to be silent— just as store workers had to put up with everything submissively. In this misogynistic imaginary, everything seemed to invite sexual demands placed on easy women. The new labor practices affirmed women's availability. As Muzilli explains, whatever the customer requested, "there is no cause for concern that any complaint will come from their lips" (1913, 20). On the contrary, in this imaginary, the prostitute's sexual client might be read as a parallel to the customer in a store, pleased with the smiles and feminine docility of the saleswoman. In the poem "Ríe" (Laugh) (*Caras y Caretas,* 17 May 11919), Luis Ventura Mohando offers a lesson on the glamour of laughter as one of the textures of identity:

> Laughter is the perfume of life. . . .
> It is the murmur of dreams. . . .
> Oh, beloved of my soul! . . . laugh, laugh. . . .
> Laughter is the hope for love!

To be loved, one has to laugh, although not in just any way: "Laugh with that soft, pure laughter / from which a cascade of tenderness flows. . . . Your laughter is a white butterfly." Although the laughter of Darío's Eulalia sparkles with mockery, and that of the "beloved of my soul" with softness, both kinds of laughter are based on the same identitary model: a permanent smile ensures that women will seduce men, whether by their eroticism or their docility.

10 PALACES OF

TEMPTATION

New marketing strategies transformed department stores into places of cultural recruitment. They brought together a wide and attractive variety of merchandise, including products that women used to make at home: "Food, clothing, soap, cosmetics ... [were] now arrayed before them in public, made available by revolutions in transportation and communication" (Leach 1984, 327). In Buenos Aires, as in the rest of modernity, the movement from shops with counters to department stores made it possible for customers to wander among consumer products. The merchandise, made more accessible, ensnared the senses of sight and smell, but especially touch, since the counter no longer separated customers from the objects of their desire. Hence the preeminence of luxury items such as sumptuous velvets and other fabrics that felt so good to touch. Along with these new marketing strategies, the spaces of consumer culture were soon globalized and copied everywhere. Department-store interiors were transformed into elegant walkways or *promenades de toilette,* where enchantment was materialized and the rewards far exceeded the realm of the market's new utopias: consumer culture filled the void left by the incipient democracies of peripheral capitalism, with their many disappointments and their lack of political representation. As William R. Leach points out in "Transformation in a Culture of Consumption," consumption responded to the desire for material self-indulgence. At the same time, it reinforced male control over the creation of fantasies for women, even as it fetishized women and promoted female consumption as a way of vindicating their mistreatment in the workplace. Unlike the Buenos Aires of today, the city then seemed to have something for everyone.

The languages and strategies of the fashion industry reached the masses, and the street became a space for cultural recruitment, thanks to the photography, visual images, and widespread circulation of newspapers. In Roberto Arlt's *Los siete locos,* Hipólita fills her servant's room with fantasies, imagining herself traveling to "Paris, France, . . . just as she had seen in the photographs . . . when she went through the streets to shop at the market" (Arlt 1981c, 1: 273). However, when Rosina and her friends, in Luis Pascarella's *El conventillo,* walk along Calle Florida, she begins to grasp the limits of her pretensions. As soon as they enter a pastry shop, "the women, above all, scrutinized her with that instinctively withering look adopted with people of the same sex. Some English women make known their disdain merely by stretching their neck" (Pascarella 1917, 179). The streets of Buenos Aires should, in principle, have been perfect, democratizing thoroughfares, just as Celedonio Flores imagined in the populist, heartfelt enthusiasm of the tango "Corrientes y Esmeralda": "Rum and gin fizz side by side, / English card games and the local *monte,* baccarat and lotteries, / drunk on grappa and stoned on coke." Rosina's experience in the Calle Florida pastry shop, however, is far from an invitation to stay and linger. Rather, she is made to feel humiliated.

It's one thing to enter, but another to remain, although between these two options the market offered the intermediate space of window shopping—which is to say, neither belonging nor staying. Department stores were the first institutions to adopt the new technologies of color, glass, and light to draw the passerby's involuntary attention. They made the alluring promises of their interiors publicly visible from outside through spectacular windows. In 1905, there were forty-one types of display cases on the market, all contributing to creating "the 'illusion' of space and abundance" (Leach 1984, 321), staging a make-believe reality through the languages of magic and sensual stimulation. The market's cultural agents (businessmen, industrialists, and even politicians, social reformers, educators, and artists) managed to assemble a long-lasting cultural paradigm in the department stores using languages and imaginaries conspicuously elevated above the basic needs of everyday life. In fact, by maximizing its offers, the market put no restraints on the virtually limitless expectations of consumption. In Discépolo's drama *Hombres de honor* (Men of Honor, 1923), Dr. Varela receives a visit from his daughter:

VARELA: How many debts do you have?

MARTA: Phew! . . . Many. The shoe store, three hats, the perfume shop, a dona-
tion of 100 pesos to the orphanage, the new carpet for my bedroom, the pin
I gave you for your birthday . . . the dressmaker. (Discépolo 1996, 69)

The father's affection for his daughter is smothered by outstanding accounts. When it comes time to pay Madame Clairon, Marta reproaches her father for not being able to pay by check: "What a pity. . . . I just love to pay by check" (70)—a detail that revealed her father's bankruptcy to contemporary audiences.

Doesn't it strike us that it was the women who spent money and the men who paid up and went broke under the frenzy of consumption? As Gail Reekie argues, given that department stores were public institutions, located in city centers and freely accessible, the gendered division of consumption they institutionalized, in complicity with applied psychology, was swiftly perceived as "natural." Women were "instinctively concerned with the care of the house and the family"; to be a purchaser was a consequence of being a mother, and the same biological determinism also explained the notion that men were "reluctant, unnatural and even 'peculiar' shoppers with a 'natural' distrust for department stores" (Reekie 1993, 366). Two main assumptions consolidated this great gender watershed. First, "women generally spent more than three times as much money as men. Overall, retailers were convinced that 'Man is essentially the earner, woman the spender'" (Reekie 1993, 37). Second, "when a man goes into a store to buy a collar he comes out with a collar. When a women goes into a store to buy a collar, she comes out with a new silk waist, a pair of gloves, ten yards of dress goods, several toilet articles, some window curtains, and a refrigerator" (qtd. in Reekie 1993, 55).

The major department stores were instrumental in establishing this gender divide. Throughout the twentieth century, "the sex of the commodity" was determined by "the sex of the customer," based on the following market strategies:

1. Matching the sex of the salesperson to the product: "Women were usually employed to sell and manage women's clothing, millinery, accessories, haberdashery and trimmings" (Reekie 1993, 65). The feminization of sales personnel among white-collar workers may be explained from an economic and political point of view as allowing the employment of cheaper and more docile workers, even if it created resentment among male employees fearful of their status and salaries. "Women's goods," Reekie explains, "especially those requiring personal fittings and therefore close bodily proximity between seller and customer, demanded women sellers" (1993, 67). Accordingly, department stores became "a cultural mediator, a vessel for sexual meaning, establishing in the store strict guidelines of heterosexual conduct" (67). *Territories* in stores were noticeably demarcated by sex, such that the presence of the other sex in certain departments produced discomfort.

2. Adjudicating the sale of objects such as tablecloths, napkins, centerpieces, and so on, as well as "lacy doilies, teapots, and silks," and other accessories, as "really not a man's occupation" because they belonged in feminine spaces. Indeed, when purchasing articles expressly semanticized as feminine, even a tablecloth, the customer was purchasing "femininity" (Reekie 1993, 69).

3. Understanding that the success of the new strategies was (and is) dependent on the sale of an idea, a concept, rather than a product. Its added symbolic and social value was masculinity, femininity, sportiness, frivolity, casualness, sensuality, or distinction, as in high fashion, which lends a touch of aristocracy to clothing set apart from the mass market of ready-to-wear (prêt-à-porter) clothing.

4. Implementing market strategies, beginning in the 1920s, that favored industrial production over manual manufacturing, which henceforth became associated with the working classes. For this reason, when the writing duo of Jorge Luis Borges and Adolfo Bioy Casares came to describe proletarian Peronists in "La fiesta del monstruo" (The Monster's Festival), they had recourse to four identitary codes: the geopolitical map of suburban Greater Buenos Aires (Cuidadela, Villa Luro, La Paternal, Villa Crespo); popular languages (Cocoliche and Lunfardo); the food consumed by the proletariat (sausage sandwiches, salami rolls, cold fried cutlets of breaded beef, Vascolet chocolate milk); and homemade knitwear (see Avellaneda 1983). By the 1940s, the pressure to consume industrial products was well established as a pattern of consumption based on the standardization of designs and

styles: "The more mass production they took, the more difficult it became for consumers to deviate from accepted notions of femininity and masculinity crystallized in the commodities they purchased" (Reekie 1993, 71). Hence, the product attained an added value consisting of an assigned identitary place in terms of class and gender.

5. Displaying the "feminine" in department-store interiors as another utopian form of self-indulgence proposed by modernity. Everything could be transformed: "Both hats and corsets bore an intimate relationship to the female body, enabling a woman to recreate her imaginary body to conform with the feminine ideal" (Reekie 1993, 73). In this respect, the corset supported one of the most profitable industries. Underwear—or *lingerie,* a word whispered in French as a shrewd marketing strategy—consisted of garments charged with redefining eroticism: "Corsets reinforced the frail, submissive and decorative nature of nineteenth-century womanhood with the suggestion that tight lacing was . . . a form of sublimated sexual expression" (Reekie 1993, 72).

How was the feminine to be adorned? Whether a *porteña* entered Harrods in Buenos Aires or in London, she easily recognized the "femininity" materialized in the shop windows and the interior of the lingerie department. These spaces were decorated in coordinated pastel shades, with white furniture, ornamental flowers, ribbons, laces, delicate curtaining in rayon or tulles, soft lighting, and abundant carpeting to eliminate the sounds of the street. She would also recognize the settings: fine and peaceful English gardens; the lavender fields of Provence; moonlit gardens; a bedroom with undergarments, dressing gowns, and nightdresses handily strewn across the bed next to delicate bouquets of flowers and pictures of women in languid, pensive poses or, perhaps, reading a book. For the first time in the commercial history of capitalism, stores separated heterosexual roles by space. From the beginning of the twentieth century, these gendered spaces were "located" on different floors and addressed through specific articles, the sex of employees, decor, interior furnishings, color, and textures. A deer's head and the tartan paper on the wall, for example, allowed the male customer to recognize that he was on the "right" floor and that his sexuality was the "correct" one.

I might add that the settings for the "feminine" also entailed a certain type of body language, consistent with the trim, laces, and lavender-filled satin cushions. We might suppose that the rules for how employees moved in the women's sections of the department stores were not overlooked in business strategies. Rather than walking, they would have been required to slip gently among the iridescent textures, to speak in sensual whispers, and of course to smile discreetly and refrain from any kind of "negative" behavior. The department store's female employees were expected to embody the coherence of new models of femininity entirely, while transculturalizing customers from different social backgrounds, especially working-class women, who viewed the saleswomen as holding enviable jobs far from the factories.[1] All the disadvantages remained hidden, however: saleswomen were required "to spend part of their income on goods of quality and smart work clothes. Retailers were themselves instrumental in creating a large body of female consumers by employing women as shop assistants" (Reekie 1993, 32).

Since lingerie lay closest to the female body, it stood for the very essence of a woman's sexual identity, eroticism, and capacity for seduction: "dainty little trifles such as ribbons, bows or floral mounts to pin in front, little silk sachet bags, ribbon garters, suspenders" (Reekie 1993, 73)—all guaranteed ardent men. To judge from Nemesio Trejo's *sainete Las mujeres lindas* (Pretty Women, 1916), such accessories must have been devilishly effective in Buenos Aires, at least in the case of a policeman who is dismayed to explain to his friends at the bar that he has had to ask for a change of post. He blames the view from his post "on the Avenida [de Mayo] and Peru, opposite a shop window full of underwear": "I went home sick every day . . . because they enticed you with wax mannequins of women in nightdresses, some of them trying on stockings, others trying out corsets, each with a figure prettier than the next, with faces like French angels that took your breath away, a seductive smile and eyes that seemed so alive they fluttered their eyelids. Obviously, the heat of the street, the heat of the crowd, the heat from being on duty, and the heat from that window gave me a fever, a feeling of nausea that left me exhausted. The doctors said it was from bottling up the excitement!" (Trejo 1977, 152). His palpitations illustrate the impact of such a public display of intimacy. Suddenly the bedroom is right in the street, with effects that go so far as to make a policeman's uniform into "an iron shield against love; I often had to call my heart to order because it was starting to dance wildly" (152). The "deceptive smile" of the mannequin is ambiguously described through desexualizing allusions to "angels" and sexualizing references to French, the language of *l'amour*. I believe that this market strategy, which exposed a sensualized and sexualized female body in public and displayed the intimacy of Buenos Aires in the transparency of shop windows, promoted a perception of the city as a space that was given over to eroticism. Between 1919 and 1939, according to Cecil Willett and Phillis Cunnington, in *The History of Underclothes,* a shift in design eroticized nightwear: "The low neck and gaping sides would reveal what was otherwise concealed by semitransparent material" (1981, 159). The lace hinted at the outline of the figure, and such a display of sensuality endorsed the availability of the female body in a city turned libidinous by the diastolic yearnings of eroticism. *Caras y Caretas* was full of advertising for lingerie, some of it surprisingly daring for the time. It seemed that eroticism and sensuality had conquered the streets of Buenos Aires, a situation that would soon draw the attention of the policing agencies of morality.

While sight certainly played a key role in the new marketing strategies, smell was also important, and the residue of the alchemy poured into the social imaginary by the *modernistas* was cleverly retrieved by the perfume industry. Alfonsina Storni's "El frasco de perfume" (The Perfume Bottle), from *La inquietud del rosal* (The Rose Tree's Disquiet, 1916), captures two moments in the life of a woman shut inside her house. In the first, she says, "I had wept copiously and without knowing why / I was neurasthenic, tired, I don't know":

> Melancholy like a dagger
> Enshrouded in my brain was hurting me so.
> I stretched out my two hands to a book I adore
> And my hands came back empty. . . .
> Then my hand rested on the vase
> And a fire rose nervously lost its petals. . . .
> Tired of this game I went to the dressing table,
> The dull ache had turned me pale. . . .
> I thought the pain was a gentle lover . . .
> And on the silvered mirror of polished glass
> I placed an icy kiss on my fatal luck. (Storni 1984, 32)

The poem here links women to neurasthenia and hysteria, dissatisfaction, weeping without reason, fatigue, and chronic depression—all symptoms of emotional instability used in market psychology to explain the *compradora compulsiva* (compulsive shopper). The poem also invokes the stereotyped formulas applied to counter female distress: reading, a flower, the dressing-table mirror, and passive waiting, none of which is able to contain a melancholy so severe it is like "a dagger / Enshrouded in my brain." It all gives way to absence, paleness, and fatal contact with the cold of the mirror, a self-reflection marked by solitude, distance, and pain. In view of the colors and temperatures evoked in the poem, the speaker's depressive confinement prefigures her withdrawal to a world with no hope of salvation. She has no companion, which meant, in the imaginaries of the time, that she is alone and therefore on the verge of death (her "fatal destiny"). Then, suddenly, the market comes to her rescue, brandishing its new talisman. As her hand is searching, "a bottle of perfume rolled to the ground / Its glass broke with a loud crash":

> Released, the perfume rose up to me.
> I sought to immerse myself entirely in its passion
> The divine miracle like a blue dragonfly
> That gave two small wings of tulle to my sorrow! . . .
> Spring! Your breath emptied into my soul
> And my defeated soul surrendered to it completely!
> And you spoke of fields, you brought them to me,
> And I laughed and laughed to myself, madly and long. (Storni 1984, 33)

The "miracle" of the perfume conquers the abyss and replaces enclosure with the "company" of its scent and dysphoria with euphoria (passion and laughter). An insubstantial product comes to the rescue, a product made of breath and pure air, with the delicate consistency of Darío's dragonfly wings and the remarkable power to transport the consumer to imaginary spaces.

Although it is the least studied sense, smell has nonetheless been the basis of one of the most prominent industries of modernity and postmodernity. Alfred Gell describes the semiotic status of perfume in "Magic, Perfume, Dream . . .": "A colour always remains the prisoner of an enclosing form; by contrast, the smell of an object always *escapes*—it is its active principle. . . . Smell is distinguished by formless-ness, indefinability and lack of clear artic-ulation. Smells are characteristically incomplete" (1977, 27; original emphasis). Perfume is ambiguous by nature, a substance that is diluted yet remains. It evaporates completely as soon as it is sensed, but its chemical/etiological matter is instantly transformed into a sign. How is it possible to retain the semiotic link that attaches matter to its sign in the fleeting moment of its ap-pearance and disappearance? Beneath its materialized and dematerialized nature lie an attraction and power quite similar to magic. Perfume "refers to, and also transforms the world" (Gell 1977, 27). It modifies concrete reality through images of different scenes—orientalist marvels, nights of passion, distant seashores, and so on—and in spite of its impalpable materiality, it alludes to contexts mediated by culture: "Smell only acquires definiteness in relation to a context, so the pleasures that this sense confers rarely appertain to the olfactory dimension *per se*" (Gell 1977, 28). Its magic works with pure absence and transports the receiver away from the everydayness of a geographic and material space to imaginary spaces and times through, for instance, the recollection of a scent from childhood, a journey to the tropics or the countryside of Provence. The odor of sanctity or of sensuality, the recollection of a fiesta through the fragrance of a garden or lavender in a meadow, are signs or semantic fields affiliated with Platonism, idealism and spiritualism, romance and alchemy, through which the immaterial acquires semiotic presence. Spirit, essence, vapor, emanation, enchantment, and aura are materialized through fragrances, meanings, and symbolic representations: "Because it does what language could *not* do—express an ideal, an archetype for wholeness . . . perfume has to do with transcendence" (Gell 1977, 30). Hence the predominant role it plays as a precious object, ether, and icon in the aesthetics of *modernismo* and art nouveau.

The convergence of crowds in the public spaces of the modern city accelerated the mass production of perfume in France as a way to "correct" the material world: the consequences of physical proximity on streets and in public transportation, the overcrowded housing, deficiencies in urban sanitation, and the sweating of bodies after a long workday. The fragrance of perfume "erupts" into the real world and instantly reterritorializes olfactory receptors into semantic fields associated, for the most part, with voluptuous sensuality and the feminine. Perfume was not much of a stretch for these imaginaries: "Obsession" (Calvin Klein), "Envy" (Gucci), "Allure" (Chanel), "Extrème" (Bulgari), "Intuition" (Estée Lauder), "Sentiment" (Escada), "Desnuda" (Emanuelle Ungaro), "Angel" (Thierry Mugler), "Lily" (Christian Dior), "Sylphide" (Lalique). Other perfumes sought to frame particular images—"Eau de Soir" (Sisley), "Romance" (Ralph Lauren), "Nuits d'amor" (Patou), "Pleasures" (Estée Lauder)—evoking orientalist imaginaries in some cases, as in "Opium" (Yves Saint Laurent), "Mahora" (Guerlain), "Jaipur Saphir" (Boucheron), "Rouge" (Hermes), and "Shalimar" (Guerlain): "a signal of retreat or surrender to the very heart and soul of love."[2] Perfumes seduce by activating imaginaries through scenarios intended to assure the wearer that they are well prepared to participate in them successfully, as in the case of "Very Valentino" (Prestige) for men. Well known to consumers in Buenos Aires, such strategies were satirized in the *sainete La vida comienza mañana* (Life Begins Tomorrow, 1927), by Pablo Suero, a *sainete* in which a Bolivian male shopper is dazed on entering a perfumery on the Calle Esmeralda "to spend a fortune . . . on 'Mine Alone,' 'Juanita's Heart,' 'Only Me' [Jené que mua], 'Blond Lover,' 'Yours,' . . . and with each perfume he asks about, [the saleswoman] blushes" (Suero 1926, 6). The French here is of the kind heard in the streets, making the strategy of marketing perfumes with hybrid, badly translated names brought from France to Argentina or Bolivia look rather careless.

In spite of perfume's ephemeral life and lack of body, "wearing perfume is a *magical* act" (Gell 1977, 31), and whoever senses it acquires "another" identity, conferred by the fragrance for as long as its effects linger. The semantics of perfumes brought about shifts of identity in bourgeois imaginaries. Perfumes enhanced notions of intimacy and the idea of women whose bodies were "caressable": exotic, pantherlike beings who belonged somewhere other than the everyday world and its opaque routines. In bourgeois morality, "to arouse desire without betraying modesty was a basic rule of the game of love" (Corbin 1986, 129). The seductiveness of perfume was therefore perfect for a game to be played at a distance. By making it possible to apply perfume directly from nature to the body, the atomizer, or *hydrofére,* allowed the industry to progress, with echoes of Baudelaire's theory of correspondences and his theme of the timelessness of perfume, Flaubert's allusion to an inventory of the flowers of the Nile, and Jules de Goncourt's reference to the baths of Turkish sultans.

The perfume industry took the market by storm in 1858, when Worth opened a house of high fashion that featured exquisitely perfumed salons. The perfumes worn by proletarian women in Buenos Aires were, by contrast, certainly cheap, cloying, or diluted, but they still suggested a metamorphosis that left behind the cultural images of the *conventillo* and its unbearable odors. Whether Gómez Carrillo liked it or not, *his* Buenos Aires smelled of the cooking of the immigrant city, as recorded in Bernardo González Arrili's "La calle, un pasadizo" (The Street, a Passageway): "[There

Muñecas Bravas *of Buenos Aires*

was] a strong smell of fried onions, rancid oil, gringo pizza" (1983, 6). Smells defined urban geographies and even identities, but the imaginaries of perfume suggested to young *porteñas* that fragrances were a way to realize their dreams.

At a time in Buenos Aires when the female body was eroticized by the extraordinary availability of sex, exposed to the public gaze, displayed in shop windows, and aroused by perfumes, the city must have been a more strategic site for the voyeur than for the flaneur. Countless texts of the time hint at intense sexual tension. The imaginaries of eroticism called upon men to intervene in two senses: the lidibinized city had to be "pacified" by sexual relations in response to its diastolic beat, or it had to be restrained through vigilance and systolic countermeasures. The tactics of the clothing industry must have reached such scandalous extremes that they rapidly became the topic of vehement parliamentary debates. New patterns of consumption in the 1930s were reinforced by the availability of credit and the appearance of women as emerging new social agents, phenomena that were explained in the discourse of business as the new consumer claiming her rights against exclusion from management of the family's financial resources.

On 8 June 1932, the socialist deputy Francisco Pérez Leirós introduced a law in the National Chamber of Deputies entitled "Freedom from En-cumbrance for Salaries under 300 Pesos," which sought to safeguard salaries and wages among the most unprotected workers against usury. Pérez Leirós made serious allegations about market practices and the strategy of taking merchandise into the street, into homes, and to workplaces: "The baker, milkman, butcher, and purveyors of . . . other items of prime necessity do not circulate through public offices, large establishments, or the premises . . . of public services offering their wares or effects on credit. Agents selling jew-elry and other equally unnecessary or dispensable items on credit circulate far too much" (Pérez Leirós 1932, 34). Given the massification of credit cards and Internet shopping today, the deputy's clear-sightedness is striking: "The seller uses every means possible to sell his product and is barely interested in collecting the monthly payments once it is sold," thanks to "the ease with which wages can be garnished and the certainty of recovering the amount of the sale" (Pérez Leirós 1932, 34). Pérez Leirós warns that "once the illu-sion of acquiring those kinds of articles has passed, their intrinsic value is much less than the amount committed in payment. People realize the decep-tion and their situation as a victim, when usury has them in its clutches" (1932,

34). Pérez Leirós argued that the most besieged and unprotected consumer was "a new kind of victim": "the female worker and employee who is increasingly pushed by capitalism into the office, the factory, and the workshop" (1932, 35). The emergence of this new social subject into the public sphere brings along the internalization of habits of luxury consumption, regardless of income, and a loss of moral integrity: "Ever open to whatever may enhance their beauty or give them the possibility of greater admiration, women are victims of heartless usury, especially in the purchase of jewels, furs, etc." (Pérez Leirós 1932, 34). The socialist newspaper *La Vanguardia* supported Pérez Leirós's proposal, while also demonstrating paternalism toward the city's "weaker" citizens: "This pernicious system, enjoying wide acceptance among women, has led to utter financial distress for many families of modest means who see their meager incomes reduced by unavoidable encumbrances processed with a speed that contrasts with the proverbial slowness of our justice system and demonstrates the powerful influence enjoyed by usurers in public office and among justices of the peace" (24 June 1932). Both Pérez Leirós and *La Vanguardia* describe the purchase of luxury items as a compulsion with long-term effects, including interest rates that, according to *La Vanguardia* (24 June 1932), ran between 10 and 20 percent a month. In the same context, gender distinctions in consumption are caustically taken up in "La ciudad" (The City; *Vida de Hoy,* 6 March 1937), in connection with a remark by the "feminist" Herminia Brumana, who stated that "a man's goal is to earn money so that his female companion can spend it": "The women who paraded along the main street . . . seemed to obey the terrible advice of that wicked writer instinctively. The windows of the jewelers with their pearls, the fashion shops with their collections of ridiculous hats . . . even the displays of birds and expensive dogs seemed . . . to say to fair and dark-haired women: 'Here we are, come in, spend your money lavishly. Isn't this why men are toiling in their offices?'" How did the model of the selfless mother give way to the insatiable, lazy woman who frequented the shops voraciously? What imaginaries sustained this leap in identity, causing such a break with the past?

11 BEAUTIES, FEMMES FATALES, TRAMPS, VAMPS, AND VAMPIRES

> An intelligent woman could be queen of the city
> if she doesn't fall in love with anyone.
>
> Roberto Arlt, *Los siete locos*

IN ITS ISSUE OF 17 FEBRUARY 1938, the city section of *Vida de hoy* posed a question:

> Why would a lady enter an elegant but vulgar bar on a downtown street? . . .
> Her unhealthy curiosity, that desire to rub shoulders with someone questionable and then be able to smile when the man is surprised at her deceit, is a sign of the time we live in. It's a time of cynical calculation, of balance between good and evil, of *incomplete satisfactions*. The *demimondaine* is in her place, but a lady. . . . There's the problem. . . . When we greet one of these sporting, resolute, muscular modern women, who would dare to kiss her hand? They deserve our devotion, and yet, they have lost it. (Emphasis added)

An ambiguous, amphibious woman who is out of her place (this is 1938) is "a sign of the time we live in"—a time of "cynical calculation" and "incomplete satisfactions." If one thing seemed clear in the confusion of the modern city, it was the danger that "men [would become] women. Women [would] become men. Gender and country were put in doubt" (Karl Miller 1987, 209). The nation had been founded on a single set of values, unified meanings, and the separation of the sexes: two nations, strictly divided. A measure of satisfaction seemed to have emerged from this situation. Anything else (i.e., sexual and identitary polymorphism) triggered alarms among those who were keeping watch.

"La cancionista" (The Songstress), in Rodolfo M. Taboada's *De la fauna porteña* (*Porteño* Wildlife, 1946), describes passages between identitary spaces: "For devotees of tango, the songstress is almost a deity . . . [who] shows signs of both sexes because she identifies as much with the saga of the abandoned girl as with the drama of a young man who has been jilted" (Lara and de Panti 1961, 334). The singer can speak from and about both sexes. With respect to ambiguous or muscular women, Francine Masiello has tracked a similar moment of discomfort in social imaginaries, reported in 1870 in *La Tribuna:* "A woman dressed in pants, waistcoat, jacket and tie and a man wearing rings, bracelets, rouge, and curls have a lot to understand. . . . They have to understand that they do not understand the rules of good taste" (qtd. in Masiello 1997, 224). With such slippages in identity, the interventionism of clothing codes was "designed to expose wayward subjects who stray from national coherence, but also to indicate the improper gendering of particular social actions" (Masiello 1997, 226). In *Difference and Pathology: Stereotypes of Sexuality, Race and Madness,* Sander L. Gilman discusses stereotypes in fin de siècle psychology in relation to sexual anarchies and explains how much Freud's theory of child sexual polymorphism was used by Steven Marcus (1905) to monitor the sexuality of the proletariat: "Children behave in the same kind of ways as an average uncultivated woman in whom the same polymorphous perverse disposition persists. Under ordinary conditions she may remain normal sexually, but if she is led on by a clever seducer she will find every sort of perversion to her taste, and will retain them as part of her sexual activities" (1985, 39). Gilman then asserts that "prostitutes exploit the same polymorphous, that is, infantile predisposition for the purpose of their profession," combining punitive imaginaries in which the correlation between childhood perversion and the sexuality of the proletarian woman in the person of the prostitute is natural. At a time when profound breaks in identity were already being seen, this was how male anxieties covered up male nightmares at being confronted with incomplete sexual satisfaction, shifting identities, and "oversexed" women—as if it were not enough that immigration had betrayed initial expectations and was following rather unforeseeable courses. The "awakening" of female eroticism was therefore processed by imaginaries and narratives that seemed reluctant to facilitate its understanding. On the contrary, eroticism was viewed as a double-edged blade: "If a woman gives in to passing happiness, she will experience pleasure but will then be abandoned because she has confirmed the proverbial truth of common morality and wisdom: a sensual woman makes an untrustworthy mother. At the same time, if she denies her fantasies and the erotic game, the poor, beautiful young woman gives up not only the pleasure of the moment but also a means to assist her objective in keeping the man she merits through her qualities, but not through her origin" (Sarlo 1985, 115).

The female body, I believe, became a crossroads where all the transitional features of modernity converged. Imaginaries of desire and social possibilism aroused the body with caresses, velvets, and intoxicating perfumes as an escape from mistreatment at home and Taylorism in the factories.[1] However, not far off, hedonism and pleasure were prohibited terms. Neutralizing them with paradigms to counter their entropic frenzy would turn back the chaos of this Babylon of sexual perversion. Yet how was it possible to combine one message with another when diastolic imaginaries incited pleasure in no uncertain terms? As a character remarks in Víctor Dolard and Armando Rillo's *El amor que no se vende* (Love Not For Sale, 1922), "That's how I want you, provocative, flighty."

Emilio Gouchón Cané's short story "Un buen empleo" (A Good Job) alludes to the insertion of women into white-collar service jobs. It tells of a young man named Liberato Arduiño who resigns from the municipality to become a typical entrepreneur in a business that's all about expansion: "General Business Enterprises. Any thing—Any size." Everything sails smoothly until his future secretary enters his office with a firm step: "I'm a woman of initiative. What counts in business is instinct, and we women, you know, are the ultimate in intuition." In view of the title of the volume of stories by Gouchón Cané in which "Un buen empleo" was first published, *Breviario satánico* (Satanic Breviary), nightmares are expected to follow, as indeed they do. Miss Peñalver has barely arrived before she takes over the office, "while Liberato is waiting in the cold and empty corridor" (Gouchón Cané 1967, 145). He ends up writing letters she dictates, and she even forbids him from inviting his friends to the office. Indeed, the transfer of power is so emphatic that Liberato has to request an appointment to find out how his company is doing: "Things are going well. I can't complain. As for you . . . you can still be useful. I'll pay you 150 a month. . . . You'll come into work in the afternoons from two until six. It's not much! Besides, we know each other and you know I'm a good boss" (144). Yet there is one more condition: "All I ask is that you pass as my husband. . . . A husband who can be seen goes over well. . . . I'll pay you double" (145). From boss to employee and husband, with decreasing degrees of power, and possessed by an increasing misogynistic horror. The theme—and the paranoia—the story conveys center on a new "enemy," who moves through the city unseen, like Satan, but whose actions are painstakingly premeditated and calculated. Gouchón Cané's misogynistic reading presents women as a group long crouched at the ready, their spectacular leap finally made possible by the crisis in social participation.

A *sainete* by Alejandro Berruti, *Cuidado con las bonitas* (Watch Out for the Pretty Ones), first performed by Olinda Bozán's company in 1931, is about the forty-five-year-old Nicola, *diventato rico,* who has come into some money and acquired a twenty-two-year-old wife—a kind of relationship that was amazingly common in the imaginaries of popular culture at that time. Margarita brings her widowed mother, her seamstress sister (Teresa), another sister working for the telephone company, and her unemployed brother all under the protection of the matrimonial roof. The *sainete* weaves three obsessions together: feminine beauty, marriage, and narcissism. The theme of beauty revolves around Margarita, who is beautiful, beloved, and married. Her husband "loves her [because] he is besotted by the beauty of his wife." As Teresa says: "She is a superficial woman, full of her own beauty. . . . I think she has a mirror for a heart, into which she peers to admire her own image" (Berruti 1973, 243). As a perfect example of self-absorption and cold calculation, Margarita needs "a rich husband like Nicola who could keep her in self-centered luxury and show off her beauty. That's why she married" (243). "Of the four women in the house," she says, "[Nicola] chose the youngest and the prettiest. Ninety percent of men would have done the same" (243). As this imaginary explains, the widow and sisters were left out of the matrimonial picture precisely because they did not enjoy perfect beauty:

> TERESA: Men generally prefer physical beauty in a woman. A perfect body, a pretty face. . . .
>
> ROBERTO: I don't think anyone has turned you down because you're not a perfect beauty.
>
> TERESA: No. But neither does anyone love me, perhaps for the same reason. (247)

Not only beauty but *perfect* beauty—and men are completely disarmed when a woman possesses it: "I'm very, very happy! She is divine! People stop and stare at her in the streets, like in the tango" (249). Nicola is a misogynist, who uses the young woman to show off in the streets, unaware that the streets and their uses are double-edged.

For early twentieth-century imaginaries, the concept of the femme fatale, inherited from Pre-Raphaelites, decadents, and symbolists like Rossetti, Burne-Jones, Gautier, Baudelaire, and Moreau, was still quite recent. This concept has several central features: a dark, fatal, and perverse eroticism; androgyny and fluctuation between sexual identities; extreme beauty, combined with complete awareness, calculation, and control of the art of seduction; sterility; fascination and disdain; and the power to take men into highly dangerous and destructive situations. To these characteristics, Virginia Mae Allen would add an erect posture and a strong, direct gaze, alternating with "lowered eyelids, sometimes a partially opened mouth, [and a] thrown back head" (1979, 7). In 1928, Enrique Cadícamo called one such woman a *muñeca brava* (brazen doll) in the lyrics of a homonymous tango he wrote to music by Luis Visca, and in the imaginaries that began to demonize her, she became a "snake" that dragged men to suicide or at least caused them to sigh with the agonizing conviction that "tomorrow is always worse" (Discépolo 1996). The new Satan of Buenos Aires was now dressed in irresistible feminine clothes.

In a remote corner of the Argentinean countryside (which will always fill a corner of the national imaginary), two characters from Nicolás Olivari's *Tedio* (Boredom, 1936) gaze at some not too distant stars, namely the beautiful women of Buenos Aires. Raúl exclaims to Juan, "When I saw those *haughty* women walking along the street as if they were queens, I was seized by a furious desire to make love!" (Olivari 1936, 8; emphasis added). If their fascination with Ela is any indication, the two of them have been struck by a new type of body language:

> JUAN: You should see her . . . how she walks. She gets to her feet and seems two feet taller. And she sways. Her lips are full and become moister and moister. . . . First she crosses one street, then another . . . and my poor heart. . . . There, there! Don't you see her? Look at her. . . . Don't you see her?
>
> RAÚL: I see her . . . I see her. . . . How beautiful she is! . . . Oh, there's no one like her! . . .

JUAN (*from deep in his hallucination*): Look at her, yes. . . . There's no one like her! . . . no one! (14)

In the densely populated misogynistic imaginary of an equally misogynistic Buenos Aires, Ela is perhaps the most perfidious and perverse femme fatale of them all. Olivari's protagonist, Juan, has reached the limits of the grotesque, driven by the "monstrous love" that has made him surrender in humiliation to a femme fatale. When the audience first sees Ela, she is absorbed with herself, fixing her nails, in an apartment paid for by Juan's untold sacrifices: "I've been imprisoned here for about ten years. . . . I paid for it all. . . . Stealing, sweating . . . down there . . . in hell. . . . Everything is mine, except for Ela" (19). At the beginning of this battle of the sexes, Juan's concept of masculinity is quite clear: every woman is "pretty and malleable, like anyone in love. It was just a matter of molding her." As time goes by, however, the soundness of the concept crumbles, soon proving outdated in the Buenos Aires of the time.

Many of the facets recycled by the fin de siècle, from classical mythology and the dichotomist world of Christianity, allow us to infer that representations of the femme fatale were constructed by men with transgressive lifestyles, but a conventional attitude toward women. They also permit us to conclude that this sudden surge of Venus Victa, sirens, Circes, cobras, Salomes, and above all poisonous Medusas with unbearably glaucous eyes must be read in the context of the emergence of feminism—of women in the public sphere and of males who have "imploded" or grown "weak":

ELA: One day a good boy . . . married me. He was a journalist, a poet. He gave up everything for me. . . . I'll never forget one particular day! His friends all came. He had just published a book. Poetry . . . I never bothered to read it. . . . Then I came in . . . serious and cold. . . . He gives me a pleading look. I know . . . he is asking for a kind word. . . . I turn to him. He is waiting like someone waiting for a death sentence, and I ask him, unmoved, almost wickedly: How much did they give you for that thing? . . . He left when he grew tired of taking so much crap from me . . . and now he's a long way from here, drinking all the time. (18)

The cynical woman is armed with "indifference and chilling remoteness from human feelings" (Allen 1979, 11) and has crossed all thresholds. This imaginary thus equates the sinister female with death, so that whoever comes

Muñecas Bravas *of Buenos Aires*

to know Ela, whether Juan, Raúl, the reader, or the spectator at the play, will be submerged in unredeeming depths: "Beside you, I'm a pig. Away from you, I'm a leprous angel. You throw me away, you drag me back. . . . Woman. . . . You tempt and enslave us in the criminal city. . . . We'll never break your bond" (24):

> ELA: The night is yours and mine. . . . This animal night, murky with shadows, where you, a poor inflamed cell, and I, an amoeba with a sex, come together in the great drama of our embrace . . . without ideas or words . . . blindly, eternally blind . . . like the night without eyes . . . like life without eyes. (25)

Hence the freezing stare of the Medusa: *a night without eyes.* Sex is death, regression to the state of amoebas and animals, a void, the end of language. In contrast to the protective woman/mother, the femme fatale abandons. She flees the *conventillo,* leaving behind the family home and her tender siblings, as in Carriego's verses. Sunk in despair, they are the dependents or children that the *milonguita* renounces. After she abandons the family home—a signifier that embodies the spatialization of the concept of motherhood—her punishment for turning her back on her family will be sterility. Abortion, barrenness, and the solitude of a woman without a family are indeed the negative, reverse side of a sexuality not intended for maternity, such as the prostitute's. In effect, such a woman's lascivious breasts are destined not to nurse infants but to ensnare her prey. Ela's words, which seem to come from the pitiless mouth of Marlene Dietrich, trace the image of a "faceless" man, like the prostitute, but the opposite of her, because he has now become just a sexual expedient. As Ela says, "You or someone else, what's the difference?" Olivari's work also uses Ela to define insatiability: "Those women bundled up in heavy fur coats . . . well-nourished women . . . kept on good food . . . who get fat with cakes and creams from the pastry shops downtown. . . . They eat enough for four, using all their teeth, [and devour] the brain, the heart, and the very soul of a man" (8). This (sexual) insatiability is responsible for the man's fall, his embezzlement, imprisonment, bankruptcy, and subsequent suicide—all for the sake of keeping a woman in luxury. It is difficult to convey the conviction and bitterness with which such imaginaries contend that the femme fatale is to blame for everything. Hence the morbid delight when she is represented as having lost her beauty. She is a cannibal who every morning devours the man with whom she has spent the night. Thus it becomes a question of survival, of being able to identify her conduct in order to spot her in the confusion of the city. Otherwise, there is a risk of reacting too late. It is especially noteworthy that the idea of cannibalism is here linked to a sexuality so rapacious that it immobilizes any defensive reaction, except the action/weapon implied by a misogynistic discourse:

> JUAN: I surrendered too much to her. Without the reserve a man should keep toward a woman's voracious sentimentality. Ela knows she just has to look at me. . . . I fall apart, I'm in pieces, and my strength all crumbles like a heap of sugar. . . . My heart ached, and my hands, ah, how my hands ran over her skin when it was taut from her laughter, because Ela would laugh, how she'd laugh! (13)

What more do we need to know to understand misogyny? In *El amor brujo* (Bewitched by Love, 1933), Roberto Arlt describes the fear of economic and sexual calculation by clever women in spheres that were formerly preserves of male dominance. The physical mobility of his female character, Irene, becomes an obsession for her lover, Balder, who calls on her mother to watch over her: "Madam, I wish to give you a warning. Don't let her go downtown on her own" (Arlt 1981c, 1: 212). If it is unwise to travel alone, however, it is worse to travel in bad company. The companion of Irene's adventures is Zulema, whom Balder considers a corrupting influence. Women who take trains. Women who cross the city from one point to another for purposes that, according to Balder, cannot be admitted. Women with aspirations and desires. The woman *in* the street is obsessively equated with the woman *of* the street. Much to Balder's dismay, it is precisely *because* gullible husbands like Zulema's maintain that "women have the same social and sexual rights as men" that she insists on becoming a singer at the Colón and leaving her marital home for a boardinghouse in the center, near the theater: "[Balder] lived in a state of agitated bewilderment and thought that the freedom enjoyed by Irene was abnormal, that the freedom Zulema took for herself was abnormal" (149). In his consternation, he doesn't doubt that they are *mujerzuelas* (loose women): "He had no proof, 'but he was certain of it'" (1: 110). Balder, Arlt's male character, reaches this equation without much effort and with little thought. Zulema goes out frequently and has professional aspirations, "incomplete desires" (tastes she would certainly like to satisfy), and a "perfumed body [that] billowed fragrances" (1: 182).

All the city's signs of chaos were caught in the net of this imaginary. Since women were beginning to enjoy "too much" mobility, imaginaries that preferred their restriction resorted to the stock-in-trade of misogyny. To have done otherwise would have meant recognizing the profound break in social practices—and taking a productive pause to reflect on the identitary searches and hopes that lay behind this break. Are social imaginaries willing to work their interpretation of the quotidian by taking into account the empirical evidence social actors draw from their own and others' experience? What is *lo acertado,* and what is *lo verdadero*? The tension in transitional Buenos Aires between social normalization and individual self-assertion, between social institutions and the spontaneous quests and improvisations of the subject, would begin to suggest the "need" to reestablish the contracts of social reproduction with amazing directness. Such contracts would, in any event, have to coexist with the new attitudes emerging from the interfaces and interstices of individuals like Zulema, ready to rethink everyday practices and to cast their lot with what they considered to be their *own* truth. What should arise from this tension is a *reflection* concerning the competence of social actors to think their own thoughts and to evaluate the effectiveness of their own way of being in the world in light of the rules of social exchange (Reguillo 1998, 107). But were *porteños* ready to undertake such a reflection in order to turn to new destinations?

The femmes fatales, lamias, and vampires are women *of a different kind,* refusing to live according to everyday routine, because the demands of their sexuality disrupt its rhythm. This imaginary sees such women as if their skin were entirely covered by a rash and they were unable to keep still. More than anything else, however, such a construction betrays its cultural agent as one severely distressed by women whose desire to inhabit "masculine" or alternative spaces is read as ambition, a yearning for power, arrogance, and obstinacy. Moreover, misogyny "confirms" the profound historical fractures in the universalist model of motherhood as a self-imposed deferment and stresses that conformity (*lo acertado*) to social reproduction is being challenged by women's new search for their own truth (*lo verdadero*). In Arlt's *El amor brujo,* Balder is on treacherous, swampy ground. Once he realizes he is an object sexually manipulated by Irene, a "very astute" young woman, well practiced in the art of male domination or the dexterity of the brothel, he experiences unbearable malaise: "'I am the object she uses to satisfy her desires. Where can she have acquired that technique for giving pleasure? Nothing surprises her; it's as if she knew everything. . . . Who can have taught her?' A shiver ran down Balder's spine" (Arlt 1981c, 185).

In a misogynistic imaginary, Pilar Pedraza argues, "the beauty of panthers is such that it allows them to hunt sheep through the strategy of petrified fascination: their splendor freezes their victims in ecstasy" (1991, 239). And they exploit that moment to strike, making no distinction for species, social class, or ideology. For example, in Samuel Eichelbaum's *El ruedo de las almas* (Circle of Souls, 1923), Guillermo de Amador is a "calm and thoughtful" lawyer with busts of Marx, Voltaire, Jaurés, Sarmiento, and Anatole France coexisting in his office. He is a deputy for a leftist party, but not even that is enough to prevent him from falling for María Angélica, a vain, aristocratic woman who is compellingly confident of her "many means of seduction." María Angélica performs the female identitary model of self-absorption. She finds Guillermo's concern for public welfare pathetic, is contemptuous of judicial authority, and ridicules parliamentary debates as much as she despises the populist inclinations of the politician. The deputy's passion predictably draws him into a cocoon, isolating him from everything unrelated to the bedroom and luxury. As a fellow party member reproaches him, he has abandoned "the responsibilities the party charged him with," his ideology, and his militancy in the name of social justice in order to follow "that woman." Transformed, he brazenly declares: "I want to live my time of love, every minute of my passion and nothing more. . . . I'm one of those who believe that life always has a sensual purpose and that we are governed by sensuality." The key word here is "governed," because on account of Guillermo's metamorphosis, "it's no longer a matter of government, but tyranny." He has betrayed the subordination of the private to the public interest—entrusted to him when he became the democratic representative of his electors—for a self-absorbing present, "my time of love, every minute of my passion."

The deputy's error also lies, I believe, in his identitary slide toward the place of the other: he speaks the cloying discourse that imaginaries attributed to women, with their talk of much passion and too much intuition, and assumes the passive role of one who has been seduced and is indeed in love. His choices are outrageous; he embodies an extraordinarily weakened model of masculinity in relation to a woman whom he addresses in the following terms: "[You are] a demonic creature playing with my life. A mysterious creature manipulating my trust and hopes like a fan you open and close at your pleasure, as if you knew all my weaknesses." Such a voluptuous flame of desire threatens to eliminate from political life any male militant touched by the mistaken bond of passion. It removes them from circulation even if they were once "doctrinaire and combative." Moreover, the condition is contagious. Guillermo's fellow party member also succumbs to the "sweet, evil force of passion," drawn to yet another woman:

> RIVADANEIRA: I tried to kill myself. For the past few days, after I'd been with her, I felt a fever running through my entire body. I asked for some cool water and drank it with feelings of anxiety and a sense of voluptuousness that were unknown to me. . . . I feel like a living flame. . . . Why doesn't [God] strike me down? Why?

In spite of her name, the disdainfully smiling María Angélica isn't much like the Virgin Mary and is even less like an angel. By removing values such as "duty, honesty, honor, and morality" from circulation, she is indeed a Satan of modernity. In fact, *El ruedo de las almas* draws attention to new threats that hang not only over the home but over the continuation of democratic life itself. How is it possible to rely on a public representative who is weakened by love, attentive only to his body temperature or to the choice of words that best express his burning feelings? Eichelbaum's drama, in conjunction with the widespread misogynist imaginaries of the time, allows the audience to anticipate the story's outcome. Only suicide can save the two debased politicians. Such is the remarkable drive displayed in the drama to turn the femme fatale into a *peligro nacional* (national threat).

In the tragicomedy *El mayor prejuicio* (The Greatest Prejudice, 1918), by José González Castillo, Coco summarizes the effects of "today's education on a woman in her youth. A fourteen-year-old fashion model who 'knows everything,' reads her brother's dirty books on the sly, and spends the day on the balcony flirting . . . such is the call of the instincts beginning to break out in her" (González Castillo 1918, 4). The full range of semantic artillery is deployed here ("the call of her instincts," "impulses," "to break out") in order to convey a sociosexual uncontrollability whose danger must be unmasked to prevent an outbreak. Let us remember that the fin de siècle portrayed its femmes fatales hidden behind veils, like those with which Louis Ernest Barrias, Audrey Beardsley, and Gustave Moreau covered Salome.

Such women wear veils because they have plenty to conceal. As Freud explained, "The erotic life of women—partly owing to the stunting effect of civilized condition and partly owing to their conventional secretiveness and insincerity—is still veiled in impenetrable obscurity" (qtd. in Showalter 1991, 144). Are women "mysterious" because of the veil or because the keys to understanding their difference are ignored or misplaced? Knowing who was a wicked woman was an obsession of Buenos Aires imaginaries. In the sexual encounter played out to unmask the wicked woman in *Amor brujo,* Balder's antagonists are women, but *mujeres de frontera,* women who cross social borders. Like mythic sirens, they draw Arlt's protagonist into the Kingdom of Quagmires, a wasteland covered "with the stench of excrement, patches of hideous thistles menstruating spiny bluish bulbs. Irene and Zulema call to him making ardent signals with hands stained with black and brown fecal matter" (Arlt 1981c, 239). Foul hands and mire, the degraded sexuality of the brothel. Balder invokes female sexuality, mixing excrement with menstrual blood, in order to speak of the death of the male and exemplary masculinity. His sensorial map may well be one of the most forceful in revealing the background of revulsion and rejection of proxemic distances between the sexes, fueled by the misogynistic imaginary of the Buenos Aires of the time. Once Balder is caught in the mire, already incapable of speech, halfway between dumbness and vocalizations (i.e., stuttering), first comes paralysis, and then comes death. However, should Balder's paralysis be attributed only to the hypersexed sirens calling to him from the mire? Because there is, perhaps, more to it than that.

Muñecas Bravas *of Buenos Aires*

12 RAGS AND REJECTS

THE THEME OF THE WET NURSE
is introduced in *El conventillo* through tensions arising between Ana María, an immigrant recently arrived from Spain, and the lady of a mansion on Calle Alvear, Angélica Gómez Salustio. The latter reproaches the nurse: "You have certainly shared the responsibilities of motherhood with me for a year, not like a woman sacrificing herself for love, however, but like a prostitute selling herself for a price" (Pascarella 1917, 256). The number of wet nurses offering themselves in the "Domestic Services" section of the *La Prensa* classifieds was in fact staggering and would remain high for the first three decades of the twentieth century. The following advertisements appeared in *La Prensa* on Thursday, 19 September 1901:

> Spanish nurse available, good milk, highly recommended. Ayacucho 772.
> French nurse available, 36 yrs. old, milk for 40 days. Laprida 680.
> Nurse available, abundant milk. Bartolomé Mitre 2106.
> Strong, young nurse available, top-quality milk. San Juan 18768.
> Italian nurse available, abundant milk, 4 months. Gorriti 668.

And the following were published on Monday, 1 April 1912, in the same newspaper:

> First-time nurse available, abundant milk, 25 days. Maza 130.
>
> Newly arrived Spanish nurse available, abundant milk, quality approved. Patagones 211.
>
> Nurse without child available, milk for 20 days, fresh, will nurse at your home. Avellaneda 348.
>
> Approved nurses, the best in Buenos Aires. Junín 577.
>
> Nurse without child required to nurse at my home. Esmeralda 1056.

María Gabriela Ini remarks that the reproductive capacity of proletarian women had acquired a social and economic value in the Buenos Aires of that time: "It was normal for poor women to hire themselves out as wet nurses. As far as the wealthy were concerned, they should have milk, but not children. Many of them stopped feeding their own children in order to work as wet nurses" (2000, 241). Commercial value in the contract between Ana María and Angélica Gómez Salustio is strictly read as maternity for cash: mercenary maternity, no subtlety about it. Moreover, the narrator of *El conventillo* distorts this negative image further by associating the immigrant woman with greed and a refusal to nurse her own child because "every suck was an amount subtracted from the total she imagined. Such is money, like the poisonous strain in certain animals, which perverts the most noble instincts and the brightest dreams" (Pascarella 1917, 142). The pages of *La Prensa* are full of advertising for this "perversion of natural instincts." From the point of view of Angélica Gómez Salustio, Ana María represents a new form of commerce, regrettably living alongside the representatives of "true" maternity, who would never, of course, sell their own milk. Unfortunate but necessary, such coexistence only enhanced the sharp contrast between the positive paradigm and the deviation: the ladies of the nation and displaced foreigners, in the person of a wet nurse who cherishes "the possibility of touching, counting, holding, and recounting the notes or metal coins that can change her life" (Pascarella 1917, 126).

Standing at the center of a circle formed by the doctor and the inhabitants of the house, Ana María is subjected, like all wet nurses, to the same "preliminary examination to which dairy cows are exposed at the County Fair" of the oligarchic Sociedad Rural:

Muñecas Bravas *of Buenos Aires*

The expression on the man examining her seemed overly severe. After scrutinizing her closely from head to toe, he placed his left index finger under her chin and with his right hand, without asking permission, looked under her eyelids. Then, continuing his task without saying a word, indicated she undo her bodice so he could examine her breasts. Ana María . . . made a gesture of modesty that any woman who has not been in a consulting room would have made, but the doctor moved to go about the task with his own hands without further ado. . . . He squeezed one of her nipples tightly to see if she had any pain in them. . . . The pain was so intense . . . that she felt a wave of heat that suffused her from the very soles of her feet. (Pascarella 1917, 147–48)

On the one hand, embarrassment and shame; on the other, the impunity of hands protected by the social privilege of the examining doctor. Wet nurses such as those offered by an agency—"Approved nurses, the best in Buenos Aires"—were guaranteed because they had passed the appropriate exam. The nudity and auscultation accompanying Ana María's exam border on pornography, set-pieces of patriarchal structures that contribute to affirming imaginaries in which the female body is abusively exposed to an unspeakable scrutiny, as in the selection of women in organized prostitution: women lined up for auction, completely naked, in front of potential buyers and subjected, as Andrés M. Carretero puts it, to "the fondling of their bodies [and] examination of their teeth . . . as if they were common animals at a fair" (1995, 120). As for the child of the *tambera* (wet nurse) hired by the Gómez Salustios, it is most convenient to remove him from the house where his mother is nursing. The doctor instructs her: "You should stay for as long as the nursing lasts. . . . You have to take your child away, and you have to come here and not leave without permission." Ana María's own baby subsequently becomes a burden to her because she must pay a good part of her own salary to another wet nurse: "Wasn't it on account of him that she wouldn't save all 100 pesos she earned every month? . . . She shook him roughly and then held him tightly to her breast so that he would be quiet, but the child kept on wailing restlessly" (Pascarella 1917, 152).

Prevalent imaginaries during these transitional times lacked understanding and would simply claim that the wet nurses' greed was responsible for the disregard and erosion of family ties, undermined within the very social place where their foundation should have been most reliable. In the *Caras y Caretas* of 5 January 1901, however, an altogether different example appears: "The dairy producer La Martona has established an annual prize of 400 pesos for the most fertile mother who has fed the most children without resorting to paid help." The prize was awarded to a mother of twenty-one children, Ángela García de Reibaud. Two others were not chosen because they had not fed their children "entirely" on mother's milk: a mother of twenty-five children, likely "the largest family in the Republic," and an Andalusian woman with twenty-three children living in Barracas. But what exactly did this competition celebrate? The numbers suggest that contraception was culturally unacceptable and unavailable in the lower-class social environment, highly organized along parameters set by the Catholic Church. In my opinion, La Martona thus effectively awarded a prize for choosing a maternity over which women exercised no choice. To think of the company's dairy products is to imagine a placid, Dutch-Argentinean cow grazing on the soft greenery of the pampas. In fact, however, La Martona had women compete as if they were dairy cows, without recognizing that motherhood is not some kind of universal and unavoidable notion. There are mothers of all kinds. The company's announcement was unbelievably unjust, insensitive to the daily drama that afflicted women without job skills of any kind or mothers raising a dozen or twenty or so children, all of different ages and with different needs. Unlike dairy cows, proletarian mothers did not find their daily struggles eased by the tranquil setting of the greenery of the pampas. With astonishing insensitivity, La Martona endorsed a discourse on maternity that praised "purity" in the form of the immaculate whiteness of the milk, without pausing a minute to notice the countless hardships posed by transitional realities in the grotesque city whose mothers were certainly a long way from the purity of the Virgin Mary's Immaculate Conception.

Another striking aspect of Buenos Aires at the time was the number of children and elderly people in the workforce. *La Prensa* carried the following classified ads on 19 September 1901:

> Older Spanish man seeks any light work, with or without meals, low wages accepted. Good references. San Juan 1636.
>
> Cook and girl of 12 yrs. seek work. Buen Orden 1520.
>
> Girl, 12 or 13 yrs., required by married couple. Azcuénaga 42, Apt. 3.
>
> Girl required for domestic service, 8–10 yrs. Independencia 758.

Boy required for domestic service by married couple, 8–9 yrs. Clothing provided, duties taught, no payment. Arenales 952.

The following appeared on 20 September 1901:

Girl, 10–12 yrs., required. Light work in exchange for clothing. Entre Ríos 2002.

Girl or boy, 10–12 yrs., required for domestic service. Piedras 1980.

And on 21 September 1901:

Orphan boy, 13, seeks work with married couple. Viamonte 947.

Each of these ads allows us to glimpse the depth of individual stories and infer the hidden hardship. They all point to a lack of safety nets and to the enormous number of illegitimate and orphaned children excluded from the metaphor of the nation's well-formed family—children who would never be among the beneficiaries of the *herencia nacional* (national inheritance).

According to Sandra F. McGee Deutsch, "about 22% of the children born in Argentina between 1914 and 1919 were brought into the world by single mothers" (1983, 236). Beatriz Sarlo alludes to a 1902 debate in Congress, led by Carlos Olivera, over "human nature, the same nature invoked by serial novels when a girl surrenders herself, outside or against social convention, pitting her desire (nature) against society and an order based on marriage" (1985, 95). Olivera, Sarlo tells us, proposed that "the rules of society should be adapted to the imperfect nature of feelings" (95). What the debate sought to alleviate were the conditions arising from "children kept hidden, broken families, double and triple liaisons, unpardonable indiscretions," and incest. For those positioned at the center of society, these strikingly frequent "accidents" or "abnormalities" were viewed as belonging to the social outskirts (*arrabales sociales*). They were the result of the empirical practices ("the imperfect nature of feelings") produced by civil society and woven by the grotesque city around formal modernity, seriously undercutting the process of bourgeois socialization. The economics and politics of global modernization gave rise to internal and external migrations; spontaneous family structures; and *suburbios sociales* (socially marginalized areas) for *mestizos/as*, blacks, mulattos, and foreigners. It also conditioned countless women to the exile of prostitution, criminalized abortions, bearing illegitimate children, as well as the "absolute" social death embodied by infanticide. It is not difficult to weigh the social consequences of such polymorphism, which was fiercely assigned to the most negative, ignominious, or uncomfortable nonspace within the systems of social categorization of formal modernity.

The widows who peopled the tango, and texts by Roberto Arlt or Evaristo Carriego, presented another social case that required surveillance. "Widow" was often used as a euphemism for the innumerable single mothers wishing to disguise their status. As Donna Guy remarks: "Left behind and often widowed, many native-born lower class women faced lives of persistent poverty unrelieved by the growth of the capital city. Among the foreign-born women, many had migrated alone. . . . To survive, some desperate women from both groups turned to prostitution" (1991, 43). Something of this sort may be detected in the following classified ads, appearing in *La Prensa* on 19 September 1901, revealing a need for widows to anticipate and prevent sexual abuse in domestic service by unscrupulous employers:

> Widow seeks work as housekeeper in responsible household, can cook desserts and make ice cream. Recommended. Suipacha 859.
>
> Young French widow, educated, seeks employment as governess or housekeeper for respectable family or reliable gentleman. Suipacha 859.
>
> Widowed lady of good family, in difficult circumstances, seeks placement with person as housekeeper or governess. Only respectable, responsible people need apply. Box S IN 38.

The frequency of "abnormal" cases causes us to think that the abnormal was not actually the exception in transitional Buenos Aires. What was seen as normal was, in reality, perhaps only a projection of the resistance of imaginaries to any recognition of what everyday life was really like. Like the grid of urban streets, indifferent to empirical geography, the *trabajo de los imaginarios* (the work of imaginaries) sought to control how events were understood. The abnormal was made invisible, in the sense that it was not permitted to interrupt the validity of predetermined responses to the spontaneity of experiential realities or to give social actors an occasion to consciously reflect on daily life and social conventions. Nevertheless, there must have been very little that was normal in this confusing Buenos Aires, which made it all the more necessary to deal promptly with any disruption or fracture.

Amid so much anguish and disruption, suicide was alarmingly prevalent. In *La Vanguardia* for 9 January 1913, we read: "Vicente Ferraiollo tried to kill himself by jumping onto the track just as a train was approaching the crossing . . . on Calle Chivilcoy. . . . He suffered serious injuries to the head and body." On Wednesday, 15 January 1913, under the general heading "Desperate People," one section of the paper reports: "José Lucíñi took his own life . . . in his home at Moreno 2467 with a single shot . . . to the right temple. Death was instantaneous." This is followed by: "Emilia Escoltini took her life last night in her home at Vidal 2840 by severing the veins in her neck with a penknife." Augusto Remo Erdosain proposes suicide to Hipólita, in *Los siete locos,* as a way of speeding up an affair that was doomed from the start: "If you asked me to kill myself right now, I'd do it willingly." Suicide is commonplace, after all, he continues: "Haven't you seen how many shopkeepers and seamstresses commit suicide together? They fall in love . . . they can't marry . . . they go to a hotel. . . . She gives herself to him, and then they kill themselves" (Arlt 1981c, 1: 266). There was, at the time, a high index of suicide and suicide attempts, especially among women. *La Vanguardia,* for example, published a striking summary for one single day, 15 January 1913: "In the Hotel Biarritz . . . María Ester López, a domestic servant, 19 years of age, tried to kill herself by taking 2 cyanide tablets"; "In her home at Corrientes 1258, Adela Martínez made an attempt on her life by drinking a solution of . . . 4 bichloride tablets. . . . She stated that she tried to kill herself because she was tired of her life"; "Isabel Petray, living at Rioja 184, tried to kill herself by drinking laudanum . . . also because she was tired of living"; "Sinfoniana Medina, 17 years of age, . . . ingested bichloride pills. She was taken to the Northern Hospital in serious condition." A similar story is taken up by Liborio Justo:

> Two women killed themselves at Santa Fe 17. Last night Gloria Méndez, Argentinean, 16 years of age, wife of Bernardo Marenco, Argentinean, aged 50, jumped from the suspension bridge into the water of the Laguna Setubal. The cause of her suicide is unknown. . . . The body of María Teresa Figueroa de Guardia, Argentinean, 23 years of age, who had married Bonifacio Guardia, aged 60, a widower and father of 7 children, only last Saturday,

has also turned up in the district of Santo Tomé. Teresa had disappeared from her home on Tuesday, and the cause of her suicide is unknown. A domestic servant killed herself by jumping from the 8th floor. . . . Of the children born in the country, 20% are to single or adolescent mothers. (qtd. in Balmaceda 1982, 31)

How did imaginaries deal with this chilling urban scene? How did the city live, day after day, with such an appalling daily toll of suicidal women—single women barely arrived in the country or married to older men and responsible for numerous children? The high index of suicide among proletarian women makes us think of the crossroads of a nonplace reached because of the following:

1. A lack of training and the inexorability of gendered conditions in the workplace. Social/labor cultures that induced agoraphobia by stigmatizing employment outside the home or family conditioned women to put up with all kinds of violence, whether in factories or at home.

2. Subhuman living conditions. Overcrowding in the *conventillos,* and the stigma of all the social ills they represented, led to physical and cultural reactions that resulted in severe claustrophobia.

3. Circles of violence. Unremitting physical exploitation, mistreatment, and submissiveness, embedded in the cultures of work at the factory, workshop, store, office, and brothel, as well as sexual violence in the home and on the street, led to violence that must have seemed inescapable.

4. Aggressive marketplace strategies of seduction clearly aimed at female consumers. The emergence of luxury goods blurred the distinction between basic and nonessential needs, between the accessible and the desirable, and new imaginaries circulated encouraging self-absorption and social possibilism.

5. Marriage as the only option open to "respectable" young women, although marriage at the same class level was considered a barrier to upward social mobility, and marriage above the lower or middle classes could entail some kind of barter.

6. Rigid patriarchal surveillance in the family environment by fathers, mothers, siblings, husbands, and neighbors, in domestic workplaces, workshops, factories, and offices. This surveillance added to the oppressive claustrophobia of the *conventillo,* compounded by the surveillance of state policing agents entrusted with enforcing patterns of socialization.

7. An abundance of imaginaries, such as the narratives of perdition, which served as reminders of what happened to those who attempted to

flout socially determined itineraries, as well as the scarce visibility of alternative imaginaries, which offered the possibility of forms of escape that did not incur punishment.

The preceding observations reveal how precarious the bonds of social laterality and empathy were among working women and within other social networks such as the family, the barrio, or the *conventillo,* and among coworkers of the same social class. Proletarian women found themselves caught in an infernal trap, a nonplace. Moreover, while proletarian men and women sought suicide as a "solution" to the oppression of poverty, they were not the only ones. The economic contortions of the times embodied capitalism's new adjustments during a dramatic new cycle of expansion. Everything was unknown; everyone was pressured to adjust, but without any empirical archive as a point of reference—hence the permanent anguish of Roberto Arlt's world. Perhaps suicide was a regressive resort, invoked when there was no "afterward"—in other words, when there were no precedents, referents, or narratives to shed light on what was to come. It was frequent in popular theater for men of the moneyed classes to opt for suicide when confronted by the shame of bankruptcy, resulting from the unstable flux of the world of finance or from their inability to pay debts incurred through wastefulness and excess. Yet the age is even better known for the suicide of highly visible public figures, such as Horacio Quiroga (1937), Alfonsina Storni (1938), Leopoldo Lugones (1938), and Senator Lisandro de la Torre (1939). In 1914, Delmira Agustini had been brutally murdered by her husband, who then killed himself. In fact, the remarkable retrospective look at Buenos Aires in the Enrique Santos Discépolo/Armando Mores tango "Cafetín de Buenos Aires" (Little Café in Buenos Aires, 1948) summarized the century thus far as "a miraculous mix of know-it-alls and suicides."

I would like to pause, however, at a suicide taken up by the urban chronicler Roberto Arlt in order to consider how his writing conveys the import of this burning issue to the residents of the city: "One morning in September 1927, as police reporter for the daily *Crítica,* I had to report on the suicide of a Spanish domestic servant, a single woman, 20 years of age, who killed herself at five in the morning by throwing herself under the wheels of a tramcar passing in front of the house where she worked" (1981c, 2: 393). The reporter/witness explains that, although he "saw corpses every day at that time," he could not erase three painful details from his mind. First, the owner of the house had told him that "on the night when she contemplated suicide, the servant didn't sleep," but remained seated on "an immigrant's sea chest. (She had arrived from Spain a year before.)" Further, she added, "The servant forgot to turn off the light when she went out to the street to throw herself under the tram" (2: 323). The tragic dimension of the suicide is thus ironically highlighted by the triviality of everyday life, which continues after the young woman has disappeared forever: "For months I walked about with the sight of this sad young girl before me sitting on the edge of her trunk, in a squalid little room with whitewashed walls, thinking of her hopeless fate, under the yellow glow of a 25-watt bulb" (2: 323).

What does this text represent with respect to daily life in Buenos Aires? Roberto Arlt wrote it specifically for the Teatro del Pueblo (People's Theater), led by his friend Leónidas Barletta, from the Boedo Group.[1] The urban chronicler comes across the body of a woman who has taken her own life. Just when he thinks he can read the scene as an ordinary event in his work as a police reporter, he decides instead to redeem it from the banality with which modernity assimilated the personal dramas it left behind in its wake. In order to achieve his purpose, Arlt needs the reader to retrieve the precise context and nuances of one particular morning in September 1927. He freezes the story and restrains it so that the reader doesn't move on, as if turning one more page of the newspaper. Instead of passing over the story as he would over a corpse, the reporter deliberately slows the pace of his chronicle to make audiences in the Teatro del Pueblo aware of suicide's excruciating social dimension. In this way, he endeavors to counteract the vertigo of the city, the way in which the mass-circulation press treats the city's many "accidents" by reducing them to just another event (just one more suicide that day). In sum, Arlt challenges the lackadaisical attitude of the mass media and the city's overall indolence. He circulates the story in another emotional space, aiming it at a demographic group close to the everyday tragedy, so they can fully touch the magnitude of its drama. Arlt's writing unbinds the pacts of silence whereby inward-looking imaginaries failed/refused to absorb the lessons of the quotidian, perhaps because daily life produces a type of knowledge and understanding that is decisively more immediate and subjective and, above all, powerful enough to reignite fading sensitivities and the bonds of social laterality.

13 REAFFIRMING
OLD PARADIGMS

MARTA E. SAVIGLIANO DESCRIBES A
choreographic figure used by *milonguitas* to "provoke a dance (call the attention of their target through their glances, figure and dancing abilities)":

> Milonguitas could challenge their male partners with the thrust and energy invested in the walks; manipulate their axis of balance by changing the distance between the bodies, the points of contact, and the strength of the embrace; play with diverse qualities of groundness in their steps; modify the "front" given to their partners, choosing to "face" them in misaligned angles of torso and hips; disrupt the cadence sought by their partners by not converting their trampling cortes at the proper musical time (thus imposing a need for skillful syncopation in order to keep up with the music); and add unexpectedly fancy ornamentations (*adornos*) of the figures "marked" by their partners. (1995, 60)

Although Savigliano stresses that the woman never "marks" or leads the dance in tango, her description nevertheless highlights the dancer's initiative, the art of attracting attention, and her skill at taking advantage of her body's movements. The verbs in Savigliano's description make us think of the dancer's active role: choosing her partner (her target); challenging him; walking with firm, energetic steps; controlling the axis along which her body is balanced, constantly changing the angle of her torso in order to draw attention to her breasts and hips; and adding adornments to lend suppleness to her movements. The verbs here—"challenge," "manipulate," "change," "play," "misalign," "disrupt," "impose"—build a semantic field that speaks of a profound awareness of how the female body can be used to destabilize and control a male partner. This choreography is specifically intended to attract the man's gaze and desire through movements strategically designed to draw attention to specific parts of the body: the hips, torso, legs, and the ever-changing profile of a sensual silhouette. Swaying hips and unpredictable slides turned *milonguitas* into enticing sirens, vampires, or medusas with piercing eyes.

Metamorphosed by Ceres—first into monstrous hybrids, half women, half birds, and then into fish with scaly tails—the classical sirens were condemned to live in the sea but were given the capacity to awaken male ardor through their irresistible singing. Whoever listened to them heard an invitation to death. Pilar Pedraza's remarkable study of the correlation between classical mythology and misogynist discourses explains that sirens engage men in a game of adulation, whereby they promise to sing of their epic deeds, to glorify the strength of their muscles, and to publicly praise their acts of bravery and valor (1991, 121). That is, they vow to honor the epics of the male's masculinity. The siren's song becomes a misogynistic—narcissistic—mirror in which the male sees his unimpeachable masculinity reflected. The male allows himself to be seduced in exchange for completing the game of love as the real seducer and the victor in the battle of the sexes. Nevertheless, as Pedraza adds, "After all, [the sirens] were not exactly trustworthy, and their hearts, if they had any, were not wrapped in sentimentality" (124). In Buenos Aires, the choreography of the *muñecas bravas* who initiated tango dances was also a premeditated invitation to the male to join in the game of responding to their movements, perhaps with the implied promise that, once launched into the dance, the men would control the female body with their skillfulness. We all know from the classical imaginary that the sirens' song hides a perverse snare that leads men to their death. Attraction, seduction, enchainment, entrapment, paralysis, and death all happen together.

The classical imagination knew what it was up to when it came to concoct-ing dark stories of sphinxes, Medusas, harpies, sirens, panthers, vampires, specters, Lamias, Gorgons, witches, ogresses, Salomes, and birds of prey—all of them women, all of them beautiful but horrifying, ready to dismember unwary men. As explained in Pilar Pedraza's fascinating work, which stresses the diabolical combination of claws and silken pleasures, misogynistic imag-inaries constructed narratives about such women intended as both a punish-ment and a warning.

From the *milonguitas'* erotic wisdom come the elements of a game whose novelty, threats, and risks must be controlled, because they disguise a search for identity that entails an irrevocable break with convention. Perhaps this is what the song of the *sirenas porteñas* hides and evades. The woman invites, like a siren, and the mere act of inviting and initiating the game is enough to arouse suspicions of an active sexuality. The choreography of the tango suggests that women understand their own pleasure and, most of all, the body and pleasure of the male. They also understand how close to get to awaken male desire. *Milonguitas* in Buenos Aires, then, had acquired a new knowledge, and they had become experts at using it. Their body language "exposed" them, and the tango allowed them to show off their new knowl-edge publicly in cabarets and *garçonières.* The tango, then, captures women's shift toward another space, characterized by active sexuality, where they turn like slippery sirens into *peces resbaladizos:* fish that are difficult to get hold of. Paranoid imaginaries detected their new knowledge and equated it with the dismembering claws of classical narratives. If Ulysses could save himself by turning away from the sirens' song—not listening to women seems to be how men remained virile—then the modern city could just as easily discover how to neutralize women's bid for new identities.

The female protagonist in Francisco DeFilippis Novoa's *El día sábado* (Saturday, 1913) protests, "All I was taught was to suffer and slave in this wretched life that gives me nothing but vain hopes in return." It is disheart-ening to see the enormous body of literary texts, popular works, tango lyrics, photographs, medical reports, and municipal bylaws that represent women as if they are a threat or danger. We must ask why "vain hopes" and women's quests for alternative identities to motherhood were automatically trans-lated, in this *porteño* imaginary, into the lethal overconfidence of the femme fatale. The Catholic Church paled but did not falter at the sight of this apocalypse. And indeed, it had good reason to take up its banners again, because the 1889 Public Education Law had brought it face to face with the secular state of Presidents Julio Argentino Roca and Miguel Juárez Celman. The Church's first political reaction was the formation of the Asociación Católica Argentina (Argentinean Catholic Association). Its second was to found the Liga Patriótica Argentina (LPA; Argentinean Patriotic League) in 1919, although it had been aligned with the Catholic Right since the founding of the Partido Autonomista Nacional (National Autonomy Party).

Between 1916, when the middle class gained power, and 1930, the year of the fascist coup, the political Right, the ultra-Right, and the Catholic Church reemerged on the political scene through nationalist organizations such as the women's branch of the LPA, known as the Comisión de Señoritas (Young Women's Committee), which instituted the Escuelas de Obreras en las Fábricas (Schools for Women Factory Workers) in 1922. This organization's declaration of principles, signed on a momentous anniversary in the nation's history (9 July), asserted that these *escuelas* would serve as "an apostolate for social harmony," founded by the Comisión de Señoritas to counteract "the extreme hostility and intransigence of workers' associations to everything Argentinean, whether or not it was related to labor, with the connivance of guilds and unions controlled by cliques intolerant to religion" ("Comisión de Señoritas" 1922, 1).[1] Under the watchful eye of the LPA's president, Manuel Carlés, this declaration referred to the LPA's own demons. On the one hand were the intransigence, hostility, intolerance, and anti-Argentinean sentiments of the workers' associations. On the other was a hagiographic discourse of social pacification, phrased in comforting words alleging that the "Señoritas" were very worthy successors of "our former, loving, and simple sovereign mothers, [who] tenderly and bravely marked out the road you follow" (2).

In order to place the Señoritas in a national(istic) narrative, the LPA's declaration—under the banner Patria y Orden (Fatherland and Order)—alluded to two historical moments from a glorious past: when the ladies of Mendoza "gave up their jewels in order to ensure the success of that momentous expedition [the crossing of the Andes by the revolutionary army, under José de San Martín] and [when] the women of Cochabamba . . . joined in the battle themselves in the name and honor of self-sacrifice" ("Comisión de Señoritas" 1922, 8). The example of the ladies of Mendoza is placed ahead of that of the women of Cochabamba, perhaps because of the LPA's zealous nationalism, as Cochabamba does not figure on the nation's maps. However,

Muñecas Bravas *of Buenos Aires*

this placement also prompts us to wonder about another discursive marker: the first example has to do with "ladies," the second with "women." The "ladies" figure in official Argentinean history because they undertake the (appropriately feminine) task of sewing flags and because they surrender their jewels, an act they perform as generous and serious patrician women, unlike those *porteñas* who are steeped in vice. By contrast, the "women" in the second example are just women from the popular classes, not so easily located on gender maps. They go into combat, like General Juana Azurduy, who gave birth in the thick of battle while instructing her troops.[2] If we are after exemplary women from history, why not mention Juana anyway?

Such a class-ridden view is systematic. The women of the LPA are "Argentinean Ladies," "Señoras," "Señoritas," or "niñas argentinas" (children of Argentina). The *obreras,* like the fighting women of Cochabamba, are just "women." Their civil status is not mentioned. There is no reference to *señoritas obreras* (unmarried working women) or to *señoras obreras* (married working women), a distinction preserved only for the Señoras and Señoritas of the LPA. The LPA's language with respect to the Señoritas revives a class privilege based on their patristic affiliation with the founding "Mothers of the Fatherland," the nation's original "mothers": "They were the patrician, heroic, virtuous, and serene women who were all fire, soul, and light in the past, when they drove the Argentinean phalanxes beyond the plains to the very foot of the slopes their grandfathers climbed in their desire for freedom" ("Comisión de Señoritas" 1922, 8). The rhetoric of self-legitimation became so prevalent that when María Lea Gastón, a worker at the Gratry factory, referred to the Señoritas in her speech at the LPA's Third Congress of Workers, she identified them as "children of the best of Buenos Aires society, descendants of Christian homes, whose mothers, Argentinean matrons of noble stock, were able to instill the beautiful Christian maxim 'Love thy neighbor as thyself' in their souls, who enlisted enthusiastically . . . and made every effort to improve the condition of working women" (20).

Of what did this improvement consist, however? The Señoritas' intervention was a reaction against the politicization of working women, the antinationalism attributed to workers' movements, widespread immorality, and alternatives for women—too many demons on the loose, indeed. Hence, Carlés fires his arrows in all directions when attempting to explain the objectives of the *escuelas de obreras:* "The eight-hour workday was so rigidly applied that this most vital task was halted by its own design at the very moment when the first bell of the last hour was struck. The workers fled in a rush from the factories as if they were escaping from prison" ("Comisión de Señoritas" 1922, 1). Although supposedly sensitive to working conditions in the factories, having said that they must be improved, Carlés speaks from the discursive position of an industrial capitalist, who is displeased when he sees workers abandon their work without a thought. He is disillusioned that the men complied with the eight-hour day to the letter and did not manage to overcome their claustrophobic impulses, which prevented them from staying in the factories any longer in order to finish their backlog. The case of working women was different: "Neither the street, with the dangers of unhealthy attentions from men, nor an evening in the *conventillo,* with the discomfort of overcrowding, were attractive alternatives for women. The poor working women even thought of killing time in the tango academies. The Señoritas of the Liga Patriótica appeared in the working-class barrios under these circumstances. The hostile guilds and unions were angry at their presence" (1).

It was a matter of great concern that the *obreras* went to tango classes. Let's recall that a femme fatale could be spotted by her body language and that the *muñecas bravas* walked differently. In the tango "Malevaje" (Ruffians, 1928), by Juan de Dios Filiberto and Enrique Santos Discépolo, the speaker confesses that his masculinity has been inhibited by the poise of a woman and her confident walk

> I saw you haughtily tangoing by
> with such a deep and sensual rhythm
> that I only had to see you to lose
> my confidence, my valor, and my desire to show off.

It was clear to the *liguistas* (LPA members) that, as a dance and a social praxis, tango, more than any other social discourse, embodied the disturbing shifts in identity and bodily conduct being shaped by Argentinean women. That rhythmical dance was an invitation to the intoxication of flagrant sexuality.

Sandra F. McGee Deutsch makes the double point that "it was the large numbers of homeless children and prostitutes and the low percentage of married adults that observers perceived as evidence of the decline of the family" (1983, 237). The *liguistas* proposed going to the rescue against a whole raft of enemies. Their schools sought to clean the dangers off the streets; shorten the time spent in the violence and overcrowding of the *conventillo;*

consolidate the two-parent, heterosexual, monogamous, married family; and save working women from the ruin of tango, with its lascivious choreography.[3] The schools "sponsored free entertainment . . . always with a nationalistic slant." They organized "celebrations of national holidays and traditions, such as folklore dances (other than tango), salutes to the flag and armed forces" (McGee Deutsch 1983, 253). In an Argentina whose essence was multicultural, the *liguistas* campaigned for Catholicism and a rabid nationalism: "And like our Divine Lord, we undertake a crusade . . . sowing the holy teachings of peace and labor in this promised land where only the idle and the wicked do not prosper. We gazed upon the inspiring, life-giving sight of the crowds eagerly awaiting the word of the Messiah that would teach them what they had forgotten, the duty of Argentineans to be faithful to their God and their country through the labor that gave them dignity and nobility" ("Comisión de Señoritas" 1922, 19). With remarkable agility, the narrative of the Crusades is suddenly connected to modern nationalism and an apology for work, although if work did give "dignity and nobility," it did so only in the case of the worker. The LPA here expresses the interests of the national industrial class, confronted by stoppages in production caused by foreign unionism, singling out the Señoritas for praise. In spite of the dangers entailed when "waiting for the *obreras* at the factory gates, that is, mingling with their foes, the good, patient Señoritas . . . were able to captivate the women with their courage and smiles in order to win their trust" (2). This discourse emphasizes how the angelic qualities of the Señoritas won over even "the most recalcitrant *obreras,*" so that all "the men and women from the factories turned up for their lessons" (3). Their objective was "to bring light to minds depressed by their own ignorance" and to improve "social and economic conditions, as is the aspiration of all men in this generous, free Republic" (4). Specifically, the LPA listed its goals as follows:

> A. To combat illiteracy among men and women workers in factories and workshops. To educate women to be the true lady of the household and the wife in her home by teaching her to sew, to mend, etc.
>
> B. To link the home to the [LPA] schools by organizing . . . periodic festivities of an educational character in order to promote respect and love of country.
>
> C. To contribute whenever possible to fulfilling any noble ideal that benefits education.
>
> D. To set up libraries in the schools. (7)

In addition to adopting Sarmiento's advocacy of literacy, the LPA sought to Argentineanize immigrants and to rechannel gender identities in traditional directions. "Basic letters and simple sewing" were the watchwords in this "struggle for life and a horizon open to victories." Carlés declares, "How fortunate you are, Señoritas, to have achieved, at such an opportune time and in such measure, the grace to enhance the blazing heroic escutcheon, this doughty shield, [which] you triumphantly inherited" (10). His epic discourse puts him on a war footing, praising the deeds of the Señoritas, which "allowed [them] to render powerless the arm raised in anger" (10). In the midst of a city whose immigrant languages transgressed against standard Spanish every minute of the day, Carlés also brought the highly diglossic *vosotros* into battle, a usage unthinkable in Latin America as a whole, let alone in Argentinean Spanish.[4]

That "Argentinean girl is no longer just an ornament in her regal drawing-rooms. . . . We know that the beings in the factories and workshops are our sisters and that our affections and hands must always be open to them. For *they* are like *us;* they suffer and love, and also harbor the illusion of a dream like a tender desire" ("Comisión de Señoritas" 1922, 12; emphasis added). The language used here ("the illusion of a dream like a tender desire") by the president of the LPA's Comisión Central de Señoritas, Josefina Cano, resembles Darío's, with suspension marks that might well express an imaginary of feminine sighs. Perhaps an imaginary is all an LPA Señorita and an *obrera* from Baley's factory have in common, given that proxemic distances and material differences of every kind were soon surfacing everywhere else. Profoundly rooted in the condescending attitude of a Christian charity that missed seeing socioeconomic class specifically as a cause of poverty, Josefina Cano is caught between treating a factory woman as a sister, as a friend (as dreamed of by María Lea Gastón), or, to use Carlés's language, as an "ignorant being" from the factory whose mind is depressed. The fluctuation between "us" and "them" therefore marks the ambivalent discursive position of the speaker and her undertaking. As the successors of the patrician Mothers of the Fatherland, the women of the LPA offered themselves as an alternative to the foreignness of feminist militancy (see McGee Deutsch 1983, 239). They were, as Carlés declared in 1927, part of the struggle against the masculinization of women and the feminization of men and were not expected to move working women away from the traditional tasks assigned by economics and gender, such as sewing, hygiene, religious duties, and preservation of moral principles. The LPA sought to use the Señoritas to indoctrinate working women so that, in the new social spaces of the street and the factories, they did not disregard "the happiness of the home and family in each phase of their lives, as daughter, wife, and mother, without which the perfection of education for women cannot be conceived" ("Comisión de Señoritas" 1922, 16). No progress beyond handicrafts was sought toward acquiring greater independence in the workforce through training and specialization.

By 1920, the women's branch of the LPA was endeavoring to use its schools to intervene in a female population that not only made up 22 percent of the workforce but was active in unions and the Socialist Party (McGee Deutsch 1983, 236). This was, according to the LPA, "a task called for by the times" ("Comisión de Señoritas" 1922, 14): working women "lived in subjugation because of their ignorance, dominated even by subversive elements that exploited their inability and discontent in order to create disorder" (4). It was necessary to depoliticize them, to remove them from the political stage as soon as possible. One sentence in particular, from María Lea Gastón, sheds light on the kind of depoliticization encouraged by the Señoritas: "The men of the Liga Patriótica Argentina brought their words of love and peace, their desires and longings, to improve the distressing condition of the worker caught and bound by the oppressive clutches of his leaders" (20). María Lea was, after all, a politicized worker herself, who believed that oppression did not come from capital but from the workers' movement, making it essential to turn a deaf ear to ideas brought from abroad to sow disorder. Class conflicts would clearly be resolved within the nationalist framework of family, tradition, and country.

Nevertheless, the LPA was not unaware that the consequences of modernity were unpredictable and dangerous. It recognized that "broader means were necessary to alleviate the misery of the poor, while preserving the essentials of the capitalist system"; even Carlés considered "possible measures [such] as social security, public housing, a national labor code, industrialization policies, and even limited land reform" (McGee Deutsch 1983, 255). When it came to making their presence known to "simple people," however, such reflections and flexibility were nowhere to be seen. On the contrary, the LPA's interventionism showed no shred of ambiguity, since its paramilitary forces participated in the bloody repressions of the Semana Trágica (January

1919), striking against "working classes and Jewish neighborhoods, destroying labor centers and beating and arresting thousands of innocent bystanders. . . . These self-styled civil guards were responsible for the many casualties of the Tragic Week, estimated at anywhere from 141 to 700 killed and between 800 and 2,000 wounded" (McGee Deutsch 1983, 238).

According to McGee Deutsch, the women's branch of the LPA "helped to camouflage those repressive acts that detracted from its respectability. In an ironic reversal of roles, women's heightened visibility helped mask the 'invisible' male ranks. . . . The dual nature of the Liga—suppressive and cooptative, invisible and visible—relied upon the participation of men and women and a sexual division of labor" (1983, 257). With "their words of love and peace, their desires and longings," the women of the LPA were also responsible for what their men carried out through speeches to Congress, ideological militancy, and brutal repression. These women represented "a model of womanhood to be imitated by upwardly mobile women" in a practice that —although antifeminist—gave the Señoritas "valuable experience in administration, voting, holding meetings, and other activities related to politics" (McGee Deutsch 1983, 257). Their message was double-edged. Women were encouraged to participate apolitically in the public sphere, while also adhering to examples of self-sacrifice.

We should not think, however, that the *liguistas* were an isolated phenomenon. On the contrary, their imaginary was strongly endorsed by their allies, some of whom were spontaneous or even involuntary, as in the case of Herminia Brumana:

> If only all the wives of all the poorest workers were able to make their eyes shine with happiness, even when they are bathed in tears, [if] they could laugh cheerfully in front of their husbands and kiss them passionately, if they could sing and read and live for their men! If only the mouths of all the women were never sullied by a reproach! If only their voices were soothing, and their fingers, still tired from work, had energy enough to caress slowly, softly, and lovingly the bowed head of the man who has come home from work ill-tempered and worried! Then, at the bottom of each glass of alcohol held in a trembling hand, there would not be . . . the stain of tears and . . . the face of a woman. (Brumana 1973, 66)

All that was needed to defeat the social epidemic of alcoholism and poverty, then, was for working-class women to ignore the minor detail of fatigue, from a long day spent working in the factory or at home, and to caress their husbands, speaking in a "soothing" voice. In contrast to Carolina Muzilli, who shared the culture of working women, Brumana represents the feminism of women who were financially well-off, completely detached from a multidimensional community whose diverse daily realities were impossible to embrace or represent as a whole. Here Brumana reveals her ignorance of the strained muscles in working bodies and her lack of consideration for deviations from the well-formed family, in spite of the fact that nonconventional families were far from unusual.

Differences of perception and different uses of time and space in the social world generate *programs of action* and *areas of interaction*. When daily life is understood in this way, it may be seen, as Rossana Reguillo points out, as characterized by zones of borrowings and exchanges—"intermediary," intersecting spaces where social exchange and even interpersonal conflicts, arising from differences of meanings and action, are negotiated and evaluated through the transfer of experiences. The potential "area of interaction" between the intellectual and the *obrera* is voided in Brumana's case, however, because Herminia simply has the latter act out a scenario (Brumana's scenario) involving soothing caresses from fingers still capable of tenderness, although worn out from work: "slowly, softly, and lovingly," Brumana instructs, the *obrera* caresses "the bowed head of the man who has come home from work ill-tempered and worried." And as if this were not enough, Brumana also charges the *obrera* with the task of eliminating alcoholism through a scene of laughter, kisses, and whispers that seem to have come directly from *modernista* imaginaries. It is not difficult to incorporate the beatific smile of María Lea Gastón herself into this scenario, as we imagine her delivering her speech to the LPA, exalting the examples of the "indefatigable and untiring" LPA Señoritas and the *obrera* who still stays behind at school after a soul-destroying day's work in the factory: "We run to class happily after working all day and there find our selfless teacher, who teaches us the glorious songs of our country while also instructing us in sewing. There we have learned to know God, of whom we were ignorant, our country, about which we knew nothing, [and] our first letters . . . to sew our clothes . . . to become, in effect, useful, contented women loving God, serving our country, and working happily" ("Comisión de Señoritas" 1922, 21). Two objectives are quite clear to María Lea: "to work," in order not to be like the idle and the wicked, who do not prosper "in this promised land," and "to work happily," singing conciliatory patriotic songs without the unyielding resentment of the anarchists and union activists. Such an imaginary of martyrdom became the social corrector against the sexual deviation, the taste for luxury, and the adultery represented by the femme fatale. One of Herminia Brumana's female characters sighs: "If women only knew the infinite pleasure of saving one whom others think of as evil! If they knew how sorrowful it is to find a good, good, good man for whom there is nothing to do but admire!" (1973, 52).

Alfredo Méndez Caldeira's appropriately titled drama *Sacrificio* (Sacrifice, 1922) is one of the many texts concerned with tensions between different models of female identity. In this play, a couple transfers to Buenos Aires because of the political future of the husband, Joaquín, who is a congressional deputy. The change is heavily accompanied by warnings ("everything is forgotten in the great capitals . . . and your heart has very little to do with life's functioning") and foreboding ("my heart foresees misfortune, and my heart is never wrong"). These somber tones undoubtedly prepare the audience for yet another trite story, all too familiar within the city's imaginaries. And indeed, the city's devastating effects are soon obvious in Luisa, who fails to remember her motherhood and delegates her responsibility to Aurora, the silent, selfless family retainer. An undisciplined "woman of fashion," Luisa is more likely to be found on Calle Florida than attending to her home. She and Aurora could not embody more opposite paradigms. Luisa goes from mother to insatiable consumer, spending hours at her dressing-table. She is a despotic coquette who is bored at the opera but attends anyway, just to show off her necklines. She is impassioned by the erotic fantasies of diastolic imaginaries, which resonate in the lascivious stares of her husband's friends. By contrast, Aurora is a counterweight to consumer culture, who educates the couple's child with wise sayings: "Good girls who have been brought up well are not interested in clothes." Aurora even gives Joaquín what little money she has saved for her dowry when he is on the verge of bankruptcy. Luisa consumes; Aurora deprives herself, thoughtfully and selflessly, sacrificing the possibility of marriage in order to cover the debts of a family not even her own. On top of this, she receives no payment for her services but is content with room and board. Such is the work ethic and the identitary space of women endured by Aurora in *Sacrificio:* "Why do I want [money]? Why do I need it? Don't I live in your house? Aren't my needs more than covered?" she asks Joaquín meekly. She incarnates motherhood as a blameless, selfless sacrifice/job, but not without the risk of being dismissed or fired by the real mother. Contrary to the imaginaries of self-absorption represented by Luisa, Méndez Caldeira's (melo)drama makes a saint of Aurora, who attends to the family's crises but pays no attention to the symptoms of a fatal illness in herself. Aurora's remark—"my heart foresees misfortune, and my heart is never wrong"—does in fact anticipate a collapse in moral and ethical values: in addition to committing adultery, Luisa goes so far as to sell her husband's political integrity for a lucrative posting in Madrid. The audience thus will evidently compare Luisa's fragmented world with the saintly pathway to heaven traced by Aurora. As E. Ann Kaplan would explain, the paradigm of "maternal sacrifice" is an attempt to restrain erotic fantasy through a patriarchal model of the feminine: "The ego-ideal for both sexes must be the Father, not the Mother, if desire is to be properly subject to the patriarchal Law" (1992, 91). *Sacrificio* suggests that men like Joaquín should be able to choose models of the female based on self-denial, including sexual self-denial. Aurora, for example, is a model of consummated/ sublimated asexuality. Like the Virgin Mary, she has not even lost her virginity, even though she is a mother.

Similarly, the female protagonist of Luis Rodríguez Acasuso's *La mal pagada* (A Woman Poorly Paid, 1937) is another model of social conduct. She is also named Aurora (meaning "dawn," the triumph of light over darkness), perhaps to clarify her affiliation with the "truth" of imaginaries that assert that women "should never abandon their post" or that women's "tenderness is, precisely, a counterweight to the dynamism of men" (Acasuso 1937, 6). Aurora "never leaves home." As a friend explains, "It troubles me to see her always shut in," not going to "theaters, dances, resorts, casinos." She is "a whitefly in an age of sporting, antipoetic women" (10). For Aurora's aunt to say, "the woman who has a husband should defend him tooth and nail" (16), allows us to infer the disquieting signs of turmoil to be found in the institution of marriage in "our turbulent times" (7). No one needs to defend what is not threatened, and in this case, the threat is Rosaura:

> AURORA: You [Rosaura] show up with your aura of elegance [and] world of adventure. . . . It certainly strikes the male imagination much more than the tender caresses and unfailing attentions of his wife. . . . She cannot compete in his fantasy with the other woman. (12)

The two women are not equally armed for the struggle. The femme fatale wields "the cynical arguments of the courtesan." She is "full of herself and such a vampire" (7). She is a figure of utter excess, oozing libido, the exact opposite of the paradigm represented by Aurora: "When we are very young, we women are blinded by our fantasies, which are embodied in our marriage, made dormant, or abandoned. It's not the same [for men]" (12); "It's human to grow tired of everything, even being happy" (12). A woman must smother and extinguish all fires of passion: "A woman who *loves seriously* . . . would find it difficult to disrupt the gentle rhythm of her home to fling herself into the whirlwind of lovers' arguments. . . . Above all, she reasons that even if she were successful in such a maelstrom of sentiments she would inevitably destroy her home, an argument that wins out over all her vanities, rights, and sorrows" (12; emphasis added). *Serious love,* and preserving "the gentle rhythm of her home" at all costs, are more important that a woman's "vanities, rights, and sorrows." They cause her to evade her own desires and to act as a counterweight to the disturbed imagination of the male.

The smoldering dilemma that anguished Buenos Aires at that time ("the age of adultery") is resolved in Aurora's case when she pardons her unfaithful husband: "I'm prepared to be understanding about everything, even the most humiliating aspects. But let's not break up our home. Think of our poor daughter sleeping nearby, a stranger to all this disgrace. Speak to me as a mother. In spite of it all, you [Enrique] never stopped being my child, my dear child" (Acasuso 1937, 28). The maneuver is as clear as it is effective. The desexualizing, desubjectivizing remedy of bourgeois morality counsels Aurora to forgive Enrique and make him her child. Now the stability of the family is guaranteed by a mother who suppresses her sorrow and rights as a woman and a husband/child who diminishes his insatiable desire for adventure in favor of a greater good: his children. Enrique repentantly exclaims in almost mystic ecstasy, "You are a saint!" (28). The Auroras of this world die as saints or live out their sanctity through forgiveness. If we were to come back down to earth for a moment, however, we would find some less than celestial subtexts: first, the economic wealth of a marriage threatened by the lavish spending of "that woman" (i.e., Rosaura) and her lover (Enrique), blinded by passion in a drama that emphasizes money matters even in its title (*La mal pagada* [A Woman Poorly Paid]); and second, imaginaries beginning to reek of the Church, dependent on a rhetoric of saints and sinners ready to repent. Against strong evidence of widespread adultery and confusing imaginaries of identity, *La mal pagada* promises women their reward in heaven "if they smile when wounded by stupidity . . . [and] hide their tears in the silence of their homes. They don't complain because their pain can only be cured by hope and by a love that is not of this world. They wait and wait forever without rebelling" (23).

Indeed, already by about 1920, it was possible to detect the widespread impact of the Church on the country's imaginaries. One *pieza de actualidad* (topical play), *La Santa Madre* (Holy Mother, 1920), by two leftist authors, José González Castillo and V. Martínez Cuitiño, takes place in the mansion of a socialist politician who has died, leaving his widow as the head of the household, responsible for his children from a previous marriage. When his son Eduardo returns from Paris, his attention is drawn to visits by members of the clergy and Catholic politicians, asking the widow for donations in money and property for "the true social defense undertaken by the Church at this time of uncertainty for the world." And their demands go further: "This home, saved by the will of God from disbelief, must defend itself against probable enemies. . . . The Church, our Holy Mother, needs homes like this one . . . in which to establish its foundations for social welfare. . . . Never has the Church been as threatened by skepticism and the dissolution of the family as it is today." Father Panard is alluding here to the social activism of the LPA. His purpose, with respect to the home, is to gradually intervene morally in the family (and, by extension, the country). His fully calculated plan is to remove the family from the clutches of the atheistic progressiveness taught by the dead socialist. The socialist's widow has already succumbed to the pressure of bishops and archbishops by sending the children to religious schools, thereby reversing the liberal spirit of the Law on Public Education.

The house will soon be "retaken" by "religious Machiavellianism," as the dead man's son Eduardo calls it. From morning until night, he finds priests conniving at winning over the widow, who has become "a servile, unconscious tool of the clergy" (19). This is not the moment for her stepson to be half-hearted: "At this particular time in the world, indecision is not the best condition. On the contrary, it's the most detrimental," Eduardo warns. During a time of shifting truths and powers, Eduardo's remarkable detection of the hidden currents that demand immediate reaction is historically accurate: "I reject dogmatism, I reject . . . conventional interpretations. . . . I reject politics in religion . . . the trafficking in faith! The church that wraps its principles in horror stories, that shrouds its practices in unverifiable dogmas, that hides from reason and science . . . that wants to govern, and seeks control and property is not a religion"(20). The stepson reproaches the widow for accepting influences alien to the house and imposing them "on persons who bear my father's name" (20). The debate in this "topical play" concerns the transfer of the dead socialist's ideological inheritance—Eduardo explains, "I'm not interested as much in my father's material inheritance as in his moral inheritance" (19)—and the right to preserve the political space of liberalism in the nation/home, while restraining the regressive advance of the political ultra-Right and the Church.

As they sought to monitor private life more closely in the disturbing polymorphism of the city, reactionary imaginaries began by uncovering the "weak" links. Any questioning of the status quo would be cut short, removed from the sight of the national audience by undermining the search for alternatives pursued by social agents interacting with the quotidian. In *La zarza ardiendo* (The Burning Bush, 1922), José González Castillo and Federico Mertens examine yet another melodramatic example of the social fragility of widowhood. The curtain rises to shock the audience with another suicide: that of María Antonieta, a wealthy widow who had married for the second time at age thirty-seven, to Gustavo, and who was the mother of the adolescent Emilia. A domestic love triangle involving stepfathers and stepdaughters was a topic frequently explored in dramas and *sainetes*. During this time of transition—1920s Buenos Aires—it was necessary to respond appropriately to the mobility of not-so-young widows, who were advised to take shelter in matrimony as soon as possible. But then it also became imperative to keep an eye on those who were living together behind closed doors, where they may well have exchanged glances and then drawn closer before intertwining their bodies in *amores equivocados* (misplaced loves):

> GUSTAVO: I confess my guilt. Emilia is as innocent as she is chaste and pure! . . . I love Emilia. . . . My affection is monstrous, criminal . . . but I've loved her for some time . . . since she began to bloom as a woman with the captivating spell of her beauty . . . temptation . . . instinct. This passion is like a hot, burning wind that passed over my soul and dried up every noble flower . . . leaving a dense growth of weeds and thorns in its passage.

The young woman feels the monstrous sexual desire of her stepfather in a way that so besieges and suffocates her, like a "stone on her chest," that she goes to the window breathless: "(*with a great sigh*) I need air . . . a lot of air." However, such is her youth, she cannot resist being "dominated by that strange force" that symbolically turns stepfather and stepdaughter into "mama's murderers":

> EMILIA: That man was not my father. . . . I felt drawn to him. . . . How often I felt spite, the pain of his kissing mama. . . . I wanted to feel my shame. . . . I wanted to tear that strange feeling from me . . . but I couldn't! . . . I loved Gustavo, I love him. . . . I condemned myself in my mother's eyes. . . . I'm as guilty as he for her suicide . . . but I can't run away, I cannot escape this cursed feeling. . . . Free me, Father! . . . I can't!

Her confessor advises her to flee from the house, but before the perversion is cleansed, the text focuses once more on the scene of forbidden love from the perspective of an eyewitness, a house servant:

> JUAN: I knew everything. . . . I saw his evil desire grow in him every day. . . . I've seen him since you were a child when he sat you on his knees and amused himself playing with your curly hair . . . with the pleasure of one who was kissing locks of burning hair. . . . I saw him, when you were grown up, kissing you on the mouth with unspeakable desires. . . . And I saw your mother, your poor mother, weeping in corners . . . swallowing her pain with tears that must have come from her terrible anguish.

Juan reveals the unspeakable passion of these intimate scenes (passion and ardor are the preserve of misguided love) to the audience of *La zarza ardiendo,* turning its members into voyeurs by triggering their morbid curiosity through a detailed account of bodily contact, the girl on her stepfather's lap. At the same time, the play converts the audience into a jury that sees the justice of the punishment for the stepfather's perversion and even extends it, perhaps, to penalize their own morbid eroticism. Emilia abandons her passion in the light of cold reason ("I've understood everything . . . it has all become clear to me"), while her stepfather opts for suicide. But this is not the end of that "bush growing on fallow land." "Our ignoble weed" is finally disposed of by the chilling specter of the dead woman herself, who "returns to claim her rights" and to throw cold water on the passions released on stage, not to mention any "bushes" still burning in the audience. Popular theater thus serves here as a searching gaze that penetrates the interior recesses of the home, revealing its secrets, shedding light on spaces where subjectivity might develop elusively, and posing those concerns that require the intervention of imaginaries set on social stabilization. *La zarza ardiendo* turns pleasure into a negative emotion. Given that passion may have a highly tragic and guilty edge, the drama gives more emphasis to its darker features than to possibilities for gratification.

Modernity in Buenos Aires opened up spaces and interstices allowing social practices to circulate, activating a profuse process of transfer and exchange between imaginaries. Everything was in full view. Bars set up their tables outside, their customers displayed in the vast showcase represented by the street. Misogynistic imaginaries trained the male gaze on female silhouettes, which women led men to appreciate by wearing close-fitting clothes and walking with the swaying, seductive gait absorbed by the choreography of tango, turning the public into a voyeur captivated by a stylized, suggestive foreplay. But the city's imaginaries were woven together in ambivalent and misleading directions. Love and desire were endorsed everywhere, but passion was a source of discomfort and always condemned, sooner or later. To live between such contradictory imaginaries must have been a truly schizophrenic experience: *mujeres de fuego* (women on fire)—smoldering embers—in contrast to purified women. Did *porteñas* have any intermediary identitary space of their own, a place more in tune with the maps of their own subjectivities?

In "Tú me quieres blanca" (You Wish Me White), from *El dulce daño* (Sweet Harm, 1916), Alfonsina Storni begins her search for such a place by challenging the socializing imaginaries embodied in Manuel Gutiérrez Nájera's "De blanco" (Dressed in White):

> You want me white
> You want me foam
> You want me pearl
> That I be a lily
> More chaste than any
> Softly perfumed
> A closed corolla. (Storni 1984, 91)

The privileges of the rakc, or *calavera,* who frequents orgies, bacchanalias, and "gardens / Dark with deception," are another matter. The lyric voice advises him:

> You who have held
> All the cups in your hand
> Of fruits and honey
> Your lips are stained . . .
> Flee to the mountains . . .
> Clean your mouth.

The women of Buenos Aires are scrutinized from head to toe, objects of patriarchal gazes of a stern and intensely claustrophobic containment. At least that is how Storni's speaker expresses the situation in "Siglo XX," in *Languidez* (Languor). The poetic voice is on the point of respiratory occlusion, fatally somatized, later, in Storni's suicide:

> I am being consumed alive
> Expending without doing anything
> Between the four symmetrical
> Walls of my house.

She pleads: "Hey, workmen! Bring your picks! / Let the walls and ceilings fall" (Storni 1984, 185). Space and posture are so predetermined (spending "the day lying down / watching from my room") they leave no room for participatory subjectivities and intersubjectivities to maneuver.

Female identity seems clumsily categorized, divided between Madonnas and Eves (Auroras and Luisas). By contrast, Alfonsina Storni had in mind women who were open to social borrowings and exchanges, surrendering to the bonds of social laterality and searching for their identity on the basis of the spontaneous unfolding of organic life:

> Woman: you the virtuous one, you the cynic,
> And you, indifferent or perverse;
> Let's look each other in the eye without fear. . . .
> We go about in our armor; if our soul
> Is too big, we cut it; if it doesn't fill
> Our armor because it is too small, then we swell it.
> We always go about with armor on our backs. (Storni 1984, 183)

What is most striking in this poem is the speaker's awareness of being enclosed in armor, fixed at the center of an identitary straitjacket that shapes and misshapes. Gender and social laterality are viewed as a way for the speaker to dismantle the triangulation induced by misogynous discourse and the rivalry fed by its gendered social geometry. Confronted with the identitary nonplace of asphyxiating walls (those of the home, of domesticity, and of socializing imaginaries), the poem proposes a sensorial/cognitive map allowing a search beyond the imprisonment of social classification. How is it possible to grow beyond the armor, or to find one's own shape within it? How is it possible to breathe? Claustrophobia is marked by a sudden sensation of losing hold of one of life's most basic biological guarantees: the ability to breathe. And yet, the claustrophobic's fear of suffocation is inseparable from the fear of restricted movement: "a) a small dark closet; b) breathing through a narrow straw, c) wearing a . . . mask that covers the entire face . . . d) lying in a construction that resemble[s] the bottom shelf of a bunkbed, and e) wearing a canvas bag that covers the torso, with an opening for the subject's head" (Rachman and Taylor 1993, 283). Wearing tight clothing or having difficulty moving (Storni's "armor") leads to desperation— desperation for air, for escape from confined spaces associated with a sensation of the imminent threat of death. Claustrophobia sufferers feel as if they are in an insecure, risky place. It is dark, without a visible exit, with pressure coming from above and from the sides, the walls closing in on the body. Such objective/subjective conditions cause tachycardia, parenthesia, tachypnea, and panic attacks, which the sufferer tries to avoid by running away (avoidance behavior).

Thus, Storni's writing and her troubled life, which ended in suicide on 25 October 1938, reveal the difficulty of finding space for flight. Indeed, prevailing imaginaries assembled an obscure identitary nonplace for odd *porteñas* such as her. The *milonguita*'s fear of the leap into the unknown combined symptoms of claustrophobia with those of agoraphobia. In fact, the sensorial/cognitive maps of Buenos Aires seem to have entangled the symptoms of agoraphobia and claustrophobia. The resulting anxiety attacks were set off by the combination of an unrelenting imperative to flee, to be able to breathe, and an unbearable fear of public spaces. The aggregate of these opposite, simultaneously experienced anxieties allows us to grasp the unsolvable nature of modernity's social spaces—what it felt like to live in Buenos Aires.

Miguel Mamone's *El obstétrico Fouschet* (Fouschet the Obstetrician, 1930) was published within months of the coup led by General José Uriburu that brought down the liberal government of Hipólito Yrigoyen. It takes place in a doctor's office visited by Flora. Several other young women also arrive at the office, and the audience soon realizes that it is part of an illegal abortion clinic. For eight years, it has served "hundreds and hundreds of young women coming to rid themselves of the stain of their sin" (Mamone 1930, 6). Clinics like this one must have appeared as chilling blots on the urban landscape to morality campaigns run by groups such as the LPA. Enrique Fouschet, a forty-five-year-old doctor and professor—an old man by the standards of the time—persuades his patients of his clinic's advantages: "There are countless people in Buenos Aires without professional scruples who constantly expose poor patients to grave risks" (6). And just to dispel any remaining hesitation in Flora's mind about the convenience of abortion, he adds:

> [Abortion allows a woman to avoid not only] the shame of her misfortune but also the physical exhaustion of being a mother. (*He sits beside her and takes her hand.*) An old-style moralist would talk to you differently, because they placed women in the following dilemma: either abstain or become a reproductive machine. . . . Both are lethal. . . . Stifling the instincts leads to serious organic disruption. . . . Motherhood exhausts, consumes, and withers women. . . . It would be a pity if you, for example (*smiling and looking at her directly*), . . . with your well-proportioned figure, . . . were to age so young. (6)

Flora must struggle with the paradox of being allowed to recover her "good reputation" through an abortion, but this is only the beginning of the tense moral dilemma she faces. The other side of Dr. Fouschet's argument is represented in the person of Dr. Gimigliano, a young physician working at the clinic in order to "achieve complete mastery of the scalpel," who reels in horror when he learns about the clinic's "criminal trade" (Mamone 1930, 9). The young doctor soon complicates Flora's decision to abort by wielding counterarguments that take issue with feminist discourse. He resorts to every argument he can muster, even a reference to the inhabitants of distant Sparta and the cliffs over which they cast physically defective newborn children. The child Flora expects will be a social defective because it will be born a bastard: "But it is unpardonable today for a being, still living in the womb, to be sacrificed to absurdly stupid social conventions. . . . Society doesn't forgive a sinful woman. . . . That's why it is in favor of loving purely, what we might call a hygienic love" (11). However, since "loving purely" is no longer possible for Flora, she must find shelter for herself in a discursive space. She must return to a time prior to the liberalizing culture of modern women, to "an earlier time, when we had not yet reached our civilized century," and embrace the traditional model of maternity (11). Gimigliano ironically comments that today's civilized age "is no more than a time of corruption in which the condition of women is worse than in the most backward periods of history" (11). The evidence of abortion in the liberal city is just one more example of the countless deformities caused by an overly permissive society: "It would be a crime not to perform a single gesture, one magnificent gesture, to show society your fertile womb where a new life is growing. . . . You must know that when every woman reaches this point, she is carrying a sacred mission and that mission is maternity. . . . To face life bravely, standing up to the scorn of hypocrites and prudes through the sublime gesture of being a mother" (12).

Gimigliano asks Flora for gestures and great deeds, to fulfill a magnificent, sacred mission. He even sublimates her pregnant body, urging her to avoid abortion and give birth: "You assume all the value of a symbol" (Mamone 1930, 12). Thus far, Flora is caught between two arguments: Dr. Fouschet's contention that maternity exhausts, withers, and ages the body, and Dr. Gimigliano's claim that motherhood elevates a woman—two males pushing for control over her body, regardless of her fears about the future. Gimigliano overlooks the social stigma that Flora's child will carry as a bastard, stressing that the child will find disfavor "only in the eyes of the law and society, not in the woman who bore and raised him" (12). The young doctor's speech is opportunely seconded by a hair-raising cry of pain from the operating room close by: "Señorita Castelar, removing a stain from her honor," he explains to Flora (11).

Miguel Mamone's work predisposes the audience *somewhat* negatively toward Dr. Fouschet by explaining that he is from France and therefore bears the marks of vice, sexual anarchy, and perversion on his face, given how France had come to be perceived by the systolic imaginaries in full sway. More to the point, audiences of *El obstétrico Fouschet* must have been simply petrified by the unusual scene in which the obstetrician's assistant, syringe in hand, "without flinching, as if he were accustomed to it, withdraws the liquid [morphine] from the vial and injects it into Fouschet's forearm" (Mamone 1930, 7). And that is not all: Dr. Fouschet seals the extortion of his patients with a satisfaction expressed in demonic laughter. This unscrupulous doctor does not perform abortions in support of feminist claims, but for money and pleasure, two signifiers demonized by descriptions of the (dystopian) liberal city in regressive, systolic imaginaries. In addition to laughing too much and too loudly, the doctor is an alcoholic and a morphine addict who has been unfaithful to his wife with innumerable patients. His new prey, Flora, "that crazy little girl," "that little dove I like so very much," will soon experience, as the audience has expected, the "fear and loathing" caused by a man "choking with desire," "drooling lasciviously," who "forcibly takes her in his arms," holds her tightly, and squeezes her while he shouts wildly: "Like this! . . . This is how I like you! . . . In my arms! . . . You'll be mine! . . . Yes! . . . Mine! . . . Mine! . . . Mine!" (14). The young woman manages to break free when others enter the scene. She asks to be removed from "that lair," far from this horrid, repugnant individual drooling over her: this "evil man! . . . a common criminal!" Yet she is soon sufficiently composed, resolved to have the "courage to show my guilt to the world! . . . Courage to cry out to society the sublime right to be a mother. And I must thank you [Dr. Gimigliano], because I did not follow through with my criminal intention, because you made me understand that it was monstrous to kill a child" (14).

Dr. Fouschet is associated with a broad spectrum of vices (drug addiction, sexual abuse, money, extortion, marital infidelity), as well as a calamitous lack of professional ethics. Not all doctors are the same: while Fouschet represents what it is to be an abortionist, Gimigliano and the author himself, also a doctor, are of quite a different color. Miguel Mamone invokes his own professional standing in order to support his fight against abortion, writing with an authority endorsed by his clinical practice. By 1930, the paradigm of free love and the right to abortion were seen as objectionable practices arrived from Paris, just like Fouschet. The text opposes the forty-five-year-old foreigner with a new young nationalist generation, which practices medicine ethically and with a moral purpose. In this "realist drama," the violence escalates so intensely that in the final scene, the abortionist is about to strangle his wife and is prevented only by the arrival of the police. The purpose of social control and vigilance in Mamone's text is for Flora to find a true refuge in maternity, removed from the detestable world of abortion clinics and other insidious trends that lead to a rejection of "the sublime right of motherhood." What, however, is the background here? In what does Mamone's play intervene?

Abortion, in fact, was not accessible to all social classes. And yet the sudden emergence of women into the public sphere, the new sociosexual practices, the lack of a culture of contraception, and feminist discourses on libertarianism made the outcome of unwanted pregnancies a cause for concern. All that and something else, as Gimigliano explains:

GIMIGLIANO: I've just read about a housemaid in the newspaper who strangled her baby girl after she gave birth.

FLORA: That's a monstrous crime, doctor!

GIMIGLIANO: Monstrous is the word for it. . . . The crime pages are full of events like that.

FLORA: And they always happen to poor people.

GIMIGLIANO: That's understandable. . . . People like that don't have the money to go to places like this. . . . What about you, are you prepared to undergo an operation? (Mamone 1930, 11)

The young doctor equates abortion with infanticide, new causes of social anxiety with old. In effect, nineteenth-century big-city newspapers were full of reports of infanticide—another of the new crimes in the burgeoning cities, monitored and apprehensively condemned by the judicial system and in the crime pages of newspapers. Where medicine could not explain it, however, other discourses intervened to account for this deviant, asocial behavior among women. The most conventional explanation could be found in *La mala reputación* (Bad Reputation, 1935), by José González Castillo and José Mazzanti.

In this drama, Clarisa is a secretary who shamefully admits her pregnancy and is questioned by César, the brother of her lover and employer:

CLARISA: The guilt is mine alone! . . . I'm the one who can't be forgiven.

CÉSAR: You know, you are turning out to be a very colorful woman? Why don't you kill yourself? Good heavens! You get on my nerves with how stupidly you give in. . . . What are you victims saving your courage, resolve, or violence for? . . . Shout for your rights! Cry out for your own destroyed life! . . . Be mothers, be women, be vengeful if you need to! Above all, be a warning against the cowardice that makes you give birth unhappily! A child should never be a matter of guilt, misfortune, or shame. A child is a right claimed in the mother's womb itself. (González Castillo and Mazzanti 1935, 10)

Clarisa accepts her guilt (extramarital sexuality has inconvenient consequences), and her virtuous conduct moves César to marry her. As his brother withdraws from the scene and rejects his paternity, César steps forward to wrap the shattered pieces of bastardy in a matrimonial embrace. At the same time, the play joins together several other loose threads. César, the typical *bacán,* has never before settled down and even abandoned a young pregnant woman in the past.[5] Now, however, he says, "In you and your child I can pay my past debts" (32), while Clarisa can claim her right to be a mother.

A *folletín* published in *Caras y Caretas* on 4 January 1908, entitled "El santo de Manolito" (Manolito's Saint), reacted against abortion as an option for the lower classes. In spite of working night and day washing clothes, here a single mother, who would not enjoy the protection of a repentant César, still has the strength to sing to her child: "If I've had a child I won't deny it, / for I was always unfortunate. / Let the world say how much I love him. / I'll always adore him madly." Seduced by the landowner's son, this mother fled to the unfamiliar city and, once resigned to accepting the feminine imperative of maternity, made a "sublime" sacrifice, which helped her resolve the contradiction of bearing a child who was "at the same time the source of her misfortune and her joy." With her eyes overcome by fatigue, in the desolation of her tiny, wretched garret, alone in the world, with no other company save that of her child, the young woman is the perfect *folletín* heroine. What, however, was to be done in the real world, where motherhood was not associated with purity and self-denial, but with rejection, the feeling of an unbearable burden, deviation, and especially violence, as in the case of infanticide?

María Gabriela Ini points out that social breakdown and infanticide were explained in the medical/psychological discourse with reference to "the complex and weak physiology of women" and to forms of social exclusion that were historically linked to witches and single mothers. Infanticide was defined as a *crimen de mujeres* (female crime), considered in the penal code as "the desperate act of women trying to safeguard personal and family honor" (Ini 2000, 239). Ini specifies that the women affected were poor, unmarried, and young, often housemaids or other members of the working class—in other words, mainly proletarian women without the resources to obtain an abortion. Poverty and its social symptoms provoked something more than disapproving looks in the big cities at a time when the new crimes were a source of bewilderment. On 19 January 1901, for example, *Caras y Caretas* commented on a "horrible drama" that had thrown "criminologists into a virtually sterile state of reflection." This was the case of "an eight-year-old girl who murdered another girl, aged two and a half," in Arremetières, a working-class suburb of Paris. Readers of the weekly's local-crime pages would have found it easy to transfer the urban geography of the Parisian suburb to their own city and thence to explain the agency of the crime, in the same way that Gimigliano explains the monstrous crime committed by a *porteña* housemaid by pointing to her social extraction.

What was the specific "truth" endorsed by such a discourse? It explains the crime in terms of the "natural" weakness of women, as a social evil derived from poverty, against which all the efforts of science were feared useless. With the morbidity of one poring over the details of a shameful and unspeakable subject, his mind closed to any form of enquiry, the dismayed *Caras y Caretas* columnist takes in the chilling details of the murder committed by the French girl and sets out to criminalize poverty by brandishing the notion of predetermined genetic conditions: "What brain of a man hardened to crime is contained in the skull of that eight-year-old girl?" Infanticide was perhaps the thorniest challenge posed to both inherited knowledge and the new scientific truths. As Ini argues, juridical clemency depended on the degree of shame shown by an accused woman (2000, 239). The more contrition she felt for her dishonor as evidence of some residual maternal feelings, the more likelihood there was of clemency. By attempting to escape the *noche social* (social darkness) of being a single mother and of giving birth to a bastard child, women who committed infanticide were drawn more deeply into the web of surveillance and punishment and were then used as cautionary arguments against active sexuality outside the bounds of marriage.

Ini cites *Criminal Law and Colonial Subject,* by Paula Bryne, who claims that "the bodies of female criminals and their history are open to public discussion; their bodies, their sexuality, and their person objects of scrutiny" (Ini 2000, 246). Such discursive practices in social control, punishment, and particularly public exposure—for example, forcing women to stand naked

Muñecas Bravas *of Buenos Aires*

in public—sought the "objective" and "neutral" arbitration of the state in order to execute sanctions against those women considered dangerous to society. The law, in conjunction with the press, would take the matter in hand. There were now "new" and stronger reasons than ever for seeing women as bodies that necessarily had to be subjected to suspicion and scrutiny for the purpose of punishment. Let us recall how the bodies of the prostitute, the wet nurse, and female "deviants," studied by socially habilitated voyeurs in the name of science and the law, were scrutinized in literature, medical photographs, and public health reports. Under the patriarchal gaze of medicine, the state, and the law, infanticide was a crime *contranatura*—against nature, entirely beyond comprehension within traditional, "natural" mechanisms of classification. And since social classification was thought of as "natural," rather than cultural, any "truth" underlying infanticide could not be heard or highlighted, because to hear it would have distracted from the enormity of the crime.

Since women were capable of crimes against nature, contrary to every societal rule, it was a terrible mistake to assume they were "naturally" inclined toward maternity. The law and the state were therefore "forced" to monitor bodily behavior much more closely and to oversee *cabezas locas* (crazy-headed women). Otherwise, what other unthinkable surprises from women and girls with inconceivable tendencies might unfold? What else might be lying in wait for the social body in Buenos Aires? But how was it possible to control, prevent, and remedy so "monstrous" a deviancy growing inside the private spheres of the city? Making the female body "public," and pointing to the consequences of decisions based on difference, subjectivity, personal interest, and excess, was perhaps the best way to contend with the complex task of standing guard over private life. Josefina Ludmer explains that, as a literary motif, crime produces fictions that "leave the criminal without a voice" (1993, 145). The criminal's utterance then becomes a sort of radical "foreignness" that legal discourse must stigmatize and deprive of "discursive descendant," voice, appeal, or explanation. Alien to the "truth" of institutional imaginaries, such utterances are to be expelled unheard, subject to malediction.

"Delicias de la paternidad" (Delights of Fatherhood), published on 26 March 1904, centers on the plight of an exhausted man who has recently become a father: "This child should be my delight / but drives me crazy / crying from nightfall / until the new day begins":

I fall into bed exhausted . . .
and he is waiting cruelly
to awaken
just when I have fallen asleep. . . .
I shout at him and he doesn't stop
but he exasperates me and forces me
to tell him in fury:
you ugly, shameless wretch!

The father spends a sleepless night "cursing my luck," the victim of a "worrying, irritating, diabolical" child whose distress is tolerable to its mother but beyond the father's cultural comprehension. How can he silence the child? "How many times have I thought, / beside myself with irritation, / of throwing him off the balcony." The illustration accompanying the poem (figure 22) shows the child's father, to the mother's horror, holding up the baby, ready to throw it violently through the window. And here there is some room for reflection: if the law is so implacably against infanticide, why make a joke of something so shocking? Why were conditions that led a parent to think of infanticide a source of humor, but only when the father was involved? And, further, why not take the occasion to recognize the exhausting work of a mother, now that the male parent has finally had to deal with it?

I believe that the law imposed punishments and controls as an afterthought, responding to the imposition of an entirely abstract, romanticized, and compulsive model of motherhood that real women in Buenos Aires and elsewhere found difficult to uphold in their everyday experience. As Reguillo states, when the structures of "plausible" (acceptable) conduct fail or go into crisis, a misalignment or break occurs between practice and structure—that is to say, in "systems of perception, evaluation, and action in the social world" (1998, 101). Empirical practice finds no echo in the symbolic universe. Hence, in a Buenos Aires undergoing so much transition, admonishing imaginaries were called on to pronounce their verdict and their punishment for social deviation and to soothe the anxieties and tremors thrown up by "accidents" in an organic and unpredictable everyday reality.

According to the patriarchal property rights written into the Civil Code of 1869, women were subjected to the authority of their father until the age of twenty-two or to their husband's authority if they were married. They were required to obey their husband or father, to live with them, and to obtain their permission for any commercial or legal activity. They had no rights of child custody unless they were widowed, and they lost these rights if they remarried. The state and the law were concerned with women who fell beyond the reach of those intent on supervising the civil status of single women, married couples, and widows. What was to be done with the population of the formless grotesque city, which increasingly escaped oversight and classification and could then claim that its sociosymbolic configurations were not in fact formless but had other forms? While wet nurses had to hide their children in order not to lose their jobs, single working women or housemaids who became pregnant feared dismissal because of the moral sanctions against lost honor. If working-class women chose to give birth, like the single mother in the *folletín* "El santo de Manolito," they could not normally count on a network of support, allowing them to care for their children, because families were constantly fragmented by the economic precariousness and hardships of the time. As a result, the emerging world of the proletariat ended up serving the polarizing imaginaries of the ruling bourgeoisie, concerned only with profiling its own enlightening "truth," in sharp contrast to the darkness of poverty and shame attributed to working-class social cases.

"La mujer en la cárcel" (Women in Jail), an account published in *Caras y Caretas* on 18 January 1908, describes the horrors of prison, where "one is overwhelmingly struck by the sight of *the irresponsibility of women*" (original emphasis). One of the article's photographs, entitled "Una infanticida antes de la condena" (Infanticide before Sentencing) (figure 23), shows an adolescent, no more than a girl, barely past puberty, staring at the camera, totally unaware of the process that will condemn her to a life behind bars. The reporter describes the "horrible cells, the dreadful rags," the isolation, and the "deafening silence." Then, drawing a comparison that flagrantly contradicts his thesis on *irresponsabilidad femenina* (the irresponsibility of women), he equates the inmates with "the child who calmly and cruelly plucks the feathers off a bird he has picked up, without understanding that he is causing it to die in terrible suffering." If women prisoners can be forgiven their lack of awareness and their childlike nature, why claim they are legally responsible? In effect, the reporter has a single agenda: contending that working-class women must be closely supervised because of their inconsistent behavior and immaturity: "Because of their weakness, anything at all can lead them to disaster. Either they are impulsive, led on by an overbearing sensuality, or victims of an inescapable atavistic inheritance. . . . Few of them have been convicted solely because they are evil or perverse, and many of those that were are tormented by guilt." If their "atavistic inheritance" was "inescapable," this was not the case with respect to the general condition of weakness among women or the lapses caused by an "impulsive," compulsive, and "overbearing sensuality" that ended in murder. By this point, the discourse wielded in the article has come far, having associated "criminality" and the "dreaded prison cells" with a sexuality outside the limits of patriarchal institutions: free sex is equal to abortion, murder of the fruit of the womb, which leads to life imprisonment.[6] From free sexuality to murder.

Why was so much attention paid to infanticide? Why was so much morbidity displayed in prosecuting a crime so narrowly defined as a *crimen de mujeres*? Arguably, highlighting this practice publicly was perhaps the most powerful way to demonize women. Among all the possible representations, why were women so overwhelmingly and viciously linked to infanticide and thereby to one of the most incomprehensible forms of *nocturnidad social*, to the darkest social margin of the time? Infanticide attracted a depth of ill feeling that recalls the treatment meted out to a fallen *milonguita*. As Ludmer points out, justice has an additional moment that the criminal lacks. In discursive positions, justice is both first and last. It is first because it exploits the advantages provided by dispositions laid out beforehand in written law, its verdicts, and its truth. It is last because it condemns and curses the guilty and makes them bear the consequences. The criminal may say what he pleases, "because he says it from his lower status outside the law," but the state and its institutions have the last word. It could be said that the subaltern is spoken of from a discursive position of intolerance, which rejects everything of which it is ignorant, ill prepared to understand, and unwilling to take either the time or the opportunity to examine thoroughly. All the unknown darkness that this position prefers not to understand, and that it deposits in an other(ness) in the form of shame, is the excess that overflows from the law's own paradigm and the limitations of its capabilities. In fact, the "truth" it seeks to impose and preserve is the self-legitimation of its own consolidated paradigms. As Jacques Donzelot points out, "the modern family is not so much an institution as a *mechanism*. It is through the disparity of the familiar configuration (the working class and the bourgeois polarity), the variance of individual interests, and the family interest that this mechanism operates" (1979, 94; original emphasis). Donzelot reads the moralizing program of the European bourgeoisie and its social technologies as the transition "from a government of families to a government through the family" (92).

In Argentina, faced by a dizzily complex social reality that defied preestablished patterns and contradicted all suppositions, the state, the law, and the imaginaries fueled by both of them declared that the world of the proletariat was a deviant ecology, crying out to the modern state for intervention regarding its immorality, its threat to public health, its gross deficiency in matters of hygiene, the blight of its housing, the crudity of its body language, the grotesqueness of its dances, the impropriety of its sexuality, the incomprehensibility of its social deviations (*casos sociales*), and even its smells. However, the bourgeois family in Buenos Aires was not entirely a panacea of morality. As depicted in *La mal pagada,* ruling-class males were also weak and also went off the rails. The foundations of morality would have to retreat, to be safeguarded somewhere else, far from the political and cultural permissiveness left behind by liberal adventurism. But where could they retreat to? The examples suggest saintly, sexless women who persist in pardoning their husbands' infidelity, but who nonetheless block the advance of the "truth" that women are as sexualized as men and put a stop to divorce and other feminist issues taken up in parliamentary debates and individual proposals, seen as a source of jeopardy to the unity of the family. Such issues had already appeared in a remarkable drama by José González Castillo, *Hermana mía . . .* (My Sister . . . , 1925), which proposed "a more positive education so that . . . [women] would be of value in themselves without needing the protection of a man . . . whether a husband or someone else." The play argues in favor of "the protection of laws granting civil status"; "institutions that defend . . . [the] rights of free [women] . . . [and] judgments that grant them equality"; "the granting of rights rather than obligations . . . [and] laws that consolidate justice" (González Castillo 1925, 8).

In my opinion, women in transitional Buenos Aires were spaces where the organic, the private, and the social intersected, where the imperatives of biological reproduction, medical/state control, and cultural recruitment by a patriarchal Church became tensely entangled. Compliance with the law (through marriage, monogamy, fidelity, heritage, and social conventions) implied the eradication of those social blights that daily life and the formless fluidity of the grotesque city had begun to spawn in spite of (or because of) noninclusive social classifications and decisions, such as the association of abortion with crime and infanticide with *monstruosidad* (monstrosity). The bodies of *milonguitas, cabareteras,* and prostitutes were the spaces of garbage and waste. The body of the *planchadora* (presser) was a map of tormented muscle, tensed and knotted by the twelve daily hours she spent on her feet, ironing clothes. A female body at large on a city street provoked sexual violence or was designed and restrained by the "armor" carefully assembled by the dream industries or by the uncertainties and anxieties endemic to a city in severe transition. Between that silent and fleeting passage where the anonymity of daily life breathes, and the space where social messages and private maps intersect, lies perhaps the clue that explains the alarming suicide rate among women. In the immense cruelty of the labor and social cultures of Buenos Aires, the proletarian woman's body was controlled by regulations stemming from Taylorism. She was also expected to be a receptacle for the male sex, which made her both a recipient of misogynistic fears and anxieties and a palliative intended to soothe feeble masculine identities. At the other extreme were either Darío's languid princesses, absorbed by their reading in cozy rooms decorated in pastel shades, or saintly women with short memories messianically dedicated to reproduction. The female body was tensed/woven by work, leisure, desire, rupture, continuity, and negotiation.

In the "truth" endorsed by *Sacrificio* (1922) and *El obstétrico Fouschet* (1930), tightly knitted bonds already announced the eruption of fascism in the political and cultural life of Argentina, long before the liberal government of Hipólito Yrigoyen was overthrown by a military coup on 6 September 1930. In *La Santa Madre* (1920), Eduardo gives meaning to the national scenario, based on such an awareness. The protagonist in this drama, by José González Castillo and Vicente Martínez Cuitiño, shrewdly reads the advance of the political ultra-Right and the Church in the struggle to define what life should be like. His most illuminating statement is, "Don't let it matter to you what people say, but what each of you does." As an agent and interpreter of daily life, he knows that the private is also political and that daily strategies and individual practices from inside the Nation House may intersect with social reproduction. The text records two significant moments: first, the "reflection" and "evaluation" of social actors concerning their own domestic and everyday environments/milieu; and second, the reaction of other social actors, who denounce attempts at social reproduction once they realize that structures of domination have moved forward and thus seek to reshape both the public sphere and private settings, where the flow of everyday life seems deceptively least offensive. As a social actor, Eduardo confronts a rising social and political imaginary that contends "that institutions are immutable, that the current structure is not susceptible to change, that every attempt at evolving toward a more harmful form of human activity brings serious dangers." The socialist Eduardo warns against the ideology of *continuismo*.[7] As a way of counteracting this ideology, he suggests listening to what the ruptures and alternatives emerging from the maps of personal subjectivities are seeking and proposing.

The Nightmare (1782–90?), Johann Heinrich Füssli

The factory: Order and silence (Archivo General de la Nación, 1912)

L'Heure du Rimel (Archivo General de la Nación, 1925)

Untitled watercolor, Sylvain Sauvage (Archivo General de la Nación, 1925)

Obrera at work (Archivo General de la Nación, 1922)

Obrera at work (Archivo General de la Nación, n.d.)

Pressers at the steam iron (Archivo General de la Nación, ca. 1905)

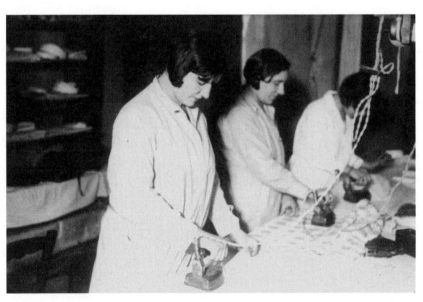

Pressing with electric irons (Archivo General de la Nación, 1929)

Jewelry-store employees (Archivo General de la Nación, 1922)

Interior of notions store (Archivo
General de la Nación, 1924)

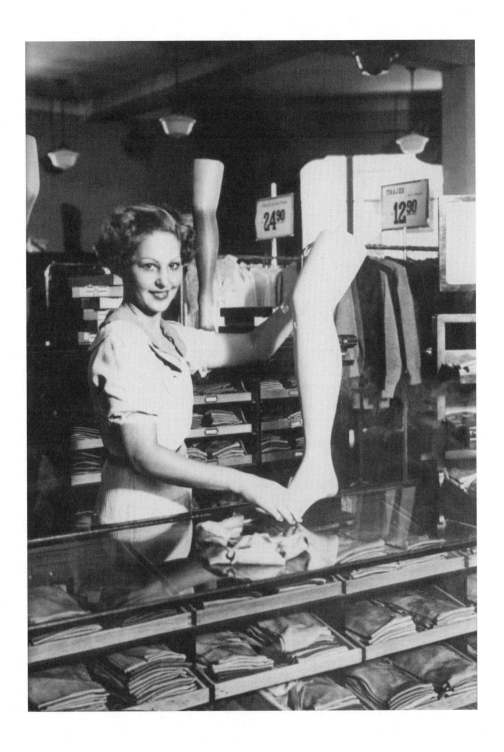

The delights of fatherhood (*Caras y Caretas,* 26 March 1904)

Infanticide before sentencing (*Caras y Caretas,* 18 January 1908)

14 NEW ALLIANCES—
OLD CAUSES

It was Saenz Peña's electoral reform that made Hipólito Yrigoyen's first government possible (1916–22), at the head of a new working- and middle-class political clientele. According to Otto Vargas, the arrival of the Unión Cívica Radical (UCR; Radical Civic Union) staved off the impact of a highly militant workers' movement without bringing about substantial changes. Yrigoyen never repealed the Residency Act (1902) or the Social Defense Act (1910), just as he never adopted policies to rein in the landowning oligarchy. On the contrary, his government included "five ministers who were members of the Sociedad Rural," drew on the support of Joaquín de Anchorena and Manuel Carlés, and turned a blind eye to the activities of right-wing unions and para-police organizations such as the LPA and the Asociación del Trabajo (Labor Association) (Vargas 1999, 21).[1] But the action that most revealed Yrigoyen's ability to maneuver in the turbulent political arena of the time was his suppression of worker militancy. The marines brutally put down strikes at the Armour and Swift packing plants in 1917, while the army perpetrated both the Semana Trágica massacres and the 1921 repression in Patagonia. Further, as Otto Vargas comments, Yrigoyen's first government coincided with "a rise in the cost of living and a drop in real incomes, which in 1918 were at the lowest they would be for the first forty years of the century. In 1919, the average wage for industrial workers . . . was 90.46 pesos [a month], while the average family budget . . . was 191.81" (1999, 23). As a result, the number of unionized workers grew. The Federación Obrera de la República Argentina (FORA; Argentinean Labor Federation) increased its affiliates from 3,427 in 1916 to 12,233 in 1917 and 35,726 in 1918. A total of 66 unions joined in 1915 and 166 in 1918. FORA added organizations for quebracho cutters and workers' associations from yerba maté plantations and Patagonian ranches.[2] Teachers throughout the country, along with state employees, millers, stevedores, railway workers, and tannin and leather workers, were among its first members. The trail of political activism sprung from Buenos Aires's factories and industries was spreading across the country's political map.

In 1917, writing in "La desocupación en la Argentina. Actual crisis del trabajo" (Unemployment in Argentina: The Current Labor Crisis), Alejandro E. Bunge wondered: "Has economic activity in the country positively absorbed that enormous wave of immigration by integrating it definitively into the labor market and production? Will the country be able to continue absorbing such a great number of immigrants? Until 1910, there was no reason to suppose otherwise. Our productivity and the future of the country, according to many, rested in the first place on an abundance of manpower. But productivity did not grow at the same rate" (1917, 4). Bunge was right to be concerned, because productivity in construction and related industries had begun to decline in 1910, unlike the number of immigrants entering the country, which remained at earlier levels. By 1914, the evidence of surplus manpower could be seen every day. As Bunge remarks, for example, the demand for home-based labor (constituting 22 percent of the workforce) was showing such a drop that workers were "idle for more than three or four days a week" (18). Yet this enforced stoppage was not recorded by surveys, which focused more on unemployment among those who worked outside the home (78 percent of the workforce). Bunge was skeptical of official census procedures, still in their infancy, but the precarious state infrastructure and the absence of labor organizations that might corroborate results did not prevent him from pointing out the "painful personal consequences of unemployment" lying at the heart of the matter. More important, one particular aspect of the unemployment figures cited by Bunge would significantly impact what followed: 82 percent of the workforce were men, 12 percent women, and 6 percent minors; of a total of 414,000 unemployed, "340,000 were men, 49,000 women, and 25,000 minors."

The events of 1919 are a milestone in the political history of Argentina. The Semana Trágica revolved around a strike by metallurgical workers from the Talleres Pedro Vasena factory, at the intersection of Cochabamba and Rioja, who were asking for a workday reduction, from eleven to eight hours; Sundays off; incremental wage increases; and the reinstatement of workers dismissed over labor conflicts. We can infer the combative nature of the unions from the name by which they were known at the time: "resistance groups" (sociedades de resistencia). The strikers' protest was violently broken up, leaving seven dead on its first day (7 January 1919) and marking the beginning of one of the nation's most dramatic confrontations between labor and capital.

In 1914, 59 percent of the working class were foreigners, who had brought political activism with them from their countries of origin. The end of the nineteenth century witnessed the rise of a vigorous union network, as evinced by the 1904 election of Alfredo Palacios as the Socialist Party's first parliamentary representative. Until the advent of Yrigoyen (1916), the state had functioned as an extension of the interests of the dominant class and thus as an impediment to organized worker movements. The Residency Act and the Social Defense Act had been promoted under the vigilant eye of the National Autonomy Party, which served the interests of the elite. Therefore, the rise of the populist/bourgeois UCR seemed to usher in a period of goodwill between the state and the working class. However, Yrigoyen must have felt the conservatives constantly at his back. His government's self-proclaimed dedication to more evenhanded administration of justice and the political integration of workers seemed to turn a page, to mark a shift away from the conservative regime, but the agenda of the Grupo Azul (Blue Group) was not long in surfacing at the very heart of the UCR, as an internal oligarchical/populist opposition led by Yrigoyen's successor, Marcelo T. de Alvear. Caught between labor conflicts, criticism from external opposition, internal dissidence, and pressures from corporations, especially English capital interests, Yrigoyen began to relinquish the role of the state as a neutral arbitrator, an attitude that subsequently led to two unprecedented trials by fire, the Semana Trágica and the bloody repression in Patagonia.

In 1917, the postwar economic crisis caused standards of living and working conditions to worsen. By 1918, unemployment had reached 10.8 percent (*Revista de economía argentina,* 1920; qtd. in Godio 1972, 14), and the total number of strikes in 1919 was 367. Strikes in Germany, Italy, and Great Britain, and the triumph of the October Revolution in Russia, filled the headlines every day in Argentinean anarchist newspapers, such as *La Protesta* (Protest) and *Bandera Roja* (Red Flag), and in the socialist *La Vanguardia.* *La Prensa,* one of the voices of the oligarchy, raised warnings about the anarchists (*maximalistas*) but, given the possibility that "worker discontent" might lead to "mass revolutionary action" (Gobio 1972, 15), was cautious enough to propose satisfying the claims of the working class within reasonable boundaries. Thus, in January 1919, the working class, now organized into two large worker organizations (FORA chapter 9, FORA chapter 5), entered the political climate of a country through which the winds of social progress and political representation were blowing, believing that the Conservative Order of 1880–1916 had been left behind.

According to *La Vanguardia,* Semana Trágica casualties amounted to seven hundred dead and two thousand injured by 14 January, while *La Nación* reported one hundred dead and more than four hundred injured. Julio Godio remarks that these numbers show how difficult it was to cover up the violence of the conflict, since they were reported by a newspaper controlled by the elite and therefore prone to reduce the number of proletarian dead. Strike leaders were pursued by the police, and anarchists became targets of the LPA, along with Jews, Germans, Russians, and Poles. Acting in "defense of national identity," the LPA viciously singled out those suspected of being *maximalistas* simply because they were "foreigners" (Godio 1972, 79). The brutal raids on proletarian barrios produced a total of fifty thousand arrests in the course of the week. Anarchists, along with activists and Jews, were murdered with impunity by xenophobic ultra-rightists, while heated parliamentarians rushed to adopt unprecedented measures, such as the declaration of a state of siege, approved with the support of members of the Radical Party, which was in power.

Promoted by the senator and writer Miguel Cané in 1899, the Residency Act was a core piece of political legislation intended "to safeguard social peace compromised by movements that were essentially subversive, not those of the . . . honorable worker or the honorable foreigner . . . but those [that promoted] violent unrest, excess, and disturbances . . . [by] individuals living within the working masses in order to exploit them, thereby abusing the generous hospitality the country has offered them" (qtd. in Oved 1978, 262). The act was intended to discourage proletarian political activism, already identified as criminal in reactionary imaginaries. The law thus redrew the social map of the nation by excising the pustule of foreign elements, whose political activism was considered dishonorable, even a betrayal of the shelter generously proffered in their new home. Miguel Cané's law equipped the state with executive police measures for implementing persecution, arrests, imprisonment, deportation, and the death penalty, its way earlier paved in the nationalist imaginary by the pungent discursive excisions of Eugenio Cambaceres's novel *En la sangre* (1887). Then, in 1910, Cané's law was endorsed even further by the Social Defense Act, which tightened the means of surveillance of foreigners and charged them with being a danger to society.

In "Después de la huelga" (After the Strike), published on 13 January 1919, *La Nación* linked the Semana Trágica with "provocateurs coming from everywhere . . . cast to the winds from their sources in Europe, fishermen on a tumbling river." *Caras y Caretas* likewise argued, on 18 January, that the unaccustomed violence was due "not just to the combination in this movement of workers fighting to impose a sheet of conditions, or socialists wanting to bring about the triumph of what they believed was their just cause, but [to] that element that has no country. . . . We mean the thugs, those men without any kind of social discipline." *Caras y Caretas* here separated the wheat from the chaff, the worker from the criminal. It printed photos tracing the violence that had begun in the streets and then invaded private spaces: "State of a neighborhood barbershop"; "Wall of a house on Calle Piperí where a resident was killed"; "Group trying to get bread at any cost from the bakery at Piedras 443." A society that had considered itself secular suddenly appeared to defend the interests of the Church: "Interior of the Church of the Eucharist attacked by mobs who burned it down and left no altar standing"; "Church of the Eucharist after the blaze; the priest's vestments are seen on the ground"; "Charred figure of Christ and piano played by attackers as they discharged their weapons before breaking it to pieces." Moreover, the rioters had even entered a girls' orphanage: "Dormitory of inmates of Home of Jesus College. Mr. Ciresa, who appears in the photo, is one of the neighbors who looked after some of the girls at the time of the attack."

It became essential to control the interpretation of chaos and to draw attention to "healthy segments of the country." This "health" was the "truth" the editorial writer for *Caras y Caretas* sought to establish by deflating the Semana Trágica massacre and redirecting collective memories toward areas untouched by the strike. A report entitled "Las simpáticas y activas telefonistas" (Telephone Operators Charming and Busy), published on 25 January 1919, explained that "during the strike . . . [the operators] struck a pleasing note by not abandoning their posts but attending to the public in excellent fashion." The photo of the operators accompanying this report is included among those showing the bloodied streets: two male figures in black stand out among the employees uniformed in white—the managers of the Cooperativa Telefónica, Mr. J. H. Swain and Mr. Antonio Pizales, supervising the work (and behavior) of their employees. The writer suggests that the operators be applauded and compensated in a way that drew attention to their "femininity": "We hope that many are grateful to them and that, after receiving their due, they may make that small ideal dreamed of by all women come true." But Christmas never comes on 25 January, and the operators' reward for services rendered in exceptional circumstances would not be in the form of financial compensation but, better yet, in the incorporation of the *telefonistas* into national imaginaries as models of social conduct. Perhaps *that* was the "*small* ideal dreamed of by all women."

A series of photos shows the employees dressed in white, sitting neatly "at the switchboard," "attending to the switches," "connecting an urgent message." Some show the operators relaxing "in the dining room during lunch break," in a room that looks like a smart restaurant. The city was seething with chaos, but the photos in *Caras y Caretas* ("Change of shift—in the cloakroom," "Break time, in the reading room") depict six employees in a pleasant lounge decorated with mirrors and plants. These images act as a not-so-subtle polemic against two of the labor movement's burning demands: that workers be provided with changing rooms and that they have time for a lunch break. In the flawless "order" of the Cooperativa Telefónica, clearly, there was no cause for such demands. The imaginary expressed in *Caras y Caretas* sees the Semana Trágica not from the perspective of workers (*obreras*), but from the perspective of employees (*empleadas*)—a choice not idly made.

In 1913, a junior saleswoman working nine, ten, or eleven hours a day earned between twenty and thirty pesos a month. By contrast, *telefonistas* (all women, since this was women's work) on the first seven-hour shift earned fifty-five pesos, while those on the third, working eight hours a day, earned eighty (Muzilli 1913, 19). Turning a blind eye to what was happening in the rest of Argentina, censuses since 1904 had drawn attention to any signs of progress that projected the image of a country unfailingly embarked on social modernization. One such unassailable sign was the growing involvement of women in the labor force. The 1909 General Census for the City of Buenos Aires interpreted the presence of women in post offices and telegraph offices, telephone exchanges, and registry offices as an indication "of great national progress . . . [an] eloquent [sign] of culture and general advancement" (qtd. in Feijoó 1990, 90), because these jobs required a certain level of education, training, and familiarity with technology and certainly entailed a shift in identity away from domesticity. But why would *Caras y Caretas* resort to this particular sector of the labor force in its depiction of the Semana Trágica? Why focus on their work as evidence of a social watershed? To begin with, the *telefonistas* are represented as if they were depoliticized and even praised for their antipolitical attitude, whereas they were not in the least antipolitical. Although the magazine does not say as much, the congenial operators who worked during the general strike were strikebreakers, or *krumiras* (scabs).

In the heat of the class struggle, *Caras y Caretas* responded as it felt it should, monitoring interpretations of the violence in the streets and the "irresponsibility" of the paralysis caused by trenches and overturned tramcars. Its imaginary suggested that on the reverse side of chaos were the spaces associated with women, especially working women sensibly seated in the workplace, so impeccably dressed in white from head to toe that they looked like schoolteachers or even nurses.[3] These were women as solicitous mothers, restoring order to the chaos of the home/nation, attending expeditiously to the responsibilities of their jobs, totally "unconcerned" by the political firestorms around them and "above" the ground-shaking events of the street. There was a new breed of professionalism at large, the female kind. As sudden protagonists in the struggle to give meaning to female and national models of identity, the magazine reports, *telefonistas* had assisted members of the fourth estate in communicating with "those from whom we have to obtain information [and] confirm stories. We have to acknowledge that journalists have been able to report news of events during the last few days because of them [the *telefonistas*] and only because of them." The reporter graciously dismisses previous complaints about telephone service, conveniently erasing them to begin with a clean slate for the country: "Indeed, we should forgive them all their shortcomings in thanks for their having contributed . . . to setting many homes at ease. We journalists know better than anyone what a good telephone service is worth. What would have become of newspaper information had it not been for that band of delightful girls . . .? Chaos." Journalists and operators here form a group whose work and duties are above any kind of disturbance. This was a moment for surprising alliances, at least at the level of imaginaries—like the alliance that equated members of the elite with scab labor. A report in *Caras y Caretas* entitled "La huelga de caddies del Golf de Mar del Plata" (Caddies Strike at Mar del Plata Golf Club; 25 January 1919) was festively subtitled "Players Stand in for Strikers," the accompanying photographs depicting certain distinguished members of this exclusive club (Messrs. Williams, Bulrich, del Solar Dorrego, and Gregory) happily toting their own golf bags to counter the effects of the general strike.

Following the example of the "delightful, working operators," women readers of *Caras y Caretas* would counter the violent events of the country's fateful hour with the professionalism of a clearly profiled national female identity: still working in the middle of a labor stoppage; agreeable in times of momentous upheaval and tense faces; unimpeachably female and professional —modern employees rather than workers. The "slight" contradictions in the pairing of social class and gender are diffused with calming phrases intended to indicate what attitude should be adopted: women were conscientiously endorsing the cleansing of the home/nation as active members of the new alliance of nationalists, who turn their backs on foreigners' strikes. They were meek employees, perfectly capable of remaining seated without the slightest complaint, smiling at the invisible speaker on the other end of the line. The photo montages—"Semana Trágica—Huelga" (Tragic Week —Strike) and "Telefonistas—Servicio" (Operators—Service)—conveyed the image of a country where the right and the legal recourse to strike were ill-advised—as unnecessary, the editorialist emphasizes, as the disruptions the city had endured. It became axiomatic that to allow conflicts between capital and labor to be worked out through strikes was just another of liberalism's historical gaffes. And even if the general strike was massive and had left the city completely deserted, the article attributed it to intrusive antisocial elements that did not even have the right to vote. This was how systolic imaginaries cobbled together a significant narrative that gave meaning to the social place and gender of the actors involved: they were guardians or criminals.

The working conditions of the *telefonistas* described by *Caras y Caretas* were far from those denounced in *La Vanguardia* on Thursday, 9 January 1913:

> Looking after 80 switches seems to be the same for the company as 100 or 120, as it is now, or 160 as it is to become shortly. . . . It is humanly impossible to respond to 120 switches for 7 hours at a stretch. Work performed in this way quickly exhausts the strength of the women and girls who have no choice but to do it. . . . Many become tubercular. . . . Many cannot stand the day's work, the nervous tension, the heat, and the weight of the headset they have to wear. . . . "The bonuses are an insult. . . . They don't understand that after so many hours, we are so tired we can no longer make out the numbers dancing wildly before our eyes. . . . When we get home, we ask for calm and silence; that's all we want."

La Vanguardia concludes: "As a matter of health, the number of switches for which each operator is responsible has to be limited. Looking after 80, 100, 120, or 160 is not the same." In Alejandro Berrutti's *Cuidado con las bonitas* (Beware the Pretty Ones), Rosalía, an employee at the Unión Telefónica, grumbles about how badly she is treated at work:

ROSALÍA: [The customers] were awful today; you've got to be patient.

JULIA: I can imagine. . . . Men are so rude!

ROSALÍA: And women too. Some of Eve's daughters are more like someone else's I could mention, the language they come out with. . . .

JULIA: The Lord's vine has everything on it.

ROSALÍA: . . . Still call it a vine, do they? It's more like a briar patch full of wild grass. People seem to have thorns. They prickle even when they talk. (Berrutti 1973, 245)

Rosalía also talks about "a man who, because I was a bit slow answering, said: 'About time you replied, you lazy slob. I'd kick your head in if you were my wife'" (246).

The feminist worker and intellectual Carolina Muzilli cites additional problems in *El trabajo femenino* (Women's Work), the remarkable report she presented to the Symposium on Social Economy in Belgium in 1913:

"How can these poor women expect to be patient and well mannered when they are condemned to wearing a heavy headset and to having a never-ending dance of numbers in front of their eyes for seven hours at a stretch with barely a ten-minute break?" (1913, 18). Muzilli's report is unwaveringly committed to inducing her readers to process its data corporeally, perhaps because she intuitively grasps the penetrating impact of understanding *from the perspective of the body*. She speaks of the weight of the equipment, the muscular effort required by the position of the head, and the nervous tension produced by unfaltering concentration over long periods of time: "It is inhuman for every operator to have to attend to between 80 and 90 lines. All her attention, all her efforts are concentrated in her mind. We can only imagine what she must be like when she's finished her shift" (18). By contrast, *Caras y Caretas* highlights a relaxed working environment with breaks for lunch, reading, and conversation. The *telefonistas'* job might well be better paid, and linked to new technologies and the romantic notion of landing "a good husband who meets our wildest dream," but the glamour of it all does not stop Rosalía, in *Cuidado con las bonitas,* from bringing the reflexes acquired on the job home with her:

> ROSALÍA (*distracted, as if at the telephone exchange*): Number please. (*Realizing her mistake.*) Sorry, Roberto, I was confused. . . . (Berrutti 1973, 249)
>
> ROSALÍA: Hang up, please, sir. Wrong number. . . . (255)
>
> ROSALÍA (*disparagingly, interrupting [Roberto]*): Hang up, please, sir! There must be a mistake. There's no one on the line. (266)

What *Caras y Caretas* cannot disguise, however, are certain details that slip through the cracks: the physical discomfort of employees hunched over switchboards in inadequate lighting, seated for seven hours at a time on chairs that—far from being ergonomic—are exactly the same as those in the company lounge. The distance between chairs is minimal, and the severe restrictions on movement must have been all the more unbearable because only one ten-minute break was allowed each shift. Such conditions explain why Muzilli's study refers to the operators as a "legion of tubercular, anemic women" (1913, 18)—tuberculosis being a pathology of the working industrial world that the militant feminist knew very well, as she later died of the disease.

Why focus on telephone operators at the height of the Semana Trágica? I asked myself this while reviewing the pages of *Caras y Caretas,* where the contrast being drawn is obscenely clear: the spotless "feminine" environment a challenge to the frantic, dark-suited men on the street, berating strike-breakers, taking bread from the mouths of families, and entering the dormitories of orphaned young women for who knows what dark purposes: "Seriously injured woman taken to Ramos Mejía Hospital," "Child with bullet wound in the forehead," "Treatment of seriously injured at Argerich Hospital," "Dead man in Triunvirato Street," "Bodies laid out in Public Health Services auditorium." A series of photographs—horrifying ("Bodies picked up in streets by Public Health Services") and melodramatic ("Family carrying relative's body to Chacarita [Cemetery] because there are no funeral companies") in turn—complete the sequence.

Another series of photographic vignettes by Alonso ("Apuntes del natural" [Notes from Life]) traces the history of the "workers' unrest" differently:

1. General strike declared

2. Subway closed

3. Tramcars attacked and abandoned [destroyed]

4. Belgrano and Lores: children playing in the trenches [in the rubble strewn across the street]

5. The first victim on foot running along the block [a sweating pedestrian in working clothes without any means of transportation]

6. Frontline troops and cavalry occupy the city [soldiers on duty]

7. Friday: the deserted city [abandoned streets and garbage on the road]

8. The last victims [the dead in the streets being picked up by Public Health Services][4]

These "Apuntes del natural" reflect a city assaulted by agitators indifferent to the public good. We should note that the final vignette ("The last victims") establishes a "truth" that justifies repression. Two others in particular are also notable. In one—"Belgrano and 24 de Noviembre: Hands up! Advance!"— two orders are given to two different passersby, one a man who is being searched by the police, the other a well-dressed woman wearing a look somewhere between disdain and offense at having been stopped by a guard who obligingly lets her go on her way. The other, entitled "A Romantic

Touch: The *Chinitas'* Gift," shows a cavalryman holding both a rifle and a flower given to him by some young *porteñas*.[5]

Were women outside political life? Certainly not. Carolina Muzilli (1889–1917?), the most influential intellectual *obrera* involved in the political education of the Socialist Party, was responsible for reports that framed the party's campaign for protective legislation in 1906. According to social historian María del Carmen Feijoó, women's struggles "neglected none of the generally known forms: boycotts, strikes, and stoppages that very clearly caught the attention of the public" (1990, 301). Women activists emerged from the nationalist Right and the Socialist Party, while anarchists seemed to avoid the feminist question: "Anarchist philosophy was basically hostile to reformist feminist objectives. . . . The role of man as protector of the family was, [anarchists] believed, being eroded by capitalist exploitation of women, and the Church was to blame too" (Carlson 1988, 123). The anarchist movement "romanticized the role of women . . . as emotional support to the alienated male worker" (Carlson 1988, 123). Women's access to the labor force "distorted the natural division of labor based on sex and prevented men from earning a living wage," while capitalist exploitation and engagement in the market economy made women corruptible. As for feminism on the Right, the LPA was opposed not just to universal male suffrage but also to women's suffrage. Under the leadership of Celia La Palma de Emory, the LPA's "feminist" branch promoted the Argentineanization of working women; patriotism; and moral education based on "the importance of patience and courtesy, of obedience to the law and to one's superior" (Carlson 1988, 164). Its adversary was the "red feminism" spawned by secular public education and a politicized immigrant population.

In addition to Muzilli, other women were also prominent in feminist socialism. Gabriela de Laperrière de Coni (1866–1906) was the first woman member of the Executive Committee of the Socialist Party and the author of naturalist novels widely read in Argentina. Fenia Chertkoff (1869–1928), who came from a socialist family from Odessa persecuted by the tsarist police, brought to the Socialist Party her knowledge of the work of the German educationalist Friedrich Fröbel (1782–1852), which she had acquired in Europe. Sara Justo (1870–1941) was a dentist, a founder of the Argentinean Association of University Women, and an activist engaged among Italian feminists in struggles against alcoholism and in favor of "the feeling of unity among women and the breaking of class boundaries" (Carlson 1988, 132). Because of her father's involvement in the 1870 Paris Commune, Alicia Moreau de Justo (1885–1986) was born in England into a family of French exiles. In collaboration with Fenia Chertkoff and Gabriela de Coni, she founded the Feminist Center of the Socialist Party (1918), bringing political education to the working women of La Boca. Like Julieta Lanteri and Elvira Rawson, she studied medicine at the University of Buenos Aires in a highly hostile atmosphere. As a feminist/suffragette, she opposed suffrage based on class, which the Conservative Order threatened to reinstate by undoing the Electoral Law. An eminent social worker and journalist, she was a longtime defender of human rights, as evinced by her position as codirector of the Radical Party's Human Rights Commission from 1978 to 1986. Justo's other concerns included the condemnation of prostitution and trafficking in women, the struggle for wage equality, a forty-four-hour workweek, and comprehensive maternity protection, including state-sponsored day care. Paulina Luisi (1875–1950), from an Italo-German family, was one of Uruguay's first women doctors. In Argentina, she promoted the feminist liberal agenda of José Batlle y Ordóñez, including the 1907 divorce law and important reforms to the civil code.[6] And Julia Lanteri's campaign for the political involvement of women, which led to vigorous street protests, was best remembered in urban imaginaries for the election run—parallel to the 1920 national election campaign— that sought to expose the political void created by the absence of women voters. Lanteri's gesture attracted supporters and provoked mockery, yet it drew the attention of the public on subways, in parks, on downtown street corners, and at factory gates.

What impact did women's militancy have on political debates? The First International Feminist Congress of the Argentine Republic (Buenos Aires, 1910) examined the condition of women from the perspective of civil law, education, science, literature, industry, and the arts. In civil law, the first Feminist Congress advocated universal suffrage; proportional representation of minorities in federal, provincial, and municipal governments; equal opportunity between the sexes in civil law; equal civil rights for legitimate and illegitimate children; state guardianship of orphaned and abandoned children; and full access to divorce. Concerning labor law, the congress pressed for a maximum six-hour workday, wage equality between men and women, laws to protect women and children at work, pensions and retirement, and paid maternity leave. In matters of education, it sought to guarantee women access to professional training; to establish centers for the deaf, the blind, and the handicapped and correctional centers for delinquent children; to reform sinister conditions in women's prisons; to abolish capital punishment; and to set up special courts for minors. Finally, in the area of public health, the congress argued for preventive action against venereal and infectious diseases; laws to protect job security; a campaign against alcoholism; the prohibition of alcohol; and the abolition of all houses of prostitution, including those regulated by health authorities.

By 1924, feminists, socialists, radicals, and even conservatives had joined forces behind Law No. 11,317, which restricted women's work to eight hours a day; granted limited maternity leave; and outlawed night shifts for women under eighteen, except those in domestic service or the entertainment industry (Carlson 1988, 165). Yet this law was systematically contravened: no means to enforce its regulations were put into place, and the state gave them no priority. Two years later, the 1926 reform of the Civil Code stipulated that married women had the same civil rights as their husbands, gave single mothers parental authority, and declared that widows had control of their property and authority over their children. It also provided for women to join the professions, enter into contracts, take up work, and dispose of their income without the consent of their husbands. However, Article VI of Law No. 11,317 required women to petition for their civil rights "through legal action": "Unless the wife demanded her share of conjugal property through the court, the husband continued to be the legal holder of this property and had no obligation to share it" (Carlson 1988, 166). Marifran Carlson explains that, in effect, "women as a whole undoubtedly either had no idea that they had been granted any rights or had no way of suing for them" (1988, 166). Public space, where feminist demands were mostly disregarded on account of a political environment totally absorbed in other debates and shaken by economic crises, was an awkward space. Unable to build a broad base of support, militant women were neutralized by the processes of political territoriality, which cast them aside or did not take them seriously. In *Caras y Caretas* (3 January 1920), for instance, suffragettes were identified with a rag doll dressed in pink, its braided hair tied up in a bun.

In more ways than one, Ivonne, the protagonist of Samuel Eichelbaum's *Nadie la conoció nunca* (No One Ever Knew Her, 1927), is a brilliant find in the monotonous heap of short works (*género chico*) penned for the popular theater. The play's action unfolds in a place easily recognized by spectators: Ricardito Iturbide's *garçonière*, where the indispensable courtesans, Odette,

Marcelle, and Ivonne, fake French accents while drinking champagne in an atmosphere "consisting of a mix of true happiness and false celebration," deep in a "life of leisure and perfume." But the party takes an unexpected turn when one of those present jokingly brings up the "incident with the Muscovite": he and his friends had stopped a Jew and humiliated him to the extent of cutting off "his beard with a penknife and [forcing him] to shout death to the Russians" (Eichelbaum 1927, 7). The episode is similar to one described in "La fiesta del monstruo" (The Monster's Party), by Jorge Luis Borges and Adolfo Bioy Casares.

The staggering anti-Semitism evidenced by those in the *garçonière* prompts the young Ivonne to reject it and confess, "I'm not Ivonne; my name's not Ivonne." Since the *garçonière*'s environment is a totally artificial one, Ivonne's cover-up corresponds exactly to the rules of the game, as her lover Ricardito explains: "What's that to me! I think it's very natural for you not to come here under your own name." But the young woman needs to reveal her identity: "I am Jewish." Her confession opens the intimacy of the *garçonière* to the streets disturbed by the Semana Trágica: Eichelbaum's transgressive authorial move allows the tight control exerted over this a highly depoliticized enclosure—a place of sexual servitude, where subjective time and historicity are annulled—to be disrupted by winds that blow in off the street. Thus, in 1919 Buenos Aires, the convulsions of the Semana Trágica are entwined with Ivonne's anguish for her family, brought on by diaspora and political/racial persecution. Although she has lost contact with her father since they fled Poland, she is able to reconstruct his last moments. She tells Ricardito that a neighbor "saw him die. I never saw him again, but tonight your friends showed me his death. I seemed to see him suffer their mockery, and I felt the torture of that humiliation on my own body" (Eichelbaum 1927, 10). What follows her anagnorisis is a calming sense of relief, along with a resignification of her identitary place: "The vision of my father's death has undone in a flash the hint of peace I always felt from this life of leisure and perfumes. . . . Much more than that, what I felt today has overturned the emptiness of my entire life like a frightening revelation. We can't live like this, accumulating hours and days and years just to hide what we are, to construct an enormous lie to flatter others" (10).

Ivonne's anagnorisis is a moment of poignant sincerity, unthinkable within the erasure of social exchange enforced by the controlling power of the *garçonière*. She causes her identity as a courtesan to waver by dwelling on her ethnic identity (as a Jewish woman), while reactivating the personal and collective memory of her race as a cognitive framework for confronting both the apathetic conformity of her life as a courtesan and the implosive de-dramatization of urban daily life. Historical time manages to break into the flow of the everyday in order to destabilize it, so that, at this point, we might anticipate Ivonne's imminent departure from the sexist, xenophobic spaces of power, especially when she recalls Ricardito's stubborn hatred for "women of my race" and his "unprecedented disdain for poor Jewish women like me." Nevertheless, Ivonne decides to stay with him because, as she says, "by your side I am sure to satisfy my instincts. That's why we've been together for several years. That's a lot for a woman of my profession, although it's not much for a woman of my race" (Eichelbaum 1927, 14). It seems that women in 1920s Buenos Aires were not free to aspire to coherent identities:

IVONNE: The worst in each of us attracts us and keeps us together.

RICARDITO: That's not true, Ivonne. It isn't the worst that binds us. Instinct doesn't reason, it levels, makes people equals. It joins a queen to a commoner ... connects a Jew to a Christian, and makes them see that by sharing their love the centuries disappear. (*Moving close to Ivonne.*) I love you! (*Embracing and ardently kissing her.*)

IVONNE (*yielding*): I love you. I don't know how, but I love you. (14)

Ivonne might be seen as the most political female character found in the *género chico,* the one who goes furthest in unveiling the naturalization of social praxis. She is perhaps the character who most intertwines the public and private spheres, history and the quotidian. Indeed, she is the one who most ardently questions the courtesan's life, from a perspective that undermines the bourgeoisie's elegant control over sexual servitude by historically recontextualizing the otherwise one-sided contract of sexual service enforced in the *garçonières.* Such a break could have anticipated a pattern whereby social agents might reflect upon the quotidian in order to give action (*their* action) a subjective meaning (*their* meaning), while establishing alternative ways for brandishing *their* truth (*lo verdadero*). Instead, the relationship between Ivonne and Ricardito remains enshrouded in the normality of what is socially acceptable (*lo acertado*), unchanged in its sordid untouchability. Ivonne will still be "la franchuta Ivonne" (Ivonne the French prostitute), not "Rebeca, Sara, Bertha, Clara, or Esther," while the discourse of passion does its best to cover up the classism, racism, and sexual domination of the almighty *bacán*. Ricardito warns her that she would have to provide "a truly serious reason" if she were to leave him. Without it, she would be "obliged" to stay with him. But where can Ivonne go with the demands she has expressed in her outburst? How can she deal with the clarity of her vision and her wounded collective memory? How can she process her doubly aggrieved experiences, as a dismissive/submissive courtesan and as a wronged Jew, when instinct persuades her to forget them? Indeed, she is perhaps not forced to leave Ricardito because, in these depoliticizing imaginaries of women, neither racism nor a historical memory is considered sufficiently serious. The courtesan's life seemed to many comfortably acceptable, capable of affording "protection" against personal or historical disruptions while allowing daily life to continue unabated, free from sudden shocks.

And how does feminism figure in *porteño* imaginaries? In *La mal pagada* (The Poorly Paid Woman, 1930), by Luis Acasuso, Mecha is "a feminist of the militant kind," the reverse of female characters normally found in the *folletines* or in sentimental literature. Before long, Mecha clarifies how she feels about her children: "For a few hours, they are a delight, but every day is sheer hell." She is eager to hear about "the thrill of divorce." She uses a needle to teach a lesson to a man on the subway who "rubbed against my shoulders like a cow against a fence," and she shocks her friends by going to a nightclub where the decor simulates a catacomb and champagne is served in skulls. She urges a friend: "Enough of cheap philosophies. I prefer bodies to souls." She goes to dramas rather than revues and explains the feminine in the following terms:

> MECHA: A hypocritical farce. We are forced to live our lives under lock and
> key, to scream when we see a mouse, to blush at a man in his shirtsleeves, and
> to use those ridiculously awful corsets that are a symbol of male barbarity.
> Do you have a cigarette, Ismael? (Acasuso 1930, 6)

Mecha is like a gender studies theorist who understands gender as a cultural performance. In Acasuso's clumsy stereotype, she is expected to smoke, using a long cigarette holder, and—unlike the angelic, redemptive woman/mother —to be an avid fan of boxing and wrestling ("It excites me, I warn you"):

> MECHA: Two huge men, almost naked, slapping and kicking each other. They
> twist each other's wrists and legs, they butt each other in the stomach and the

back of the head, and they poke each other in the eyes. . . . A German was fighting the other night, and he . . . fouled my favorite. . . . So I took off a shoe and threw it at his head.

AURORA: No! You didn't! How could you be so uncivilized?

MECHA: I got a great round of applause from the crowd that . . . made my husband's face go red. (6–7)

The existence of this kind of feminist, the *sainete* seems to argue, is conducive of a disconcerting sort of upset that turns husbands into delicate, ardent admirers of poetry and of orchids "of shimmering pearl, something marvelous . . . worthy of the dream of a symbolist poet" (8). But there are no advantages to be had from such feminism. Since Acasuso's text is an apology for monogamy and bourgeois stability, the restoration of balance to the institution of marriage will end up restricting social spaces even more severely, especially sexual identity. Aurora's adulterous husband, the feminist, and the demasculinized male are part of the new ecology of sexual chaos that has overturned heterosexual certainties. To reassert the balance of social conventions, "feminists" like Ivonne will go back to the romance of monogamy, husbands will admire flowers less passionately, and adulterers will fall on their knees and beg for forgiveness.

The first act of Julio Escobar's *La mujer que odiaba a los hombres* (The Woman Who Hated Men, 1927) takes place in "the main room of the luxury store La Famosa," where an employee, Margarita, is having to fend off the advances of the owner, Señor Duble:

DUBLE: Let others do the work for you. . . .

MARGARITA: No, sir. . . . I prefer to live in my modest rooms, not in a luxury apartment paid for differently.

DUBLE: Those are old-fashioned ideas.

MARGARITA: Old-fashioned? Respectable . . . ideas that allow me to walk with my head held high. Your other ideas are like lead and make me walk with my head bowed. (Escobar 1927, 3)

In an imaginary whose answers hold no surprises and that naturalizes whatever it touches, Margarita is a challenge for La Famosa's owner. He boasts: "Nearly all the employees have been through my hands. . . . But that one . . . is getting away from me. She is honest." Yet because of the unfailing culture of sexual abuse in the workplace, Margarita will not be long in following in the footsteps of Susana, a former store employee who has traded her eight-hour workday and eighty pesos a month for the twenty-five hundred pesos provided by her new millionaire friend. The process of seduction involves treachery; complex strategizing; the sinister complicity of others; and even a potion slipped in the champagne that Margarita is made to drink called "elixir of love, a concoction from *cántira,* guaranteed to make a tiger affectionate." There follows the rape of the limp tiger's/woman's body, which is unable to resist.

The next scene finds the deceived woman, now known as Margot, in her sumptuous house, dressed in a Chinese robe. There are syringes and morphine, cocaine and opium in abundance. Given her addiction, one year after the scene of her rape, Margarita/Margot is no longer a "healthy, likable young woman," but "a pale, heavy-eyed, haggard-looking woman who evidently leads an unending life of vice. She dresses lavishly and is weighed down with diamonds" (Escobar 1927, 18). As the drama's title (*La mujer que odiaba a los hombres*) and its imaginary anticipate, Margot is a woman who hates men. Aside from injecting herself with morphine, her only goal in life is revenge. As she explains to her friends Antonio and Rico, as well as the audience: "For a year, since that swine changed my life . . . I have been contemplating my revenge. . . . Today, I think it will be achieved. . . . In the meantime, I assure you that I've not rested from doing harm to men" (20). Although her former employer doesn't yet know it, Margot has enslaved his son, a young man reduced to nothing by his humiliating devotion to her. He steals and shoots up for her, and when his father finds him in this condition, her long wait ends in revenge. A cold, evil Margot proclaims to the man who raped her, "You made a sinful woman of me; I have turned your son into an addict and a thief."

Escobar's is yet one more story of perdition and revenge among the many imaginaries obsessed with femmes fatales—untamed, angry women of fire and sin. And to what social models might venomous women like Margarita/Margot refer, according to the "truth" of this misogynist imaginary?

RICO: They are right to call you "the woman who hates men."
MARGARITA: Hate them? . . . I bring them to justice. . . . Go to any place where there's corruption, and the majority of women you find were driven there

after being abandoned by the man who seduced them. . . . There are no rights for women, only duties. While everything in the world progresses . . . only she is still the legal slave of men. . . . And their tyranny is so brutish that a man who will not leave his car in the street, will abandon his mother, sisters, wife, and children there.

Rico: You sound like Dr. Lanteri.

Antonio: I'll vote for you in the next elections. (18)

Margot makes feminist claims and behaves like a femme fatale brewing her poison, while Rico pairs her with the suffragette Julieta Lanteri, a self-declared candidate in the 1920 election campaign, as we may recall. Neither Antonio nor Margarita could have voted for her, however, because there were no women presidential candidates until Estela Martínez de Perón ran in 1973, and because Margarita, like all Argentinean women, would have to wait until Perón's first presidency before being qualified to vote in elections at all (27 September 1947).

It is significant that *La mujer que odiaba a los hombres* connects feminist movements with an "androgynous" woman who carries both an indisputably tango nickname (Celedonio Flores's "Margot") and too many pacts centered on morphine and anger. Escobar's writing is enough to induce proxemic distances of flight in the audience. Margot's truth—speaking of equal justice, women's rights, and the indifference of men more attentive to their cars—appears alongside the nocturnality of the pernicious space of an opium den. As Josefina Ludmer points out, in the order imposed by true-crime writing, nicknames imply the lack of a name or a missing name, as in the case of illegitimate children (1993, 148). The suffragette Margots appear side by side with the vengeful, tango Margots. They are perceived as bodies and identities moving toward some indiscernible, concealed goal that the misogynist imaginary believed would be achieved after a long period of sullen waiting, when the fatal, irreversible blow would come. A similar bitterness was later attributed to the *bastardismo*/feminism of Eva Perón. In Julio Escobar's chain of logic, Lanteri's sought-after right to woman's suffrage seems to be represented as an act of revenge, steeped in the unyielding memory of dark feelings of resentment.

15 PUTTING

OUT FIRES

BLAS MATAMORO HAS ARGUED THAT
the passive, nostalgic attitude in the lyric voice of tango is related to the
conformist imaginaries of the Acuerdismo (Social Contract) of the Radical
Party's second term in office, but I believe that the slowdown in sociopolitical activism did not begin with the presidency of "Marcelino" T. Alvear
(1922–28). The Radical Party's political alliances may instead be traced to
Hipólito Yrigoyen's first presidency (1916–22). Yrigoyenism benefited from
a broad political base, as the first multiclass alliance to succeed in bringing
together a far-reaching, complex imaginary of enabling narratives on national
unity. Yrigoyen's policy of cooling the political fervor of the times can be detected in two of Miles's editorials for *Caras y Caretas,* published on 4 October
1919 and 18 October 1919, barely eight months after the Semana Trágica.
In addition to instituting an all-embracing social contract for the nation,
Yrigoyenism also endeavored to insert Argentina into the global political
geography that had been fashioned after the Great War. Miles explains: "An
intense desire for 'social peace,' under which all elements of society can live

together in fraternal harmony, is a feature of all civilized countries. The agitators, those with a revolutionary spirit, who cannot conceive of anything
useful without convulsions and upheavals, would like catastrophes like the
one the Russian people are still suffering to be repeated in all civilized countries. But they are a minority, and if the majority does not provide the ladder
for them to climb to power, as happened in Russia, they will not overcome
their impotence."

The editorialist's eagerness to quantify his argument is reflected in the
percentages he cites to isolate the minority unconcerned with "social peace."
These "unconcerned" members of the nation are scarce and are in decided
retreat, in light of "the universal movement of civilized nations." "Civilization" in this context turned out to be comparable to a disregard for political
activism, which was rendered ineffective by an imaginary that was claiming,
after all, to have taken on the fight to "improve living conditions for social
categories least favored by fortune, that is to say, those who have to work to
earn their own and their family's sustenance." Not surprisingly, in order to
escape the repercussions of the Semana Trágica, Miles knowingly sidesteps
politicized terminology in his discourse. Instead of social "class," he refers
to social "category," and "poverty" is mentioned in positive terms (as the
plight of those *least* favored), so as to leave intact the allure of the edifice of
promised progress, soon to be in everyone's grasp: "Our *conventillo* has to
disappear. . . . That form of communal life has the worst of moral consequences. . . . It is to be feared that it will cause the dissolution of the family
among our working classes if it is prolonged too long. . . . The task is neither
easy nor cheap, but must be pursued resolutely without delay . . . both by state
authorities and in public opinion. Every family in its home should be the basic
principle underlying 'social peace.'" Yrigoyen's new social contract seemed
disposed to rid the geography of Buenos Aires of one of its deepest scars. The
conventillos are cast as moral and housing blights, and the working class, it is
declared, will die out without decisive intervention. In addition to the *conventillos,* at least in the terms of its imaginary, this discourse makes social class
disappear from the city, along with anything outside bourgeois morality or
tainted with the unpleasant smell of anarchism and workers' strikes.

The title of Francisco DeFilippis Novoa's drama *Puerto Madero* (1924)
refers to a space heavily politicized by dockworkers' unions. The play opens
in a *conventillo* in La Boca on the day of a general strike. One of the char-

acters, who earlier witnessed events at Santa Cruz in Patagonia, describes the strike's outcome: with the advance of strikebreakers, arrests, and home invasions, it was "a real massacre . . . rotting bodies. . . . Dozens of dead, hundreds injured." Pietro, an Italian anarchist, a father and alcoholic whose adulterous wife has left him, is waiting for news of his two anarchist sons. When Juan is killed in a clash with the police, Miguel, Pietro's other son and secretary of the dockworkers' union, loses control: "Taking out my revolver, I fired in a fit of rage, without aiming or thinking of anything. . . . Two policemen went down" (DeFilippis Novoa 1977b, 183). Without further ado, to judge from all the tears shed by Pietro's daughter, the audience at *Puerto Madero* might well have guessed that more tragedy was to come. Rosa is in floods of tears for many reasons. As a seamstress sunk in poverty, in constant danger of losing her honor in the promiscuity of the *conventillo,* she keeps the home afloat while putting up with her father's alcoholism and her brothers' dangerous militancy. In her, all the torments of proletarian life are compressed into one single, heartbreaking emotional space. Miguel defends the right to strike, but the public dimension of his political declamations is in sharp contrast to his personal failures:

> MIGUEL: That's how it is, Rosa. . . . We don't know how to make a home or a family, such a small and easy thing to do with a little love and sacrifice . . . and we want to make the world right! Oh, how many times I've thought that old, worn-out drunkard, who no longer lives even for himself, is to blame for it all.
>
> ROSA: We're all to blame, Miguel.

The brothers, conscious that something has broken forever, face loss with the fatalistic self-destruction that so often haunts the reactive imaginaries of melodrama:

> MIGUEL: Nothing can be done now . . . nothing!
>
> ROSA (*embracing him*): Perhaps not everything is lost. . . . Who knows if this may serve as a lesson to us . . . for Pop . . . you . . . me.
>
> MIGUEL: No . . . no . . . it's late. . . . It's already too late . . . (*Rosa . . . bursts into tears on her brother's chest.*) Don't cry, sis, . . . don't cry. It's also too late for tears. (190)

Rosa and Miguel are right: it is too late to undo what the strike has unleashed, but there is still the possibility that the violence might "serve as a lesson"—that it might at least prove useful in turning political upheaval into a *negative* model value, which is precisely what DeFilippis Novoa's drama, a social text about closures, seeks to establish. Moreover, *Puerto Madero* asserts that treason and denunciation are rife in the social ecology of the *conventillo,* as in Miguel's perplexing betrayal by his own father. Could there be anything more heartrending than Miguel's capture in the final scene?

> MIGUEL: So it was you . . . you who sold me out. (*He charges at Pietro and tries to choke him with his manacled hands. The police pull them apart.*) My father . . . my own father. . . . Take me away! . . . Take me away. . . . Goodbye, sis. . . . Goodbye! . . .
>
> ROSA (*trying to cling to Miguel*): Brother! . . . (*. . . falls to her knees weeping . . .*)
>
> PIETRO: Don't cry, child . . . don't cry. . . . That's how the world is! [Cosí é il mondo!]
>
> ROSA: What world! It was you. . . . You were the one who couldn't keep his home together . . . and you want to make the world right. . . . (*She weeps bitterly.*) (DeFilippis Novoa 1977b, 194)

The curtain falls on Rosa as the eternally despoiled woman facing what is left of a shattered family. Pietro, the seed of anarchism transplanted from Italy to La Boca, has failed entirely as head of the family. The "truth" endorsed by this imaginary is that he "couldn't keep his home together," perhaps symmetrically suggesting anarchism's failure to construct an Argentinean family. The state had succeeded in eliminating the "discursive descendants" (*descendencia discursiva*) of the anarchist family, rendering anarchism a political legacy that would not continue into the next generation, its alleged attempt at instigating social disintegration truncated. In Josefina Ludmer's terms, it could be said that anarchism is here placed in the "secondary social position" (*secundaridad social*) of the criminal, meaning that it is looked upon from the perspective of the "primary social position" (*primeridad social*) until it has been totally disfigured or rendered mute (1993, 148). After all, who would be willing to open the old wounds of past deaths and political struggles that demanded violence in reply? In order to save the working-class family, therefore, it was necessary to gain the utmost distance from the social ecology of the *conventillo* and tear out the social roots of anarchism, found in poverty, alcoholism, adulterous mothers, family breakup, and betrayal. The social ills of the city had all ripened in one ignominious space. Thus, Yrigoyenism promised the first generation of Argentinean children of immigrants the panacea of private property in the suburban barrio. By 1919, as the new utopia, the barrios implied overcoming the adversity of the *conventillo*, an erasure that might finally give new meaning to the dramatic immolation of Rosa and Miguel. Like the *conventillo*, the brothers in DeFilippis Novoa's play had to disappear from the mnemonic geography of the city if the new Buenos Aires of Acuerdismo was to be born.

As suggested, then, Acuerdismo was not confined to Alvear's term of office. Its imaginaries can already be traced, working at full speed, to the moment when Yrigoyen showed that democratic governments were also prepared to suppress workers' movements brutally. Given their capacity for political maneuver, democratic imaginaries harbored no doubts of their growing strength, although Yrigoyen actually weakened his political stance by zealously heeding the oligarchy's demands and political extortion. In DeFilippis Novoa's drama, the Puerto Madero of the time is sacrificed in order to strive for a nonviolent, depoliticized Argentinean family that has no need for tears. Today Puerto Madero is an enclave of postmodern recycling in the urban geography of neoliberal Buenos Aires. Its transformation has provided a new skin for the old warehouses and coupled the port to the architectural clones of globalization. Anyone strolling among its expensive restaurants today is far from imagining the clamor of workers' struggles at the beginning of the twentieth century. I believe that the city's imaginaries began to erase the historical memory through works like DeFelippis Novoa's drama and its sanction against ill-conceived political action that left young women devastated, without a lifeline, but with an alcoholic father, one brother killed, and another condemned to death. As the epitome of Argentina's most radically resistant political agency, then, anarchism was left with no "discursive descendants"—indeed, with no descendants of any kind.

Returning to *Caras y Caretas*, Miles also updates a fundamental concept of Argentinean modernity: "Alberdi said, 'to govern is to populate,' and was right at the time *when he said it*, but the problem is now becoming more complicated every day" (emphasis added).[1] In Miles's discursive maneuver, we see the political countermarches of modernity at work: the time had come to erase Alberdi's words and to write new ones—such as "Let every family have its own home," a slogan unimaginable in the Argentina of the Generation of 1880 or the Centennial Generation. Yrigoyen's social contract struck notes hitherto unsounded. Not in vain was it competing with the Conservative Order, and even the Liberals, and it was thus imperative to suggest a true break: "It's all very well to populate, but the big issue is for the population to be happy." And if the state appointed itself as an overseer of all sectors of society—as an arbiter of social justice, attentive to the happiness of its citizens—what was the sense of engaging in politics? The notion of the citizens' "happiness" would later fully crystallize in Alvear's Acuerdismo, thanks to a remarkable economic boom. In the meantime, however, as Miles explains, "There are no basic reasons for discontent in the Republic of Argentina as there are in other countries." Social duty, then, consists of making "the differences that lifestyles have brought into society disappear . . . to be replaced by reciprocal cooperation." The reward—the elimination of social classes—represents such a spectacular rupture that it is cause for suspicion: we can guess that something valuable will have to be given up in exchange. And Miles spells it out: "The secret [of the future] is sacrifice in the present." But in what part of the social body would the pain of sacrifice be felt? "It is unwise," Miles tells us, "just to think about today. Many generations will come after us and we have to prepare the way. . . . The tactic of 'Après moi le déluge' is simply shameful, as well as dangerous, because sometimes the deluge comes before we expect it. And this is precisely what we should try to avoid . . . as a matter of general interest in which all personal egos are suppressed." Prudence, saving, betting on future generations, and deposing "personal egos"—these emphases politically define a good part of barrio culture in Buenos Aires. In order to save the nation from the biblical flood, *Caras y Caretas* tackles the voracious culture of luxury of the Centennial elites, undertaking a serious evaluation of the social cost of irresponsible waste. It was not by chance that the worst effects of this waste—suicides and the social death of bankruptcy—were dramatized over and over again in popular theater. Two of its demons had already been identified by the systolic pulse of Yrigoyen's imaginary, which withdrew its support for the invigorating winds of liberalism's political permissibility and poured cold water on the glitter of conspicuous waste. Austerity puts a damper on the notion of carpe diem, because enjoyment of the present must be sacrificed for the future. Single *obreras* and *obreros* would become prudent parents.

They would live in the suburban barrios of Buenos Aires and strengthen the political clientele of Acuerdismo. From the safety of the barrios and the lesser epics of everyday life, they would ignore, like Ulysses, the sirens' songs of the Buenos Aires of consumption and luxury, promiscuity, adultery, and liberated sexuality. The Yrigoyenist imaginary of *la casa propia* (home ownership) made the economic rise of the middle class accessible but brought about the depoliticization of the nation/home, an aspect examined later in this chapter.

Miles's 18 October 1919 editorial justifies government repression of a railway strike in Great Britain: "It was a matter of saving the community from a positively unjust and inconsiderate attack, from a surreptitiously revolutionary movement." Yrigoyen had been instrumental as the Argentinean mediator for British capital, and Great Britain now served once more as the mirror into which the Argentinean state gazed, in order to embrace the wisdom of a nation with a much longer tradition of civilization: "The [British] public . . . understood the situation and cooperated without distinction of [social] categories from the beginning of the government's action by first placing at the government's disposal its firm and sincere will to submit to whatever restrictions were judged necessary to impose and then immediately making every means of transport available, from the millionaire's luxury automobile to the most unstylish bicycle. . . . Where movements . . . against society are involved *all the social categories threatened* must combine their forces and make common sacrifices to defeat the danger" (emphasis added). Once more, Miles steers clear of politically charged terms, although he does allude to social class, as in the worker's unstylish bicycle. The new social pact was endorsed by a strident charitable collection that included a perplexing alliance of millionaires willing to share their luxury cars. In Great Britain, a new concept of the nation, founded entirely on individual philanthropy and bigheartedness, passed for social peace; this new concept would soon find its echo in the city on the River Plate. Perhaps María Eva Duarte de Perón would later have those well-publicized pictures of the charitable collections in mind when she called on the ladies of the oligarchy to "cooperate" with their jewels and furs. After all, she was following the metropolis irreproachably.

In Buenos Aires, the Gran Colecta Nacional (Great National Fund Raiser) was held in the sumptuous Salón Príncipe Jorge in October 1919.[2] It featured the participation of "distinguished women from our society" and amassed the "fabulous sum" of ten million pesos. Monsignor Miguel De Andrea stands in the foreground of the photo illustrating the event in *Caras y Caretas,* a symbol of the intensification of activity on the ultra-Right: it was thanks to "his initiative," the caption tells us, "that the great success of the Fund Raiser is owed." And what name was given to the fund raiser's executive committee? The "General Command," as if it were a military body: "Monsignors Bazán and Ussher, . . . *Artillery General* Dr. Francisco Sagasti, *Marshal* Dr. Ignacio Olmedo, . . . *Air Force General* Dr. G. B. Prack . . . , Dr. R. Parborell, *Cavalry General,* and Engineer Alejandro Bunge" (original emphasis). In other words, these civilians were also, or perhaps above all, soldiers. Something was quietly growing here unseen, beneath the water: an increasingly militarized society already approaching coups d'état. In 1919, Miles's editorials were already advancing the *golpista* imaginary that would interrupt Yrigoyen's second government (1928–30).[3]

Two characters in the drama *La Santa Madre* (Holy Mother) detect the event's political manipulation:

> FEDERICO: Concerning public collections, La Gran Colecta is contemptuous of the government because it abrogates its exclusive responsibility for social peace. . . .
>
> EDUARDO: It recognizes that social peace is disturbed just by wanting to intervene in it. In this case, it abrogates a right that doesn't correspond [to the Church], but belongs only to the state, the government, within whose jurisdiction [no other institution] can take on the role of social redeemer.
>
> FEDERICO: On the other hand, who can give the donors of those millions any guarantee . . . about how they will be used? Is their purpose social or political? Neither the government nor the people know. (González Castillo and Martínez Cuitiño 1920)

La Santa Madre raises questions and sounds the alarm, having detected the political maneuvers through which the Church was beginning to intervene in political life, its role overlapping with that of the state. An 11 October 1919 *Caras y Caretas* cartoon, "La Competencia" (The Competition), shows a suburban street in Buenos Aires with two businesses standing opposite each other (figure 24). One is the "Old Socialist Store," with a worker dressed in red sitting at the door. The other is the *new* "Social Peace Store. Capital:

13,200,000 pesos," with a priest (Monsignor De Andrea) standing outside it. What does this cartoon let slip? The Church was capitalizing on the events of the Semana Trágica, taking up the interests of working people, and even disputing the Left's ability to represent the popular classes. The illustration advises shopping henceforth at Monsignor De Andrea's new store, which is doubly backed—on the one hand by the material capital amassed through charity fund raisers, and on the other by the nonmaterial capital of its "great spirituality."

The impact of the retrogressive vocabulary of this imaginary must have been extraordinarily successful. The nostalgic, deflated men of the tango are conscious of their marginality and failure, for which they blame themselves and/or treacherous women, rather than facing the real cause of their abrupt displacement: the dissymmetry between the enabling narratives that tantalize them and the disappointing realities of everyday life. How was it possible to be so out of tune with a nation refounded on the confidence that everything would soon be well? It had become tolerable to burst into tears but objectionable to resort to the violence of strikes. Miles asks his readers: "How can we speak of partiality when looking after the interests and very life of the nation is involved? *Et nunc, reges, erudimini."*[4] In the shift of imaginaries, the anarchist meetings held by stevedores, bakers, metalworkers, and stokers, photographed so often at the beginning of the century, had become part of the discourse of social criminality. What had happened to the Buenos Aires of 1904, so open to social modernity that it had deemed anarchism to be in the social vanguard?: "Whatever you think [of anarchism], it is impossible to overlook the importance of the present moment in relation to the march and progress of our community, a heterogeneous assemblage, . . . as the enormous development of the most advanced ideas in sociology convincingly shows" (*Caras y Caretas,* 9 January 1904). In 1904, *Caras y Caretas* inclined toward a discursive middle ground between "bosses and workers, the police, the army, and the general public—that is to say, between capital and labor, the state or the law and the armed forces, the consumer and the intermediary." *Caras y Caretas* had also reacted quite differently in "El anarquismo en el Río de la Plata" (Anarchism on the River Plate, 1900), when it diligently lectured its readers on the social revolution, "which, according to the tenets of Bakunin, will happen today or tomorrow, once minds are sufficiently evolved and prejudices have in part been set aside, as [the anarchists] advocate in their philosophical publications, at the same time as they combat alcoholism, idleness, and crime" (qtd. in Ruffinelli 1968, 105–6).[5]

Yrigoyen's intricate alliances not only coalesced cultural imaginaries but also combined with military and political repression, as in the 1921–22 strikes in the province of Santa Cruz, stifled through massive deportations and the massacre of Argentinean and Chilean militants, including indigenous people, as well as European immigrants, mostly anarchists. This display of state intervention, known as Patagonia Trágica, epitomized the political/military triumph of the Patagonian landowners over labor and strengthened semi-feudal social structures in the region, while confirming the landowning oligarchy as the dominant political force for the rest of the twentieth century. But in Buenos Aires, the Semana Trágica was a difficult break to underestimate. It revealed the political use of urban space by modernity's new social actors, as well as the growth in "union organization [and] the influence of anarchism and rising communism" (Vargas 1999, 106). Because of its impact, dominant imaginaries promptly reacted to the quotidian by promoting political repression, xenophobia, classism, and sexism. As for the anarchists, Julio Godio argues that after 1919, "on the basis of this defeat, not only would they begin a march toward their irreversible decline, but a new workers' movement would emerge, now marked by the effective supremacy of reformist factions, . . . reduced . . . to a purely union activity. This supremacy would remain until the middle of the thirties" (1972, 81). As Luis Alberto Romero remarks, the image that Argentinean society held of itself, based on the expansion of social mobility, was confirmed by the middle classes' access to power: "The [image] of an open society with opportunities for all shaped a decidedly integrationist and reforming attitude. . . . The popular sectors . . . identified themselves in terms that were much less classist (than those of the workers won over by anarchists) and much more popular" (1985, 67). We might suppose, however, that the political implosion alluded to by Godio and Romero was perhaps more indicative of the effectual working of imaginaries, swiftly assembling readings of the quotidian that blocked the impact of events, while steering the public's attention to Acuerdismo's new social contract. Although these processes entailed the slow collapse of political combativeness, as embodied in anarchism, they did not imply an end to proletarian activism. They merely indicated that everyday events were habitually represented as swallowed up by stabilizing imaginaries. Anarchism, then, was the first *desaparecido* (disappeared) of the modern Argentinean imaginary. Nevertheless, Otto Vargas proposes to separate facts from their outcomes by disregarding theories that endeavor to "understand processes" without giving importance to facts (1999, 11)—an approach that reverses the semantic maneuvers of imaginaries (their selective interpretations, their ignoring and denial of hidden currents) and grants a central stage to facts as a source whose meanings have been obscured.

Between 1921 and 1922, there occurred a savage repression of strikes in Santa Cruz, followed by Kurt Gustav Wilckens's assassination of Lieutenant-Colonel Varela in 1923, José Pérez Millán Temperley's assassination of Kurt Gustav Wilckens in 1925, and José Pérez Millán Temperley's own subsequent death—all sequels and adjustments in the class struggle. Kurt Gustav Wilckens, a miner from Silesia, had been deported from the United States for political activism. In Argentina, he worked as a stevedore in Ingeniero White and Bahía Blanca, as a rural laborer in Alto Valle del Río Negro, and as a correspondent for Hamburg's *Alarm* and Berlin's *Der Syndicalist* (Vargas 1999, 142). All the common signs of a diaspora fed by hunger, unemployment, and politicization triggered by crises of adjustment to capitalism converged in his life. Although he was an adherent of Tolstoy's pacifism, Wilckens killed Varela, the officer charged with putting down the strikes in Patagonia, because he was animated by a desire "to wound through him the brazen idol of a criminal system" (Vargas 1999, 142). Wilckens was himself killed in jail by José Pérez Millán Temperley, a young man from an aristocratic family belonging to the Patriotic Association of Argentina. News of Wilckens's death led to a general dock strike, the burning of streetcars, arrests, death, and injury, while also achieving "an incredible miracle: unifying the divided working class in Argentina" (Vargas 1999, 143). The Argentinean Federation of Unions supported the strike "in belligerent speeches but left the anarchist FORA isolated" (Vargas 1999, 143). In June 1921, parliamentary representatives debated a law giving the state the power to control unions, declare strikes illegal, and reimpose the ten-hour workday. This proposal provoked popular condemnation in a demonstration supported on all sides, followed by a general strike and a state of siege.

On 23 August 1927, Nicola Sacco and Bartolomeo Vanzetti died in the electric chair in the United States.[6] During the lengthy wait leading up to their execution (1921–26), the dismay their sentencing caused in Argentina was expressed in general strikes (on 5, 6, 10, and 22 August 1927), organized by three unions in Buenos Aires and Rosario, in which "workers came out into the streets without previously declaring themselves on strike" (Vargas 1999, 355). On 3 May 1930, Pedro Gómez Grimau published his drama *Sacco y Vanzetti* (Sacco and Vanzetti) in the theater review *Bambalinas*. Gómez Grimau's apparently urgent need to remember Sacco and Vanzetti just a few months before José Uriburu's military coup, and the unusual authorial comments in his drama, are quite remarkable. To begin with, Gómez Grimau explains his refusal of any royalties and urges that his play "be performed for the benefit of schools or workers' libraries" (Gómez Grimau 1930, 2). Elsewhere, he remarks: "Comic actors: Remember not to perform your clowning or balloon tricks in this drama. . . . I beg you most sincerely to keep them for when you are working in the circus ring where you can paint your faces heavily . . . and roll on the floor if you want. Here I ask for a little respect" (7–8). The drama itself includes a detailed floor plan describing the *cámara de la muerte* (execution block); the location of the electric chair; the cells of Vanzetti, Sacco, and Madeiro (a third anarchist held with them); and the *depósito de cadáveres* (morgue). The authorial note at the beginning of scene 5 is addressed to the director: "Dear Director: There is a breed of ill-intentioned half-wits in the theater that loves to joke during a performance . . . and a dimwit to celebrate the fool is never amiss. You will surely have spotted them both. Try not to let them perform in my play, especially this scene. In brief, I want the companies who put on my play to consist of 'decent actors.' . . . And you, my dear director, if you cannot command respect or have no confidence in your cast, do not put on the play. Please!" (15). Gómez Grimau asks for respect, professional seriousness, and wishes his work to be staged *de otro modo* (differently), even during rehearsals. No doubt he adds these directions because he has no confidence of finding the proper respect for his work amid the circus of productions put on by busy theatrical impresarios. His play itself records Sacco's and Vanzetti's last hours—their last actions and their final look at the world. By urging understanding ("Please!") for *Sacco y Vanzetti* as a very special play, drawn from an abominable real-life event, Gómez Grimau's directions convey an emotion that the performance must also communicate. Somehow, perhaps because he correctly realized that his drama would be performed in a context that seemingly did not allow anything to be heard, he had to raise his own voice so that the audience would listen to what the characters needed to say.

What was this context, in which Gómez Grimau deemed it indispensable to write such telling directions calling for silence and respect? What was the *noise* with which he was forced to contend? Gómez Grimau's poignant drama was published in *Bambalinas* (1930), along with other examples of the *género chico*, such as *Milanesa* (Schnitzel), *La culpa la tiene el gallego del frente* (The *Gallego* Opposite Is to Blame), *Se alborotó el avispero* (The Hornet's Nest Was Stirred Up), *Pacífico torbellino* (Peaceful Whirlwind), *El dinero de mi mujer* (My Wife's Money), *El Gigoló* (Gigolo), *Como las mariposas* (Like Butterflies), *¡Te has lucido Belisario!* (You've Outshone Yourself, Belisario!), *Porque te quiero te aporrio* (I Beat You because I Love You), *Cascabelito* (Jingle Bell), *El sultán de la oficina* (The Office Sultan), and *Miss Argentina, Miss Universo* (Miss Argentina, Miss Universe). This list alone reveals the characteristics of the eye-popping works on offer and the direction generally taken by the *género chico*, as the main fare of popular theater. Gómez Grimau somehow understood that if he didn't interrupt the tone of this riotous flood of triviality, his work would go unnoticed amid the strident *cocoliche* characters of popular theater: the coquettish women, racy love affairs, sighing lovers, and starstruck beauty queens. Perhaps he thought that if he did not remark on his play in a way that made it stand out, his solemn homage would amount only to preaching in the wilderness. For readers of *Bambalina*, as well as for spectators of the *género chico*, it was more than likely that *Sacco y Vanzetti* would be diluted by the impressive weight of the popular theater's imaginaries and their unwavering proclivity to turn their back on injuries and crises in favor of middle-class conformism and consumerism. Gómez Grimau's social drama had to swim against the tide of *pochades* (comedies), *sainetes*, comic shows, *estudiantinas* (student musicals), farces, and gaucho romances.

Alongside *Caras y Caretas*, *Bambalinas* was basic to establishing the culture industry and putting mass imaginaries within reach of the hands and pockets of the reader. Its advertising urged, "Do not miss the next issue of *Bambalinas* . . . ask for it at the subway and newsstands." By 1930, dramas and *grotescos* had given way to works like *Hay casorio en el barrio* (Barrio

Wedding), *El milagro de Peppino* (Peppino's Miracle), *El perfume del pecado* (Scent of Sin), *El pecado de todas* (Every Woman's Sin), *Tro-la-ró-la-rá* (Tra-la-la-la), *El bailarín de la señora* (The Lady's Dance Partner)—all published in 1925. *La bailarina del Empire Theater* (The Ballerina from the Empire), *Los varones somos muchos* (We Are Many Men), *¡Hay que tener clase!* (You Need Class!), and *Los muchachos de antes no usaban Avanti* (Young Men of Old Didn't Use Avanti) appeared in 1928. And in 1937, readers found *Seré como tú quieras* (I'll Be What You Want), *Besos perdidos* (Lost Kisses), *El gato con botas* (Puss-in-Boots), *Como gustéis* (What You Will), *Tus razones y las mías* (Your Reasons and Mine), *Antes del desayuno* (Before Breakfast), *Otra vez el diablo* (Return of the Devil), and *Boite rusa* (Russian Cabaret), as well as translated works unconcerned with local issues.

I believe that by 1930, popular theater's imaginaries had managed to confine both anarchism and political activism to a mute space, in favor of flamboyant promises such as "tomorrow's another day." But the process of erasure was a slow and lengthy one. Even when the anarchist movement was at its height, the anarchist dramatist José González Castillo had the father in *El mayor prejuicio* (The Greatest Prejudice, 1918) complain that his two sons were living off him, one an anarchist, the other an idle good-for-nothing:

> Pereira: Not a cent. . . . Roberto has picked up . . . anarchist ideas and refused to become fodder for exploitation while eating and clothing himself at my expense. . . . The other . . . a "high-lifer," full of aristocratic airs, is more concerned about his clothes and hasn't given a cent to help look after his mother. (González Castillo 1918, 7)

In Alejandro Berruti's *Cosas de la vida* (That's Life, 1926), a woman berates her anarchist husband:

> Leopolda: What I do know . . . is that men, not women, should support families.
>
> Julio: Provided men have no other mission to fulfill as important as work.
>
> Leopolda: And what is your mission? Hanging about cafés and street corners talking nonsense, creating trouble, and shouting abuse at society?
>
> Julio: "I am a spokesman for public opinion," regardless of your poor judgment.
>
> Leopolda: You're a layabout with the gift of the gab and a rattle for a brain. It's a big joke (*laughing loudly*) that a nobody like you should go about promising happiness to everyone. I don't suppose anyone'll take you seriously. (Berruti 1912, 39–40)

Gender and Politics

In *El fuego del Vesubio* (Fires of Vesuvius, 1930), by Angel Curotto and Carlos César Lenzi, a character explains why he is unemployed: "I worked in the docks . . . but then the strike came and I lost my job. . . . Now my kids are sick." Political activism is either squarely to blame or a gesture out of step with the times. In *Mañana será otro día* (Tomorrow's Another Day, 1930), by Alberto Vacarezza, Alejandro Berruti, and González Castillo, the anarchist militancy of the Catalan Miriñac (an appropriate caricature) is disavowed by the typical rhetoric inherited from the new social contract of Acuerdismo, explained by the Italian Cataldo: "We are all peaceful . . . let harmony continue to reign among us." And when the "Catalan dynamiter" Miriñac suggests a new definition of the concept of liberty, he is questioned by his neighbors:

> CATALDO: And if you like freedom so much, why not leave me the freedom to think what I like? . . . I live very well here! . . . Each of us in his own way lives relatively happily in this house. . . . I with my deep personal philosophy . . . my wife with her dreams of grandeur, our *compadre* over there with his attachment to the *milonga,* the *gallego* from Andalusia with his addiction to gambling, the *gallego* from Galicia with his craziness for amorous adventures. . . . You're the only discordant note in this harmonious family group living here. (Vacarezza, Berruti, and González Castillo 1930, 3)

The anarchist is already out of place, out of sync with the "harmonious family group living here." "Here" refers to the imaginary space of a republic ironically less than six months away from ceasing to be a republic, thanks to Uriburu's coup.

El fuego del Vesubio and *Mañana será otro día* were both published in 1930, the same year as the "misplaced" plea in *Sacco y Vanzetti*. Cataldo's sagacious speech alludes to various social actors whose profile had visibly changed with Acuerdismo. On the one hand, this immigrant tramcar driver, with his philosophizing—or *filosofería personal,* as he calls it—finds logic to explain his new happiness, in contrast to his colleague in Discépolo's *El viaje aquel/ El guarda 323*. Here we find women caught in dreams of grandeur and consumption—"tea at Harrods, summers at Mar del Plata"; a *compadrito* whose nostalgia for the *milonga* gives him some sort of sense of identity; a *gallego* who gambles on chance; and a seducer who puts all his energy into an insatiable thirst for conquest. *Los casados son los peores* (Married Men Are the Worst), a *sainete* by Alfredo E. Bertonasco and Domingo L. Martignone, appeared in the same issue of *Bambalinas*.

In *Mañana será otro día,* Vacarezza, Berruti, and González Castillo assemble a cultural map that shows how stabilizing imaginaries rendered the contradictions and tensions of modernity opaque, dispelling them through the conformist and "harmonious family group living here." Each person is in his or her place, everyone in an imaginary space where illusions and longings are actively fostered and political resentments are actively dispersed. *Mañana será otro día* traces this displacement of identity. The Catalan Miriñac forgets anarchism and "humanitarian feelings," instead finding paradise in his share of the fat sum won by the *conventillo* as first prize in the lottery. Henceforth, his only concern (a few months before the Wall Street crash) is, "What bank will assure us it won't go bust tomorrow? . . . We must find a bank that offers better guarantees and higher interest. I demand security and performance."

To judge from the above, it is not, after all, surprising to find a *mujer de fuego* (ardent woman) in Carlos R. de Paoli's *La culpa la tiene el gallego de enfrente* who suggests in 1930 that "a smile is the formula for happiness." Nor is it surprising for her to date the moment at which happiness begins exactly at a dramatic turning point in Argentinean history: "Today, on 12 January, a new life begins in this house." In the year of Argentina's first coup d'état, dominant imaginaries seemed compelled to relegitimize the beginnings of military and discursive repression during the Semana Trágica. The events of 1919 and 1930 were thus entwined in the *golpistas'* imaginaries of a long-lasting, slow process of formation:

> Nélida: Smile, gentlemen! . . . The embittered die victims of their own bile! . . .
> It's the optimist who triumphs in this life. . . . Smiling should be the watch-
> word in this house. . . . Smile in the heat and the cold, in good times and
> in bad. . . . Today, on 12 January [1930], a new life begins in this house.
> (Paoli 1930)

From Nélida's mouth comes a paradox: her tone of caustic conformism is linked to words that reveal what was considered *acertado* (correct) in Argentinean political life. Both *Mañana será otro día* and *La culpa la tiene el gallego de enfrente* were written just as the military coup was about to break. But of what did the "new life" consist in 1930? Ronald H. Dolkart has examined the trajectory of the Argentinean political Right during a period deservedly called *la década infame* (the villainous decade). Along with the atrocious social costs of the 1929 depression, Argentineans had to endure Uriburu's drastic turn to the Right in political and cultural life. In their struggle against the country's incipient democratic tradition, the *golpistas* were fueled by the fascist Europe of Hitler and Mussolini. Yet the *golpistas'* struggle did not go unresisted, and Dolkart alludes to violent confrontations in the streets of Buenos Aires. The coup, however, made the high level of politicization of the armed forces in Argentina tangible, while marking the beginning of a long and brutal history of similar military interventions perpetrated to "rescue" the nation.

Uriburu (1930–32) came to power through an alliance of the new nationalist Right and old conservatives from the National Democratic Party, landowners, exporters, and bankers, who held that Argentina's devastated economy could only be revived through beef and wheat exports. The sudden explosion of ultra-rightist organizations leads us to infer that these factions had long been in a constant state of alert, lying just below the surface—forging alliances that gradually took shape during both Radical governments and moving into relevant areas of social life: the Legión Cívica Argentina (LCA; Argentinean Civic Legion), "paramilitary units . . . trained regularly by the army" (Dolkart 1993, 68), the Milicia Cívica Nacionalista (Nationalist Civic Militia), the Alianza de la Juventud Nacionalista (Alliance of Nationalist Youth), the Asociación de Damas Argentinas (Association of Argentinean Women), the Unión Nacionalista Universitaria (Nationalist University Union), the Acción Nacionalista Argentina (ANA; Nationalist Action of Argentina), the Federación Obrera Nacionalista Argentina (Federation of Nationalist Workers of Argentina), the Corporación Nacionalista de Maestros (Nationalist Guild of Teachers), and so on. Based on the premise that activating forces was just a matter of founding organizations, even Leopoldo Lugones was planning an "Argentinean Guard," although he committed suicide before he could carry out his plan.[7] These organizations saw the coup as the only way of safeguarding the moral, political, and economic well-being of the country. They were thus responsible for the immense subsequent public instability, repression, and violation of human and constitutional rights, perpetrated against their political opponents with full impunity. Uriburu was barely in power when he tried to abolish the secret ballot that had brought the Radical Party to power, but he was opposed by his rival Agustín P. Justo (1932–38). Indeed, recent history had shown that abolishing the secret ballot was not necessary: "The upper class favored the constitutional and institutional structure that it had created as the 'liberal' oligarchy of the nineteenth century, using the mechanism of fraudulent elections and corrupt payoffs to maintain control behind a façade of representative government" (Dolkart 1993, 65). The September Revolution that had unified the Argentinean Right gradually played its hand, sheltering behind electoral fraud. The Radicals opposed the Right as they had before, in two ways: through a policy of abstentionism and through the Civil Alliance, led by Lisandro de la Torre. In 1930, given the political abstention of the Radicals, the absence of alternatives, electoral fraud, and the agro-exporting oligarchy's rigid monopoly over the country, much suggested a sense of déjà vu in an Argentina returned to the time of the Conservative Order. The nationalists' first attack had two targets in its sights. In *Acerca de una política nacional* (Concerning National Policy, 1936), Ramón Doll alleged that the permissive demagogy of liberalism had unleashed communism (Dolkart 1993, 76) and set the political stage for a foreign element not even able to speak Castilian. In this context, then, Matías Sánchez Sorondo promptly brought forward a law to suppress communism, including a penalty of five years' imprisonment for using phrases such as "dictatorship of the proletariat," "collectivism," and "abolition of private property." He gave examples of these phrases as they had appeared in 127 supposedly communist publications, including *El Centinela Gastronómico* (The Gastronomist's Watchman) and *Boletín de la Cruz Roja* (Red Cross Bulletin), speaking almost continuously during thirteen parliamentary debates, after which the law went into effect. The censors monopolized the right to speak and usurped the space for debate in service to their own cause.

Anarchism had certainly disappeared from the national scene since 1919, and had Yrigoyen's new social contract been successful in proposing that there was no need for politicking, the 1930 coup would not have occurred. David Rock has traced the formation of Argentinean nationalism in the political activism of Manuel Gálvez, Leopoldo Lugones, Juan A. Cafferata, Monsignor Miguel de Andrea, Alejandro Bunge, and Ricardo Rojas, not all of whom always found themselves, incidentally, in entirely agreeable company.[8] In view of the confusion and bafflement resulting from the immigrant mosaic, it was imperative to create a strong sense of nationalism based on "nativism," oriented toward an encounter with the country's internal borders. Not all the nation's borders were included, however. In the construction of "authentically" Argentinean myths—the invention of a tradition—

gaucho literature was instrumental in counteracting the cosmopolitan life of liberal Buenos Aires. This was a nativism without indigenous peoples, but with gauchos from the oligarchy's pampas landholdings—a literary theme legitimized in written culture; established in cultural systems; and disseminated in "the *folletín* . . . lyric poetry, occasional songs, drama [and] circus performances" (Prieto 1988, 15). This new nativism began with *El gaucho Martín Fierro* and *La vuelta de Martín Fierro* (The Return of Martín Fierro) and then went through innumerable versions: *Juan Moreira, Santos Vega, El gaucho Buenaventura, El gaucho Hormiga Negra, Juan Cuello, El gaucho Pancho Bravo, El gaucho Picardía, El gaucho Paja Brava, El gaucho Agapito,* and so on. The gaucho's urban descendant, the marginal, amphibious *compadrito,* appeared in the work of Fray Mocho (José S. Alvarez), Evaristo Carriego, Manuel Pinedo, Jorge Luis Borges, Leopoldo Lugones, and Ezequiel Martínez Estrada.

On the other hand, the impact of the crisis of capitalism on Argentina's dependent modernity was cause for thought for Alejandro Bunge, who argued in favor of "the need for a major effort to reduce the country's strong dependence on foreign markets" and foresaw that if international markets collapsed, so would Argentina: "The solution to these problems . . . lay in a program of economic diversification: the substitution of imports, the planned colonization of the land, the growth of construction and manufacturing, increased investment, especially in new technical skills, and the expansion of the state in the economy" (Rock 1993, 70). The "truth" of this nationalist imaginary supported an economic and cultural policy aimed at intervening in the flow of international capital—and its cultural identity—so that the symbolic location of the nation could be kept at home—hence the romanticization of the countryside and the *arrabales* as a counterweight to the stigmatized, evil Buenos Aires. Nationalists perceived the city as a house disfigured by immigration and the unbridled spending of the liberal oligarchy, a perfect space in which to perform disciplinary "corrections." The goals had been clear ever since the Semana Trágica. For Lugones, the focus must be on the struggle between the nation and the foreign enemy: "There could be 'no civil war against foreigners . . . because all wars with foreigners are national wars' requiring a full-scale military mobilization. The citizens of Argentina exercised absolute dominion over the foreigners resident in the country. . . . In exercising the right of command, citizens had an obligation to root out the foreigners" (Rock 1993, 71). In the combination of Alejandro Bunge's outward-looking economy and Lugones's xenophobic, fascist diatribes, the nationalists of the time wielded a need to bring the country back to traditional models and to carefully scrutinize liberal values. Hence the 1930s marked a profound break in the historic continuity of the ascent of the middle and proletarian classes.

The Uriburu coup was backed by massive repression, with the help of professional torturers whose methods and effectiveness were later perfected during the presidencies of Agustín P. Justo (1932–38) and Roberto M. Ortiz (1938–42). Fraudulent elections (1932, 1938), in addition to imprisonment and torture, were complemented by the reorganization of the Central Bank into a public company with English capital, the much-disputed Roca-Runciman Pact, "scandals in the purchase of armaments . . . and beef, [and] a memorable debate led by Lisandro de la Torre . . . in the course of which Senator Bordabehere was murdered on the Senate floor itself" (José Luis Romero 1983b, 215).[9] Senator Lisandro de la Torre, leader of the opposition, killed himself in his apartment on Esmeralda Street. Maneuvers to reestablish the oligarchy's monopoly progressed, but not without dissent. In the meantime, the seasons at the Colón Theater were ever more brilliant, the theaters on Corrientes Street sparkled with packed houses, and Florida Street remained the city's elegant cultural and social heart, while the prestigious periodicals *Sur* and *Martín Fierro,* linked to the Florida literary group, succeeded in setting learned tastes and giving them their avant-garde seal. By contrast, in the *other* Buenos Aires,

> there were layoffs in the public-service and the private sectors. Unemployment became noticeable in the center in the shine on old suits and, in more dramatic forms, in the popular barrios: in the hunger of the unemployed, which was not relieved by the "soup kitchens," or in having to abandon a room in the *conventillo,* which led its inhabitants to [the shantytown of] Villa Esperanza, which had sprung up in Puerto Nuevo. Looking for work or "enough money to eat" was the daily concern of many, and [Enrique Santos] Discépolo expressed the general feeling of frustration and cynicism amid the poverty [*mishiadura*] that had overcome the middle and popular classes. (José Luis Romero 1983b, 215)[10]

In the year of the Russian Revolution, the oligarchy was warned, in the tango "Se viene la maroma" (Here Comes Trouble), by Mario Battistella and Manuel Romero, that "the communist row is ready . . . you'll have to work if you want to eat":

> Puppy-dog good-for-nothing
> go get on the train
> today the wealthy are standing
> at the edge of the platform

But no such revolution came. Through repression, self-affirming or conciliatory imaginaries, or Grandes Colectas, reactionary imaginaries, their convictions strengthened since the Semana Trágica, managed to discourage political mobilization and new collective identities. Every failure or difficulty in reaching the goals laid out on the cultural horizon was attributed to individual flaws. The 1930s saw three destabilizing and interconnected kinds of coups in social life: military, economic, and identitary. Conflicts had been resolved democratically before Uriburu's coup, but henceforth the armed forces would act out of the conviction that the country needed their attentive response and their ever-vigilant arms. In the fifty-three years between 1930 and 1983, then, Argentina "experienced 21 years of military governments emerging from coups d'état [and] more than 15 years of elected governments . . . with presidents of military origin . . . who . . . 'inherited' the military governments that immediately preceded them" (Itzcovitz 1986, 6).

Women, through all of these upheavals, were depicted as compliant workers, emblematic of national conciliation, while men were politically immobilized. Both were equally feeble. As anarchism had disappeared from the city's imaginaries, the strength for combat also vanished, along with all sense of drama. With drama gone, then, it seemed that what was left behind was melodrama, whose matters are deliberately saturated to dilute confrontation and dissent. What remained were the tango and its narrator, who would hardly find much to smile at, even when, according to *La culpa la tiene el gallego de enfrente,* "smile in the heat and the cold, in good times and in bad," was the "watchword in this house."

16 FRACTURED IDENTITIES AND ECONOMIC DISLOCATION

The good times are all over for me,
my sick body can take no more.

César Vedani, "Adiós muchachos," 1927

SENSORIAL MAPS ARE VERY VALUABLE
for beginning to understand what it was like to live in working-class Buenos
Aires. Dr. Carlos Carreño, a university professor and state health inspector
of factories, enumerated the most pressing work-related illnesses of his day
in *La higiene en los talleres* (Health in the Factories, 1931), linked to "lead,
mercury, arsenic, and phosphorous poisoning, anthrax, tuberculosis, apathy,
syphilis, and worms." He warned against pathologies from dust in unregulated factories "that penetrates the lungs and causes pneumocomiosis or gets
into the digestive system and leads to enterocomiosis" (Carreño 1931, 48).
Workers exposed to mineral dust included potters; grinders; plasterers; metal
polishers; cutters; stone and glass engravers; and employees in the cement,
ceramic, and porcelain industries. Vegetable dust was absorbed by textile
workers handling flax, cotton, and hemp and by workers in the tobacco and
cereal industries. Handlers of horsehair and manufacturers of cosmetic creams
and powders suffered "the effects of dust from animal products. The rates
of absorption for 10 hours work are 0.10 grams of organic particles at a saw,

o.12 in an iron foundry, and 1.08 in a phosphate mill" (Carreño 1931, 49). State inspectors commonly identified poor ventilation and lighting and high levels of heat as targets for improvement in working conditions, although requirements were different for each factory.

Reports crafted during the first three decades of the twentieth century collected impressive data on skin sensitivity, blood pressure, heart rate, the oxygenation of hemoglobin, and the metabolization of carbohydrates and proteins in relation to three factors: heat, humidity, and air. Law No. 9,688 set no limits for factory heat and humidity, while the requirement for breathable air was a minimum of ten cubic meters per worker, although the particulars of each form of production made this amount relative. As Carreño points out, in a lime factory, "it was impossible to stay for more than a few minutes because the lime dust hanging in the air made it unbreathable. A complaint to the foreman led to a mask being produced after a long search (although it was useless because it was too basic), and the workers refused to wear it, according to the foreman, because it only made them hot and brought out sores on their skin . . . where lime and sweat were mixed" (1931, 8). For this reason, dry sweeping was replaced by wet sweeping; factories were cleaned at the end of the workday instead of in the morning; and breathing masks were regulated by Article 63 of Law No. 9,688, which also required that "dust, fumes, or gases given off during work had to be vented . . . to the outside in a way that did not harm the surrounding area" (Carreño 1931, 51). But health regulations were studiously ignored. For example, Mirta Lobato reports a complaint made by neighbors in Berisso, an area affected by the Swift and Armour meatpacking plants, where industrial waste was held in "lakes of foul water, and the stench of the guano processing 'more than once stopped families from sitting down to eat'" (1990, 333).

The issue of ventilation brought state legislation into conflict with industry over air quality; reduced oxygen levels; the presence of toxins and impurities from factory work—smoke, fumes, gases, and dust; and the need to maintain humidity levels and optimum temperatures during production. Carlos Carreño followed British geneticist John Burdon Sanderson Haldane in pointing out the perniciousness of stale air in confined spaces. The poisoning of the air in workshops, factories, and home worksites, arising from combustion and human breath, increased levels of carbon dioxide, nitrous ammonium, formaldehyde, and ptomaines. It also reduced oxygen levels (Carreño

1931, 22), causing discomfort, severe headaches, dizziness, and nausea—physical symptoms that could result in death if conditions went unchanged. As in the crowded spaces of ships' holds, the only remedy was improved air circulation.

Carreño recommended not exceeding "the number of persons that the capacity [of an enclosed space] allows, in relation to the amount of breathable air at 10 cubic meters per person" (1931, 24), and suggested artificial ventilation to renew the air at least three times an hour. Articles 14 and 20 of Law No. 9,688 required the clothing industry to use mechanical means to renew the air at least twice an hour and specified that when gas irons "are used, measures must be taken to prevent unignited gas from leaking into the air" (26). He advised abundant fresh air, suggesting that wire mesh be installed on the windows and doors of some factories, such as those making mattresses, "to prevent the dust and materials produced by the carding machines from getting out of the factory" (27). He asserted that air circulation allows high humidity levels and temperatures to be reduced—these being the principal causes of the confinement often felt in dry-cleaning plants, textile factories, and mines: "An animal kept for six hours in a humid (90% relative humidity) and hot (33° Celsius) atmosphere loses a quarter of its energy, measured ergographically, . . . and develops anemia" (28).

Spinning and weaving factories in the wool industry required a hygrometric level of 60 to 70 percent for production and up to 80 or 90 percent humidity. But their air, Carreño stressed, should not be more than 70 percent saturated if workers were to breathe it without harm: "Rubner has shown that pulmonary and cutaneous evaporation is made difficult in proportion to the heaviness of air humidity, and cases of poisoning have been confirmed caused by a hot and humid atmosphere that prevented sweating" (1931, 29). Thus, hot, stagnant air easily becomes highly toxic: "By removing heat from the skin, the evaporation of sweat causes body temperature to drop and allows the body to protect itself. . . . [When ambient temperatures and humidity are high,] neither the lungs nor the skin can release sufficient moisture into the air, given that moisture is abundant when at rest and increased when working. Under such conditions, changes to the mucous membranes of the respiratory system and their susceptibility to germs . . . are not long in following" (Carreño 1931, 30).

What Carreño described here was the prelude to tuberculosis, *the* disease of early industrialization. During this period, scientists contemplated a reality that was taking shape for the first time, in the full process of evolution. New industrial diseases, and physical conditions whose etiology still needed to be determined, began to affect working bodies, but researchers' attention was awakened only by symptomatic evidence—when pathology had already reached an advanced stage and, in many cases, was irreversible. Carreño noted countless harmful effects of industrialization, only some of them summarized here to illustrate how, as industrialization took root, every aspect of its physical and cultural implementation produced destructive sequel techno-pathologies. Industrialization opened Pandora's Box, and experts in industrial medicine were left to read the bad news on the sick bodies of their patients.

The father in Carlos Mauricio Pacheco's *sainete El diablo en el conventillo* (The Devil in the Tenement, 1916) comes home weary from the factory every day: "How d'you expect me to be. . . . Stuck between pulleys from morning until night, my arms ache, my legs ache, and I can't show up at home looking as if I'm ready for a party. Besides, I'm not destined for happiness" (Pacheco 1977a, 107). References to excruciating physical pain abound in the literature of the time, recording the severe violence of physical labor. And although industrial medicine was gradually producing studies to support remedial legislation, there were absolutely no guarantees it would be implemented. Carreño wrote *La higiene de los talleres* in 1931, but how many workers' bodies had already suffered irreversibly by then from the conditions he described?

The Socialist senator Alfredo Palacios wrote *La fatiga y sus proyecciones sociales* (Fatigue and Its Social Consequences) in order to counteract the possibility of lengthening the workday. Furnished with a laboratory equipped with an ergograph and Patrizzi's experimental devices, he conducted studies on psychometric rates of attention in July 1921, at the worksite of Talleres Riachuelo. This investigation was his contribution to Congress's debate on Taylorism, spurred by the fact that Frederic Taylor's calculation of productivity applied the same criteria to human and machine labor, totally ignoring (or intentionally excluding) any consideration of how the human body operated under fatigue. The goal of Taylorism was "to make human actions predictable and precise and dependable like machinery" (Eberle 1985, 12)—to eliminate as much as possible the efforts associated with useless movements.

In *Los hombres de la ribera* (Men of the Waterfront, 1922), a drama by Eugenio López and Antonio López Azcona, one character recalls a workmate who had been "crushed between two bumpers" that morning. He goes on to describe with remarkable vividness the effects of the rate of work maintained on the docks, "where the amount required of the laborer is a disgrace, and the conditions in which he has to do his work are sheer punishment":

> Diamonte: The stevedore's lot is not work; he is exhausted by the time the day is done, and he's no longer a man but a limp rag. His body's worn out, and he's dismissed because they can't get any more out of him. The day is never done! Up and down the ramp, almost doubled over, unendingly, with 70-kilo sacks, under the punishing eye of the foreman and the insults of his shouted orders . . . loading everything into the holds! . . . Our wheat! Our meat! Our blood! Everything of ours! . . . The sacks keep coming and never stop! Sack after sack after sack! Nothing but sacks! Until we are broken! . . . We move along aimlessly . . . in an uncontrolled throng, pushed on by the horror of the supply and demand [of manpower], bumping into one another, hoping to be picked and separated from the flock like sheep! This isn't what a man was meant to be! This is making us beasts of burden, machines, starving dogs with loading ramps for a muzzle. . . . Beasts! Dogs!

The unforgiving pace of work among stevedores at Puerto Madero could be traced to the triumph of Frederic Taylor's criteria and calculations. Taylor's greatest contribution to the interests of capitalism was his understanding of the nature of weight, in particular the relation between the time when a worker is bearing weight and the time when he is at rest. Taylor observed workers at Bethlehem Steel unloading train wagons; stacking material; loading furnaces; and collecting ingots, incandescent sheet metal, and sheet rollers. He concluded that with ninety-pound loads, a worker did not put in "more than 43% of a day's work, carrying nothing for the remaining 57%." Thus, Taylor, choosing the strongest men, did not allow workers to pick up and put down loads at will, but paced them through the verbal commands of foremen, who set the periods for work and rest. As a result, the same workers moved forty-seven and a half tons a day instead of twelve and a half (Palacios n.d., 69).

Palacios wanted his contemporaries in Argentina to think about what happened to workers' bodies subjected to Taylor's rationalization of labor. Even when "inferior" or physically disadvantaged workers were made useless as a labor force, condemned to unemployment because the system replaced the weak with the strong, the harm done to the bodies of healthy workers soon became clear. These workers were subjected to a drastic change in the pattern of labor, based on the optimization of time and a sustained rate of work. Palacios cited Upton Sinclair, who observed, at the end of the nineteenth century, that "the speed [of life] was increasing daily, although in ways that were not felt." Sinclair was referring specifically to Jurjis, a Lithuanian metalworker who increased working rates, "repudiated the union, and condemned the weak, so that even his own father . . . was reduced to misery . . . begging for a chance to earn a crust of bread" (Palacios n.d., 99). Taylor even used himself as a model, recalling how, when he worked as a mechanic, "the other workers suggested I slow down . . . by half, under threat of being thrown out of the factory" (qtd. in Palacios n.d., 99). But if Taylor's pragmatism was intended to suggest that the optimization of labor began at home, with him, he was hardly in a position to measure its further effects. After doing manual work, he graduated as an engineer, then became a factory manager and later a capitalist technocrat. Hence, he had no opportunity to measure the effects of labor on his own body.

In *El pobre hombre* (The Poor Man, 1920), a "drama about contemporary life" by José González Castillo, the Old Man cannot find work, to the shame of his son:

> OLD MAN: Where? I'm good for nothing. . . . I'm old, half blind, with all these aches and pains. . . . After three days they'd throw me out anywhere . . . like they threw me out of Sanfuertes after twenty-five years. (González Castillo 1920, 9)

Lost or damaged eyesight was a frequent techno-pathology, since natural light shifted in the factories and workshops along with the seasons, the time of day, and weather conditions. Industrial health inspector Carlos Carreño gave no precise indications for each case, but he did stress the importance of illuminating all the corners, corridors, and passages in the complex and hardly ergonomic factories: "Whether natural or artificial, light should be measured by its intensity. . . . Artificial lighting should be sufficiently intense to produce a light comparable to daylight, be constant and uniform, and not dazzle or cast shadows across the space" (1931, 18). However, the lack of precise regulations gave factory owners a free hand to do as they pleased. Complaints caused by poorly illuminated workplaces ranged from "frequent blinking, watering, photophobia, and tiredness," to "asthenopia, myopia, and eye conditions such as nystagmus that lead to blindness": "Deprived of the benefit of natural light, our blood grows weak in hemoglobin and induces pallor and particular weaknesses, especially those reported in print-shop workers, watchmakers, lithographers, engravers, goldsmiths, tailors, and seamstresses" (Carreño 1931, 18).

The hazards of unregulated work are given center stage in Francisco DeFilippis Novoa's drama *Los desventurados* (The Unlucky Ones, 1923). The foundry worker Eulogio describes his working conditions: "The bar shoots out red hot in front of you like a sword. There's hardly time to cut it. Woosh! I'd already counted seventeen on my side this afternoon when I see one more coming out the other furnace. I was about to count eighteen when Pepin shouts out 'Look out' and . . . God help my feeble body and eyes" (DeFilippis Novoa 1923, 7). Here, for the first time in Argentinean culture, a male confesses fear and anxiety at the thought of losing his strength, realizing that his body cannot take it anymore. To declare this fear openly, or to cover it up through some kind of ruse, became perplexing constants of industrialization. On the one hand, there was no time for *cuerpos transicionales* (transitional bodies), caught up in the changes, to adjust to the new rhythms of work whose brutality was perceived with even greater sensitivity precisely because of its sudden imposition. On the other hand, failure to keep up with the pace of work produced bodies unfit to be hired. They were broken models, weakened and discarded, far removed from exemplary masculinity's paradigms for whole, vigorous bodies. Eulogio's account also highlights the constant need for adjustment to sensorial/corporeal maps, made all the more exhausting because it involves concentration, staying alert and attuned to three areas (the senses, the muscles, and cognition). In addition to keeping themselves ready to dodge out of the way throughout the entire workday, laborers also faced the dangers of high temperatures and molten materials. Foundry workers were exposed to heat, and those most affected were precisely those most adaptable to the high temperatures of the furnaces. This was why specialists in industrial medicine recommended "breaking the day into shifts . . . two hours work alternating with two hours rest" (Mordeglia and Francone 1940, 55) and even reducing the workweek—a notion that went against the interests of standardizing industrial practices.

There are no texts quite like Roberto Arlt's for retrieving the impact of the rhythm of the industrial city on men's bodies. The characters in *Los siete locos* (Seven Madmen) and *Los lanzallamas* (The Flamethrowers) display symptoms of severe somatization, defining themselves either as suffering bodies or as bodies that have gone beyond the point of feeling, to the extreme that Erdosain is described as having "a body . . . he saw only when he brought it in front of a mirror" (Arlt 1981c, 1: 191). Perhaps this is why Erdosain suggests that, in the infernal city, "you had to forget your body in order not to suffer" (1: 319): "Every question . . . resonates in his brain; every thought is transformed into physical pain. Erdosain listens to the din of these pains reverberating in the phalanges of his fingers, in the knots of his muscles and the warm recesses of his intestines. . . . He squeezes his temples, crushes them with his fists; he is at the black center of the world; he is the suffering, carnal core of a pain that radiates three hundred and sixty degrees" (1: 329). The symptoms of stress include panic attacks, high blood pressure, cardiac arrhythmia, vertigo, insomnia, migraines, muscular tension, digestive upsets (gastritis, dyspepsia, ulcers), tremors, and feelings of claustrophobic oppression (Last and Hersen 1989, 520). Erdosain feels all these symptoms: pounding migraines, a body wracked by contorted muscles ("The knot that connects his band of thoughts"), anxiety attacks related to respiratory difficulty: "authentic voids," "armor that plates his life," "caged beasts prowling around his hovel against the indestructible bars of his rambling" (Arlt 1981c, 1: 343). His pain makes him feel every inch of his body as if it is but a passive surface on which the city's abuse has left marks, having held him in its grip: "[The pain] is like a triangle, its apex reaching to his neck and its base in his stomach, while from its frozen sides there emanates the rounded emptiness of uncertainty toward his brain. . . . They've made maps of the muscles and arteries, but how will they make *maps of the pain* that spreads throughout our poor bodies?" (1: 342; emphasis added).

Urban maps in Arlt's world are literally "maps of pain," and the body of each of his characters is the "core of a pain that radiates three hundred and sixty degrees." Maryse Renau argues that in Arlt's writing, "the masses . . . unconsciously plead for relief from their anxiety" (1989, 213): "Erdosain tosses impatiently in bed. He has no strength left either to breathe heavily or to bellow in pain. It feels like his wrists are bound by metal straps. He rubs their insides nervously, and it feels like the links of a chain have ensnared his hands. He turns over slowly in bed, changing the position of the pillow. . . . The terrible question that swings like a clapper inside the triangular hollow of his chest and evaporates . . . into the bladder that is his brain is pumped out inexorably by a millstone through the ventricles of his heart" (Arlt 1981c, 1: 342). Yet Buenos Aires could not possibly contain the sleepless anguish of the masses, because its own languages and imaginaries had already triggered a frenetic flow of blood through its streets, as if transferring the pressure and speed of the rhythms of industrial production to the body of the city itself. But where did this anguish come from?

Elías Castelnuovo's "El delirio" (Delirium, 1934) follows a man's "dialogue" with his wife, a delirious conversation held while his wife sleeps: "Forgive me, Antonia. Understand that if I bring no money for food . . . I see the baby's thin. I understand you too are more and more worn out. . . . But you must see I'm not to blame. You must understand the suffering, the bitterness of a man who never stops walking all day long to bring something home and after walking so much shows up, like me now, with empty hands" (Castelnuovo 1968, 77). The transitional city still has no place for the understanding for which the man pleads. Antonia is certainly not his interlocutor. In fact, he is confronting his own gendered expectations, which hound him with specters of failure and humiliation and pitilessly strip him of his virile identity:

> (*Beginning to get angry again.*) I should earn some money if I don't want to let my son die of hunger? . . . And how should I do that? Working? . . . Give me some work? I should look for it? And what am I doing out of the house all the time? What d'you think I'm doing? . . . Sunning myself on a bench in the park? I should change trades? Well today I asked for work washing wool! Can you believe it? That's what I did! A mechanic like me offering to wash sheep's wool. How sickening! . . . Everything is so corrupt . . . those on top can't even hire those beneath them. . . . I should beg? Antonia! Did I hear you right? . . . Me? A man like me? A grown man? Healthy like me? I'd rather rob, kill, strangle someone! I'd much rather! It's more dignifying. (77)

A skilled *obrero* "lowering" himself to work at washing, just like a proletarian woman? A man pushed to the edge of his manliness.

The story "El chino de Dock Sur" (The Chinaman on the South Dock, 1920), by Héctor Pedro Blomberg, contains an advertisement placed in *La Nación* and the *Buenos Aires Herald* by Juan Wang: "Young Chinaman, knows how to cook, sew, wash clothes of any kind. Only speaks English." How he earns his living provokes amusement and scorn among the women of his sordid *conventillo* in La Boca, especially a prostitute: "The sight of a man washing clothes from dawn until dusk seemed so comical [to Lola]" (Blomberg 1920, 73). But the Chinese immigrant is flexible when it comes to work and identity, which allows him to survive the turbulent flood of an unyielding, pragmatic modernity, which produced unheard-of sights—like long queues of unemployed hungry men at soup kitchens (figure 25). Juan Wang is a man, but he joins the workforce as a woman. He is an unskilled proletarian who cannot even speak the national language, a Chinese immigrant in a country expecting skilled, fair-skinned northern Europeans. He is a margin on the margin. In the confusion of an eminently transitional milieu, however, Juan Wang takes advantage of the pickings available to the quick and the ready, choosing not to comply with compulsive masculine identities. Castelnuovo's tortured character in "El delirio" is an entirely different kettle of fish. He confronts the economic/identitary dislocation of unemployment without bending, with no room to maneuver, constantly haunted by the imaginary being that, in reality, he only carries inside himself: "Antonia, I beg you, please. Don't laugh! . . . Don't give me those *snake's eyes* again. Don't you see there's nothing for anyone anymore?" (Castelnuovo 1968, 78–79; emphasis added).

In the immense corpus of social texts on violence of that time, Castelnuovo's narrative is particularly striking for its capacity to capture the trajectory of a crucial transference: a powerless man resorts to violence as a social remedy, in order to restore to himself something of the identitary wholeness of manliness. As he drowns in the pit of his anguish and desperation, his wife appears to him with "snake's eyes": "It's true. I don't deny it. I beat you. And why do I do it? Because you are terrible, Antonia! . . . I come in off the street half crazed, and you drive me completely crazy. . . . (*Just as he turns toward the closed bedroom door, the baby's cry is heard. . . .*) Why is he crying? . . . From hunger? . . . Is he crying from hunger? . . . Through my fault? You're lying, you wretch! . . . What a fate! What a mean woman! Don't you see that I haven't eaten either? Don't you see, you miserable, filthy, down-and-out bitch . . . ? Don't you see I'm still a man? Are you laughing? You're laughing again? Watch it, I'll break your spirit!" (79). This character foresees a time when "not even women will have to think of anything but money and food, like animals." In the meantime, as long as "there's nothing for anyone," interpersonal dynamics will transfer violence from the public sphere to the private, from the economic and political to relations between the sexes. He reproaches Antonia for her mockery of him because she—a "miserable, filthy, down-and-out bitch"—fails to see that he is "still a man."

"Thirty million unemployed, two million of them in Argentina. . . . there seems to be a terrible poverty in the world. A crisis the likes of which was never seen before. No one says anything so as not to frighten people" (Arlt 1981a, 188). Thus wrote Arlt in "Aguinaldo inesperado" (Unexpected Christmas Gift; 12 December 1931), a chronicle relating the effects of the 1929 global crisis. In "Busca trabajo a las cuatro de la mañana" (Looking for Work at Four A.M.), Arlt follows the steps of an unemployed man, "his overcoat almost stiff with dirt . . . a grim expression on his face . . . and his tie twisted like a hangman's noose": "He is the lonely, waiting man, to use a term from Scalabrini Ortiz. The man of the lost hours, as Nalé Roxlo would say. Nobody takes pity on him because people look at his sturdy frame and thick wrists and say to themselves: 'Let him work in the docks,' without realizing there are no jobs for anyone in the docks" (Arlt 1981a, 189). "Look! Look at my feet! They are ruined from so much walking! Worn out! Even Christ had no feet like these," exclaims the main character in "El delirio" (Castelnuovo 1968, 99). A similar comment may be found in Arlt's *Las aguafuertes porteñas* (*Porteño* Sketches, 1928–33), in "Lo tragicómico: El botín con la suela desprendida" (Tragicomedy: The Boot with the Loose Sole; 1 February 1929): "Jesus was not made to walk along the road to Calvary with a sole hanging loose from one of his boots. If he had, his *via crucis* would have been more bitter." At every step, "the sole gets in the way [of the unemployed walker]; you can't stand your boot, and that tongue trips you up however much you raise your foot as you step; it rolls up on itself . . . so that you have a kind of wheel under your foot that unrolls as you lift it and folds over on itself as you lower it" (Arlt 1981a, 210). As in the rest of Arlt's world, unforgiving looks unsurprisingly return the marginalized subject to the hell of humiliation, where he belongs: "Now . . . even the blind stare at you. You glance around you like one who is shipwrecked. . . . A heroic remedy is called for in such circumstances . . . like asking the owner [of a delicatessen or butcher's shop] for the loan of a knife, not to kill yourself, although you are not without reasons, but to cut off the sole" (Arlt 1981a, 211).

Cast into the street by one crisis of capitalist adjustment after another, these wanderers are experts at disguising "the torn seat of a pair of pants" or "the hole in the felt of a black hat," at hiding "a dirty or threadbare shirt cuff" or calculating "how to bend their leg when their pants are horribly baggy around the knees," if only to delay the discovery of their "downfall and poverty" for a moment. "Reality is the plazas packed with the unemployed," the "crowds of bearded men, poorly dressed . . . willing to work just for food . . . for whatever the boss will pay. . . . People go to all the places like these, giving their labor away." The writing in *Las aguafuertes porteñas* itself seems to choke at the sight of "Plaza Once, at four in the afternoon, without a single empty bench. . . . Go into any café on Avenida de Mayo, and you witness a drama. An unhappy soul of indefinably advanced age goes by hawking ties . . . the one selling garters moves on, and another with umbrellas comes by" (Arlt 1981a, 185). The bustle acquires a very different form in the bars described in *Las aguafertes porteñas,* where it is more like a sorrowful stage of unemployment: "I feel affection [for these bars] because at their tables . . . the men whose feet are swollen from so much walking take a break; they collapse like exhausted horses after empty miles of unsuccessfully peddling their wares": "I think of those boys having to take to the street without yet being men. By eleven in the morning, discouraged and fed up with walking, they drop like exhausted mules and order a coffee gazing into the distance at a happy country that doesn't exist. . . . This is life in the raw, life in this city of unemployment in quick time and layoffs every few months. This is the life of almost all the sons of a proletarian family without a trade, advantage, or job" (Arlt 1981a, 151).

Arlt's chronicles are likely the most revealing record of the impact of the Wall Street collapse on peripheral modernity. They seem to have been written from the perspective of the bodies of those who "drop like exhausted mules," beaten down by the weight of their discouragement, "gazing into the distance at a happy country that doesn't exist." They portray sensorial maps of Buenos Aires through worn-out shoes, swollen feet, the exhaustion of walking, and the relief of sitting down for a quick coffee. Their titles are like cinematic images of the city: "Begging on Avenida de Mayo," "The Terrifying Employment Agency," "The Man Ashamed of Lunching on Milk Coffee," "The Tragedy of the Man Looking for Work," "On the Different

Ways of Sleeping in Our City," "The Man in the Wet Undershirt," "The Man Who Stretches His Money," "The Pleasure of Drifting," "The Sentimental Silliness of Suicide," "The Man Who Does Boys' Work," "So, Let's Talk about the Unemployed," "The Messenger's Humble and Tragic Life," "Don't Get Sick if You're Poor," "To Be in Bad Straits," "Furnished Room with Full Board," "Night Shift," "Soliloquy of an Unemployed Man Who Never Had a Job," "Soliloquy of a Man Expecting to Be Fired," "Looking for a Handout."

I would like to address cultural environments where the effects of the economic crises that afflicted Argentina from the beginning of the century may be traced. I will begin with a *grotesco* by Carlos de Paoli, *Los chicos de Pérez* (Pérez's Children, 1916), concerning the numerous family of an "everyman" named Juan Pérez living in a modest apartment. All on the same day, Juan becomes unemployed; one of his daughters is expelled from school; his daughter Bertha puts off her wedding because her fiancé has been out of work for three months; his son loses his glasses in a fight; and his sister, from whom he had hoped to borrow fifty pesos to avoid eviction, takes refuge in his home because she has been evicted herself. The moneylender Rabowisky, who turns up to collect back payments on old debts, tells him: "Do y'know, you're a really cheeky one?" Moreover, in the adjoining room, his wife has had premature triplets, which—to cap it all off—Rabowisky suggests are not Juan's. In such a scenario, a stage direction reads: *"Don Juan leans against the door in order not to collapse. It's not happening to him, but is all in his imagination. . . . His face shows him to be the unhappiest man on earth."* Meanwhile his children cry, run, fall about, play, and fight. Rat poison crosses his mind:

> JUAN: My poor head! I can't take any more! What if I end it once and for all! . . .
> My downfall . . . without a job and more children . . . what can I do with this
> lousy life? (*Runs to the Lysol, then . . . downs the contents of the bottle.*) I've done
> it. . . . *Consumatum est.* . . . In ten minutes I'll go up like a rocket. . . . My God!
> . . . Kill me quickly, please! (Paoli 1977, 125)

Juan later appears on stage wearing "a strange apron belonging to his wife," carrying one of the triplets on his arm while "holding a feeding bottle in the hand of the same arm. He has a frying pan in the other hand since he's come from the kitchen." While trying to maintain order ("Cretinous kids. . . . Your father's slaving in the kitchen, and you're roaring around like pigs!

Sardanápalos!"), he wipes his hands on the apron and announces that "dinner is ready" (134). In other words, he is doing "women's" work:

JUAN: My child, . . . you have plenty of what many men are lacking. . . . Character . . .

BERTHA: You're a good man, Daddy.

JUAN: I'm good for nothing, child.

FELIBERTO: Of course, he's a nobody! (*Bursts out crying.*) He'd like to be a man. (133)

It is "natural" for Juan's daughter Bertha to cry because she is female: "*She crosses to the machine and begins to sew. . . . She dries a tear with the sleeve of her blouse*" (134). But something is decidedly wrong from the moment when Juan also weeps: "*A tear he has not been able to hold in wells up, and he wipes it with the palm of his hand*" (136). From the start, Paoli's play shows no distinction between father and daughter: "*he crosses to the machine, picks up the sewing. . . . Two tears well up in his eyes, and he dries them with the sleeve of his shirt*" (118). Juan weeps from the cumulative melodrama of losses and woe that has been his life. His tears remind us of the tearful storytellers of tango, who are perhaps also weeping for something *other* than abandonment by a treacherous woman.

In a remarkable document entitled *Vidas: Apuntes de una visitadora* (Lives: Notes of a Welfare Visitor), the social worker Pilar de Algarra describes her interviews with proletarian families in the 1930s. One of the houses she visited offers a familiar picture of the never-ending crises in male employment. The woman interviewed, who works at home for a fine lingerie store, "had set up her workshop in her spotless kitchen." "They paid her quite well," Algarra notes, which surprised her, because "it is not common for stores to pay . . . equitably." Algarra perceives the woman's justifiable pride in the success that has crowned her demanding piecework: "Señora, I have to feed and clothe seven hungry children": "I asked her if she was a widow, and she motioned toward a man sitting in a chair at one end of the room as she told me she was not. . . . The [magazine] he was reading covered his face. I am not sure whether he seemed not to hear what his wife was saying out of shame or indifference" (Algarra 1943, 60). The social worker enters the furthest corners of the home, where she sees a shadowy being—a man—killing time during working hours. This was a new but common social phenomenon at a time when inclusion in the formal economy was tough. The unemployed male was an "evident irony" (60), an equivocal version of hardened masculinity—apathetic men, "idle fathers." Discursive positions are here reversed: now the man is the one observed. The two women talk about him as if he were a "case," highlighting his deviant condition. One of the women is a laborer, the other a professional. Both have doubtless overcome the obstacles to entering the female labor market, as is evident in the productive efficiency of the sewing workshop and, in the social worker's case, the writing of a professional report that evinces her contribution to the public record and her participation in public administration. From the perspective of long-established identitary imaginaries, however, this new species of male had no social place: he was an object without remedy.

Victor J. Seidler invites us to consider masculinity not from an essentialist point of view, but as the experience of specific historical moments. If modernity conceived of "masculinity as power invisible, for the rule of men is simply taken as an expression of reason and 'normality'" (Siedler 1989, 4), it is easy to understand why the unemployed father hides his face. The woman interviewed explains: "He didn't last in any job, and every time they let him go he got upset, so I prefer him to stay home. He's only good for taking my sewing to the store, and I have to give him a small commission for doing that" (Algarra 1943, 60). The social worker, on the other hand, is concerned that, having become his wife's errand boy, this man implies the end of proper balance and the persistence of a bad example: "There seems to be no cure for these apathetic men; their most immediate error is being a harmful example to their children, who grow up without encouragement or awareness of the responsibilities they must take on in the future" (60). Algarra also makes note of cases in which families "are forced to vacate a dwelling because the rent is unpaid, and yet the woman admits that her husband gambles away everything he has.... This vice is spreading like wildfire and ends up corrupting all sense of morality" (60).

In *Vidas,* Algarra conveys the feeling that she is watching daily life in transition. There was as yet no record of such a life, and when she is faced with it, she does not remain neutral: "The women are the ones who work and look after the entire family. Their husbands, stretched out on the bed, only get up to drink maté. And, when their self-esteem surfaces, on account of their conduct, they argue that it is difficult to find work, that they are not

Gender and Politics

taken on once they are past a certain age" (Algarra 1943, 59). In the dark en-
closures of their kitchens, with exhausting efforts, women manage to feed
their families while their husbands "fail." Searching for some light in order
to bear the struggles of present, the woman interviewed by Algarra dreams
of the future: "Pulling back a curtain . . . she shows me an unexpected scene.
A girl dressed in black tights and wearing pointed slippers is dancing on
tiptoe to the sound of a vitrola. . . . My little girl is studying dancing at the
National Conservatory and wants to dance at the Colón Theater. . . . Don't
you think, Señora, . . . she looks a little Russian? . . . Of course, we'd have
to change her name to a Russian one. . . . Many ballerinas are Italian, and
they take on Russian names" (51). Algarra's writing itself carefully opens
a crack in the curtain. The social worker highlights both the dreams born
of a mother's despair and her blind spots. This "poor mother" sees in her
daughter what is not there: "I looked at the young girl and only saw in her
something of a gypsy type with olive skin, black eyes, and curly hair of the
same color." The text reverses the deluded imaginaries of Buenos Aires. While
such imaginaries make it possible to see what is *not* there, *Vidas* sees exactly
what *is* there, reinserting whatever has been hushed up by self-enabling narratives. The reader feels that, with or without a Russian pseudonym, far from
becoming another Pavlova, the future ballerina will most likely never make
it to the Colón. She may, in fact, be drawn into the vast, faceless crowd of
cabareteras, tonadilleras, and tango dancers. There is also a remarkable identitary shift perceptible here: the child's mother has dismissed the man of the
house. He has become invisible, and she has placed her hope for social mobility in the next generation of women, while still remaining ignorant of the
fact that diastolic dreams do not always come true in that "happy country"
filled with "splendors" (Arlt 1981c, 1: 157).

17 THE *GARÇONIÈRES* AND THE SEX OF POWER

<small>Cabarets like the Palais de la</small> Glace, Pabellón de las Rosas, Armenonville, and Hansen were passageways in the cultural geographies of Buenos Aires between the elite and the tango of the urban underworld. In 1912, Baron Antonio de Marchi (Demarchi) organized a party at the Palais de la Glace that acclimated tango to the upper-class salons of the capital (Calcagno et al. 1992, 111). Both cabarets and *garçonières* were highly revealing cultural spaces, allowing us a glimpse of how the upper and lower classes mixed and how certain rules of the social game evolved, particularly those concerned with sexual servitude. More so than cabarets, however, which were, after all, public spaces, *garçonières* spatialized the symbolic capital and power of the elite with respect to the sexuality of the city.

In the Eduardo de Labar/Luis César Amadori tango "Portero, suba y diga" (Doorman, Go Up and Tell Her, 1928), the speaker has followed his lover or wife (the text does not specify their exact relationship) to the place of her amorous assignations. Since angry, violent scenes might soon unfold, he assures the doorman guarding the entrance to the building:

Don't worry,
don't you see I'm calm?
I followed her
just to see
if it is true
she debases my affection
with those young men [*niños*] in that *garçonière*.

The speaker stops once the woman has crossed the threshold of an apartment belonging to a *niño bien,* aware he can go no further, and asks the doorman to "go up and tell that ingrate / that I have come / to charge her with treachery."[1] That is, he sends a messenger because he cannot penetrate the building himself to confront the abductors. "Portero, suba y diga," then, shows us a powerless subject, stranded and blocked at a doorway he cannot possibly cross, because the *garçonière* belongs, in effect, to a class of private, exclusive spaces jealously protected against any incursion from the street. If anyone can go up to the apartment, aside from its residents, the doorman can, because of his job, as can the occasional visitor and the woman who makes herself sexually available to the *bacanes.* The speaker, however, must resort to a servant of the privileged to convey a message that can only be delivered by a mediator:

And tell those cowards . . .
there's a man out here
if they have the courage;
and tell her, my friend,
I'm waiting for her here,
I'm here dying
of love for her.

The speaker invites the *bacanes* to come down from the *garçonière* "if they have the courage." In other words, he challenges them to come down to his level, calling them out, as in a case of ritual bravery. But duels in Buenos Aires were either a matter for the residual culture of valor of the *compadrito* or affairs between equals, gentlemen. Although duels had been made illegal in 1922, the speaker challenges the *bacanes* in 1928, perhaps as a way of returning to a world already lost, built on other values. Yet as modernity's strongest social actors, the *bacanes* would never consent to a duel with a contender who was not their equal; further, the weapons they carried were not swords or pistols, but of a rather different nature: the new factories and the old commonplaces of fraud, political swindling, and sexual privilege. A duel would also imply an unthinkable condescension/descent in relation to an inferior who, not for nothing, was to be kept "outside." The *bacanes* had no need to *go down,* in any case, because the woman had *come up* to the *garçonière* in her capacity as courtesan and sexual servant.

In *Sociabilidad en Buenos Aires: Hombres, honor y cafés, 1862–1910* (Social Life in Buenos Aires: Men, Honor, and Cafés, 1862–1910), Sandra Gayol highlights the importance of honor in disputes among social actors during the transitional times at the turn of the century: "Virtue did not depend exclusively on the sexual behavior of women," but on a complex system of social opinion concerning competition and conduct in the public sphere: "Although male honor consisted of exerting male authority, in compliance with the precepts of patriarchy, and winning over women belonging to other men as proof of virility, masculinity was also defined by courage and cold-bloodedness, strength and valor. The ability to protect a woman doubtless counted, but it was clearly not enough without bodily strength, honesty, a sense of duty, and a knowledge of some essentially manual skills" (2000, 246). Nevertheless, the muscular strength of the injured speaker in "Portero, suba y diga" will not help him restore his social space in the public sphere. Nor will his honesty or sense of duty have much impact on the armor of symbolic languages, in the new forms of social barter and transactions. Since the language of courage had become a code without currency or echo in the modern city, the speaker in "Portero, suba y diga" is left with his word alone—to speak in a tango, to ask someone to speak for him, or to have the tango speak for him. I believe that the explicit indirectness evident in "Portero, suba y diga" reveals the mediated nature of the discursive positions of middle-class and proletarian social actors. The powerlessness of its speaker may be read as a sign of the gradual implosion in political representation within the trajectory of incipient democracy in Argentina, a void that may well have been imprinted/embossed on the nonaffirming discourse of tango and the desire to weep. At the same time, this ventriloquism is symmetrical to a lamentably irreversible rarefaction in communication between the impotent proletarian man and a woman who abandons the ecology of the *conventillo* because she sees freedom in the mirages and silken flights of fancy of the *garçonière.*

The break occurs precisely when traditional interaction between the sexes is overturned. For the subaltern male, to speak or to gain access to a woman, socially and sexually, is no longer a tacit matter of reassuring conventional gendered hierarchies, but of uncharted territory, without the guidance of maps, empirical archives, or sources of reference. He must accept the shifting identities: an aspiring woman and a beaten man. The moment the woman in "Portero, suba y diga" accesses the physical/symbolic space of the *garçonière,* she performs new proxemic distances by turning a deaf ear to the spoken and sexual message of her subaltern equal, while she opens her body to the oligarchic *bacán.* Let us recall that the speaker asks the doorman to address two different groups: "those young men in that *garçonière*" and the woman herself ("tell her, my friend, / I'm waiting for her"), emphasizing his passive ("waiting") and subordinate (below) position in relation to her.

The proletarian male and the oligarchic, landowning male here confront the new class struggle armed with old weapons. The *bacán* owns the *garçonière* in the same way he owns the means of production. The proletarian woman who goes up to the *garçonière* is yet another extension of the elite's symbolic capital and the class struggle: she is the elites' "booty of war." What the speaker in the tango disputes is the sexual territory. It has clearly been confiscated by upper-class males, and his ability to reverse other kinds of dislocation —political repression, economic and cultural marginalization, the plunder of his body weakened by the pace of work, unemployment, and other identitary slippages—is equally doubtful. As for the woman, she goes up to the *bacán,* who, as a member of a parasitic oligarchy, does not have to do much to win her. Buenos Aires had trapped the proletarian woman between the devastation of the *conventillo* and the violence of the factories. The compensatory imaginaries of the marketplace had played their part in conferring a positive meaning on the wrench of separation from family, home, and proletarian or middle-class equals. The speaker in the tango is the powerless figure of the void and the inclemency of the street; the woman embodies identitary displacement; and the *bacán*—that figure waiting unhurriedly, without effort or concern, to see her enter the space/property of his *garçonière* —is the vampire.

To what extent is the doorman the tango speaker's interlocutor or perlocutor? We might say that the lyric voice seeks out the doorman as his interlocutor ("tell her, my friend"). In the imaginary of the profound crisis in male identity, the complicity that might arise from common experiences should cause these two to join forces, given that abandonment by a woman (*amuramiento*) was widespread at the time. Moreover, the doorman, like the speaker, is a man and "a working stiff." Yet, because he earns his keep by serving the señorito in the *garçonière,* he has a foot in two cultural camps. How can we imagine him going upstairs to the bachelor's apartment to repeat the two messages—"Tell those cowards . . . / there's a man out here" and "tell her . . . / I'm here dying / of love for her"? The doorman bears a declaration of defeat in a struggle that has transpired "in other places."

In the syntax of the city, different types of buildings—factory, hospital, school, marketplace—are defined by their function as part of a whole that allows them to be understood. At the level of collective space, architecture brings the (collective) body of the city together as a totality. What, then, was the function of the *garçonière* in collective space? In principle, the *garçonière* was a space in the modern city where all the imaginaries of Buenos Aires intersected profusely. On the one hand were the languages of power expressed through the oligarchy's sexuality and economic vampiric/parasitic power. On the other were the languages of powerlessness and loss of manliness spoken by middle-class and proletarian males no longer able to compete for a woman against such an unequal rival. The fact that the speaker in Amadori's lyrics here is unable to voice his complaint on his own behalf reveals his sexual impotence with respect to the oligarchy's many "virile" spaces. Silvio Astier bitterly understands that the homes/treasure chests of the elite guard the symbolic capital of privilege, including the sexuality of Buenos Aires's "beautiful women." Thus, in the sexual powerlessness of the tango speaker, I read a corollary of his political powerlessness and economic exclusion. Only the *bacán*'s equals were welcome in the *garçonière.* Women entered only to surrender their bodies.

I believe that tango is an abundant source of chatter and relentless complaint about sexual, political, and economic impotence. The voice of the speaker in "Portero suba y diga," and what he has to say, are always exposed to the risks of the indirectness and misrepresentation of ventriloquism. I further believe that a symmetry exists between the enforced indirectness of the subaltern voice of the tango, asking another to address the elite on his behalf, and the mediating political representation of Yrigoyen and Alvear, whose imaginaries had a propensity to deflate crises and social fractures. According to *La culpa la tiene el gallego del frente* (The *Gallego* Opposite Is to Blame): "You must laugh, gentlemen! . . . The bitter die from their own bile!" In *Mañana será otro día* (Tomorrow's Another Day), anyone opening a wound is criticized: "You're the only discordant note in this harmonious family group living here." The speaker in "Portero, suba y diga" strikes the same discordant note: he is out of step, claiming the moral authority of his own *personal* drama, which the closed doors of the *garçonière* will render invisible in the trivializing euphoria of the city. Nevertheless, tangos like those by Armando Discépolo would contribute to redramatizing the city, thereby preserving its last tragic traces.

Even Rubén Darío had something to say about the sinisterness of sexual appropriation in "*Garçonière*" (1896):

> It was a friendly bachelor nest
> of laughter, poems, and rowdy pleasures;
> every gentleman was inspired
> by blue dreams and golden wine. (Darío 1977, 195)

Darío's bachelor is not the cowardly *bacán* of "Portero, suba y diga," but a *caballero* (a gentleman), who alternates pleasure with poetry and laughter:

> A fair-haired man spoke sententious lines:
> refusing, then loving the eternal muses;
> a dark-haired man recites a poem like a rose,
> in rounded rhymes and tender words.

In 1929, Hermina Brumana had warned: "Ah, the young men who write verses! How women have always allowed themselves to be lulled by their words!" (1973, 47). Ensnared by the ambiguity of love and possession, Darío's "white doves of the *garçonière*" hover between happiness and a "veiled" melancholy: "sadness moved on, veiled and confused; / happiness snowed roses and orange blossom." What was to be expected of the *garçonière*? Was it the *caballero*'s place of love or his place of power? From the *bacán*'s point of view, at least, the smiles of the muse "who brings pleasure and carries off pain" should prevail. Yet Darío's speaker both wants and does not want to reveal the darkness of the "friendly bachelor nest," opting for the distance provided by classical mythology in order to speak of sexual violence, thereby dissociating it from the savage crime reports and sexual mistreatment of everyday life in Buenos Aires: "And around their brows kissed by laurel . . . / the satyr and centaur joyfully wear / the noble joy of the golden wine." Sons of Bacchus, fauns, Sylvanus, and Pan, the satyrs and centaurs are associated with the rape and abduction of virgins, unrestrained pursuit, and insatiable sexuality. Darío's euphemism here allows us to glimpse his ambiguous discursive position, unmasking the *bacán* as a *caballero*-rapist (half man, half beast), a hybrid whose aggression/generosity is hidden/revealed through the complicity of ample payment to the woman who surrenders herself.

The *garçonière* combined the double domination of economic and sexual violence, perpetrated by oligarchs and men. Its nature was dual, like that of the centaur: it provided a space for love and slavery. This is how Federico Mertens must have understood the *garçonière* when he titled a *sainete La casa donde no entró el amor* (The House Where Love Didn't Enter, 1920). As Sandra Gayol remarks, "Women were a source of satisfaction and prestige . . . part of one's patrimony . . . a factor that raised or lowered a man's personal capital" (2000, 188). At the imaginary level, all *porteño* men likely desired to live in a *garçonière* and ensure for themselves the *bacán*'s active sexuality, which neither the castrated Astrologer in Arlt's *Los siete locos* nor Silvio Astier would ever enjoy. The *garçonière* was never a neutral place, never a dialogic site allowing the spontaneous revision of interactions among social actors. It was a space where the female body was exploited during modernity's class struggles, used to confirm the masculinity of elite men. No wonder a working-class man in Carlos Morganti's horse-racing *sainete Primero en la colorada* (First Past the Post, 1926) complains to his boss:

> LANGOSTA (*disdainfully, to Rivas*): That's what you [*bacanes*] are like. Riding high on your social standing, you don't hesitate to bring down a poor man's woman, as if neither of them had any right to be happy. (Morganti 1926, 24)

Similarly, in Nemesio Trejo's *sainete Las mujeres lindas* (Pretty Women), Julio describes the new amorous relations: "Poor men like us are dismissed by those in command, by those who hold the reins of power. . . . They take no notice of us, we annoy them if we approach to ask for something; but if it's a pretty woman, especially one of those whose look or smile commands instead of begs, the magnate, the big tycoon, the government minister, or whatever he is, goes as soft as a sponge and grants the favor while harboring a dream like someone with bad intentions or hopes like a criminal on the lookout" (Trejo 1977, 146).

Donatella Mazzoleni defines architecture as: "(1) an extension of the body, a way in which the body speaks, attempting to satisfy the need for totality; (2) a metaphor of the body, a way in which the body speaks in order to symbolize itself. A double and an accomplice" (1985, 12). A replica and a double of the body. If architecture is an extension of the body, then we must ask not only of what body Buenos Aires is an echo and extension but, above all, how the interior space of the *garçonière* acquires its shape. In the domain of the body, the design and manufacture of objects establish a nonverbal communication: the curvature of a doorknob reproduces the concavity of the hand: "The gesture of gathering; the sharp tools, the nails; the gesture of dividing; the tools of weaving and writing, the finger joints; the gesture of uniting. To the proxemic spheres of body movements, these are the greatest tools: those of rest and love (the bed), of nutrition (the kitchen), of conviviality (the table with chairs around it)" (Mazzoleni 1985, 14). Although the spaces of the modern city can be defined in terms of their function (hospital, school, factory), Mazzoleni argues that "they are none other than the separate, gigantic organs of a primordial house." Since Buenos Aires's urban reform was in the oligarchy's own writing, the city served as an extension of the body of the elite, a space tailored to the body for which it had been created, like a glove for a hand, a shirt for a torso, or a hat for a head. By the same token, the *garçonières* were ergonomically disposed to reaffirm social spaces in the sexuality of the city and to accommodate sexual fantasies in a private darkness that had a very public side to it.

Working with a staggering number of radiating and intersecting notions, urban imaginaries in Buenos Aires succeeded in muffling dissonant voices. Such voices spoke other types of language. They spoke, perhaps, through nonverbal languages and gestures that dominant imaginaries considered tangential, sly, or perversely deviant, unable to make themselves heard because of their hermetic and nonconventional configuration. How was it possible, for example, to detect the place where a woman in a *garçonière* resisted, so as not to become what the glove is to the hand? Once desire had been awakened, a slippage in identity and courtesan lust followed. Was there anything to intercept the completion of this circle of chains? If there were, perhaps it could be found in the ambivalent place of resistance/surrender occupied by the courtesan's imposture. In *Muñecos de trapo* (Rag Dolls, 1926), by Ricardo Villarán and E. González Cadavid, women are advised, "You have to be an actress on stage, but above all *off stage.*" In *Nadie la conoció nunca* (No One Ever Knew Her), Ivonne explains to the *bacán* she lives with, "That's how I've loved you, without feelings, as women like us learn to love; by living for pleasure, we are also its prisoners and give up everything for it." The courtesan's "skin"—her cynicism, her caustic disdain, her sarcastic resistance/surrender—allowed her to maintain her distance from the two identitary spaces of her proletarian origin and the cabaret/*garçonière,* becoming emotionally detached because she certainly knew she would always lose in these spaces. Her "resistance to love," therefore, was the space she kept just for herself, a hollow that refused to be molded concavely to conform to the shape of another. Perhaps this was the only enclosure where she went untouched—by the insatiable stares on the street; by the avid hands of the lover in a *garçonière;* by the customer in a cabaret, in a brothel, or picked up in the street. In that silent space, in the hollow space of her love, the courtesan would reconstruct herself through the hermetic configuration of a language that, like Lunfardo and *vesre,* served as imposture, premeditation, and transgression, as well as self-defense. In a city that did not belong to her, because it had been built by and for another, inside an individual body forced to be part of the city's public body, and intended for another, her "skin"—her distance—allowed her perhaps her only secure space, the only space where she could cease to "belong to another." Only inside this space could she remain unreachable, like a femme fatale. She could critique or invalidate the practices of dominant imaginaries through a "comeback" (*revancha*), to use Rossana Reguillo's term (1988, 108), as an evanescent being wizth no identitary mold that could truly contain her, or through reactive cunning, even if it led nowhere. However, the very skin/*revancha* that may have protected her against feeling also became the motive that fueled the violence of the misogyny that was directed against her.

18 IN-BETWEEN IDENTITIES, PERIPHERAL SEXUALITIES

It's always the women who kill the dream.

Juan Carlos Cobián and Enrique Cadícamo,
"La casita de mis viejos," 1931

I can forgive a man any crime.
Except not being a man.

Alfredo F. Lliri, *Castillos en el aire,* 1922

In a boardinghouse in *Los primeros fríos* (The First Frosts, 1910), a *sainete* by Alberto Novión, Sarita points something out to her friend:

Sarita: I've never heard you have a single kind word for men. . . .

Mercedes: I like to be alone, free, independent, the opposite of most girls who let themselves be dominated by men. Unlike them, I like to dominate men, play with them, laugh at their woes, make them suffer, torture them, despise them, make them my puppets, my puppies, my slaves. (Novión 1977, 53)

Transitional Buenos Aires exposed many fissures where intermediary spaces of identity went far beyond the stereotype of the femme fatale. Eduardo Mallea's eponymous character in "Serena Barcos" is an excellent example, described as "a skinny, strong woman, aged thirty-two. Laughter seemed not to agree with her unsociable face. . . . She had the look of a surly woman with jealous eyes." She is a university professional who works "with cold dedication" in a laboratory: "She had left home at seven, as she did every morning, and after crossing Reconquista and the poor neighborhood, had entered the laboratory, changed the gray, tailored jacket, with the shoulders just a little too wide, for a cotton pinafore . . . [and was] beginning to lay out the test tubes and burners for her task" (Mallea 1939, 323).

Serena takes refuge in the routines of her job during a time she reads as marked by "social uncertainty and the loss of status of all hierarchies" (Mallea 1939, 326). The ordered laboratory provides a kind of filter, allowing her to avoid a particularly crucial possibility: contact with men. As the narrator explains, "During almost all that time, her existence unfolded without any regard for men in anything having to do with a sentimental life; her contacts with them were strict, simple, and professional" (325). It is striking how closely her fear recalls that of Emma Zunz. Borges's narrator mentions that, with her friend "Elsa and the better Kronfusses, [Emma] discussed what cinema they would go to on Sunday afternoon. Then they talked about their boyfriends, and no one expected Emma to say anything. She would turn nineteen in April, but men still brought out a pathological horror" (Borges 1974, 1: 565). The narrator emphasizes Emma's "pathological horror" in particular, causing us to wonder what might have motivated it. The immediate origin of Serena's preventive proxemic distance lies in her response to the "rather dirty and unacceptable way those men" treated their girlfriends: "Those men tried to exploit their purely physical side and took exception when met with a contrary reaction, whether through feelings of chastity or just indifference to sex. And it was precisely at about that time when that business occurred with Bertha, a young woman . . . [who was] whipped by a wealthy, lecherous, unmarried man behind an apartment building" (Mallea 1939, 326). Mallea's character cannot avoid feeling "a wave of disgust and disdain for conventional relations between the two sexes." Like Emma Zunz, she prefers just to go out with her girlfriends and avoid "the poisonous, thankless presence of beings whose features never failed in the end to display an element of revolting bestiality" (326). Serena's haptic systems process the physical proximity of the male body from a highly defensive geography, its gradations increasing from dislike to disdain and disgust, until she foresees a fatal danger ("poisonous") and opts to retreat: "Like certain organisms that contract instinctively, she withdrew more and more into herself" (326).

As Elaine Showalter reminds us, feminists and suffragettes saw celibacy as a "silent strike against oppressive relations with men . . . as a political response to men's corrupt sexual behaviour" (1991, 22). Sexuality in "Emma Zunz" is associated with concentric spaces that have no exit. When posing as a prostitute, Emma Zunz is led by a sailor to "a door and then to a murky hallway and then to a winding stairway and then to a lobby . . . and then to a passageway and then to a door that closed behind her" (Borges 1974, 1: 566). No escape can be easily engineered from such a winding, labyrinthine space, which triggers feelings of vertigo and nausea. Sexuality is represented in "Emma Zunz" both through the pursuit by a male body whose physical anxiety inflicts relentless violence and through the unyieldingly unbearable proximity of another body, a sort of centripetal and claustrophobic space. With respect to Serena, all her energy is directed precisely at forestalling that inner deepening of oppression as a way of preventing the compulsion of hetero-sexual coupling: "By dwelling obsessively on the deception that seemed to live at the very heart of every man, her conflict with everything male was aggravated" (Mallea 1939, 326). Nevertheless, her phobic strategies do not always protect her entirely, because her walk through the streets after work —along the lock gates and Plaza Británica—inevitably exposes her to un-desirable contacts: "Sometimes a man followed her. Or he came up to her, with devious, gallant words, and she looked at him . . . with restrained fury and contempt" (330). The streets are problematic because public spaces are sites that reaffirm identitary places of conventional masculinity. Only in her own subjective space can Serena create areas of identity safeguarded from "the uncontained physical voracity" of men (330), that "male spirit of un-yielding domination in relation to women, their carnal plaything" (332). Whenever she talks with her boss, "with the slightest thing the man said, just because he was a man, it was not long before the caustic presence of a woman arose in her again, ready with cold determination to take her revenge . . . against the criminal delight she had seen exercised by so many men over certain pitiful, submissive female natures" (333).

In the misogynist imaginary of Mallea's story, her distance and critical re-actions are simply "vengeance." The woman's resistance consists in not be-coming "food for that hunger" (Mallea 1939, 335), in avoiding the male will "to create servitude under his dominion" (335). Serena becomes a social agent able to evaluate everyday social life, capable of maneuvering more freely among other models of subjectivity that had begun to surface in the polymorphous space of the city: "She looked at the working women and the men in the streets . . . she looked at the somnolent attitudes of the entire bourgeoisie alongside them and felt herself increasingly on the side of the former, preoccupied by . . . publications and news concerned with the fate of those people—just like anyone who might accompany in spirit someone painfully struggling for her own life in the next room" (331). To shape an alternative sexuality and to *move* herself into "the next room" are identitary shifts that allow her to engage in social interaction, while displacing Sylvain Sauvage's listless paradigm of self-absorption. But alternative models confronted the bewilderment they raised, as explained in the prologue to *44 horas semanales* (44 Hours a Week), by the feminist writer Josefina Marpons: "It is a difficult and confusing time for the new women, a painful moment, like any beginning, but through the pain of the moment runs a fertile, generous femininity, like a thin, stubborn thread of water seeking a safe channel for its ideal of a better humanity" (1936, 6).

According to Mallea's imaginary, Serena is a deviant who threatens conventional behavior. She belongs to an unprecedented collective of professional women, and her concern for social justice is seen as antagonistic to an acritical "women's place": "Those who heard her . . . took those rebellious ideas badly in a beautiful woman whose deportment and character were distinguished by nature . . . and they were left silenced and confused by the contempt this young woman appeared to profess for any falsehood or abuse of life" (Mallea 1939, 329). Serena smokes. She adopts an upright stance next to men, and even her clothing is cause for suspicion: "her felt hat and raincoat with its wide shoulders and pockets so low they made her stretch her arms to reach them" (333). She would certainly pay a very high price for her choice of identity, and the narrator dwells on the *escena de la solitaria* (scene of the lonely woman), on long silent walks beside the river at nightfall in the cold *porteño* winter, in order to indicate the scale of her transgression. When Mallea's character stops at a shop window, the glass reflects, "as well as the dark breath of the air, a face in which fatigue and a growing fear of her arid future were beginning to show their ravages" (338). The narrator goes even further: "What a rare, unwavering love hers was for a humanity she did not know" (333).

A deviation from the norm or, in any event, a transgressive slippage toward social configurations as yet unrecorded in the city's empirical archives, Serena is associated with the inflexible, the lean, and the rough. She is a target singled out by watchful eyes on the street, especially if we recall the expectations of the man in Discépolo's tramcar in *El viaje aquel* (That Journey), who sees swaying feminine silhouettes whenever he sees women: "Ah, what a slender woman, what a snake of a woman!" Serena tries to avoid the paradigms of sociability in a city that, emerging almost entirely from the immigration of single men of a sexually active age, made natural phenomena of prostitution and the availability of the female body in order to reinforce an essentialist view of masculinity. Jorge Salessi argues that dominant imaginaries trained "the 'masculine,' bourgeois male [to be] a purchaser and 'possessor' of the 'feminine' woman" (1991, 46). But since Serena is not a "'feminine' woman," she will have to carry the burden of being an *otredad inapropiada* (an inappropriate other): "Without joy in her chores, her friends, in the day that dawned with a new *burden* of inflexible responsibility and work . . . it was useless to consult the trees . . . the solitude of objects. . . . They would not answer her. Nobody knew exactly when it would end, the feeling that had concerned her for years, and to which she still *sacrificed* so much, that *bitter* vocation for justice and vindication" (Mallea 1939, 337; emphasis added). Her professional status, her political militancy (as probably a feminist socialist), her unyielding stand against misogynist masculinity, and her questioning of a passive, conformist femininity condemn Serena Barcos to exile from (heterosexual) pleasure. Why is she "without joy"? What is her "burden"? As a "beautiful woman whose deportment and character were distinguished by nature," she should have identified with the dominant, joyful imaginaries of the city.

As Showalter reminds us, "Sexual anarchy began with odd women. . . . Odd women were a social problem" (1991, 19). The socializing resources of cultural formation, such as Mallea's text, stigmatized the perplexing, oppositional paradigms endorsed by subjects like Serena, based on a typical, turn-of-the-century attitude. Serena embodies an unprecedented identitary space, uncomfortable within conventional binarisms. Where else should degenerate "sexual anarchies" be confined, but to ignominy? As Showalter observes, "If different races can be kept in their places, if the various classes can be held in their proper district of the cities, and if men and women can be fixed in their separate spheres, many hope, Apocalypse can be prevented" (1991, 4). However, when the Apocalypse already seems imminent, Mallea resorts to the same strategies utilized in discourses on crime. When the author "opens up" his character, he dissects her, turning her into a "case" whose odd nature triggers anxiety for a swift resolution, in the same way that an emotionally detached observer, repelled by what he sees, coldly proceeds to use a scalpel. What discursive maneuver was called for by such measures of social control? Serena is a *femme seule* (single woman), an odd woman, and for turn-of-the-century imaginaries, "the odd woman was the one left over, the uneven number . . . an odd glove," an asymmetry that mathematically exceeded binary categories.

"Why this sudden attention to single women?" asks Showalter (1991, 20). The answer must be sought in the coalescing of feminist imaginaries, in "the period's construction of unmarried women as a new political and sexual group, not just an absence or cipher in the social body, but a constituency with potential opportunities, power and rights" (Showalter 1991, 21). Toward the end of the nineteenth century, female sexual desire had already been recognized in obstetrics as a biological necessity, with the warning that abstinence could have "evil results" (Showalter 1991, 21). Sexual activity outside marriage, masturbation, and lesbianism were the feared responses to a contested heterosexuality. Mallea's text addresses these margins, outside the boundaries of heterosexuality, by penalizing Serena with expulsion from the only happiness that seems possible: "heterosexual happiness." A *femme seule,* she ruins her chance for such happiness in an incomprehensible exchange, instead choosing the "burden" of a "bitter vocation for justice and vindication," which "had concerned her for years and to which she still *sacrificed* so much."

Emma Zunz is also a double deviant, as a murderer and as a female with an unidentifiable sexuality. Why does Emma need to kill? Why does she willingly prostitute herself? Both Serena and Emma walk where they walk and do what they do after imagining an emotional and identitary space for themselves that is an alternative to heterosexual compulsion. There is something of flight in all of this, deliberately planned flight, and something of excess and the disquiet/restlessness of feelings that need to find rest and serenity in *another place.* Ela, the venomous and egotistical female character in Nicolás Olivari's *Tedio* (Boredom), describes solitude as the only bridge connecting her to her own subjectivity, in a statement that at first sight seems perfidious, as it generally appears to be, but that opens a window on her tenderness when viewed in a different light: "It was always a celebration for me to go bed alone. To take off my stockings in a silent room. Alone with myself and my hatred for everything. . . . I am more alive to myself going to bed alone" (Olivari 1936, 18). For heterosexual imaginaries, Ela exudes nothing but absolute abrasiveness, while Serena is soon consumed by "her arid future . . . beginning to show [its] ravages" (Mallea 1939, 338).

Josefina Marpons's emphatic depiction of the new femininity as "fertile" and "generous" may be seen as an attempt to counteract an imaginary that fiercely linked single women to aridity and sterility. In fact, Ela, Emma, and Serena *deliberately* renounce maternity, making their audiences reflect both on the negative value attributed to their drastic decision and on the social burden the three women carry like a life sentence. Emma, the *obrera,* is only nineteen. Serena, the biochemist, is in her thirties. Judging from the fact that the two stories associate both women with sacrifices, we can deduce how intensely the transgressive female population in Buenos Aires must have felt they were taking an irreversible leap into the void. According to this imaginary, if there was no heterosexual sexuality, there was no sexuality at all, so that the sacrifice of both women may have consisted, precisely, of their renunciation of sexuality.

Feminism found it especially difficult to find resonance in the imaginaries of Buenos Aires—because it was not framed as a political party but also because of a public ready to hastily dismiss problematizing claims. All manifestations of alternative sexualities were seen as shrouded in the shame of the cases detailed in police reports and *crónicas rojas* (newspaper crime pages), which were aimed, after all, at normalizing heterosexuality in order to overcome the crisis in gender, by controlling both the female body and the formation of the symbolic. Heterosexuality was reinforced in transitional Buenos Aires by the "naturalization" of sexual violence, whose unpunished virulence was arrogantly flaunted. To reject heterosexuality head-on was to go too far —reason enough for the feminist Herminia Brumana, writing in *Mosaico* (1923), to advise caution to her female readership:

> Consider carefully, woman: you should not be anything except what you must be. One fine, sunny morning when you wake up, consider: is this life I lead the one I dreamed of in my youth? . . . And if your conscience answers: "no!", then let out a cry of protest, not to governments, because governments are useless for that; not to men, for your pain may be indifferent to them; not to women, for your pain may give them happiness; not to your parents, for those

poor folks . . . are also cowards. *Raise your protest against yourself,* break with your prejudices, rise above the tyranny of "what will people say," and be what you want to be. But don't forget that, as a woman, you must only be just. Listen well: just; that is to say, work according to your conscience, without looking back and stepping over those who fall in your way. (1973, 45–46; original emphasis)

Rather than the soaring winds of freedom, Brumana introduces a note of hesitation into the search for new identitary spaces, positioning herself on the borderline between reactionary and habilitating imaginaries. Brumana begins by launching new identitary maps: "you should not be anything except what you must be"; "break with your prejudices"; "be what you want to be." She proposes a break, inviting her reader to undertake reflection and evaluation so that she can carefully redefine the "meanings of life" according to her own subjectivity: "One fine, sunny morning when you wake up, consider: is this life I lead the one I dreamed of in my youth? . . . And if your conscience answers: 'no!', then let out a cry of protest." Nevertheless, the stirring images of new dawns and "sunny morning[s]" are soon neutralized by adverse restrictions and conditions: "*But* don't forget that, *as a woman . . .*" Where should her audience locate a discourse that appeals both to rights and to desire, only to extinguish them with duties and demands? Lime on the one hand, sand on the other. Then, adding ambiguity to ambiguity, Brumana retreats from her drive for subjectivity with an admonishing countermove: "*You must* only be just. *Listen well:* just; that is to say, work according to your conscience." With that, she abandons her reader. Where are subjective "truth" (*lo verdadero*) and social "correctness" (*lo acertado*) to be found? How is the instruction "work according to your conscience" to be read? The phrase "you should not be anything except *what you must be*" summarizes the slippery discursive position of Brumana's statement. In transitional Buenos Aires, *lo acertado* would not make it easy to see *lo verdadero,* because, on subjective maps, *lo verdadero* was being negotiated through the fractured, resemanticized maps of *lo acertado.* Brumana's writing is a remarkable place from which to imagine what the identitary searches and improvisations pursued by the Serenas of Buenos Aires must have felt like within such closely guarded social and discursive contexts.

In the case of "Emma Zunz," "having" to kill Loewenthal "in self-defense" is the device Emma uses to stage her departure from heterosexuality: her boss

Gender and Politics

tried to rape her; she had to kill him. Through the prostitution of her sexuality and the murder of her boss, Emma makes her terror of men become real. Thereafter, following the "rape," she enjoys the compassionate silence of her friends: how could she be reproached for not having a boyfriend or marrying? The female characters in "Emma Zunz" and "Serena" avoid conventional heterosexuality in different ways. Emma's ruse consists of the "sacrifice" of spoiling things for herself in the worst possible way, through two pure deceptions, fictionalizations. The first story she acts out, devised for public consumption, is aimed at making her sexuality appear to have been spoiled by the "rape scene" in Loewenthal's office—a sexual abuse that never took place. The logic underlying this fictionalization remains publicly inaccessible but allows the young woman to justify (to herself) the killing of Loewenthal as revenge for her father. In the second story Emma acts out, her sexuality is spoiled by the disgust and nausea she feels at prostituting herself with a faceless sailor, none of whose words she understands. With the ignominy derived from this story/enactment, she gathers the strength needed to discharge "the heavy revolver" three times. Nonetheless, her action takes place *somewhere else*. Borges's narrator describes the moment of intercourse as a "confused disorder of disconnected, appalling sensations": "[Emma] thought (she couldn't think) that her father had done this horrible thing to her mother that was now being done to her" (Borges 1974, 1: 566). And yet the "negative" sexuality derived from the atrocious sexuality of prostitution is not the only sexuality to cause revulsion. Emma's repugnance for heterosexual sexuality seems to originate *earlier* and from *elsewhere*. Too many displacements and plays of substitution make us suspect that revenge, as a justification, is as much a concealment and disguise as is Loewenthal's nonexistent sexual abuse and as much a strategy of deferral as Emma's surrender to the sailor. In fact, Emma's "truth" lies in none of these performances, which is how a deferred, hidden meaning begins to surface. Emma "performs" Loewenthal's violence for the city's imaginaries. She "performs" her surrender to the sailor and, through both, "performs" revenge (for her father/herself). But what "truth" does Emma hide in both enactments?

We can all agree that the plan of escape from heterosexuality that Emma orchestrates is somewhat lurid, but the slim margins for maneuver in her case, allowed by a sociability based on a compulsion to heterosexuality, can be easily figured out. How could she explain to her friends the difference of a subjective gender identity that dispenses with heterosexuality? How could she explain *lo verdadero* (alternative sexuality) when confronted with the "truth" of *lo acertado* (heterosexuality)? Given the social surveillance embodied by her friends, perhaps Emma's *deliberately* publicized story of sexual violence is the only recourse open to her to justify her subsequent withdrawal from (hetero)sexuality. She thus gives new meaning to the narrator's observation that when her friends "talked about their boyfriends . . . no one expected Emma to say anything." The young woman gambles on her story to provoke soothing words that will "rehabilitate" her sexual difference by interpreting it from the perspective of the trauma of rape. When considered in light of the tension between the compulsion to heterosexuality and alternative sexualities, woven into the fabric of transitional Buenos Aires, the story of her rape might be devious and convoluted, but Emma achieves something truly exceptional because of it. She is able to live by her "truth" (*lo verdadero*), without the gaze of social "correctness" (*lo acertado*) casting suspicion on her. Most likely she is condemned to be pitied, but at least this probably allows her to live in peace, understanding that Brumana's resounding directive "be what you want to be" is not as easy as it seems. After all, in the city's imaginaries, habilitation is closely followed by admonition: "Consider *carefully, woman:* you should not be anything except *what you must be*" (emphasis added).

Serena's escape from the compulsion to heterosexuality brings unhappiness, loneliness, barrenness, and emptiness in its wake. However, the paradigm of embitterment affirmed in "Serena Barcos" also proposes lateral turns and a female culture that is both more generous and more attuned to the transitional upheavals of the times—a kind of solidarity among women "increasingly supportive" of working men and women, as Josefina Marpons remarks. Looked at today, although Mallea's aim was to make clear what *lo acertado* was all about, Serena's choice of identity suggests the visibility achieved by a social agent who reflects on her political and social agency, drawing her "truth" and the meaning of life from her own subjectivity. What stands out in this context is the semantic productivity of a story unable to cover up its own refraction of the subject it presents. No matter how contrary it is to the author's control, Serena's identitary model still surfaces as a visible, stubborn margin, an asymmetry that resists absorption by the normalizing logic of the story. "Serena Barcos" was written in an attempt to thwart

Gender and Politics

alternative socializations precisely because they were already undermining the armor-plated inexorability of *lo acertado*.

In the section "Semana al día" (This Week) in *Caras y Caretas* (10 May 1919), a photo shows six upper-class young women taking their morning walk, with the caption: "On the hotel terrace—Señoritas Iturralde, Gracia-rena, Morgan, Spaolaza, and Imaz on a morning stroll." Images of this kind, of women walking arm in arm, should not attract attention except when their frequency makes them significant. At the beginning of the 1930s, an amateur photographer captured a group of women out walking along a street in central Buenos Aires (figure 26). The photo shows five women advancing arm in arm, as if forming a protective wall with their bodies. In the first *Caras y Caretas* photo, the women are posing for a society column; in the second, they are not posing, and the only woman looking at the photographer does so warily. The rest hide their faces behind their hats, three of them avoiding the photographer altogether. More photos of similar scenes lead me to believe that the existence of so many such images is not coincidental. Another photo from the time shows three working women leaving a factory arm in arm (figure 27). They are so attached to each other that they seem as one, as if movement through public space required them to form a collective body against the inclemency of open spaces. Such a formation prompts us to recall studies on female agoraphobia by Helene Deutsch and her statement that this anxiety disorder "either disappears or becomes far less acute if the patient has somebody with her" (1929, 51). A third photograph shows a line of women workers standing close to each another as they wait to enter the factory (figure 28).

From such images, we can see a stable signifier in the body language of women in the public spaces of modernity: bodies so close together they form a real collective. The resemanticization of the body through group laterality is understandable if we keep in mind that women gain access to public space when they enter the world of work and that they enter it as a collective. Their identity as working women emerges as a spectacularly massive physical presence, one woman beside another, in the vast factory sheds (figure 29). I wonder how many extraordinary forms of interaction and alliances among proletarian women could have come about because of how women were brought together in public spaces.

How should we read the way *porteñas* walked along the streets warily, with evasive glances, protecting each other? Were they evidencing symptoms of agoraphobia, fear of the street, or insecurity in the new public spaces that they had to face? All of this—and perhaps much more. Iris Goldstein Fodor links the fear of socializing to gender: "For males, socialization tends to enhance experimental options. . . . For women the socialization process tends to reinforce the nurturant, docile, submissive and conservative aspects of the traditionally defined female role and discourage personal qualities conventionally defined as masculine: self-assertiveness, achievement, orientation, and independence" (1974, 141). Goldstein Fodor discusses how boys are often shown in active poses, while girls "appear to have agoraphobia. . . . Their bodies are rigid with their hands held tightly to their bodies or behind their back" (143): "passivity and pseudo-dependency, altruism, goal restriction and rehearsal of domesticity, incompetence and mishaps" (144) are reserved for women. Girls are consequently three times more likely to express fear than boys. They feel uncomfortable and deliberately "withdraw from active competition and master substituting instead romantic notions of finding the right man who will . . . take care of them" (Goldstein Fodor 1974, 148).

Development psychology places the emergence of agoraphobia/sociophobia at the point of transition between dependence and autonomy, when the subject accesses the public domain and social interaction. Gender socialization is a culturally reinforced threshold at which agoraphobia makes it possible to exaggerate "female" roles of submission and defenselessness for women: "The phobias represent a holding on to their frightened little-girl roles" (Goldstein Fodor 1974, 148). Was there any reason for agoraphobic conduct in this Buenos Aires? The fact that Helene Deutsch researched agoraphobia in 1929 is directly related to the appearance of modernity and to the hyperventilation and connectivity of the public spaces it created. A section of the *Vademecum de la Liga del Honor* (Handbook of the League of Honor, 1910) on the "suppression of immorality" by the federal police chief repeats a police ordinance of 23 November 1907, which addressed "looking out for morality and good manners, by preventing anyone from being troubled by words or actions offensive to their modesty [and] by acting with the utmost rigor when women, girls, the elderly, and persons of religion are assaulted" (*Vademecum* 1910, 10). "Obscene words," spoken in the street, "should be suppressed by the proper means, especially when they might be heard by women or girls" (7). The ordinance also specified that attacks, words, actions, and obscene gestures against "women and persons of religion" should be challenged "inexorably through the application of penalties" and by arresting the offenders (11). The *Vademecum* makes it possible to see that public space in Buenos Aires was secular, sexist, and notoriously aggressive. Why would the ordinance of 1910 repeat the ordinance of 1907, and why was the latter itself a reissue of another, by Colonel Ramón L. Falcón, of 28 December 1906, which itself could be traced to an ordinance of 10 April 1889? The written letter of the law went unobserved in daily practice: the legal statute was resisted by the state of events, just as it was resisted by Angel Villoldo's tango "Cuidado con los cincuenta" (Beware the Fifty-Peso Fine, 1907), which made light of a form of harassment that must have been quite violent:

> A man must refrain from saying
> sweet nothings to a woman.
> When we see a beautiful woman approach
> we cannot even offer her a compliment,
> and can do nothing except look in silence
> if we value our freedom.

In Villoldo's tango, Pascual, a spokesman for men in the audience, receives a disproportionate reply to an innocent compliment ("Good day, goddess, divine angel"). The woman he addresses "saw red, / gave the poor man a slap / and marched him off to the police" (Gobello 1980, 24). In reality, however, much more than compliments were at stake. A 1903 *sainete* by Enrique de María, *Bohemia criolla* (Creole Bohemia), alludes to the counterpart of the docile woman. An immigrant Galician named José, who also manages a *conventillo,* argues heatedly with his wife:

FRANCISCA: You're sap and a sop! . . . Galician booby (*punching him*).

JOSÉ: Ouch! . . . My darling Francisca . . . are you a woman or a man? (María 1980, 62)

Francisca reproaches José for his spinelessness when collecting the *conventillo* rents, although he promises revenge:

JOSÉ (*angrily*):
¡ . . . I'm gonna get that woman
whose worser than deathly cholera

and . . . bubonic plague,
to tell you frankly . . .
I've gone cannibal
and I'm gonna eat up
her liver and kidneys,
her brains and tongue. . . .
Oh! . . . Saint Joseph! . . . Saint Joseph!
My blessed namesake, save this poor man! (64)

José's Spanish combines Galician and criollo-gauchesque terms (*güesos, pior, entuavía, volvido*), but the greater sources of confusion are slippages in transitional identities: the wife punches her husband and demands he collect the rents mercilessly, while he commends himself to the saints. Francisca's imperious manner would have put the audience on José's side as a completely untypical *conventillo* manager, given that such managers were usually unforgiving vultures. José even turns to anthropophagy, to eating his wife as if she were a cow, and lays his complaint before a public that is doubly sympathetic because he is both the woman's victim and a compassionate *conventillo* manager. This insignificant husband describes a spine-chilling process step by step: "I'm gonna eat up / her liver and kidneys, / her brains and tongue." Audiences must have laughed in complicity, wishing with every grisly mouthful that José would get back *his* masculinity and that Francisca would return to *her* place as a woman, not a man.

Identitary shifts, like those of the effeminate male, were cause for both hilarity and serious pronouncements in popular theater, but however they are treated, the fact that they appear so problematically, and so frequently, reveals that they had become an obsession. José María, a character in *La mal pagada* (The Poorly Paid Woman), is a delicate man, who "weeps like a Magdalena," reads affected literature, and "admires beauty": "A fabulous collection from Brazil, of all possible colors, sizes, shapes, unlikely designs. I was transfixed. More than flowers, they seemed like sensitive beings who even had souls. There were some orchids the color of a baby's skin with overtones of pearl. It was rather marvelous, fantastic, worthy of the dream of a symbolist poet" (Acasuso 1937, 8). José María is attentive to silks and velvets. "The soul of men and women is in their clothes" (20), he says of fashion. He is an "immaculate, fastidious" man, "soft as a flower . . . so delicate!" (24). Of all the texts, however, *Los invertidos* (The Other Way Round, 1914), by the anarchist writer José González Castillo, from La Boca, by far had the most impact. *Los invertidos* is a paradigmatic naturalist drama set in a *garçonière,* behind whose closed doors male sexual "deviancy" is hidden. The sexuality of proletarian and middle-class women is conventionally brought into the *garçonière,* where the circulation of prostitutes is institutionalized, taken off the streets and reserved for the pleasure of wealthy men. González Castillo also alludes to the *garçonière* as a receptacle for "lustful sensualisms," "vehement passions," "insatiable desires," and "the excess of pleasures" (1991, 15). Such phrases do not refer to female sexuality, however, but to the "symbolic fires that consumed Sodom"—that is, to the "insatiable desires" of homo-eroticism, a remarkably surprising thematic undertaking for 1914.

In an imaginary profoundly fearful of transitional shifts in identity, homo-sexuality was another shadow that slipped by like a panther's silhouette. It took a swipe when least expected, even turning up in the most emblematic cultural space of conventional male masculinity, the *garçonière.* González Castillo's text even exploits the social surveillance embedded in forensic discourse, through which the courts and criminology vent their intolerance against a favorite hobbyhorse: "The accused Calixto, Your Honor, . . . [is] one of those interesting cases of sexual inversion . . . that have been precisely described pathologically in an infinite number of books on the subject": "After a thorough physical examination, he has not shown the physiological deformities that . . . characterize . . . such cases . . . but his decidedly feminine habits, the fineness of his mannerisms . . . that same fineness that makes women so charming, the soft, caressing tone of voice, [and] the same constant display of an indefinable female coquetry make us believe that we are in the presence of one of those strange cases of sensual duality that results from a perversion of the instincts, exaggerated by the excesses of pleasure, rather than from an aberration of sex" (González Castillo 1991, 11). The forensic expert Dr. Flórez explains that homosexuals "are generally normal individuals, usually healthy, manly, and young, as in the case of the man about whom I am giving evidence, who killed the other man with the Herculean strength of his own hands. . . . [They are] individuals endowed with all the virile qualities of ordinary men" (17). Moreover, homosexuality is the face of a monster just around the corner, with the capacity to change "ordinary men" with virile characters not only into "deformed . . . unfortunate" beings but even into murderers whose greatest crime may well be replacing the

Herculean strength of their arms with affected voices. As the audience soon discovers, Dr. Flórez has himself taken that *mal paso* (wicked step), although he behaves as if it has nothing to do with him:

> FLÓREZ: And when they are caught in a moment of action we would call "critical," especially at night, they turn into women, into less than women, with all their peculiarities, all their fancies and passions, as if a marvelous and monstrous transformation were performed in that instant . . . (*as if possessed*). (17)

In the misogynist, homophobic imaginaries of Buenos Aires, the theory of "excesses of pleasure" says it all. It turns *porteñas* into sexually and economically insatiable predators and homosexuals into vampires and murderers. Both groups operate under cover of social obscurity. They are restless beings, worried and worrying, forever slipping out of view, huddled hybrids whose dual nature sets the determined desire for control of the new order on edge. The demonization of active sexuality in women associates them with new subjective maps based on an untraceable process that leaves them warped, while paradigmatic masculinity in "cases" of homosexuality was considered to have collapsed so far it has turned men "into less than women." Transvestitism also caused the rigidity of social categories to waver and become confused, the frontiers of demarcation having collapsed. The *garçonière* in *Los invertidos* becomes a space for sexual inversion, transvestitism, bisexuality, hermaphroditism, and the manwoman (*manflorismo*). It is a space for queers, feminization, and the uncontrolled other. The source of all the trouble is the confusion of identitary crossings and passages, where the infallibility of "socially correct truths" is challenged by the "whim" of subjective truths.

When Dr. Flórez explains Calixto's homosexuality in his expert report, he is also talking about himself, thereby occupying two discursive positions at the same time. He embodies both the law and the deviant, both the legal expert/scientist and the object of his expertise. "Pathology" and "normality," the "case" and the "sentence," are entwined in Flórez's two-faced identity. His concealed homosexuality approaches the same dangerous and inexorable level as that felt by the defendant Calixto when murdering his partner. At night, Flórez frequents the *garçonière* owned by Pérez, his lover, the "masculine" partner in his relationship and the one who incites him to vice. *Los invertidos* presents homosexuality as vampirism, as an attack against the healthy reproductive sexuality of the nation: "One of the abiding arguments against homosexuality is that, in addition to representing a constellation of unnatural (perverse, sinful) forms of sexual behavior, it involves the seduction of the innocent by the already corrupt or perverted" (Foster 1989, 10). According to David W. Foster, González Castillo read the homosexuality of the *garçonière* owned by the *bacán porteño* in terms of the Romantic legend of Count Dracula: as "a result of a degenerative bourgeoisie or a rotten aristocracy" (Foster 1989, 21).

Hence, social danger also simmered among the upper class. Clara, the central character of *Los invertidos,* discovers the "horror" of male homosexuality in her own marriage but promptly nullifies any possibility of homosexuality's truth and discursive descendant by urging her husband to kill himself: "Like Clara, the audience must accept the bitter truth about the existence and activities like the vampires that pervert the morally healthy" (Foster 1989, 27):

> CLARA: This is all so disgusting! Oh, those wretched, wretched men. . . . And to think of the bitterness those unhappy people will spread in their homes! To think of the moral poverty of the homes where such vices are picked up! What a stigma for their children: what a school for them, what an example! . . . It doesn't bear thinking of: the pure and the innocent receiving such a heritage! . . . Oh, no! It cannot be! It just cannot be! (González Castillo 1991, 52)

Since "it cannot be," González Castillo's text proposes to wipe out deviancy through a double means: suicide and the eradication of its social discourses, *Los invertidos* itself being a remarkably pioneering example: "There is a secret, strange, fatal law that always imposes justice on such people, tragically removing them when life weighs them down like a burden. . . . They are unredeemable. . . . Suicide is 'their last, their good outcome' . . . as Verlaine would say" (18)

Although the theme of *Los invertidos* is that sexual "inversion" is a vice because it consumes, degenerates, and infects exemplary gender spaces, I believe the play was principally intended to warn about the hidden nature of the *doble vida* (double life). In such a tricky city as Buenos Aires, carnival and masks have always been cause for suspicion, covering up the permissiveness and secrets fostered by the anonymity of the city in all its corners, far beyond carnival time: "The night seems to infuse them with new life, as if in the mystery of its shadow a miraculous sex transfusion were performed.

They become women then, just as they have been men by day" (González Castillo 1991, 30). By day, Dr. Flórez is a prominent and respectable heterosexual jurist; by night he is homoerotic. He is therefore bisexual. Similarly, Pérez "is a blasé, elegant, self-assured, conversational, and disdainful aristocrat by day." He "wears an impeccable morning coat," but he is a vampire by night. Nothing is what it seems in this tantalizing game of concealment and deception. Fernández's homosexuality is unthinkable: he is "tall, athletic, vigorous. . . . He speaks slowly and deliberately, like one confident of his physical strength" (19). He practices hunting, rowing, and fencing and is always ready for a duel, like any good example of virility.

Referring to the fin de siècle, Elaine Showalter alludes to this site where conventional categories are undermined as "Dr. Jekyll's closet": "a secret but active subculture, with its own language, styles, practices, and meeting places" (1991, 107). The decorum practiced by day is rent in two by the "female" hysteria of the night, when a city riddled with doubleness yields to dissoluteness and chaos. In *The Strange Case of Dr. Jekyll and Mr. Hyde*, R. L. Stevenson's double alternately hides and reveals repressed emotions, especially "the homosexual self." Imaginaries of the time had begun to recognize the evasive but firm shifts performed by these identitary transvestitisms and did not underestimate their potential impact as forms of displacement. As if to create antibodies against this social nocturnality, the ending of *Los invertidos* arouses the audience's homophobia through an explicitly homoerotic scene between Pérez and Dr. Flórez:

> PÉREZ: . . . I'm not leaving. I want you to be docile, as you've always been, submissive, feminine, your true self . . . that's it . . . forget you are a man and let your own disgrace be your dark happiness. (*Caressing him.*) Yes . . . like that . . . like you were as a child . . . and like you'll be for the rest of your life, unredeemable and unchanging. (*Leaning toward him, brushing his collar with his lips. Clara has appeared at the door. . . . She seems to lean in to listen, anxiously. As the dialogue reaches its climax . . . she softly opens the drawer to the writing desk and takes out a gun.*) . . . Go back to being what you always were. . . . (*A long, slow kiss is heard. Clara turns on the light quickly. The two men, startled, try to stand up.*) (González Castillo 1991, 63)

As Clara is the center of the play's "truth," where she goes, the audience goes too. Through her furtive entry onto the stage, the audience perceives the scene's secrets, disguised sexuality, and monstrous embraces. When

Clara *"turns on the light quickly,"* she is also lighting up, for Argentina's social imaginary as a whole, the ignominious, unsuspected darkness contained in Pérez's *garçonière,* as well as in the nocturnal whispers of the grotesque city, always on the point of getting out of hand. Fin de siècle sexual discourse fluently exposed what lay behind closed doors, revealing deception with "images of forced penetration through locked doors into private cabinets, rooms, closets . . . the breaking down of doors, learning the secrets behind them" (Showalter 1991, 110). Clara (and González Castillo) owes the audience this necessary, prophylactic revelation—hence her name. Once more the means of social control endeavor to penetrate the identitary ruptures and secrets of private life, where social space was most intractable. Pérez, Fernández, Emilio, Juanita ("a beautiful-faced, twenty-year-old youth with almond-shaped eyes"), Dr. Flórez, Benito, and Princess Borbón ("a pretty boy . . . an ephebe," although a "petty thief") slip between bisexuality and transvestitism and back again. The source of the threat is in what desire unleashes, a crossover into an eminently transgressive realm where the characters reveal lavish sexualities:

JUANA: Oh, to have been born a man!

PRINCESA: Oh, to have been born a woman, rather!

EMILIO: Don't complain. . . . After all, better than being just a man or a woman is being both at the same time, and neither of you can complain about that. (González Castillo 1991, 32)

Aníbal Ford and Nora Mazzioti point out that González Castillo's anarchist, Tolstoyan work comes to the defense of "divorce, the rights of single mothers and of women in general . . . the protection of children born out of wedlock, and labor law, [and that it] attacks the penal system, the administration of justice, and the structure of the law" (1991, 79). González Castillo was an intellectual attentive to the hybrid nature of transitional cultures: "a friend of thieves, prostitutes, tramps, and drunkards, [who] knew about the life of the poor; with some exceptions, as in *Los invertidos,* he got away from mechanistic explanations . . . positivism, social Darwinism . . . [and] the boom in criminology in which the culture of the time was steeped" (Ford and Mazzioti 1991, 79). Foster agrees that "anarchism was not . . . opposed to 'healthy' sexual responses" (1989, 20). Hence, *Los invertidos* endorses other *sainetes* associated with bourgeois sociosexual norms. Pérez, the "vampire," proclaims, with predictable arrogance, "You know our sin is eminently democratic" (González Castillo 1991, 25). When confronted with the tentacles and expansiveness of vice, *Los invertidos* prescribes homophobia and heterosexuality, as well as female rehabilitation in the figure of Clara, who is to be the bearer of social normativity. That is to say, women are the pillars of "truth" to the extent that they are able to "cleanse" themselves, steering clear of adultery and limiting themselves to the asexuality of motherhood. Once the father has disappeared and social nocturnality has been excised, Clara becomes the matrix around which the Argentinean family unites. All unnoticed wounds are closed, while Clara keeps watch over the social body.

It will fall to Clara, of course, to put all her efforts into heading off the stigma of deviancy in order to rescue her son Julián: "What a school for them, what an example! . . . It doesn't bear thinking of: the pure and the innocent receiving such a heritage! . . . Oh, no! It cannot be! It just cannot be!" (González Castillo 1991, 52). This is not an easy task for this selfless mother. Even with her husband's suicide, Clara cannot yet rest easy, as public health theory gruesomely stressed the hereditary nature of homosexuality—the "secret, unsuspected, hereditary instincts . . . the cry of vice, the imperious call of reproductive decline" (González Castillo 1991, 17). *Los invertidos* confirms the theory that "it is too late . . . [that] what is received by blood or learned in childhood is neither forgotten nor abandoned, except through death" (62). If González Castillo's text, as the work of an anarchist, places blame on the upper classes, what did he intend with his enigmatic drama? To demonize homosexuality as an alternative identity or as a metaphor for the vampirism of the elite? If we believe he resorted to homosexuality in order to address the hereditary marks of the aristocracy—the "reproductive decline inherited by a decrepit, exhausted organism"—how can we explain his tracing its "evil" origin to the "material and spiritual poverty of the past"? Such social determinism would have to include the proletariat. According to Juan José Sebreli, the theory of homosexuality as degeneracy was used by police doctors to explain its rise among the lumpen, where it was thought to be congenital and hereditary, while it was viewed as a learned behavior among the upper classes, brought in by laborers on country estates or by other perverse influences (1997, 295). González Castillo alludes to homosexuality in order to speak about social blights, but what comes through most powerfully is his disdain for anything having to do with the world of women. As Alberta Ure remarks, "There do not seem to be many men in this work . . . who desire another man: there are men who want to be women" (1991, 68). In other words, men who incur the "madness" of crossing from the affirmative culture of masculinity to the inferior social spaces associated with female hysteria and gossip:

> Pérez: Look . . . you'd better keep quiet. . . . Otherwise, to be honest, you appear unbecoming. . . . Good heavens! Or now are you going to get jealous . . . like a common, vulgar woman? . . . Answer me. (González Castillo 1991, 16)

One wonders what fears *Los invertidos* addresses. In my opinion, what González Castillo is most concerned with is the risk of "proximity." His text warns obsessively against the untraceable conditions that make a secretive crossover to homosexuality possible. Any strapping athlete, even if he knows how to handle weapons and practices sports, could end up being a traitor to "genuine" maleness. How can homosexuals be detected? It is akin to the difficulty of diagnosing decency in *porteñas:* how can you possibly spot the signs and stay clear of the tentacles of homosexuals' vampirism, especially when they are "in all the schools . . . especially the boarding schools" (González Castillo 1991, 52)?

> Petrona: Manphrodite . . . Bah! . . . Doctors and judges are always having to invent names for simple things. . . . In my day, we just called them fags, or queers, which was clearer. . . . I've known more than a hundred of them.
>
> Julián: You? . . . Where?
>
> Petrona: Where else? . . . Out in the world! What did you think? There are many more of them . . . than there seem. (12)

According to Foster, Petrona's remark would have disturbed "bourgeois wishful thinking . . . that homosexuality involves only a minuscule number beyond the pale of decent society" (1989, 27). But transvestitism had already alarmed Juan Manual Rosas. In Afro-Argentinean neighborhoods, it was forbidden, during the 1836 carnival, "to dress in clothes that did not correspond to your sex" (Sebreli 1997, 281). The modern city was much more confusing, beginning with the fact that tango was initially danced between men, in close embrace (figure 30). In any case, identity-crossing was to be expected in a disproportionately male population. Sebreli explains that Pepita Avellaneda, the first woman tango singer, used to dress as a man and rivaled

Carlos Gardel for the love of Madame Jeanne. But the mannerisms of deviancy were minutely scrutinized. The urban chronicler Vicente Rossi was dismayed at *compadritos* walking like women in tight clothing, while Sebastián Tallón emphasized that their gait was "somewhat affected, if not effeminate" (figure 31), unable to resist remarking that "they dressed with the evidently sexual and suspiciously exaggerated narcissism of a woman" (Sebreli 1997, 285). Moreover, homosexuals even had their own meeting places, their own city within the city: Paseo de Julio and Plaza Mazzini, a name taken by Cambaceres in *En la sangre* in order to link homosexuality and Italian immigrants (Sebreli 1997, 284; Salessi 1991, 38). I believe that sexuality was one of the most genuinely open social spaces in Buenos Aires, one proof of which is the choreography of the tango: "a lascivious dance . . . that comes close to belly dancing . . . the absolute representation of a feigned eroticism" (Salessi 1991, 47). And if these contacts were worrying when the dancers were a heterosexual couple, we can just imagine the concern when both were men. In effect, according to Salessi, when tango was danced by men, it was a secretive simulation of homoeroticism (1991, 46).

By 1902, Manón, Cielo Imperio, Princesa de Borbón (Luis Fernández), Bella Otero (Culpido Alvarez), and Blanca Nieves Abratte were sashaying through the streets and soirees of Buenos Aires, spreading transvestitism and colliding with heterosexual binarism. Because of homosexuality, the body was no longer a source of "truth" and "natural" correspondence (as between a male body and masculinity), as alleged by heterosexual culture, but of "concealment" and "prevarication" (Ben 2000, 262). Pablo Ben maintains that cases of hermaphroditism were studied by a medical specialty called teratology (from the Greek *teras:* monster), interested only in determining the "true" sex of the person affected: "Hermaphrodites were in general condemned to silence and were given an identity different from the one in which they had been raised" (Ben 2000, 262). But transitional Buenos Aires seems to have been more deviant than normal. Tango itself shuffled all the paradigms, both of men shaped by an exemplary masculinity and of docile, feminine women: elegant, knife-wielding *compadritos* walking with a supple sway; songsters singing male tango lyrics in a man's voice, for the tango speaker is almost always male; men dressed as women and vampires on the lookout for the unwary. Inside the city was yet another city, densely populated, a city out of reach.

Gender and Politics

In Samuel Eichebaum's *El ruedo de las almas* (Circle of Souls, 1923), a socialist deputy betrays the political trust conferred on him by the electorate by opting for the chaos of his passions and the collapse of institutional authority, brought down by the sarcastic laughter of María Angélica, the femme fatale who, like a vampire, steals him from his peers and public activity. In *Los invertidos,* the danger of deviancy touches the figure/body of justice itself with homoeroticism. How is it possible to maintain the very authority from which verdict, sentence, and discipline derive when justice is represented in the figure of Dr. Flórez? On his head lies the guarantee of paradigms of the absolute, with their ability to surpass the uncertainties of the transition and dismiss the grotesque with an unequivocal "truth." But the jurist in *Los invertidos* is more attentive to other identitary areas of his body. He is absorbed by divided loyalties and amphibious spaces. If minotaurs, centaurs, harpies, sphynxes, femmes fatales, and sirens are metaphors of a Western horror of double identities, homosexuality and lesbianism are spaces of excess, hyperventilation, and social chaos. Elaine Showalter explains their ramifications: "These identifications also made possible a number of ways for individuals to position themselves, as well as a fluid and diverse set of political and aesthetic alliances, groups" (1991, 172). "Decadence" was a euphemism used at the fin de siècle to name homosexuality, and Flórez is undoubtedly a "decadent" judge. His last name—which is not quite proper for the authority/ masculinity residing in him—anticipates as much, with its many ambiguous meanings and errors that are not just in the spelling. In *Male Subjectivity at the Margin,* Kaja Silverman's Lacanian vision claims homosexuality as the "end of reality," or at least the end of the mechanisms of recognition (*vraisemblance*) that support the whole edifice of the symbolic order: "If ideology is central to the maintenance of classic masculinity, the affirmation of classic masculinity is equally central to the maintenance of our governing 'reality.' Because of the pivotal status of the phallus, more than sexual difference is sustained through the alignment of that signifier with the male sexual organ. Within every society, hegemony is keyed to certain privileged terms, around which there is a kind of doubling up of belief. Since everything that successfully passes for 'reality' within a given social formation is articulated in relation to these terms, they represent ideological stress points" (1992, 16).

It was clear to many people that, with so much confusion, the Apocalypse had indeed reached Buenos Aires. Leopoldo Lugones was so convinced that he included an epigraph from Leviticus (26:19) in "La lluvia de fuego" (Rain of Fire, 1906): "And I will make your heaven as iron and your earth as brass." Here the narrator lives in a "vast libertine city," Gomorrah, a city awaiting God's imminent punishment. He looks out over the decadent city, where "the pleasure people color the streets more numerously than ever," and he lists the symptoms that will be its downfall: "a dubious youth, whose tunic was hitched up to his thighs, . . . allowed his shaven legs to be seen"; "courtesans paraded their indolence, sweating perfumes, with a naked breast in the latest fashion"; exogamy and sexual chaos are reflected in an old pimp's carriage, decorated "with appropriate paintings showing the monstrous couplings of beasts: lizards with swans, a monkey and a seal, a young maiden covered by the rapturous jewels of a peacock." He sees drugs, opium and asafetida, and a eunuch whose "morbidity was predictable" (Lugones 1926, 32). In Lugones's Gomorrah there are no couples dancing tango, but a black man uncovers secret, forbidden, pornographic scenes as he dances. The well-deserved storm of fire and infernal rain pours down on Gomorrah/Buenos Aires, which certainly suffers enormously: "Its roaring was asking something . . . of that tremendous thing that caused its suffering. Ah . . . that roaring, the one element of grandeur those beasts still had" (36). Thus does this imaginary resolve the cataclysm that has arisen from its own incoherence, attributing it to the new quests for identity in the grotesque city.

Adela, a character in Armando Discépolo's drama *Entre el hierro* (Between Two Swords, 1910), is torn between an "other" space and being forced to remain a female subject: "I was born a woman, and I take my role seriously" (Discépolo 1987a, 96). Although she is still at the threshold, Adela opens a way into this alternative space between fissures and transitional slippages. She urges the audience to allow her to desire from the perspective of her subjectivity, "to do as my free will dictates, [and accept] a contrary appetite," while she claims her right from León to desire "not to see you, to be alone, happy, free!" (99):

> Adela: Allow my heart not to beat to the same rhythm as yours!
>
> León: You're crazy!
>
> Adela: Have you never stopped to think what you would do in such a situation?
>
> León (*clutching her in his arms*): I would kill you, Adela! . . . I want you to be submissive, as you were until today, as you should be all your life. . . . Forever! (99–100).

The dialogue shows the level of social obscurity surrounding this identitary *nonplace:*

> PEDRO: That viper's tongue!
>
> ADELA (*exploding*): And, so what! Viper! Viper! Or do you think that just because I'm here my pulse doesn't beat, my nerves don't function? What do they want of me? What? . . . For me to kiss them, to caress them? Whatever next! No, my heart isn't here; it's nowhere. . . . I have no heart, you have all consumed it and still believe I'm complaining. . . . I'm not complaining, it's an insult. (109)

Like the hearts of so many others, Adela's heart seems to find no place to rest in Buenos Aires: "My heart isn't here; it's *nowhere.* . . . I have no heart, you have all consumed it" (emphasis added).

19 THE WEAK,

THE VIOLENT,

AND

THE TEARFUL

No one asked about routes and stations.

Roberto Arlt, *Los siete locos*

ANOTHER "INAPPROPRIATE" PERIPH-
eral identity that severely tests the strategies used in categorizations of social
stability is that of the male who has lost the most reliable of masculine certainties: his virility. His is the voice of the tango. What is to be done with
him? In Horacio Zuviría's "Enfundá la bandolina" (Put Away Your Mandolin), we read:

> What d'you expect, Cipriano,
> the fifty Springs
> you bear on your back
> have nothing left.
> As well as the hair
> that has left your head
> you've lost your good looks
> never to return.
> Leave the girls
> for the boys;
> such wholesome dishes

are not for you.
Avoid the early morning dew
and go to bed
or tomorrow
you'll wake with a cough.

The speaker has several reasons for advising Cipriano to retire from society—"to withdraw to winter quarters / alongside the fire and your memories / in the shadow of a corner": he has lost his looks and his hair, his virility has waned, and his health is shaky. He should go to bed early, not stay out until morning, to avoid the chills and a cough. The speaker finds it unbearable to see him(self) "waiting for a woman / with the look of old Mateo, / long-faced, put out to pasture." The intertextuality with Armando Discépolo's *grotesco Mateo* links the horse pulling the anachronistic cart with self-conscious men who have lost their usefulness. Cipriano, whose name is associated with the forgotten Argentine countryside and its "decline" as a source of production, should "withdraw to winter quarters," metaphorically "put away . . . [his] mandolin," and adjust to the "rhythm of the calendar": "there's nothing else for it, you're already old . . . / the girls don't look at you anymore / and if one of them speaks to you / it's to ask for advice." He is now a grandfather, no longer a *galán* (suitor), and the text discreetly alludes to his sexual impotence: Cipriano must understand that his "stock has fallen." In brief, he must resign himself just to speaking words of wisdom to young women and set aside his impulse for philandering. The motif is the same in Evaristo Carriego's "Una sorpresa" (A Surprise), where the lyric voice reacts to the possibility of his wife's return: "I advise you, / don't come back, you'll feel a bitter / disappointment: you'll find me old" (Carriego 1985, 99).

The notion of active female sexuality as vampirism had been appearing in medical discourse since the end of the nineteenth century and had played a part in shaping public health legislation and regulation. In a five-hundred-page study in 1881, the French doctor Pierre Garnier linked male impotence to obesity, venereal and nervous diseases, and toxic substances in factories (mercury, carbon sulfate, lead), before addressing it as a consequence of the new sexual attitudes among women: the woman, he opined, "tastes the surplus voluptuous feelings more in her heart and soul. The normal role of women during copulation is much more moral than physical. Otherwise it would only be an unequal battle between unequal organs" (Kern 1985,

105–6). As Garnier explained to his reader, "the overly aggressive woman might diminish his pleasure." He predicted that a new generation of "voluptuous women" was "challenging male sexual ability" (Kern 1985, 106). Although it was difficult to determine whether sexual practices were actually changing, "the evidence shows that . . . [they were] believed to be changing. The several warnings that a lively and sensuous woman could damage a man by rendering him impotent are telltale signs that those changes were taking place in the popular imagination" (Kern 1985, 108).

In 1908, in *Die Weidergeburt der Kraft* (The Rebirth of Power), Emil Peters examined sexual impotence as a cause of suicide among men, although no statistics really link the two. Nevertheless, the German doctor noticed a "severe" reconfiguration of sexual roles as a corollary of the labor, economic, legal, and sexual agency promoted by feminist imaginaries, drawing a conclusion that, to him, was obvious: "A lively and passionate woman can severely damage a man, causing impotence" (qtd. in Kern 1985, 107). The antidote, "pure women and superb men," was very simple: "To maintain the ideal of female chastity and restrict women to a passive sexual role in marriage required great pressure to keep women from acknowledging or indulging their sexual impulses. Most of the medical literature helped to impose the idea that the male sexual impulse was natural and acceptable, while the female sexual impulse was unnatural or even pathological" (Kern 1985, 100).

The "awakening" of female sexuality was thus seen as leading to a threatening situation and identitary confusion. The remarkable proliferation of writings on sexual impotence at the time demonstrates the contemporary concern for maintaining the essentialism of a male identity able to ride out the new, hazardous times untouched. Feminist discourse did not appear to deal with the sexual activity of women directly, although it is easy to conclude that its arguments would eventually have steered it in that direction. In the first decade of the twentieth century, the German sexologist Edward Fuchs asserted that the ideal male was "the fully potent husband and father": "The complete man should be energetic, strong-willed, self-confident, with an upright posture and a firm grip . . . sexually energetic, strong-willed and confident—constant, upright, and firm" (qtd. in Kern 1985, 104). In 1905, the German biologist Rudolf Virchow argued that "all the characteristics of women's body and mind—nutrition and nervous activity, the sweet tenderness and curves of her limbs, the development of her bosom, her posture and voice—in short, everything that we revere in women is dependent on the activity of her ovaries" (qtd. in Kern 1985, 98). The biological/sexual determinism of Virchow's "anatomy is destiny" theory, which ignored socio-symbolic formations, was disputed by Rosa Mayreder in the same year. Her reading of the female condition as a social construct cunningly contested *Studies in Hysteria* (1895), in which Sigmund Freud connected sexual disorders to the female anatomy's *two* erogenous zones. By contrast, having just *one* genital area, Freud believed, "men are less prone to disturbance . . . because of the relative simplicity of their sex life" (Kern 1985, 186). Stephen Kern asks: "Why . . . not conclude that two is better than one? Why is sexual female complexity necessarily a detriment?" "Women's greater physical capacity for sex," Kern observes, "her capacity to have multiple orgasms, and the increase in her sexual appetite in her late twenties, all contrast with a more limited physical capacity in man. He can have sex less frequently than a woman, he is generally capable of single orgasms only, and his sexual powers begin to decline when women's are still on the rise" (1985, 187). Nevertheless, once the biologically plural nature of female sexuality was recognized, anxiety and confusion gave rise to corrective "truths" based on *Studies in Hysteria*. The "differences" in the devilish physiology of women served to stigmatize the emergence of the new social group. According to Kern, the biological theory of the greater sexual complexity of women was superimposed on the theory of their sexual superiority. Socializing imaginaries would hence swathe female sexual superiority in negativity. In 1905, the Goncourt brothers asserted that "women tended to excess in everything." Johann Jakob Bachofen "found them dominated by instinct," while Laura Marholm argued for "women's natural flightiness and unreliability" (qtd. in Kern 1985, 98). The "truths" of these socializing imaginaries constructed women as loose, unruly, cynical, unfaithful, and always treacherous. With respect to the theory of female sexual superiority, suppressed entirely in this imaginary, Kern formulates questions that would surely have scandalized public health doctors, tango lyricists, and popular theater dramatists in transitional Buenos Aires: Why not recognize the advantage of women? Why not allow them "a wider range of sexual feeling and a greater capacity to make do with the necessary limitations of monogamous sexual relations?" (1985, 186). One of the male characters in *La mal pagada* (A Woman Poorly Paid) muses on these identity changes:

ISMAEL: Women have driven us men into brutalizing ourselves.

MECHA: And what have we done to you?

ISMAEL: You think it's nothing to have dispelled the poetic myth of your weakness? How can a man care when he knows a woman is quite capable even of swimming the English Channel? . . . Our mistake was to discover it. Women's weakness was the only thing that kept us going. (Acasuso 1937, 6)

In 1900's *The Virile Power of Superb Manhood,* Bernard McFadden sought to raise consciousness of masculinity by urging his fellows who lacked true masculinity that "their first duty was to acquire it": "If you are not a man, you are nothing but a nonentity" (qtd. in Kern 1985, 104). McFadden was convinced that the combination of "physical health, muscular strength, and sexual potency" was the essence of a unique, exemplary masculinity, regardless of the radical changes of the times. How could a trembling employee in Roberto Mariani's *Cuentos de la Oficina* (Office Stories) or an unemployed man on the soup line in Puerto Madero (figure 32) be "energetic, strong-willed, self-confident, with an upright posture and a firm grip"? The pages of *Caras y Caretas* were literally packed with advertisements providing advice for men feeling disconsolately low:

No life is more useless than that of a man . . . without
the necessary energy and manly strength, whose vitality is low . . .

IPERBIOTINA MALESCI
Gives a new outlook on life. It makes youth bloom again, fortifies the nerves and the mind, stimulates the vital organs, purifies the blood and builds a NEW HUMAN MACHINE from a body worn out, tired, or old before its time.

On sale in drug stores and pharmacies.
                    (Caras y Caretas, 6 March 1920; emphasis added)

The advertisement resorts to euphemisms because it must deal with a highly delicate, unprecedented subject: male feelings of uselessness, inadequacy, lack of vitality, chronic fatigue, and aging. Male biological decline is alluded to in many terms and displaced to other areas of meaning, the first of which is unemployment. The man shown in the advertisement is represented inside a house, in an attitude of defeat, and his decline may combine with other kinds of impotence—economic, sexual, and political.

In the same issue of *Caras y Caretas,* an advertisement from the Dr. Sanden Company offers help "to you who suffer from nervous debilitation, who are lacking strength, vigor, and vitality"—an electric girdle. Another advertisement explains: "I always felt weak and was fearful when I had to exert myself, but now I can lift any weight without a problem, and my spirit for work has been raised considerably" (*Caras y Caretas,* 6 March 1920). An advertisement for "Hierro Nuxado" (Nutty Iron) depicts a young man sitting on the edge of a bed, bent over, holding his head in his hands. He is overwhelmed. But along with an abundance of red corpuscles, the advertisement promises "Strong Muscles, taut Nerves, and clear Intelligence," all of which will create "Strong, Daring, Vigorous Men—Men with the Energy and Power Necessary to Triumph in all Aspects of Their Life" (*Caras y Caretas,* 8 March 1919). Why so much talk of weakness, tiredness, and intellectual fog? What is happening here? What comes through is the confusion and bewilderment felt by males confronted with industrialization's new languages and values, set alongside new Darwinian physical, intellectual, and emotional demands. Such market strategies, unfortunately, promoted affirmative models of masculinity, based on the purest paradigms of "Victorious" men, while simultaneously polarizing the fractured, disconnected negative models still further.

Another advertisement for Dr. T. A. Sanden's girdles advises that "that lack of self-confidence, that shyness, that indecision and lack of energy hindering your material advance have a source: nervous debility. . . . Now the means to become vigorous, robust, and energetic and recover the physical endurance necessary to triumph in life's struggle is available." Such telling advertisements put the new uncertainties into words and promised recovery. Yet while recovery was on its way, imaginaries continued to produce antidotes to their own obsessions. Violence was still tolerated as a first measure of defense in a ritual of survival aimed at reestablishing gender hierarchies and reversing territorial losses. If the 1929 crisis demolished the certainties of capitalism, it also spectacularly exposed the crisis/fracture in exemplary masculinity: "Men do not think of themselves as cases to be opened up. Instead, they open up a woman as a substitute for self-knowledge, both maintaining the illusion of their own invulnerability and destroying the terrifying female reminder of their impotence and uncertainty" (Showalter 1991, 134).

Roberto Arlt's narrator in "Las fieras" (Beasts) is a pimp from a city far below the level of the river, like a jail, with "walls surrounded by other surrounding walls, cellars dug out beneath the cement floor of other cellars, [where], for a minute, my life covered the space of a century at the bottom of these dungeons" (Arlt 1939, 40). Emphasizing the compactness of a scene that extends downward and outward, this space is described with claustrophobic sensitivity, heightened by the oppression of concentric underground chambers, similar to the brothels without an exit in "Emma Zunz" or *Historia de arrabal:* "Those in the room [were] without a bed, except for a palliasse thrown onto the brick floor, and [there were] women with lips perforated by syphilitic cankers. . . . There were black women there, in the corners, cradling in one arm a newborn child nursing at their breast, while removing the pants from a lascivious drunk with their free hand so as not to lose time" (43). A barracks, a factory, or a brothel—they are all the same: punitive geographies designed to increase the simultaneity and superimposition of functions. Literally at the same time, the woman is both a mother and a prostitute: a black, syphilitic, sexual servant. The environment is oppressive because it is inescapable. For the black woman, there is no other place in which she can be solely a mother, just as there is no escape from her syphilis. This accretion of subaltern identities comes together to label/define life, consolidating the oppressiveness and unyielding synchronism of the social ghettos.

The male characters in "Las fieras" meet in bars in a ritual that begins in passive lethargy: "At night, they come listlessly to the table beside the counter, sit, give a sidelong greeting to the girl on the vitrola, order a coffee, and remain in the same position where they have sat for hours and hours, staring through the window with an anguished look at the people going by" (Arlt 1939, 44). The group is depicted in light of "the ferocity in us all, oppressed and oppressors." They are violent (oppressors), at the same time as they are reacting to the violence that marginalizes them (the oppressed). All of them are "as implacable as executioners . . . until the day we fall beneath an enemy's blade or from the bullet of someone waiting for us for a long time in the shadows." They have all robbed, have all turned to crime, "have ruined a woman's life, have despicable memories, and wear cynical, painful masks" (44). Violence draws ever-widening circles around those from whom any possible meaning rebounds. One member of the group cannot explain why he brutalizes his wife: "How should I know? It must be because I'm bored." Another, named Uñas de Oro (Golden Fingernails), tells how "he stabbed the palm of a woman's hand with a penknife" as "a sign of love." Negro Cipriano says that "he prostitutes minors under 14, handing them over to the voracity of fearful magistrates and aged magnates." In the brothel, he is "charged with using a whip to tattoo purple stripes on the buttocks of disobedient prostitutes." He also joins in the rape of minors: "A boy held down by five thieves, who pressed him against the floor, covering his mouth; then the curdling scream that shuddered through the restrained body like an electric shock . . . and the row of men who . . . awaited their turn while the boy's body, penetrated by a terrible pain, arched and then fell lifeless" (45). Sickening scenes like this punctuated daily life and filled the reports of police doctors and personnel from the state, prisons, and reformatories, such as *Menores delincuentes: Su psicopatología sexual* (Juvenile Delinquents: Their Sexual Psychopathology, 1919) and *La infancia abandonada y delincuente y la ley Agote* (Abandonment and Delinquency in Childhood and Agote's Law, 1932), both by Dr. Carlos de Arenaza.

How does the narrator justify the violence committed in "Las fieras"? "The thing is," he says, "we all have a terrible boredom inside us, an evil word that's pent up, a blow that doesn't know where to unleash itself, and if the Clockmaker unloads it on his wife, it's because a pain like the unease of a nerve in a rotten tooth bottles up his soul in the dirty night of his room" (Arlt 1939, 49). Violence is concealed under an externalizing logic as a purely biological reflex bound to an involuntary impulse. It should be noted that the characters' narrations of their crimes are not unproductive: their accounts intensify the wretchedness of their memories and their morbid delight in their crimes: "And when that pain, which no one knows how to put into words, explodes . . . whoever has kept quiet splutters a curse, to which the others re-soundingly reply and the table that until then had seemed to be a circle of sleeping people is immediately animated by terrible allegations and irrational hatreds" (49). The narrator speaks of "a blow *that doesn't know where to unleash itself*" (emphasis added). Stories about violence as inescapable give a second wind to its naturalization and reinforce equally inexorable paradigms of predatory masculinity. They account for the obstruction of other models of interaction between the genders or a transformative sensibility toward women:

A sickening state of happiness explodes in each of the beasts in the group, and they talk with the impulse of an inexplicable vanity, a devilish pride. . . . If they talk, it is of hunting for women in the heart of the city, of pursuing them in their clandestine hideouts outside the city limits. . . . If they talk, it is of the procedures of judges to whom they are sold, of the [police] investigations and their ferocity, interrogations, confrontations in court. . . . If they talk, it is of punishment, pain, torture, blows to the face, punches to the stomach, twisted testicles, kicks to the shins . . . squashed fingers, wrenched hands. . . . If they talk, it is of women who are murdered, robbed, on the run, beaten with a stick. (50)

Then the gaze of the group "falls on the girl at the vitrola. . . . A smile curls someone's lip, and it is already known to whom the poor girl will fall; the one who will chase her is already anticipating how many beatings he will give her" (50).

Josefina Ludmer would say that the criminal is able to be open about his crimes because his discursive position lies at the lowest edge of society (1993, 151). Yet, while the chroniclers of infanticides had the benefit of additional time in which to accommodate their crime to a sequence of meaning that "straightened" it out, Arlt's text seems to refuse any attempt to contain violence, perhaps trying to leave its burning questions unanswered. The ubiquitousness of violence in Buenos Aires was simply disheartening. The public ran across it in cafés or when passing a sidewalk kiosk; when thumbing through the crime reports in newspapers and magazines; or in the silent language of photography, which had no reservations about portraying decapitated heads, decomposing corpses, bodies cut up by expert slaughtermen, faces disfigured by an axe, or the body of "a woman of the night," such as that of Eugenia Fougère on her bloodstained bed (*Caras y Caretas,* 1 January 1904).[1] The popular press contributed to the slipping of violence into the city's imaginaries, to the extreme of turning it into a habit of everyday private life and a "natural" part of the maps of mistreatment at the factories and on the streets, behind the closed doors of *conventillos,* brothels, apartments and *garçonières,* orphanages and prisons.

Arlt's Melancholy Pimp, Manuel Gálvez's pimp, and Borges's Eduardo and Cristián Nilsen all come from the same imaginary. In "La intrusa" (The Interloper), the Nilsen brothers hand Juliana Burgos over to a brothel madam in order to remove her from the burning love they both have for her. Yet what will really save them as brothers is to kill her, which is what they proceed to do: "To work, brother. The owls will clean up afterward. I killed her today. Let her stay here with her belongings. She'll not give us any more trouble" (Borges 1974, 1: 1028). To what does Cristián Nilsen refer when he talks of the "trouble" caused by Juliana? What do the brothers really destroy when they murder the young woman? How are Buenos Aires's social texts of violence rooted in "La intrusa"? Beyond the story it tells, Borges's text states that there is "no place for love": love inexorably involves threat, risk, instability and pain, lack of control, and vulnerability. The two Nilsens both love Juliana. Thus, not only the seamstresses but the men of Buenos Aires take a *mal paso de amor* (false step through love), perpetrating the same imprudent error, the same unsafe act that the tango men lament so disconsolately as the result of an unbearable, irreversible fatal calculation. The duel in "La intrusa" is the most horrendous in all of Borges's writing. It pits Juliana against the Nilsens, two adult men, practiced at handling switchblades and knives, who have killed before—and whose business is the killing and quartering of animals. It is a profoundly unsymmetrical duel. The slaughtermen kill Juliana, a young, defenseless woman, doubly subaltern as the brothers' housemaid and sexual servant.

Told from the perspective of the Nilsens' incestuous pact, "La intrusa" avoids focalizing the narrative from Juliana's point of view and thus blocks the reader from the horror of the moment when she is stabbed by Cristián. Juliana never speaks. The Nilsens speak for her and decide her life and death. In the vastness of the Argentinean pampas, she has nowhere to flee. She is isolated, rendered mute by the double silence imposed by the brothers and by the text. She does not speak while she is alive, and her murder makes her muteness absolute. How many women are represented by Juliana! With her death, the Nilsens—along with the imaginaries of social stability—reassert the alliances in male misogyny, precluding any breach in the solidarity among men. The two opening sentences of "Las fieras"—"I am lost for a long time," and "I think of you, the one I've lost forever"—could have come from a tango or from the necrophiliac embrace of the Nilsen brothers after Juliana's death: "They embraced each other, almost in tears. Now they were bound by another tie: the woman sadly sacrificed and the obligation to forget her" (Borges 1974, 1: 1028). For the Nilsens, the young woman represented love and fear at the same time. Or, perhaps, the fear of love.

In Evaristo Carriego's poem "El amasijo" (Dough), from *El alma del suburbio* (Soul of the Suburb), masculinity is heightened by the violence as a ritual that maintains gender hierarchies. A man stops beating his wife because he is "finally worn out"

> from repeating the brutal assault
> that he'll later narrate, congratulating himself,
> in the rude circle of his fellows. . . .
> The sound of voices grows in the little café
> where they are discussing what has happened
> and, in answer to them all, someone insists
> that right belongs only to a husband. (Carriego 1985, 41)

Meanwhile, "the poor, beaten woman tries / to hide her dark, timid shame. . . . / She tends to her injuries, weeping over her bruises, / marks of pain on her stricken body . . . / this is why she is resigned / like an animal in the throes of death under a whip" (41–42). As the foundational text of tango poetry, this work, with its reference to sexual violence, must have served to naturalize such practices without questioning their truth. In "En el barrio" (In the Neighborhood), a *payador/tanguero* embroiders the story of a slit throat:

> a verse that tells a tale of dark passions
> of alcohol and blood, cruel punishments,
> mortal offenses,
> and violent deaths of unfaithful lovers. (Carriego 1985, 43)

"Finura," by José Luis Lanuza, is chronologically located during the Centennial celebrations of 1910, in a dancehall called El Pasatiempo, where "you had to be careful what you said and where you looked": "People looked at each other furtively, and it meant something if a woman lingered on someone with her eyes." In the case of Finura, the flute player, "His work prevented him from complimenting the dancers. So he looked at them. He had gazer's eyes and could make himself understood just by looking" (Lanuza 1939, 293). Through looks alone, he wins Nélida, a dark-skinned woman accompanying the *guapo* Nuñez, wearing her hair in "a big, heavy, black bun that made her lean her head back as if searching for cushions in the air." Finura feels that "something in her escapes me," something indefinite, but does not understand what it is until Nélida reappears with Nuñez. The space of Nélida's "treachery" is the space of a woman's slippage toward an agency that would certainly be dimmed through violence with the regularity of clockwork. In "A la luz del candil" (By the Light of a Candle), we read:

> If I am a criminal
> may God forgive me. . . .
> They betrayed me, Lord,
> and I killed them both. (Qtd. in Pelletieri 1992, 240)

I believe that the only way to understand the anxiety caused by the presence of a woman in the streets, and the signs of her incipient agency, is to grasp the full gravity of the social text of violence. Women were physically close, while emotionally removing themselves. They were close in the tight spaces of buses or subways or when exposing their bodies in the factory changing room. Their bodies were within sight and reach. Nevertheless, they were also distant, sheltered by the dawn of new polymorphous maps of subjectivity, alliances, and lateralities.

According to sensorial geography, urbanism is the solidification of space through the widening of the radius of interpersonal, social contact. It is always perceived from the position of a particular body, as Donatella Mazzoleni explains, "because the dynamic of urban traffics all occurs on the scale of the movements of the natural locomotion of individual bodies" (1985, 16). This means that each of us processes what we see as a social actor and a coinhabitant of the city and that what we process becomes part of our cognitive map of urban space. This is a public space filled with social agents who are mobilized and displaced and who travel with us. Neither the observer nor the person observed is static. Established interactions between observer and observed give shape to rules of exchange arising from mutual displacement. The male speaker moves through the streets of Buenos Aires. There are moments he discards and others on which he confers relevance: details, images, gestures, silences, bodies, rhythms. But the gestures of the "other" that catch his attention have as much to do with the object in motion as with himself, with his own *displacement* somewhere or his own *emplacement*— not solely in terms of geographical displacement, but in terms of his own socioidentitary displacement. What are the moving points that catch the attention of this speaker, given that *porteñas* are not all that move through the

streets of Buenos Aires? As Néstor García Canclini remarks, "Urban journeys undertaken daily are associated with the experience and imaginary of
habitation" (García Canclini, Castellanos, and Mantecón 1996, 12). Thus,
social actors in Buenos Aires engage in an identitary "crossing" that identifies
the mobility of others in relation to their own.

Although the remedies prescribed for these depressed men—the central
theme of the weeping in tango—were tonics for the blood or electric girdles,
I believe that the symptoms of their depression were to be found in less
evident places. I propose that they might instead most powerfully be located
in three areas of displacement: first, in the profound economic dissymmetry
between place and identity; second, in the crisis in the paradigm of exemplary masculinity, caught between essentialism and the vicissitudes of everyday reality that disturbed it; and third, in the gradual evidence of a lack of
political representation. This formation of the symbolic developed against the
background of political processes that went from the Conservative Order, to
Radicalism, to fascist dictatorship. "I am castrated," is the Astrologer's shocking phrase, which perhaps explains the madness and ultra-marginalization
explored in *Los siete locos*. When it comes to castrations and slippages, however, nothing is more revealing than the point of view of Hipólita, a prostitute from "the dregs of Buenos Aires": "I gave myself to the first young man
who came by. . . . What a surprise, when he collapsed like an animal after
satisfying himself! At first, I thought he was ill . . . But when someone else
explained it was natural in all men, I couldn't resist the desire to laugh. So
men whose strength seems as great as a bull's . . . imagine" (Arlt 1981c, 1:
265). Before leaving him, Erdosain's wife gives herself to him, "but with revulsion, disillusioned. . . . And he knelt at the head of his bed begging her
to give him a minute more, but his wife answered him almost shouting in
a voice thick with impatience: Leave me alone! Don't you see you revolt
me?" (Arlt 1981c, 1: 190). Hipólita's declarations and her sensorial body language rub salt into a bleeding wound: male weakness seen from the perspective of female disenchantment, the end of the paradigm of hierarchies and
certainties that had long depended on the game of static recognition and fore-
knowledge. Arlt's place is an identitary nonplace, from which, unfortunately,
no *new* identitary place is extracted. In fact, his fictional worlds refuse to
envision second chances within hybrid identities arisen from marginaliza-

Gender and Politics

tion and inadequacy. They also decline to believe in the flashy promises of empowering imaginaries.

It was not enough to be a man to be included in paradigms of masculinity in Buenos Aires. Unemployed and unknown in the wretched boardinghouses of the *mishiadura,* Arlt's men and *tangueros* embody expulsion.[2] Hipólita is quick to detect this: "[Erdosain] will do nothing all his life save complain and suffer. What use is a boy like that to me? . . . I've yet to find one among them worthy of cutting the others' throats or of being a tyrant. They're pitiful" (Arlt 1981c, 1: 271). Nothing saddens Hipólita more than knowing that, of all the men she meets, none "had the drive to become a tyrant or conqueror of new lands" (1: 270). She has never met any lions anywhere, "just mangy dogs; and her most adventurous knights wore the cross of the fork and were mystics of the cooking pot. She drew back in revulsion" (1: 271). Hipólita's refusal to visualize the laterality that joins her to failures such as Erdosain could be read as a reaction/revenge against the social subalternality of women, but I read it instead as an ardent fidelity to exemplary masculinity and its strong, triumphant identities. Hipólita cries out for violent men willing to slit throats, for tyrants and *conquistadores.* In fact, in the sordid, claustrophobic city of brothels, she reproduces the Darwinian act of expelling the weak. The general and the dictator to whom Hipólita calls in her disenchantment when she finds no manly men are two paradigms of nationalist imaginaries. The first is commended by Leopoldo Lugones in the chapter "Los constructores" (The Builders), in his *Historia de Roca* (History of Roca); the second would spring onto the national stage with the coup headed by General José Félix Uriburu, on 6 September 1930—that is to say, less than a year after the publication of *Los siete locos* (in October 1929). Hipólita longs for dictators, paradigms self-legitimized by violence, as in the theory of the coup espoused by authoritarian states. She displays her desire for a society that believes it has lost its forceful leaders and needs to reorder its convictions by violent means.

The drama *El ruedo de las almas* (Circle of Souls), we recall, warns that the heart of danger lies not in the phantoms encased in the silhouette of a woman, but elsewhere. As if in a tango, here a leftist politician declines into a lover drained by a femme fatale who betrays him. A worker in the politician's party reproaches him for having abandoned the voters. He politicizes the term *treason*—a signifier restricted by stabilizing imaginaries to the bedroom and the fires of desire. Treasons of all kinds coexist:

> MUCCHETTI: . . . Our party no longer is what it once was; it seems unreal that
> something so spotless should become what it is today, something so unclean.
> Everyone is given up to a loathsome, ambitious struggle. I, as one who has
> given you so little—what could a worker without learning and intelligence
> give—feel myself victimized. . . . There are no ideals anymore. It all comes
> down to who climbs highest.

At the opposite end of the political spectrum, a major in the army stationed in Temperley to advise seven madmen anticipates the logic that would justify Uriburu's coup. In 1920s Buenos Aires, political representatives pursued "a career of lies . . . a life outside the rules and truth": "In our chambers of deputies and senators are people accused of extortion and homicide, bandits who have sold out to foreign companies, and individuals with such crass ignorance that parliamentary politics has turned into the most grotesque comedy that could ever degrade a country. Presidential elections are fought with American capital on the basis of promises of concessions to be granted a company interested in exploiting our national wealth" (Arlt 1981c, 1: 223). In his nationalistic harangue, the major declares, "The fight between political parties in our country is nothing more than a squabble among businessmen willing to sell the country at any price." After explaining that *Los siete locos* was published *before* the 1930 coup, Arlt's "Author's Note" states, "It is curious that the declarations of the September 6 revolutionaries coincide so exactly with those of the major" (1: 223). In fact, the military coup was perpetrated by "officers disillusioned by theories of democracy." Arlt's writing must have picked up what was being said on the streets. Without going any further, it was the same reading of the void in political representation expressed by the worker in 1923 in *El ruedo de las almas*.

In *La patria fuerte* (1930), at the request of the officers' cultural and social club—the Círculo Militar Argentino—Lugones collected a series of articles first published in *La Nación*. This book was intended for the young officer corps, meant to substantiate the nationalist reaction implied by the coup: "the complete citizen is defined by the soldier" because there is no greater calling. This paradigm of identity is founded on the idea that "the Argentinean Fatherland is not the child of politics, but of the sword" (Lugones 1930, 8). Convinced of the virile character of the nation's destiny, Lugones denounces the cowardice and lack of manliness (*falta de hombría*) underlying liberalism's bland permissiveness, which he calls a "socioradical freak": "Fear of death is in turn transformed into pacifism, espousing the conviction that 'war is bad business,' a maxim we hear repeated by all contemporary statesmen. But this dual 'devirilizing' process . . . consisting of an exclusive cult of well-being and life without risk, has organic consequences: the fall in the birth rate unfailingly promoted by urban life. Pacifism, humanitarianism, and sterility tip the balance, slowly but surely bringing to its knees the potency whose excessive vitality disturbs tranquility" (115). This strong identification—the protagonist of dominant paradigms—of an eminently military and necrophiliac nature, like all fascist discourses, would have been neutralized by the more relaxed condition of democratic life. On the contrary, *golpismo* (the prevailing ideology of the coup) would reinstate the virile "tension" and "potency" needed to recharge the tumultuous "social condition of our country." Here was a paradigm of forceful masculinity worthy of attention if what was needed was a strong fatherland: "To be useful to yourself and to others you must be strong in all areas of strength" (Lugones 1930, 116). Challenging those debilitated males in the *Caras y Caretas* advertisements, the lachrymose men of the tango, and other deviations, this discourse proposed instead a new virility, militarization, and vitality: "Only the weak are nothing, which is why the desire to consign the world to its decline, by proclaiming the fallacy of equality, is senseless" (Lugones 1930, 116). *La patria fuerte* brings together the military ideology and the fascist politics of "the hour of the sword." In other words, General Uriburu's coup, led by a "strongman," was the reverse of the error and "fallacy of equality," unmasked by Herculean men who would save the Babylonian city from chaos.

The fluidity of transitional cultures turns the *questioning* of the paradigm into the *end* of the paradigm: "When the prototypical male subject is unable to recognize 'himself' within its conjuration of masculine sufficiency, our society suffers from a profound sense of 'ideological fatigue.' Our entire 'world,' then, depends upon the alignment of phallus and penis" (Kaja Silverman 1992, 16). The coup's imaginary uses violence for the same reasons as does the *compadrito* from the *arrabal* when he mistreats a woman who is longing to move away. Hence Lugones's writing endorses the strong state (Estado Fuerte) for imposing "capital punishment on the rebel," "carrying out enforced or voluntary expatriation," and reaffirming "its principle of power": "The nation exerts hierarchical empire over all individuals who inhabit it . . . for sovereignty includes . . . the power to unconditionally suppress or vary those limitations," while anarchy is "the subordination of the nation to the individual" (1930, 45). Who would be the virile men of Argentina? Henceforth, they would be the men of the military, preordained by the sword and capable of inflicting "necessary wounds" on the social body with prophylactic coldness and conviction: "'Exemplary' male subjectivity cannot be thought apart from ideology, not only because ideology holds out the mirror within which that subjectivity is constructed, but because the latter depends upon a kind of collective make-believe in the commensurability of penis and phallus" (Kaja Silverman 1992, 15). Whoever would be virile could exercise the sexuality of power and, of course, power itself. Not like that crowd of those melodramatic Buenos Aires males who had made tango a good place in which to shamelessly weep and sigh, protected by the fact that, deceitfully detached from their own problems, they were only singing somebody else's sad stories.

20 BARRIOS AND MELODRAMAS

Of Love and Consternation

Never expect any help, a hand or a favor.

Enrique Santos Discépolo, "Yira . . . yira," 1930

It's not love but consternation that unites us;
maybe that's why I love it so much.

Jorge Luis Borges, "Buenos Aires," 1964

BETWEEN 1910 AND 1930, BUENOS
Aires's suburban areas were shaped by a wide diversity of nationalities, languages, and proletarian or middle-class backgrounds (workers, small businessmen, teachers); by long-term connections to barrio mutual societies or
ethnic/national associations; by high job turnover; by scant demand for
skilled labor; and by varied personal successes as social modernity moved
some groups up and left others behind (Romero and Gutiérrez 1995, 10).
The legitimation of the Radical Party state and its political consensus was
constructed on two fundamental axes: the culture of the barrios, and education as a means to Argentineanize the children of immigrants. Evaristo
Carriego, Jorge Luis Borges, Boedo writers, popular theater, and the tango
made it possible to create consensual meanings and give a local name to everyday life by representing how it was lived in the barrios. These were the cultural spaces where collective Argentinean identities were forged. Suburban
barrio culture was a product of expansion and real estate speculation in the city
center, extension and improvement to the railway system, and the relocation

of workers able to buy lots on vacant land. It promoted a strong spirit of collectivism through pragmatic projects, such as paved streets, drainage, and primary schools. Because such projects were pursued by the community, they fueled a sense of social laterality, but the consolidation of the suburban barrio as a space of symbolic integration was also possible thanks to the mass written culture of newspapers, *folletines,* popular novels, and cheap publications, as well as radio, the entertainment industry, and national cinema—all connecting the suburbs to the city center and then to global culture through the rise of Hollywood. The proliferation of promotional societies (*sociedades de fomento*) and popular libraries was impressive. Lectures and locally published leaflets, along with the cultural activism of barrio intellectuals, provided a bridge allowing the circulation of cultural and political ideas. The local thus developed into a culture (*localismo*).

José Moya has discussed two functions of national immigrant organizations: "to deal with the challenges of the new setting . . . [and so ease] adaptation to the host country," and to aid in maintaining "Old World ways and mentalities and a sense of separateness among the arrivals" (1998, 327). Yet while national organizations began by developing sociocultural activities intended to ensure the continuation of cultures of origin, they soon redefined their objectives. Xosé M. Núñez Seixas indicates, with respect to immigration from Galicia, that in 1923 sixteen associations affiliated with the Casa de Galicia were dedicated to helping new arrivals, providing aid in cases of illness or unemployment, repatriating members who were sick or without resources, or covering funeral and burial costs for the deceased (1999, 223). Even if differing sociopolitical objectives and class interests gradually altered their goals, they would all share the assumption—like the Sociedad Unión Progresista del Distrito de Salvatierra de Miño (Progressive Union Society of the Salvatierra de Miño District)—that "individual efforts" were fruitless (Núñez Seixas 1999, 226). Every collective undertaking was to have two main purposes: to preserve the common bonds of national origin and to locate the community in the more immediate contexts of suburban development and Argentineanization.

The Centro Vecinal Barrio Nazca (Neighborhood Center of the Barrio of Nazca) was founded by "responsible residents," public service workers who donated their expertise in public administration. Most of its members were Yrigoyen supporters (its weekly newspaper was called *Yrigoyen*), and it had to contend with a population that had no collective experience in promoting community interests through cultural activities and sports; improving housing by building affordable homes; or pursuing other priorities— including opening streets, repairing infrastructure, or lighting the streets (Gonzalez 1990, 101). The progress in the process of adjustment could be seen in the Galician associations and in the Centro Nazca. Immigrants' associations gave way in due course to those representing the barrio and its most emblematic cultural function: leading the predominantly foreign working-class population into "becoming Argentinean" (*farsi argentini*).

Hence the city's periphery ceased to be a dormitory-suburb, becoming instead the suburban barrio where the first generation of immigrants were forming families whose children would contribute to the Argentineanization of the family unit, and thanks to the leisure time gained from the reduction in the workday, suburban families could gradually develop a deeper relationship with the barrio. At the same time, a consensus on social and political order was also being built within barrio culture, cemented by two major promises that could not be lightly dismissed: the expectation of economic improvement and a rise in the quality of local life. A well-placed facilitator would serve the interests of suburban culture well. Local barrio interests and activities were steadily endorsed by the populist, democratic ideology of the UCR as a way to channel the political participation of its clientele and to engage them in a dialogue sought by a government that would insistently project itself as committed to social justice. Consequently, when Yrigoyen's UCR came to power in 1916, and when Acuerdismo, in 1919, laid the foundations for imaginaries based on conciliation and surrogate political representation, they found their most attentive partners in the barrios. Henceforth, the government would endeavor to take seriously whatever the trade associations, unions, and barrio and mutual societies asked of it.

When looked at this way, with the city as a whole in mind, the suburban world seemed to provide a space for integration that was, precisely, everything the urban world was not. Just as the urban spaces of the center had been stamped throughout with the signature of the dominant class, the barrios seemed to be a place for democratic culture. Having said this, however, there must be a reason why Enrique Santos Discépolo's tango "Yira . . . yira" warned, in 1930, "Never expect any help, a hand or a favor." This amounted to claiming that the precariousness of the *yiranta* (street prostitute) was a condition spread far and wide and that the social network as a whole was broken by "the indifference of the world / —that is both deaf and dumb." Something had been seriously derailed, the collective identity developed in the barrio seeming to have collapsed at one point without a sound. The causes of the collapse were certainly not to be found in the barrio itself, but in the conditions of peripheral capitalism and the world crisis of 1929 and in the overthrow of Yrigoyen, with the subsequent interruption in democratic life that lasted until Perón. In 1930, the oligarchy regained its power to defend corporate interests, while the political parties, neutralized by a fraudulent democratic system, "lost their reason for being" (González 1990, 119). The repression silenced militant workers, while unemployment also played a big part in the class struggle. These were not times to put one's job at risk through political militancy. While political and union parties were not exactly absent, they were at least conspicuously lukewarm and reticent, just at the time when the working and middle classes needed their intervention most. This void, and the resulting lack of political representation, explain the common terms *década infame* (decade of infamy) and *mishiadura* (indigence)— the former referring to the impunity with which the oligarchy regained political power and the latter to the defenselessness and powerlessness of the working class.

Like any crisis in economic readjustment, the 1929 crisis required both a break in the political paradigm in Argentina (hence Uriburu's coup) and an economic (and therefore political) slowdown among social sectors that the democratic experience had mobilized. Luis Alberto Romero and Leandro Gutiérrez contend that, with routes to the grand political stage closed off, libraries and social and sports clubs were left to contain collective identity, although soccer and basketball clubs could not channel collective interests related to the quotidian. In the first phase of *golpismo,* elitism, bureaucratization, and authoritarianism seemed able to turn the page on the Argentinean democratic paradigm. Political and union institutions then reacted gradually until, in 1936, the General Workers Union, under the leadership of socialists and communists, renewed its activism in the context of structural changes brought on by the development of the second wave of industrialization (exportation) in the light of World War II.

The activities of barrio associations worked very well to cement suburban laterality, while its imaginaries did likewise. Evaristo Carriego's poems/

chronicles of daily life in the suburbs were undoubtedly the most important cultural synthesizers of collective barrio identity. According to Osvaldo Pellettieri, Carriego's texts were "genuine producers of new texts" and continued to be imbibed until well into the 1950s (1992, 228). The imaginaries responsible for constructing the quotidian in the barrio redefined proxemic distances by emphasizing a high sense of intimacy and social laterality. Carriego's *El alma del suburbio* turns the absolutely soulless open grounds of unoccupied lots and wastelands into a true place/identity. It creates a unique cultural landscape that makes possible everything the city does not: an identity that stems from mutual recognition and a sense of belonging. The suburban barrio, then, gradually Argentineanized, adopting the patois of the popular and middle classes (Cocoliche and Lunfardo), while immigrant accents and habits tended to melt into a homogenized *national* identity.

How does a collective identity come about? It comes about, I suppose, in many ways, but I believe that melodrama is one of the most effective. In *The Life of Melodrama,* Eric Bentley asks, "What does it mean: to weep?" (1967, 197). The tears of the stormy sea of sentimentality remained unexplored until Bentley examined them from the perspective of a Victorian-era need to bring together the fragments dispersed by the city. Self-pity is, without a doubt, the heart of melodrama, along with a tacit agreement to confront the fear of emotions, to delve into the self, but as if the experience always belongs to another. The door to melodrama was opened by Sigmund Freud's and Josef Breuer's explanations of where emotions go when they are too tightly contained. Henceforth, the melodramatic became "grandiose," fulfilling a cathartic "need" (Bentley 1967, 199). I would call melodrama's grandiosity "necessary," because it captures the emergence of social laterality as a powerful identitary strategy able to ignite collective emotions regardless of attempts to socially control them. Melodrama draws out the audience's pity and fears. It works with the audience's worst fears and most unattainable dreams, setting them against each other in order to maximize the impact of the melodramatic moment. This emotional polarization propitiates an overstated accumulation of bad luck and misfortunes of every kind. Nevertheless, the unprecedented experiences of everyday modern life in Buenos Aires forged the emergence of new discourses. Melodrama was a discursive strategy that endorsed the socially correct (*lo acertado*)—absolute social control. At the same time, however, it did not refrain from capturing the anguish of belonging to a city without roots, a city of which few people felt themselves a part. To narrate the "minor" epics of daily life, ignoring the grander stories and settings, is both the role and the shame of melodrama.

In Carriego's barrio, one neighbor advises another, "No salgas resfriado" (Don't Go Out with a Cold). People are curious about rumors and tittle-tattle, as well as concerned about the pain of a neighboring *obrera.* Buenos Aires's imaginaries portrayed the suburban barrios as a community that cared, a collective body and home: what need was there, after all, to go to the city center? The barrio exorcises all the demons of the center and the sloth of those who rule over it: perdition and enslaved sexuality; unrestrained consumption; and the bombastic, symbolic spaces of oligarchic privilege that remind suburban residents of painful exclusions.

The poem "El alma del suburbio" constructs connecting spaces at odds with the fragmentation of the city center. Everything here smacks of an embracing, gossipy closeness and intimacy, as if the barrio were a corporeal bubble so inclusive and indiscriminate that it could shelter all its inhabitants. Gaslight (electricity reached the suburbs much later) and the eternally open windows, giving an interior view of seamstresses bent over their work or the working man's wife exhausted from her double shift, in the factory and at home, add to this intimacy. Women spill onto the streets to listen: while Carriego's barrio may be visual, it is auditory above all. It picks up everything "shouted on street corners": "the (celebrated) late edition" brought into the *conventillo* by "one boy or other / spreading the crier's news." The news is never that new. It has already been heard, consisting of crimes of passion whose stories are told and retold by *vecinas* (neighborhood women) so that they reverberate throughout the barrio. Like the tale of the murderer "who recites his adventures from prison," turning his private story into public history for the attentive audience in the bars:

> The barrio women talk about it together
> and philosophize on fate . . .
> while the unmovable men try
> to defend the lover who turned into a murderer. (Carriego 1985, 30)

Evaristo Carriego's imaginaries assert the symbolic formation of collective places and social habits in at least three ways. First, his versified urban chronicles proceed as if filmed, the focus shifting to bring in intersecting zones: a view from the interior of a house coincides with that of a passerby on the street, looking in through the open window. The ensuing combination of points of view creates a collection of loose-tongued, insufferable gossipers drawn into the suburban barrio as part of its imaginary "connectivity." Second, verbal/auditory repetition ensures the recognition of stories and events shared by all members of the barrio. Like packs of used cards and common coins, collective experiences—such as illness, unemployment, or widowhood —serve to "normalize" the grim avatars of everyday. Third, common rituals give meaning to and consolidate the quotidian. At night, for example, the barrio "sleeps like a saint," sensing "the slow, clicking heels of passersby," the police on their rounds, the barking of dogs listened to by cats, "quiet and disdainful / on inaccessible balconies," and a gringo singing to himself on his way home from work. Everything is in its place in this perfectly reassuring imaginary scenario.

Daily social habits are the cultural spaces that best forge social laterality. Carriego appeals to common praxes and recurring experiences in order to gain the social laterality of an audience much less concerned with information than with recognition. "El otoño, muchachos" (Autumn, My Friends) traces the changes in the barrio with the coming of the season: "people / leave their doors earlier. / They leave them silently." As the cold arrives, Carriego's much-celebrated blind man sings "less frequently the tune his organ stammers / on the street corner." Even the depression caused by the loss of daylight is evident in a woman "who, for days now, / has been feeling down" (Carriego 1985, 120).

Neighbors see themselves "in" each other when they perform common rituals, celebrating them as mechanisms of identitary recognition: a family gathers at teatime, "remembering / who knows what family joke" (Carriego 1985, 90), while the children carry on playing; a boy "finishes the annoying essay on carelessness / given him as punishment at school" (93); the tea grows cold beside a book being read (102), and the dog dozes (*hace fiacca*). The heaviness and laziness of this representation of domesticity cast its lassitude over everything. There is an evident benefit to believing life is like this. "Cuando hace mal tiempo" (When the Weather Is Bad) describes the inside of a house when it is raining and cold outside. The speaker comments: "I doze in the delightful softness / of such warm winter idleness" (105). Every routine is conducive to relaxation, even the "whimsical views" through cigarette smoke:

"in the blue cloud, things / take on unreal shapes." Everything is a celebration of domesticity and inactivity. The barrio is a breathing space for the everyday unknown warrior of the factories:

> How good the sofa is on these cold
> afternoons! . . . How good you feel, stretched out like this,
> in heavy sensuality! . . . I'd like never
> to move from here! If we could only live eternally drowsy! (106)

In the imaginary of the barrio, a man finds peace and shelter in the domestic setting. In fact, he seems to enjoy domestication, which might raise some eyebrows about this peculiar masculinity. Agoraphobia was a female matter, after all, for women seeking refuge from the inclemency of life in the shelter of domesticity. As Diane L. Chambless has indicated, fear of open spaces is actually "fear of being away from home and familiarity—places and people that provide psychological security" (Chambless and Goldstein 1982b, 2), while Leo Salzman points out that the phobia originates from "being away from an established location . . . viewed as safe, and inviolable. Thus, the fear of going out of one's home is that of distance, not open space" (1982, 28).

Notwithstanding such feelings, in "De sobremesa" (After Supper), alongside the custom of reflection, once "supper is over / while savoring the bitter coffee" (Carriego 1985, 106), a fissure may also be glimpsed: "as if by some unusual virtue / I don't look badly on life / even during the most irksome hours." This "unusual" (and "doubtful") virtue consists in placating frustrations with settling ceremonies derived from imaginaries of self-deferment: "so many things / can be well hidden in the breast!" (106). And what does the speaker's heart hide? This "unusual" virtue and silenced heart are eminently melodramatic. Directly related to naturalism, "the melodramatic vision is in one sense simply normal. It corresponds to an important aspect of reality. It is the spontaneous, uninhibited way of seeing things. . . . It is drama in its elemental form" (Bentley 1967, 216). Melodrama permeated popular theater in Buenos Aires precisely as a compilation of the events of daily life, allowing audiences to retrieve their quotidian experiences and recognize themselves. But melodrama is also the vehicle in which polarity and moral stereotyping are dramatized and theatricalized: "extreme states of being, situations, actions; overt villainy, persecution of the good and final reward of virtue . . . dark plotting, suspense, breathtaking periphery" (Bentley 1967,

216). If the barrios were the other side of the rationalist, functional city, their emotional excess linked them to the Romantic tradition and the feminine, for melodrama allowed barrio and tango men to weep, thereby feminizing entire zones of the city.

The *feminine* is fundamental to melodramatic discourse because it functions to stress bewildering ruptures, falls, fractures, and interruptions within the flow of everyday normality. In this respect, Carriego's female characters are emblematic: "unlucky seamstresses who took a wrong turn" (*costureritas que dieron el mal paso*), on the one hand, and, on the other, aged mothers, widows, single women, tubercular working women, and anachronistic spinsters so agoraphobic they never leave home. In other words, weakness predominates as the most effective means of inciting the tears and relief of collective emotions because the people portrayed—those left behind by the city—were the most vulnerable. Bowed by the misfortunes carefully listed in melodrama, these female paradigms seem, in principle, to contrast with the revolt represented in the abandonment of men and family by women on their way to becoming *milonguitas*. In contrast, these women are far removed from the upright pose of the *muñecas bravas* and the search for sexual and identitary agency by lascivious femmes fatales, who can toy with the love of unwary men but whose hours are just as numbered as those of aged or tubercular women.

In "La viejecita" (Little Old Woman), published in 1919, an old woman drags her exhausted body ("her cross demands it") through the barrio streets:

> The old woman goes by, inconsolably,
> she is not much more than a castoff
> of misfortune, her pitiful
> body worn out through sacrifice. (Carriego 1985, 33)

The old woman is a "useless reject," "a sorrowful psalm from the Gospel of Poverty," but she sacrifices herself to take on others' troubles, establishing an identitary model that lateralizes social destitution in the barrio: yours and another's affairs are intertwined. Although she has only "a crust that doesn't fill her," she decides to take in a girl, "the child of others": "Without ever having been loved, / she feels herself a mother to those who cry out," welcoming "that child who is not her child." Melodrama ordains the fate of barrio residents, the *costurerita que dió el mal paso:* prison, the crime of passion, sickness, the fateful premonition, the self-sacrificing and heroic but useless gesture. Both Carriego's writing and tango approach this determinism through characters located on the margins, in extremis, with no way out. The little old woman is a woman without a man, in old age, and therefore stripped of sexuality. She is poor and, to cap it all off, stigmatized for being "an old spinster." Hence the pity evoked by the diminutive (*viejecita*) amid the "dead years" of her life:

> For the poor woman never knew
> love, whether great or small,
> to inspire her; it was not given
> to her to dream a dream about life. (33)

Such a portrait arises in the context of compulsive heterosexuality. The old woman's years are "dead" from the perspective of patriarchal structures. Her spinsterhood is alluded to as a wretched fate because she had no "love . . . to inspire her." By contrast, what does destiny have in store for the young girl? Stabilizing imaginaries do not foresee a solitary, sexually deprived, poverty-stricken life for her:

> That young child at her side
> will tomorrow be her support,
> a flower of the heartbroken suburb,
> a lily from the ferns that sprouted in a stream. (Carriego 1985, 33)

Stabilizing imaginaries ordain that this girl, "later a beautiful, desirable woman," will inevitably become "Inés, the sweet, seduced nun / of the tavern Tenorios"—a sad end like those awaiting other Ofelias, the "poor, unknown heroines of those dramas," or the consumptive "Ladies with the Camelias." Next to them, Carriego's old woman, "a naked mother in rags / a covering of love from the lowly barrio," will become just another "daydream / overturned by reality!" Since her "first cradle was already an abyss," there is no reason to suppose that in old age she will cast off the heavy frown of one "obsessed by cruelty," looking "the image of madness incarnate."

In Carriego's world, all roads traveled by women from working-class barrios lead to silent, collective dramas, downfalls, and abysses. A woman is either a woman of the mire (*mujer de fango*) or "the consumptive across the street [who] cherishes a sweet nostalgia / for that beloved but forgotten verse /

once sung to her by a gallant minstrel." Or she is that "working man's tired and dirty wife,"

> mending her son's clothes .
> heartbroken to believe her husband, as always,
> will likely come home drunk. (Carriego 1985, 37)

Suburban barrios are represented by defeated women who transfer their fall to agoraphobic men with hearts in pain, stifled by fears of life's sudden changes. The barrios were an intensely paradoxical, bipolar identitary space. They offered the relief of belonging to a space for common rituals, certainties, and sorrows, but at the same time, they constituted a cartography of identitary refraction, because of that heart repressed by an "unusual virtue."

The sacred spaces in Jorge Luis Borges's Buenos Aires are strictly regulated, like the predictable interior of a house where no furniture changes place in order to facilitate rituals and customs, or even the movements of a blind man. "El ciego" (The Blind Man), from *El oro de los tigres* (The Tigers' Gold), advises the caution of prevention: "Unevenness lies in wait. Every step / may lead to a fall" (Borges 1974, 1: 1098). How to deal with the outdoors, where unevenness, downfall, and the material city lurk? There is a tension between going outside and staying inside, filling Borges's imaginary with lonely people, claustrophiliacs, and sociophobes intimidated by open public spaces. Clearly, wild horses could not move Asterión from the solitude of his huge mansion. The protagonist of "La espera" (The Wait), from *El Aleph,* doesn't leave the house either: "when four weeks or so were up, he took to going out for a while at nightfall" (1974, 1: 609), but he prefers rather closed and dark spaces, like the cinema. In Evaristo Carriego's "Historia de jinetes" (A Story of Horsemen, 1930), a horse breaker is taken to Buenos Aires by his boss: "He went to look for him three days later [and] found him sipping maté in his room. . . . He asked what he thought of Buenos Aires, and it turned out the man hadn't once gone out onto the street" (Carriego 1985, 152). Examples of "avoidance behavior" as a shelter from the inclemency of the city abound in Borges: "The nomads [Moguls] didn't know what to do with a big city," and of course, "gauchos fear the city" (1974, 1: 152). How can this agoraphobia be explained?

In principle, Borges seems to find it sufficient to refer loosely to indistinguishable streets or barrios in order to territorialize urban space as his own.

Such is the case with "a corner in the South," Recoleta, Palermo or Chacarita, and Maldonado. Borges's cultural geography then specifies corners and particular blocks—"the barrio of Villa Alvear: between Nicaragua, Arroyo Maldonado, Canning and Rivera Streets"; "la Plaza Garay"; "Serrano, Canning, Coronel" (1974, 1: 108)—and even locates "the ghost that haunted one side of the Calle Agüero" or the "wall in Recoleta against which one of my majors was shot by firing squad" (1: 1009). If Borges finds it necessary to use his writing as a surface allowing personal inscriptions on the cultural maps of Buenos Aires "before it is too late," this is because he is fully conscious of new cultural agents already marking their own urban maps, as in the cartography of tango, which places the "Café de los Angelitos" at Rivadavia and Rincón (in "Isla de Flores," by Román Machado and Arturo César Senez) and expressly locates the secrets of "Corrientes three-four-eight" and "Juncal twelve-twenty-four," as revealed in "A media luz" (In the Dimmed Light), by Edgardo Donato and Carlos Lenzi. Beatriz Sarlo has stressed how "the heterogeneity of this public space—accentuated . . . by the new cultural and social mixtures provoked by the pressing demographic changes—put different levels of literary production in contact with each other, establishing an extremely fluid system of aesthetic circulation and borrowing" (1993, 13). Just as Borges named the barrio of Palermo in order to make it *his* territory, Homero Manzi did likewise with San Juan and Old Boedo, Nicolás Olivari specified "the old store 'To the City of Genoa'" on Cangallo and Ombú, César Tiempo marked out Junín and Lavalle (in "Canturria" [Song]), and Celedonio Flores claimed the corner of Corrientes and Esmeralda, thereby establishing the legend of Buenos Aires's celebrated nightlife.

These cultural agents were all engaged in the hurried construction of cognitive maps of the city. Yet since the center had become an unfamiliar place, permeated by privilege and global culture, the suburban barrios, on the periphery, would function as nodes of identity. Paradoxically, however, they were fleeting anchorages of personal identity, writings from very different discursive positions speaking of Villa Crespo (Tagle Lara, Vacarezza), "Sur" (Manzi, Borges), San Telmo (Horacio Armani), Barrio Belgrano (Lugones, Borges, Mastronardi, Petit de Murat, Pondal Ríos, Elba de Lóizaga, García Jiménez), Flores (Girondo, Luis Cané, Cordoba Iturburu, Gaudino), Palermo–Barrio Norte (Lugones, Carriego, Borges), Almagro (De Lellis, Derlis, Martini), Barrio Boedo and Pompeya (Castelpoggi, Manzi), Once (de la Púa), and so on. Such a collection of writing and chatter is notoriously unhierarchical, and the collapse of the divide between high and popular culture it signals brings together tango poets, authors of *folletines* and *sainetes,* and intellectuals from the Boedo and Florida groups—all mingling in a porous and surprisingly interactive cultural space of the modern city.

Popular culture in the barrios was instrumental in the massification of tango, so that whatever the voice in tango talked about—the suburb and lost identity—was echoed in *sainetes, folletines,* and the cinema. The secrets of the speakers' heavy hearts were no longer chastely private, but shamelessly disseminated through the shrill, public sound of radio. And the secret that made their hearts heaviest was the loss of the barrio and identity, as Florencio Escardó laments:

> On what corner shall I find you, Buenos Aires?
> Not on Corrientes and Esmeralda
> where *porteños* are not alone and do not wait. . . .
> Callao and Quintana is another land,
> perhaps on Matadero,
> at the corner
> where a cowhand counts the miles he traveled,
> or near Florencio's statue,
> or along Salguero on the way to the market
> where Gardel sang tangos. (Escardó 1971, 127)

A similar question is raised in "Puente Alsina," the 1929 tango cited in Borges's *Evaristo Carriego* (1930): "Where is my barrio / my beloved cradle / my hideaway / my shelter of yesteryear?" Fernández Moreno asks, in the verses of his *Décimas,* "Where is the land we dreamed? / Where the silent, perfumed city of enchantment? (Fernández Moreno 1928, 37), and Borges enquires, in "El tango," from *El otro, el mismo* (The Other, the Same, 1964):

> Where (I repeat) are the *malevos*
> who founded in deep, dirt
> alleys or in lost towns
> the sect of the knife and bravado? (1974, 1: 888)

The same obsessive question reappears in "¿Dónde se han ido?" (Where Have They Gone?), from *Para las seis cuerdas* (For Six Strings, 1965):

Where are those who left
to free the nations
or fought in the South
the spears of the Indian raiders? ...
Where are the intrepid
commoners who trod this land? ...
Did they live, as in the war,
in the North like the Murañas
and in the South like the Iberras? (Borges 1974, 1: 957).

Texts of the time speak of a perplexing search that would last for decades:

Tango *barrio* ...
distant streets ...
old friends ...
what's become of them,
where can they be!
(Homero Manzi, "Barrio de tango,"
   1942)

Where's the gang from back then?
Where's the old group of yesteryear? ...
Where are those women,
strong-hearted, loyal girls?
(Manuel Romero, "Tiempos viejos"
   [Old Times], 1926)

You sing no more, my boy!
Where did you end up?
(Edmundo Bianchi,
   "Ya no cantás chingolo," 1926)

I seek you in my memories ...
I spend hours at a time
wondering: where did she go?
(Atilio Supparo, "Por dónde andará," 1932)

Where are you? Where are you?
Where have you gone?
Where are the feathers of my nest?
(Homero Expósito, "Yuyo verde"
   [Green Weed], 1944)

Now you are dead, I wonder:
What will you do, Don Nicanor,
in a heaven without horses,
without debt, stakes, or scores?
(Jorge Luis Borges, "Milonga de don
   Nicanor Paredes," 1965)

These verses all speak of a collective disorientation. They seem to come
from individuals *perdidos en la ciudad* (lost in the city), subjects who do not
know where they are, afraid to take a wrong step or to fall because there seem
to be no maps available to explain the city or to guide their way. These are
decidedly lost males (figure 33), confused and groping their way, as if somehow blind. Conscious of the losses caused by such identitary dislocation,
Borges's texts seek a fixed, sacred spot in the mnemonics of the forgetful

city and find it, strangely, in the tango as a net that brings memories together and retains everything: "Death, those departed, are alive in tango" ("El tango," Borges 1974, 1: 889). Identitary shifts are endured in "1929," from *El oro de los tigres,* by one of the most prominent figures of Borges's pantheon, the *compadrito.* Already in decline in modern Buenos Aires, he is barely able to withstand the lethargy of his depression: "drinking maté and waiting. / Another empty day, like all of them. / And still his ulcer burns" (1974, 1: 1124). Borges's character crosses an unrecognizable city, Rivera Street now named Córdoba, and has become an "other" himself:

> Everything has changed.
> He trips on a sidewalk. Hears the jokes
> of some lads. . . .
> Now he's walking more slowly.
> Suddenly he stops. Something has happened.
> There where the ice cream parlor stands
> used to be a bar called Figura
> (History is half a century old). (1974, 1: 1125).

An ice cream parlor has erased the old taverns of his beloved *arrabales* (suburbs). He will have to walk more slowly, careful to avoid tripping or falling, now that the landscape is no longer a stable map of identity, but a space of fractures, breaks, and unrecognizable sites. Melodrama resorts to female figures to represent breakage, falls, and fractures, but the seamstresses were not the only ones to take a wrong turn or the only ones to trip. Buenos Aires's males fell and suffered downfalls.

As we know, the "hollow" remaining in the cultural geography of the city is the core of tango—a speaker obsessively wondering where to find the "Café de los angelitos" (Angel Café), or the bar in "Adios, mi barrio" (Farewell, My Barrio), or "the inconsolable old blind man in the line by Carriego," in "El último organito" (The Last Barrel Organ). What was happening to the suburbs of Buenos Aires? A line in *Evaristo Carriego* alludes to "the conversion of the troublesome or needy barrios to middle-class decency" (Borges 1974, 1: 164). According to Borges, the downfall of the *arrabales* must be located in material and historical mutations so radical they accounted for the substitution of the epic of the insolent *compadrito* with the melodrama of flat middle-class conformity. Thus, it becomes a little complicated to look for identitary references in a city that betrays personal sacred corners. I believe that a sense of place-identity was not to be found in this totally unrecognizable city by either the patrician oligarchy, to which Borges belonged, or the immigrant voices of the tango. They were all lost in a city dressed in evening wear and given to self-indulgence through a gaudy appetite for consumerism and unbridled madness. *Their* city had become evanescent, leaving them unsheltered—unless we consider the nature of that evanescent place-identity as a place-identity in itself.

The emergence of a popular culture expressed through Yrigoyen's politics resulted from the recent arrival of mass-circulation media (radio and cinema), which rapidly developed an audience and spawned an unprecedented culture industry. Modernization made city life more complex. Social differences were expressed in the field of culture through multiple aesthetic and institutional agendas synchronically adjacent to each other. Once the new cultural agents had come into the open, the domain of culture, formerly guarded by the elite, was turned into an intersecting battleground. Various cultural fields fed into the tango: the mazurka, the quadrille, the polka, and the *milonga* (a genre popularized by the guitars of *payadores* like the Afro-Argentinean Gabino Ezeiza); the creole *género chico,* which became a mass theater phenomenon; *poesía rufianesca* (literally, "pimp poetry"), which spread among *compadritos* in the suburbs; and popular gaucho poetry (Eduardo Romero 1983, 94). In chronological terms, the efforts of cultural agents like the *payadores, cantantes cupletistas* (female singers of variety songs), and *tonadilleras* (female singers of popular songs), as well as female dancers from Italy, changed the choreography of the "smooth" tango, not adapting to the movement *criollos* imposed on it (Gobello 1980, 37). Paulina, a dancer at the Salón Scudo de Italia, stood out in this respect, and from Pascual Contursi's "Mi noche triste" onward (1916–17), an Italian accent gave tango a melancholic, melodramatic, and shamelessly sentimental tone.[1] The Italian population, especially its women, left their mark on the rich cultural archive of tango.

This Italianized cultural product also engaged with other foreign groups and native-born cultures, such as the rural and the Afro-Argentinean, in the same way that Spanish migration had transferred the foundation of the Spanish *zarzuela* to the *sainete.* Broken-down individuals, *malevos, compadres, compadrones* and *compadritos, guapos,* city dwellers, early industrialization's *obreras* and *obreros,* aristocrats, hoodlums, prostitutes, show-business types, journalists, transvestites, countless seamstresses, newspaper boys, office workers, *sainete* performers, the lumpen, the *conventillo* dwellers, and even residents of *petits hôtels:* all intersected in the cultural node of tango. The tango's hybridity comes from the nostalgic simplicity of short-lived suburban barrios: the tango was shaped by Evaristo Carriego; appropriated by the *folletín;* reflected in the humor of the *sainete;* performed in circus tents; plagiarized and replagiarized through the title changes of tangos broadcast on the radio; touched up by elites for export; made decent for the middle class; transformed into gloomy tales of the margins by Enrique Santos Discépolo; processed through news columns, entertainment pages, and crime reports; disseminated via radio; and turned into film—and vice versa. I see the tango as the most spectacular cross-sectional, intersecting space in all Argentinean culture, the most inclusive grouping of cultural agents and discursive positions, the most ostensibly cultural excess or "hyperventilation," able to touch the entire city in one way or another through the fickleness of its cultural passages, borrowings, and transferals.

The whole city spoke of barrios and of women lost forever. The slippage of women toward sociosexual agency began with the growing availability of alternatives for life and for relations between the sexes, new paradigms for families of the future, birth control, adultery, and divorce. These were viewed as a break with a monogamous view of marriage, giving rise to debate and legislative proposals. Women were on the loose out there, and the nature of the devices misogynist imaginaries used to culturally construct them is thus highly revealing. These are "good women turned into serpents," warns Santa, in Armando Discépolo's *La fragua* (The Forge). In the tango "Allá en el Bajo" (Down in the Slums), by Ismael Aguilar and Martinelli Massa, one such woman is described as follows:

> Out in the dance
> this crafty one
> only remembers she is a woman . . .
> And to the rhythms
> of the bellows
> her body sways
> provocatively;
> she is the serpent

who has the poison
of passion
in her eyes.

Passion here is dissociated from love, and love is certainly expelled from the female's gaze. Where has love gone? In order to stigmatize women's passion as antisocial, misogynist discourse describes it through a demonizing, biblical vocabulary ("crafty," "provocatively," "poison"), working to counter an active sexuality that must be contained within the discipline of the patriarchal sexual binary. The alternative would drive exemplary masculinity into crisis and presage its fall. If this were not so, then to what else could the speaker of the tango "Como abrazao a un rencor" (As if Clinging to Rancor) be referring when he admits that his vigor as a male has been brought low by love?

My worst memories
make a mess of my head:
a childhood without toys,
a past without honor,
the pain from the shackles
still burning my wrists,
and a *mina* [young woman] *who brings*
my vigor as a male
to its knees. (Emphasis added)

The tango "Tomo y obligo" (I Take and Oblige, 1931), by Carlos Gardel and Manuel Romero, describes a similar inversion of gendered social places with equal melodrama: "How I loved her, how feverishly I adored her, / how many times, in a tremble, I've gone down on my knees." Once passion had been placed at the center of imaginaries aimed at women, how could its disruptions be controlled? How could its excesses be corrected? How was it possible to discipline active love, or love that was "out of place" and that caused identities to shift? Above all, how could the love felt by men be disciplined?

I believe that the imaginaries of stability began this disciplining by demonizing love through passion, its most biological facet and the most likely cause of "downfall." The character Don Mardoqueo explains this view condescendingly in *La mala reputación* (The Bad Reputation, 1920): "I understand that a young, beautiful, and healthy woman has the right, even the physical need, I might say, to love . . . to be loved. . . . But when you are poor, humble, like you, you have to use a bit of common sense in what you do. . . . You have aspirations. . . . Your education, your gentleness itself, will bring you to desire something better than the men of your class you could choose" (González Castillo and Mazzanti 1935, 22). However, a woman's "right" and "physical need . . . to love" are spoken of with sarcasm. As stated by one of the characters in *Muñecos de trapo* (Rag Dolls, 1926), by Ricardo Villarán and E. González Cadavid, a woman is "like the stage at a variety show, open to the curiosity and desire of every man." Similarly, "another puppet," a male character in *Las mujeres lindas* (Beautiful Women, 1916), comments on the difficulty of keeping a woman: "There are men with a beautiful wife who have the misfortune of struggling constantly over the beauty of their better half. He goes for a walk, rides a tram, or goes to a dance, and everyone looks at her and praises her. It drives him crazy and his heart is crushed" (Trejo 1977, 148).

Buenos Aires is a libidinous city of many crushed hearts. It is striking that nobody speaks of love, at least not requited love: love is a signifier displaced to other imaginaries, according to which "love is an article in a bazaar" (Trejo 1977, 142), while "sexualized" women see themselves from the perspective of their "inferiority, the evil inside, [their] unhealthy, perverse condition as a wretched female" (Olivari 1936, 17). Active female sexuality is thus associated with *cálculo amatorio* (amorous manipulation). Where love is concerned, everything is deviancy, ill-fated interaction between the parties involved. Yet it should be noted that, if active female sexuality is condemned, this is to prevent, at all costs, the scene of the man brought to his knees by love—that is to say, by a *misplaced* love. In defense of this posture, Oliverio Girondo's poem "Exvoto" (1920) constructs male desire as a persistent imposition already voided of love. Women are mere receptacles, bodies on display who go to the plaza "so men can ejaculate words into their ears and so their fluorescent nipples can glow and fade like fireflies."

Where was love in Buenos Aires? What were the symbolic formations on which any social actor could base interpersonal relations? The following quotations capture the vast polyphony of an imaginary that proposed the nonexistence of love anywhere. This imaginary portrayed interpersonal relations based only on distance and distrust. Love was a mistaken attitude: there were good reasons for caution, for rejecting proxemic distances, the lack of correspondence located not just between the sexes but in the socio-political sphere itself. What were the characteristics of this imaginary?

The negativity or impossibility of love

One always has bad luck in love, my girl. (Ricardo Villarán and E. González Cadavid, *Muñecos de trapo*)[2]

It's all the same to me. I can't love anymore. (Alfredo E. Bertonasco and Domingo L. Martignone, *Un amor imposible* [An Impossible Love])

It's so difficult to be happy. (Félix Gandéra, *El marido de mi novia* [My Girlfriend's Husband])

Love / is an old enemy / it inflames punishment / and teaches tears. (Enrique Santos Discépolo, "Canción desesperada" [Song of Despair])

She can love me no more. (José Manuel Curat Dubarry, *La tristeza de los viejos* [The Old Folks' Sorrow])

The pleasure of love lasts an hour. The pain of love lasts a lifetime. (Félix Gandéra, *El marido de mi novia*)

You'll see all is a lie, you'll see love is nothing (Enrique Santos Discépolo, "Yira . . . yira")

JAIME: Now they can love and understand each other.

SILVIA: It's too late. (Pablo Suero, *La vida comienza mañana* [Life Begins Tomorrow])

Misogynist opinions of women

What woman doesn't think of another man? (Munier and Montignac, *Tenemos que divorciarnos* [We Must Divorce])

Antonio had learned that women are perverse, that you had to dominate them forcibly for them to love. That's how he won over his conquests. He was evil, selfish, brutal, and women gave in to him. (Herminia Brumana, *Obras completas*)

You have always betrayed me, you have ruined my life . . . you have condemned me *(falls weeping on table)* forever. (Carlos Morganti, *Primero en la colorada* [First Past the Post])

RAÚL: You never really knew that woman. What a difference between her face and her soul! It was terrible for me: to learn the great capacity for pretense and deceit the transparent eyes of a woman can hide. (Félix Gandéra, *El marido de mi novia*)

MARCOS: They're not all the same.

RAÚL: But how do you tell the one that is from the one that isn't? That adventure was painful for me . . . the seed of distrust it planted in me forever. Unable to believe in love! You don't know what that is. (Félix Gandéra, *El marido de mi novia*)

IVONNE: That's how I loved you, without feelings, as women like us learn to love; by living for pleasure, we are also its prisoners and give up everything for it. (Samuel Eichelbaum, *Nadie la conoció nunca* [No One Ever Knew Her])

You have to be a stage actress, above all off-stage. (Ricardo Villarán and E. González Cadavid, *Muñecos de trapo*)

Femmes fatales, flighty women, vampires

I'm a bandit. I have the soul of a vampire . . . (*laughing*). Don't pay me any attention. (Jorge Salessi, *El bandoneón*)

That's how I want you, provocative, flighty. (Victor Dolard and Armando B. Rillo, *El amor que no se vende* [Love Not for Sale])

All dolls, the cheap and the pricey, are the same: porcelain eyes and empty inside. (Félix Gandéra, *El marido de mi novia*)

There are women . . . who give you vertigo. (Alberto E. Godel, *El farruco Manolo* [Manolo the Spaniard])

The female soul has recesses where simple, pure souls cannot go. (Jorge Salessi, *El bandoneón*)

Silence, you snake, don't spit more venom . . . or I'll cut out your tongue. (Alberto E. Godel, *El farruco Manolo*)

I'm different. The naive Silvia who believed in love is gone. Now I believe only in pleasure, money, and champagne (*loudly and with false happiness*). (Pablo Suero, *La vida comienza mañana*)

RICARDO: The fiery passion, the flaming passion, the passion that demands everything, that consumes everything. Ever since you became my wife, I knew that the moment would come in your life when love would sear your soul with a kiss and that kiss would not be mine. . . . I have lived . . . in great anguish, waiting for the day, the hour, the minute when your eyes would not look at me with the purity and innocence with which they always looked at me, when your arms would not reach out to me with longing, but with rejection. Now the day has arrived, the hour has chimed, for death in my heart and for paradise in yours. (Armando Moock, *Canción de amor* [Song of Love])

RAÚL: When a woman fools you, the time for you to fool is gone, and the time to be fooled has come. (Félix Gandéra, *El marido de mi novia*)

What a tramp . . . she's begging the gawkers to feed her on kisses. (Carlos Morganti, *Primero en la colorada*)

ELENA: . . . A deceived woman, victim of a man, should not waste the opportunity to give something back in return. What have men ever given me? Lies to steal my honor, a pittance to be my lover, a pittance with no more meaning than the misery of a hospital or a dissecting room. And you call that love? Well, I'll get my own back on them. They'll have no more of me than the paint on my lips, my perfumes, and my hairpieces—in a word, the appearance of me that I'll make them worship, show off in public, and take pride in exhibiting. (Alberto E. Godel, *El farruco Manolo*)

ELENA: The falls and deceptions have turned my heart into a strongbox. I've worked out my own kind of philosophy that's selfish, or vengeful, if you like, and my happiness consists in carrying it out. (Alberto E. Godel, *El farruco Manolo*)

RICARDO: Enough, Magdala, enough. The naive little girl has already learned to lie. (Armando Moock, *Canción de amor*)

The best of women are not worth a minute of unease in a man. . . . A banker is the best complement to a modern woman. You have so many enchantments and are worth so many gifts! (Ricardo Villarán and E. González Cadavid, *Muñecos de trapo*)

Love is affected

However romantic a woman is, she'll yawn at a prolonged bout of idealism. (Ricardo Villarán and E. González Cadavid, *Muñecos de trapo*)

Affectation is the style of sincerity. (Diego Ortiz Grognet, *Los vegetarianos* [The Vegetarians])

You're in love with me? Don't be affected, Señor Martín Figueredo. Have you forgotten a woman who once loved you with all her heart said the same thing and you replied: "That's in bad taste. I can only think of love as something between my valet and my lover's chambermaid"? (Pablo Suero, *La vida comienza mañana*)

GIRL: I let myself go . . . How can you control yourself? I love you.

RAÚL: That's your downfall, my dear. . . . (Nicolás Olivari, *Tedio* [Tedium])

Incredible! Incredible! Falling in love like a seamstress. (Alfredo E. Bertonasco and Domingo L. Martignone, *Un amor imposible*)

PERALTA: My heart beat impassively. (Ricardo Villarán and E. González Cadavid, *Muñecos de trapo*)

How you have given body and life to that vulgar instinct you call love. (José González Castillo, *El pobre hombre* [The Poor Man])

I would not want it said of Enrique, one of the most brilliant figures of the next generation, that he took his own life like a lovesick seamstress or a bankrupt tradesman. (Alcibiades Biffi, *La hoja de hiedra* [Leaf of the Ivy])

Love, money, and marriage

Yes, you must marry, child, you must marry. It's what's expected of good, pretty girls. (Alcibiades Biffi, *La hoja de hiedra*)

CRISPÍN: But who's talking about love! I'm talking about marriage. Love is the cherry on the top of marriage. But you can also marry without the cherry. (Jorge Salessi, *El bandoneón*)

I tell you, Mamá Rosa, I was more scared signing the register than a check for ten thousand pesos. (Ricardo Villarán and E. González Cadavid, *Muñecos de trapo*)

I've come here to sell myself to my friend. To sell myself. Yes, to sell myself. . . . Now I'm the worst of them all and the most expensive of those who sell themselves. (Pablo Suero, *La vida comienza mañana*)

Interpersonal closeness is discouraged with "proofs" and "evidence" provided from stories of treachery and disencounter, misplaced love, and women capable of sexual or matrimonial calculation and deserving of violence: "Women are farmyard birds to be eaten, to be killed intentionally and mercilessly plucked" (*Puerto nuevo* [New Port]; Bassi and Botta 1922). A young woman in *Entre el hierro* (Between Two Swords) is warned: "Be quiet. You're more stubborn than iron and must be broken" (Discépolo 1987a, 109). David W. Foster reminds us, however, that "romantic love is not a choice, but it is an obligation, whether as part of an ideology based on the need to perpetuate the species . . . or as part of a need to affirm sexual allegiance. Such a need, under the broad aegis of masculinism, is always an imperative for men, for they must demonstrate not only that they are 'real' men, but that they are not queer" (1998, 57–58). Remarks like this reveal how imaginaries dealing with questions of love regulated the "confusion" and "accidents" arising from transitional slippages in gender.

"Mi noche triste" (1916–17) recorded the waiting and the first tears of the *amurado* (abandoned male), an unprecedented form of masculinity:

> When I go to bed at night
> I can't close the door
> because by leaving it open
> I can believe you'll come back.

In "La última cita" (The Last Meeting), by Agustín Bardi and Francisco García Jiménez, "too late, sick, and defeated," the speaker recalls "the fatal meeting / for our unjust 'End.' . . . / I'll never forget / that I lost you then / that my life went astray." From the choice of words, it may be deduced that, although romantic love was a paradigm of obligatory social correctness (*lo acertado*), it competed with the practices of relationships and imaginaries that were already attaining shape and meaning within the social body. As one of the women characters of *La mala reputación* explains: "You have aspirations. . . . Your education, your gentleness itself, will lead you to desire something better than the men of your class you could choose"—thereby authorizing a woman to slip away from her barrio. This radical shift left exemplary masculinity with nowhere to turn. Women no longer wept or waited patiently in the shelter of domesticity. They neither sighed nor died of love.

The pragmatics of transitional times and the structures that promote rupture moved in a different direction, while the paradigms of social correctness drifted without much hold on the practice of social relations. However, romantic love was still a male imperative. To the extent that men "must demonstrate not only that they are 'real' men, but that they are not queer," it had to be strengthened, even if this meant finding an accommodating space between paradigms and pragmatics. Misogynist imaginaries of the time showed an extraordinary ability for maneuvering discursive positions with respect to an identitary break that had clearly already played its hand. The abandoned speaker, both in tango and in other social imaginaries, seems not to know how to process/feel his pain, a fire burning so intensely he cannot stop *talking about it.* He seems not to know where to place himself either. He is a misogynistic, violent male, a tearful victim, a forgiving soul, or even one who laughs at whatever weighs on his heart. The astute speaker of "Mi noche triste" disguises it all with humor, enclosing his passivity within his home and immersing himself in an inventory of undeniably "feminine" actions and items: waiting and weeping, matching colors, and looking inconsolably at a photo of his lost lover; gluttony, ribbons, and bottles of perfume:

> I always buy biscuits
> to eat with maté
> like when you were here. . . .
> When I go to my room,
> I see it in disarray,
> so sad and abandoned,
> it makes me want to cry,
> and I spend a long time
> looking at your picture
> trying to console myself.
> The room no longer has
> those pretty bottles
> tied with bows
> all the same color.
> And the mirror is misted over;
> it seems to have wept
> because your love is gone.

The speaker here is ridiculous, as well as affected: sitting down alone to the ceremony of taking maté and biscuits only deepens his irremediable loss of the shared ritual. In Samuel Linnig's "Melenita de oro" (Goldilocks), a male speaker chokes on his own contradictions:

> Like a blond stain on the pillow,
> I imagine I'm kissing your absent head. . . .
> Let me be; no, I don't want your caresses,
> the paint from your lips will leave a mark on me;
> they are still warm from another assignation.
> I can see you've just put lipstick on again. . . .
> I don't want to see you anymore, detested woman.
> Leave me alone, alone with my pain;
> I don't want to see you anymore . . . come back tomorrow.

Nevertheless, the difficulties of openly occupying the position of the *amurado* give way to the burning search for more dignified places. In Juan B.

Reyes's "¿Te fuiste? ¡Ja, Ja!" (You're Gone? Ha-ha!), the emptiness left behind by the woman turns into a noisy celebration of the bachelor's much-desired recovery of his freedom:

> My room looks much better,
> my friend, more airy and ventilated,
> with my clothes strewn on the floor,
> in a fine state of disorder.
> Now I have no one to get me into a fight
> or little dog to bite and bark.
> I want to thank you, you gullible woman,
> for having abandoned me.

In Discépolo's tango "¡Victoria!" the speaker even *thanks* the traitor because her departure has allowed him to go back to living with his mother:

> I can't believe it
> living again
> after six years. . . .
> See my friends again
> live with *mamá* once more.

And there are many more advantages and comforts, as described in "¿Te fuiste? ¡Ja, Ja!":

> Because the bed
> is so big
> I've not missed you
> I assure you;
> your absence is noticed
> only because I sleep
> sprawled out. . . .
> I wake up happy
> and I laugh
> and when I see you are gone
> I start to sing.

One of the characters in *Tedio* also lists the benefits of freedom from social formality and restraint: "And afterward there you are, just you. Alone! To sleep as late as you like. . . . To eat any time of day. . . . Go about with no shoes. Free. . . . Free! To look at the birds as if you had wings. . . . To live in a nest so free, so completely yours you know you can take it apart in a blow if you wanted to" (Olivari 1936, 22).

This search for a more graceful discursive position cannot fail to reveal the pain and rupture, however, especially when it lets us see through the cracks in the man's facade. The lyric voice in "Cuesta abajo" (Downhill) no longer warns the woman who betrayed him of a foreseeable future in the mire, old age, and ruin, as ordained in misogynist imaginaries. Significantly, his discursive position represents a truly substantial change, because he no longer talks "about" female otherness as something to be always watched over and open to examination and punishment:

> Under the brim of my hat
> how often under cover
> a tear welled up
> I could not contain.
> Although I wandered
> like a pariah that fate
> was determined to undo . . .
> I just want it to be understood . . .
> what courage it takes to love.

It is surprising that courage is defined here by the act of loving and that the test of masculinity is no longer a matter of duels and knives but of the ability to come through the pain of betrayal in love. Speaking of separations, and without going further than the fear of loving or the fear of loving when imaginaries assert that love is the same as consternation, many of love's re-cluses may be found in Borges. In a poem cryptically titled "1964," the lyric voice proclaims: "The world is magical no more. You have been left. You'll no longer share the bright moon / or the lingering gardens" (Borges 1974, 1: 920). Borges's most spectacular love poem, "El amenazado" (Under Threat), from *El oro de los tigres,* ends shamelessly: "the name of a woman informs against me. / A woman aches in my entire body" (1974, 1: 1107). This poem seems to openly echo tango melodrama, as if the speakers in both cases were singing in unison, expressing intimacy unreservedly with loud, naked cries, with no qualms about publicizing it. The discourse of tango seems to have freed speakers from the stigma of male affectation, so they could give voice to the weakened, "feminine" masculinities expelled from the formal city.

Eduardo P. Archetti alludes to gender theorists Andrea Cornwall and Nancy Lindisfarne, for whom "the different images and forms of behavior contained in the notion of masculinity are not always coherent and can appear as contradictory and undetermined. In this sense, it is important to capture the diversity of signs and forms of behaviors by understanding that masculinity cannot be treated as something fixed and universal" (1996, 34). At first sight, it might seem that the speaker in the tango "Cuesta abajo" is, literally, "downhill," but it is important to note the elevated side of his "fall." He is a subject who, once he has abandoned the privilege of codifying and objectifying female otherness, has also abandoned the misogynist discursive position that passes sentence in the "case" of the *traidora* (female traitor) from the point of view of social correctness (*lo acertado*) and closes its eyes to her "truths." *The paradigm he proposes redefines masculinity on the basis of the act of love.* This male does not appear to fear his own feelings or to disguise his wounds with humor. He has ceased to talk about an otherness whose flight has given everything new meaning, including his own identity. The imaginaries surrounding the identitary crisis expressed in tango are a heteroglossic space of ventriloquial, muffled, refractory, and negotiating voices. For those who want to hear, they express the punishment for women who leave the suburbs out of unbridled ambition for "jewelry, / fashionable clothes, / and champagne parties" ("Flor de fango" [Fower of the Mire]), only to be implacably overcome by tears, "so many, so many until returning," or to be left "without a tear until bleeding" ("Margo"). Other horrors are described in "Pobre paica" (Poor Girl), "Carne de cabaret" (Cabaret Fodder), "Pobre milonga" (Poor *Milonga*), "Tu pálido final" (Your Pale Demise), "No salgas de tu barrio" (Don't Leave the Barrio), and countless others.

These imaginaries of the crisis in masculinity constituted an ambiguous, misogynist frontier, where women are an other with no voice or right of discursive outlet and where a defective masculinity is exhibited. The only male with any sexual and political power is a *bacán;* while he enjoys his *garçonière* to the full, however, an injured masculinity awaits below at the door, expressing his impotence/tango to the doorman. By the same token, the reticent Borges of "El Aleph" does not enjoy a comfortable or conformable position either. Let us recall that Carlos Argentino Daneri, Borges's flamboyant, affected rival in "El Aleph," is the emblematic subject of an expanding modernity in Buenos Aires, who still speaks with an Italianized *s* and has begun to corral the two major symbols of privilege of the patrician elite: their women and their *national* prize for literature. Perhaps now Borges has begun *to talk about himself,* his inadequacy, and his disjuncture, without even realizing it. Confronted with the urgency of exorcizing otherness through distances and disciplinary measures, he ends up finding himself at the center of his own powerlessness. Cast onto the periphery of the paradigm of exemplary masculinity, his anxieties, uncertainties, and hesitations allow him to catch sight of other paradigms whose imprecision, fluctuations ("a stubborn question"), and inventory of failures bolster still further the masculinity embodied in the *garçonières*/nation. In Carlos Bahr and Armando Pontier's "Cada día te extraño más" (Each Day I Miss You More), none of the male identitary strategies works, and the situation shows all the signs of going from bad to worse:

> I've tried to silence my feelings
> by showing indifference, diminishing the memory of you.
> I've tried to stifle . . .
> the cry of the love I keep secret
> and tonight, breaking my determination,
> the voice of my heart has broken my silence.

Silencing and stifling feelings, censoring memories, and keeping secrets are ill-fated undertakings. This confessional chatter betrays the secrets of the male heart, above all, opening the wound, and voluntarily surrendering its intimacy. A being, recognizing he is broken, injured, fractured, gives a subjective and melodramatic turn to his discourse in an undertone, as in the tangos "Pobre corazón mío" (Poor Heart of Mine), "Soledad" (Solitude), "Mi noche triste" (My Sad Night), "Se va la vida" (Life Goes By), "Como abrazao a un rencor" (As if Clinging to Rancor), "Que nadie se entere" (Let Nobody Know), "Cuando el corazón" (When the Heart), "Corazón" (Heart), "Sólo se quiere una vez" (You Only Love Once), "Qué falta que me hacés" (How I Miss You), and "Canción desesperada" (Song of Despair), as well as many more. Cast off from the pragmatic weightiness of judgments attached to exemplary masculinity, this male otherness is set adrift in relation to the maps of *lo acertado,* which remain in the possession of the *garçonière*'s disdainful male and the impassive military.

The poetry of tango could have been about to give a second identitary life to other masculinities, but unfortunately, these were never stabilized. The speaker was left confused by the gnawing confirmation of his identitary break, without the ability to entirely reassemble new series of meanings except by resorting to the old misogynist inventory most at hand. What has changed? What is the profound displacement that tango has glimpsed? According to Blas Matamora, "Just as radicalism accepted an agreement [with other political groupings], tango accepted its respectability and left the suburb, losing its early hermeticism" (1982, 73). For this reason, Matamoro reads tango lyrics as "passive responses to a heavily codified and solidified social reality between whose social classes there is no mobility whatsoever. . . . The society that tango reveals is an immobile society" (117). By contrast, Pablo Vila sees movement and agency in the tango's dealings in social construction, which "not only entailed a social recognition of an actor previously scorned . . . [but] allowed the popular sectors to handle their everyday life in a manner that also included opposition to the dominant project" (1991, 112).

The speaker in "Mi noche triste" finds some relief to help him bear the emptiness of the loss and absence of the *traidora:* "I feel like crying / and I spend a long time / looking at your picture / trying to console myself." Borges's willful, flighty Beatriz, in "El Aleph," is a traitor on two counts: first, because she rudely ignores Borges while she is alive, preferring his rival, Carlos Danieri; second, because she dies. Borges acknowledges "the futility of his devotion" on both counts. Yet all *amurados* in Buenos Aires seem to opt to linger in the space where they best feel the pain caused by the woman's absence, paradoxically sheltered by their own hollowness—namely their wounds, which at least fill, somehow, the hollowness left behind by the elusive beloved:

> Beside the flowerless vase on the useless piano smiled . . . the unskillfully colored, large photo of Beatriz. No one could see us, and in tender desperation I drew close to the photo and said:
> "Beatriz, Beatriz Elena, Beatriz Elena Viterbo, beloved Beatriz, Beatriz gone forever, it's me, it's Borges." (Borges 1974, 1: 628)

In these embarrassing, "affected" men who talk to photos of their beloved, it is perhaps possible to see new paradigms of masculinity emerging, even when struggling just with photos of loved and troubling women represents a far more convenient protection from a more physical interaction and organic "contact" with the city and its women. A feminized subject thus appears at the same time as misogynist violence, opening a third identitary space:

an agoraphobic, uterine male who is turned inward. Tango reflects the profound crisis in exemplary masculinity: rejected males and frivolous, phallic women, standing so erect that Johann Heinrich Füssli's misogynist scene has no further resonance. For women to move from their places causes an entire system of correspondences to collapse. These are lackadaisical women who dispense with their equals (proletarian men, unemployed office workers, or insipid poets) because they are more interested in fur coats or Paris hats—women without hearts, something these males seem to have in excess. But was love the only standard where a lack of correspondence was to be recorded?

We might say for the moment that imaginaries of the crisis in exemplary masculinity speak vividly to their own anguish over the combined loss of that identitary space of both the city and love, as explained in Borges's "Elegía" (Elegy), from *El otro, el mismo,* in relation to the "face of a Buenos Aires girl / a face that doesn't want to be remembered by me. / Oh, Borges' fate, perhaps no stranger than yours" (1974, 1: 933). Buenos Aires is again associated with a woman, untimely love, and a speaker perplexed by his fate at being rejected and left with no resort but lamentation/writing. Buenos Aires (or its modernity) is the city/woman, place/identity that arbitrarily abandons him, provoking, as in Pascual Contursi's "En esta tarde gris" (This Gray Afternoon), "a desire to weep this gray afternoon. . . . / No, I cannot live this way / this love piercing me / like a curse." The ruin remaining after the break resembles a deserted house whose inhabitants have left forever; the house is a void, and yet one returns to its emptiness as the only identitary point of reference. In Borges's work, there are so many *amurados* who disguise/display their rejection. In "El Aleph" and "El Zahir," Borges is spurned by unattainable cities and implacably decisive women—the Buenos Aires/woman retreating from him. The *amurado* in "Alguien" (Someone) searches for "the memory of a woman who has left him / so many years ago now" (1974, 1: 926), and the one in "H.O." cries out for death and oblivion, although the changes in urban space always arise to bind lost love and the city together as "those things [that] are no more":

> On a certain street is a certain sturdy door
> with its bell and exact number.
> And a feel of paradise lost. . . .
> At the end of my daily work

a hopeful voice would await me
in the disintegration of each day
and in the peace of the loving night.
Those things are no more. My fate is something else. . . .
I only beg
for two abstract dates and oblivion. (1974, 1: 1102; emphasis added)

This is not unlike the fate of another *amurado,* in "El centinela" (The Sentry), whom "some woman or other has rejected and whose grief I must share" (1974, 1: 1115). Similarly, the speaker in "1964" concludes:

Mirror of solitude, suffering sun.
Farewell to mutual hands and brows,
that love drew near. Today you have only
the faithful memory and deserted days. . . .
The happiness you gave me
and took from me must be erased. . . .
Only the joy of being sad remains. (1974, 1: 920)

That ephemeral city of innate, anchorless exile has drawn all these men together through melodramatic affectations that cry out in identitary sorrow and rootlessness. Hence *el amor y el espanto* (love and consternation).

Carriego's imaginary highlights the impressive centripetal force of an agoraphobic culture as a prophylactic against the risks of leaving the barrio/family/political space. What was the benefit of this culture? I believe it lay in the collectivization of the everyday rituals of bars, neighborly greetings, and footsteps on the cobbles at night. Along with stories of deviancy, failure, and ruin, it naturalized resignation and strengthened the suspicion that no other reality existed except for the one that brought down hopes and dreams. Such was the fine work of inhibiting imaginaries as they gave meaning to life in the suburban world of Buenos Aires. As a new identitary space, the suburban barrio of the tango accommodated those aspiring to the middle class in an imaginary that embraced desexualization; an apology for simplistic, conformist politics; and a social passivity that had no faith in enabling utopias to be realized by offspring, because the wounded male had no descendants, no children or family.

In Borges's poem "La Plaza San Martín," there is a reference to the evening, "grave as the posture of a man in mourning." The man is likely "grave" because he is widowed. He might also be asexual or celibate, not having to face the risks of social exchange, perhaps to save himself from being *amurado* or from the unpredictability of organic life. A depoliticized and depoliticizing world seemed to incline to impotence. In one way or another, the barrio writings of Baldomero Fernández Moreno, Evaristo Carriego, and Jorge Luis Borges, and the poetry of tango, sublimate the simplicity of the everyday, basic culture (anticonsumerism), the margins, powerlessness, and political and sexual isolation. Their sublimation of the suburban barrio coincided with the tango's sublimation of the crisis in masculine identity, because both idealized a depoliticizing and desexualizing barrio as an agoraphobic and domestic place of refuge. Turned into a powerful cultural space and a center for collective meanings, they would end up resemanticizing the very desolation and featurelessness of urban anonymity. In a city belonging to everyone and to no one, the evanescent was sublimated. Hence the gnawing centrality of the margins, a nonplace that, notwithstanding, became some sort of identitary anchorage. If the center and its strong/busy identities embodied the ill-fated core of the city, with its pressing materiality and abandoning woman, the barrio's imaginaries and the male crisis of the tango were represented as paradoxical nonplaces, thanks to writings actually perceived as *inscriptions of disappearances*. Materiality and evanescence tautened the imaginaries of the moment, and nostalgia became an agoraphobic, narcissistic stubbornness that refused to let go: "I'll never love another now"; "only the joy of being sad remains" (Borges 1974, 1: 920). The identity strategy consisted in not changing place, because to do so would betray the only identitary space accessible to the greater population of the city.

We might say that the imaginaries of the crisis in masculinity speak to the rootlessness arising from loss of both the city and love were it not for the fact that there were other events and registers in which to locate failures and falls. Was Uriburu's military coup initiated by university students? *Caras y Caretas* (13 September 1930) suggests as much: "The tragic death of the student [Juvencio] Aguilar is the first spark of the revolution," unleashing intervention by the armed forces against student demonstrations in the street demanding Yrigoyen's resignation. The city figures as the great protagonist of the 1930 coup and the military intervention as the respectful response to popular will, as old signatures and some new ones show up in *Caras y Caretas* (20 September 1930).[3] Similarly, the next issue of the weekly opens with a greeting to the armed forces from the president of the Liga Patriótica Argentina, Dr. Manuel Carlés: "Worthy sons of the heroes who gave us country and glory a century ago . . . just as the warriors of the heroic campaigns won freedom in America against the tyrants, you will give the people back the freedom outraged by despotism." His objectives are, first, to legitimize members of the coup by associating them with the founding generation of the fatherland, and with a "refoundation"; second, to turn the de facto government into the country's rescuer from Yrigoyen's despotism; and third, to tell the story of the coup as a peaceful political event. This deepest wound on the constitutional body thus became part of national life thanks to the people of Buenos Aires, "who stood together, at the ready, quietly resolved. The close togetherness that defines a people could be seen in their attitude of quiet strength. It was a revolution of the people in solidarity with the armies of the Republic. There had to be a nation in order for it to come about, which is to say that it had to succeed in bringing its citizens together in a common feeling about the most fundamental aspects of life."

Wherever members of the armed forces appear in photos in *Caras y Caretas,* members of the Catholic Church and Monsignor De Andrea's curia may also be found. All sectors of society are also included in a military parade, where the people "wrap the heroic ranks of the army in a giant embrace." *Caras y Caretas* reports from a building site where "the workers stand in symbolic homage and in silence pay their respects to the Revolution and its dead" (20 September 1930). Beginning with the issue of 13 September, the weekly's reports capitalize on *porteñas* offering "smiles and shouts of encouragement to the soldiers, certain of their victorious return." And the ladies are not long in visiting the new president: "Support from women. Surrounded by a group of ladies and girls, Lieutenant-General Uriburu displays the satisfaction of those who added a softer tone to the heroic movement of September" (4 October 1930). Again, Hipólita, in *Los siete locos,* was evidently not the only one calling for dictators.

Caras y Caretas militarized its covers, displaying officers of the armed forces, ministers, and federal and provincial military administrators, all in uniform, in images conveying unity and solidity (figure 34). It showed army parades and naval reviews and flybys. "Why are so many planes flying over?" asks a boy in the children's section, to which Adela Di Carlo thoughtfully replies, "To let the people know their rights are defended even from the air and to advise calm" (18 October 1930). Judging from the photos, the whole country was in uniform or spellbound by military paraphernalia. As for civil life, *Caras y Caretas* showed those condemned to death under martial law, running one caption in particular that sealed matters once and for all: "Police dragnet for Severino Di Giovanni and Paulino Scarfó," "ringleaders of a gang of criminals who, after terrorizing . . . the public, paid with their lives for the long series of crimes to which martial law . . . brought an end" (7 February 1931). The events would not have aroused national expectations (and eight pages in *Caras y Caretas*) had Severino not been a "fearful anarchist." The same issue describes attacks allegedly perpetrated by Severino, in which both police and civilians were killed. It also highlights that, when the time for their executions came, the criminal anarchists refused "to accept the spiritual support offered by Christian priests." Martial law would make certain of the triumph of the necessary rigor of its arms over the darkness in the social body.

Following the military coup, *Caras y Caretas* launched a new section under the aristocratic Juan José de Soiza Reilley, whose editorial agenda was to win back the city's popular barrios and include them in the "new founding of the Fatherland." La Boca was more than significant, in view of its history of foreign proletarian militancy and economic marginality: "Beneath its Genoese exterior lurks a *criollo* spirit, so *criollo* that foreigners learn to become Argentineans there. . . . It is the pot where, within half a century, the different races that will become our future race are melted together" (19 October 1930). As for Boedo, the new imaginaries would try to relocate it in the city's new cultural geography by disassociating it from the lower-middle-class, leftist militancy of Castelnuovo, Mariani, Yunque, César Tiempo, and Barletta. It had become an animated, easygoing "miracle of progress": "The streets are full of people. Businesses are booming. There are no empty seats in theaters and cafés. Progress can be seen on the terrace roofs. It rises through every floor. It illuminates the tallest cornices with blazing signs, like golden rain. . . . I counted seventy-eight cafés in six blocks . . . places to buy drinks, milk bars, vending machines, pizzerias, pastry shops, trattorias . . . nine cinemas, bazaars, variety theaters, and a classic theater, The Boedo, where artists the likes of Luis Arata first took to the stage" (11 October 1930).

The description of La Boca proposed imaginaries of regeneration for the barrio and, by extension, the country, while the picture of Boedo drew attention to small businessmen, who could have confirmed that the vitality and economic boom of the center were now obtainable in the barrio. The newly born middle class had to form new political alliances. Popular barrios were "appropriated" by makers of the new national image, giving them a new face that resemanticized even some of the city's most prominent landmarks of the Left, such as Boedo Theater. Before the suburban barrios were developed, the urban barrios had been inhabited by workers and militants, especially anarchists and socialists. The former united laborers in small factories, mechanics, bakers, masons, shoemakers, and tradesmen closer to the old artisans than to industrial workers. The unions brought together longshoremen and dockworkers, while socialists organized skilled factory workers such as machinists and stokers (Gutiérrez 1983a, 91). These militants led the workers in strikes whose scope and violence ensured that the "social question" figured on the agenda of the government and the ruling class.

The creation of the suburban periphery began in 1857, with the first railway line between Plaza Lavalle and Flores. By 1887, it filled the perimeter of the federal district, and by 1910, it had begun to reach into what would become greater Buenos Aires. This gradual process of expansion relieved the overcrowded housing of the end of the nineteenth and beginning of the twentieth centuries, but it also erased collective memories from urban maps. The center had been the setting for the soup kitchens in Puerto Madero and innumerable strikes, as well as the tenants' strike of 1907, protesting inhumane conditions in the *conventillos*. The urban periphery developed rhizomatically. Its spread weakened the concentration of political strength in the center, adding to the political implosion brought about by the harsh repressions during the Semana Trágica and in Patagonia. Additional factors included the new culture endorsed by the Radical government, based on the family and access to home ownership, and the social reconciliation of the two Radical administrations. Their ideological party line was never intended as an attack against industrial capitalism and its allies, the members of the agro-exporting oligarchy defended by the army. As Cerruti Costa points out, moreover, the period between 1922 and 1930 was one of notable reverses for the working class, an observation with which the anarchist Diego Abad de Santillán agreed (see Gutiérrez 1983a, 77). Far from the paradigm for men envisaged in mobilizations of the working class, the male represented in the tango embodied an exclusionary modernity, evidence of the profound disjuncture between the uplifting promises and imaginaries of modernity and everyday life's hardships and frustrations. From an economic point of view, the new wave in the uncompromising insertion of capitalism produced an uninterrupted series of crises in unemployment or forced stoppages in 1890, 1891, 1900–1901, and 1907. By 1917, unemployment had become structural (Gutiérrez 1983a, 72), dealing a serious blow to the popular classes in the years leading up to the world crisis of 1929 and the years that followed, especially 1932. The tango's imaginary recorded an ill-fated or restricted modernity whose male population had no family or children, lacked the economic capacity to be husbands and fathers, and were powerless to keep themselves socially and sexually anchored.

By 1937, the coup as a political expedient, and the "truth" of the rightness of its arms, had been legitimized in the national imaginary. Agustín P. Justo (1932–38) was endorsed internationally by fascist Europe. *Caras y Caretas* had already launched (6 November 1937) a meticulous series of covers featuring Adolf Hitler: reviewing the Hitler Youth, at a torchlight procession in Nuremburg before the multitudes in the Zeppelinfeld, and so on. The weekly magazine thus began to educate the Argentinean public about Germany— its history; the arts in its cities; the powerful monopoly of I. G. Farben Industrie, the Bitterfeld factories, and the Bayer Cross; its leadership in industry, armaments, finance, and even pharmaceuticals. In order not to appear too biased, perhaps, the weekly also published long comments from Argentinean army generals with details of the Italian war in Ethiopia, giving readers cause to ponder the military strategy of the Harrar raid, General Gaziani's Southern Front, and Maltrioti's handsome troops marching bare-chested in shorts across the open desert. At the same time, La Dama Duende was attentive to the elite's social events, to which the black robes of the priests lent sobriety and where recipes for "the perfect wife" were exchanged. Petrona C. de Gandulfo began publishing kitchen recipes, showing that housewives could stand out through skills learned in and for the home. Women had returned to their place. The soup kitchens run by the Federation of Circles of Catholic Workers and charity or benefit events filled page after page of *Caras y Caretas.* The sweltering summer drew proletarian *porteños,* not exactly to the increasingly aristocratic area of Palermo but to the overcrowded congestion of the municipal beaches. Hollywood was already a sparkling imaginary that made it possible to dispel everyday local realities, as in the popular outpouring during Clark Gable's visit. Thus, by 1937, *Caras y Caretas* had become a highly predictable public space for parades, political discourse, charity balls, kitchen recipes, blond stars of the screen, and convertibles.

After the liberal adventure, the "house" had been retaken, but Uriburu's coup could not freeze Argentinean history. It entailed above all a beginning to the institutionalization of the role of the armed forces as a mechanism for political deceleration that would last throughout the twentieth century. Nevertheless, popular struggles would soon reawaken. These struggles would realize some of their most spectacular mass achievements in Peronism; in the impressive advances made by the Left in the 1970s; and in the unyielding mobilization of mothers and grandmothers with homemade placards in the Plaza de Mayo, claiming the rights of their relatives, victims who had disappeared in clandestine concentration camps and death flights during the period of military fascism (1976–83). Finally, these struggles would also resurface in the *escraches* held to unmask the decades of impunity legalized under the Ley de Punto Final (1986) and the Ley de Obediencia (1987), as well as more recent popular activism by HIJOS, *piqueteros,* retired citizens, and countless organizations from civil society, against impunity and the deadly readjustment policies imposed in the name of neoliberalism and the International Monetary Fund.[4]

CARAS y CARETAS

De Andrea. — Casa nueva y bien surtida, ésta principia muy bien. Creo que el otro almacén

LA COMPETENCIA

Justo. — Mi antiguo establecimiento va a seguir perfectamente, pero la casa de enfrente

The competition (*Caras y Caretas,* 11 October 1919)

Soup line (Archivo General de la Nación, n.d.)

A stroll down the street
(Archivo General de la
Nación, 1929)

Obreras leaving the factory
(Archivo General de la
Nación, 1926)

Obreras clocking in at the factory (Archivo General de la Nación, 1929)

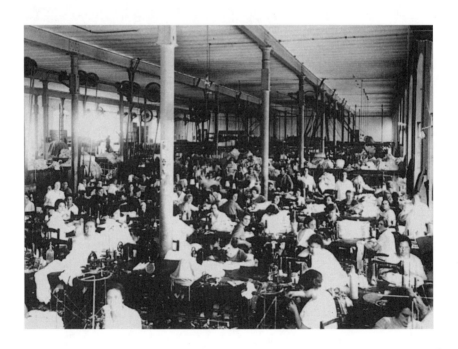

Inside Pirovano Hospital (*Caras y Caretas,* 24 January 1920, and Archivo General de la Nación)

View of the factory (Archivo General de la Nación, n.d.)

Compadrito (Archivo General de la Nación, 1922)

Unemployed men in Puerto Madero (Archivo General de la Nación, ca. 1933)

Man at the Exhibition Hall (Archivo General de la Nación, 1917)

Lieutenant Colonel Pedro J. Rocco (*Caras y Caretas,* 7 February 1931)

Arm in arm: strike and demonstration by employees of city-center stores (Archivo General de la Nación, 1919)

CONCLUSION

Your tangos are abandoned children.

Homero Manzi, "Malena," 1940

LEOPOLDO LUGONES'S SHORT STORY
"Los caballos de Abdera" (The Horses of Abdera) may well be one of the
best places from which to understand the second half of the nineteenth century and the first half of the twentieth in Argentina. Although published
in 1906, it alludes to the trajectory of Argentinean history from Sarmiento's
nonauthoritarian liberalism, symbolized by the 1869 Education Law, to Sáenz
Peña's Electoral Law (1912) and Uriburu's coup (1930). As a prophetic, con-
spiratorial text, it details with chilling foresight what would happen in 1930.
Lugones's short story tells of the humanization of horses by Abdera's liberal
citizens. The horses represent the workforce; the nobles; the liberal wing
of the Argentinean oligarchy; and the promoters of free, obligatory public
education, electoral law, and imaginaries of upward social mobility. The
narrator belongs to a group in silent disagreement with the lords of the city,
who take pride in educating their horses. Thanks to such eccentricity, the
animals acquire speech, their "intelligence is developed on a par with their
consciousness," and they are left "in freedom whenever the packsaddle or

415

harness does not require them" (Lugones 1926, 110). However, alarming passions and disturbing signs soon begin to appear, such as an increase in the incidence of infanticide, which "it was necessary to correct by bringing in some old adoptive mules" (111). Nevertheless, blinded by their arrogance, the lords of Abdera insist on "developing close relations between the animals and their owners, even to the extreme of allowing horses at the table" (110), which permits them to enter the city's mansions and lust after whatever they see. The narrator sees this permissiveness with misogynist eyes, so that the mares develop the same narcissistic self-indulgence as bourgeois women: after entering a mansion, one of them demands "mirrors for her stall, tearing one out of her owner's bedroom with her teeth" (111). When the great rebellion occurs, "the herds got into the rooms intent only on jewels and shiny trinkets." Thanks to the nobles' liberality, an egalitarian market culture is made accessible to all. With respect to one of the male horses, the narrator relates that "Balio . . . had just died of love for a lady. She was the wife of a general . . . and certainly did not hide the occurrence. She even believed it flattered her vanity" (111). Perhaps, in Lugones's xenophobic/misogynist mind, this is what women like Máxima would have felt when making their bodies, class privilege, and wealth available to uncouth upstarts like Genaro in *En la sangre*.

When the time for rebellion arrives, the males, "corrupted by the refinements of a good table," attack the wine cellars. But that is a mere detail in comparison with the embrace between upstarts and noblewomen entangled in "monstrous lovemaking," before which the xenophobic gaze of the narrator pales: "Women [were] assaulted and pinned in their own beds by bestial ardor. There was even a noble maiden who wept as she told of her terror . . . waking up in her bedroom . . . her lips caressed by the ignoble snout of a black stallion snorting with pleasure and showing his disgusting teeth . . . his eyes burning with lewdness in a human, malevolent gleam" (Lugones 1926, 114).

"Los caballos de Abdera" allegorizes the proletariat's growing political awareness, mobilizations, and strikes, in a struggle for improved working conditions that—in the story—leads to the great rebellion, a highly anticipatory allusion to the general strike of 1919. As the narrator explains: "The horses increasingly resisted being harnessed and yoked. . . . Some animals would not accept a particular harness. . . . One day . . . they did not respond to the sound of the horn, and it was necessary to constrain them by force" (Lugones 1926, 112). They aspire to better food and less work in order to fully enjoy their "feminine" caprices. When the rebellion comes, "the broken-down doors lay on the ground. . . . Blood had flowed, for not a few towns-people had been crushed under the hooves and teeth of the gang" (114). The destruction is almost total, since the horses have taken over the army's weapons, which they have secretly learned to use. When it seems that noth-ing will stop the devastating advance of the wild horses, Hercules appears, charged with halting their "long-lived wrong-headedness" (109) and restor-ing the order that existed prior to the liberal adventure. The narrator be-comes less a mere scribe than a decisive character in his own story, a faithful servant of the cause who backstabs an insurgent animal caught crushing an unguarded young nobleman. The punitive act of this savior of the noble-woman (and the nation) foreshadows Lugones's later activism as a writer and ideologue of the 1930 fascist coup: in his fictional world, an authoritarian, xenophobic, misogynist masculinity regains control of the nation. Hercules's blow represents everything that Uriburu's coup would achieve: the reestab-lishment of the hierarchies of class, xenophobia, and patriarchy.

My study has sought to trace the profound and violent transformations the implementation of modernity brought about in the physical city of Buenos Aires and in its symbolic formations, in debates on national identity, in the languages and paradigms of interpersonal relations, and in the transitional bodies of citizens and those yet to become citizens. I have also endeavored to describe how the new culture of modernity became entwined in every aspect of the city's daily life, through the simultaneous workings of many different kinds of imaginaries. These imaginaries were countless and di-verse. Some were based on aristocratic or paternalistic privilege, on liberal or populist social reconciliation. Others radiated models of renovation, rup-ture, self-restraint, or conformism. They included anarchism, market- and goal-oriented imaginaries, feminism, populism, sexism, xenophobic imag-inaries, imaginaries related to parenthood and motherhood, nationalist imaginaries, *golpista* imaginaries, imaginaries derived from the identities of alternative genders, imaginaries that inspired dreams of social ascent, *delirios de grandeza* (delusions of grandeur), and/or imaginaries that punished the *malos pasos* of both women and men. I believe that, one way or another, they all fall to pieces and all intersect, as in the hopeless dislocation of the speaker in the tango "Malena," who refers to the *other* modernity, a world of "abandoned children." Armando Discépolo's character Adela, in *Entre el hierro* (1910), cries out, "No, my heart isn't here; it's nowhere . . . I have no heart," while Fermín announces, "I'm leaving . . . I don't feel comfortable anywhere . . . I'm leaving." Such imaginaries seem to have been the uneven edges, where modernity oozed dissymmetry and unease and the subject's needs and subjectivities were negotiated by its colossal and implacable gravitation.

The tango may well provide the best window into daily life during Argentina's first stage of industrialization. Like the monumental symbolic ground plan of the city, tango became a complex cultural space composed of intersections, impurity, clashes, and most of all displacement: "Nothing appears in tango that shows adherence to tradition or the land, because *porteños* are detached from the land, even their 'beloved' city/port" (Pérez Amuchástegui 1984, 131). The tango speaker seems to have found a secure place/identity in "Mi Buenos Aires querido" (My Beloved Buenos Aires). Although the city is distant, he is confident that "when I see you again / there'll be no more sorrow or oblivion." But in the meantime, the city and all it encompasses are so remote and evanescent that he is fated not only to feel forgotten by the woman but to experience an unbearable sense of uncertainty and despair. I believe that the identitary displacement that tango obsessively focuses on the heartless city and on women might well be addressing a signifier embedded *elsewhere*. In other words, it might well come from another field of the social.

In the *folletín* "Todo se conversa" (Everything Open for Discussion), by C. Correa Luna, published in *Caras y Caretas* in 1904, at the dawn of modernity's promises of social progress, the guests at a house party are gathered in a mansion greenhouse, where members of parliament and elegant young women comment on the one event of the day: a strike that has shaken the city. Confronting criticism of the strike ("a government weakness . . . Where else could a crowd of second-rate foreigners come and tell us what to do?"), Enriqueta replies: "Perhaps the strike is not evil. We've had a former striker here as a gardener since yesterday. It's sad to hear him. . . . They worked like animals and lived in worse conditions. . . . Honestly, sometimes I think, although we're lucky to be protected, not everything is as it should be." The greenhouse functions as passageway, a space of convergence in the mansion as well as in the city. It bridges the social distance between Enriqueta and the striker-become-gardener, the elite woman and the worker, Argentina and foreigners, capital and labor. The text concludes: "At that moment, a tall, broad-shouldered Italian crossed the patio. It was the gardener, and . . . [Enriqueta's eyes] followed him with a look of curiosity . . . immediately turned into another more intense look, from one heart to another" (*Caras y Caretas,* 9 January 1904). Correa Luna's *folletín* seems to endorse paternalism, even exogamy, on the grounds of a porous and interactive social sphere. But by 1930, *that* city was nowhere to be found. Whatever became of that Buenos Aires where exchanges between social actors and spaces allowed people to speak "from one heart to another"?

My study has attempted to trace what happened to Buenos Aires during the early twentieth century, especially how the day's events were processed and decanted through the working of Buenos Aires's imaginaries and their semanticization of daily life, its conflicts, differences, and transitional detours and maneuvers: how they read the in-between social spaces that began to spring up from the material and organic nature of the city; how they narrated the interstices that contested the claustrophobia of the regimes of social control, the seduction of the marketplace, and the insensitive capitalist culture of labor; how the maps of women's corporeal geographies and women's subjectivity sought to process an identitary space beyond the asphyxiating walls of homes, factories, and workshops and the equally oppressive lights of the city center.

I believe that the monumental polymorphism of modernity's transition was processed by imaginaries mostly "incapable" of understanding the transformation brought by modernity and only too ready to sanction what they were unable to interpret because of the rigidity of their monochromatic points of reference and interests. I also believe that such rigidity was an effect of a systematic reticence and political refusal to extract from daily life in Buenos Aires the immanence of organic processes and cultures in motion. But even when the events of the organic city were absorbed, their selection was never random. I have tried to trace how, beginning with essentialist definitions of life, socializing imaginaries managed to select and process events even from the organic, grotesque quotidian, with the purpose of polarizing the city's dreams and nightmares and neutralizing the *acontecimiento,* pivotal event, ground-breaking subjective meanings, and actions undertaken by social actors. Roberto Arlt found it necessary to draw attention to suicide when he understood that its drama failed to shock the audience of the mass-circulation newspapers, forcing his contemporaries to pause to imagine the last hours of a young immigrant woman. What Arlt attempted to reverse here was the distance induced by socializing imaginaries aimed at countering the impact of urban intimacy and the potential laterality or empathic sensitivity among *porteños*.

Diastolic, enabling, socializing, stabilizing, conservative, inhibiting, and revolutionary impulses reflected the hyperventilation of the polymorphous, hysterical, vulgar, stylish, dramatic, and melodramatic Buenos Aires. The city set sail inspired by the winds of novelty and did not hesitate to propose new, impure, and bastardized linguistic registers, as well as insolent, open sexual identities. Systolic or socializing impulses offered irritated interpretations of the new cognitive and emotional maps to emerge from *porteños'* subjectivity and proceeded to judge them based on "truths" centered on regaining a unified semanticization of the country. Fatherland, Argentineanness, and family became social values defended by a xenophobic religiosity, reproductive morality, and strict vigilance over the new public/private political languages and models of subjective and interpersonal intimacy. The prostitute, the femme fatale, the homosexual, the adulterous or odd woman, the unemployed man, the anarchist, the woman who aborted, and the unfathomable secrets of the infanticide represented deviant bodies and a social nocturnality that contrasted with the social order of the Catholic, nationalist, bourgeois family. In the meantime, tango continued to allude bluntly to passion, touch, and bodily contact with a choreography that was at once both homoerotic and heterosexual.

I have also attempted to call attention to the sensorial maps of bodies at work, with their clenched muscles, nausea, and stress from the risks and rigors of ten-hour workdays. The sustained rhythm of the industrial mode of production was relentless in its impact on the unwary bodies of the working women, men, and children of Buenos Aires, causing technopathologies completely unknown at the time and only discovered when they had reached an advanced stage. What identitary place could be forged with respect to the ethics of the body? A new kind of cultural right, arising to counteract the depredations of industrial Taylorism, or an ethics swiftly capitalized on by the market and resemanticized in giddy perfumes and caressing velvets? Even so, I am convinced that social actors in Buenos Aires found new social values in their quest for healing imaginaries and social praxes for the bodies and identities brutally despoiled by modernity's darkest sides. One of capitalism's most successful logics is aimed at concealing its immense social cost. To reveal it would lead to exposing capitalism's flagrant disregard for the ethics of the body. Nelly Richard draws attention to the epistemic wealth to be found in the interstices of fissures, areas of tension and conflict, "symbolic/ cultural formations of deposits and sedimentations where the fragments of meaning that tend to be left out or discarded by social rationalization are gathered," so that "whatever is secondary and non-integrated is able to displace the force of meaning toward the outer regions" (1998, 11). Such a reversal of the logic of capitalism's maneuvers may well be achieved by tracing the full process of production, from the end to the beginning, from front to back, and always from below—in other words, by retrieving the body/ grotesque edge of the city effaced in the anonymous rush of daily life in Buenos Aires. Those sensorial geographies and maps of subjectivities, once unveiled and reversed, might well be instrumental in invoking collective resources and social laterality. The feminist worker Carolina Muzilli knew this very well. I understand what she was trying to accomplish when she conceived such an unveiling strategy as creating a powerful bridge, enabling a compelling exchange between her reading/public audience and an ignored, concealed, albeit essential text: *los cuerpos del trabajo* (bodies at work). For this reason, I elected to follow Carolina's path.

Another invitation to follow the sensorial and cognitive maps drawn by the body comes from Armando Discépolo's tram conductor and his resistance to the sociophobia of proxemic distances and positions dictated by the new urban sociability. He suggests two revolutionary maneuvers instead: evaluating every aspect of modernity's culture from the perspective of individual subjectivity, and transforming its sociability through eye contact and spontaneous dialogue in the closeness of the barrio or the tramcar. He is confident that such intimacy will strengthen social empathy and facilitate proximity, touching and embracing within the collective body of the city. Turned into a cultural agent, he contests the condition of the unavoidability of induced paranoia, agoraphobia, or fear. After all, touching also implies being touched. The body is also a problematical space in Alfonsina Storni's anguished invitation to Argentinean women to substitute their oppressive identitary armor with spontaneous interpersonal relations that correspond better to their subjectivity. These imaginaries give central stage to the body, calling for a more caring and a protecting relationship within (and in spite of) the demands enforced by modernity's structures of work culture, sociability, and affectivity.

Together with utopian propositions for resensitizing modern sociability, imaginaries of all kinds, from the private spheres of everyday life to the organizing narratives of historical and public events, engaged in the struggle for control of how life should be defined. There were imaginaries that contributed to affirming the social text of violence in both the domestic and political spheres, with fearful beatings in the home, the institutionalized violence of the world of prostitution, coups d'état, massacres, honor killings, deportations, and state terrorism; there were imaginaries that encouraged cultural assimilation, others that inspired rupture, and some that gambled on proxemic distances of irreconciliation, such as tango and the thesis that "love is a lie." I believe that the thesis of *la mentira del amor* (love is a lie), and the devastating grief it caused, must also be traced elsewhere, and that tango itself is the struggle to find interstices where it is acceptable to sigh and to weep at will whenever needed, whether or not the reason is known. Such is the case with many speakers in tango, who, in their confusion, do not know the cause of their tears.

Where did the need to weep come from? The origin of much of the urge to weep—and not only on gloomy, rainy Sunday afternoons—can be found, I believe, in Argentina's political and cultural landmarks, such as the Conservative Order's monopoly and deception, the political demobilization following the Semana Trágica, and Uriburu's coup d'état. Yet Acuerdismo, under Yrigoyen and Alvear, wove its democratic/conciliatory imaginaries from the conformist suburban barrios that, it should be remembered, had been intended by urban planners to relieve the intense congestion of political life in the center, the port, and other proletarian zones. Urban spaces, as custodians of many stories imbued with a sense of drama, had previously been able to trigger an immediate social and political laterality from the audience. Once this specific urban setting and its drama disappeared, however, what remained was a recourse to melodrama and the tango as melodrama's form/ voice for mass culture. The dramatism attributed by Klauss Scherpe to modern thought feeds off *acontecimientos,* or pivotal events, longing for the moment that activates the state of emergency whose subsequent resemanticization of life will be able to reposition social actors (Scherpe 1988, 351). In modernity, all the productive capacity of evaluation and action mobilized by the dramatic event is placed at the disposal of the power of history and, therefore, of the historical dialectic. By contrast, the implosion represented by melodrama and tango survives on the basis of the absence of the event and the relinquishing of historical reference. Interestingly enough, the effect of melodrama coincides with the objective of stabilizing imaginaries of protection from *acontecimientos*. Social rupture has lost its power of attraction: all of the fascination of the *acontecimiento* has lost its power to mobilize, so that what remains seems to be fascination with recognition of the habits and rituals of everyday life. New imaginaries constantly tend to rebuild a safe way out by consolidating new essentialisms.

What were they, then, these new essentialisms of modern homogenization? I believe that the fascination with the word/lament in tango resides in a discourse whose only *acontecimiento* is its own repetition, the inertia of its nonmovement. Its ultimate satisfaction seems to lie in the self-reflecting recognition of this repetition, as if recognition were the only identitary space left in the desolation of the modern city. If modernity is a state of loyalty to another way of being (progress, future, utopia), then melodrama and tango seem to have lost the capacity to imagine the other space, that dramatic space that could bring the *acontecimiento* and the state of commotion it triggers back to life. Hence the commitment, in tango and melodrama, to déjà vu, the closure of purpose, and that uterine subject who was unquestionably best suited to Uriburu's coup.

I read abandonment in tango lyrics as a figure for the displacement of meaning, a metaphor that speaks of socioeconomic, sexual displacements, as well as political dislocations. Expressed through the theme of a love always lost, it structured relations and presupposed formulas based on interpersonal distance and distrust. The failure of love, as well as the violence of the time, could also be read as the failure of diversity in homogeneity, contrary to the great myth of an encompassing Argentine nation. Distance and violence materialize a fundamentalist defense of sameness. Why not propose some other fortune for the *intrusa,* the Borgesian female character viciously murdered by the Nilsens and their flagrant fear of otherness? Perhaps because it was not convenient to openly propose love and social coexistence when what was imperative was to control the social sphere and dilute how much the inhabitants of Buenos Aires had to learn from otherness, how much they had in common with each other, particularly during the heavy seas of transitional times and its many shipwrecks.

Eduardo Archetti argues for the need to analyze, first, cultural arenas where masculinity is always produced and reproduced as a complement and in opposition to femininity; second, how the eminently masculine is defined when "relevant others are men—different types of men"; and third, how the masculine is articulated and negotiated in relation to the construction of national identity (1996, 34). In Argentina, the *bacán* in his *garçonière* may have been the "strong identity" paradigm to counter men displaced by modernity, but the nationalist/xenophobic/patriarchal discourse of 1930 would depose this masculine icon, embodied by the self-indulgent/dissipated bachelor of the oligarchy, and replace it with a paterfamilias. The paterfamilias had a better sense of the historical undertaking and a strong sense of masculinity purely based on Catholic morality. By 1930, both the positive paradigm of the past (the *bacán* in his *garçonière*) and the negative (the hurting men discombobulated by love and the modern city) were finished. I believe, however, that what tango always represented was a retreat to private life and subjectivity. We could say that tango was a code that transferred/detoured the impact of the public onto the private by redirecting claims that could have been vociferously made in the public/political sphere into a personal, agoraphobic, self-embarrassing lament. Yet at the same time, in spite of its crass misogyny, the voice in the tango stands at the threshold of a masculine subjectivity deeply moved by the affectivity, sights, weaknesses, and failures he cries over, turning these voids into some sort of identitary anchor, albeit one that noticeably feminizes him.

I have endeavored to examine how imaginaries in Buenos Aires worked on the basis of highly complex intersections, interweavings, and superimpositions, able to create spaces of great density and thickness through countless social texts of every kind. Like enormous icebergs, these imaginaries gathered material, processed it, and elaborated it, returning it to the surface with ready-made meanings. What were the stabilizing, socializing imaginaries that intervened in the definitions of life in this contradictory Buenos Aires? From a synchronic point of view, they were those related to cultural/urban geography, medical/juridical discourse, journalism, the marketplace, misogynist imaginaries, and political and social repression. They seem to have continued to function throughout the political transformations of the period as stable, cognitive frameworks responsible for the reallocation of social places and the symbolic formation of modern and nationalist values. In Discépolo's 1925 *grotesco Babilonia,* a fifty-five-year-old Neapolitan chef named Don Piccione concludes: "This is unheard of. . . . It's unseen anywhere in the world. . . . We are in the land of *carbonara:* salted, spicy, sour, sweet, bitter, poisonous, explosive. . . . Christ, what a Babylon! . . . 'Señor Citizen, everyone hang on with whatever nails you've got; it's all about hanging on.' Are you hanging on? . . . What an intelligent man! Bravo! Bravo! What a phantasmagorical country! They respect nothing . . . they turn everything topsy-turvy on you, they change everything" (Discépolo 1996, 173).

For some, such a process of cultural recruitment ("it's all about hanging on") made it possible to draw interpretative maps that calmed the annoyance of living among unknown people in a talkative, heteroglossic, polyglot space. New rites and exclusions gave names and meanings to the quotidian, making essentialist much of what was really contingency, exploration, testing, and improvisation. Legal and public health discourses contributed to defining two of the most crucial axes of the social: public and private proxemic distances regarding interpersonal relationships, social laterality, sexuality. They were ratified even through the mediation of the new languages of the modern city, such as electric lighting, the layout of streets, tramway maps, the zoning of cafés and theaters, palaces, *conventillos,* the social use of public parks, the location of bordellos, garbage incinerators, barrios, and so on. That is to say, urbanism, zoning, lighting, transportation, and housing turned the urban ground plan into a written surface that the inhabitants of Buenos Aires learned to read—although not entirely on their own or just with their own wit, but with the help of texts that had already been underlined. An array of multidiscursive texts—police reports, public transportation routes, newspapers, literature, photographs, *folletines,* and so on—played a major role in adding symbolic values to urban spaces, as well as their social actors, their actions, and their languages. These social agents were clearly on the move, for urban space in Buenos Aires was indeed the setting for all the transitional configurations of modernity's socialization and its new political, relational, urban, judicial, sensorial, sexual, and gastronomic practices. At the same time, the culture of the marketplace brought a series of substitutions in identity into play, thereby exacerbating the tension women felt between their original social background and their new aspirations. Yet this "other" identity place was not seen in any way as a secure port of arrival. On the contrary, misogynist imaginaries elaborated on a daunting interpretation of women's journey, although the anguish released, in spite of them, by women's movements in social and urban space added to the devastating effects of the economic crises suffered by the male population.

From a diachronic point of view, the Generation of 1880 and the Centennial Generation exploited their pompous city of privilege, as well as the newspapers they owned, in order to draw public attention to their private deeds, rituals, architecture, clubs, art collections, women, and lifestyle. This symbolic capital contributed to the delineation of social distances, beginning with the elites' own residences and the sexual politics of their *garçonières*. But not everybody would long for the material and symbolic capital of the elite, which Silvio Astier and Erdosain felt so compelled to caress. Parodic imitations, or irreverent antibodies like Homero Manzi's rewriting of Palermo Park, synthesized what the dowdier sectors of the city felt about it all.

With respect to the two stages of Radicalism, alongside the discourse of violence surrounding the Semana Trágica, Radical imaginaries struck a new chord worth listening to: a rejuvenating confidence in the possibility of overcoming social backwardness. Hence the miraculous ring that reaches out from the palace to habilitate the immigrant *turco,* or the young single mother socially redeemed by the marriage proposal from the brother of the lover who abandoned her and her illegitimate child. Such imaginaries seemed to fortify the premises of an all-inclusive and participatory democracy: equal access to consumer culture, the impression of leaving behind the unyielding city of the Conservative Order, and the opportunity to remedy the social and economic breaks caused by modernity and industrialization. These imaginaries stretched the trust in state institutions as agents of social mediation, to the detriment of civil society's activism, although the means for public delivery of welfare services were not yet available, as in the case of social networks able to evaluate empirical reality in ways that went further than merely invoking sanctions and repression. In Francisco DeFilippis Novoa's drama *María la tonta* (Crazy Mary, 1927), a doctor describes a hospital patient as an idiot "picked up by the police at night off the street, hungry and poverty-stricken, not knowing if she was a beggar or a prostitute." The physician then decides "to remove her child . . . because . . . what would this irresponsible woman do with a boy!" (1927, 27). Along the same lines, the extreme Right, in alliance with the Catholic Church, was sliding almost imperceptibly in a similar direction by intervening in reproduction, inheritance, and the conduct of proletarian life—not only replacing the democratic Yrigoyenist state but, more important, initiating a mechanism historically intended to void the legacy and the children of the popular struggles and to make them disappear.

I would like to highlight the eminently intersecting nature of the imaginaries considered here, based on how they behaved. Tango intersected with at least five fields of imaginaries: (1) those related to the city's cultural geography that polarized the exact location of its paradises and infernos; (2) misogynist imaginaries that severely stigmatized women's search for new gender and social identities and their resolute questioning of conventional ones; (3) imaginaries that reinforced the *milonguita*'s preference for the *bacán,* leaving behind proletarian men who were their equals in terms of social extraction, and the appropriation of *porteñas*' sexuality in the *garçonière,* read as a loss of (proletarian) male territoriality and part of the symbolic formation of class struggle; (4) imaginaries that found nothing worth learning in poverty, unemployment, layoffs, and economic instability: after all, these conditions utterly inverted the *identidades fuertes* (strong identities) of enabling imaginaries and mechanically implied a painful, veiled conclusion concerning the male's personal failure—in the forefront of tango's imaginaries, men always fail through unruly women, never through personal deficiencies, never as a consequence of capitalism's new crisis of economic adjustment and its pressing demand for specialized labor (hence the uniqueness of tangos like Discépolo's "Yira . . . yira" and "Cambalache" [Pawn Shop], which pinpoint the other social contexts where downfall occurred); and (5) imaginaries that naturalized the repression of the Conservative Order, Radicalism, and fascism, which gradually declared the purpose of political activism to be outmoded and left the popular classes and some sectors of the middle classes without political representation.

Working women in Buenos Aires would have learned to maneuver between meager salaries and other types of harassment and the dreams of grandeur stimulated by modernity's desire industries, paradigms of *ensimismamiento* (self-absorption), the tantalizing glitter of the courtesan's life, economic and *deudas emocionales* (emotional debts) of all kinds, such as a romanticized femininity based on sacrifice and self-deferral and new identitary quests that could shelter women's *ilusiones útiles* (conducive hopes). They had learned to imagine their bodies from the perspective of places less sinister than *conventillo* rooms. The imaginaries of Buenos Aires's cultural geography inspired them to fantasize in "other" places, but their bodies were trapped at a cultural crossroads, between at least two contrasting discourses: the hedonism of the market and the harassment of the labor culture. Market imaginaries set out to mitigate the harm done to bodies by piecework, countering brutality with the soft, gauzy textures of dreamy goods and the flimsy postures of department store mannequins. Yet while market imaginaries seemed to grant an agency focused on gender, by giving central stage to women as purchasers, the gendered division of political activism inclined to eliminate them from the public sphere. Stabilizing imaginaries saw women as mere pegs: receiving the deeds of knights with swords, on whom they in turn bestowed their gentleness and solicitous concern. There was no question of listening to the suffragettes or of vindicating their quest for new social positions. Their concerns were seen as evidencing a watchful, erect posture that brought to mind the phallic ambition and the *mala pasión* (boisterous passion) of the femme fatale. Innumerable *porteñas* found a solution to survival in their bodies. They thought that the body was all they had, and in the strict terms of the labor market, they were quite right: training and specialized labor were unimaginable for them. As prostitutes they sold their bodies, as nursemaids the milk from their breasts. Similarly, new market strategies required saleswomen to wear permanent smiles for nine hours a day and to keep their bodies in languorous poses, as if they had just stretched, regardless of fatigue and the ever-eventful biology of a woman's body. I also believe that the choreography of tango played a crucial role in giving women a new sensuality, body language, and opportunity for sensorial/cultural explorations, although reactive imaginaries promptly read these as paradigms of social negativity. It was not for nothing that the Liga Patriótica Argentina had this unpredictable collective space of the search for identity in its insomniac sights.

The bodies of women and homosexuals in transitional Buenos Aires were intersecting spaces scrutinized by multiple discourses that disclosed their secrets, while seeking to map the social danger released by the grotesque city. Biological and psychological paranoia would attribute their bodies to the hysteria and disorder of active, peripheral sexualities. The homoerotic city was a troublesome point of flight from social control. Imaginaries of classic masculinity saw this city as a vampire advancing with crafty calculation, recruiting docile followers in settings of social normality, but slithering under cover of darkness and secrecy. Like the vampire, the femme fatale was also the sign of a forked city. She was double, elusive. She aspired to have her own heart, but the one crystallized for her by stabilizing imaginaries was homogenizing and submissive. Claustrophobic syndromes revealed in women an urge for air and for unconfined, unbound spaces, as a reaction to the oppression of *identidades acertadas* (socially correct identities), but conservative imaginaries would heavily induce women's agoraphobia. "Don't leave your barrio," warns the tango, only to describe the *milonguita's* decrepitude and fall from the aspirations of her daring flight—women sullied by moral ignominy and disease, dying alone in poverty and desolation in hospital. In a city taking shape as it progressed, it was important to find truths, purity, and certainties, or at least transactions with the socially correct (*lo acertado*). Hence the calming function of the narratives of perdition and their implied recognition of and apology for woman's domesticity, as well as the equally reassuring word of the law, whether constitutional or de facto. Uriburu's coup redefined masculinity/nationality, just as the Ley de Residencia had set up the political limits binding foreigners. Thus, the polyglot, decadent Babel might, after all, avoid a raucous identitary crisis by resorting to militarism/virility, a recourse that Roberto Arlt's Hipólita knows well enough when she expresses her disgust at those frightened, pathetic men who never stop thinking about suicide. Only in this way can it be understood why she cries out for dictators, *varones de verdad* (true men).

I am left with the impression that it was not in the least bit easy to live in that Buenos Aires. In *Las mujeres lindas* (Pretty Women), Julio remarks: "But the smart woman becomes a juggler with the intentions of a wolf when she plays. She is a cunning litigant, who denies her debt when the time comes to pay. Everyone, brother, is two-faced. In politics, business, and social life every man changes his face to suit the occasion, and it's just the same for women; whether pretending love, honesty, or status, their lies are disguised as truth" (Trejo 1977, 146). Nemesio Trejo's play captures both the intersecting fluidity of imaginaries in the process of configuring new definitions of meaning and the failed potential of the new social explorations revealed by the city. Social laterality among women in the factories was neutralized by the triangle of classic masculinity, against which Alfonsina Storni vehemently dissented. But it was also defeated by the cultural departure of the *milonguita* who abandoned the cotton clothing (*percal*) of the factory for the furs and jewelry given her by a *bacán*. Without the backing of a political party, feminism had no hold—not even in anarchism, the most combative of the political movements of the time, where such intergender alliances were eventually deflected by misogynist anxieties and sidestepped by the urgency of continuous political turmoil. Who better to understand the claustrophobic need for air among proletarian working women than their male companions in the factory, who were also severely beaten down by unregulated industrialization? Yet the misogynist imaginary surrounding the crisis in masculinity seems to have read the steps "toward freedom" taken by the *muñecas bravas* as betrayal and unfortunately did not hesitate to respond brutally and even viciously through the physical violence of lovers and husbands, fathers, brothers, employers, and coworkers, as well as in the narratives of perdition obsessively told in tangos and *folletines*. The wounds of a failing masculinity were supposed to be staunched by misogynist gestures. To be a male was not a matter of abstract, ahistorical essentialism. It was a matter of power and money. And violence.

Consumerism and the cultural/sexual practices modeled after those of the elite fueled much of the *obrera*'s drive to escape the ghetto and the culture of industrial labor. For the elite, sexuality acted as just one more antagonistic means in the class struggle against the working classes. As for the *obreras,* it was a matter of necessity to break from the ecology of poverty of the barrio, its males, and everything it implied, even including abandoning "your mother, poor mother / [who] washes clothes all week / to earn a life / of Franciscan poverty / in a miserable *conventillo* / illuminated by kerosene" (Celedonio Flores, "Margot"). When looked at today, we could say that the only space for the development of female subjectivity was monopolized by the market. But subjectivity and femininity were defined by market imaginaries as equivalent to individualism, self-indulgence, and self-absorption. Regarding interpersonal contact, and judging from restrictions on the social use of public parks, the stigmatization of the *conventillo* community, and the staged depoliticization of the barrios, it could be said that there were not too many spaces where collective subjectivities could develop and interact.

I have no doubt that a life saturated with violence and destitution caused the factory worker, the saleswoman, and the courtesan to grow a thick, anesthetizing skin that was supposed to prevent her from hesitating or even feeling. "You have no heart anymore" ("Flor de fango") was the recrimination most frequently thrown at *milonguitas* impassive to males who had failed or had not managed "to hang on." Imaginaries of class and gender "recruited" the operators as counterweights to their male peers who were on strike for labor rights that might well have also benefited them. The space resulting from overlapping imaginaries of class, gender, and ethnicity holds the key to why Samuel Eichelbaum's Ivonne/Rebeca renounces her Jewishness and even condescends to anti-Semitism, set on retaining her upward economic mobility and the feminine spaces that were becoming socially acceptable for women, as in the case of the courtesan. As for men, socializing imaginaries countered economic insecurity and crumbling falls from identity by allowing the unmanly men stranded on the fringes of classic masculinity to survive in the discourse of tango.

I read the agoraphobic intimacy of the tango as the *cuarteles de invierno* (winter quarters) of a male population that had been cast aside, drowning, ashamed of their beleaguered bodies and minds unable to withstand the relentless rhythm of industrial culture. Bodies as well as identities thus became the surfaces on which the new culture of labor imprinted its unilateral contracts. White-collar workers in the urban center felt the impact of this culture too, as "Balada de la oficina" (Office Ballad), by Roberto Mariani, illustrates only too well:

> Come in. Enter my belly. It's not dark, see how many Osram lamps there are with their sulfurous, luminous eyes. . . . Enter my flesh, and you'll be safeguarded from the burning sun and the buffeting wind. . . . Come in. Then you'll be sure to have bread every day for your mouth and the mouths of your little ones. . . . Don't be afraid. So long as you're in my bosom and don't break any of the rules. . . . Life is Duty . . . you must work. Modern life is as tangled as a ball of wool a kitten has played with. . . . Nobody dies from working eight hours a day. . . . You have fulfilled your Duty. . . . You have to be serious, honest, with no vices. Come back tomorrow and every day . . . later, if you haven't died of consumption, I'll allow you to retire. Then you'll enjoy the sun and will die the day after. (1925, 14–15)

In sum, I suggest that the new spaces so openly displayed by modernity's habilitating imaginaries held all the conditions necessary to foster many kinds of new alliances, resources, networks in social laterality, and creative interpersonal relations among the multicultural groups involved. Yet spontaneous improvisation in the grotesque city was not simply monitored but prevented in many cases by the work of constricting imaginaries whose weight was wide-ranging. In addition to public environments, detection and vigilance over emerging formations also focused on private everyday social practices. Private life is the most secret laboratory for molding new subjectivities, a social space hard to reach through social surveillance. Issues at the core of class, ethnicity, and gender were put to the test, and in my opinion, the results of such a field of intersections played a neutralizing role in attempts to break with the conventions of the socially acceptable. Adaptation appears to have prevailed over subjective improvisation. The indeterminacy of the open city was negotiated in order to stabilize social normalization, but such transactions did not necessarily mitigate the struggle of its tensions. Perhaps this is what is pointedly alluded to by two of the remarks in Trejo's play—"Everyone, brother, is two-faced," and "Lies are disguised as truth" —as well as by Borges's stubborn diligence in narrating the struggling nature of the double.

The scenario of social reproduction tended to disregard pluralism in interactions, meanings, and symbols by enforcing its sense of social time and space, anchored in the repetition of social practices, but the conflictive political and cultural divide could not fail to trigger tensions so conspicuous and hard to dismiss that they hastened the rise of fascism and the Uriburu coup. Above and beyond the interpretative working of stabilizing imaginaries, social modernization had already permitted social actors to make the constituted order function in a different way. Rossana Reguillo argues that alongside the normalizing purpose of power, it is important to notice the practices of "micropowers": "It is a question of little retaliations whereby social actors subvert what is designed for them and assert their existence as 'authors' by stamping the mark of their own actions on socially shared practices" (1998, 109). In this sense, the subsequent sedimentation of historical events gave continuity to what the coup's imaginaries had sought to exorcise forever. Buenos Aires's workers had learned the rules of active agency and would invoke them again in successive popular political mobilizations. This was also true of women activists, who contested conventional gender formations daily in their public and private lives (figure 35). Neither of these groups turned back but would henceforth march forward, having learned from the collective consensus and the value of their own subjective actions and empirical evidence. Modernity had unleashed strategies of social hyperventilation that would continue to enable possibilities beyond the barriers of its restrictive imaginaries. Such was the case with the political activism that led to Peronism and leftist mobilizations throughout the twentieth century, in favor of a much broader political agency.

I believe that Buenos Aires must have been a fiendishly contradictory city and that its inhabitants, like Borges, were deeply bound to it by *amor y espanto* (love and consternation). I think of the photo of immigrants newly arrived at the port of Buenos Aires, only allowed to remain in the immigrants' hostel for five days. After those five days, they were on their own. Anguish and expectancy are revealed on their faces, none of them knowing what the city, still without personal maps, would hold for them. But the rest of the inhabitants of Buenos Aires were equally lost. The city's daily life seemed to be permanently caught in the frenzy of its beginning. It slid dizzily and unpredictably, never ceasing to challenge all conventional categories, identitary maps and subjectivities, and the ability of bodies to adjust. I also think the Buenos Aires of that time was a perplexing city, immersed in fears and surprises, regimentation and laxity, legal verdicts and gaps in the law, learning and anxieties of all kinds, and above all culture in motion —questions, reflections, searches, experiments, and changes so energizing and radical that many feared the Apocalypse. In the intense intertwining of meanings, cultural maps were as much polysemic as overlapping. *Mapas del dolor* (maps of pain) seemed to fill the same spaces as those of desire and enabling dreams. For the despairing *milonguita,* the urban center was a dazzling space, shining with hope, but the working man despondently watched her leave enthralled by its lights, fearing her departure held no promise of return.

I am also left with the impression that Buenos Aires was a loveless city, because it was not envisaged for everyone. Nevertheless, it was also a space where *actores sociales chapuceros* (slapdash social actors) lived through improvisation, surviving in spite of their own inadequacy and informality. The grotesque is also laughter and untidiness, the expansion of whatever is unique, and a space for writing second cultural lives. In such conditions, social actors reaccommodated, rearranging rites and codes in their own way. These social agents asserted their existence as "authors" "by stamping the mark of their own actions on socially shared practices." I keep thinking about how much the Cocoliche-speaking Italian immigrant must have laughed when, still not fully convinced of what he was doing, he ventured into using the adaptations and perplexing distortions of his own language, into speaking a new language—as new for him as for everyone else in Buenos Aires. A language that had literally been born in jest and that he, in turn, would also transform because it would become *his* new surface for inscription and identity. I also think of how much the immigrant from Salamanca or the *criollo/a* would have been amused at hearing him- or herself speaking a freewheeling Castilian-Cocoliche in which everything meant and sounded like the Castilian spoken by the children of Genoa. I am quite aware that not even a lifetime is enough to understand a city, especially one so caught in the middle of its own motion and metamorphosis as was the Buenos Aires of that time, but this is my attempt to trace the silent messages of its spaces; the watchful work of its socializing imaginaries; the pain and illusions of its bodies; and above all its feelings and reflections, its sighs, and its empowering dreams.

NOTES

Introduction

1. The "Generation of 1880" includes the members of the ruling oligarchy who came to power that year, with Julio Argentino Roca's election to the presidency (translator's note).

2. The "Generation of the Centennial" includes those individuals who held power in 1910, the centenary of Argentina's declaration of self-government (translator's note).

3. The "Conservative Order" refers to the landowning oligarchy that ruled Argentina between 1880 and 1916 and to their conservative ideology, which persisted long after their demise (translator's note).

4. An analysis of the period's cinematic production is left for another occasion.

1. The Jockey Club

1. The indigenous people of the Frontera Sur had been defeated by 1879.

2. The terms *modernista* (modernist) and *modernismo* (modernism) refer to the aesthetic movement that flourished in Latin America in the early twentieth century (translator's note).

3. Julio Ramos defines the "chronicle" as "a weak, minor literary form [that] expands the discursive networks emerging from the encounter of the literary with 'low,' 'anti-aesthetic' discourses [by absorbing] aspects of everyday capitalism that . . . are beyond the thematic range of canonical, codified forms of literature" (1989, 112). (The term *chronicle* is used henceforth as a translation of the Spanish *crónica,* the genre defined by Ramos, which refers to a newspaper report or commentary on everyday events [translator's note]).

4. The term *porteño* is synonymous with Buenos Aires, reflecting the character of the city as a port (*puerto*) and the fact that many of its citizens arrived on boats coming into the port. It is used both as an adjective and as a noun, referring to persons, male or female (*porteño/a*), who come from the city (translator's note).

5. Palermo was at that time (and still is) an upscale district in Barrio Norte.

6. The term *arrabal,* typically translated as "suburb," refers to the city's outlying districts (translator's note).

2. Palaces and Residences

1. Please note that most publications of the period, especially the popular ones, did not paginate their issues. Pagination is cited where it is available.

2. Manuel Ugarte (1878–1951) and Enrique Larreta (1875–1961) were both writers. The latter is best known for his historical novel *La gloria de don Ramiro* (The Glory of Don Ramiro, 1904), set in the time of Felipe II of Spain (translator's note).

3. The first fenced-in estates appeared in 1868, in the division of Las Flores (Bioy 1958, 52).

4. *Costumbrista* writers focused on social customs and manners (translator's note).

5. "*Caras y Caretas* . . . appeared for the first time in 1898 as a virtual introduction to art nouveau by way of its graphic art. . . . Their advance in style was possibly due to the capacity and quality of the journal's illustrators, a number of whom came from Barcelona" (Peña 1992, 224).

6. A *garçonière* was an apartment owned by a man as a place to keep a lover or hold wild parties; see chapter 17 (translator's note).

7. "Grotesque theater" features themes based on the everyday life of the popular classes, often from a tragicomic or cynical point of view. Works of theater in this vein are often referred to as *grotescos* (translator's note).

4. Passages, Public Spaces, and Cultural Crossings

1. A *folletín* is a *feuilleton,* or work of fiction, published in a newspaper or magazine, often in serial form (translator's note).

2. Adela Di Carlo writes, "un pobre inmigrante de nacionalidad turca." The term *turco* (i.e., Turk, Turkish) came to refer, generically and somewhat pejoratively, to all immigrants from the Middle East or from nations belonging to the Ottoman Empire, in much the same way as the term *gallego* (Galician) referred to all Spaniards (translator's note).

3. The first of the *villas miserias* was Villa Esperanza, in Puerto Nuevo (1936).

4. Concerning the obsession provoked by the underground tunnels found in south and central Buenos Aires, see Jorge Larroca's "El misterio de los túneles coloniales" (The Mystery of the Colonial Tunnels, 1977).

5. The expression *voluntad de la forma* alludes to a utopian trend that deemed homogeneity, control, and contention pivotal to the triumph of form over barbarism.

6. The *vosotros* form of the imperative is also associated with Iberian Spanish (translator's note).

7. *Laterality* here refers to the sense of identity individuals feel toward others of the same social environment or class (translator's note).

8. *Payadores* are singer-songwriters associated with the rural culture of the Argentinean pampa (translator's note).

9. See Serrano Anguita 1936: *Siete puñales* (Seven Daggers).

10. The moment of this revisionism is captured in *Historias del comer y del beber en Buenos Aires* (Stories of Eating and Drinking in Buenos Aires): "Our gauchos were dynamic, bloodthirsty, savage, and above all carnivorous; civilized people . . . were vegetarian, peaceful, sedentary, and intellectual" (Schávelzon 2000, 92).

11. Diego Ortiz Grognet's *sainete Los vegetarianos* (The Vegetarians, 1922) addresses the debates over vegetarian and meat-based diets.

12. See Prieto 1988: *El discurso criollista en la formación de la Argentina moderna* (Creole Discourse in the Formation of Modern Argentina).

5. Theaters and Cafés

1. I discuss several types of phobias in Borges's writing in *Haciendo camino: Pactos de la escritura en la obra de Jorge Luis Borges* (Bergero 1998).

6. Conventillos

1. The phrase "yo también porto" (I'll also contribute) also plays on the similarity of the verb *porto* (from *aportar,* "to contribute") to the name of the Portuguese city of Porto, which many of the Galicians portrayed in the *sainetes* would claim as their place of origin in order to appear more sophisticated.

2. The term *caballo de vuelta* (literally, "returning horse") refers to words and phrases that are switched back and forth between languages and changed each time they are switched (see Meo Zilio and Rossi 1970, xv).

3. The terms used by Reguillo are *lo acertado* ("what is appropriate") and *lo verdadero* ("what is true"). The former alludes to social conformity and to what society considers "correct"; the latter refers to individual subjectivity and fidelity to the self. They will be cited parenthetically henceforth in order to signify the concepts embodied by Reguillo's terminology (translator's note).

7. Paradigms and Deviations

1. *El matadero* was written between 1838 and 1840 and published in 1871 by Juan María Gutiérrez.

2. The war with Paraguay (1865–70), also known as the War of the Triple Alliance, set Brazil, Argentina, and Brazil against Paraguay after Paraguay reacted to the 1864 Brazilian invasion of Uruguay.

3. Part of this paragraph was suppressed in the first edition of the novel, but it was retrieved by Jorge Lafforgue in his notes to *Historia de arrabal* (Gálvez 1989, 75–76).

4. Specifically, an article by Anita Lagouardette denounces the activist F. Denanbride for killing his girlfriend when she wanted to leave him.

5. All tangos cited in this study may be found at http://www.todotango.com. This very comprehensive online archive includes recordings, historical commentary, sheet music, and lyrics from over thirty-four hundred songs. Tango texts may be searched by title, composer, or lyricist.

6. The name change (from Teresita to Teresa) is made obvious to the audience through changes in the actor's performance.

9. Chains of Desire

1. The terms *diastolic* and *systolic* are used throughout to express different moods and forms of desire. The "diastolic" refers to the expansive desire of self-realization and fulfillment. By contrast, the "systolic" refers to restraint and the desire to ensure conformity with established conventions (translator's note).

10. Palaces of Temptation

1. Aside from the commercial sector, the feminization of the labor market for the middle classes also occurred in service (white-collar) sectors, in secretarial work (stenography and typing), and in tertiary sectors (state employees, teachers, nurses, and—probably because women were thought to chatter—telephone operators).

2. The quote is from "What's in the Air" (Saks Fifth Avenue catalog, 2001, 10). The majority of these companies still exist today, and some, such as Guerlain, Lalique, Dior, Chanel, and Patou, date from the 1930s.

11. Beauties, Femmes Fatales, Tramps, Vamps, and Vampires

1. The term *possibilism* is used to signify an attitude hopeful of social success and upward mobility that is often illusory or the product of self-affirming imaginaries.

12. Rags and Rejects

1. The group, named for Boedo Street, in the working-class area of the city, espoused social realism in its writing. Its counterpart, the Florida Group, was associated with the avant-garde and with the more fashionable side of the city (translator's note).

13. Reaffirming Old Paradigms

1. On 9 July 1816, a meeting of Congress at Tucumán declared the independence of the United Provinces of the River Plate, the region that, in due course, would become Uruguay and Argentina.

2. General Juana Azurduy commanded an army against the royalists during the war for Upper Peru in the nineteenth century.

3. The first schools were in the Bagley factory, the Avanti tobacco works, and the Grether shirt factory, and they then spread to other areas of the city (Barracas, Belgrano, Matadero, Palermo).

4. By this time in Argentina, as elsewhere in Spanish America, the plural form of address *vosotros* commonly indicated an archaic or Iberian usage. The more usual form in Spanish America was *ustedes*. The use of *vosotros* had commonly disappeared, although, abbreviated to *vos* in Argentinean Spanish, it was already a popular form of address in the singular (translator's note).

5. A *bacán* is a playboy who is wealthy or pretends to have money.

6. The chronicle ends its review of inmates with the description of an old woman serving a life sentence.

7. The word *continuismo* alludes to a practice in Latin America whereby governments remain in power beyond their constitutional term. Here it refers to the continued ideological predominance of the political Right (translator's note).

14. New Alliances—Old Causes

1. Like the Jockey Club, the Sociedad Rural Argentina (Rural Association of Argentina) was an association that brought together the leading families in Argentina, connected to large landholdings, ranching, and industry (translator's note).

2. The bark of the native Argentinean quebracho tree was an important source of tannin and dye (translator's note).

3. The operators' uniform, in the summer of the southern hemisphere, consisted of a stark white pinafore, stockings, and, shoes. Public health discourse had successfully equated the whiteness of the hospital with the purity and reliability of new measures in social welfare. Interestingly, *Caras y Caretas* proposed an example of altruism by dedicating one of its covers to "los abnegados de la semana" (the selfless heroes of the week): the emergency medical staff who had attended "to the public tirelessly" (18 Jan. 1919).

4. The author has added the comments in brackets to clarify the photos' contents (translator's note).

5. The term *chinita* refers to a young *mestiza* (translator's note).

6. José Batlle y Ordóñez (1856–1929) was twice president of Uruguay (1903–7, 1911–15). He introduced radical legislation to increase public welfare and implement political reform, including universal male suffrage and laws governing labor practices (translator's note).

15. Putting Out Fires

1. Juan Bautista Alberdi (1810–84) was a celebrated political philosopher, diplomat and patriot, and early contributor to the foundation of modern Argentina (translator's note).

2. Although the word *national* figured in the organization's title, there is nothing to suggest that the charity collection was active elsewhere in Argentina.

3. The term *golpista* refers to a coup d'état—from the Spanish *golpe de estado* (translator's note).

4. From Psalms 2:10: "Et nunc reges intelligite erudimini qui iudicati terram" (And now, kings, understand: be instructed, you who have judged the Earth) (translator's note).

5. Mikhail Bakunin (1814–76) was one of the intellectual founders of anarchism (translator's note).

6. Sacco and Vanzetti were immigrant anarchists arrested and tried in 1921 for the murder of a shoe-factory paymaster and guard. The trial, which took place in a climate of antianarchist sentiment, provoked widespread international protest (translator's note).

7. Leopoldo Lugones (1874–1938), a distinguished poet and man of letters, became one of the principal spokespersons of fascism (translator's note).

8. Manuel Gálvez's remarkable comment is worth repeating: "I've spent an hour talking with Lugones and am left with the impression of having been in touch with a viper" (qtd. in Itzcovitz 1986, 9).

9. Signed in 1932, the Roca-Runciman Pact gave important trade concessions to Great Britain, especially regarding beef (translator's note).

10. The Spanish for "enough money to eat" is "el mango que te haga morfar," a line adapted from lyrics written by Enrique Santos Discépolo for the tango "Yira . . . yira" (translator's note).

17. The Garçonières and the Sex of Power

1. A *niño bien* is the son of a wealthy, upper-class family, given to high living (translator's note).

19. The Weak, the Violent, and the Tearful

1. Another issue of *Caras y Caretas* combines photos of aristocratic nightlife by "La Dama Duende" and the fanciful oil painting *Gasas y plumas* (Gauzes and Feathers), by R. Rivero, with horrifying photos of "the chauffeur's premeditated murder" (6 Sept. 1919).

2. The Lunfardo term *mishiadura* not only means "poverty" or "indigence" but defines a prevailing condition of the times (translator's note).

20. Barrios and Melodramas: Of Love and Consternation

1. "Mi noche triste," the first sung tango, was popularized by Carlos Gardel.

2. Except for two tangos by Discépolo, this quotation and those that follow are all from works included in the bibliography. They are cited here by authors' names and titles in order to highlight the pertinence of the titles themselves.

3. The new names found in *Caras y Caretas* are Enrique Blanch, Arturo Cancela, Roberto Gache, Roberto Giusti, Alberto Grochonoff, and Constancio C. Vigil, with Leopoldo Lugones regularly mentioned.

4. The word *escraches* is from the Italian *scraciare,* meaning "to reveal or uncover." An *escrache* is a popular form of political demonstration intended to highlight the presence in society of unpunished military perpetrators involved in the dictatorship's genocide. The Ley de Punto Final and the Ley de Obediencia were enacted to protect perpetrators of crimes during the military dictatorship of 1976–83. The first put an end to investigations and prosecutions; the second made a response to an order from a superior officer a legitimate defense for actions carried out by members of the armed forces. HIJOS is an organization of the children of those "disappeared" during the last dictatorship in Argentina. *Piqueteros* are literally members of a picket or squad. The term generally refers to unemployed workers and to disruptive tactics used to force the government to remedy social grievances (translator's note).

REFERENCES

Acasuso, Luis R[odríguez]. 1930. *Poker de almas. Bambalinas: Revista Teatral* 13, no. 639.
———. 1937. *La mal pagada. Argentores: Revista Teatral* 14, no. 148.
Agnew, John A., John Mercer, and David E. Sopher, eds. 1984. *The City in Cultural Context.* Boston: Allen and Unwin.
Agrest, Diana, Patricia Conway, and Leslie Kanes Weisman, eds. 1996. *The Sex of Architecture.* New York: Harry N. Abrams.
Algarra, Pilar de. 1943. *Vidas: Apuntes de una visitadora.* Buenos Aires: Editorial Araujo.
Allen, Virginia Mae. 1979. *The Femme Fatale: A Study of the Early Development of the Concept in Mid-Nineteenth Century Poetry and Painting.* Ann Arbor: University Microfilms International.
Antología de cuentistas rioplatenses. 1939. Ed. Julia Prilutzky Fary. Buenos Aires: Editorial Vértice.
Antología del género chico criollo. 1977. Sel. Susana Marcó, Abel Posadas, Marta Speroni, and Griselda Vignolo. Buenos Aires: EUDEBA.
Archetti, Eduardo. 1996. "Playing Styles of Masculine Virtue in Argentine Football." In Marit Melhuus and Kristi A. Stolen, eds., *Machos, Mistress and Madonnas: Contesting the Power of Latin American Gender Imagery,* 34–55. New York: Verso.
Argentina, la otra patria de los italianos/Argentina, l'altra patria degli italiani. 1983. Buenos Aires: Manrique Zago Ediciones.
Arlt, Roberto. 1939. "Las fieras." In *Antología de cuentistas rioplatenses* 1939, 38–52.
———. 1981a. *Las Aguafuertes porteñas de Roberto Arlt.* Ed. and intro. Daniel C. Scroggins. Buenos Aires: Ediciones Culturales Argentinas.
———. 1981b. *El juguete rabioso.* Madrid: Editorial Bruguera.
———. 1981c. *Obras completas.* 2 vols. Prol. Julio Cortázar. Buenos Aires: Ediciones Carlos Lohlé.
Armont and Bousquet. 1925. *El bailarín de la señora. Bambalinas: Revista Teatral* 8, no. 382. (Adapted by Julio F. Escobar.)
Armus, Diego, ed. 1990. *Mundo urbano y cultura popular: Estudios de historia social argentina.* Buenos Aires: Editorial Sudamericana.
Avellaneda, Andrés. 1983. *El habla de las ideologías: Modos de la réplica literaria en la Argentina.* Buenos Aires: Sudamericana.
Balmaceda, Rodolfo, ed. 1982. *Condición obrera y despilfarro oligárquico.* Buenos Aires: Ediciones del Mar Dulce.
Balmori, Diana. 1991. "Public Space, Public Life." *Modulus: Politics and Architecture* 21: 84–95.
Barnestone, Willis. 1982. *Borges at Eighty: Conversations.* Bloomington: Indiana University Press.
Barranco, Dora. 1990. "Anarquismo y sexualidad." In Armus 1990, 7–37.
Bassi, Antonio de, and Antonio Botta. 1922. *Puerto Nuevo. Bambalinas: Revista Teatral* 9, no. 457.

Bataille, Georges. 1986. *Eroticism, Death and Sensuality*. San Francisco: City Lights Books.

Ben, Pablo. 2000. "Cuerpos femeninos y cuerpos abyectos: Construcción anatómica de la femineidad en la Medicina argentina." In Gil Lozano, Pita, and Ini 2000, 252–71.

Benjamin, Walter. 1986. "Paris, Capital of the Nineteenth Century." In *Reflections, Essays, Aphorisms, Autobiographical Writings,* 146–62. New York: Schocken Books.

Bentley, Eric. 1967. *The Life of Melodrama*. New York: Atheneum.

Bergero, Adriana J. 1998. *Haciendo camino: Pactos de la escritura en la obra de Jorge Luis Borges*. México: UNAM.

Berruti, Alejandro E. 1912. *Historietas de don Alejandro*. Buenos Aires: Ediciones Talía.

———. 1920. *Madre Tierra. La Escena: Revista Teatral* 3, no. 127.

———. 1973. *Cuidado con las bonitas*. In *Comedias y sainetes argentinos* 1973, 239–66.

Berruti, José J. 1930. *Como las mariposas. Bambalinas: Revista Teatral* 13, no. 634.

Bertonasco, Alfredo E., and Domingo L. Martignone. 1926. *Un amor imposible. Bambalinas: Revista Teatral* 9, no. 453.

Biffi, Alcibiades. 1922a. *La hoja de hiedra. Bambalinas: Revista Teatral* 5, no. 201.

———. 1922b. *Jaque mate. Bambalinas: Revista Teatral* 5, no. 201.

Bioy, Adolfo. 1958. *Antes del novecientos: Recuerdos*. Buenos Aires: Cía. Impresora Argentina.

Birabeau, André. 1936. *Besos perdidos. Argentores: Revista Teatral* 3, no. 132.

Blomberg, Héctor Pedro. 1920. *Las puertas de Babel*. Prol. Manuel Gálvez. Buenos Aires: Agencia General de Librería y Publicaciones.

Bloomer, Kent C., and Charles W. Moore. 1977. *Body, Memory, and Architecture*. New Haven and London: Yale University Press.

Bobbio, Norberto, and Nicola Matteucci. 1985. *Diccionario de política*. Mexico: Siglo XXI Editores.

Borges, Jorge Luis. 1974. *Obras completas*. 2 vols. Buenos Aires: Editorial Emecé.

———. 1985. *Los conjurados*. Madrid, Alianza Editorial.

———. 1993. *El tamaño de mi esperanza*. Buenos Aires: María Kodama/Compañía Editora Espasa Calpe/Seix Barral.

Borlenghi, Angel G. 1934. *Beneficios del nuevo Artículo 157 del Código de Comercio: Lo que todo empleado debe saber*. Buenos Aires: Confederación General de Empleados de Comercio de la República Argentina.

Botana, Natalio. 1977. *El orden conservador: La política argentina entre 1880 y 1916*. Buenos Aires: Editorial Sudamericana.

———. 1983. "Conservadores, radicales y socialistas." In Romero and Romero 1983, 107–19.

Bourdieu, Pierre. 1990. *The Logic of Practice*. Stanford: Stanford University Press.

———. 1996. *Distinction: A Social Critique of the Judgement of Taste*. Cambridge: Harvard University Press.

Brooks, Peter. 1976. *The Melodramatic Imagination*. New Haven and London: Yale University Press.

Brumana, Herminia. 1973. *Obras completas*. Comp. and prol. José Rodríguez Tarditi. Buenos Aires: Ediciones Amigos de Herminia Brumana.

Bucich, Antonio J. 1962. *Rasgos y perfiles en la historia boquense*. Buenos Aires: Editorial Ergon.

Buenos Aires: De la fundación a la angustia (antología). 1967. Sel. Julio Cortázar, Félix Luna, Leopoldo Marechal, et al. Buenos Aires: Ediciones de la Flor.

Bullrich, Francisco J. 1983. "La arquitectura: El eclecticismo." In Romero and Romero 1983, 201–12.

Bunge, Alejandro E. 1917. "La desocupación en la Argentina. Actual crisis del trabajo." In *Revista estudios*. Buenos Aires: R. Herrando & Cía.

Calcagno, Lucía E., Marta Feijoó de Llamas, et al. 1992. *Guía de la arquitectura de Buenos Aires: Itinerario, Barrio Norte-Recoleta*. Buenos Aires: Ediciones de Arte Gaglianone.

Cambaceres, Eugenio. 1956. *Obras completas*. Santa Fe, Argentina: Editorial Castellvi.

Carella, Tulio, ed. 1957. *El sainete criollo: Antología*. Buenos Aires: Hachette.

Carlson, Marifran. 1988. *¡Feminismo! The Woman's Movement in Argentina from Its Beginnings to Eva Perón*. Chicago: Academy Chicago.

Cárrega, Hemilce. 1997. *Aspectos del inmigrante en la narrativa argentina*. Buenos Aires: El Francotirador Ediciones.

Carreño, Carlos. 1931. *La higiene en los talleres*. *La Semana Médica* (Buenos Aires), no. 15.

Carretero, Andrés M. 1974. *Orden, paz, entrega (1880–1886)*. Buenos Aires: Ediciones La Bastilla.

———. 1995. *Prostitución en Buenos Aires*. Buenos Aires: Ediciones Corregidor.

Carriego, Evaristo. 1985. *La canción del barrio y otros poemas*. Sel. and intro. Javier Adúriz. Buenos Aires: Editorial Biblos.

"Carta orgánica de la Unión Gastronómica Argentina." 1926. Buenos Aires: n.p.

Carter, Erica, James Donald, and Judith Squires, eds. 1993. *Space and Place: Theory of Identity and Location*. London: Lawrence and Wishart.

Caruso, Juan A. 1924. *La garçonnière*. *Bambalinas: Revista Teatral* 7, no. 395.

Castell, Manuel. 1983. *The City and Its Grassroots: A Cross-Cultural Theory of Urban Social Movements*. Berkeley and Los Angeles: University of California Press.

Castelnuovo, Elías. 1934. *Vidas proletarias*. Buenos Aires: Editorial Victoria.

———. 1968. "El delirio." In Lubrano Zas, ed., *Palabras con Elías Castelnuovo: Reportaje y antología,* 75–79. Buenos Aires: Carlos Pérez Editor.

Castro, Donald S. 1991. *The Argentine Tango as Social History, 1880–1955: The Soul of the People*. Lewiston, N.Y.: Edwin Mellen Press.

Cayol, Roberto. 1920. *La casa donde no entró el amor*. *La Escena. Revista Teatral* 3, no. 10.

———. 1921. *La chica de la guantería*. *La Escena: Revista Teatral* 4, no. 29.

Chambless, Diane L., and Alan J. Goldstein, eds. 1982a. *Agoraphobia: Multiple Perspectives on Theory and Treatment*. New York: John Wiley and Son.

———. 1982b. "Characteristics of Agoraphobia." In Chambless and Goldstein 1982a, 1–18.

Chiarello, Enrique. 1929. *Así se escriben los tangos*. *Bambalinas: Revista Teatral* 12, no. 603.

Colomina, Beatriz. 1992. "The Split Wall: Domestic Voyeurism." In Beatriz Colomina, ed., *Sexuality and Space,* 73–128. New York: Princeton Architectural Press.

Comedias y sainetes argentinos I: Antología. 1973. Buenos Aires: Ediciones Colihue.

"Comisión de Señoritas de la Liga Patriótica Argentina: Sus escuelas de obreras en las fábricas." 1922. Pamphlet. Buenos Aires.

Conde, Oscar. 1998. *Diccionario etimológico del lunfardo*. Buenos Aires: Bitácora.

Corbin, Alain. 1986. *The Foul and the Fragrant: Odor and the French Social Imagination.* Cambridge: Harvard University Press.

Cortés Conde, Roberto. 1983. "Riqueza y especulación." In Romero and Romero 1983, 31–44.

Curat Dubarry, José Manuel. 1927. *La tristeza de los viejos. Bambalinas: Revista Teatral* 9, no. 462.

Curotto, Angel. 1927. *La vida buena. Bambalinas: Revista Teatral* 9, no. 466.

Curotto, Angel, and Carlos César Lenzi. 1930. *El fuego del Vesubio. Bambalinas: Revista Teatral* 7, no. 626.

Darío, Ruben. 1977. *Poesía.* Caracas: Biblioteca Ayacucho.

———. 1986. *Cuentos.* Sel. and intro. José Emilio Balladares. San José, Costa Rica: Libro Libre.

Darthés, Damel. 1922. *La pipa de yeso. Bambalinas: Revista Teatral* 5, no. 202.

DeFilippis Novoa, Francisco. 1922. *El turbión. Bambalinas: Revista Teatral* 5, no. 219.

———. 1923. *Los desventurados. Bambalinas: Revista Teatral* 6, no. 257.

———. 1930. *Nosotros dos. Bambalinas: Revista Teatral* 7, no. 630.

———. 1977a. *El día sábado.* In *Antología del género chico criollo* 1977, 83–113.

———. 1977b. *Puerto Madero.* In *Antología del género chico criollo* 1977, 177–94.

———. 1980. *María la tonta.* In *El teatro argentino* 1980, 8.

Deutsch, Helene. 1929. "The Genesis of Agoraphobia." *International Journal of Psycho-Analysis* 10: 52–69.

Díaz Olazábal, Adriano. 1922. *Castillo en el aire. Bambalinas: Revista Teatral* 5, no. 205.

Diego, Jacobo A. de. 1983. "El teatro: El gauchesco y el sainete." In Romero and Romero 1983, 143–53.

Discépolo, Armando. 1969. *Mustafá.* In *Obras escogidas,* 246–83. Buenos Aires: Editorial Jorge Alvarez.

———. 1987a. *Obra dramática de Armando Discépolo.* Vol. 1. Ed. Osvaldo Pelletieri. Buenos Aires: EUDEBA.

———. 1987b. *Armando Discépolo. Obra dramática: Teatro.* Vol. 2. Ed. Osvaldo Pelletieri. Buenos Aires: EUDEBA/Editorial Galerna.

———. 1996. *Armando Discépolo. Obra dramática: Teatro.* Vol. 3. Ed. Osvaldo Pellettieri. Buenos Aires: Editorial Galerna.

Discépolo, Armando, and Rafael José de Rosa. 1987a. *El guarda.* In Discépolo 1987b, 251–42.

———. 1987b. *El movimiento continuo.* In Discépolo 1987b, 295–354.

———. 1987c. *El viaje aquel.* In Discépolo 1987b, 77–109.

Discépolo, Armando, Rafael José de Rosa, and Mario Folco. 1987. *El novio de mamá.* In Discépolo 1987b, 121–71.

Dolard, Víctor, and Armando B. Rillo. 1922. *El amor que no se vende. Bambalinas: Revista Teatral* 5, no. 211.

Dolkart, Ronald H. 1993. "The Right in the Década Infame, 1930–1943." In McGee Deutsch and Dolkart 1993, 65–98.

Donzelot, Jacques. 1979. *The Policing of Families.* Intro. Gilles Deleuze. New York: Phanteon Books.

Downton, Jorge. 1925. *La fiesta del odio. Bambalinas: Revista Teatral* 8, no. 381.

Dworkin, Andrea. 1989. *Pornography: Men Possessing Women.* New York: E. P. Dutton.

Eberle, Scott Gerard. 1985. *The Human Factor: Mental Hygiene and the Retreat of Taylorism.* Ann Arbor: University Microfilms International.

Echeverría, Esteban. 1963. *El matadero.* Buenos Aires: Edición Cina-Cina.

Edwards, Susan S. M. 1993. "Selling the Body, Keeping the Soul: Sexuality, Power, the Theories and Realities of Prostitution." In Sue Scott and David Morgan, eds., *Body Matters: Essays on the Sociology of the Body,* 89–104. London and Washington, D.C.: Falmer Press.

Eichelbaum, Samuel. 1923. *El ruedo de las almas. La Escena: Revista Teatral* 6, no. 259.

———. 1927. *Nadie la conoció nunca. Bambalinas: Revista Teatral* 9, no. 461.

Elguera, Alberto, and Carlos Boaglio. 1997. *La vida porteña en los años veinte.* Prol. María Sáenz Quesada. Buenos Aires: Grupo Editor Latinoamericano S.R.L.

Escardó, Florencio. 1971. *Nueva Geografía de Buenos Aires.* Buenos Aires: Editorial Américalee.

Escobar, Julio F. 1927. *La mujer que odiaba a los hombres. Bambalinas: Revista Teatral* 10, no. 474.

Evans, Caroline, and Minna Thornton. 1989. *Women and Fashion: A New Look.* London and New York: Quartet Books.

Feijoó, María del Carmen. 1990. "Las trabajadoras porteñas a comienzos de siglo." In Armus 1990, 283–311.

Fernández, Alejandro E., and José Moya, eds. 1999. *La inmigración española en la Argentina.* Buenos Aires: Editorial Biblos.

Fernández Moreno, Bartolomé. 1921. *Nuevos poemas: Ciudad, Intermedio provinciano. Campo argentino.* Buenos Aires: Editorial Biblos.

———. 1928. *Décimas.* Buenos Aires: L. J. Rosso Ediciones.

Fimiani, Maripaola. 1985. "Cartografie." In Donatella Mazzoleni, ed., *La cittá e l'imaginario,* 227–34. Roma: Officina Edizione.

Ford, Aníbal, and Nora Mazzioti. 1991. "José González Castillo: Cine mudo, fábricas y garçonières." In González Castillo 1991, 77–96.

Foster, David W. 1986. *Social Realism in the Argentine Narrative.* Chapel Hill: University of North Carolina, Department of Romance Languages.

———. 1989. "José González Castillo's *Los invertidos* and the Vampire Theory of Homosexuality." *Latin American Theater Review* 2, no. 22: 19–29.

———. 1990. *The Argentine Generation of 1880: Ideology and Cultural Texts.* Columbia: University of Missouri Press.

———. 1998. *Buenos Aires: Perspectives on the City and Cultural Production.* Gainesville: University Press of Florida.

F. P. L. and Arsuaga. 1923. *Esperar haciendo bien (entremés en verso). Bambalinas: Revista Teatral* 6, no. 271.

Franco, Jean. 1989. *Plotting Women: Gender and Representation in Mexico.* New York: Columbia University Press.

Fraser, Howard M. 1987. *Magazines and Marks: Caras y Caretas as a Reflection of Buenos Aires, 1898–1908.* Tempe: Arizona State University.

Furlán, Luis Ricardo. 1995. *Esquema de la poesía lunfardesca.* Buenos Aires: Torres Agüero Editor.

Gache, Roberto. 1919. *Glosario de la farsa urbana.* Buenos Aires: Cooperativa Editorial Limitada.

Gallo, Blas Raúl. 1970. *Historia del sainete nacional.* Buenos Aires: Editorial Buenos Aires Leyendo.

Gálvez, Manuel. 1950. *Nacha Regules.* Buenos Aires: Editorial Losada.

———. 1989. *Historia de arrabal.* Notes by Jorge Lafforgue. Buenos Aires: Centro Editor de América Latina.

Gandéra, Félix. 1927. *El marido de mi novia (A tout . . . coeur!). Bambalinas: Revista Teatral* 9, no. 459.

García Canclini, Néstor, Alejandro Castellanos, and Ana Rosa Mantecón. 1996. *La ciudad de los viajeros: Travesías e imaginarios urbanos, México, 1940–2000.* México, D.F.: Editorial Grijalbo.

García de D'Agostino, Rebok-Asato-López. 1981. *Imagen de Buenos Aires a través de los viajeros, 1870–1910.* Buenos Aires: Universidad de Buenos Aires.

Gatti, Gabriel. 1999. "Habitando (astutamente) las ruinas del mapa: El Aleph, la nación, los cronopios y las modalidades débiles de la identidad colectiva." *Política y Sociedad* 30: 39–52.

Gayol, Sandra. 2000. *Sociabilidad en Buenos Aires: Hombres, honor y cafés, 1862–1910.* Buenos Aires: Editorial Signo/Colección Plural.

Gell, Alfred. 1977. "Magic, Perfume, Dream . . ." In Ioan Lewis, ed., *Symbols and Sentiments: Cross-cultural Studies in Symbolism,* 24–36. London and New York: Academic Press.

Ghiraldo, Alberto. 1922. *Doña Modesta Pizarro. Bambalinas: Revista Teatral* 5, no. 213.

Giddens, Anthony. 1999. *The Consequences of Modernity.* Cambridge: Polity.

Gil Lozano, Fernanda, Valeria Silvina Pita, and María Gabriela Ini, eds. 2000. *Historia de las mujeres en la Argentina.* Vol. 1, *Colonia y Siglo XIX.* Coord. Mercedes Sacchi. Buenos Aires: Taurus, Santillana Editorial.

Gilman, Sander L. 1985. *Difference and Pathology: Stereotypes of Sexuality, Race and Madness.* Ithaca and New York: Cornell University Press.

Gipsy, Stear. 1925. *El perfume del pecado. Bambalinas: Revista Teatral* 8, no. 379.

Girondo, Oliverio. 2001. *Oliverio Girondo. Textos Selectos. Muestra Individual.* Buenos Aires: Corregidor.

Gobello, José, ed. 1969. *El tango: Antología—capítulo oriental.* Montevideo: Biblioteca Uruguaya Fundamental.

———. 1980. *Crónica general del tango.* Buenos Aires: Editorial Fraterna.

Godel, Alberto E. 1926. *El farruco Manolo. Bambalinas: Revista Teatral* 9, no. 452.

Godio, Julio. 1972. *La Semana Trágica de enero de 1919.* Buenos Aires: Granica Editorial.

Goldstein Fodor, Iris. 1974. "The Phobic Syndrome in Women: Implications for Treatment." In Violet Franks and Vasanti Burtle, eds., *Women in Therapy: New Psychotherapies for a Changing Society,* 132–68. New York: Brunner/Mazel.

Gómez, José. 1923. *El dinero de mi mujer. Bambalinas: Revista Teatral* 7, no. 258.

Gómez Carrillo, Enrique. 1919. *La mujer y la moda. El teatro de Pierrot (La moda y Pierrot).* Madrid: Editorial Mundo Latino.

———. 1921. *El encanto de Buenos Aires.* Madrid: Editorial Mundo Latino.

Gómez Grimau, Pedro. 1930. *Sacco y Vanzetti. Bambalinas: Revista Teatral* 7, no. 629.

González, Ricardo. 1990. "Lo propio y lo ajeno: Actividades culturales y fomentismo en una asociación cultural de Barrio Nazca (1925–1930)." In Armus 1990, 93–128.

González Arrili, Bernardo. 1967. "La calle, un pasadizo." In Buenos Aires 1967, 75–78.

———. 1983. Ayer no más: Calle Corrientes entre Suipacha y Esmeralda. Buenos Aires: Academia Argentina de Letras.

González Castillo, José. 1918. El mayor prejuicio. La Escena: Revista Teatral 1, no.12.

———. 1920. El pobre hombre. Teatro Popular: Revista Teatral 2, no. 36.

———. 1925. Hermana mía . . . Buenos Aires: Editorial Claridad.

———. 1991. Los invertidos. Buenos Aires: Punto Sur Editores.

González Castillo, José, and Vicente Martínez Cuitiño. 1920. La Santa Madre. Teatro Popular: Revista Teatral 2, no. 13.

González Castillo, José, and José Mazzanti. 1935. La mala reputación. Argentores: Revista Teatral 2, no. 42.

González Castillo, José, and Federico Mertens. 1922. La zarza ardiendo. La Escena: Revista Teatral 5, no. 232.

González Stephan, Beatriz. 1995. "Modernización y disciplinamiento: La formación del ciudadano, del espacio público al espacio privado." In González Stephan et al. 1995, 431–55.

González Stephan, Beatriz, et al., eds. 1995. Esplendores y miserias del siglo XIX: Cultura y sociedad en América Latina. Caracas: Monte Avila Editores/Latinoamericana Equinoccio, Ediciones de la Universidad Simón Bolívar.

González Tuñón, Enrique. 1999. "Camas desde un peso." In Pedro Orgambide, comp., Los desocupados: Una tipología de la pobreza en la literatura argentina, 53–54. Buenos Aires: Universidad Nacional de Quilmes.

Gorelik, Adrián. 1998. La grilla y el parque: Espacio público y cultura urbana en Buenos Aires, 1887–1936. Buenos Aires: Universidad Nacional de Quilmes.

Gouchón Cané, Emilio. 1967. "Un buen empleo." In Buenos Aires 1967, 141–48.

Gutiérrez, Eliseo, and León Alberti. 1927. Yo me hago el loco. Bambalinas: Revista Teatral 9, no. 460.

Gutiérrez, Leandro H. 1983a. "La mala vida." In Romero and Romero 1983, 85–92.

———. 1983b. "Los trabajadores y sus luchas." In Romero and Romero 1983, 67–83.

Gutman, Margarita, and Jorge Enrique Hardoy. 1992. Buenos Aires: Historia urbana del área metropolitana. Buenos Aires: Editorial Mapfre.

Guy, Donna. 1991. Sex and Danger in Buenos Aires: Prostitution, Family, and Nation. Lincoln and London: University of Nebraska Press.

Hall, Edward T. 1985. La Dimensión Oculta. México: Siglo XXI Editores.

Harvey, David. 1993. "From Space to Place and Going Back Again." In Jon Bird, Barry Curtis, et al., eds., Mapping the Future: Local Cultures, Global Changes, 3–29. London and New York: Routledge.

Hurst Vose, Ruth. 1981. Agoraphobia. London and Boston: Yale University Press.

Iglesias Paz, César. 1919. Buenos Aires. La Escena: Revista Teatral 2, no. 40.

Ini, María Gabriela. 2000. "Infanticidios: Construcción de la verdad y control de género en el discurso judicial." In Gil Lozano, Pita, and Ina 2000, 234–51.

Itzcovitz, Victoria. 1986. "La ideología golpista antes de 1930: Los escritos de Leopoldo Lugones." El Bimestre Político y Económico, no. 30: 5–14.

Jitrik, Noé. 1978. *Las contradicciones del modernismo: Productividad poética y situación sociológica*. México: El Colegio de México.

Justo, Liborio. 1974. *Masas y balas*. Buenos Aires: Ediciones de la Flor.

Kaplan, E. Ann. 1992. *Motherhood and Representation: The Mother in Popular Culture and Melodrama*. London and New York: Routledge.

Kern, Stephen. 1975. *Anatomy and Destiny: A Cultural Study of the Human Body*. Indianapolis and New York: Bobbs-Merrill Company.

Korn, Francis. 1983a. "La aventura del ascenso." In Romero and Romero 1983, 57–66.

———. 1983b. "La gente distinguida." In Romero and Romero 1983, 45–55.

Lafforgue, Jorge, sel. 1979. *Canillita y otras obras (Sánchez, Trejo, Pacheco, Disceepolo, Dragún)*. Buenos Aires: Centro Editor de América Latina.

———. 1983. "La literatura: El naturalismo y los vanguardistas." In Romero and Romero 1983, 155–60.

———. 1989. "Notas." In Gálvez 1989, 73–77.

Lanuza, José Luis. "Finura." In *Antología de cuentistas rioplatenses* 1939, 288–96.

Lara, Tomás de, and Inés Leonilda Roncetti de Panti. 1961. *El tango en la literatura argentina*. Buenos Aires: Ediciones Culturales Argentinas-Ministerio de Educación y Justicia, Dirección General de Cultura.

Larroca, Jorge. 1977. "El misterio de los túneles coloniales." In Larroca et al. 1977, 7–21.

Larroca, Jorge, Luis Soler Cañas, Miguel Angel Scenna, et al., eds. 1997. *Crónicas de Buenos Aires*. Buenos Aires: Todo es Historia.

Last, Cynthia, and Michel Hersen. 1989. *Handbook of Anxiety Disorders*. New York: Pengamon Books.

Leach, William R. 1984. "Transformation in a Culture of Consumption: Women and Department Stores, 1890–1925." *Journal of American History* 71, no. 2: 319–42.

Lefebvre, Henri. 1995. *The Production of Space*. Oxford and Cambridge: Blackwell.

LeGates, Richard T., and Frederic Stout, eds. 1996. *The City Reader*. London and New York: Routledge.

Leland, C. Towne. 1984. *The Last Happy Men: The Generation of 1922, Fiction and the Argentine Reality*. Syracuse: Syracuse University Press.

Liernur, Jorge F., and Graciela Silvestri. 1993. *El umbral de la metrópolis: Transformaciones técnicas y cultura en la modernización de Buenos Aires (1870–1930)*. Buenos Aires: Editorial Sudamericana.

Linnig, Samuel. 1925. *Puente Alsina. Bambalinas: Revista Teatral* 8, no. 392.

Lliri, Alfredo F. 1922. *Castillos en el aire. Bambalinas Revista Teatral* 5, no. 205.

Lobato, Mirta Zaida. 1990. "Una visión del mundo del trabajo: El caso de los obreros de la industria frigorífica Berisso, 1900–1930." In Armus 1990, 313–37.

———. 1997. "Women Workers in the 'Cathedrals of Corned Beef': Structure and Subjectivity in the Argentine Meatpacking Industry." In John D. French and Daniel James, eds., *The Gendered Worlds of Latin American Women Workers*, 53–71. Durham and London: Duke University Press.

Lobato, Mirta Zaida, and Juan Suriano. 2000. *Nueva historia argentina*. Buenos Aires: Editorial Sudamericana.

López, Eugenio, and Antonio López Azcona. 1922. *Los hombres de la ribera. Bambalinas: Revista Teatral* 5, no. 212.

Ludmer, Josefina. 1993. "El delito: Ficciones de exclusión y sueños de justicia." *Revista de Crítica Literaria Latinoamericana* 19, no. 36: 145–53.

Lugones, Leopoldo. 1897. "El himno de las torres." In *Las montañas del Oro,* 131–52. Buenos Aires: Premia Editora.

———. 1926. *Las fuerzas extrañas.* Buenos Aires: M. Gleizer Editor.

———. 1930. *La patria fuerte.* Buenos Aires: Círculo Militar, Biblioteca del Oficial.

Luisi, Paulina. 1919. *A propósito de los Proyectos sobre moralidad.* Buenos Aires: Talleres Gráficos y Casa Editorial "J. Perrotti."

Lynch, Kevin. 1996. "The City Image and Its Elements." In LeGates and Stout 1996, 98–102.

Mallea, Eduardo. 1939. "Serena Barco." In *Antología de cuentistas rioplatenses* 1939, 322–37.

Mamone, Miguel. 1930. *El obstétrico Fouschet. Bambalinas: Revista Teatral* 13, no. 640.

Marechal, Leopoldo. 1967. *Historia de la Calle Corrientes.* Buenos Aires: Paidós.

María, Enrique de. 1980. *Bohemia criolla.* In *El teatro argentino* 1980, 7–61.

Mariani, Roberto. 1925. *Cuentos de la oficina.* Buenos Aires: Editorial Deucalión.

Marling, Karal Ann. 1997. "Imagineering the Disney Theme Parks." In Karal Ann Marling, ed., *Designing Disney's Theme Parks: The Architecture of Theme Parks,* 29–177. Montreal: Centre Candien d'Architecture/Canadian Centre for Architecture-Flammarion.

Marmol, Arsenio. 1930. *Milanesa. Bambalinas: Revista Teatral* 7, no. 631.

Marpons, Josefina. 1936. *44 horas semanales.* Buenos Aires: Editorial Vanguardia.

Martel, Julián. 1979. *La Bolsa.* Buenos Aires: IMPRIMA Editores.

Martinez Cuitiño, Vicente. 1924. *Teatro: La mala siembra/El derrumbe/Nuevo mundo.* Buenos Aires: M. Gleizer, Editor.

Martínez Estrada, Ezequiel. 1940. *La cabeza de Goliath: Microscopía de Buenos Aires.* Buenos Aires: Club del Libro.

Martinez Sierra, Gregorio. 1936. *Sólo para mujeres. Argentores: Revista Teatral* 3, no. 131.

Masiello, Francine. 1986. *Lenguaje e ideología: Las escuelas argentinas de vanguardia.* Buenos Aires: Libreria Hachette, S.A.

———. 1995. "Horror y lágrimas: Sexo y nación en la cultura de fin de siglo." In González Stephan et al. 1995, 447–72.

———. 1997. "Gender, Dress and Market: The Commerce of Citizenship in Latin America." In Daniel Balderston and Donna J. Guy, eds., *Sex and Sexuality in Latin America,* 219–33. New York and London: New York University Press.

Matamoro, Blas. 1982. *La ciudad del tango: Tango histórico y social.* Buenos Aires: Editorial Galerna.

Mazzei, Angel. 1971. *He nacido en Buenos Aires: Poemas de la ciudad.* Buenos Aires: Ediciones SADE, Sociedad Argentina de Escritores.

Mazziotti, Nora. 1990. "*Bambalinas*: El auge de una modalidad teatral-periodística." In Armus 1990, 71–89.

Mazzoleni, Donatella, ed. 1985. *La città e l'immaginario.* Roma: Officina Edizioni.

———. 1993. "The City and the Imaginary." In Carter, Donald, and Squires 1993, 285–301.

McGee Deutsch, Sandra F. 1984. "The Visible and the Invisible Liga Patriótica Argentina, 1919–28: Gender Roles and the Right Wing." *Hispanic American Review* 64, no. 2: 233–58.

———. 1993. "The Right under Radicalism, 1916–1930." In McGee Deutsch and Dolkart 1993, 35–63.

McGee Deutsch, Sandra F., and Ronald H. Dolkart. 1993. *The Argentine Right: Its History and Intellectual Origins, 1910 to the Present.* Washington, D.C.: Scholarly Resources.

Melhuus, Marit, and Kristi Anne Stolen, eds. 1996. *Machos, Mistresses and Madonnas: Contesting the Power of Latin American Gender Imagery.* London and New York: Verso.

Méndez Caldeira, Alfredo. 1922. *Sacrificio. Bambalinas: Revista Teatral* 5, no. 207.

Meo Zilio, Giovanni, and Ettore Rossi. 1970. *El elemento italiano en el habla de Buenos Aires y Montevideo.* Firenze: Valmartina Editore.

Miller, Karl. 1987. *Doubles: Studies in Literary History.* London: Oxford University Press.

Miller, Michael B. 1981. *The Bon Marché: Bourgeois Culture and the Department Store, 1869–1920.* Princeton: Princeton University Press.

Ministerio de Industrias y Trabajo. Instituto Nacional de Trabajo y Servicios Anexados. 1935. *Uso de sillas para el descanso de empleadas y obreras/Trabajo nocturno/Salario mínimo rural.* Montevideo: Imprenta Nacional.

Mirande, Ives de, and André Picard. 1927. *El hombre del frac. Bambalinas: Revista Teatral* 9, no. 468.

Molyneux, Maxine. 1986. "No God, No Boss, No Husband: Anarchist Feminism in Nineteenth-Century Argentina." *Latin American Perspectives* 13, no. 48: 119–45.

Moock, Armando. 1927. *Canción de amor. Bambalinas: Revista Teatral* 9, no. 465.

Morales, Isaac. 1922. *El ultimo tango. Bambalinas: Revista Teatral* 5, no. 202.

Mordeglia, Miguel, and Mario P. Francone. 1940. *Tecnopatías: Enfermedades profesionales.* Buenos Aires: Librería y Editorial El Ateneo.

Moreira, Elena. 1992. "High Fashion: The Search for a Style." *Journal of Decorative Art,* no. 18: 170–87.

Morely, David, and Kevin Robins. 1993. "No Place like Heimat: Images of Home(land) in European Culture." In Carter, Donald, and Squires 1993, 3–31.

Moreno, Artemio. 1924. *Niñez abandonada y delincuencia en Buenos Aires.* Ed. Valerio Abeledo. Buenos Aires: Librería Jurídica.

Morganti, Carlos. 1926. *Primero en la colorada. Bambalinas: Revista Teatral* 9, no. 455.

Mosse, George L. 1985. *Nationalism and Sexuality: Respectability and Abnormal Sexuality in Modern Europe.* New York: Howard Fertig.

Moya, José C. 1998. *Cousins and Strangers: Spanish Immigrants in Buenos Aires, 1850–1930.* Berkeley and Los Angeles: University of California Press.

Moya, José C., and Alejandro Fernández, eds. 1999. *La imagen española en la Argentina.* Buenos Aires: Biblos.

Munier and Montignac. 1927. *Tenemos que divorciarnos. Bambalinas: Revista Teatral* 9, no. 462.

Muzilli, Carolina. 1913. *El trabajo femenino.* Buenos Aires: L. J. Rosso y Cía.

Navas, Miguel. 1932a. *Los dependientes de almacén y la jornada de trabajo.* Buenos Aires: Establecimiento Gráfico Fernández y Poccollo.

———. 1932b. *El sábado inglés a través del reportaje.* Buenos Aires: Establecimiento Gráfico Fernández y Poccollo.

Newton, Jorge, and Lily Newton. 1966. *Historia del Jockey Club de Buenos Aires.* Buenos Aires: Ediciones L. N.

Notari, Humberto. 1923. *Aquellas señoras. Bambalinas: Revista Teatral* 6, no. 271.

Novión, Alberto. 1977a. *Los primeros fríos.* In *Antología del género chico criollo* 1977, 47–63.

———. 1977b. *El rincón de los caranchos.* In *Antología del género chico criollo* 1977, 67–79.

Nuñez Seixas, Xosé M. 1999. "Asociacionismo local y movilización sociopolítica: Notas sobre los gallegos en Buenos Aires." In Alejandro E. Fernández and José Moya, eds., *La inmigración española en la Argentina,* 195–233. Buenos Aires: Editorial Biblos.

Ochoa, Jorge, and Eduardo Valdés. 1991. *¿Dónde durmieron nuestros abuelos? Los Hoteles de inmigrantes en la capital federal.* Buenos Aires: Fundación Urbe.

Oficina de Servicio Doméstico. 1887. "Libreta de Inscripción." Pamphlet. Buenos Aires: Imprenta Europea.

Olivari, Nicolás. 1936. *Tedio. Argentores: Revista Teatral* (Buenos Aires) 3, no. 131.

Ordaz, Luis, et al. 1982. *Historia del teatro argentino.* Buenos Aires: Centro Editor de América Latina.

Ortiz, R. I. 1967. "El Barrio de las Ranas." In *Buenos Aires* 1967, 79–84.

Ortiz Grognet, Diego. 1922. *Los vegetarianos. Bambalinas: Revista Teatral* 5, no. 209.

Ostuni, Ricardo A., and Oscar B. Himschoot. 1994. *Los cafés de la Avenida de Mayo.* Buenos Aires: Ediciones Club del Tango.

Oved, Iaacov. 1978. *El anarquismo y el movimiento obrero en Argentina.* México: Siglo XXI.

Pacheco, Carlos Mauricio. 1921. *La quinta de los reyes. Teatro Popular: Revista teatral* 3, no. 72.

———. 1964. *Los disfrazados y otros sainetes.* Buenos Aires: EUDEBA.

———. 1977a. *El diablo en el conventillo.* In *Antología del género chico criollo* 1977, 99–113.

———. 1977b. *Los tristes o la gente oscura.* In *Antología del género chico criollo* 1977, 33–44.

———. 1979. *Los disfrazados.* In Lafforgue 1979, 73–102.

Palacios, Alfredo L. n.d. *La fatiga y sus proyecciones sociales.* Buenos Aires: Editorial Claridad.

Paoli, Carlos R. de. 1930. *La culpa la tiene el gallego de enfrente. Bambalinas: Revista Teatral* 13, no. 632.

———. 1977. *Los chicos de Pérez.* In *Antología del género chico criollo* 1977, 117–37.

Pascarella, Luis. 1917. *El conventillo: Costumbres bonaerenses.* Buenos Aires: La Lectura.

Pedraza, Pilar. 1991. *La bella, enigma y pesadilla, esfinge, medusa, pantera.* Barcelona: Editorial Tusquet.

Pellarollo, Silvia. 1997. *Sainete criollo, democracia y representación: El caso de Nemesio Trejo.* Buenos Aires: Corregidor.

Pellettieri, Osvaldo, ed. 1987. *Obra dramática de Armando Discépolo I.* Buenos Aires: EUDEBA.

———. 1992. "La mujer argentina entre el tango y el sainete (1917–1935)." *Diógenes: Anuario Crítico del Teatro Hispanoamericano,* 227–70.

Peña, José María. 1992. "Art-Nouveau Stained Glass and Ironwork." *Journal of Decorative and Propaganda Arts,* no. 18: 222–41.

Pereira, Susana. 1979. *Literatura testimonial de los años treinta.* Buenos Aires: Peña Lillo Editor.

Pérez Amuchástegui, Antonio J. 1984. *Mentalidades argentinas, 1860–1930.* Buenos Aires: EUDEBA.

Pérez Leirós, Francisco. 1932. Sesión del 8 de Junio de 1932 de la Cámara de Diputados de la Nación Argentina. Asunto: "Inembargabilidad de sueldos menores de $300 pesos." Buenos Aires: Imprenta de Rivadavia 2150.

Pike, Burton. 1996. "The City as Image." In LeGates and Stout 1996, 242–49.

Piore, Oscar del, and Irene Amuchástegui. 1998. *Cien tangos fundamentales.* Buenos Aires: Aguilar, Altea, Taurus, Alfaguara S.A.

Portela, Mario J. 1914. *El sweating system: Definición, origen, importancia del mismo.* Buenos Aires: Colección Candioti.

Posada, Abel, Marta Speroni, and Griselda Vignolo. 1982. "El sainete." In Luis Ordaz, et al., *Historia del teatro argentino.* Buenos Aires: Centro Editor de América Latina.

Potash, Robert A. 1982. *El ejército y la política en la Argentina, 1928–1945: De Yrigoyen a Perón.* Buenos Aires: Sudamericana.

Prieto, Adolfo. 1988. *El discurso criollista en la formación de la Argentina moderna.* Buenos Aires: Editorial Sudamericana.

Pronsato, Carlos. 1940. *Lumgabos y ciáticas del trabajo.* Buenos Aires: Ediciones Mercatali.

Quesada, José. 1925. *El pecado de todas. Bambalinas: Revista Teatral* 8, no. 398.

Rachman, S., and Steve Taylor. 1993. "Analysis of Claustrophobia." *Journal of Anxiety Disorder* 7, no. 4: 281–91.

Ramos, Julio. 1989. *Desencuentros de la Modernidad en América Latina.* México: Fondo de Cultura Económica.

Reekie, Gail. 1991. "Impulsive Women, Predictable Men: Psychological Constructions of Sexual Difference in Sale Literature to 1930." *Australian Historical Studies* 21, no. 97: 359–77.

———. 1993. *Temptations: Sex, Selling and the Department Stores.* Sydney: Allen and Unwin.

Reguillo, Rossana. 1998. "La clandestina centralidad de la vida cotidiana." *Causas y Azares: Los Lenguajes de la Comunicación y la Cultura en (la) Crisis,* no. 7: 98–110.

Renau, Maryse. 1989. "La ciudad babilónica o los entretelones del mundo urbano en *Los siete locos* y *Los lanzallamas.*" In Rosalba Campra, coord., *La selva en el damero: Espacio literario y espacio urbano en América Latina,* 195–213. Pisa: Giardini Editori e Stampatori.

Richard, Nelly. 1998. *Residuos y metáforas: Ensayos de crítica cultural sobre el Chile de la Transición.* Providencia: Santiago, Editorial Cuarto Propio.

Rock, David. 1987. *Argentina 1516–1987: From Spanish Colonization to Alfonsín.* Berkeley and Los Angeles: University of California Press.

———. 1993. *Authoritarian Argentina and the Nationalist Movement: Its History and Its Impact.* Berkeley: University of California Press.

Rodaway, Paul. 1994. *Sensuous Geographies: Body, Sense and Place.* London and New York: Routledge.

Rojas, Eduardo. 1913. "El sweating system: Su importancia en Buenos Aires." Ph.D. diss., Facultad de Derecho y Ciencias Sociales, Universidad Nacional de Buenos Aires.

Rojas, Ricardo. 1922. *La restauración nacionalista.* Buenos Aires: Librería La Facultad.

Romero, Eduardo. 1983. *Sobre poesía popular argentina.* Buenos Aires: Centro Editor de América Latina.

Romero, José Luis. 1983a. "La ciudad burguesa." In Romero and Romero 1983, 9–18.

———. 1983b. "La ciudad de masas." In Romero and Romero 1983, 215–22.

Romero, José Luis, and Luis Alberto Romero, eds. 1983. *Buenos Aires: Historia de cuatro siglos.* Buenos Aires: Editorial Abril.

Romero, Luis Alberto. 1985. "Sectores populares, participación democrática: El caso de Buenos Aires." *Pensamiento Iberoamericano,* no. 7: 57–91.

Romero, Luis Alberto, and Leandro Gutiérrez. 1995. *Sectores populares, política y cultura.* Buenos Aires: Editorial Sudamericana.

Rossler, Osvaldo. 1981. *Cantores y trágicos de Buenos Aires.* Buenos Aires: Ediciones Tres Tiempos.

Rotenberg, Robert, and Gary McDonogh. 1993. *The Cultural Meaning of Urban Space.* Westport and London: Bergin and Garvey/Greenwood Publishing Group.

Ruffinelli, Jorge. 1968. *La revista* Caras y Caretas. Buenos Aires: Editorial Galerna.

Saisselin, Rémy G. 1984. *The Bourgeois and the Bibelot.* London: Thames and Hudson.

Salas, Horacio. 1968. *La poesía de Buenos Aires.* Buenos Aires: Pleamar.

Saldías, José Antonio. 1922. *¡Siga el corso! Bambalinas: Revista Teatral* 5, no. 220.

———. 1927. *Primavera en otoño. Bambalinas: Revista Teatral* 9, no. 469.

Salessi, Jorge. 1926. *El bandoneon. Bambalinas: Revista Teatral* 9, no. 451.

Salessi, Jorge. 1991. "Tango, nacionalismo y sexualidad: Buenos Aires, 1880–1914." *Hispamérica* 20, no. 60: 33–53.

Salzman, Leo. 1982. "Obsessions and Agoraphobia." In Chambless and Goldstein 1982a, 19–42.

Sanguinetti, Carlos. 1937. "La ciudad." *Buenos Aires* 2, no. 4.

Sarlo, Beatriz, ed. 1969. *Martín Fierro (1924–1927): Antología.* Buenos Aires: Carlos Pérez Editor, S.A.

———. 1985. *El imperio de los sentimientos: Narraciones de la circulación periódica en la Argentina (1917–1927).* Buenos Aires: Catálogos Editora.

———. 1993. *Jorge Luis Borges: A Writer on the Edge.* London and New York: Verso.

Sarmiento, Domingo Faustino. 1993. *Facundo: Civilización y barbarie.* Madrid: Editorial Cátedra.

Sau, Victoria. 2000. *Diccionario ideológico feminista.* Barcelona: Editorial Icaria.

Savigliano, Marta E. 1995. *Tango and the Political Economy of Passion.* Boulder, San Francisco, and Oxford: Westview Press.

Scenna, Miguel Angel. 1977. "Los cafés, una institución." In Larroca et al. 1997, 93–135.

Schávelzon, Daniel. 2000. *Historias del comer y del beber en Buenos Aires: Arqueología histórica de la vajilla de mesa.* Buenos Aires: Aguilar, Altea, Taurus, Alfaguara, S.A.

Scherpe, Klauss R. 1988. "Dramatización y des—dramatización de 'el fin': La conciencia apocalíptica de la modernidad y post-modernidad." In Josep Picó, ed. *Modernidad y Postmodernidad,* 349–85. Barcelona: Alianza Editorial.

Scobie, James R. 1971. *Argentina: A City and a Nation.* New York and London: Oxford University Press.

———. 1974. *Buenos Aires: Plaza to Suburb, 1870–1910.* New York: Oxford University Press.

Scobie, James R., and Aurora Ravina de Luzzi. 1983a. "El centro, los barrios y el suburbio." In Romero and Romero 1983, 173–99.

———. 1983b. "El puerto y los ferrocarriles." In Romero and Romero 1983, 19–30.

Scott, Sue, and David Morgan, eds. 1993. *Body Matters: Essays on the Sociology of the Body.* London and Washington, D.C.: Palmer Press.

Sebreli, Juan José. 1986. *Buenos Aires, vida cotidiana y alienación.* Buenos Aires: Hispamérica Ediciones Argentina, S.A.

———. 1997. *Escritos sobre escritos, ciudades bajo ciudades 1950–1997.* Buenos Aires: Editorial Sudamericana.

Seibel, Beatriz. 1985. *Los artistas trashumantes: Testimonios del circo criollo y radioteatro.* Buenos Aires: Ediciones de la Pluma.

Seidler, Victor J. 1989. *Discovering Masculinity: Reason, Language and Sexuality.* London and New York: Routledge.

Sennett, Richard. 1994. *Flesh and Stone: The Body and the City in Western Civilization.* New York and London: W. W. Norton.

Serrano Anguita, Francisco. 1936. *Siete puñales. Argentores: Revista Teatral* 3, no. 128.

Shakespeare, William. 1937. *Como gustéis.* Trans. Luis Astrana Marín. *Argentores: Revista Teatral* 4, no. 147.

Showalter, Elaine. 1991. *Sexual Anarchy: Gender and Culture at the Fin de Siècle.* New York and London: Penguin Books.

Siegrist de Gentile, Nora, and María Haydée Martín. 1981. *Geopolítica, ciencia y técnica a través de la Campaña del Desierto: Lucha de fronteras con el indio.* Buenos Aires: EUDEBA.

Siete sainetes porteños. 1958. Intro. and notes by Luis de Ordaz. Buenos Aires: Ediciones Losange.

Silverman, Debora L. 1989. *Art Nouveau in Fin-de-Siècle France: Politics, Psychology and Style.* Berkeley: University of California Press.

Silverman, Kaja. 1992. *Male Subjectivity at the Margin.* New York and London: Routledge.

Simmel, George. 1945. *Filosofía de la coquetería, filosofía de la moda: Lo masculino y lo femenino.* Madrid: Revista de Occidente.

Skirius, John, ed. 1981. *El ensayo hispanoamericano del siglo XX.* México: Fondo de Cultura Económica.

Sommer, R. 1969. *Personal Space: The Behavioural Basis of Design.* Englewood Cliffs, N.J.: Prentice Hall.

Sorensen Goodrich, Diana. 1996. *Facundo and the Construction of Argentine Culture.* Austin: University of Texas Press.

Steele, Valerie. 1985. *Fashion and Eroticism: Ideals of Feminine Beauty from the Victorian Era to the Jazz Age.* New York and Oxford: Oxford University Press.

Stilman, Eduardo. 1983. "El nacimiento del tango." In Romero and Romero 1983, 165–72.

Storni, Alfonsina. 1927. *El amo del mundo. Bambalinas: Revista Teatral* 9, no. 470.

———. 1984. *Obras escogidas: Poesía.* Buenos Aires: Sociedad Editora de Latinoamérica.

Strindberg, Juan Augusto. 1925. *El padre. Bambalinas: Revista Teatral* 8, no. 378.

Suero, Pablo. 1927. *La vida comienza mañana. Bambalinas: Revista Teatral* 9, no. 456.

Suriano, Juan. 1990. "Niños trabajadores: Una aproximación al trabajo infantil en la industria porteña de comienzos del siglo." In Armus 1990, 253–79.

Tabanillo. 1927. *La moral del gringo. Bambalinas: Revista Teatral* 9, no. 464.

Talice, Roberto, and Raúl Valentini. 1930. *Miss Argentina, Miss Universo. Bambalinas: Revista Teatral* 13, no. 642.

El teatro argentino. 1980. Buenos Aires: Capítulo-Centro Editor de América Latina.

Teruggi, Mario E. 1978. *Panorama del lunfardo: Génesis y esencia de las lenguas coloquiales urbanas.* Buenos Aires: Editorial Sudamericana.

Torre, Juan Carlos. 1983. "La ciudad y los obreros." In Romero and Romero 1983, 275–86.

Torre, Lidia de la. 1983. "La ciudad residual." In Romero and Romero 1983, 287–97.

Torre, Mariano de la. 1927. *El Gallego Mondoñedo. Bambalinas: Revista Teatral* 19, no. 467.

Tosoni, Feruccio. 1922. *En un rincón de la quema. Bambalinas: Revista Teatral* 5, no. 223.

Trejo, Nemesio. 1912. *Los inquilinos. Dramas y Comedias* 2, no. 18.

———. 1957. *Los devotos.* In Tulio Carella, ed., *El sainete criollo: Antología,* 73–105. Buenos Aires: Hachette.

———. 1977. *Las mujeres lindas.* In *Antología del género chico criollo* 1977, 141–58.

———. 1979. *Los políticos.* In Lafforgue 1979, 10–43.

Troncoso, Oscar A. 1983. "Las formas del ocio." In Romero and Romero 1983, 95–104.

Ulla, Noemí. 1982. *Tango, rebelión y nostalgia.* Buenos Aires: Centro Editor de América Latina.

Unsain, Alejandro M. 1942. *Trabajo a domicilio: Exposición y comentario a la Ley N. 12.713.* Buenos Aires: Librería Jurídica.

Ure, Alberto. 1991. "La realidad del escenario: Notas sobre la puesta en escena de *Los invertidos.*" In González Castillo 1991, 65–75.

Vacarezza, Alberto, Alejandro Berruti, and José González Castillo. 1930. *Mañana será otro día. Bambalinas: Revista Teatral* 8, no. 627.

Vademecum de la Liga de Honor aprobado por la Jefatura de la Policía de la Capital Federal. 1910. Buenos Aires: n.p.

Vargas, Otto. 1999. *El marxismo y la revolución argentina.* Buenos Aires: Editorial Agora.

Vazquez, José María, and Salvador Riese. 1930. *Se alboroto el avispero. Bambalinas: Revista Teatral* 13, no. 633.

Velasco y Arias, María. 1937. *Juana Paula Manso: Vida y acción.* Buenos Aires: Taller Porter Hermanos.

Vila, Pablo. 1991. "Tango to Folk: Hegemony Construction and Popular Identities in Argentina." *Studies in Latin American Popular Culture* 10: 107–39.

Vilariño, Idea. 1981. *El tango cantado: Prólogo y antología.* Montevideo: Editorial Calicanto.

Villarán, Ricardo, and E. González Cadavid. 1926. *Muñecos de trapo. Bambalinas: Revista Teatral* 9, no. 454.

Viñas, David. 1973. *Grotesco, inmigración y fracaso: Armando Discépolo.* Buenos Aires: Corregidor.

Wainerman, Catalina H., and Rebeca Barck de Raijman. 1984. *La division sexual del trabajo en los libros de lectura de la escuela primaria argentina: Un caso de inmutabilidad.* Buenos Aires: Cuaderno del CENEP, no. 32.

Whitelow, Guillermo. 1992. "José María Sert in Buenos Aires." *Journal of Decorative and Propaganda Arts,* no. 18: 76–89.

Wilde, Eduardo. 1899. *Prometeo y compañía.* Buenos Aires: Ediciones Jacobo Peuser.

Willett, Cecil, and Phillis Cunnington. 1981. *The History of Underclothes.* London and Boston: Faber and Faber.

Williams, Raymond. 1980. *Problems in Materialism and Culture.* London: New Left Books.

Zago, Manrique, José María Peña, et al. 1984. *Buenos Aires ayer/Buenos Aires Yesterday. Testimonios gráficos de una ciudad/A City in Pictures 1910–1930.* Buenos Aires: Manrique Zago Ediciones.

Zas, Lubrano. 1968. *Palabras con Elías Castelnuovo: Reportaje y antología.* Buenos Aires: Carlos Pérez Editor.

Zocchi, Juan. 1937. *Martín Vega. Argentores: Revista Teatral* 4, no. 149.

INDEX

Note: Page numbers in italic type indicate illustrations.

"A media luz" (tango), 380
Abad de Santillán, Diego, 404
abortion, 237–42
Academia Porteña del Lunfardo, 97
Acasuso, Luis Rodríguez, *La mal pagada*,
  229–31, 247, 277–78, 340, 355–56
lo acertado (social correctness): defined,
  437n3 (ch. 6); gender roles, 397; love,
  392; politics, 296; power of, 429; sexuality, 276, 336–37; *el verdadero* versus,
  106, 203; women's role, 116, 334;
  women's sexuality, 139–40
acontecimientos (pivotal events), 422–23
activism, political, 294–95, 432–33
Acuerdismo (Social Contract), 55, 281,
  285–87, 290, 295, 371, 422
"Adios, mi barrio" (tango), 383
advertisements, 22–23, 153–54, 169, 189,
  356–57
aesthetics. See *modernismo*
Afro-Argentinians: language of, 96–97;
  mutual aid societies of, 75; and transvestitism,
agoraphobia, 53, 85, 214, 236, 337–38, 376,
  379, 400, 429
Aguilar, Ismael, "Allá en el Bajo," 135,
  385–86
Aguilar, Juvencio, 401
Agustini, Delmira, 215
air quality, 303–4
Alberdi, Juan Bautista, 285, 439n1 (ch. 15)
Alberti, León, *Yo me hago el loco*, 99
alcahuetas (procurers), 122
Alcorta, Rosita, 24
Algarra, Pilar de, *Vidas. Apuntes de una
  visitadora*, 315–17
Alianza de la Juventud Nacionalista
  (Alliance of Nationalist Youth), 297

"Allá en el Bajo" (tango), 135, 385–86
Allen, Virginia Mae, 199
Alma recta (textbook), 116–17
Alsina, Alfonso, 125
Alvarez, Culpido. See Otero, Bella
Alvarez, José S. See Mocho, Fray
Alvear de Errázurriz, Josefina, 27–28
Alvear, Marcelo T. de, 2, 5, 27, 55, 263, 281,
  286, 322, 422
Alvear Palace Hotel, 26
Alvear, Torcuato de, 41
Alzaga Unzué Casares Residence, 26
Amadori, Luis César, "Portero, suba y
  diga," 318–23
amurados (abandoned males), 392–400
anarchism, 133–34, 264, 272, 284–85,
  289–95, 345, 404, 430
Anchorena, Joaquín de, 261
Anchorena Palace, 26
Anglo-Argentina Company, 67
"Aquel tapado de armiño" (tango), 171–72
Arata, Luis, 403
Archetti, Eduardo P., 396, 424
architecture: of Barrio Norte, 15, 26, 41;
  body and, 324–25; class and, 37–40, 61;
  of department stores, 50; *modernista*, 32;
  of palaces, 26, 30, 37–40
Arena, Luis, *Hermanito*, 115
Arenaza, Carlos de: *La infancia abandon-
  ada y delincuente y la ley Agote*, 359;
  Menores delincuentes, 359
Argentina: identity of, 3, 6, 21, 298–300;
  imaginaries of, 3, 6, 15, 17, 54, 56, 97,
  128, 290–91. See also nationalism
Argentina Railway, 66
Argentinean Association of University
  Women, 272
Argentinean Federation of Unions, 291

argot, 96
aristocracy. *See* elites
Arlt, Roberto, 54, 84, 86–87, 89, 212, 215–16,
    419–20, 429; *Las aguafuertes porteñas*, 87,
    312–14; "Aguinaldo inesperado," 312;
    El amor brujo, 202–4, 206; "Busca tra-
    bajo a las cuatro de la mañana," 312;
    "Las fieras," 358–60; *El jorobadito*, 19;
    El juguete rabioso, 19, 57–58, 94; *Los
    lanzallamas*, 309–10; *Los siete locos*,
    51–53, 56–57, 153, 166–67, 180, 184,
    195, 213, 309–10, 352, 364–66; "Lo
    tragicómico," 312; "La tristeza del
    sábado inglés," 87–88
Armour company, 151, 261, 303
arrabales: avant-garde and, 63; and cattle
    industry, 128; characteristics of, 75;
    defined, 435n6; language of, 96, 98, 103,
    125; representation of, 118–19, 124,
    126–36; tango and, 74. *See also* suburbs
art. *See modernismo*
art nouveau, 32–34, 160–61, 170, 175. *See
    also modernismo*
artificial flowers, 176
Asociación Católica Argentina (Argentin-
    ian Catholic Association), 220
Asociación de Damas Argentinas (Associa-
    tion of Argentinean Women), 297
Asociación del Trabajo (Labor Associa-
    tion), 261
associations, barrio, 372
Au Bon Marché, 50
automobiles, 65
avant-garde, 61, 63
Avellaneda, Nicolás, 45
Avellaneda, Pepita, 347
Avenida Alvear, 41–42
Avenida de Mayo, 82, 125
Azurduy, Juana, 221

bacanes (playboys), 73, 76, 277, 318–26, 396,
    424, 427, 438n5
Bachofen, Johann Jakob, 355
Bahr, Carlos, "Cada día te extraño más,"
    397
Bakhtin, Mikhail, 7
Bakunin, Mikhail, 125, 439n5 (ch. 15)

Balmori, Diana, 41
Balzac, Honoré de, 86
Bambalinas (theater review publication),
    292–93
Bandera Roja (newspaper), 264
Barbier, George, 170; *Shéhérazade*, 169
Bardi, Agustín, "La última cita," 392
Barletta, Leónidas, 216
Barolo building, 33
Barrias, Louis Ernest, 205
barrio associations, 372
Barrio Norte: architecture of, 15, 26; cul-
    tural significance of, 15; elite residential
    area of, 15; public space in, 23, 41–43
barrios. *See arrabales*; suburbs
bars. *See* cafés
Bassi, Arturo de, *Otra cosa es con la
    guitarra*, 122
Bastos, María Luisa, 32
Basualdo de Becú, Magdalena Ortiz, 24,
    107
Batlle y Ordóñez, José, 273, 439n5 (ch. 14)
Battistella, Mario, "Se viene la maroma,"
    300
Baudelaire, Charles, 86, 192, 199
Beardsley, Aubrey, 205
beauty, 162, 165, 168–70, 198–99
Beckers, Jeanne Marie Charlotte. *See*
    Paquin, Jeanne
beggars, 118–19
behaviorist theory, 149
Ben, Pablo, 348
Bentley, Eric, *The Life of Melodrama*, 373
Bergero, Sofía Isabel. *See* Bozán, Sofía
Berruti, Alejandro: *Cosas de la vida*, 294;
    Cuidado con las bonitas, 103, 198–99,
    269–70; *Madre tierra*, 156; *Mañana será
    otro día*, 101–2, 295–96, 322–23
Bertonasco, Alfredo E.: *Un amor imposible*,
    388, 390; *Los casados son los peores*, 295
Bianchi, Edmundo, "Ya no cantás chin-
    golo," 382
bibelots, 168–69
Biffi, Acibiades, *La hoja de hiedra*, 391
Bill 1420 (1884), 25
"Bill Posting Prohibited," *111*
Bioy, Adolfo: *Antes del novecientos*, 13

Claramunt, Teresa de, 134

class: cultural crossings, 51–60; fashion and, 154–55, 165–67; feminism and, 227; homosexuality and, 346; identity and, 166; Jockey Club and, 16–21; language and, 40, 103–4; and literature, 49, 60; *modernismo* and, 60; modernization and, 14–15; power and, 319–24; public space and, 42–43, 45–49; residential architecture and, 37–40; sexuality and, 126, 318–26; and social mobility, 54–57; theater and, 81. *See also* bourgeoisie; elites; "other" Buenos Aires; workers

claustrophobia/claustrophilia, 32, 36, 39, 85, 236, 429

clothing, industrial versus handmade, 186–87. *See also* fashion

Cobián, Juan Carlos, "La casita de mis viejos," 327

Coca-Cola, 73

Cocoliche, 95, 98–99, 102–3, 434

Cocoliche, Antonio, 99

cocottes (mistresses), 121

cognitive maps, 43–44

Colomina, Beatriz, 37

Comisión de Señoritas (Young Women's Committee), 220–26

communism, 298

"Como abrazao a un rencor" (tango), 386, 397

compadritos, 90, 299, 319, 348, 383, *412*

"La Competencia" (cartoon), 288, *407*

Conference of the Trades Unions of the Confederation of Danish Unions (1919), 72

Conference of Trades Unions (Leeds, 1916), 72

Confitería del Molino (The Windmill Café), 33

confiterías, 84–85

Congress of Workers (Baltimore, 1916), 72

Coni, Emilio, 121

Coni, Gabriela Laperrière de, 272–73

Conquest of the Desert, 3

Conservative Order, 4–5, 15, 38, 55, 104, 264, 273, 298, 422, 426, 427, 435n3 (introduction)

consumer culture, 153–94, 430

continuismo, 249, 438n7

contraception, 210

Contursi, Pascual: "En esta tarde gris," 399; "Mi noche triste," 384, 392–93, 397, 398, 440n1 (ch. 20)

conventillos, 90–106; Argentine nation and, 105–6; conditions in, 92–94, *112*; critique of, 282–85; cultural representations of, 92–95; and identity, 94–95, 104, 167–68; interpersonal relations in, 93–94; and language, 95–96; and prostitution, 119; removal of, 63; residents of, 92–93; sanitation and disease in, 91–93, 126–27, 131; strikes by inhabitants of, 79–80, 91, *111*; and upward mobility, 90; urban-rural mixture in, 71

Cooperativa Telefónica, 266

"Corazón" (tango), 397

Cordiviola, Cleopatra, "Las chicas de enfrente," 174

Cornwall, Andrea, 396

Corporación Nacionalista de Maestros (Nationalist Guild of Teachers), 297

Correa Luna, C., "Todo se conversa," 418–19

Corrientes Street, 63, 77, 300

"Corrientes y Esmeralda" (tango), 184

Cortázar, Julio, 61

La Cosechera, 84

cosmetics, 29

Costa, Cerruti, 404

countryside, 31

coups, 237, 248, 292, 295–97, 301, 365–68, 401–2, 405, 417, 422, 429

courtesans, 274–77, 320, 325–26, 430–31

creoles, food of, 20

Crítica (newspaper), 215

crime: foreigners as perpetrators of, 265–66; language and, 96; women as perpetrators of, 240–46

criollismo, 75

Croatian Committee of the Federation of Employers in Industry and Commerce, 72

crowds, 83

"Cuando el corazón" (tango), 397

"Cuesta abajo" (tango), 395–96
"Cuidado con los cincuenta" (tango), 339
cultural crossings, 51–60, 73–74, 84–86
culture: in Buenos Aires, 71–72, 77–89; imaginaries and, 89; of suburbs, 75. *See also* cafés; literature; tango; theater
Cunnington, Phillis, *The History of Underclothes*, 189
Curat Dubarry, Juan Manuel, *La tristeza de los viejos*, 160, 388
Curotto, Angel, *El fuego del Vesugio*, 295

daily life. *See* everyday life
Daireaux, Emilio, *Vida y costumbres en el Plata*, 118–19
Darío, Rubén, 27, 33, 59–60, 84, 96, 182; "Era un aire suave," 161; "*Garçonière*," 323–24; "In Memoriam: Bartolomé Mitre," 29; *Oda a Mitre*, 31; "El rey burgués," 31
De Andrea, Miguel, 288, 289, 298, 402
década infame (decade of infamy), 296–97, 372
death: femmes fatales and, 200–201; sirens and, 218
debt, 193–94
DeFilippis Novoa, Francisco: *Los desventurados*, 308; *El día sábado*, 219; *María la tonta*, 426–27; *Puerto Madero*, 282–85; *La vendedora*, 81
Del Clé, Eçe, "Del Buenos Aires exótico," 136
"Delicias de la paternidad" (illustration), 258
"Delicias de la paternidad" (poem), 243–44
"The delights of fatherhood" (illustration), 258
Dellepiani, Antonio, 96
Department of Public Health, 91
department stores, 50, 180–81, 183–89
desire: consumer culture and, 177–78, 430; diastolic, 154, 165, 170, 174, 189, 193, 197, 228, 317, 420, 437n1 (ch. 9); femininity and, 165–77; systolic, 174, 193, 238–39, 420, 437n1 (ch. 9); working women and, 156, 164, 430

Deutsch, Helene, 337, 338
Di Carlo, Adela, 402; "Justa recompensa," 54–56
Di Giovanni, Severino, 403
Diagonal Norte, *110*
El Diario (newspaper), 16
diastolic desire, 154, 165, 170, 174, 189, 193, 197, 228, 317, 420, 437n1 (ch. 9)
Díaz, Porfirio, 130
Díaz, Teófilo E., 16
Dickens, Charles, 86
Dickman, Enrique, 87
Dietrich, Marlene, 201
Dios Filiberto, Juan de, "Malevaje," 222
Discépolo, Armando, 323, 353; *Babilonia*, 38–39, 425; "Cambalache," 427; *Entre el hierro*, 350–51, 391, 418; *La fragua*, 159, 385; *El guarda 323*, 67–70, 103, 105, 295, 421 (see also *El viaje aquel*); *Hombres de honor*, 185; *Mateo*, 65–66; *El movimiento continuo*, 34; *Mustafá*, 106; *El novio de mamá*, 100–101; *El vértigo*, 175; *El viaje aquel*, 67, 105, 295, 331 (see also *El guarda 323*); "¡Victoria!," 394; "Yira . . . yira," 427
Discépolo, Enrique Santos, 385; "Canción desesperada," 388; "Yira . . . yira," 369, 371, 388
discursive nodes, 7
disguise, 71, 83. *See also* carnival
distance. *See* proxemic distance
Dolard, Víctor, *El amor que no se vende*, 197, 389
Dolkart, Ronald H., 296–97
Doll, Ramón, *Acerca de una política nacional*, 298
domestic service, 36, 38–39, 115–17, 130
Donato, Edgardo, "A media luz," 380
Donovan (police chief), 118
Donzelot, Jacques, 246–47
Dostoyevsky, Fyodor, 86
Drago, Luis María, 96
dressing tables, 168–69
Dubois, Jules, 58
duels, 319–20
dust exposure, 302–3

Echeverría, Esteban, 73; *El matadero*, 127–28

economy: Buenos Aires as attraction based on, 93; capitalism and, 4; crises in, 93, 313–14, 372, 405; modernization and, 4; nationalism and, 299; during Yrigoyen government, 262–64

education: liberalism and, 415–16; public, 25; textbooks, 115–17; working women and, 220–25

Education Law (1869), 415

Edwards, Susan S. M., 121

Eichelbaum, Samuel: *Nadie la conoció nunca*, 274–77, 325–26, 389, 431; *El ruedo de las almas*, 204–5, 349, 365–66

elderly, as labor, 210

Electoral Law (1912), 415

electric girdles, 357

elites: Buenos Aires and, 15–25; characteristics of, 33; chronicles and, 21–24; and Jockey Club, 16–21; and *modernismo*, 21–24, 27–29, 32–33; and modernity, 16, 21–25; newspapers and, 17, 21, 26–30; palaces of, 26–32, 35–40; parks of, 43–48; plazas of, 48; politics and economics of, 4–5; public cultural display of, 21–25, 48–49, 51–53, 426; and tango, 318; women of, 22–24, 28. *See also* class

emotion, 373, 377

empirical geography, 8

"En esta tarde gris" (tango), 399

"Enfundá la bandolina" (tango), 352–53

English Saturday, 87–88

Enlightenment, 41

L'Épatant, Paris, France, 18

Escardó, Florencio, 381

Escobar, Julio, *La mujer que odiaba a los hombres*, 278–80

escraches, 406, 440n4

Escuelas de Obreras en las Fábricas (Schools for Women Factory Workers), 220–25

Estrada, Martínez, *La cabeza de Goliat*, 3

ethnicity, and tango, 75–76

everyday life: capitalism and, 8; exchanges in, 227; habits of, 105; historical nature

of, 105; imaginaries and, 89; melodrama and, 376; significance of, 8; tango and, 418; in theater, 80

Expósito, Homero, "Yuyo verde," 382

eyesight, damage to, 307–8

Ezeiza, Gabino, 384

factories, 117, 151, *251*, 302–8. See also *frigoríficos* (meatpacking plants); textile industry

"The Factory: Order and Silence" (illustration), 146, *251*

fairy tales, 29–30

Falcón, Ada, 97

Falcón, Ramón L., 339

Falguière, Alexandre, 16

family: breakdown of, 139; unemployment's effect on, 315–17

fascism, 220, 248, 297, 405–6

fashion, 24–25, 153–94

fashion industry, 164–65, 184

Federación Obrera de la República Argentina (FORA; Argentinean Labor Federation), 262, 291

Federación Obrera Nacionalista Argentina (Federation of Nationalist Workers of Argentina), 297

Federation of Circles of Catholic Workers, 405

Feijoó, María del Carmen, 158, 272

Femina (magazine), 170

femininity: art and, 160–61; characteristics of, 161–62; consumer goods and, 165, 186–87; fashion and, 23–24, 187; lingerie and, 188; melodrama and, 377; and self-absorption, 168–70, 430

feminism: anarchism and, 134, 272, 430; class and, 227; femmes fatales and, 200; imaginaries of, 332, 354; political right and, 272; and politics, 273–74; *porteño* imaginaries and, 277–80; socialism and, 272–73

Feminist Center of the Socialist party, 273

femmes fatales, 199–206, 230, 279–80, 389–90, 429

Fernández, Luis. See Borbón, Princesa de

Generation of 1880, 4, 15, 25, 55, 125, 426, 435n1 (introduction)

género chico, 78, 81, 98, 274, 276, 293, 384

genocide, 3, 4, 18

geography: cognitive mapping and, 43–44; sensorial, 6, 85, 150, 363; sensuous, 43–44, 93

Gerchunoff, Alberto, 84

germanía, 96

Germany, 405

Gilman, Sander L., *Difference and Pathology*, 196

Girondo, Oliverio: "Exvoto," 387; *Kodak desafiante*, 63

Gobello, José, 75, 97

Godel, Alberto E., *El farruco Manolo*, 389–90

Godio, Julio, 264, 290

Goldstein Fodor, Iris, 338

golpismo, 367, 372

golpistas, 296–97, 439n3 (ch. 15)

Gómez Carrillo, Enrique, 21–24, 31, 33, 50, 54, 153, 155, 165, 169, 170, 172, 173; *El encanto de Buenos Aires*, 22, 28, 162, 177–78

Gómez Grimau, Pedro, *Sacco y Vanzetti*, 292–93

Gómez, Indalecio, 5

Gómez Salustio, Angélico, 208

Goncourt, Edmund de, 355

Goncourt, Jules de, 192, 355

González Arrili, Bernardo, "La calle, un pasadizo," 192–93

González Cadavid, E., *Muñecos de trapo*, 325, 387, 388–91

González Castillo, José: *Hermana mía*, 247; *Los invertidos*, 340–49; *La mala reputación*, 240–41, 386–87, 392; *Mañana será otro día*, 101–2, 295–96, 322–23; *El mayor prejuicio*, 205, 294; *El pobre hombre*, 307, 391; *La Santa Madre*, 231, 248–49, 288; *La zarza ardiendo*, 232–34

González Stephan, Beatriz, 35

González Tuñón, Enrique, "Camas desde un peso," 93–94

Gorelik, Adrián, 45, 62

Gouchón Cané, Emilio, "Un buen empleo," 197–98

Gourmont, Remy, 95

Gran Aldea (Great Village), 15, 16, 37

Gran Colecta Nacional (Great National Fund Raiser), 287–88

Great Britain, 287

Great Depression, 93

grotesco, 81

grotesque city, 15, 46–48, 55, 59–61, 69, 118, 124, 125, 132, 211, 245, 248, 345, 350, 428, 432. *See also* "other" Buenos Aires

Grupo Azul (Blue Group), 263

Guijarro, Juan, 89; "Mozo de café," 86, 87

Gustavo, Soledad (pseudonym of Teresa Mañé), 134

Gutiérrez, Leandro, 372

Gutiérrez, Eliseo, *Yo me hago el loco*, 99

Gutiérrez Nájera, Manuel, "De blanco," 234

Guy, Donna, 132, 152, 212

habits, 105, 375

Haldane, John Burdon Sanderson, 303

Hall, Edward, 39

Harper's Bazaar (magazine), 170

Harrods, 50

Harvey, David, 41

Haussmann, Georges, 42, 61, 91; *Memoires*, 45

health: *conventillos* and, 91–93, 126–27, 131; factories and, 151–52, 302–8; labor and, 151–52, 159–60, 176–77, 180, 269–70, 302–8; sweatshops and, 159–60. *See also* public health

hermaphroditism, 348

Herreros, Pedro, 84; "Paseo de Julio," 135–36

heterosexuality, as norm, 332–36, 346

"L'Heure du Rimme" label, 168–70, 252

HIJOS, 440n4

Hispanism, 28

historias de perdición, 116, 140, 429

historicism, 6

Hitler, Adolf, 297, 405

Hollywood, 405

home ownership, 285, 287

media, 384
melodrama, 373–74, 376–77, 422–23
men and masculinity: abandoned males,
 392–400; crisis in, 357, 364–67, 396–401;
 exemplary masculinity, 206, 308, 348,
 356–57, 364–65, 368, 386, 392, 397, 399,
 424; and fatherhood, 243–44; and
 homosexuality, 341–49; and honor, 320;
 imaginaries of, 331; and labor, 310–11,
 315–17; love, 386, 391–400; in meatpacking industry, 146–47; modernity
 and, 316; nationalism and, 366–68, 424;
 sexuality, 121, 328–29, 352–56; sirens
 and, 218; tango and, 347–48, 377, 386,
 392, 394–401, 404–5, *411*, 424, 427; violence, 357–62, 430; virility, 352–57,
 367–68; and weakness, 357, 365, 367.
 See also gender
Méndez, Evar, 59, 60
Mertens, Federico: *La casa donde no entró
 el amor*, 324; *La zarza ardiendo*, 232–34
"Mi Buenos Aires querido" (tango), 418
"Mi noche triste" (tango), 384, 392–93, 397,
 398, 440n1 (ch. 20)
micropowers, 432
Miles (editor), 281–82, 285–89
Milicia Cívica Nacionalista (Nationalist
 Civic Militia), 297
militarization of society, 288, 402–3
military governments, 301, 366–68, 401–2,
 406
milonguitas (tango dancers), 59, 121, 122,
 171, 217–19, 377, 427, 430, 431
Mirande, Ives de, *El hombre del frac*, 73–74
mishiadura (indigence), 365, 372, 440n2
 (ch. 19)
misogyny, 141–42, 182, 198–206, 218–19,
 234, 279–80, 326, 329, 361, 385–86,
 388–89, 392, 416, 426, 427, 430
Mitre, Bartolomé, 29
Mocho, Fray (pseudonym of José S.
 Alvarez), 299
modernismo: architecture and, 32; chronicles and, 21–24; class and, 60; defined,
 435n2 (ch. 1); elite culture and, 21–24,
 27–29, 32–33; and the feminine, 160–62;
 literary, 32–33. *See also* art nouveau

modernity and modernization: advent of,
 3–4; aesthetics of (see *modernismo*);
 chronicles and, 21–24; city and, 24; class
 and, 14–15; effects of, 2–4, 7, 8, 417;
 elites and, 16, 21–25; historical agents
 of, 3; identity and, 5–6, 69–70, 187;
 imaginaries of, 71, 73, 165, 176, 417,
 419; law versus capitalism in, 152; masculinity and, 316; mixture as characteristic of, 85; newspapers and, 27; theater
 and, 78; voting and, 5; women's role in,
 116, 338; working women and, 267
Moller and Müller (architects), 37
Mondongo, 75
Mones Ruiz, Antonio, *Otra cosa es con la
 guitarra*, 122
Montaner, Domènech i, 33
Moock, Armando, *Canción de amor*, 389–90
morality: bourgeois, 192, 230, 247; in
 Buenos Aires, 83; public, 338–39
Moreau de Justo, Alicia, 273
Moreau, Gustave, 199, 205
Moreno, Artemio, *Niñez abandonada y
 delincuencia en Buenos Aires*, 151–52
Mores, Armando, "Cafetín de Buenos
 Aires," 215
Morganti, Carlos, *Primero en la colorada*,
 324, 388, 390
"La morocha" (tango), 80
Moya, José, 28, 370
Mozzoni, Maria, 134
Mucha, Adolphe, 161
"Muñeca brava" (tango), 199
muñecas bravas, 218, 222, 377, 430
Mussolini, Benito, 297
Muzilli, Carolina, 179–82, 227, 272, 421; *El
 trabajo femenino*, 176–77, 269–70

La Nación (newspaper), 1, 21, 22, 29, 31,
 55, 86, 96, 264, 265, 366
Nalé Roxlo, Conrado, 83–84
narrativas de perdición, 116, 140, 429
Nash, John, 42
National Autonomy Party, 263
National Democratic Party, 297
national identity: formation of, 6, 21; Frontera Sur and, 3; language and, 95–97

national immigrant organizations, 370–71

nationalism: and barrios, 403–4; Buenos Aires as target of, 299; growth of, 220; LPA and, 223–24, 272; and masculinity, 366–68, 424; and morality, 239; nativism and, 298–300; police powers and, 265; targets of, 298; unions and, 220–21, 223, 268

nativism, 298–300

naturalism, 123–24, 142, 376

Navas, Miguel, 87

newspapers: crime reporting of, 240; as cultural intermediaries, 17, 21, 27, 29–30; elite culture and, 17, 21–24, 26–30; fashion industry and, 184; strike coverage by, 264–68, 271. *See also* chronicles

Nieves Abratte, Blanca, 348

"9 de Julio" (tango), 167

"No salgas de tu barrio" (tango), 396

Noda, Pedro, "Allá en el Bajo," 135

Notari, Humberto, *Aquellas señoras*, 58–59

notas sociales. *See* society columns

La novela femenina (folletín), 78

La novela para todos (folletín), 436n1 (ch. 4)

La novela semanal (folletín), 78

La novela universitaria (folletín), 78

Novión, Alberto: *El rincón de los caranchos*, 103; *Los primeros fríos*, 104, 327

Núñez Seixas, Xosé M., 370

obreras. *See* working women

Ocampo, Victoria, 24

Olbrich, Joseph Maria, 161

oligarchy. *See* elites

Olivari, Nicolás, 380; *Tedio*, 199–202, 332–33, 390, 394–95

Olivera, Carlos, 211

Ordinance Regulating Domestic Service, 36

Ortíz, Fernando, 75

Ortiz, Grognet, Diego, *Los vegetarianos*, 390

Ortiz, R. I., 128

Ortiz, Roberto M., 300

Otero, Bella (pseudonym of Culpido Alvarez), 348

"other" Buenos Aires: elite versus, 17, 25, 118; and public space, 45–47; urban appearance of, 15, 46–47; during Uriburu

government, 300; variety within, 74; and work, 49. *See also* grotesque city

Pacheco, Carlos Mauricio: *El diablo en el conventillo*, 64–65, 157, 305; *Los disfrazados*, 71; *La patota*, 60; *Tangos, tongos y tungos*, 122–23, 143; *Los tristes o gente oscura*, 64, 140–42

packing plants. *See frigoríficos* (meatpacking plants)

Padula, José Luis, "9 de Julio," 167

pain, of workers, 177, 305, 309

palaces, 26–32, 35–40, 53–54

Palacios, Alfredo, 84, 263, 305–7; *La fatiga y sus proyecciones sociales*, 72, 144, 305

Palermo, Barrio Norte, 22–23, 41–43, 45–48

Paoli, Carlos R. de: *Los chicos de Pérez*, 314–15; *La culpa la tiene el gallego de enfrente*, 296, 301, 322

Paquin, Jeanne (pseudonym of Jeanne Marie Charlotte Beckers), 161

paradigms, 105

Paris Commune, 91

Paris, France, 15, 16, 18–21, 24–25, 42, 45, 50

parks, 43–48

Partido Autonomista Nacional (National Autonomy Party), 220

Pascarella, Luis, *El conventillo*, 63, 126–27, 155–56, 165–67, 184, 207–9

Paseo de Julio, 135–37, 348

passion, 234, 386–87. *See also* love

Pasteur, Louis, 91

Patagonia, repression in, 262, 264, 290

Patagonia Trágica, 290

Pater, Pablo, 58

paterfamilias, 424

Patria y Orden (Fatherland and Order), 220

patriarchy, 244–45, 424

Paz Social (Social Peace), 5

Pérez Leirós, Francisco, 193–94

Pedraza, Pilar, 204, 218–19

Pellegrini, Carlos, 16–21, 25

Pellettieri, Osvaldo, 69, 373

Peña, José María, 33

Pereda, Celedonio, 33

Pereda Palace, 26, *107*
perfume, 150, 189–93
Perón, María Eva Duarte de, 27, 280, 287
Peronism, 66, 406, 433
personal space, 148–49
Peters, Emil, *Die Weidergeburt der Kraft*, 354
petits hôtels. See palaces
photography, and fashion industry, 184
Piazzolla, Astor, 97
Picard, André, *El hombre del frac*, 73–74
Pike, Burton, 6, 86
Pinedo, Manuel, 299
piqueteros, 440n4
Pirovano Hospital, *411*
Pizales, Antonio, 266
plague, 91–92
Plaza de Mayo, 406
Plaza Mazzini, 348
Plaza Pellegrini, 41
Plaza San Martín, 48
plazas, 43
pleasure, 342
"Pobre corazón mío" (tango), 397
"Pobre milonga" (tango), 396
"Pobre paica" (tango), 396
Podestá, José, 99
poesía rufianesca (pimp poetry), 384
Poli, Manolita, 97
police and policing, 118–19, 338–39
politics: activism in, 294–95, 432–33;
    Catholic Church and, 219–20, 231–32,
    248, 288–89, 402, 427; elites and, 4–5;
    immigrants and, 263, 265; interactive
    nature of, 72–73; and internationalism,
    72; labor and, 262–65; military govern-
    ments, 301, 366–68, 401–2, 406; and
    suburbs, 371–72, 404; transitions in,
    4–5; Uriburu government (1930–1932),
    297–300; women and, 267, 272–74, 428,
    432; Yrigoyen government (1916–1922),
    261–63, 281, 285–87. *See also* coups
Pontier, Armando, "Cada día te extraño
    más," 397
popular culture: *conventillos* and, 92–93;
    media and, 384; tango and, 381; in the-
    ater, 35, 78–81

popular theater: class in, 81; contemporary
    references in, 78–81; cultural signifi-
    cance of, 78, 80–81; Golden Age of,
    77–81; imaginaries of, 99, 293–94, 296;
    and interior decor, 35; melodrama and,
    376; modernity and, 78; palace decor
    represented in, 35; political activism
    as represented in, 294–95; prostitution
    as represented in, 138–40; supporting
    structure of, 78; topics in, 140, 215, 234,
    286
pornography, 141, 209
Portela, Mario J., "El *Sweating System*,"
    159–60
porteños(as): class and, 22–23, 170; and con-
    sumer culture, 178; defined, 435n4 (ch.
    1); and feminism, 277–78; and interper-
    sonal relations in city, 70; and language,
    98; public space for *porteñas*, 338; sexu-
    ality of, 427; and urban planning, 62
"Portero, suba y diga" (tango), 318–23
Posada, Abel, 80
poverty, 61. *See also conventillos*; workers
power: class and, 319–24; men and, 368;
    micropowers and, 432; tango and, 322
La Prensa (newspaper), 21, 43, 79, 86, 207–8,
    210–12, 264
Pre-Raphaelites, 199
proletarian women, social imaginaries of,
    115–43, 152, 154, 156–57, 160, 162–68,
    214–15, 321, 427–28
proletariat. *See* workers
property rights, 244–45, 274
prostibularias (bordello prostitutes), 121
prostitutas libres (unattached prostitutes),
    122
prostitution, 119–23, 129–31, 135–43,
    181–82, 196, 209
La Protesta (newspaper), 264
proxemic distance: architecture and, 32, 37,
    53, 57; in Buenos Aires, 87, 126; cities
    and, 70; defined, 14; elite establishment
    of, 19, 23, 38, 129, 426; ghettos and, 129;
    men-women and, 206, 321, 328; public
    health and, 92. *See also* interpersonal
    relations; social laterality
Pua, Carlos de la, 84

Public Education Law (1889), 220, 231
public health, 91–93, 126, 131, 142
public space: class and, 21–25, 42–43, 45–49;
    meaning of, 41–42; regulation of, 42,
    47, 61–62, 66–70, 118–19; women and,
    23, 337–39. *See also* parks; plazas
public transportation, 42–43, 47, 66–70
"Puente Alsina" (tango), 381
Puerto Madero, 285, *412*

quarantine, 91–92
"Que nadie se entere" (tango), 397
"Qué falta que me hacés" (tango), 397
Quesada, Vicente G. *See* Gálvez, Víctor
Quiroga, Horacio, 84, 215
Quiroga, Rosita, 97

race. *See* Afro-Argentinians; ethnicity
Radical Party, 54–55, 273, 281, 297–98, 369,
    404
Radicalism, 104, 426, 427
radio, 96–97
Raijman, Rebeca Barck de, 115
railways, 66–67, 404
Ramos, Julio, 23–24, 32, 435n3 (ch. 1)
rape, 323–24
Rawson, Elvira, 273
razza forte (mighty breed), 81
Recoleta, 41, 44
red, 127–28
Reekie, Gail, 185–86
Regent's Park, London, England, 42
Reguillo, Rossana, 8, 105, 227, 244, 326, 432
Renau, Maryse, 309
repression, state, 225–26, 262, 264, 287,
    290–91, 296–97, 300–301, 367–68
Residency Act (1902), 4, 5, 134, 261, 263–65,
    429
residential architecture: and class, 37–40;
    and gender, 37–38; placement of, 53,
    109; and sexuality, 37–38. See also *con-
    ventillos*
El Revolucionario Español, 85
Reyes, Juan B., "¿Te fuiste? ¡Ja, Ja!," 394
Richard, Nelly, *421*
Right, political, 296–98. *See also* ultra-
    Right

Rillo, Armando, *El amor que no se vende*,
    197, 389
Rivera, Castro, 34
roads. *See* streets and roads
Roca, Julio Argentino, 17, 93, 220, 435n1
    (introduction)
Roca-Runciman Pact, 300, 439n9 (ch. 15)
Rocco, Pedro J., *414*
Rock, David, 298
Rodaway, Paul, 38, 40, 52, 149; *Sensuous
    Geographies*, 43–44
Rojas, Eduardo, 162; "El *Sweating System*,"
    158–60
Rojas, Ricardo, 84, 97, 298; *La restauración,
    nacionalista*, 95
Romay, Francisco, 75
Romero, Luis Alberto, 290, 372
Romero, Manuel: "Aquel tapado de
    armiño," 171–72; "Se viene la
    maroma," 300; "Tiempos viejos," 382;
    "Tomo y obligo," 386
Rosa, Rafael José de la: *El guarda 323*,
    67–70; *El novio de mamá*, 100–101
Rosas, Juan Manuel de, 127–28, 347
Rossetti, Dante Gabriel, 199
Rossi, Vicente, 348
Rousseau, Jean-Jacques, 73
Rouvier, Charlotte, 29

Sánchez Sorondo, Matías, 298
Saborino, Enrique, "La morocha," 80
Sacco, Nicola, 291, 439n6 (ch. 15)
Sade, Marquis de, 141
sado-misogynism, 142
Sáenz Peña, Roque, 5, 261, *415*
sainetes (popular farces), 59–60, 82–84, 157;
    characteristics of, 81; and consumer
    culture, 192; contemporary references
    in, 79–81; and gender relations, 198;
    and Health Department, 91; and immi-
    gration, 80; language of, 98, 99; and
    public transportation, 67–70
Saisselin, Rémy G., 168
Saldías, José Antonio, 86; *¡Siga el corso!*, 178
salespersons, 178–82, 186–88, 267
Salessi, Jorge, 331; *El bandoneón*, 389, 391
Salzman, Leo, 376

San Martín, José de, 220
Sánchez, Florencio, 84
Sanden, T. A., 357
Sandoz, Gerard, 161
Sanguinetti, Carlos, 65
"El santo de Manolito" (*folletín*), 241
Santos Discépolo, Enrique: "Cafetín de Buenos Aires," 215; "Malevaje," 222
Sarlo, Beatriz, 211, 380
Sarmiento, Domingo Faustino, 3, 25, 62, 73, 415; *Facundo*, 3, 128
Sauvage, Sylvain, 330; untitled watercolor, 170, *253*
Sauvrey, Laurentine, 134
Savigliano, Marta E., 217–18
scab labor, 267–68
Scarfó, Paulino, 403
Scarpino, Alejandro, "Canaro en París," 167
Scherpe, Klauss, 422
Schiaparelli, Elsa, 161
Scobie, James, 66–67
"Se va la vida" (tango), 397
"Se viene la maroma" (tango), 300
seamstresses, 158, *410*
Sebreli, Juan José, 346, 347
Seidler, Victor J., 316
Semana Roja (Red Week), 4
Semana Trágica, 225, 262–66, 275, 281, 289–90, 296, 422, 426
Senez, Arturo César, "Isla de Flores," 380
Sennett, Richard, 30, 42, 61, 70, 71; *Flesh and Stone*, 129
sensorial geography, 6, 85, 150, 363. *See also* sensuous geography
sensory experience: in advanced cultures, 40; of domestic servants, 39; in factories, 147–50; geography and, 43–44; of green spaces, 44
sensuous geography, 43–44, 93. *See also* sensorial geography
September Revolution, 298
Sert, José María, 33
sexual harassment, 138, 150, 179–80, 278–79
sexuality: alternate, 330–36; bourgeois, 192; bourgeois residential architecture and, 37–38; in Buenos Aires, 348; class and, 126, 318–26; consumer culture and,

193; femmes fatales and, 199–206; *garçonières* and, 318–26, 341, 427; heteronormativity, 332–36, 346; men's, 121, 328–29, 352–56; polymorphous, 196; tango and, 219, 222, 348; underwear and, 188–89; women's, 122, 139, 141, 196–97, 205–6, 328–30, 332, 353–55, 385–87. *See also* homosexuality
Showalter, Elaine, 328, 331–32, 344, 349; *Sexual Anarchy*, 142
silence, 145–46
Silverman, Kaja, *Male Subjectivity at the Margin*, 349
Simmel, Georg, 172; *Filosofía de la coquetería*, 155
Sinclair, Upton, 307
single mothers, 211, 245
single women, 332–33
sirens, 218–19
slaughterhouses. See *frigoríficos* (meatpacking plants)
smells, 149–50. *See also* perfume
"Sólo se quiere una vez" (tango), 397
Social Defense Act (1910), 261, 263, 265
social distance. *See* proxemic distance
social laterality, 39, 69, 80, 94, 215, 216, 235, 370, 373, 375, 377, 429. *See also* interpersonal relations
social mobility: Argentine, 290; *conventillos* and, 90, 168; immigrants and, 54–57; and impostors, 165–66; prostitution and, 122–23; of women, 175–76
social peace, 281–82, 287–88
social rituals, 35
socialism: Catholic Church versus, 231–32; feminism and, 272–73; workers organized by, 404
Socialist Party, 263, 272–73
Sociedad Rural Argentina, 261, 439n1 (ch. 14)
Sociedad Unión Progresista del Distrito de Salvatierra de Miño (Progressive Union Society of the Salvatierra de Miño District), 370
society columns, 17, 21, 27–29
Soiza Reilley, Juan José de, 403
"Soledad" (tango), 397